A

SUPPLEMENT

TO THE

LAWS AND ORDINANCES

OF THE

CITY OF BOSTON.

PREPARED AND PRINTED UNDER THE DIRECTI
COMMITTEE ON ORDINANCES.

BOSTON:
J. E. FARWELL & COMPANY, PRINTERS TO THE CITY.
37 CONGRESS STREET,
1866.

PREFACE.

THIS "Supplement to the Laws and Ordinances" has been prepared in pursuance of a design entertained by the Committee under whose supervision the last edition of the Ordinances was published, and announced by them, in a report to the City Council, as a proposition to "print a supplementary volume to embrace the rules and regulations of the different institutions and departments, various orders of a permanent character, and some of the City contracts, which, being periodically renewed, it is convenient to have accessible to those who are responsible for their faithful performance. Several acts and resolves of the Legislature, for temporary objects will also be given. The volume will contain, in addition, an explanatory list of the special laws passed for the benefit of the City, as also of the cases decided in the Supreme Court upon points of Municipal interest."

The work of preparing this volume was not entered upon until 1865; and it has been found by the Committee on Ordinances, expedient to change the construction of it to some extent, rather increasing its scope and value. It comprises

1.—Rules and Regulations of the different departments. Under this head will be found fourteen articles, all corrected up to the date of publication. Like the Ordinances, they are subject to occasional alteration, but it is believed that this collection of the details of the administration of the outside branches of the City Government will be found permanently useful.

2.—Special Acts, incorporating companies to hold large amounts of real estate within the City limits, and to maintain rights which affect the public health and convenience.

3.—Agreements, chiefly between the City of Boston and other corporations and parties, in respect to the new lands of the Back Bay, the legislation and litigation concerning which will doubtless be, for many years, most vital to the welfare of the corporation and the community.

4.—Trusts: being a memorandum of the wills investing the City of Boston with valuable charitable and educational trust funds.

5.—Decisions of the Supreme Court on Municipal Law: very carefully prepared by a competent legal hand; being an epitome of all the decisions on questions affecting Municipal rights, duties, and obligations made by the Supreme Court.

6.—An alphabetical index, topically arranged, of all the printed City Documents.

It seems to be unnecessary to compile a list of the "Special laws for the benefit of the City," for the reason that the "Laws and Ordinances" contain all those which are of substantial importance, and may easily be referred to there.

It is believed that the contents include all the matters relating to the Municipal affairs which are not readily accessible elsewhere; but the volume is without precedent, and omissions and imperfections will doubtless be observed. These can be remedied in the next edition, to be published whenever the Ordinances are again revised.

H. T. R.

CONTENTS.

RULES AND REGULATIONS.

PAGE.

Fireworks 1

Gunpowder 2

City Hospital 6

Public Institutions 17

House of Industry 19

House of Reformation 25

House of Correction 29

Lunatic Hospital 38

Public Library 47

Market 57

Overseers of the Poor 65

Police 68

School-houses 151

Street Watering 153

Telegraphic Fire Alarm 154

Water Board 156

SPECIAL ACTS.

Boston Mill Corporation 162

Boston and Roxbury Mill Corporation 166

Boston Water Power Company 176

Boston Gas Light Company 179

Boston Wharf Company 182

Eastern Avenue Corporation 189

South Bay Company 195

PAGE.
South Cove Corporation.................................... 196
Tremont Improvement Company........................... 203
Mass. Institute of Technology............................ 205

AGREEMENTS.
City of Boston, Edward Tuckerman and others and the Boston and Roxbury Mill Corporation 209
City of Boston and Boston and Roxbury Mill Corporation........ 214
Ephraim Marsh and others and the Boston and Roxbury Mill Corporation 218
Boston and Roxbury Mill Corporation and Boston Water Power Company 222
Same.. 229
Ephraim Marsh, Francis C. Lowell, and the Boston Water Power Company 231
The Commonwealth and the Boston Water Power Company...... 234
The Commonwealth and the Boston and Roxbury Mill Corporation 245
The Commonwealth and the Boston Water Power Company 250
Same.. 254
The Commonwealth, the Boston Water Power Company, and the City of Boston, (The "Tripartite Indenture.").............. 258
The Commonwealth and the Boston Water Power Company..... 271
The Commonwealth and the Boston and Roxbury Mill Corporation, Dec. 30, 1856.................................... 275
The City of Roxbury and the Boston Water Power Company.... 281
The City of Boston and J. E. and N. Brown................... 284
The Commonwealth, the Boston Water Power Company, and the City of Boston, ("New Tripartite Agreement.")............ 288
City of Boston and the Boston and Worcester R. R. Corporation.. 293
Jacob Ulman and others and the Boston Water Power Company..
The City of Boston and the Boston Water Power Company...... 303
Commonwealth of Massachusetts and the City of Boston........ 306
The Boston Water Power Company and the City of Boston 307

TRUSTS.
Franklin Fund, for the encouragement of Young Mechanics..... 311
Franklin School Medal Fund 312
Lawrence High School Fund.................................. 312
Lawrence Latin School Fund.................................. 312

CONTENTS.

PAGE.
Latin School Prize Fund.. 313
Webb's Franklin School Fund.................................. 313
Smith Fund.. 313
Poor Widows' Fund... 314
Library Fund.. 314
Phillips' Street Fund... 317
City Hospital Funds... 317
Funds for the Poor.. 318
ORIGIN OF THE HOUSE OF INDUSTRY................................ 323
HISTORICAL REFERENCES
To the Legislation and Municipal Action respecting the Back Bay and adjacent territory.. 331

APPENDIX.

A DIGEST OF DECISIONS of Municipal interest of Supreme Judicial Court.
AN INDEX to the City Documents.

RULES AND REGULATIONS.

FIREWORKS.

RULES AND REGULATIONS.
1. Charged pieces not to be exposed.
2. Explosive pieces to be kept in tight covered cases.
3. Licenses to be recorded.
4. Application for license to be made at the Chief Engineer's Office.

RULES AND REGULATIONS.[1]

SECTION 1. Any person or persons licensed to sell Fireworks by wholesale or retail, shall not be allowed to keep any charged pieces of Fireworks exposed in any windows. Charged pieces not to be exposed.

SECT. 2. All Rockets, Bombs, Shells, Mines, or other explosive pieces, shall be kept in tight covered cases; said cases shall always be kept closed except when putting in or taking out Fireworks, which shall be done as expeditiously as is consistent with proper care. Explosive pieces to be kept in tight covered cases.

SECT. 3. The Board of Engineers shall keep a record of all Licenses granted and renewals thereof, and shall designate how, and in what manner Fireworks shall be kept, and no alteration shall be made unless by consent of the Board. Any change made by removal shall be indorsed on the License, and no Record of Licenses.

[1] Rules and regulations made and established April 29, 1853, by the Board of Engineers of the City of Boston, relative to the sale, storage, and safe-keeping of Fireworks in said city, in conformity with a law of this Commonwealth, made and passed on the 14th day of April, A. D. 1853. See Laws and Ordinances, p. 209.

License shall be valid for any other place of business, unless so indorsed by the Chief Engineer or Secretary of the Board.

Application for licenses.

SECT. 4. Licenses will be granted on application to the office of the Chief Engineer of the Fire Department.

GUNPOWDER.

RULES AND REGULATIONS.

1. Vessels laden with gunpowder not to lie at any wharf except as provided.
2. Gunpowder may be loaded at certain wharves; but not elsewhere without permission.
3. Boats conveying gunpowder to be approved.
4. Vessels receiving powder to leave the wharf within three hours.
5. Powder carriages to be approved and marked, and the powder protected.
6. Transportation of powder through the city prevents the use of boats.
7. Licenses.
8. Retailers; their stock; how and where kept.
9. Whosesale dealers; their stock; how and where kept.
10. Stock at "wholesale or retail."
11. Licensed dealers to expose a sign.
12. Powder not to be kept except as here provided.
13. Magazines at Spectacle Island.
14. Record of licenses.
15. Repeal of inconsistent rules.

RULES AND REGULATIONS.[1]

Vessels laden with gunpowder not to lie at any wharf.

SECTION 1. No ship or other vessel, on board of which gunpowder shall be laden, shall lie at any wharf in the City of Boston, nor within two hundred yards of any wharf or landing-place, except as hereinafter provided.

Gunpowder may be loaded at certain wharves.

SECT. 2. Gunpowder may be landed at Tileston's Wharf, Long Wharf, and Commercial Wharf; and no gunpowder shall be landed at any other wharf, quay or place, in said city, without a written permit from one or more engineers; but in no case shall powder be allowed to remain on the above-named wharves for a longer time than is necessary for its removal.

---

[1] Rules and regulations made and established April 7, 1837, by the Board of Engineers of the City of Boston, relative to the sale, storage, safe-keeping, and transportation of gunpowder, in said city. See Laws and Ordinances, pp. 216, 230–38.

SECT. 3. All boats employed in the conveyance of gunpowder, shall be examined and approved by the Chief Engineer, and shall have displayed at the stern or bow, a red flag, so long as there is any gunpowder on board. And all powder so conveyed, shall be covered over with canvas or other suitable covering.

Boats conveying gunpowder to be approved.

SECT. 4. Gunpowder in any quantity (not exceeding six quarter casks) may be put on board of any vessel lying at any wharf in the City of Boston, from any approved powder boat, according to the foregoing section, provided that no vessel shall remain at the wharf more than three hours, nor shall such vessel be allowed to ground or remain after sunset, with powder on board. And it shall be the duty of all dealers to deliver the captain a copy of this section, at their own expense, at the time the powder is shipped.

Vessels receiving powder to leave the wharf within three hours.

SECT. 5. No gunpowder shall be conveyed through the city in any other than a carriage closely covered with leather or canvas, and without any iron or steel on any part thereof, such carriage first having been approved by the Chief Engineer, and marked on each side, in capitals, with the words "Approved Powder Carriage," excepting, however, that a quantity not exceeding in the whole four quarter casks, of twenty-five pounds each, may be transported through, or removed in this city, and shall be in tight casks, each of which shall be put into a strong leather bag, closely tied, on which bag shall be legibly marked the word "Gunpowder," and shall so remain in said bags, whilst within the bounds of the city. And in no case shall powder so carried, be suffered to remain on board any vehicle for a longer time than is necessary for its removal.

Powder carriages to be approved and marked, and the powder protected.

SECT. 6. Gunpowder in any quantity may be conveyed through the city, for shipment, when ice renders it impossible to put it on board from boats, provided a special permit is obtained from one or more Engineers, one of whom shall personally superintend the conveyance and shipment of the same; and provided also, that the vehicle used to convey the same, shall

Transportation of powder through the city when ice prevents the use of boats.

be lined at the bottom and sides, with leather, so as to prevent the escape of any particle of powder, and shall be entirely covered with canvas, to prevent the possibility of any fire or sparks communicating with the same; and provided also, that no vessel shall remain at the wharf more than three hours, nor shall such vessel be allowed to ground or remain after sunset, with powder on board.

Licenses.

SECT. 7. Licenses will be granted on application to the Chief Engineer, and all persons so licensed shall be required to sign these rules and regulations kept in a book for that purpose.

Retailers; their stock; how and where kept.

SECT. 8. Any person or firm, who may be licensed to sell gunpowder by retail, shall be allowed to have on hand thirty pounds at any one time, and no more, which shall always be kept in tin or copper canisters, which shall always be kept in a copper, tin, or zinc chest approved by the Chief Engineer, which shall always be kept at the right side and within eight feet of the door, over which the sign provided in article 11th is placed.

Wholesalers; their stock; how and where kept.

SECT. 9. Any person or firm who may be licensed to sell gunpowder by wholesale, shall be allowed to have on hand a quantity not exceeding at any one time, four quarter casks, of twenty-five pounds each, which shall be deposited in a copper chest, with two handles, and a tight cover furnished with hinges, and secured with a padlock, all of copper, which shall be always kept locked, except when opened to put in or take out powder, which shall always be done in as little time as shall be consistent with proper care, and placed on the lower floor, at the right side of and within six feet of the principal door or entrance from the street, over which the sign provided in Article 11th is placed, and such chest shall not be kept in any other part of the building, unless by permission, which shall be expressed in such license. Each cask so deposited shall be kept in a leather bag, closely tied, and under no circumstances shall a cask of powder be allowed to be opened by any person or firm holding such license.

Stock at wholesale or retail, &c.

SECT. 10. Any person or firm, who shall be licensed to sell

by "wholesale or retail," shall be allowed to keep on hand three quarter casks of gunpowder, at any one time, of twenty-five pounds each, and no more, which shall always be deposited and kept as provided in section 9; provided, however, that such person or firm may be allowed to keep on hand, in addition to the above, such quantity as is required for retailing, which shall not exceed, at any one time, twenty-five pounds, which shall be kept in tin or copper canisters, with a top or cover fastened thereto, which canisters shall always be kept in the copper chest, together with the above-named three quarter casks.

SECT. 11. Every person or firm, licensed to sell gunpowder, shall have and keep a signboard placed over the outside of the door or principal entrance from the street, of the building in which such powder is kept, on which shall be painted in capitals, the words "Licensed to keep and sell gunpowder."

Licensed dealers to expose a sign.

SECT. 12. No gunpowder shall be kept otherwise than as before provided for licensed dealers, at any place within the city, except in the magazines at Spectacle Island, and such other places as shall be from time to time designated, and which are hereby established as places of deposit for gunpowder.

Powder not to be kept, except as here provided.

SECT. 13. The Board of Engineers shall have the superintendence of the said magazines, whose duty it shall be, annually, to appoint a suitable person or persons to receive such quantity of powder as may from time to time be considered necessary by the Board of Engineers, and to deliver the same to the order of the owners thereof, who shall pay to such person or persons such fees for receiving, storing, and delivering the same as the Engineers shall direct: and such person or persons, so appointed, shall hold their office during the year, and until others are appointed, subject always to be removed at the pleasure of the Board.

Magazines at Spectacle Island.

SECT. 14. The Chief Engineer shall keep a record of all licenses granted, and renewals thereof, and of the place designated for keeping and selling gunpowder, which place shall not be altered or changed unless by consent of this Board,

Record of Licenses.

which shall be expressed in their license; and all persons who may receive a license, shall sign their names, respectively, to these rules and regulations, as evidence of their assent to, and obligation faithfully to comply with, and perform the same.

SECT. 15. All rules and regulations heretofore made and adopted, inconsistent with the foregoing, are hereby repealed.

CITY HOSPITAL.

GENERAL RULES.

The Trustees to have charge of the Hospital; to hold stated meetings and keep records; to appoint Physicians, Surgeons, and other officers; may remove officers at pleasure; to appoint subordinate officers; to make an Annual Report; to keep an account of Donations, and manage them; may establish minor rules; to designate the hospital wards.

The Superintendent; his powers; to report delinquencies; to make purchases; to keep accounts; to make collections and take charge of patient's property; to keep an inventory of furniture; to provide the diet of patients; to examine purchases; to submit bills and pay-rolls monthly; to visit all departments daily; to ascertain the settlement of patients; to oversee autopsies; to keep full records of patients; to assign beds.

The Physicians and Surgeons; their term and order of service; to report patients for discharge; and make suggestions; to keep records of treatment; to procure substitutes in case, &c.; to make regular morning visits; to have consultation before capital operations.

The Students and others may be admitted to the amphitheatre.

The Resident Graduates to be nominated by the board of physicians and surgeons; two of them to be constantly present; their duties; their number may be increased; they shall not exchange departments without consent; their general duties; private practice prohibited; to examine claims for admission when requested; to attend patients on admission.

The Librarian to have the care of books, &c.

The Apothecary to purchase and prepare medicines, &c.

A dispensary may be established for out-door patients.

The Matron; her duties.

The Nurses; their duties

The Gate-keeper; his duties.

Applications for admission to be made at Hospital. Parties unable to apply in person to be visited. Trustees or physicians may give permits in case of emergency. Permits to be approved by visiting committee; powers of the visiting committee.

Certificates of discharge and decease.

Paying patients.
Disbursements, monthly bills, &c.

HOUSE RULES.

Hours of patients.
Free patients to give assistance.
Passes required for leaving the grounds or the wards.
Purchases by patients; officers not to receive fees.
Indecorum prohibited.
Incurable, infectious, and contagious cases not to be admitted.
Acute syphilitic diseases and *mania-a-potu* not to be treated without compensation.
Patients may choose their religious attendants.
Rules to be obeyed.
Visitors not allowed except by permission.
Friends may visit patients once a week; but must not eat or sleep in the Hospital, nor give articles to patients without permission.
Nurses to be on duty each morning to choose clothing for patients in the wards.
All employés to be in place during their hours of duty.
Smoking prohibited.
Meals of employés.
Students may be admitted by the Trustees; subject to revocation of privilege.
Forms of application, admission, &c.

GENERAL RULES.[1]

The Board of Trustees, under the Statutes, Ordinances, and these Rules and Regulations, shall have the charge, management, and custody of the Hospital, as well as the control and direction of its employés and inmates. *Powers of Trustees.*

A meeting of the Board shall be held at least once in each month at the Hospital, and records of their proceedings shall be kept, which shall always be open to the inspection of the City Council. *Meetings and records.*

Annually, as soon after the organization of the Board as shall be convenient, there shall be chosen by ballot three consulting physicians, three consulting surgeons, six visiting physicians, six visiting surgeons, one ophthalmic surgeon, four resident graduates, an apothecary, librarian, matron, and such other officers as they may think necessary, whose term of service shall expire in one year from the first Monday of the following April, or as soon after as their successors shall be chosen. A Superintendent shall be elected annually in the month of February, and whenever a vacancy may occur. *Physicians and other officers.*

---

[1] Rules and Regulations of the Hospital, approved by the City Council, May 20, 1864. See Laws and Ordinances, p. 324; Ordinances of 1864, p. 24.

Removal of officers.

They may remove any officer so chosen at their pleasure; and shall fill vacancies, from whatever cause, for the residue of the term.

Subordinate officers.

They shall appoint and discharge all subordinate officers, attendants, and domestics, and shall fix the compensation of all persons employed, excepting that of the Superintendent.

Annual report.

Annually in the month of January, the Board shall make a Report of their proceedings to the City Council, and shall furnish statistics of the Hospital, embodying in such blanks as may be adopted, details concerning the operations of the year. They shall also furnish a statement of the various items of expense, with estimates of the amount of appropriations necessary for the coming year.

Donations.

The Board of Trustees shall keep a book containing an account of all donations and bequests to the Hospital, and shall manage such property in accordance with Sections 1, 2, and 3 of the City Ordinance relating to that object.

Minor rules.

The Trustees shall be authorized to establish from time to time such minor rules for the government of persons on the premises, for the regulation of the internal police of the wards, and other parts of the Hospital, the appointment of hours, and the arrangement of diet tables, as may to them seem expedient.

Designation of wards.

They shall designate each ward in the Hospital by a letter, or by the name of some benefactor, and shall number the beds in order.

The *Superintendent*; his power.

The Superintendent, under the direction of the Board of Trustees, shall have the general control of all departments of the Hospital; of all subordinate officers, attendants, and domestics; of the patients, and the charge of the grounds, buildings, and appurtenances.

Delinquencies of employés.

He shall see that there is no waste or carelessness in any department, and shall report to the Trustees omissions of duty, or disorderly conduct on the part of employés.

Purchases.

He shall, under the direction of the Trustees, purchase the provisions, stores, and fuel, shall have the charge thereof, and shall be responsible for their proper and economical use. He shall make monthly returns of the consumption of fuel and gas.

He shall keep regular accounts of all moneys received and disbursed by him, on behalf of the Hospital, in books provided by the Trustees, with a record of all contracts, and shall submit the same to the Board at their monthly meetings. Accounts.

He shall, when required, collect all sums due to the Hospital, and shall take charge of money or other property not in use belonging to patients, and keep a record of the same. Collections; property of patients.

He shall keep an inventory of all furniture, and other property belonging to the Hospital, and shall make a quarterly report of articles injured, destroyed, or missing. Furniture.

He shall provide the diet of patients, as may be directed by the physicians and surgeons, and for the persons employed shall furnish such provisions as the Trustees may direct. Diet of patients.

He shall examine all articles purchased as to their quality, quantity, and price. Examination of purchases.

He shall make no purchase exceeding one hundred dollars, or of an unusual nature, without the sanction of the Trustees or of the Committee on supplies. Purchases over $100.00.

All bills, together with the pay-rolls, shall be submitted to the Board on the third Tuesday of each month. Monthly bills and pay-rolls.

He shall daily visit and inspect the wards, kitchen, laundry, engine room, and all other departments of the Institution. Daily visit to all departments.

It shall be his duty to ascertain the settlement or residence of patients, and when belonging to other places than Boston, to correspond with the authorities of such places, and make the necessary arrangements for the reimbursement of expenses incurred. He shall have charge of the correspondence of patients, and shall communicate to their friends information of their condition or decease. He shall see that autopsies are decently made, but shall allow no such autopsy, if objected to by the immediate relatives of the deceased. He shall cause the bodies of the deceased to be delivered to their friends, or, if not claimed by them, to the proper authorities. Settlement of patients, &c. Autopsies.

He shall keep for the inspection of the Trustees a record of the names of all patients, with their age, residence, employment, date of admission, discharge, elopement, or death, and result of treatment. Records of patients.

Assignment of beds.

He shall assign a bed to each patient on admission, subject to the approval of the physician or surgeon in attendance.

The *Physicians* and *Surgeons*; their term and order of service.

As soon after their election as possible, the physicians and surgeons shall be notified by the Trustees to meet for the purpose of arranging their term and order of service, which arrangement shall be made subject to the approval of the Trustees.

Reports of patients for discharge; suggestions.

They shall weekly, or oftener, report the names of such patients as they think should be discharged, and shall make any suggestions or remarks which may tend to promote the interests of the Hospital or its inmates.

Record of treatment.

They shall keep or shall cause to be kept by the resident graduates in permanent volumes, in such form as may be provided by the Trustees, full records of the cases and treatment of all patients in both medical and surgical departments. No volume of such records shall be taken from the premises, and no extracts shall be made from them by persons not connected with the Hospital.

Substitutes in case of absence.

Regular morning visits.

If any physician or surgeon shall be prevented from attending in his term, he shall procure one of the other physicians or surgeons to attend in his stead. The regular morning visit to patients shall be made between the hours of eight and eleven.

Capital operations.

Except in case of emergency, no capital or important operation shall be performed without a previous consultation, of which all the surgeons shall have due notice.

Admission of *Students*.

Students and other persons shall be admitted to the wards and the amphitheatre of the Hospital, in such numbers and with such restrictions as the Trustees may from time to time deem expedient.

Choice of four *Resident Graduates*.

The Resident Graduates shall be chosen on the nomination of the Board of Visiting Physicians and Surgeons, whose duty it shall be to report such nomination to the Trustees on or before the first day of April in each year. The names thus reported shall be those of the four persons who, in the opinion of the said Board, after a rigid examination in the various branches of medicine and surgery, shall seem most competent to fulfil the duties required of them.

Two of the Resident Graduates shall reside constantly at the Hospital, and shall not absent themselves without the consent of the Superintendent, and in no case shall both be absent from their posts at the same time. The year shall be divided among them as shall be agreed upon by themselves, subject to the approval of the Trustees.

Two to reside at hospital.

Their duties shall be assigned them by the visiting physicians and surgeons, who shall, in the case of absence of either of them by sickness or other causes, appoint a temporary substitute, subject to the approval of the Visiting Committee.

Assignments of duties; substitutes.

If more than four Resident Graduates be required, the Trustees may appoint the same and permit them to reside on the premises or elsewhere.

Increase of the number.

They shall in no case make an exchange of their respective departments without the consent of the visiting physician or surgeon under whom they serve, and the sanction of the Visiting Committee.

Exchange of departments.

They shall accompany their superiors in their daily visits, shall make the necessary record of treatment and diet of patients, and shall see that their directions are complied with. They shall, when requested by the physician or surgeon, make autopsies and other pathological examinations; and the Resident Graduate in the Surgical Department shall take charge of the instruments and apparatus, none of which shall be taken from the Hospital without the consent of the Superintendent.

General duties.

The Resident Graduates shall not engage in private practice during their term of service.

Private practice prohibited.

They shall, when requested by the Superintendent or Visiting Committee, investigate the claims of applicants for admission, whether made at the Hospital or from the city.

To examine claims for admission, when requested.

They shall attend to patients on their admission, and give the necessary directions for their comfort, before they are seen by their regular medical attendant, and shall make a daily evening visit to each patient.

To attend patients on admission.

The Librarian shall have the charge of all books belonging to the Hospital, and of the casts, models, anatomical prepara-

The *Librarian* to have care of books, models, &c.

tions, and prints, under such regulations as may be prescribed by the Trustees.

The *Apothecary* to purchase and prepare medicines, &c.

The Apothecary shall reside on the premises, and shall not absent himself except at such hours as may be authorized by the Superintendent. He shall purchase all medicines under the direction of the Committee on the Medical Department, and shall keep exact accounts of quantities, qualities, and prices. He shall compound medicines, prepare prescriptions, perform chemical analyses, and such other duties as may be prescribed by the Trustees or the Superintendent.

Dispensary for out-door patients.

The Trustees may establish a dispensary department for out-door patients who are unable to pay fees for medical attendance at their houses, with such restrictions and under such regulations as they may from time to time deem expedient.

The *Matrons*; their duties.

The Matron shall have the general direction of all female nurses and servants, see that they perform their several duties, and report all instances of inattention and neglect of duty. She shall be responsible for the neatness and order of every part of the establishment; shall superintend the kitchen and laundry, and cause to be kept an accurate account of bedding, clothing, table, and other furniture. She shall perform such other duties as may be required.

The *Nurses*; their duties.

The Chief Nurse of each ward, under the direction of the Matron, shall have charge of the same with the convalescents room attached thereto. She shall keep a ward book, containing a list of patients, and an inventory of furniture, bedding, and other articles, and on each Tuesday shall make a return to the Matron of all occupants of the ward during the week. She shall keep, in a suitable book, a list of all parcels or property belonging to patients in her ward not in use, which property shall be deposited in a suitable room, under the charge of the Superintendent. She shall also keep a list of articles sent to the laundry, and if not returned in good condition report the same to the Matron. She shall perform such other duties as may be required.

The *Gatekeeper*; his duties.

The Gatekeeper shall allow no one to enter or leave the premises unless duly authorized.

He shall examine all permits, and, when so instructed, record the names of persons passing the gate. He shall keep in good order the grounds, walks, and borders surrounding the Hospital, shall take care of horses and vehicles in the sheds, and shall perform such other duties as may be required of him.

Applications for admission of patients shall be made at the Hospital on each day of the week, at such hours as the Trustees may appoint. Applications for admission.

Whenever able, the patient should apply in person. When not able to appear in person, application may be made by a friend, and the patient shall be visited by one of the Resident Graduates, or by some physician designated by the Trustees. Patients unable to appear in person, to be visited.

Any Trustee or either of the physicians or surgeons in attendance may, in case of emergency, send a patient in the first instance to the Hospital by written permit, and the Visiting Committee shall, on the certificate of one of the medical officers designated for the purpose, decide as soon as may be afterwards whether such patient shall remain. Permits in case of emergency.

Persons accidentally wounded or otherwise disabled or injured, shall be received at all hours, subject to such rules as the Trustees may from time to time enact. Admission of persons accidentally injured.

Permits for admission shall be subject to the approval of the Visiting Committee for the time being, or, in their absence, to that of the Superintendent. Approval of permits.

The Visiting Committee, however, shall have the power at any time to require the Superintendent to report to them the names of applicants before admitting them, and may dismiss any patient whom they think improperly admitted. Powers of visiting committee.

Patients discharged on the recommendation of the physicians or surgeons, shall be provided with a certificate stating their condition at the time of discharge, whether cured, relieved, or not relieved, which certificate shall be signed by the Superintendent. Certificates of discharge and decease.

In case of the decease of any patient, the Superintendent shall sign a certificate to that effect, and shall furnish the City Registrar with a copy of the same. He shall also state the time and cause of death, the disposition made of body, whether delivered to friends or buried from the Hospital. In the last case he shall mention the place of interment.

Paying patients.

Patients may be admitted by the Trustees to the privileges of the Hospital, at such rates of board as they may from time to time determine; such board being secured by their friends, or by the authorities of the place to which they belong.

In all cases where in the opinion of the Trustees the circumstances of the patient will warrant it, the whole or a part of the board shall be paid. If separate apartments or articles not usually furnished at the Hospital are provided, such payment shall be made therefor as the Trustees shall deem reasonable.

Disbursements.

On or before the twentieth day of each month, the Superintendent shall submit to the Trustees the order and bill book, and all bills approved by any of the committees, with a schedule of the same, and also the pay-roll for salaries and wages, containing the names of the persons entitled to payment, with the amounts due to them respectively; and, if approved by the Board, said schedule shall be signed by the President, and with the pay-roll and bills shall be sent, on or before the twentieth day of each month, to the Auditor of Accounts for payment by the Treasurer.

House Rules.

Hours of patients.

Patients must be in their proper places in the wards during the visit of the physicians and surgeons, and always by 9, P. M. unless specially exempted by the Superintendent.

Free patients to give assistance.

Those free patients who are able, are expected to assist in nursing, and in such other services as may be reasonably required of them.

Pass required for leaving the premises.

Patients shall not leave the Hospital Grounds without a pass from the Superintendent, nor their respective wards without the consent of the nurse in attendance.

Purchases by patients: fees to officers.

No patient shall purchase, or cause any member of the household to purchase for him, any article of food whatsoever, nor any other article, without the consent of the Superintendent. Nor shall any officer or servant of the Hospital receive a gift or fee from a patient.

Profane or obscene language, loud talking, and incivility, are prohibited. Decorum.

No person shall be admitted to the Hospital whose case is judged to be incurable, unless there be urgent symptoms which in the opinion of the physician or surgeon are capable of being relieved. Nor shall any one be admitted having an infectious or contagious disease. Incurable, infectious, and contagious cases.

No patient having acute syphilitic disease, or *mania-a-potu*, shall be admitted as a charity patient, or at a lower rate than twenty-five dollars a week for the former, and fifteen dollars for the latter. Acute syphilitic disease, and mania-a-potu.

Patients may be visited by clergymen of their own selection, and where there is a wish for the performance of any particular religious rite, it shall be indulged when practicable. Religious attendants.

It is expected that patients will implicitly obey the rules of the Hospital. Complaints, for whatever cause, may be made to the Superintendent or Visiting Committee, and when reasonable shall be by them reported to the Trustees. Obedience to rules; complaints.

No person shall visit any part of the premises, except on business, or at such times as may be fixed for the reception of visitors, without the permission of the Superintendent, or of some one of the Trustees. Visitors require permits.

On each day of the week, Sundays excepted, from two to four o'clock P. M. friends may be permitted to visit patients, though no patient shall receive more than one visitor at the same time. In all cases, however, the trustees or Superintendent may exercise discretionary powers as to excluding or admitting visitors. Friends may visit patients, but must not eat or sleep in the hospital; nor give articles to patients, without permission.

No visitor will be permitted to take any meal in the Hospital, or pass the night therein, without permission from the Superintendent.

No visitor shall be allowed to give any article of food or drink to a patient, unless by permission of the nurse; and any article sent to the patients shall be left with the Superintendent.

Nurses are required to be in their several wards each morning ready for duty, before the night watchers leave the same. Hours of nurses.

Nurses are to decide what clothing or other articles patients are to retain in the ward. Clothing of patients.

General hours. All employés must be in their respective places during their hours of duty. The doors and gates of the Hospital will be closed at $9\frac{3}{4}$ P. M. at which time all are expected to be quiet, and those not on duty, in their own rooms.

Smoking prohibited. The smoking of tobacco is prohibited within the Hospital, also the use of wine and intoxicating liquors, unless prescribed by a physician.

Meals. The Matron, Resident Graduates, and Apothecary shall take their meals with the Superintendent; all other employés in the dining-room provided for them.

Admission of students. The Trustees may grant any practitioner or student of medicine of one year's standing, on the joint recommendation of the Physician and Surgeon in attendance, a ticket of admission to follow the practice of the Hospital for not more than one year. Before receiving this ticket, the applicant shall sign an obligation to obey in all respects the By-Laws and Regulations of the Hospital. The privilege thus granted may be modified or revoked.

No student shall be entitled to admission except at the regular hours for visiting, operation, or lecture.

Every student when requested shall show his ticket to the porter at the gate, and shall conduct himself with decorum and propriety. It shall be the duty of the Superintendent to report any infringement of the rules to the Visiting Committee.

Forms of application, admission, &c. The form of application for admission shall be as follows.

Boston City Hospital.

The undersigned, inhabitant of   for the last
and now residing at   Born in   being
years of age, by employment a   married and ill of
requests to be admitted to the City Hospital.

Boston,   , 186

Certificate of Admitting Physician.

Having examined the condition of the said applicant, I find it a suitable case for admission to the City Hospital.

——— ———, M. D.

TO BE SIGNED BY SUPERINTENDENT.

Admit to the Hospital.
Said is assigned to ward bed
Extra payment, $ Transferred to ward bed
Said is discharged, 186
—— ——, *Superintendent.*

PUBLIC INSTITUTIONS.

RULES AND REGULATIONS FOR THE SEVERAL INSTITUTIONS.

Officers to be appointed annually; subject to removal; their compensation.

House of Industry.

Officers of House of Industry.
Superintendent to nominate subordinate officers; to make rules for them; to enforce the orders of the Board; to suspend officers for cause; to make requisitions and give receipts; to examine persons admitted, attend to their cleanliness, and care for the infirm and children; to enforce discipline; to punish infraction of rules; to register inmates and make daily and weekly detailed reports.
Assistant Superintendent to aid the Superintendent, and act in his absence.
Resident Physician to have charge of dispensary; visit the sick daily; make medical reports; supervise the nurses, and to regulate the diet of the sick; may take students: to notify the Board before performing surgical operations.
Clerk to keep the register and books; to have charge of the stores.
Receiving officer to receive the males; instruct them as to rules; see to their clothing, &c.; to have charge of the male dining halls.
Chaplain.
Engineer.
Teacher.
Female Supervisor.
Chief Matron.
First Assistant Matron.
Second Assistant Matron.
Third Assistant Matron.

House of Reformation.

Officers of the House of Reformation.
Superintendent to have general charge; to enforce the rules; may suspend delinquent officers; to make requisitions, see to cleanliness, &c.; to keep records of inmates; to make daily reports and annual report; may delegate his powers.
Superintendent of Schools.
Teachers.
Physician.
Chaplain.
Female Supervisor.
Matrons.

General Rules for the Houses of Industry and Reformation.

Absence of employés; corporal punishment; clothing for discharged persons; permits to visit; rules for visitors; contractors and agents; watchmen.

House of Correction.

Officers.

Master to control the institution; to enforce the regulations; to see that prisoners are properly cleansed, located, &c.; to make rules and appoint subordinates; to punish infraction of rules; to require daily medical visits to prisoners in "solitary;" to see that the food and clothing are good and plentiful; to cause accounts to be kept; to make requisitions and certify bills; to keep a register of inmates in detail; to make daily and weekly reports, and annual report.

Deputy Master to have charge in absence of Master; to receive the convicts, and enforce obedience; not to inflict excessive punishments; to make daily report of punishments.

Receiving officer; his duties.

Clerk.

Physician.

Chaplain.

General Instructions for the officers and matrons; deportment; discipline; corporal punishment, &c.

General Regulations; disposition of convicts; their labor: food; clothing; stimulants; perquisites; visitors; punishments, &c.; contractors; visitors.

Lunatic Hospital.

Officers.

Superintendent to appoint subordinates; to visit patients daily; see to their food, cleanliness, warmth, &c.; to make requisitions and receipts; to keep a register of patients; to make daily reports and an annual report; to notify the Board of patients ready for discharge, and of surgical operations to be performed.

Assistant Superintendent to act in the absence of Superintendent.

Chaplain.

Male Supervisor.

Female Supervisor.

Housekeeper.

Seamstress.

Laundress.

General Attendant.

Watchmen.

Duties of attendants, and general remarks.

General rules; permits; suspension of rules.

RULES AND REGULATIONS.[1]

Officers to be appointed annually. Subject to removal; their compensation.

The officers for the Institutions hereafter named shall be chosen or appointed annually, and whenever vacancies may occur, by the Board, unless otherwise provided by statute, ordinance, or these Rules, and shall hold their offices subject to removal at any time by vote of the Board, and shall receive such compensation as may from time to time be determined upon.

---

[1] Rules and Regulations for the several institutions of the City of Boston, adopted February 22, 1861; amended August 16, 1864. See Laws and Ordinances, page 369; also chap. 241, statutes of 1865.

HOUSE OF INDUSTRY.[1]

The officers of the House of Industry shall be a Superintendent, Assistant Superintendent, Resident Physician, Clerk, Receiving Officer, Chaplain, Engineer, Teacher, Female Supervisor, Matron, Assistant Matrons, and such other subordinates and employés as may be required. Officers of House of Industry.

The Superintendent of the House of Industry, who may also be the Superintendent of the House of Reformation, if so elected, shall be chosen annually in the months of April or May, and whenever a vacancy may occur, and shall reside at the Island, in apartments assigned for his use. He shall, subject to the orders of the Board, have charge of the Institution in all its departments, and of all officers and employés, except as hereafter provided. He shall nominate the subordinate officers and employés, unless otherwise determined, subject to the approval of the Board. *Superintendent* of House of Industry, to nominate subordinate officers.

He shall have a code of rules not inconsistent with these Rules, the ordinances of the city, or the statutes of the Commonwealth, for the government of the subordinate officers and inmates, to be approved by the Board. To make rules for subordinates.

It shall be his duty to see that all regulations and orders of the Board are strictly enforced, and that all the officers and employés are diligent in the discharge of their duties. To enforce the orders of the Board.

In case of neglect of duty, or disobedience of orders, by any subordinate, or for any proper cause, the Superintendent shall have authority at once to suspend such officer from duty, and shall immediately make special report of the same to the Board, with a statement of the cause. He shall make requisitions for all articles needed, and receipt at once for all articles received, according to forms prescribed by the Board, and shall certify bills of articles received. To suspend officers for cause. To make requisitions and give receipts.

He shall examine all persons admitted to the Institution, noting on the permit, or mittimus, such information as it is important to preserve, and in all cases where there is a probability of a settlement in the State by any one of them. He shall report to the Board a full description of such inmate. He shall To examine persons admitted, attend to their cleanliness, and care for the infirm and children.

[1] See *post.* history of the House of Industry.

see that all inmates are properly cleansed and clothed upon their admission, and that thereafter they have a bath of the whole person at least once a week, and as much oftener as he may deem necessary. He shall be especially careful that the infirm and children are treated with considerate care and kindness by those placed over them.

To enforce discipline; to punish infraction of rules.

He shall enforce obedience on the part of the inmates, to the rules prescribed for them, and shall see that those able to perform labor are constantly employed. He shall have power to punish all wilful infractions of the rules, but shall communicate the facts in relation thereto on the next daily report.

To register inmates, and make daily and weekly detailed reports.

He shall keep a register of all inmates admitted and discharged, and make daily and weekly reports, according to forms prescribed by the Board, giving the names of all persons admitted or discharged, and when sentenced, the offence for which committed, and the term of sentence, the births and deaths at the Institution, the punishments, and the causes thereof, and such other information as is worthy of remark.

Upon the daily report he shall give the Physician's report of the sick, and on the weekly report a statement of the employment of the inmates. He shall annually, on the first day of January, submit a Report of the condition of the Institution, giving the number of inmates therein, and in which department, with the number of admissions thereto and discharges therefrom, and the births and deaths therein during the year, and such information and suggestions as he may deem important, or the Board may direct.

Assistant Superintendent, to aid the Superintendent, and act in his absence.

The Assistant Superintendent shall be chosen by the Board annually in the months of April or May, and whenever a vacancy may occur, and shall reside at the Island in apartments assigned him, and shall, subject to the rules and orders of the Board, aid the Superintendent in the discharge of his duties, and in case of his absence, sickness, or disability, act as Superintendent. He shall attend the services in the Chapel on Sunday, and see that good order and decorum are maintained, and shall at all times perform such duties as may be required of him by the Superintendent. When directed by the Superintendent of the House of Reformation, he shall, under his direction, also act as Assistant Superintendent of that Institution.

Resident Physician to have charge of Dispensary.

The Resident Physician shall be elected by the Board annually, in the months of April or May, and whenever a vacancy may occur, and shall reside at the Island in apartments assigned him. He may be Superintendent of the House of Industry and House of Reformation, if so elected. He shall have charge of the Dispensary, and all surgical or other instruments belonging to the medical department, and shall keep an account thereof, and be responsible therefor, and shall make requisitions upon the Superintendent for all medicines or other articles needed for the department.

To visit the sick daily; make medical reports.

It shall be his duty to give careful attention to the sick in each Institution at the Island, visiting them once in each day, and as much oftener as shall be necessary, and shall keep a record of the names and diseases of each invalid, and of their treatment and the results, and daily to report to the Superintendent the name, disease, and condition of each patient in the hospital.

Supervise the nurses.

He shall see that the nurses faithfully discharge their duties, and shall report to the Superintendent any neglect or improper conduct on the part of any nurse or patient, and also give him notice of all convalescents able to perform labor, so that they may be employed.

Regulate the diet of the sick.

The sustenance and diet of those in the hospitals shall be regulated by him, through requisitions therefor upon the Superintendent, which must be in writing, and given daily.

May take students.

He shall be allowed, if thought necessary by the Board, to take students, who may have charge of the Dispensary, but shall not have access to other apartments than the hospitals, nor hold communication with any inmates, except in pursuance of his medical duty.

To notify the Board before performing surgical operations.

He shall not perform, or allow to be performed, any important surgical operation, without having previously notified the Board. Whenever he may deem it necessary or expedient to call a consultation of physicians, he shall give notice to the Board.

Clerk to keep the registers and books.

The Clerk shall be elected by the Board annually in the months of April or May, and whenever a vacancy may occur, and shall reside at the Island. It shall be his duty, under the direction of the Superintendent, to keep the registers and other books of the Institutions at the Island, and render such other services as may, from time to time, be required.

To have charge of stores.

He shall be the Storekeeper; and it shall be his duty, under the Superintendent, to have charge of all stores, and other movable property (except for the medical department), to the receipt and distribution of which he shall personally attend, making deliveries only on the written order of the Superintendent, which he shall preserve as vouchers for the disposal of the property.

He shall keep a record of all articles furnished to the Sewing Department, and of the number of garments returned from the same. In the absence of both Superintendent and Assistant he shall act as Superintendent.

Receiving officer to receive the males; instruct them as to rules; see to their clothing, &c.

The Receiving Officer shall, under the direction of the Superintendent, have special charge of the male receiving room, and attend to cleansing the male inmates on their reception to the Institution, and at other times. He shall read and explain the rules of the Institution for the government of inmates to all paupers and prisoners upon their admission. He shall have special charge of the clothing worn by the male inmates on their entrance, and after so much of it as is worth saving has been thoroughly cleansed, shall keep such record of the same as will insure its return to the inmate on his discharge.

He shall, at proper and stated times, have the clothing and bedclothes changed, and replaced with clean, and see that the articles which have been in use are conveyed to the laundry to be cleansed. He shall aid in the charge and oversight of the male dining halls, and generally perform such other duties as may be required of him.

To have charge of the male dining-halls.

Chaplain.

The Chaplain, who shall be Chaplain to the several Institutions at the Island, shall be elected by the Board, and shall hold religious services in the Chapel at least once on every Sabbath, and as much oftener as the Board may direct, at such hours as the Superintendent may appoint, and shall, at all times, visit such sick or dying inmates as may desire his ministration, or as the Superintendent may direct. He shall not be allowed to exchange or send any substitute without the consent of the Superintendent, or the Board.

The Engineer shall, subject to the order of the Superintendent, have charge of the engine-house, boilers, engine, and apparatus connected with the heating of the building and furnishing steam for cooking and bathing. He may examine the different parts of the building, heated by steam, to see if the temperature agrees with the directions of the Superintendent, but for no other purpose unless specially so directed, and must not hold communication with any of the inmates, except in pursuance of his duty. He must not be absent from the Island without first giving notice to the Superintendent, and obtaining his consent. Engineer.

The Teacher, and such assistants as may from time to time be necessary, shall be required to instruct the children in such elementary branches of an English education and otherwise, as the Board may direct, to advance them in the knowledge best fitted to enable them to make their own way in life; and also to impress upon them, by all proper means, the duties of temperance, frugality, and honesty, and the ruinous consequences of vice. It shall also be the duty of the Teacher to take charge of the children during service in the Chapel, and give them religious instruction in the schoolroom for at least one hour of each Sunday. Teacher.

The Female Supervisor shall, under the Superintendent, have the general oversight of the domestic management of the Institution, and the direction of the matrons and female employés, and shall report any case of negligence, inefficiency, or mismanagement to the Superintendent, whenever it is discovered. Female Supervisor.

The Chief Matron shall, subject to the orders of the Female Supervisor, have charge and oversight of the female inmates, and see that they are properly provided for and detailed to the several branches of labor, assigning to each such kind as, under the circumstances, she is best fitted to perform. She shall have Chief Matron.

special charge of the sewing-room and the direction of the women employed therein, and apply to the Superintendent for the material necessary for making up clothing and for other purposes connected with her department, and attend to the distribution of articles so made, or deposit them with the storekeeper. She shall, at proper and stated times, have the clothing and bedding of the females changed and replaced with clean apparel, and see that the portion which has been used is properly cleansed, and that all clothing and bedding that may require it, is thoroughly repaired, after having passed through the laundry, before being again distributed for use. She shall be vigilant over every part of the Institution assigned to her charge, especially in regard to cleanliness, and to the daily ablution and occasionally bathing of the whole person of each of the female inmates.

First Assistant Matron.

The First Assistant Matron shall, subject to the orders of the Female Supervisor, have direction of the operations of the kitchen in the preparation of food for the inmates, and see that strict economy is exercised, and that the meals are properly served at the appointed hours. She shall see that cleanliness and good order and decorum are at all times observed in her department, and generally perform such other duties as may be required.

Second Assistant Matron.

The Second Assistant Matron shall, subject to the orders of the Female Supervisor, have special charge of the female pauper's department, and shall see that proper order and cleanliness are maintained in the several wards, and that such inmates as are able are constantly employed at some proper work.

She shall have charge of the female pauper dining-hall, and superintend the distribution of food prepared for the several meals, and see that no waste is permitted, and shall generally perform such other duties as may be required.

Third Assistant Matron.

The Third Assistant Matron shall, subject to the order of the Female Supervisor, have special charge of the laundry and the operations therein. She shall have charge of the female receiving room, and attend to the cleansing of the women and children upon their admission, and during their stay.

She shall have special charge of the clothing worn upon their entrance, and after so much of it as is worth saving has been cleansed, shall keep such record of the same as will insure its return to the inmates upon discharge. She shall generally perform such other duties as may be required.

HOUSE OF REFORMATION.

Officers.

The Officers of the House of Reformation shall be a Superintendent, Chaplain, Physician, Superintendent of Schools, Teachers, Female Supervisor, Matrons, and such watchmen and employés as the Board may deem necessary.

Superintendent of the House of Reformation.

The Superintendent of the House of Reformation shall be chosen by the Board annually, in the months of April or May, and whenever a vacancy may occur, and may be the same person as the Superintendent of the House of Industry, who shall reside at the Island in apartments assigned him.

To have general charge.

He shall, subject to the orders of the Board, have the general charge of the several branches of the Institution, and of the inmates committed thereto, and the subordinate officers thereof, except as may hereafter be provided. He shall nominate the subordinate officers and employés, unless otherwise provided, subject to the approval of the Board.

Enforce the rules, and suspend delinquent officers.

He shall have a code of rules for conducting the Institution, to be approved by the Board, and it shall be his duty to see that all rules and regulations are strictly enforced, and that the employés are diligent in the discharge of their duties. In case of neglect of duty or disobedience of orders by any subordinate, or for any other proper cause, he shall have authority to suspend such officer from duty, and shall immediately report the same to the Board, with a statement of the cause.

To make requisitions; see to cleanliness, &c.

He shall make requisitions, through the Superintendent of the House of Industry, for all articles needed. He shall see that every inmate is thoroughly cleansed, and properly clothed, upon admission, and that they have a bath of the whole person once in each week, and as much oftener as he may deem necessary, and are taught generally to be cleanly in their persons, and attentive to their studies, and that such of the boys as are capable are employed at work on the farm or otherwise.

To keep record of inmates.

He shall keep a register, according to plans adopted by the Board, of the name, age, and birthplace of every inmate committed to the Institution, with the date of admission, the court from which sent, and the term of sentence. He shall also keep a record of the names, birthplace, residence, occupation, and habits of the parents of the inmates as far as they can be obtained, together with such other information connected with the history of the inmates, as may be important.

To make daily reports.

He shall make daily reports to the Board, according to forms prescribed, giving the admissions, discharges, deaths, punishments, with the cause thereof, and the Physician's report of the sick, together with information of all occurrences of the Institution worthy of remark.

Annual Report.

He shall annually, on the first of January, submit a Report, embracing the reports of the teachers, containing a statement of the number of inmates admitted and discharged during the year, with the number remaining, and the condition of the Institution at the close of the year, with such other information and suggestions as he may deem important, or the Board may require.

May delegate his powers.

He may delegate his powers to the Assistant Superintendent of the House of Industry, or other person, to act as Superintendent during his absence from the Institutions.

Superintendent of Schools.

The Superintendent of Schools, who may be the Chaplain, if so appointed, shall have supervision of the teachers of both the male and female departments. He shall have charge of the discipline of the children, with authority to punish minor offences, subject to the direction of the Superintendent. He shall do such teaching as the Superintendent may direct. In the month of December, annually, he shall report to the Superintendent the condition of the schools in the Institution, with such information and suggestions in relation thereto as he may deem important.

Teachers.

There shall be such male and female teachers as the Board may deem necessary, who shall reside at the Island, in apartments assigned them. It shall be their duty to see that the inmates under their charge are instructed in such manner as the Superintendent may direct, and that their physical, moral, and religious improvement is properly regarded. They shall attend to the enforcement of all rules and directions, and in every way aid in securing cleanliness of the premises, and the cleanliness, order, and obedience of the inmates.

Physician. The duties of Physician shall be performed by the Resident Physician, under the general powers conferred on him, who shall daily report the condition of the sick to the Superintendent.

Chaplain. The duties of Chaplain shall be performed by the Chaplain of the House of Industry.

Female Supervisor. The duties of Female Supervisor shall be performed by the Female Supervisor of the House of Industry, subject to the same duties, and with the same general powers, as conferred on her by the rules of the House of Industry.

Matrons. The Matrons, under the direction of the Female Supervisor, shall exercise general oversight of the cleansing of the apartments, particularly the sleeping rooms, and perform such other duties as may be required of them.

General Rules for the Houses of Industry and Reformation.[1]

Absence of employés. The whole time of the employés belongs to the Institution, and no one of them shall be absent from the Island without the consent of the Superintendent, or permission of the Board.

Corporal punishment. No employé shall be allowed to inflict corporal punishment, or otherwise maltreat any inmate, nor shall any punishment be allowed, except by direction of the Superintendent. No spirituous liquors or tobacco shall be furnished to any sentenced

---

[1] The houses of Industry and Reformation being located in the same building, the general Rules apply to the officers of both.

inmate, except by order of the Physician, and smoking by the inmates is strictly prohibited.

Clothing for discharged persons.

Paupers and prisoners about to be discharged in need of comfortable clothing, shall be furnished by the Institution, notice having been given to the Board by the Superintendent a week beforehand, to that effect.

Permits to visit.

Persons visiting the Institutions, except members of the City Council, must have a permit from some member of the Board, or the Mayor of the city, or have the assent of the Superintendent. Such visitors (except members of the City Council), unless accompanied by a director, shall not be allowed to go over any building, or around the grounds, unless accompanied by an officer, who, when the visit is completed, shall return them to the office on the wharf.

Rules for visitors.

Visitors shall not be allowed any communication with the inmates, or to furnish them any articles, except by permission of the Superintendent, or a director.

Visitors shall be required to place their names on the register kept at the office on the wharf for that purpose, and the Superintendent shall, on his next daily report, submit the names of such visitors, and by whom permitted. As far as practicable, visiting to sentenced inmates shall be at the reception room on the wharf.

Contractors and agents.

Contractors who may hire the labor of inmates, and agents of such contractors, shall not be permitted to have any conversation with the inmates, but such as may be necessary to instruct them in their work, or to give directions in relation thereto; nor shall they be permitted to visit any other parts of the Institutions than those assigned them. They shall be subject to the rules and regulations of the Institution, and such agents shall be removable at the pleasure of the Superintendent.

Contractors or their agents shall not be allowed to carry into or use any spirituous liquors at the Institution, nor shall they give any perquisite, overstint money, or reward of any kind to convicts in their employ, or grant them any favor inconsistent with the rules and regulations of the Institution.

The watchmen shall keep watch during the night, in such manner and for such periods as the Superintendent shall direct, and during the daytime perform such duties as may be required. Watchmen.

HOUSE OF CORRECTION.

The officers of the House of Correction shall be a Master, Deputy Master, Receiving Officer, Clerk, Physician, Chaplain, and such number of male and female assistants as the Board may from time to time deem necessary. Officers.

The Master of the House of Correction, subject to the orders of the Board, shall have the control and management of all who are employed at the Institution. He shall have the entire management and control of the convicts, subject to the laws defining the powers and duties of Masters of Houses of Correction, and such directions not inconsistent therewith, or the Ordinances of the city, as he may receive from the Board. He shall reside at the Institution in apartments assigned him. *Master* to control the Institution.

It shall be his duty to see that the police and other regulations for the management of the Institution and the employment of the inmates, and all orders of the Board, are duly enforced, and that the subordinate officers and others employed faithfully discharge their duties. To enforce the regulations.

He shall examine all persons committed to the Institution, noting on the mittimus such facts as it is important to preserve, and cause them to be thoroughly cleansed and suitably located, and see that the rules for insuring cleanliness by daily ablution and the weekly bathing of the whole persons are strictly observed. To see that prisoners are properly cleansed, located, &c.

He shall have a code of rules for conducting the Institution, to be approved by the Board, and such parts as relate to the prisoners shall be read to them in the Chapel at least once a month. He "shall appoint all subordinate assistants, employés, and officers for whom he shall be responsible," and at once report the same to the Board. To make rules and appoint subordinates.

To punish infraction of rules.

He shall enforce obedience on the part of the inmates to the rules prescribed for them, and shall have power at his discretion to punish according to law all wilful infractions, such punishments and the cause thereof to be reported to the Board on the next daily report after the occurrence.

To require daily medical visits to prisoners in solitary.

It shall be his duty to have all prisoners while in solitary confinement visited by the Physician once in each day during such confinement.

To see that the food and clothing is good and plentiful.

He shall see that the provisions furnished to the inmates are of good quality and in sufficient quantity, and that no waste is allowed, and also that every part of the premises is kept clean, and the several apartments are properly warmed and ventilated, and such of the inmates as are able to labor are constantly employed. In case any prisoner going out may require clothing, he shall make report thereof to the Board at least one week before his discharge, so that he may be suitably provided with the same; and should pecuniary aid be thought proper in any case, the Master may grant it to an amount not exceeding five dollars.

To cause accounts to be kept.

He shall cause regular books to be kept, showing the quality and amount of articles received at the Institution for the supply of the same, and also of the money received for the sales of produce or otherwise, which books shall at all times be open to the examination of the Board.

To make requisitions and certify bills.

He shall make requisitions on the Board for all articles needed, and receipt at once for all articles received, according to forms prescribed, and also certify the bills of such articles.

To keep a register of inmates in detail; make daily and weekly reports.

He shall keep a Register of all inmates admitted or discharged, embracing the term of sentence and the offence for which committed, and make daily and weekly reports, according to forms prescribed, giving the names of all persons admitted or discharged, the offence for which committed, and the term of sentence, — the births and deaths, — the Physician's report of the sick, — the punishments and the causes thereof, and such other information as is worthy of remark. Upon the weekly report he shall also give a statement of the employment of the inmates.

He shall annually, on the first of January, submit a report of the condition of the Institution, and number of inmates, giving the number of admissions thereto and discharges therefrom, — the births, deaths, and number of inmates therein during the year, with such information and suggestions as he may deem important or the Board may require. To make an annual report.

During the absence of the Master, or his sickness or other disability, the charge of the Institution shall devolve upon the Deputy, and he shall be responsible for its good order and the preservation of its discipline, and shall not absent himself from the prison during the time the convicts are out of the cells, without permission of the Master. *Deputy Master* to act in the absence of the Master.

He shall, subject to the directions of the Master, have a general and superintending care of the prison, especially its police and discipline, and see that all the rules and regulations, and orders of the Master are strictly observed. He shall be constantly about the establishment, visiting frequently the workshops, kitchen, hospitals, and all departments of the prison, and must, if possible, always be present at the opening and closing of the prison, and also attend in the Chapel during the performance of religious services.

On receiving convicts he shall cause to be read and explained to them such extracts from the rules of the prison as may be necessary to enable them to understand their duty and the discipline to which they are to be subjected. He shall assign them their cells, and shall station them in the department of labor directed by the Master. To receive convicts.

He shall enforce obedience to the officers on the part of the convicts, and report to the Master all violations of discipline, or rectify them in a prompt and decisive manner. When he feels the least doubt as to the proper course to be pursued, he shall, if possible, not act without consultation with the Master. Enforce obedience.

In deciding on the propriety and extent of punishment necessary to be inflicted during the absence of the Master, he shall be governed by previous examples, always keeping within the limits of a sound discretion, and the laws of the Commonwealth, making due allowance for possible ignorance of duty, or of mental imbecility, on the part of the convict, and Not to inflict excessive punishments.

ever exercising a just degree of lenity, without shrinking from the discharge of a highly responsible and very unpleasant duty.

To make daily report of punishments.

He shall present to the Master, on the morning of every day, a report, closed at 7 o'clock of the previous day, stating therein all cases of punishment, and the occasion of them, and the number in solitary confinement — the names, duty, and stations of the officers composing the prior night guard, together with any important occurrences that may have taken place within the Institution during the preceding twenty-four hours.

To give notice of "first bell;" leaves of absence.

He shall give notice on the Bulletin Board, every Saturday afternoon, of the time for ringing the first bell in the morning, of the ensuing week, as directed by the Master. He shall not grant leave of absence to any officer without consulting the Master, nor himself be absent at the same time as the Master, except in cases of great emergency.

Receiving officer; his duties.

The Receiving Officer shall take charge of all convicts on their admission, conducting the females to the proper Matron of the female department, and examining all males at the receiving room, where he shall cause them to be stripped and thoroughly cleansed, and have their beard and whiskers shaven off, and their hair cut if necessary.

He shall make an entry, in a book, kept for the purpose, of the clothing and all articles belonging to the inmates, and shall have such part of the clothing as is worth preserving cleansed and placed away, to be restored to them upon their discharge.

He shall aid the Deputy Master in a superintending care of the prison, hospital, and yard, and be careful that they are kept in proper order, and shall discharge male convicts on the expiration of their sentence, according to a list furnished to him monthly.

He shall distribute rations to those in solitary confinement and shall regularly attend upon the Physician during his visits to the sick, and attend to the delivery of the medicines, and the treatment he may prescribe for the patients.

He shall, if desired, be present in the yard when the female prisoners are passing to or from the Prison or Chapel, and perform such other duties as may be required of him.

In the absence of the Master and Deputy Master, or their

sickness or disability to act, he shall have charge of the Institution.

The Clerk shall keep the books of the Institution conformably to the laws and such plans as may be adopted by the Board. He shall keep a distinct account with each department of the prison, so as readily to know the result of their operations, and attend to the subsidiary books of the different departments, and make up the daily and weekly reports, and perform all necessary writing for the prison. Clerk.

He shall be present during the hours of labor, unless excused by the Master, and receive the reports of the officers of divisions on locking up at night. He shall give constant attention to the interests of the Institution and the duties of his office, and perform such other duties as may be required.

The Physician shall be elected by the Board annually, in the months of April or May, and whenever a vacancy may occur. It shall be his duty to visit the Institution once each day, and as much oftener as may be necessary, and to examine carefully into every case of sickness or inability to labor, and prescribe such medicines and course of diet or treatment as he may deem proper, and notify the Master of all convalescents able to perform labor. He shall, from time to time, furnish the Master a list of such medicines as may be needed for the Dispensary, and report to him any neglect or improper conduct on the part of the nurses or those in attendance that may come to his knowledge. Physician.

The sustenance and diet of those in the hospitals shall be regulated by him, through requisitions therefor upon the Master, which must be in writing, and given daily.

He shall keep a record of patients in the hospitals, designating the time of admission thereto, with the nature of the disease and the treatment, and the date of discharge or death, and shall make a daily report, in writing, to the Master, of each person in the hospital, and their condition. No critical surgical operation shall be performed, except in cases of urgent necessity, without the sanction of the Board.

The Chaplain shall be elected by the Board, annually, in the Chaplain.

months of April or May, and whenever a vacancy may occur. It shall be his duty to perform divine service on the Sabbath, and such other times as may be set apart by the Board for religious exercises, and shall visit the sick, instruct the inmates in their moral and religious duties, and counsel and advise them prior to their discharge, and perform such other duty in his capacity as the Board or the Master may require. He shall not be allowed to exchange or send any substitute without the consent of the Superintendent or the Board.

General Instructions for the Officers and Matrons.

The Officers and Matrons shall strictly observe all orders that they may receive from the Master or Deputy Master.

Deportment; discipline, corporal punishment, &c.

As the reputation of the officers is more or less affected by the good order and discipline of the prison, it is incumbent upon all to conduct themselves with correctness of deportment as well without as within the Institution.

In the presence of convicts, it is important and necessary to show due respect for the opinions and orders of each other and observe the utmost propriety of demeanor and language. In all intercourse with convicts, the most uniform evenness of temper and deep interest in the prosecution of the labors or duties of which they may have charge should be exhibited, evincing those examples which are more salutary than precept, and at the same time manifesting firmness and forbearance, to look down the lazy and vicious, and kindly regard those who conduct with propriety.

All orders to the convicts should be given with the utmost possible distinctness, so as to be clearly understood. Every officer immediately engaged in the government of the inmates must notice and report to the Master or Deputy all cases of violation of the Rules that may fall under his observation. Should a convict refuse or hesitate to obey the orders of an officer, he shall be admonished and informed of the consequences of disobedience; if he still persists, the officer shall send for the Master or Deputy, or, if they are absent, the receiving officer, or shall take such measures as the emergency may require to enforce obedience for the time being, and report the same to the Master or Deputy as soon as may be.

No officer shall be allowed to inflict corporal punishment, or otherwise maltreat any convict, nor shall any punishment be allowed except by authority of the Master or Deputy; but in case of a rebellion, or insubordination, the officer in charge shall use his own discretion, with such means as he may have at command to quell it.

No officer or matron, in any case, shall use insulting or irritating language towards the convicts. If there is any talking or noise in the shops or prison, the officers must ascertain where the same is made, and see who the person is, speaking in a low tone, in such manner, if possible, that the convict next will not hear. At night, the outside doors of the prison shall be locked as soon as the convicts are in their cells, and particular care shall be taken of the keys until they are delivered to the Master or Deputy. The male prison cells must not be unlocked during the night, unless ordered by the Master or his Deputy, nor in the morning without three officers being present, nor the female prison cells without two Matrons being present. The officers are reminded that they must not talk with each other, with visitors, or with agents and contractors, or superintendents, in the hearing of the convicts. On all occasions, as little conversation shall be permitted in the prison while the convicts are there, as the duty required will admit of, and that in a low tone of voice; common conversation with the convicts is inconsistent with the dignity of an officer, and is not allowed.

The Officers and Matrons are required to see that the public property is not wasted or misapplied, and that all complaints by the convicts to the officers, respecting food, clothing, or ill treatment, are communicated to the Master or Deputy without delay.

The Watchman shall keep watch during the night time in such manner, and for such periods, as the Master or Deputy shall determine; and during the daytime, perform such other duties as may be required.

General Regulations.

Disposition of convicts, their labor; food; clothing; stimulants; visitors; perquisites; punishments, &c.

The convicts, during the whole time when they are not taken out for work, or other purposes, by order of the Master, shall be kept locked in their several cells, in no case more than one being allowed to each cell, except in cases of special emergency, and while so shut up, shall preserve perfect silence, except in cases of illness, when they shall be allowed to speak to the officer then in charge of the cells. They shall be taken out for work on all days but Sundays and holidays, at sunrise, and shall labor at the work assigned them through the day, with the exception of a half hour's respite for each meal, when they shall be reconducted to their cells, receiving their rations at some convenient place as they go.

On Sundays, the prisoners shall be conducted to the Chapel, at the times of public worship, and seated in such manner as the Master may direct. During the times when they are moving to and from the Chapel, or to and from the workshops, entire silence, and the most perfect order and decorum, shall be maintained. Their food shall be such as the Board may, from time to time, determine.

The convicts shall have clean clothes as often as once a week, and as much oftener as the Master shall direct. No spirituous liquors or tobacco shall be furnished to any prisoner, except by order of the Physician. No trafficking shall be allowed between the officers and convicts, nor shall any officer be allowed to receive any perquisite, in any shape, in addition to the compensation allowed him by the Board. Trafficking among the convicts is prohibited, and they shall not be allowed to receive anything from without the premises, or hold any intercourse with persons outside, without express permission of the Master, or the Board.

When visitors are present, no convict shall be allowed to address them, without permission, except in answer to such questions as may be asked by a Director, or members of the City Government authorized to examine into the state of the Institution.

For every failure to comply with the foregoing requirements, or for any insolent or insubordinate behavior, or neglect or refusal to obey the orders of the Master, or those having charge by his direction, or for gross or profane language towards the officers, or each other, or defacing the cells, or any of the furniture thereof, or any part of the premises, and for any want of decent and proper deportment in the Chapel, or in the presence of the Chaplain, the convicts so offending shall be punished by being kept on bread and water in solitary confinement, for a term not exceeding ten days; and it shall be the duty of the Master to have every such convict visited by the Physician once a day during such confinement.

Contractors who hire convicts may have agents, removable at the pleasure of the Master, to oversee their business, or direct the convicts in their labor; but neither the contractors nor the agents shall be allowed to hold any conversation with the convicts, but such as is necessary to instruct them in their work, or give them directions in relation thereto. **Contractors.**

The contractors, their agents, and all persons who may visit the prison on their account, shall be subject to the rules and regulations of the Institution. Teamsters, or other persons in the employ of contractors, who may occasionally visit the prison, shall not be allowed to speak to a convict, without permission of the Master, nor shall they be allowed the privileges granted to the contractors and their agents.

Contractors, or their agents, shall not allow any perquisite, overstint money, or reward of any kind, to the convicts, while in their employ, nor be permitted to give them anything, or grant them any favor inconsistent with the rules and regulations of the Institution, or be allowed to have any conversation with an officer while on duty, but such as may be in relation to convicts employed by them.

The contractors, their agents, or persons employed by them, if spoken to by a convict on subjects other than those relating to the work or business in which they may be engaged, shall report such convict to the officer in charge, or to the Master, or Deputy Master, without delay.

Visitors.

No persons, except the City Council, shall enter the premises without a permit from a member of the Board, or the Mayor of the city, or have permission of the Superintendent.

Visitors cannot be admitted, except in extraordinary cases, or on business, before 8 o'clock in the morning, nor at the dinner hour, between 11¾ o'clock and 1 o'clock, nor after one hour previous to sunset, and are prohibited from conversing with the convicts without permission of the Master, or some member of the Board first obtained. Visitors shall be required to place their names on the Register kept at the office for that purpose, and the Master shall, in his next daily report, submit the names of all such visitors, and by whom permitted. Female visitors can only be admitted to the premises assigned to female convicts. The time for visiting convicts shall be on the fourth Wednesday of each month.

LUNATIC HOSPITAL.

Officers.

The officers of the Lunatic Hospital shall be a Superintendent, Assistant Superintendent, Chaplain, Male Supervisor, Female Supervisor, Housekeeper, Seamstress, Laundress, and Watchman, and such male and female attendants and employés as the Board may, from time to time, deem necessary.

Superintendent.

The Superintendent of the Lunatic Hospital, who must be a Physician, shall be elected in the month of February, or whenever a vacancy may occur, and shall reside at the Institution. He shall, subject to the rules and orders of the Board, have charge and control over all the departments of the Institution, and all persons employed at the same, and shall have authority, unless otherwise provided, to appoint all subordinate officers and employés, subject to approval of the Board, and to remove the same, and shall also perform the duties of Physician to such other institutions under the charge of the Board as they shall require.

To appoint subordinates.

To visit patients daily.

He shall visit all the patients at least once on each day, and as much oftener as may be necessary, giving his personal attention to their mental and physical condition, and calling consultations whenever it may be necessary and expedient. He shall see that the food furnished is of good quality, and sufficient in quantity, that the premises are kept clean and in order, and that the halls and apartments are properly warmed and ventilated, and generally see that the affairs of the Institution are conducted in accordance with these Rules.

See to food; cleanliness, warmth, &c.

He shall make requisitions for all articles needed for the Institution, and receipt at once for all articles received, according to forms prescribed by the Board, and certify the bills of such articles. He shall keep a register of the names, age, and, as far as can be ascertained, the birthplace, and nature and cause of their insanity, with the date of admission and discharge of all patients, and how or by whom admitted.

To make requisitions and receipts, and keep a register of patients.

He shall make daily reports to the Board, according to forms prescribed, showing the admissions, and discharges, and condition of the sick, and, in case of death, the probable immediate cause, and the disposition made or to be made of the body, with such other information as may be necessary to keep them fully advised of the condition of the Institution. He shall annually on the first of January, submit a Report of the condition of the Institution, embracing a statement of the number of inmates, with the number admitted thereto and discharged therefrom, and births and deaths therein during the year, with such other information and suggestions as he may think proper, or the Board may require.

To make daily reports, and an annual report.

When a patient is in condition to be discharged, he shall notify the Board thereof, that they may act upon the same at their next meeting. In case he desires to be absent from the Institution for more than twenty-four hours at any one time, due notice shall be given to the Board, so that they may act upon the same as the welfare of the Institution may require.

To notify the Board of patients ready for discharge, and of surgical operations to be performed.

He shall not perform, or allow to be performed, any important surgical operation without having previously notified the Board.

The Assistant Superintendent, who must be a Physician, shall be elected by the Board annually in the months of April,

Assistant Superintendent.

or May, and whenever a vacancy may occur, and shall reside at the Institution, and, in the absence of the Superintendent, shall have charge. It shall be his duty, acting under orders of the Superintendent, to aid him in the discharge of his duties; have charge of the Dispensary, and perform the writing for the Institution, if required, and generally see that the rules and regulations and orders of the Superintendent are strictly complied with, and also perform such other duties in his said capacity as may be required. His absence from the Institution at the same time as the Superintendent is strictly prohibited.

To act in absence of Superintendent.

Chaplain.

The Chaplain shall be elected by the Board annually in the months of April or May, and whenever a vacancy may occur, and shall conduct divine service in the Chapel on each Sunday, at such hour as the Superintendent may arrange, and shall perform such other official services during the week as may be required of him.

Male Supervisor.

The Male Supervisor shall devote his whole time and attention to the interests of the Institution, and perform such duty as the Superintendent may require. It shall be his duty to see that personal cleanliness is maintained among the male patients; that all the premises are kept clean and in order, and the apartments properly warmed and ventilated; that the clothes and bedding of the patients are suitable and clean, and that the inmates are faithfully cared for and kindly treated by the attendants and persons placed over them.

He shall attend in the dining-hall of the male patients at meal hours, to see that the food is in proper condition when received from the kitchen, and that it is equitably served and properly distributed. He shall note, in a memorandum book kept for that purpose, any remissness on the part of the attendants or other persons employed, or occurrences coming to his notice, that may in any degree affect the general welfare of the Institution, and report the same immediately or daily to the Superintendent. In case of the absence of the Superintendent and Assistant Superintendent, he shall have charge of the Institution.

Female Supervisor.

The Female Supervisor shall, as far as practicable, be the

counterpart of the Male Supervisor, and shall exercise special oversight of the female attendants, and the patients, and their apartments, and perform such other duties as the Superintendent may require.

The Housekeeper shall see that the internal arrangements of the household, other than the patients' apartments, are properly conducted; that all parts of the house are kept clean and in good order; and to report to the Superintendent any remissness of duty on the part of persons employed therein. She shall superintend the cooking for the patients, and for the household, and attend to its regular distribution from the kitchen at such hour as may be designated by the Superintendent, and perform such other duties as may be required. Housekeeper.

The Seamstress shall have charge of the sewing-room, and of making and repairing the clothing and bedding of the patients; and shall furnish employment therein for as many of the female patients as can be profitably and safely employed. She shall keep the Superintendent apprised of all wants as they may occur in the clothing department, and also of any negligence in the use or custody of garments or bedding, and perform such other services as may be required. Seamstress.

The Laundress shall have charge of the washing and ironing department, and see that the clothing of the patients and of the household is duly received, attended to, and returned; that order and neatness prevail among those under her direction, and that as many of the patients as can be made serviceable in her department are at all times employed. She shall, from time to time, confer with the Seamstress, Supervisors, and Housekeeper, respecting the condition of the clothing and bedding, as they come to and go from her department, and shall generally perform such other duties as the Superintendent may require. Laundress.

The General Attendant shall, subject to the orders of the Superintendent, have charge of all duties outside of the Hospital, including the stable, grounds, and buildings thereon, and shall have oversight of patients employed upon the grounds, General Attendant.

and generally make himself useful in performing such other duties as may be required.

Watchman.

The Watchman shall faithfully watch and guard the buildings and grounds during the night, beginning, going, and leaving his rounds as the Superintendent may direct, and during the day perform such other services as may be required.

Duties of Attendants, and general remarks.

The whole time of the attendants belongs to the Institution; and it is required that every one shall promptly and cheerfully obey all the directions given, and perform all the duties required by the Superintendent, Assistant Superintendent, or either Supervisor; and that each of these officers shall, on all occasions, be treated with courtesy and respect. The subordinate officers are to eat at one table, and punctuality at meals is enjoined upon all.

Conversations between officers or attendants, in relation to the discipline or management of the Institution, must not be made in the hearing of any patient.

No one employed in the Hospital shall convey any letters or messages from the patients to any one out of the Asylum, without leave of the Superintendent.

No subordinate officer or stranger shall enter the female halls, without permission from the Superintendent.

Each one will be held responsible for the duties of his or her department, and should be ambitious to discharge those duties in a satisfactory manner.

The attendants are not allowed to take any article of property from the house. A Book shall be kept by the Superintendent, in which it shall be the duty of the Supervisors to enter all articles wanted in their respective apartments, with the date of each entry.

Self-respect is especially enjoined upon all; and as the patients will naturally imitate the manners and habits of the attendants, it is of the greatest importance in these respects, as in all others, that a good example should be set before them.

The dress of the attendants should always be neat and

clean; and their intercourse with each other, and with the patients, must be marked with kindness and courtesy. Whenever it becomes necessary for an attendant to speak to an officer or visitor concerning a patient who is present, it should be done in such a manner as not to excite suspicion on the part of the patient that he is the subject of conversation.

Under all circumstances, the patients are to be treated with kindness and forbearance; they must be spoken to in a mild and gentle tone of voice, soothed and calmed when irritated, encouraged and cheered when melancholy and depressed. They must never be ridiculed or mocked, nor their extravagances or delusions be made the subject of jest or sport.

The patients are never to be considered or treated as servants; on the contrary, whenever they are employed by the attendants, they are to be regarded as assistants.

Every patient, within twenty-four hours after admission, is to be washed, and observations made of any swelling on the body, or sores, spots, or vermin on the skin, and the fact immediately reported to the Superintendent. To this the Supervisors will give their particular attention.

Whenever the patients engage in any controversy, or in any improper or exciting subject of conversation, the attendant must interfere and check them; and must shut them up in their respective rooms, if the quiet and good order of the halls can in no other way be preserved, and promptly report the same to the Superintendent. No other restraint shall be applied, or, when applied, be remitted, unless by order of the Superintendent.

When the attendants receive insult and abuse, they must forbear to recriminate, scold, threaten, or to dictate in the language of authority.

Violent hands are never to be laid on the patients, except in self-defence, or to prevent injury to themselves or others. They must not be rudely handled, to induce them to obey; it will rarely happen that gentle and persuasive measures will not prevail; whenever these fail, the Superintendent is to be informed.

Every patient must be in the charge of some responsible person at all times (unless permitted to be at large by the Superintendent), and such person shall be held responsible for the safe-keeping of such patient, till returned to the hall, or intrusted to the care of another.

The attendants shall not retire to their rooms and close their doors while the patients are in the halls, but shall pass as much of their time in the halls with the patients as possible during the day, endeavoring to encourage and amuse them, and, so far as practicable, incite them to habits of industry.

No patient shall be permitted to go out of the halls without the consent of the Superintendent.

All persons who have duties to perform in the Hospital, will rise at the ringing of the bell. At ten o'clock in the evening, the labor of the house shall cease, the lights in the dining-room, kitchen, entries, and galleries shall be extinguished, and all persons shall retire to their respective rooms.

Every attendant shall keep a lamp burning, in a small lantern, through the night.

The attendants shall see that the patients rise at the same hour with themselves, that they are properly washed, their hair combed, and their dresses suitably arranged in season for breakfast.

The dress of the patients should at all times be neat and whole. The beds must be made, the halls, entries, and stairs swept, and the water-closets cleansed as early as possible. Every apartment in the wings must be thoroughly ventilated every morning, and as often through the day as may be necessary, by opening the windows, &c.

One or more attendants, as may be directed by the Superintendent, shall remain in the wing and move through the galleries, while the others are occupied in providing the meals of the patients, or in taking their own.

The attendants (with the exception of those on guard in the wings) shall be present at the meals, to distribute the food in a proper and equitable manner; particular care must be taken that the patients return to their respective galleries after meals;

their having left the dining-rooms is not sufficient evidence of this; they are to be immediately followed, seen to be in their proper places, and the gallery doors locked.

The attendants must be watchful lest any knives or forks or articles of food be carried to the rooms of the patients, no one of whom may be absent from the regular meals (excepting in cases of sickness or high excitement), without permission from the Superintendent.

Patients shall never be allowed to have a razor, penknife, or a dangerous weapon of any kind, without permission from the Superintendent. Especial care shall be taken that no such weapons get into their possession, and the beds, clothes, &c. of any suspicious patient must be frequently searched, if it is known or suspected that any such instrument is in the possession of a patient; and, if it cannot be found, immediate information must be given to the Superintendent.

No person connected with the Hospital shall be allowed to use ardent spirit or tobacco, in any form, unless prescribed or permitted by the Superintendent.

The attendants shall not leave their halls, nor visit the galleries, the kitchen, or other rooms in the house, without particular business; nor shall they give up their keys, or admit visitors to the halls, without permission from the Superintendent. The attendants must not leave the Hospital without permission from the Superintendent, and must always return by ten o'clock, P. M. unless leave be expressly given to remain out later; and when abroad, they must not report the conduct or conversations of the patients.

The patients must retire at the usual hour, and their bedroom doors be locked, care being taken to hear the slipping of the bolt.

The gallery doors, and especially the dining-room and outer doors, must be kept *locked* at all times. If these precautions are observed, escapes can rarely happen.

All persons employed in the Hospital, who are well, and can be spared from the duties in the house and halls, shall attend the religious services on the Sabbath, in the Chapel of the Hospital, unless leave of absence be granted.

Each person employed in the Hospital shall give notice, thirty days before leaving, of his or her intention to leave; and it is understood, in all contracts for services with attendants and other officers, that they may be discharged upon one week's notice, or upon shorter notice if occasion so requires, and that their salaries will be computed accordingly.

In case of the sickness of any of the sub-officers, no wages will be allowed them after a fortnight's absence from their duty.

No subordinate officer shall be absent from the Hospital for the purpose of visiting or recreation, during more than two consecutive days, between the first day of May and the first day of November in any year, the services of all employés being required in warm weather.

General Rules.

Permits. Persons visiting the Institution must have a permit from a Director, or the Mayor of the city, or have the assent of the Superintendent, it being always understood that the Superintendent may refuse admission to any one having a permit whenever, in his judgment, the welfare of the Institution requires, he reporting at once to the Board such refusal, and the reason therefor. Visiting as a matter of curiosity is denounced.

Suspension of rules. Either of these rules may be suspended in individual cases by vote of the Board, or they may make such other Rules and Regulations as circumstances may require, provided the same are not inconsistent with these Rules, or the City Ordinances, or the laws of the Commonwealth.

PUBLIC LIBRARY.

RULES AND REGULATIONS.

Chapter 1.

1. Reading Rooms to be open every day, except Sundays and Holidays.
2. Persons who may have access thereto.
3. Books may be used in Reading Rooms.
4. Card to be furnished, how used.
5. Return of Pamphlets and Books.
6. Decorum.
7. Persons who abuse their privileges may be excluded.
8. Lists of persons using Reading Rooms.

Chapter 2.

1. Books for home use; persons who may borrow them.
2. Hours for taking books from Upper Hall.
3. Hours for taking books from Lower Hall.
4. Books not to be taken from shelves.
5. Cards for borrowers; how used.
6. Number of books which may be borrowed.
7. Books not to be lent out of household of borrower.
8. Lists of persons using Library.
9. Applications for books not in Library.
10. Fines for undue detention of books.
11. Books to be sent for when unduly detained.
12. Books of reference and rare volumes to be used only in Library.
13. Injuries to, and losses of, books to be made good.
14. Annual examination.
15. Strangers may use the Library.
16. Persons abusing their privileges may be excluded.

Appendix.

FORMS: (1) Certificate for a minor: (2) notice to a person responsible for a delinquent: (3) Card for the use of books in the building: (4) Voucher for a person wishing to borrow books for home use: (5) Certificate for a pupil in Girls' High and Normal School: (6) Certificate for medal Scholars and others of merit: (7) Receipt for deposit money: (8) Card for borrowing books from Library: (9) Card for books wanted, but not in the Library: (10) Circular for recalling books unduly detained: (11) Special privilege to take out rare books.

RULES AND REGULATIONS.[1]

Chapter 1. — *Of the Use of the Reading Rooms.*

ARTICLE 1. The Reading Rooms shall be open from nine o'clock in the morning until ten o'clock in the evening of all secular days throughout the year, except the Seventeenth of Reading rooms to be open every day, except Sundays and holidays.

[1] Rules and Regulations for the use of the Public Library of the City of Boston, adopted by the Board of Trustees, Nov. 8, 1853; amended Aug. 18, 1863.

See Laws and Ordinances, pp. 393–396; also Ordinance passed July 11, 1865.

June, and the five legal holidays, viz: Washington's Birthday; Fast Day; Independence Day; Thanksgiving Day, and Christmas Day; — provided always, that the President may direct the Library to be closed for a part or the whole of any one day, reporting the fact and his reasons for it, in writing, to the Trustees at their next meeting.

Persons who may have access thereto.

ART. 2. All inhabitants of Boston above the age of sixteen years, of respectable character, and of such orderly conduct and condition as not to interfere with the occupations and comfort of others, shall have free access to the Reading Rooms during all the regular hours, first signing a promise that they will observe all the existing rules and regulations, and all that may be subsequently prescribed by due authority; — provided always, that minors shall bring certificates from their parents or guardians, in a form to be furnished by the Superintendent, setting forth that they are persons who ought to enjoy the privileges of the Public Reading Rooms, and that such parents or guardians become responsible for their conduct while there. See Appendix, (1,) and (2.)

Books may be used in Reading Rooms.

ART. 3. All books belonging to the Library may, at the discretion of the Superintendent or Librarian, be used in the Reading Rooms, — a discretion which they are required by the Trustees to exercise, especially in the case of minors, and in regard to books of great value or rarity.

Cards to be furnished: how used.

ART. 4. Every person entitled to use, in the Reading Rooms, the books of the Library, shall be furnished with a printed card, on which such person shall designate the particular book asked for, by entering, in blanks left for that purpose, the number of the shelf, on which it stands, the number of the book on the shelf, and, if it be part of a set, the number of the particular volume, — all which numbers can be easily ascertained from the copies of the catalogue always on the tables of the Reading Rooms; — and this card, which must be presented whenever a book is asked for to be used in the Reading Rooms, will be retained so long as its owner retains the book; but no book, so received, shall, for any reason whatever, be removed from the Reading Rooms by the person receiving it. See Appendix, (3.)

ART. 5. Every person who may visit the Reading Rooms shall return each of the pamphlets and periodicals such person may have used, to its proper place, and shall return each of the books used to the attendant.

Return of pamphlets and books.

ART. 6. All conversation and conduct inconsistent with the quiet and orderly use of the Reading Rooms by the persons resorting to them are prohibited.

Decorum.

ART. 7. Any person abusing the privileges of the Reading Rooms by unbecoming conduct or by the violation of any of the regulations, by intentional defacement of a book by writing in it, or in any other way, shall be reported to the Trustees as soon as may be, and by them excluded from the Library for a time, or permanently, according to the nature and degree of the delinquency or default; but, in case of any gross offence, the Superintendent or Librarian shall act summarily in the matter, and cause the offender to be, at once, excluded from the rooms, reporting the case to the Trustees as soon as possible, in writing, for their final decision. See Appendix, (2.)

Persons who abuse their privileges may be excluded.

ART. 8. An alphabetical list of the names of all the persons enjoying the privileges of the Reading Rooms, shall be kept in the Library, the residence of each person being noted in it.

Lists of persons using reading rooms.

Chapter 2. — *Of the Use of the Library.*

ARTICLE 1. The following persons shall be entitled to borrow books from the Library *for home use*, upon signing a promise to obey its Rules and Regulations.

Books for home use.

First. All inhabitants of Boston above the age of eighteen years, known to the Officers of the Library as proper persons to enjoy its privileges, or so recommended by some responsible citizen, who shall thus make himself liable for any loss resulting therefrom. See Appendix, (4.)

Persons who may borrow them.

Second. All clergymen and teachers having regular occupations in the city, all members of the Girls' High and Normal School, and all medal scholars, and such others as shall have received Lawrence Prizes, with such others each year (not exceeding in number the medal scholars of each school for the said year), as may be selected by the Chairman of its Sub-Committee to receive this reward for proficiency in their studies and for excellence of character. See Appendix, (5,) (6.)

Third. Any other inhabitant of Boston depositing the value of the volume asked for, if permitted to circulate (or of the set to which it may belong), for which a receipt will be given; which sum shall be repaid, whenever the book and receipt are returned, after any fines incurred for injury to the book or its improper detention have been deducted. See Appendix, (7.)

Hours for taking books from upper hall.

ART. 2. The upper hall in the Library shall be open from ten o'clock, A. M. until one half hour before sunset; and the books belonging to that portion of the Library must in all cases be applied for, and returned, within those hours, and in the upper hall.

Hours for taking books from lower hall.

ART. 3. The lower hall of the Library shall be open for the delivery of books for home use from ten o'clock in the morning until eight o'clock in the evening and for use in the Reading Rooms from nine o'clock in the morning to ten in the evening, on all the days when the Reading Rooms are open, except on such days as the Trustees may designate, immediately before the annual examination of the Library.

Books not to be taken from shelves.

ART. 4. No books shall be taken from the shelves in any part of the Library by any person not employed in the service of the Library, except such books as are deposited in the Reading Rooms for reference.

Cards for borrowers: how used.

ART. 5. Books desired for home use must be designated by their numbers on a printed card to be given to the borrower for that purpose; and this card will be returned to its owner as soon as the book is charged, or if it cannot be furnished. See Appendix, (8.)

Number of books which may be borrowed.

ART. 6. No person shall have for home use more than one volume from each hall on any one day, or more than two volumes at a time from both; and no book shall be retained by the person borrowing it more than fourteen days; provided always, that any book may be borrowed twice by the same person, but not more than twice, until it shall have been returned to the Library, and shall have remained there at least one full Library day.

Books not to be lent out of household of borrower.

Art. 7. No person who has borrowed a book from the Library, shall lend it to any one not a member of the same household.

Lists of persons using Library.

Art. 8. A list of all persons entering their names for the purpose of borrowing books shall be kept in the Library; the residence of each individual, and the page where the loans are recorded, being inserted against the name.

Applications for books not in Library.

Art. 9. Whenever a book wanted by any one using the Library, does not belong to it, such person is particularly requested to enter the title of the book on a card furnished for the purpose, to which the person's name and residence shall be added. See Appendix, (9.)

Fines for undue detention of books.

Art. 10. To protect the Library against loss, and to secure to all a just and equitable share in its benefits, any person detaining an imperial octavo or larger volume longer than the regulations permit, shall be fined three cents for each day of detention, and two cents a day for the detention of a smaller volume; the Librarian being charged with the collection of these and all other dues to the Library.

Books to be sent for when unduly detained.

Art. 11. Any book detained one week beyond the time limited by these regulations, shall be sent for by the Librarian, and the expense thus incurred shall be paid by the person who has so detained it. See Appendix, (10.)

Books of reference, and rare volumes, to be used only in Library.

Art. 12. Encyclopædias, dictionaries, and other books needed for reference in the Library building; books not easily to be replaced, in consequence of their rarity or value; books expressly given for reference only; and books deemed by the Trustees to be unsuited for general circulation, shall be used only in the building; provided, nevertheless, that, in order to allow the widest practicable use of the Library consistent with its greatest efficiency, a person desiring to borrow any book whatever (except such books as may have been given on condition that they should not be taken from the Library), and stating the reasons for it in writing to the Trustees, shall, if the reasons are deemed sufficient, be permitted to borrow it on proper conditions. See Appendix, (11.)

Injuries to, and losses of books, to be made good.

ART. 13. All injuries to books beyond a reasonable wear, and all losses, shall be made good to the satisfaction of the Superintendent by the persons liable; every book detained above three months being held to be lost.

Annual examination.

ART. 14. All books must be returned to the Library at such time before the annual examination as may be required by the Trustees, under penalty of a fine of one dollar for each volume detained; but seasonable notice of the time of returning them shall be given in the newspapers that advertise for the city.

Strangers may use Library.

ART. 15. Any stranger or person visiting the city for the purpose of literary or scientific investigation, may, on being properly recommended, temporarily receive the benefits of the Reading Rooms, and the use of the books within the Library building, by signing the Strangers' Book.

Persons abusing their privileges may be excluded.

ART. 16. Any person abusing the privilege of taking books from the Library, by the violation of any of the regulations, by intentional defacement of a book by writing in it, or in any other way, shall be immediately reported to the Trustees, who shall, if they think the case requires it, exclude such person, for a time or permanently, from the Library, according to the nature and degree of the delinquency or default. See Appendix, (2.)

Appendix.

Forms.

Forms that will be needed in the administration of the Library according to the preceding Rules, and which shall always be furnished at the Library free of expense.

(1.)

CERTIFICATE to be given by a parent or guardian to a *Minor*, over sixteen years old, who wishes to frequent the *Reading Rooms* of the Public Library. (See Rules, 1, 2.)

BOSTON, 18

Certificate for a minor.

The subscriber requests permission for , a *Minor*, residing at No. in Street, to frequent the *Reading Rooms of the Public Library*, and will become responsible for said Minor's observance of the Rules of the Library, and for any damage that may accrue to the Library in consequence of granting such permission.

Signed, *Parent*, [*or Guardian.*]

Residing at No. in Street.

(2.)

NOTICE to a person responsible for one who has failed to observe the Regulations of the Library. (See Rules 1, 2, and 7, and II. 16.)

BOSTON, 18

To , residing at No. in Street.

Notice to a person responsible for a delinquent.

A. B. residing at No. in Street, for whose observance of the Regulations of the Public Library you became surety on the day of 18 , has failed to observe them, and the *privilege is therefore withdrawn* by order of the Trustees.

Signed, *Librarian.*

(3.)

CARD *indispensable* for those who wish to read books belonging to the Public Library *in the building;* — which card, when its blanks are filled up, is to be returned to the Librarian, and another one issued by him in lieu of it. (See Rules I. 4.)

Books asked for *to be used only in the Library Building,*

Card for the use of books in the building.

By residing No. in Street.

SHELF.	NO.	VOL.	SHELF.	NO.	VOL.

(4.)

VOUCHER for any person who, under the assurance of a respectable and responsible citizen, wishes *to borrow books* from the Public Library *for home use.* (See Rules II. 1.)

BOSTON, 18

Voucher for a person wishing to borrow books for home use.

I, the subscriber, hereby certify that , residing at No. in Street, is *a fit person to enjoy the privileges of the Public Library,* and that I will be responsible for the observance, by said , of the Rules of the Library, and will make good any injury or loss the Library may sustain from the permission that may be given in consequence of this certificate.

Signed,

Residing at No. in Street.

(5.)

CERTIFICATE for a pupil in the *Girls' High and Normal School.* (See Rules, II. 1.)

BOSTON, 18

Certificate for a pupil in Girls' High and Normal Schools.

This certifies that the bearer , residing at No. in Street, is a pupil of the *Girls' High and Normal School,* of the city of Boston, and, as such, entitled to the privileges of the Public Library,

Signed,

Master of the Girls' High and Normal School.

(6.)

CERTIFICATE for medal scholars and others, selected on account of their merit, to receive the privileges of the Library. (See Rules, II. 1.)

BOSTON, 18

Certificate for medal scholars and others, of merit.

This certifies that the bearer, , residing at No. in Street, and *graduated with distinction at one of the public schools* of the city of Boston, in 18 , is, for proficiency in studies, and for good personal character, entitled to enjoy the privileges of the Public Library.

Signed, *Chairman of the Sub-Committee of School.*

(7.)

RECEIPT given by the Librarian on taking a *deposit of money* as a pledge for the safe return of books borrowed from the Library. (See Rules, II. 1.)

PUBLIC LIBRARY, BOSTON, 18

Received of , residing at No. , the sum of *in deposit,* as a pledge for the safe return of books taken from the Library for home use; and the same is to be repaid on the delivery of this Receipt, after deducting any amount incurred for fines, unreasonable damage, or other dues.

Receipt for deposit money.

Signed, *Librarian.*

(8.)

CARD for those who wish to *borrow* books from the Library, which card is to be renewed whenever its blanks have been filled, and it has been returned to the Librarian. *It is indispensable* to those who ask for books for *home use.* (See Rules, II. 5.)

Card for borrowing books from the Library.

TAKEN FROM THE PUBLIC LIBRARY

By..

Residing..........................*Page*......

SHELF.	NO.	VOL.	SHELF.	NO.	VOL.

(9.)

CARD for books *wanted,* but not in the Library. (See Rules, II. 9.)

BOSTON, 18 .

The subscriber recommends that a book entitled in vols. in printed at in the year be procured for the Public Library of the city of Boston.

Card for books wanted but not in Library.

Signed

Residing at No. in Street.

(10.)

For recalling a book that has been detained too long. (See Rules II. 11.)

Public Library, Boston, 18

Circular for recalling books unduly detained.

To , residing at No. in Street.

You are requested to deliver to the bearer borrowed by you from the Public Library, *and which has been retained beyond the time allowed by the regulations of the Library.*

Librarian.

(11.)

Special privilege to take out books not commonly circulated. (See Rules, II. 12.)

Special privilege to take out rare books.

To the Librarian of the Public Library.

The bearer, residing at No. in Street, is authorized to take out and retain the same for the space of weeks.

Signed, *Committee on Special Permissions.*

MARKET.

CONDITIONS.

1. Lessee to obey ordinances.
2. To keep premises in order.
3. Not to place articles in the passageways.
4. Not to smoke on the premises.
5. Not to underlet without assent of Board of Aldermen.
6. To remove all offal and dirt.
7. Stalls, when vacated, or when regulations are violated, to revert to the city.
8. Market-house to be closed on legal holidays.
9. Rent to be paid monthly.
10. Objectionable persons not to be employed.
11. If lessee becomes insolvent, stall to revert to city.
12. No stall to be occupied by more than one person except as copartners.
13. Violation of conditions forfeits the lease.

General lease conditions.

CONDITIONS.[1]

1. That the Lessee shall obey all the provisions of the city ordinances, and orders of the Board of Aldermen relating to the Market. *Lessee to obey ordinances.*

2. That the several stalls or cellars shall be kept in repair at the expense of the Lessee. *To keep premises in repair.*

3. That the Lessee shall not place, or suffer to be placed, any box, cask, or other articles in the passageway before his stall or cellar, or within it so as to project into any part of the passageway, or in the cross passageway, unless by consent of the Superintendent of the Market. *Not to place articles in passageways.*

4. That the Lessee shall not smoke, nor have in his possession any lighted pipe or cigar, within the limits of the Market. Nor shall he suffer or allow any other person to smoke upon his premises in the Market. *Not to smoke on premises.*

5. Said stall or cellar shall not be underlet to any person by said Lessee, or be occupied by any person except said Lessee, without the assent of the Board of Aldermen previously obtained. *Not to underlet without assent.*

---

[1] Conditions prescribed by the Board of Aldermen, for Lessees of Faneuil Hall Market, May 3, 1852, and since amended verbally. They were last fixed June 30, 1864.

See Laws and Ordinances, pp. 172–73.

To remove all offal and dirt.

6. Said Lessee shall not throw, or permit to be thrown, or to remain within the precincts of his stall or cellar, any offal, animal substance, scrapings, or any kind of dirt, filth, or useless matter, but shall forthwith remove the same, or cause the same to be deposited in some tight vessel, to be approved by the Superintendent of the Market; and to be removed by said Lessee, as the Superintendent or either of his deputies shall direct.

Stalls, when vacated, or when regulations are violated, to revert to city.

7. When the Lessee of any stall or occupant of any cellar in said Market-house shall from any cause whatever vacate the same, or shall receive notice from the Board of Aldermen to vacate the same, or shall neglect or refuse to pay his rent for the space of twenty-four hours, or shall neglect or refuse to comply with any regulations established for the good order and cleanliness of the said Market-house, and its entries, passage-ways, sidewalks, and the streets adjoining said house, the stall or stalls and cellar or cellars of such Lessee, shall thereupon revert to the city, and be at the disposal of the Board of Aldermen.

Market-house to be closed on legal holidays.

8. The Market-house to be closed on Washington's Birthday (22d of February), and on Christmas Day; also, on the day of the Celebration of the Declaration of Independence, unless said occasion occurs on Saturday or on Monday, when said Market shall be closed at 9 o'clock, A.M.; said Market shall also be closed on the 17th of June at 9 o'clock, A.M.

Rent to be paid monthly.

9. That the rent shall be paid monthly to the Superintendent of the Market, unless otherwise provided by indorsement on the lease.

Objectionable persons shall not be employed.

10. The Lessee shall not employ any person within the limits of Faneuil Hall Market who shall be objectionable to the Market Committee.

If Lessee becomes insolvent, stall to revert to city.

11. In case of the insolvency of the occupant of any stall or cellar before his term expires, the lease shall revert immediately to the city, and shall be subject to the disposition of the Market Committee for the remainder of the term.

No stall to be occupied by more than one person, except as copartners.

12. No stall shall be occupied by more than one individual unless the same shall be occupied by such parties as *Copartners*.

13. In case of any violation of the preceding conditions, the Lessee shall be subject to a forfeiture of his stall or cellar and of his lease. Violation of conditions forfeits the lease.

And the said Lessee doth accept the lease of the said stall or cellar on the conditions aforesaid, and doth promise to pay the said rent in monthly payments, on the first day of each and every month, to the Superintendent of the Market as aforesaid, and to quit and deliver up the said premises to the Board of Aldermen of the city of Boston, or the Superintendent of the said Market, peaceably and quietly, at the end of the term, in as good order and condition as the same now is, or may be put into by the said Lessors; that the Lessors, by the said Superintendent of the Market, may always enter upon to view the said premises, and make repairs and improvements of the same, to expel the Lessee forcibly if necessary, if shall fail to pay rent as aforesaid, or make any waste or destruction to the said stall or cellar, or otherwise forfeit this lease by virtue of the conditions which are hereinbefore contained. General lease conditions.

MOUNT HOPE CEMETERY.

BY-LAWS.

1. Annual meeting of *Trustees;* choice of Chairman and Superintendent; appointment of committees, &c.
2. The *Chairman:* his duties.
3. The *Secretary;* his duties.
4. The *Superintendent;* his duties.
5. Committee on Accounts.
6. Committee on Grounds.
7. Committee on Lots, sales, transfers, &c.
8. Committee on Interments.
9. Interments not to be made without due permission, nor until fees are paid; the fees prescribed.
10. Lots and spaces; to be laid out by Superintendent; prices of lots.
11. Lots in Cypress Vale; price of interments therein.
12. Sales and conveyances; fees for deeds.
13. Trees may be removed, to be in charge of Committee on Grounds.
14. Tombs.
15. Receiving Tombs; fees for deposit.
16. Monuments, fences, &c.
17. Funerals.
18. Teams, carts, &c.
19. Alteration of by-laws.

BY-LAWS.[1]

Annual meeting of *Trustees*; choice of Chairman and Supt.; appointment of Committees, etc.

ART. 1. The Annual Meeting of the Trustees shall be held on the first Tuesday in February. At this meeting there shall be chosen by ballot a Chairman, and a Superintendent for the ensuing year. At the succeeding meeting the Chairman shall nominate a Committee on Accounts, a Committee on Grounds, a Committee on Lots, and a Committee on Interments. The regular meetings of the Trustees shall be held on the first and third Tuesdays in each month, and a majority of the Board shall constitute a quorum. The chairman shall call a special meeting when requested to do so by two Trustees.

The *Chairman*; his duties.

ART. 2. The Chairman shall preside at the meetings of the Trustees. He shall determine the hour and place for the meetings. He shall, unless otherwise ordered, nominate all committees; — he shall sign the deeds of conveyance of lots; — he shall make the annual and other reports to the City Council, and perform such other duties as are required by the ordinance of the city. All bills on account of the Cemetery shall be approved by him before they are presented to the city for payment. In the absence of the Chairman, his duties shall be performed by the senior Trustee present.

The *Secretary*; his duties.

ART. 3. The Secretary shall notify and attend all meetings, and record the doings of the Board. He shall have charge of the plans belonging to the Cemetery, and all legal instruments, reports, catalogues, and other publications of the Trustees. He shall receive and record all applications for lots and graves; and prepare, countersign, and record, in a book kept for the purpose, all deeds of conveyance for lots. He shall pay into the City Treasury, monthly, all moneys received by him on account of the Cemetery.

The *Superintendent*; his duties.

ART. 4. The Superintendent shall reside near the Cemetery, and under the direction of the Trustees, shall have the general supervision and custody thereof; shall keep the avenues, paths,

---

[1] By-laws of the Trustees of Mount Hope Cemetery, adopted by them March 23, 1858. Revised March 7, 1865.

See Laws and Ordinances, page 412.

and grounds, in neat and satisfactory order; and, as agent for the Trustees, shall have the sole power to engage and discharge workmen on the ground; also to order and arrange their respective duties, and to pay their wages at such times and in such manner as the Trustees shall direct. He shall see that all regulations with regard to interments and the construction of tombs, monuments, and fences are complied with. He shall see that the rights of the city and the regulations of the Trustees are respected by artists, mechanics, and laborers employed on the ground by individual proprietors. He shall fulfil all contracts made with proprietors for the repair of lots, and perform such other duties as the Trustees may require. He shall have power to remove from the Cemetery improper and disorderly persons, to abate nuisances, and remove rubbish and unnecessary incumbrances. He shall keep, in books provided for the purpose, regular and accurate records of all interments, including the names and ages of the persons interred, and the place and date of their interment; also of all monuments erected, and lots enclosed, sodded, or otherwise improved. Also of all moneys received or disbursed by him, whether for wages, fees, improvement of lots, sales of any kind, purchases made, or services rendered. On the first Tuesday of every month, or oftener if required by the Trustees, he shall render to the Secretary, copies of said accounts, with proper vouchers, and pay over to him all moneys remaining in his hands. The compensation of the Superintendent shall be a salary, to be fixed by the Trustees, and the use of the dwelling-house connected with the Cemetery, and no other perquisites; and he may be removed for cause by a vote of the majority of the Board.

Committee on Accounts.

ART. 5. The Committee on Accounts shall consist of two Trustees. They shall act as auditors, and examine and satisfy themselves of the correctness of all the accounts rendered by the Secretary, Superintendent, Committees or others connected with the Cemetery. And all bills payable on account of the Cemetery shall be indorsed as correct by one of the Committee on Accounts, and submitted to the Board for their approval.

Committee on Grounds.

ART. 6. The Committee on Grounds shall consist of three

Trustees. They shall have the general charge of the grounds, trees, avenues, and paths in the Cemetery, with power to make such alterations, repairs, and improvements therein as they shall deem expedient. But no avenues or paths shall be changed in situation, without a vote of the Trustees.

Committee on Lots; sales, transfers, etc.

ART. 7. The Committee on Lots shall consist of three Trustees. They shall have the general supervision of all sales, locations, and enlargements of lots; also of all questions of right between individual proprietors, or between proprietors and the officers of the Cemetery. No transfer or conveyance of land shall take place without the approval of a majority of the Committee. The Committee on Lots shall have power, subject to the concurrence of the Trustees, to contract with any proprietor for the repair of his lot, and shall see that the contract is duly executed.

Committee on Interments.

ART. 8. The Committee on Interments shall consist of two Trustees. They shall superintend the general subject of interments, and see that they are made in conformity with the laws of the Commonwealth, and the rules and regulations of the Cemetery. They shall, from time to time, inspect the records and accounts of the Superintendent relative to interments, and see that the same are properly kept.

Interments: not to be made without due permission, nor until fees are paid; fees prescribed.

ART. 9. No interment shall be made at Mount Hope until such a permit as may be required by the laws of the State, or of the city or town from which the deceased may be brought, together with an order from the proprietor of the lot in which the interment is to be made, or from his legal representative, shall be presented to the Superintendent, *nor until the fees have been paid*.

Until otherwise ordered, three dollars shall be charged for digging a grave and making an interment. A deduction of fifty cents shall be made from the above charges for a child under ten years of age. In all burials in Cypress Vale, but one adult body, or two children under the age of ten years, shall be interred in each grave-lot at the usual price of digging the graves. If the grave is reopened for the purpose of burying a second body, except that of an infant, the price for such reopening and interment shall be five dollars. For each interment in a tomb, a charge shall be made by the Superintendent according to the amount of service rendered in the case.

Lots & spaces; to be laid out by Supt.; prices of lots.

ART. 10. Lots shall be laid out by the Superintendent, subject to the approval of the Committee on Lots. In future sales of lots, a space of not less than two nor more than four feet in width, at the discretion of the Committee on Lots, shall be reserved between the fence limits of different lots, which spaces shall forever be kept open, and within which there shall be no interments.

The price of a full lot of three hundred square feet, including grading, and six eight-inch stones for the fence, shall be one hundred and twenty-five dollars. The price of a half-lot, of one hundred and fifty square feet, including grading and six eight-inch stones for the fence, shall be seventy-five dollars. Enlarged lots and small lots will be sold at a corresponding rate per foot. No lots shall be sold without including the grading in the price. A proper allowance may be made when the *usual* fence stones are not used or desired.

Lots in Cypress Vale; price of interments therein.

ART. 11. The price of graves in Cypress Vale shall be eight dollars. No slab, monument, or fence shall be erected upon or around such graves without the approval of the Committee on Lots.

ART. 12. Lots applied for by purchasers may be laid out and graded by the Superintendent, subject to the approval of the Committee on Lots. If the sale is approved by the Committee, the purchaser shall then pay to the Secretary the customary or stipulated price of the lot sold him, and the fee of one dollar for the deed, and shall receive a certificate therefor, which shall be returned to the Secretary when the deed is delivered. No deed of any lot shall be issued to more than one grantee, nor, to any person as trustee, executor, or administrator, except by vote of the Trustees. One dollar shall be paid to the Secretary for recording any deed of transfer, and giving a certificate of the same.

Sales and conveyances; fees for deeds.

Trees may be removed; to be in charge of Committee on Grounds.

ART. 13. Trees standing within lots can be removed if desired, by an application by the proprietor to the Superintendent, subject to the approval of the Committee on Grounds. The Committee on Grounds have, also, charge of the general subject of introducing and cultivating, trimming, and removing trees and shrubs in other parts of the Cemetery.

Tombs.

ART. 14. Lots for tombs may be sold in places approved by the Trustees, and at prices fixed by them. Such tombs shall be constructed in a strong, tight, and durable manner, and shall be in every part to the satisfaction of the Committee on Lots.

Receiving tombs; fees for deposit.

ART. 15. Bodies may be deposited in the receiving tombs on payment of ten dollars to the Superintendent. But if within four months after interment the deposited body shall be removed to any part of Mount Hope Cemetery, five dollars of the above sum shall be refunded; otherwise the whole shall be forfeited to the city, and the Superintendent shall remove the body to such place as shall be designated by the Committee on Lots. But the friends or relatives may, in a legal way, remove the body from the Cemetery, at their own expense.

Monuments, fences, etc.

ART. 16. Proprietors have a right to erect on their lots fences, monuments, and stones of appropriate character. Wooden fences are not permitted. Live hedges of small or moderate size are allowed.

Funerals.

ART. 17. Early notice of funerals should be given to the Superintendent at the Cemetery, who will make all the arrangements for the interment. In military funerals, no firing of volleys will be allowed within the Cemetery.

Teams, carts, etc.

ART. 18. No teams or carts, except those used on the grounds, or omnibuses, will be allowed to drive into the Cemetery, without a special vote of the Trustees.

Alteration of By-laws.

ART. 19. No addition to or alteration in the By-Laws shall be made at the same meeting at which it is proposed, nor unless adopted by a vote of the majority of the Trustees.

OVERSEERS OF THE POOR.

RULES.

1. Officers of the Board not to be interested in any contract or supplies.
2. Meetings of the Board.
3. Central office: co-operation with charitable societies.
4. Relief not to be granted except after visit.
5. Applications for relief; temporary aid in cases of necessity; prompt visits to be made and results recorded.
6. Committee of Investigation and Relief.
7. Appeal from officers and the Committee to the Board.
8. Subordinate officers.
9. Any citizen may refer claims to the Board.
10. Standing Committees; purchase and delivery of supplies, bills.
11. Meals and lodgings at Temporary Home and Station-houses.
12. Temporary lodgings and relief at Station-houses, and visits thereto.

RULES.[1]

1. The officers of the Board shall be a Chairman, Secretary, and Treasurer, together with the Visitors hereafter named; and such clerks or agents as the business may require; and no paid officer shall be a member of the Board. No one of the Overseers, nor any individual in their employ, shall be interested in a private capacity, directly or indirectly, in any contract or agreement for labor, or for articles furnished by direction of said Overseers, unless the same be expressly authorized by a recorded vote of the Board. *Officers of the Board. Not to be interested in any contract or supplies.*

2. A stated meeting of the Board shall be held on the first Monday of each month during the year. At the stated meeting in April, the Board shall proceed to the election of a Chairman from its own number. At the same meeting the Board shall also proceed to elect a Treasurer and a Secretary, and fix the Secretary's salary. *Meetings of the Board.*

3. A central office shall be established, in a convenient situ- *Central office.*

---

[1] Rules adopted by the Overseers of the Poor, August 15, 1864. See Laws and Ordinances, pp. 433-60; also Ordinances of 1864, pp. 43.8.

ation, with ample accommodations to receive the applications of the poor; and for this purpose such office shall be open to applicants every day in the year, at such hours as the Board from time to time shall appoint. It shall be recommended to the city to provide a building to contain the central office, and as many of the offices of charitable societies as can be accommodated with convenience and advantage, and as can render services to the Board, which may be an equivalent for their rent. It is designed that the Overseers and their officers shall consult and coöperate with such societies.

Co-operation with charitable societies.

Relief not to be granted except after visit.

4. Except in cases of pressing necessity, no relief shall be afforded to any person who has not been previously visited by some member of the Board, or by some person authorized by the Board, and the case recorded at the central office.

Applications for relief.

5. There shall be in attendance at such office, during the hours appointed, the Secretary of the Board, or some officer or member thereof, whose duty it shall be promptly to hear every application for relief, and to cause the same to be recorded with all useful particularity, in conformity with the city Ordinance, in a book to be kept for that purpose. In cases of pressing necessity, it shall be the duty of the officer receiving such application, to afford such temporary aid as may at the time be necessary. And in every case, it shall be the duty of some officer of the Board promptly to visit the applicant and to record in a book, to be kept for that purpose at said office, the facts observed or obtained upon such visit, and the opinion of the visitor as to the necessity and nature of aid or relief, which records shall be properly arranged and indexed.

Temporary aid in cases of necessity.

Prompt visits to be made and results recorded.

Investigation and relief.

6. All applications and reports which in their nature and circumstances admit of it, shall be referred to a Committee of the Board, to consist of five members, to be called the Committee of Investigation and Relief, of whom three shall be a quorum, who shall decide whether any relief be given, and if any, the nature and extent of the same, which decision shall be recorded, and shall be promptly carried into effect by the Secretary, or other officer, for that purpose designated by the Board. The meetings of said Committee shall be held at

the central office, and shall be sufficiently frequent to afford to the poor seasonable hearing and aid.

7. Any person aggrieved by the decision of any officer of the Board, or of the Committee, shall have an opportunity to be heard by the Board, at convenient times, to be hereafter appointed.

Appeals from officers and the Committee to the Board.

8. In addition to the officers specifically named in the statute, the Board shall appoint suitable subordinate officers, who shall be called Visitors, whose duty it shall be personally to visit the applicants for relief, and to make the report hereinbefore provided, and who shall be paid for such service, at such rates as shall be determined by a vote of the Board.

Subordinate officers.

9. Any citizen of Boston shall be at liberty to refer to the Board for investigation and relief, if needed, such cases as he may deem suitable for relief or inquiry.

Any citizen may refer cases to the Board.

10. The Board shall appoint the following Standing Committees, in addition to that named in Article VI. to wit: A Committee of Finance and Accounts, to consist of three members; a Committee on Employment, Settlements, and Removals, to consist of three members; whose duty it shall be, in addition to ascertaining settlements and attending to removals, to assist the poor, who are able to work, in obtaining employment; a Committee on the Temporary Home, to consist of three members; and a Committee on Supplies, to consist of three members, who shall superintend the purchase, deposit, and delivery of all food, clothing, fuel and other articles for distribution, other than those of the Temporary Home, subject to such rules as may be adopted by the Board. No bills shall be paid by the Treasurer without a vote of the Board authorizing the same.

Standing Commitees.

Purchase and delivery of supplies.

Bills.

11. Tickets may be issued according to rules adopted by the Board, entitling the holders to a meal at the Temporary Home; or to a lodging, according to their sex, at the Home, or at the police station.

Meals and lodgings at Temporary Home and station-houses.

12. It shall also be recommended to the city that the police stations be used, as at present, for temporary lodgings; and food be given there to the destitute at night and on Sun-

Temporary lodgings and relief at station-houses, and visits thereto

days, so that persons asking relief in the streets may always be sent, at those times, to the nearest station-house, and at others, to the central office. Reports of the names, residences, and occupations of all persons lodged or fed at the stations, shall be sent daily to the central office. And if the Board shall, at any time, deem it expedient, a Visitor or member may attend at the several police stations, at fixed hours, for the purpose of receiving applications, which shall be recorded, and the applicants visited, as if received at the central office.

POLICE.

RULES AND REGULATIONS.

1. *Chief of Police* to be responsible for the Department.
2. To keep statistical books.
3. To keep books of accounts.
4. To visit station-houses.
5. To instruct captains.
6. To cause military drills.
7. To keep complaint book.
8. To keep records of special officers.
9. May suspend officers and grant furloughs.
10. To give information to prosecuting officers.
11. To provide station-houses with books.
12. To keep a meteorological diary.
13. To publish ordinances.
14. To keep record of defects in highway, and accidents therefrom.
15. To keep record of licensed dealers and places, and suspected wrong-doers.
16. Messages for the central office.
17. The *Deputy Chief* to assist the Chief, and officiate in his absence.
18. To supervise the City Prison.

19, 20. *Qualifications of Officers,* to consist of — (1) citizenship; (2) residence and taxpaying; (3) suitable age; (4) health, temperance, etc.; (5) ability to read and write; (6) application in handwriting.

21. Officers to be physically examined.
22. Reference of nominations.
23. Oath of office.
24. *Officers,* to give their whole time to their duty.
25. To be punctual, obedient, etc.
26. To be decorous and energetic.
27. Not to drink liquor while on duty, or enter drinking places except in performance of duty; nor smoke except as provided.
28. Not to receive rewards or gifts, nor extra compensation without approval.
29. To be punished or discharged for cause.
30. To have charges against them made in writing; and may have inquiry before the Committee on Police, and may be discharged with approval of the Mayor.

31. When discharged, to surrender property.
32. To co-operate in cases of danger.
33. Not to apply for warrants for assault, or make complaint for damages without consent of Chief.
34. Not to belong to fire or military companies, serve on juries, or form associations without consent of the Board of Aldermen.
35. Not to disclose affairs of department without permission.
36. To avoid political and religious discussions, and not interfere in elections.
37. Watch to be set at the hour after sunset.
38. *Detectives* to have certain hours.
39. To visit public places and take note of suspected places and persons.
40. To visit thronged thoroughfares and endeavor to prevent crime.
41. To perform any duty required by the Chief or Deputy.
42. May go out of the city with permission.
43. To bring persons arrested to the central office, note their description, etc., and leave their property with the Chief.
44. Shall inform the Chief of all matters.
45. To keep private records, to be inspected by superiors.
46. *Superintendent of Carriages* to supervise licensed carriages; record complaints; report on applications for license, etc.
47. To record all licenses and collect the fees; and perform other duties required by the Chief.
48-52. *Superintendent of Trucks*, to supervise vehicles licensed to transport merchandise; to keep records, collect fees, etc.
53. *Superintendent of Pawnbrokerage* to supervise pawnbrokers and second-hand dealers.
54. To record all persons coming under his supervision.
55. To examine books of such persons and report suspected cases.
56. To complain of unlicensed dealers.
57. Police officers may examine books and property of second-hand dealers when directed.
58. Superintendents shall report weekly to the Chief.
59. To be at his office daily.
60. *Clerk of Police* to keep books of central office, etc.
61. *Captains of Police* to be at station-house during the day, and have charge of the house.
62. To keep station-house open and properly attended.
63. To have charge of his district, and note matters requiring attention; report cases of contagion and danger from fire.
64. To have control of men attached to his station; to inspect the men; report neglect or insubordination; instruct men in drill and duty, and divide the district into beats.
65. To receive and keep all persons arrested, remove them to the City Prison, etc.
66. To make proper records of arrest; to search prisoners, etc.
67. To record lodgers.
68. To make proper disposition of property taken by the police.
69. To record offences and other police matters.
70. To record and report the duty done by men, with bills incurred, etc.
71. To make daily, monthly, and yearly reports of all matters.
72. To record all licenses and suspected persons and places.
73. To detail officers for duty at fires, etc.
74. To have control at fires of all police present.

75. To suppress riots.
76. To give military instruction to officers.
77. Not to permit improper persons or conduct in station-houses, and to report irregularities.
78. To use gas and fuel economically.
79. *Lieutenants* to have same powers and duties as the Captain in his absence.
80. To alternate in duty.
81. To report delinquencies to the Captain.
82, 83. *Sergeants of Police* to perform such duties as directed.
84, 85. To have charge of, and instruct men; patrol the dis trict and report the conduct of men.
86. *Patrolmen* may be called into service at any time; not to receive extra pay or fees without approval.
87. To be courteous to superiors, report neglect, be obedient, etc.
88. To be present at roll-call unless excused.
89. To patrol their beats once an hour, and confine themselves to their beat except in specified cases.
90. Not to communicate with one another or other persons unless in the line of duty.
91. To inform themselves of the inhabitants on their beats.
92. To give information and aid consistent with duty, keep his number in sight, etc.
93. To direct strangers and give assistance to other officers.
94. To restore lost children; to note cause of contagion or sudden death, etc.
95. To warn crowds as to pickpockets.
96. To watch persons of bad character and prevent assaults, crimes, etc.
97. To note and report licensed and suspected places and persons.
98. To note and report obstructions and defects in the streets; insecure coal holes; defective lamps; unsafe buildings; nuisances, etc.
99. To examine doors, grates, etc., and secure those left open; to be vigilant in respect to fires, waste of water, the state of sidewalks, nuisances in the streets, and report parties violating the ordinances.
100. To request loiterers to move on, and report those who refuse.
101. To note beggars, and if in distress, direct them to Overseers of Poor or charitable associations.
102. To note fast driving, brutality, to animals, violations of law in respect to carriages.
103. To assist to disentangle blocked teams, and protect foot passengers.
104. To quell disturbances and arrest offenders.
105. To arrest on warrants and make proper returns; may arrest persons reasonably suspected, and night-walkers, and may examine persons abroad at unreasonable hours.
106. To require accusers of crime to go with the accused to the station.
107. Not to use unnecessary force in making arrests, or abuse prisoners.
108. To carefully preserve all property taken from prisoners.
109. Not to act in civil cases except by authority.
110. To be paid for time lost by injury while on duty, and by sickness for ten days.
111. To give alarm of fire and note circumstances.

112. To protect lives and property at fires; officer first arriving to have control until superiors arrive.
113. To keep private record of all matters of duty.
114. To make day reports.
115. May be suspended for not wearing uniform and badge.
116-119. *Harbor Police*, divided into two districts.
120. To visit the powder-boats and oyster-beds.
121. To pay particular attention to cases of drowning.
122. To board foreign vessels, keep boats away, and challenge strange boats.
123. To render aid on the wharves.
124. To have certain signals.
125. To be relieved at certain hours; shall keep boats and firearms in order.
126. Time of the different watches.
127. Officers on the sail boat.
128. To familiarize themselves with all vessels in port.
129. To co-operate with U. S. officers and Harbor Master, in enforcing the laws.
130. Roll-call.
131. *Special Police* to wear a badge.
132. To conform to the rules.
133. To make weekly returns of duty.
134. To be removed for delinquency.
135. *Police Property* — to be under charge of Committee on Police.

APPENDIX.

1. *Police Uniform.*
2. Summer uniform.
3. Winter uniform.
4. *Specifications;* Overcoat.
5. Coat.
6. Vest.
7. Pantaloons.
8. Buttons on Coat.
9. Boatmen's uniform.
10. Cape for wet weather.
11. Uniform to be worn when on duty.
12. Clubs, belts, etc.
13. *Badges ;* of the Chief.
14. Of the Deputy.
15. Of Captains and Lieutenants.
16. Of Sergeants.
17. Of Patrolmen.

RULES AND REGULATIONS.

Chief of Police.

1. The Chief of Police shall be the Chief Executive Officer of the police department, and shall be responsible for its discipline and efficiency. He shall report all instances of wilful disobedience or neglect of duty to the Committee on Police, who shall investigate the same. *Chief of Police to be responsible for the department.*

2. He shall keep a book, alphabetically arranged, in which shall be entered the name, age, birthplace, date of service, district, and occasions of censure, or punishment of every member of the department. *To keep statistical books.*

To keep books of accounts.

3. All the accounts and expenses of the department shall be audited and entered in proper books, to be kept in his office for the inspection of the Mayor and Board of Aldermen, and it shall be his duty to see that the utmost economy is practised throughout the service.

To visit station-houses.

4. He shall visit each station-house as often as his other duties will permit, and inspect the drill of the men, the books of the station, and see that the houses are properly conducted and kept in good order.

To instruct captains.

5. He shall instruct the captains in all branches of their duty, and see that they give similar instructions to their men.

To cause military drill.

6. He shall, as often as opportunity permits, cause as large a number of the members of the department as can be spared from their other duties, to be drilled together in military movements and evolutions, so that they may act efficiently in concert when called upon to suppress riots or disorders.

To keep complaint book.

7. He shall keep a book in which complaints may be made by citizens against members of the department, and another in which violations of the laws and ordinances, robberies, burglaries, articles lost, and other similar matters when brought to his knowledge may be entered, and he shall cause prompt attention to be paid to such complaints or information.

To keep records of special officers.

8. He shall keep a list of all special officers, with their names, ages, residences, birthplaces, and the names of their employers, and the extent of their powers; as also of any omission to make report of their doings as hereinafter provided.*

May suspend officers and grant furloughs.

9. He may suspend from duty and stop the pay of any member of the department for a time not longer than one week, for cause, and may grant furloughs to any one member for the same period, making report thereof to the Committee on Police for approval.

To give information to prosecuting officers.

10. He shall keep the city solicitor and prosecuting officers of the county informed of all matters that pertain to their several offices relating to the police or interests of the city, or to any breach of the laws or ordinances. He shall prescribe rules for

---

*Rule 133.

the entry of all complaints and prosecutions for violations of the laws and ordinances, and use his best efforts to bring offenders to punishment. He shall make report to the Committee on Police, every morning, of his doings for the preceding twenty-four hours, and send a duplicate of such report to the Mayor.

To provide station-houses with books.

11. He shall cause the station-houses to be provided with copies of the "General Statutes," the "Ordinances of the City," the "Municipal Register," "Boston Directory," some system of drill, an "English Dictionary," and the "Bible," and each member of the department with a copy of the "Rules and Regulations."

To keep meteorological diary.

12. He shall cause a meteorological diary to be kept in his office, with the state of the weather at eight in the morning, at noon, and at sunset.

To publish ordinances.

13. Whenever a disregard of any law, ordinance, or order prevails to any extent prejudicial to the well-being of the city, he shall cause the said law, ordinance, or order to be published in the newspapers of the city, or in handbills or circulars, calling thereto the attention of the public.

To keep record of defects in highway, and accidents therefrom.

14. He shall record in a book reports from the several stations, of all defects in the highway, violation of the building laws, causes of nuisance, and take measures to have the same corrected, and keep a record of all accidents whereby the city may become chargeable, with the circumstances, names of witnesses, and a particular description of the locality.

To keep record of licensed dealers and places, and suspected wrong-doers.

15. He shall keep a record of all intelligence offices, junk shops, and dealers in second-hand articles, pawnbrokers, theatres, and other places of amusement licensed by law, and see that they observe the laws, ordinances, and rules for their government, and of all suspected gambling-houses, drinking-saloons, and houses of ill repute, as also of all convicted persons who may become dangerous to the community.

Messages for central office.

16. The central office shall be open day and night, where all messages must be sent and applications made.

Deputy Chief.

***The Deputy Chief* to assist**

17. The deputy chief shall be under the immediate direction

Chief and officiate in his absence. of the chief, assist him in his duties, and officiate for him in his absence.

To supervise City Prison. 18. It shall be his especial duty to supervise the city prison, be responsible for its good order and cleanliness, and cause all the rules and orders for its government to be rigidly enforced.

Qualifications of Members.

19. It is the design of the appointing power to select men for office with a view to their fitness for the position and usefulness in the service of the department. No officer can necessarily expect to retain his office unless his conduct be such as to secure the good will of the respectable portion of the community, and to command respect from the unfortunate and vicious.

Qualifications of officers, consist of— 20. The following qualifications shall be necessary for any one to be eligible as a member of the department:—

1. Citizenship. *First.* To be a citizen of the United States.

2. Residence and tax paying. *Second.* To have been a resident of Boston and paid taxes there for the two years next preceding his appointment.

3. Suitable age. *Third.* To be not under twenty-one nor over forty years of age when first appointed.

4. Health, temperance, etc. *Fourth.* To be of sound health and vigor, of unquestionable energy and courage, of temperate and industrious habits, of peaceable and courteous manners, decorous and cleanly in his person and dress, respectful to superiors, prompt and decided in action, and diposed to be zealous in the service.

5. Ability to read and write. *Fifth.* To be intelligent, and able to read and write the English language.

6. Application in handwriting. *Sixth.* All applications for appointment shall be made in the handwriting of the applicant.

Officers to be physically examined. 21. It shall be the duty of the city physician, or of such other regular physician as may be duly appointed by the board of aldermen for that purpose, to examine and report on the physical condition of candidates (when not already on the force) for police officers, and to perform such other professional duty as may enable such physician to certify to the chief of police as to the cause of sickness or disability of members of the department, of their physical fitness to perform police duty, and also to the length of time they shall have been disqualified for service by such sickness or disability; and before a nomination is made of a police officer to the board of aldermen for confirmation, a certificate of the city physician, or of such other regular physician, that the candidate is physically qualified, shall be furnished to the mayor.

Reference of nominations.

22. Nominations shall be referred to the Committee on Police, who shall report as soon as practicable to the board of aldermen for confirmation or rejection.

Oath of office.

23. Before entering upon the discharge of their duties, the members appointed on the police department shall take and subscribe to the following *oath* before the City Clerk.

I, ————, do solemnly swear that I will faithfully and impartially discharge and perform all the duties incumbent upon me as a Police Officer of the city of Boston, so long as I shall be such officer. So help me God.

General Rules.

Officers to give theirwhole time to their duty.

24. Each member of the police force shall devote his whole time and attention to the business of the department, and he is expressly prohibited from following any other calling, or being employed in any other business. Although certain hours are allotted to the respective members for the performance of duty on ordinary occasions, yet at all times they must be prepared to act immediately on notice that their services are required.

To be punctual, obedient, etc.

25. Punctual attendance, prompt obedience to orders, and conformity to the rules of the department, shall be rigidly enforced.

To be decorous and energetic.

26. Each member, in his conduct and deportment, must be quiet, civil, and orderly in the performance of his duty; he must be attentive and zealous, control his temper, and exercise the utmost patience and discretion. He must at all times refrain from harsh, violent, coarse, and profane language, and, when circumstances require, act with energy and decision.

Not to drink while on duty, or enter drinking places, ex-

27. No member of the department shall, in the station-house or elsewhere, while on duty, drink any kind of intoxicating liquor, or smoke, or, except in the immediate performance of

cept in performance of duty; nor smoke except as provided.

his duty, enter any place in which intoxicating drinks are sold or furnished. No intoxicating drink shall be introduced upon any pretext into the station-houses, except when advised by a physician. Smoking shall not be allowed in the station-house, except in apartments designated by the captain, with the approbation of the chief.

Not to receive rewards or gifts, nor extra compensation without approval.

28. No member shall, directly or indirectly, accept from any person, either liable to be arrested or to complaint, or in custody, or after he has been discharged, or from any of his friends, any gratuity, reward, or gift whatsoever; nor from any person money or other compensation for services rendered or damages sustained while on duty; nor any extra compensation whatsoever, without the approval of the committee on police.

To be punished or discharged for cause.

29. Any member of the department, for intoxication, wilful disobedience of order,s indecent, profane, or harsh language, disrespect to a superior, unnecessary violence to any prisoner or citizen, neglect in paying his just debts for rent or necessaries, or any breach of the "Rules and Regulations," shall be subject to reprimand, suspension, deductions from his pay, or to discharge, according to the nature or aggravation of the offence.

To have charges against them made in writing; and may have inquiry before the Committee on Police, and may be discharged with approval of the Mayor.

30. All complaints made against any member of the department by any other member thereof, or by any other person not of the force, shall be reduced to writing, with specifications, and shall be signed by the party making the complaint before the same shall be investigated. For minor offences the measure of punishment shall be determined by the chief of police, subject, however to an appeal to the committee on police. The investigation of all important charges shall be before the committee on police, and the evidence shall be taken down by a clerk; and when they find the officer guilty of any irregularity not sufficient to warrant his removal from the force, they shall state what deduction shall be made therefor from his compensation, and such deduction shall accordingly be made. No officer shall be removed from the force unless so recommended by said committee, and his removal approved by the Mayor.

When dis charged, to surrender property.

31. Whenever any member of the department resigns or is discharged, or in any way vacates his office, he shall surrender

to the captain of the station to which he belongs, his badge, number, book of regulations, memorandum books, club, police buttons, belt, and other equipments.

32. Coolness and firmness will be expected in all cases, of every officer, and in times of extreme peril the police must be careful to act together, and to protect each other in the restoration of peace; whoever shrinks from danger or responsibility, at such a moment, should be discharged as unworthy of a place in the service.

To coöperate in cases of danger.

33. No member of the department will be permitted to apply for a warrant for an assault upon himself, or make a complaint for damages, or adjust the same without consent of the chief.

Not to apply for warrants for assault, or make complaint for damages without consent of Chief.

34. No member of the department shall belong to any fire or military company, nor shall he serve on a coroner's jury nor perform any similar service. No association shall be formed within the department, of members thereof, without the assent of the board of aldermen.

Not to belong to fire or military companies, serve on juries, or form associations without consent

35. No member of the department is allowed to communicate any information respecting orders or regulations or any other business of the department whatever, or which has been procured in its service, except by special permission of a superior officer.

Not to disclose affairs of department with-permission.

36. No one will be appointed on the police for his religious or political opinions, and officers will avoid all religious or political discussions in the station-houses; they shall not interfere or make use of the influence of their office in elections, but may quietly exercise the right of suffrage as other citizens.

To avoid political and religious discussions, and not interfere in elections.

37. By statute of 1833, chap. 62, the mayor and board of aldermen were authorized to set the watch at such time after sunset as they shall deem expedient; it is ordered that the watch shall be set one hour next after sunset.

Watch to be set at the hour after sunset.

Detective Police.

38. The head-quarters of the detective police shall be at the central office, and their office hours from 9 to 10 A. M. and from 2 to 3 P. M. each day, or at such other times as the chief may

Detectives to have certain hours.

direct. Some one of their number shall be, when practicable, at the office at all hours, from 9 A. M. to 6 P. M.

To visit public places and take note of suspected places and persons.

39. They shall, as often as practicable, visit the railroad stations, theatres, and places of amusement, all public gatherings and other places where large numbers of persons collect, take note of all gaming-houses and houses of ill-repute, and all persons who may reasonably be suspected of crime or evil design, whether residents or strangers, and keep a list of all persons convicted of crime, who are likely to be dangerous to the community.

To visit thronged thoroughfares and endeavor to prevent crime.

40. When no other business engages their attention, they shall visit the most thronged thoroughfares in the city, noting persons and transactions which may be of service to them in the discharge of their duties; and they shall not only use their best efforts to detect the criminal, but also to prevent the commission of crime.

To perform any duty required by the Chief or Deputy.

41. Being the only force at the immediate command of the chief, they will at all times hold themselves in readiness to answer any calls made by the chief or the deputy to perform any duties connected with the business of the department.

To go out of the city with permission.

42. Should there be occasion to send one of their number out of the city, county, or State, in pursuit of any fugitive from justice,—this may be allowed by permission of the chief or the committee on police. But all his expenses and a reasonable compensation may be required by the department of the parties interested in the apprehension of the criminal, as a condition of such permission.

To bring persons arrested to the central office, note their description, etc. and leave their property with the Chief.

43. When any person is taken into custody, he shall, if practicable, be brought to the central office, and a full description of his person, and the time and cause of his arrest, his name, and that of the arresting officer, with the amount and description of property taken from his person, shall be recorded on the book kept for that purpose; and if he is to be locked up, he shall be placed in the city prison, and a *mittimus* left with the keeper. All property taken from any person shall be put together, carefully marked, and left with the chief of police.

44. They shall at all times keep the chief informed of all matters coming to their knowledge relating to the interest of the department, and they shall not undertake the investigation of any case without the knowledge and consent of the chief or the deputy.

To inform the Chief of all matters.

45. They shall each keep a private record of their doings in a book kept at the central office for that purpose, always open for inspection by superior officers.

To keep private records to be inspected by superiors.

Superintendent of Carriages.

46. The superintendent of carriages shall devote his whole time to the business of the department. He shall have the general supervision of all carriages licensed for the conveyance of passengers in the city of Boston. He shall keep a book for the entry of complaints against parties licensed, made for demanding or receiving illegal fares, or for not having their numbers in a conspicuous place, or other irregularities, and examine and report the same to the committee on licenses. He shall investigate and report to the chairman of said committee upon all applications for carriage licenses, and the names of all persons occupying carriage stands in the city of Boston, or carrying passengers for a compensation, who are not duly licensed, or who do not fully comply with the rules and regulations in relation thereto.

Superintendent of Carriages to supervise licensed carriages; record complaints; report on applications for license, etc.

47. The superintendent of carriages shall keep an accurate record of the names of the owners of all licensed carriages, and the number of the license. He shall collect all dues for licenses granted, and pay over the same to the chief of police, and he shall also perform such other duties as may be required by the chief of police. He shall be at his office from 9 to 10 o'clock, A. M. and from 2 to 3 o'clock, P. M., each day, for the transaction of business belonging to his branch of the department.

To record all licenses and collect the fees; and perform other duties required by Chief.

Superintendent of Trucks.

Superintendent of Trucks to supervise vehicles licensed to transport mer-

48. The superintendent of trucks shall devote his whole time to the business of the department. He shall have the

chandise; to keep records, collect fees, etc.

generāl superintendence of all vehicles licensed for the transportation of merchandise in the city of Boston.

49. He shall investigate and report to the chairman of the committee on licenses, upon all applications for license of vehicles for transportation of merchandise, as also for street stands, and shall see that all vehicles of that kind are properly licensed and numbered, and that the proprietors conform to the rules and regulations prescribed in their respective licenses.

50. The superintendent of trucks shall keep an accurate record of the names and number of each license. He shall collect all dues for such granted licenses, and pay over the same to the chief of police; and he shall perform such other duties as may be required by the chief of police.

51. He shall keep a book at his office in which complaints may be entered, and he shall promptly investigate the same, and all other irregularities in his department that come to his knowledge, and make report thereon to the chief and to the committee on licenses.

52. He shall be at his office from 9 to 10 o'clock A. M. and from 2 to 3 o'clock P. M. each day, for the transaction of business connected with his branch of the department.

Superintendent of Pawnbrokerage.

Superintendent of Pawnbrokerage to supervise pawnbrokers and second-hand dealers.

53. The superintendent of pawnbrokerage shall devote his whole time to the business of the department. Under the direction of the chief of police he shall have the general supervision of all matters appertaining to the license of pawnbrokers, intelligence offices, dealers in junk, and second-hand articles, throughout the city.

To record all persons coming under his supervision.

54. He shall keep a book in which he shall register alphabetically the names of all pawnbrokers and all dealers in junk or second-hand articles, together with the name and number of the street where they are doing business, and he shall see that each is furnished with a copy of the ordinance relating to his branch of trade.

55. He shall also keep a book in which he shall register alphabetically the names of all who have taken out licenses, or to whom, on petition, license has not been granted, and also those to whom license has been granted, but subsequently revoked, with the name and number of the street where each carries on business; and he shall see that all such persons duly licensed, keep the requisite books, and in all things conform to the requirements of the laws and ordinances regulating their trade; and he shall inspect said books from time to time, as often at least as once a month, making note of such facts as are deemed of importance, and if suspicions are reasonably connected with any property falling under his observation, he shall immediately report the same to the chief of police.

To examine books of such persons, and report suspected cases.

56. In all cases where persons carry on either of the above trades without license, he shall cause such persons, under direction of the chief, to be complained against, and attend to their prosecution.

To complain of unlicensed dealers.

57. Members of the police department, when so directed by the chief, may enter the shop of any pawnbroker or dealer in junk or second-hand articles, and examine their books and the articles therein, and if resisted, or refused permission to so do, the case shall be reported to the chief, and by him to the superintendent and committee on licenses, and if the circumstances justify it, the license shall be revoked.

Police officers may examine books and property of second-hand dealers, when directed.

58. The superintendent of pawnbrokerage shall submit to the chief of police, on each Monday morning, a written report of his doings for the previous week.

Superintendent shall report weekly to the chief.

59. He shall be at his office from 9 to 10 A. M. and from 2 to 3 P. M. each day, for the transaction of business connected with his branch of the department.

Clerk of Police.

60. The clerk of police shall devote his whole time to the business of the department. He shall keep fully and accurately all books, records, papers, or reports appertaining to the central office, under the direction of the chief of police or the deputy, and perform all such other clerical service as they shall order.

Clerk of Police to keep books of central office, etc.

Captains of Police.

Captain of Police to be at station-house during the day, and have charge of the same.

61. The captain of police shall be at his station-house at all times during the day, unless absent on official duty. He shall have the general charge of his station-house, and be held responsible for the cleanliness, good order, and proper condition of the same.

To keep station-house open, and properly attended.

62. He shall see that his station-house is kept open at all times, and in his absence shall detail a lieutenant or sergeant, to be constantly in charge thereof, to receive prisoners, attend to calls, answer the applications of citizens, or to attend to other business properly belonging to the department.

To have charge of his district, and note matters requiring attention; report cases of contagion and danger from fire, and may order inquests.

63. He shall have the general charge of his district, visiting every part of it as often as once each week, noting the condition of the streets, sidewalks, street-lights, obstructions, nuisances, and non-compliances with the city ordinances, and all other matters requiring the attention of the police in his district. He shall report to the chief all cases of contagiuos disease, and any negligence which may expose the city to danger from fire, all mat ters within the line of the duty of the superintendents of streets or internal health.

To have control of men attached to his station.

64. He shall have immediate control of the officers and patrolmen detailed for duty at his station, and shall carefully note their conduct, condition, faithfulness, and efficiency. He shall call the roll at 6 P. M. each day — then communicating all necessary information and orders, and at such other times as the chief shall order, noting and reporting every absence. He shall daily inspect his men, and reform any negligence in attire, want of cleanliness or of neatness, or other improper personal habit, and report to the chief every case of sickness, misconduct, insubordination, neglect, or unfitness for duty, and establish such rules for the government of the station-house as the chief shall approve. He shall, as often as once a week, at roll-call, put the men through the simple military formations-in-line and evolutions, and once each week instruct them as to their conduct at fires or riots, in making arrests or complaints, as to defects in the highway, nuisances, and accidents, in procuring information, or

To inspect the men; report neglect or insubordination; instruct men in drill and duty, and divide the district into beats.

other matters pertaining to their duty. He shall see that each has his copy of the "Rules and Regulations," and duly observes them. He shall divide, with the approval of the chief, his district into beats for day, and also for night, so arranged that the whole territory shall be covered at all times by officers on duty, except at roll-call, and as circumstances require, placing each officer, as far as practicable, where he will be most useful and efficient.

65. He shall receive into his custody and safely keep all persons arrested in his district for any criminal offence, and unless otherwise lawfully disposed of, shall, before the opening of the next session of the police court, cause all such prisoners to be conveyed to the city prison, there to await the action of the court or the order of the chief of police; and it shall be his duty, or that of one of the lieutenants or sergeants, to be present at the police court each morning, when required, after making his morning report, to attend to cases from his station.

To receive and keep all persons arrested; remove them to the City Prison, etc.

66. He shall cause all persons brought into his station-house, before they are committed to the cells, to be first brought into the dock, where the officer in charge shall then enter in the blotter his own name, the name of the arresting officer, also the name, nation, age, height, complexion, weight, residence, and offence of the prisoner, and the number of his cell; the prisoner shall be properly searched, and whatever is taken for safe-keeping be properly entered on the book. He shall post daily from the blotter to a register, alphabetically arranged, the name and description of criminals so arrested, with their sentence in court, of which he shall inform himself.

To make proper records of arrests.

To search prisoners, etc.

67. He shall also enter on his blotter and post into a register the name and description of all persons furnished with lodgings at the station-house.

To record lodgers.

68. He shall receive and keep all property coming into the possession of officers of the station by virtue of their office; mark, and keep together and separate, the property taken from each person, and keep a record of the same; and property holden for evidence shall be delivered by order of court, and all other property holden shall, as soon as possible, be delivered to the lawful owner, a receipt being taken therefor; and all

To make proper disposition of property taken by the police.

property remaining at the close of each quarter shall be delivered or reported to the chief.

To record offences, and other police matters.

69. He shall keep a daily record of burglaries, robberies, larcenies, amount of property lost or stolen, assaults, disturbances, lost children, fires, dangerous places, and accidents, with the cause and proofs, and of all other matters appertaining to the business of the department in his district, for reference.

To record and report the duty done by men, with bills incurred, etc.

70. He shall keep a daily account of the regular and extra duties done by his men, and on the eighteenth of each month submit to the chief a full and accurate account against the name of each member of his station, the number of days on duty, number of days absent without pay, or from sickness; all stoppages, amount due for extra work, and total amount due for the month preceding, with the requisite certified bills, certificates, and vouchers for the same; also all other bills necessarily incurred at the station for the current month, approved by him.

To make daily, monthly, and yearly reports of all matters.

71. He shall daily transcribe from his blotter and journal to his morning report, a true copy of all matters of importance there recorded for the twenty-four hours ending at 8 o'clock, A. M., and present said report to the chief at 9 o'clock A. M. of the same day. He shall, on the last day of each month, transmit to the chief a full and correct synopsis of all the police work done in his district for the current month; and on the last day of each year he shall submit to the chief a full synopsis of all the police work done in his district for the current year.

To record all licensed and suspected persons and places.

72. He shall keep a record of all pawnbrokers, second-hand dealers, junk shops, intelligence offices, licensed places of amusement within his district, and cause the laws and ordinances concerning them to be observed. He shall keep a record of all suspected drinking-saloons, gambling-houses, or houses of ill-fame, and of all places where idlers, tipplers, gamblers, sellers of lottery-tickets, thieves, and other disorderly and suspicious persons congregate.

To detail officers for duty at fires, etc.

73. In case of an alarm of fire the two officers on street duty nearest the fire shall repair at once to the fire and act as fire-police, the officers on beats adjoining to cover those left vacant. The captain will detail from the reserve at the station,

with a sergeant, to repair to the fire, sufficient men to keep the streets clear and protect property, that the officers on street duty may return as soon as practicable to their beats.

74. In case of fire or other emergency, the captain or superior officer of the district present shall have direction not only of his own men, but also of patrolmen of other stations within call. To have control at fires of all police present.

75. In case of any riot or sudden emergency, requiring the services of the police, on notice being given, the captain of the district in which such riot may occur shall forthwith proceed to the scene of disturbance, with the whole police force he can muster, and be vigilant in suppressing the disorder. Should the captain have any doubt of his ability to preserve the peace, or to restore order, he will immediately send notice to the chief of police or the deputy chief. To suppress riots.

76. He shall cause the members of his command to be thoroughly instructed in the "School of the Soldier and Company," excepting those parts which relate exclusively to the manual of arms. To give military instruction to officers.

77. No person shall be permitted to remain at the station-house without permission of the officer in charge, except members of the department detailed for service, members of the city council, and persons having official business there. The use of spirituous liquors or wines, gambling, boisterous or indecent language or conduct, and profanity, are strictly prohibited at the station-house, and it is the duty of the captain to report any disobedience of the rules or other irregularity, that comes to his knowledge, to the chief. Not to permit improper persons or conduct in station-houses, and to report irrrgularities.

78. He shall observe the strictest economy in the use of fuel and gas at the station-house, consistent with a due regard to the comfort of the men, and see that the furniture and other property belonging to the same is neither destroyed nor injured. To use gas and fuel economically.

Lieutenants.

79. The lieutenants shall be detailed two to each district, and in the absence of the captain and in charge of the station, *Lieutenant* to have same powers and duties

as the Captain, in his absence. shall have and exercise all his powers and duties, and be held to the like responsibility.

To alternate in duty. 80. They shall rank first and second as named in their appointment. They shall alternate their duties, spending day and night such hours at the station-house and such hours in the examination of the district, and perform such other duties as shall from time to time be ordered by their captain or by the chief.

To report delinquencies to the Captain. 81. While on duty, or in the absence of a superior officer, their orders shall be respected and obeyed, and they shall report to the captain every instance of violation of duty or of disobedience to orders.

Sergeants.

Sergeants of Police to perform such duty as directed. 82. Sergeants of police shall be detailed two to each station, except No. 8 and No. 4, to each of which shall be attached three.

83. They shall rank first and second, and, under the orders of their respective captains, shall perform such duties and at such hours of day and night as shall be directed by the chief of police.

To have charge of and instruct men; patrol the district and report the conduct of men. 84. They shall have the general charge of the men on their beats, and shall instruct and assist them in their duties. When on duty and not otherwise detailed, they shall constantly and faithfully patrol their respective districts, visiting each beat as often as twice in each term of service, ascertaining the presence of each man at his proper place, and aiding in the enforcement of every duty.

85. They shall carefully note, and impartially report to the captain or lieutenant, every officer found on duty, by name and number, and the case of every officer absent from his beat, or other neglect of discipline or duty; and their failure so to report shall be sufficient cause for suspension or discharge from service.

Patrolmen.

Patrolmen may be called into service at any time. 86. The districts will be divided into beats, and the rounds of regular service will be from time to time specified; but it is clearly to be understood that when occasion requires, officers are liable to be called into service for any portion of the day, if necessary. The ordinary sphere of their duty is the city of Boston and the harbor with its islands. But as officers clothed with the criminal powers of constables, they may be required to go into any other part of the State to arrest criminals, or for other duties. No compensation will be allowed beyond their pay for extra service, except upon such bills as are approved by the mayor and the committee on police, and all fees as witnesses in court shall be deducted from their pay, except as provided in the seventh section of the ordinance; and they must report to the captain all fees so received, who shall report the same to the chief, to be deducted from the next month's payment.

Not to receive extra pay or fees without approval.

87. The patrolman will hold himself in readiness, at all times, to answer the calls, and to obey the orders of his superior officers. He shall treat them with respect, and in his demeanor to his associates, on the force, be courteous and considerate, guarding himself against envy, jealousy, or other unfriendly feeling, and refraining from all communications to their discredit, except to his superior officers, whom it is his duty to inform of every neglect or disobedience of orders on their part that may come to his knowledge. He shall conform to the rules and regulations of the department, observe the laws and ordinances, and render his services to the city with zeal, courage, discretion, and fidelity. Any violation of the rules of the department will be punished by reprimand, suspension, deductions from pay, or discharge.

To be courteous to superiors, report neglect, be obedient, etc.

88. He shall be present at the daily roll-calls, and attend at the station-house at the times appointed him, and if absent, except by permission, or for sufficient reason, deductions shall be made from his pay.

To be present at roll-call unless excused.

89. Immediately after roll-calls, the patrolmen going out on duty shall each repair to his beat, and continually patrol every part thereof, as often as once each hour if practicable, and he shall confine his patrol within the limits of his beat, except in case of fire, arrest of a prisoner, or other necessary ab-

To patrol their beats once an hour, and confine themselves to their beat, except in specified cases.

sence on duty, until the time assigned for the expiration of his tour of duty, and he is regularly relieved.

Not to communicate with one another or other persons, unless in the line of duty.

90. Policemen must not walk together, or talk with each other, or with any other person on their beats, unless it be to communicate information pertaining to the department, or in the line of their duty, and such communication must be as brief as possible.

To inform themselves of the inhabitants on their beats.

91. As far as he can, without intrusion upon the privacy of individuals, he must note all removals from or into the limits of his beat, and acquire such a knowledge of the inhabitants as will enable him to recognize them.

To give information and aid, consistent with duty, keep his number in sight, etc.

92. He shall furnish such information and render such aid to all persons, when requested, as is consistent with his duty, and he shall keep his number in sight and give his name and number to all persons who inquire.

To direct strangers, and give assistance to other officers.

93. He must direct strangers and others, when requested, the nearest and safest way to their places of destination, and, when necessary, cause them to be accompanied thither by one of the police, but shall not leave his beat for that purpose, but pass such persons from his beat to the next. If he hear the cry of watch, or other call for assistance, he shall proceed to render aid with all despatch, taking every practical precaution for the protection of his beat, when he leaves it for this or any other purpose.

To restore lost children.

94. He shall cause all children who have strayed, or infants who have been abandoned, to be taken to the residence of their parents, if known, and within the bounds of his beat, and if not, to the station-house. Children or families without home shall be directed or sent to the City Temporary Home, 36 Charles Street.

To note cases of contagion, or sudden death, etc.

He shall take note of all cases of contagious disease, or sudden death, where there is reasonable ground to suspect criminality, and render immediate aid in cases of accident or illness in the streets, ascertaining all important particulars connected therewith, and making record thereof.

To warn crowds as to pickpockets.

95. When he discovers a pickpocket in a crowd at railroad stations, theatres, or any other thronged place, he shall give suitable warning.

96. He must strictly watch the conduct of all persons of known bad character, in such manner that it will be evident to them that they are watched, fixing in his mind such impressions as will enable him to recognize persons whom he frequently meets in the streets at night, and to the utmost of his power, prevent the commission of assaults, breaches of the peace, and all other crimes about to be committed.

To watch persons of bad character and prevent assaults, crimes, etc.

97. He must note all junk-shops and shops of second-hand dealers and pawnbrokers, all places of amusement, and all licensed persons and places within his beat, and also all suspected gambling-houses, public saloons for drinking, dancing, or prize-fighting, mock-auction rooms, venders of lottery tickets, houses of ill-fame, and all other suspicious persons and places therein, keep a list thereof in his book for reference, and report the same to his captain.

To note and report licensed and suspected places and persons.

98. While on duty he shall note all street and sidewalk obstructions, all defects therein from which accidents may occur, removing them when practicable; all places for which temporary permits are granted for building, or where openings or excavations are being made, and not suffer them to be continued without examining the permits authorizing the same, and shall cause suitable accommodations to be provided for the public travel; all coal-holes left exposed or insecure; all street lamps not lighted at proper times, or too early extinguished, where not clean, or not giving sufficient light; all wooden buildings erected or being erected contrary to law, or any building defectively built or become unsafe, or where any noisome, dangerous, or unwholesome trade is carried on; and all nuisances, and other matters relating to the safety and convenience of the public or to the interests of the city, which may exist or occur on his beat, *and shall make report thereof without delay in writing to his captain.*

To note and report obstructions and defects in the streets; insecure coal-holes; defective lamps; unsafe buildings, nuisances, etc.

98. He shall examine in the night-time all doors, gates, and windows of dwellings and stores, to see that they are properly secured, and if not give notice to the inmates, if any, and where not, make the same fast and notify the owner in the morning. He must watch vacant houses, to prevent depredations, be vigi-

To examine doors, gates, etc. and secure those left open.

To be vigilant in respect to

fires, waste of water, the state of sidewalks, nuisances in the streets; and report parties violating the ordinances.

lant to prevent fire or waste of Cochituate water, call the attention of abutters to the state of their sidewalks, where by snow, ice, or other cause they are rendered dangerous, or when obstructed by fuel, boxes, or other incumbrance, or with goods, or signs extending more than a foot over the same: take note of all ashes, garbage, dead animals, or other nuisance thrown into the street, or where the street is used for washing carriages or horses, or improperly obstructed thereby, or where the laws and ordinances, orders, rules, and regulations for the government of such cases, upon notice given, are not forthwith obeyed, the officer shall do what he can himself to make the way safe and convenient, ascertain the names of the parties offending, and report the same for complaint and prosecution.

To request loiterers to move on, and report those who refuse.

100. Whenever any person remains upon any one part of the sidewalk longer than is allowed by law, it shall be the duty of the officer to request him courteously to move on; and if any such person unreasonably persists in remaining so as to incommode other passengers, the officer shall endeavor to ascertain the name of such person, and report the same for prosecution.

To note beggars, and if in distress, direct them to Overseers of the Poor or Charitable Associations.

101. When any person begs in the street or goes from door to door soliciting alms, it shall be the duty of the officer to inquire the name and abode of such person, and note the same for record, and to direct such person, if in distress, to the Overseers of the Poor or to any charitable association to his knowledge affording relief in similar cases.

To note fast driving, brutality to animals, violations of law in respect to carriages.

102. He shall note all cases of fast driving, brutality to animals, horses or vehicles left unattended more than five minutes, or standing more than twenty, or going upon the sidewalk, or taking the wrong side in passing or meeting, all cases where the drivers of licensed vehicles are uncivil, or demand illegal fares, or where rail cars or omnibuses stop opposite the intersection of streets or on crossings or do not conform to any other lawful provision made for their regulation.

To assist to disentangle blocked teams, and protect foot passengers.

103. When any way becomes blocked, he shall use his best efforts to aid the drivers in disentangling the same, and when the stream of travel is continuous, open the way for foot-travel-

lers wishing to cross, attending women, children, and aged persons, who would be otherwise exposed to danger.

To quell disturbances, and arrest offenders.

104. When a disturbance occurs, he shall instantly repair to the spot, and use his best efforts to restore quiet. If any person has committed a felonious assault, or any other felonious crime, or by loud outcries, or otherwise, persists in disturbing the peace, any one so offending shall be taken into custody, and conveyed to the station-house to await the order of the captain. If he is opposed in the performance of his duty, he shall spring his rattle, and the policemen who hear it shall answer the same, by forthwith proceeding to his assistance.

To arrest on warrants, and make proper returns; may arrest persons reasonably suspected, and night-walkers, and may examine persons abroad at unseasonable hours.

105. When holding a warrant against a party, he shall arrest him, and safely keep him in custody, and carry him before the next session of the police, or other court, to which the warrant is returnable, making the proper returns thereon over his own signature as a police officer. He may also arrest, without a warrant, any person riding or driving through the streets at a rate of speed inconsistent with the public safety or convenience, any person reasonably suspected of having committed a felony, or seen committing a breach of the peace, or being unduly armed with a dangerous weapon, and also nightwalkers; but in every case of arrest without a warrant, complaints must be made at the next session of the police court. He may also examine any person whom he shall see walking abroad in the night after the watch is set, and whom he shall have reason to suspect of any unlawful design, and may demand of him his business abroad and whither he is going.

To require accusers of crime to go with the accused to the station.

106. When any party charges another with crime, and insists that the party so charged shall be taken into custody, he shall require the accuser, if unknown to him, or there is any other sufficient reason for it, to go with the accused to the station.

Not to use unnecessary force in making arrests or abuse prisoners.

107. When it becomes necessary to take a party into custody, he shall do so in as easy and quiet a manner as possible, only using sufficient force to secure the prisoner, and no more, and in no instance shall he strike the prisoner, except in self-defence. When in custody, he shall see that the prisoner is

properly dealt with and cared for, until disposed of from his custody according to law, and any unnecessary deprivations or abuse to prisoners while in custody, will be met with reproof and punishment.

To carefully preserve all property taken from prisoners.

108. The property coming into his possession in his official capacity he shall carefully preserve, mark and place in the hands of his captain, and whatever is taken from each person while in his custody shall be kept together, and separate from other property.

Not to act in civil cases, except by authority.

109. As by virtue of his appointment he can act officially in criminal matters only, he will not render assistance in any civil case whatever, except to prevent a breach of the peace, or to suppress a disturbance actually commenced, nor serve any warrant of search, without permission of the chief, deputy chief, or his captain.

To be paid for time lost by injuries while on duty, and by sickness for ten days.

110. Policemen wounded, or otherwise disabled while in the performance of their official duty, and those rendered ill in consequence of unusual or extraordinary hardship, or exposure beyond the regular line of their duty, shall receive pay for their period of service necessarily lost in recovering, when duly certified by the city physician, or other physician appointed by their respective captains for them, upon approval of the committee on police. In cases of ordinary sickness, pay will be allowed for three days upon the voucher of the captain, and for ten days, and never more, when certified to by his own or the city physician.

To give alarms of fire, and note circumstances.

111. On discovering a fire, the officer shall first ascertain if it can be extinguished without alarm, if not, he shall at once repair to the nearest signal-box and give the alarm. In the night-time, upon an alarm of fire, officers shall pass quickly over their beats, springing their rattles, crying fire, and giving the number of the district and the number and location of the box. He shall note the time, and his position when he gives an alarm or hears one, and any circumstances connected therewith which seem to be suspicious.

To protect lives and property at fires; officer

112. At an alarm of fire the officers who are detailed for fire police at the station, shall quickly repair to the fire, to ren-

der such assistance as practicable in securing and protecting lives and property, under the direction of the engineers of the fire department. The officer first arriving shall have precedence and control of the other officers who may be present, until a superior officer arrives.

first arriving to have control until superiors arrive.

113. It shall be the duty of the police officer to keep a private record of his work, with day and date, and he shall enter therein all matters of any importance in all work in which he is engaged in his official capacity, whether at court, on his beat, or elsewhere, and also any other matter of importance that comes to his knowledge, connected with the police of the city; and when his book is full, it shall be carefully preserved for future use or reference, and he shall commence another.

To keep private record of all matters of duty.

114. He shall each day, at such time as shall be appointed, make report to thé captain of all that he has done, or which has come to his knowledge, during the previous twenty-four hours, or since his last report, exhibiting his book to the captain if requested.

To make daily reports.

115. Any officer who neglects to wear his badge and uniform when on duty, or in court, without permission from the chief, or his captain, will be suspended from the department.

May be suspended for not wearing uniform and badge.

Harbor Police.

116. The water police district will be divided into two beats, to be called the north and south districts.

Harbor Police divided into two districts.

117. The north district will comprise all the docks, wharves, and shipping north of Union Wharf to Charlestown Bridge, including East Boston.

118. The south district will comprise all the docks, wharves, and shipping south of Union Wharf, India Wharf to the water to South Boston Bridge, including South Boston.

119. If it become necessary in the performance of their duty, to go farther north or south than the districts above described, they will do so.

120. The south district will visit the powder boats every hour, and see that all is safe; also the oyster beds once in each

To visit the powder boats and oyster beds.

watch, and as much oftener as practicable, to see that they are not disturbed.

To pay particular attention to cases of drowning.

121. They will pay particular attention to all cases of drowning coming under their observation, using every means in their power, regardless of time or cost, to resuscitate persons taken from the water.

To board foreign vessels, keep boats away, and challenge strange boats.

122. They will board all foreign vessels on their arrival, supplying them with a copy of the "Harbor Regulations," keeping away all boats, and allow no person to board said vessel without permission, until such vessel has been made fast to the wharf. They will also, after ten o'clock in the evening, challenge all strange boats, satisfying themselves that there is nothing wrong.

To render aid on the wharves.

123. Should the cry of watch be made on the wharf, or a disturbance of the peace, the boatmen shall take notice thereof, and render such aid as the circumstances may require.

To have certain signals.

124. The following signals shall govern either watch when they may be wanted: For the watch on the north district one shot will be fired from a pistol at the end of Union Wharf.

For the watch of the south district two shots will be fired in quick succession from the same place, — when the boat so signalized shall come directly to Union Wharf.

In addition to the above, the north watch will be at the end of Union Wharf at the following hours: seven, nine, eleven, one, three, five, and seven, — and the south watch at eight, ten, twelve, two, four, and six.

To be relieved at certain hours; to keep boats, and firearms in order.

125. The relieving time will be five minutes before one and five minutes before eight in the morning, and five minutes before six in the evening, when the watch to be relieved will be at their relieving post.

It will be expected of the eight o'clock morning watch and the six o'clock evening watch to have their boat washed and left clean, and everything in order for the next watch — the fire-arms kept clean and in order, and loaded and in their proper place.

Time of the different watches.

126. The time for the morning watch will be at three and half-past three o'clock, the north watch coming in at three to

be on duty at half-past three o'clock, during which time the south watch will have charge of both districts. The south watch will come in at half-past three to be on duty at four o'clock, during which time the north watch will take charge of both districts.

127. It will be expected of the officers belonging to the sail boat, unless otherwise ordered, to be on board the boat during their hours of duty; and the officer detailed whose night watch is aboard the boat will be on board at nine o'clock in the evening. **Officers on the sail boat.**

128. The officers shall instruct their men to familiarize themselves with all vessels belonging to Boston, as well as with vessels from other places frequenting the port. **To familiarize themselves with all vessels in port.**

129. They shall, under the direction of the chief of police, co-operate with the officers of the custom-house, the marshal of the district, and the harbor master, in enforcing the laws of the Commonwealth and the United States. **To co-operate with U. S. Officers and the Harbor Master enforcing the laws.**

130. All officers will be present at roll-call — day officers to be punctual at five minutes before eight in the morning; night officers at five minutes before six in the evening. **Roll-call.**

Special Police.

131. Persons who hold warrants as special police officers without pay, must wear the badge required by the chief of police. ***Special Police* to wear a badge.**

132. Such officers must conform to the rules and regular tions of the police department, so far as relates to their habits, conduct, mode of performing police duty, and in every particular in which they may be applied. **To conform to the rules.**

133. Every special police officer shall make a return every week to the captain of the district within which his duties lay, of all the official acts which he has performed in the week preceding. **To make weekly returns of duty.**

134. Special police officers who abuse their trusts, who violate the rules of the department, or who are unfit for duty, will be deprived of their warrants. **To be removed for delinquency.**

Police Property.

Police Property to be under charge of Committee on Police.

136. The committee on police shall have a general superintendence of all property belonging to the city used by the police department, and shall have power to authorize the sale or exchange thereof, when in their judgment expedient: and within the limits of the appropriation made for the same, to authorize the purchase of what is needed therefor.

APPENDIX.

Police Uniform

Police uniform.

1. The Chief of police, the Deputy Chief, the Captains, Lieutenants, Sergeants, and Patrolmen, shall wear a dark blue sack frock coat, dark blue pants, and dark blue vest, and police hat, like the pattern at the Chief's Office. On public occasions the Chief, Deputy Chief, the Captains and Lieutenants, may wear a buff vest, with police buttons.

Summer uniform.

2. From the tenth day of June until the first day of October, in each year, the police shall wear a skeleton sack coat, and pants made of dark blue flannel, like the pattern at the Chief's office.

Winter uniform.

3. When the weather is cold, the police may wear a dark blue overcoat, like the pattern at the Chief's office.

Overcoat.

4. Overcoat, surtout pattern, double breasted, with short rolling collar, made to button close up in the neck: the waist to be two and one half inches below the natural waist; the length of the skirt to be four inches below the knee-pan, one pocket in the left breast upon the outside, one in the right breast upon the inside and one in each skirt; two rows of police buttons, six in a row, upon the breast, four buttons behind with side edge, and three small police buttons on each cuff.

5. Sack frock, single breasted, with rolling collar, made to button up to within six inches of the neck; waist to be one and one half inches below the natural waist; length of skirt to be within one inch of the knee-pan, the coat to be bound with narrow silk binding, four police buttons on the front, four upon the back with side edge, and two small police buttons upon each cuff. Coat.

6. Vest, single breasted, made without collar, to button up within three inches of the neck, with seven police buttons on front. Vest.

7. Pantaloons, to be made like the pattern at the Chief's office. Pantaloons.

8. The sack frocks, when worn, will be buttoned at the top button alone, unless otherwise ordered by a superior officer; the skeleton sacks, when worn, will be buttoned up with four police buttons. Buttons on coat.

9. The boatmen's undress uniform, when on duty on board their boats, shall consist of a single breasted "reef jacket," and pants made of dark blue cloth; the jacket will have four police buttons on the front, and be buttoned close up, and they will wear the police hat and badge like the patrolmen; in stormy or wet weather they may wear suitable clothing to protect them from its inclemency, under the direction of their Captain. Boatmen's uniform.

10. In wet or stormy weather the patrolmen may wear a portable cape of cloth or rubber. Cape for wet weather.

11. The police uniform shall be worn by the officers when on duty before the public, and when at court, unless by permission of the Chief, Deputy Chief, or the Captain of the district from which he is detailed for detective purposes. Uniform to be worn on duty.

12. Clubs, belts, and white gloves, will be worn whenever the Chief or Deputy Chief orders. Clubs, belts, &c.

13. The Chief of Police shall wear upon the front of his hat a gold-embroidered wreath, with the word CHIEF embroidered therein, in old English letters with silver bullion, and the same insignia upon each shoulder. *Badges*, of the Chief.

14. The Deputy Chief of Police shall wear on the front of his hat, and upon each shoulder, a wreath like the Chief, with Of the Deputy.

Deputy Chief, in old English letters, embroidered therein, in silver bullion.

Of Captains and Lieutenants. 15. Captains and Lieutenants of Police shall wear upon their hats and their shoulders, a wreath like the Chief, with the word Captain or Lieutenant, in old English letters, embroidered therein, in silver bullion, and above the wreath the number of their district.

Of Sergeants. 16. Sergeants of Police shall wear upon their hats a gold wreath, with Sergeant embroidered therein, in silver bullion, over which will be their letter, upon each shoulder the number of their district, and upon each arm, above the elbow, a strap with the word Sergeant, in silver bullion.

Of Patrolmen. 17. Patrolmen shall wear upon their hats a gold wreath like the sergeants, with the number of the man embroidered therein, in silver bullion, and upon each shoulder the number of the district to which they are attached.

SCHOOLS.

RULES AND REGULATIONS.

Chapter 1.

1. Organization of the Board.
2. Standing Committees.
3. Districts; district committees.
4. Chairmen of sub-committees.
5. Annual and quarterly meetings.
6. Quorum.
7. Vacancies in the Board.

Chapter 2.

1. Opening of meetings; order of business.
2, 3, 4. Duties of the President.
5. Committee of the whole.
6. Yeas and nays.
7. Motions.
8. Motion to adjourn.
9. Previous question.
10. Call of special meetings.
11. Appointment on committees.

Chapter 3.

1. Duties of members in debate.
2. Call to order.
3. Violation of rules.
4. Rules of debate.
5. Motions.
6. Order of motions.
7. Reconsideration.
8. Members to vote.
9. Commitments.
10. Division of a question.
11. Reading of a paper when called for.
12. Suspension of rules.
13. Repeal or amendment of rules.

Chapter 4.

1. Committee on elections.
2. Committee on rules and regulations.
3. Committee on accounts.
4. Mover of a motion, etc., to be notified of the time of its consideration.
5. Committee on schoolhouses: — warming and ventilation of schoolhouses.
6. Committee on salaries.
7. Committee on text-books.
8. Introduction of new books.
9. Committee on music.
10. Committee on printing.
11. Committees on high schools.
12. Organization of district committees.
13. Duties of district committees; classification of pupils; care of primary schools.
14. Additional primary schools.
15. Quarterly examinations.
16. Quarterly reports.
17. Medals and certificates.
18. Pupils to attend school in section where they reside.
19. Teacher of sewing.
20. Examination of teachers; teachers advanced to another grade to be examined; reappointed teachers to be considered as new teachers.
21. Names of well-qualified candidates at examinations to be preserved.
22. Canvassing the lists of teachers; nomination of teachers for re-election.
23. District committees shall give advice to instructors, etc.; district committees may make temporary arrangements.
24. Transfer of primary schools and teachers; notice to be sent to Secretary of the Board; transfer of teachers by the Board.

25. Annual examinations; annual reports.

Chapter 5.

1. School year.
2. Annual election of teachers.
3. Mode of choosing instructors.
4, 5, 6. Election of a *new* master.
7. Examining committee's report.
8. Instructors to hold their offices for one year.

Chapter 6.

1. Records and files.
2. Notices to be given.
3. Report to Secretary of State.
4. Votes to be transmitted.
5. Medals to be provided.
6. Examination of bills.

Chapter 7.

1. Election of Superintendent; salary.
2. His general duties.
3. Visiting schools; meetings of primary school teachers; meetings of grammar school teachers.
4. State scholarships; absentees from school.
5. Assistance to committees.
6. Building and altering of schoolhouses; school expenses.
7. To attend meetings of Board: semi-annual report.
8. Record of names of applicants.

Chapter 8.

1. Teachers to observe the school regulations.
2. General duties of teachers.
3. Schoolhouses.
4. Teachers and pupils to be at school early.
5. Opening the schools.
6. Moral instruction.
7. School register and records.
8. Blanks for schools.
9. Masters to examine their schools.
10. Semi-annual returns.
11. Notices to be given to Secretary.
12. Teachers visiting schools.
13. Corporal punishment.
14. Exclusion of a pupil.
15. Suspension and restoration of pupils.
16. Absence of pupils.
17. Instructors, in cases of difficulty, to apply to district committees.
18. Absentees must pay their substitutes.
19. Temperature and ventilation.
20. Examination of cellars and unoccupied rooms in season of fires.
21. Recesses.
22. Physical exercise in schools.
23. Care of school premises.
24. Things not allowed.
25. Presents; contributions.
26. No advertisement to be read to the pupils; no agent to exhibit articles in school.
27. Authorized books and studies.
28. Pupils must have the books and utensils required.
29. Books, &c., for indigent children.
30, 31. Children entitled to attend the public schools.
32. Certificate of vaccination.
33. Cleanliness of pupils required.
34. Tardiness and absence of pupils; dismission of pupils before the close of the session; truancy.
35. Annual exhibitions; school festival.
36. Holidays and vacations.
37. Reading of Washington's Farewell Address.

Chapter 9.

1. Admission of pupils to primary schools.
2. Transfer of pupils.
3. Promotion to grammar schools.
4. Schools for special instruction.
5. School on Western Avenue.
6. Proper care of the pupils in school; recesses for primary schools in grammar school buildings.

7. Number of pupils to a school; classes.
8. Sewing; singing.
9. Order of studies; text-books.
10. Promotions.

Chapter 10.

1. Second grade of instruction; list of grammar schools.
2. Instructors in boys' schools; in girls' schools; in mixed schools.
3. Number of pupils to a teacher.
4. Qualifications for admission to the grammar schools.
5. Examination of primary scholars for promotion to the grammar School; certificates of admission.
6. Times of admitting pupils to Grammar Schools.
7. Out-of-school lessons.
8. Classes and sections.
9. Text-books.
10. Permitted books.
11. Arithmetic.
12. Instruction in music; examination in music.
13. Arrangement of the studies and recitations.
14. Committees to superintend the organization of the first class; no pupils to be retained who should join the High Schools.

Chapter 11.

1. English High School established, and its object.
2. Instructors.
3. Time of examining candidates for admission.
4. Annual examination of candidates.
5. Division of pupils; advancement; term to be only four years.
6. Reviews.
7. School hours.
8, 9. Course of studies and text-books.
10. Diplomas to graduates.

Chapter 12.

1. Establishment and object of the girls' High and Normal School.
2. Instructors.
3, 4, 5. Admission of pupils.
6. Course of instruction.
7. School hours.
8. Visitations by parents and friends.
9. Pupils may remain three years.
10. Diploma.

Chapter 13.

1. Latin School.
2. Objects of the school.
3, 4. Instructors.
5. Candidates for admission.
6. Time of examining candidates for admission.
7. Pupils may remain six years.
8. School hours.
9. Classes.
10. Examination by master.
11. Course of studies and text-books.
12. Translations and keys forbidden.
13. Penmanship, reading, etc.
14. Diploma.

RULES.[1]

Chapter 1. — *Organization of the Board.*

SECTION 1. At all meetings of the Board of School Committee, the Mayor, styled President, shall preside; in his **Organization of the Board.**

[1] Rules of the Board of School Committee, as in force 1865. The first three Chapters relate chiefly to the parliamentary rules of the Board in session, and are given for the reason that it is difficult to separate them from the body of the Rules.

For the composition, powers, &c. of School Committee, see Laws and Ordinances, pp. 22–3, 631–50.

absence, the President of the Common Council shall preside; and in the absence of both the Mayor and President of the Common Council, a President *pro tempore* shall be chosen by ballot.

Standing Committees.

SECT. 2. At the first meeting in each year, the Board shall elect a Secretary by ballot, and fix his salary for the ensuing year; and the President shall appoint, subject to the approval of the Board, the following Standing Committees of five members each, viz: 1. On Elections; — 2. On Rules and Regulations; — 3. On Accounts; — 4. On Schoolhouses; — 5. On Salaries; — 6. On Text-Books; — 7. On Music; — 8. On Printing;[1] — and the following, of thirteen members each, one member to be selected from each of the twelve wards of the city, viz: 1. On the Latin School; — 2. On the English High School; — 3. On the Girls' High and Normal School.

Districts.

District Committees.

SECT. 3. For convenience in the management of the Grammar and Primary Schools; the city shall be divided into as many Districts as it has Grammar Schools; each District shall take its name from the Grammar School within its boundaries; the President shall appoint, at the first meeting of the Board in each year, and subject to its approval, a Standing Committee on each District, whose number, in each case, shall be proportionate to the number of schools in the District.

Chairmen of sub-committees.

SECT. 4. The member first named on any committee, shall be the chairman thereof; except that the Committee on the Latin School, on the English High School, on the Girls' High and Normal School, and each District Committee, shall respectively elect its own Chairman.

Annual and quarterly meetings.

SECT. 5. The Board shall hold its annual meeting for the election of teachers on the second Tuesday in June, and three other stated quarterly meetings on the second Tuesday in March, September, and December, at seven and a half o'clock, P. M., at such place as the President may appoint; and the Board may hold special meetings whenever they are deemed necessary.

Quorum.

SECT. 6. For a quorum, a majority of the Board must be present; but a less number may vote to send for absent members, and to adjourn. Whenever the Board is obliged to wait,

---

[1] See note on page 109.

after the hour appointed for the meeting, for a quorum to begin business, or whenever it has to suspend business and adjourn for want of a quorum, the roll shall be called and the names of the absentees recorded by the Secretary.

Vacancies in the Board.

SECT. 7. Whenever a vacancy occurs in this Board, a Committee shall be appointed, consisting of three members from the ward in which the vacancy exists, and two at large, who shall consult with the Aldermen of said ward, or with the Chairman of the Board of Aldermen, in case the ward is not represented in that branch, and report to this Board, on or before the day of election, the name of a suitable candidate to fill said vacancy.

Chapter 2. — *Powers and Duties of the President.*

Opening of meetings.

SECTION 1. The President shall take the chair precisely at the hour appointed for the meeting of the Board, and shall call the members to order, and, on the appearance of a quorum, he shall cause the records of the last meeting to be read, and shall proceed to business in the following order, and shall not depart from it unless authorized by a vote of the Board.

Order of business.

1. Papers from the City Council;
2. Unfinished business of preceding meetings;
3. Nomination and Confirmation of Teachers;
4. Reports of Committees;
5. Motions, Orders, Resolutions, Petitions, &c.

The Nomination and Confirmation of Teachers shall be called for in the order of the districts.

Duties of the President.

SECT. 2. The President shall preserve order and decorum in the meetings; he may speak to points of order in preference to other members, and shall decide all questions of order, subject to an appeal to the Board, on motion of any member regularly seconded, and no other business shall be in order till the question on the appeal shall have been decided.

Same.

SECT. 3. When two or more members rise to speak at the same time, the President shall name the member who may speak first.

Same.

SECT. 4. He shall rise to address the Board, and to put a

question, but may read sitting. He shall declare all votes; but if any member doubt the vote, the President, without debate, shall require the members voting to rise and stand until they are counted, and he shall declare the result.

Committee of the Whole.

SECT. 5. The President shall appoint the chairman when the Board goes into Committee of the Whole; at any other time he may call any member to the chair, but such substitution shall not continue longer than one meeting. He may express his opinion on any subject under debate; but in such case, he shall leave the chair, and shall not resume it while the same question is pending; but he may state facts, and give his opinion on questions of order, without leaving his place.

Yeas and nays.

SECT. 6. The President shall take the sense of the Board by *Yeas* and *Nays* whenever *one fifth* of the members present sustain a motion therefor.

Motions.

SECT. 7. All questions shall be propounded by the President in the order in which they are moved, unless the subsequent motion shall be previous in its nature; except that in naming sums and fixing times, the largest sum and the longest time shall be put first. After a motion is seconded, and stated by the President, it shall be disposed of by vote of the Board, unless the mover withdraw it before a decision or an amendment.

Motion to adjourn.

SECT. 8. The President shall consider a motion to adjourn as always in order, except when a member has the floor, or when a question has been put and not decided; and motions to adjourn, to lay upon the table, to take from the table, and for the previous question, shall be decided without debate. Any member who moves to adjourn to a day certain, shall assign his reasons for so doing.

Previous question.

SECT. 9. He shall put the previous question in the following form: "Shall the main question be now put?" and all debate shall be suspended until the previous question shall have been decided. The adoption of the previous question shall put an end to all debate, to bring the Board to a direct vote upon pending amendments, if any, in their regular order, and then upon the main question.

SECT. 10. Whenever in his opinion it is necessary, the President *may*, and at the written request of any five members, he *shall* call a special meeting of the Board; but no meeting of the Board shall be called on shorter notice than twenty-four hours. Call of special meetings.

SECT. 11. All Committees shall be nominated by the President, unless otherwise ordered by the Board. Appointment of committees.

Chapter 3. — Rights and Duties of Members.

SECTION 1. When any member is about to speak in debate, or to present any matter to the Board, he shall rise in his place, and respectfully address the President; shall confine himself to the question under debate, and avoid personality. No member in debate shall mention another by his name, but may describe him by the ward he represents, the place he sits in, or such other designation as may be intelligible and respectful. Duties of members in debate.

SECT. 2. No member while speaking shall be interrupted by another, but by rising to call to order, or to correct a mistake. But if any member, in speaking or otherwise, transgress the rules of the Board, the President *shall*, or any member *may*, call him to order; in which case the member so called to order shall immediately sit down, unless permitted to explain; and the Board, if appealed to, shall decide on the case, but without debate. Call to order.

SECT. 3. If the Board shall determine that a member has violated any of its Rules, he shall not be allowed to speak unless by way of excuse for the same, until he shall have made satisfaction therefor. Violation of Rules.

SECT. 4. No member shall speak more than twice to the same question, without leave of the Board; nor more than once until all other members choosing to speak shall have spoken. Rules of debate.

SECT. 5. No motion shall be considered by the Board unless seconded. Every motion shall be submitted in writing, if the President direct, or any other member of the Board request it. Motions.

SECT. 6. When a question is under debate, no motion shall be received but to adjourn; to lay on the table; for the previous Order of motions.

question; to postpone to a day certain; to commit; to amend; or to postpone indefinitely; which several motions shall have precedence in the order above stated.

Reconsideration.

SECT. 7. When a question has once been decided, any member voting in the majority may move a reconsideration; such motion, if made at the same meeting with the decision, shall prevail if a majority of the members present sustain it; but if made at the subsequent meeting, it shall not prevail unless a majority of the whole Board vote for it; and only *one* motion for the reconsideration of any vote shall be permitted.

Members to vote.

SECT. 8. Every member present when a question is put, shall give his vote unless excused by the Board.

SECT. 9. All motions and reports may be committed and recommitted at the pleasure of the Board.

Division of a question.

SECT. 10. The division of a question may be called for, when the sense will admit of it.

Reading of a paper, when called for.

SECT. 11. When the reading of a paper is called for, and the same is objected to by any member, it shall be determined by a vote of the Board.

Suspension of Rules.

SECT. 12. The consent of *three fourths* of the members present at any meeting shall be requisite for the suspension of any standing Rule of the Board, or Regulation of the Schools, unless the proposal for the same shall have lain upon the table for at least one week.

Repeal or amendment of Rules.

SECT. 13. Whenever any proposition is submitted by a member to amend or repeal any Rule of the Board, or involving the amendment or repeal of any Regulation of the Public Schools, said proposition, before any action thereon, shall be referred to the Committee on Rules and Regulations, or to such other committee, standing or special, as the Board may designate, who shall report thereupon, in writing, and said report, together with such recommendations or orders as may be therein contained shall be open to immediate consideration and action.

Chapter 4. — *Duties of Standing Committees.*

SECTION 1. Immediately after the appointment of the Standing Committees, at the meeting for organization, the Committee on Elections shall receive the certificates of election of the members, and examine them, and report the result of their examination without any unnecessary delay. Whenever any person shall be elected to fill any vacancy that may have occurred in the Board, this Committee shall examine his certificate of election, and report as above provided, and said committee shall hear and report on all cases of contested elections. Committee on Elections.

SECT. 2. The Committee on Rules and Regulations shall take into careful consideration every proposition presented to the Board, to repeal or to amend any Rule or Regulation, whenever the same shall be referred to them, and shall report in writing, stating their reasons for or against the proposed alteration. Committee on Rules and Regulations.

SECT. 3. Whenever any proposition is submitted to this Board, involving the payment of money for any other purpose than the payment of salaries, or the establishment of a new school, such proposition shall not be acted upon before it has been referred to the Committee on Accounts. Said Committee shall have power to authorize the purchase of all stationery, record books, and blanks for the use of the schools, and a further supply, when called for, of any apparatus, globes, maps, or books of reference, or other conveniences, which this Board may have authorized the use of as means of illustrating the studies of the school. No Sub-Committee, nor any other persons connected with this Board, shall expend any money for these supplies, without authority from this Committee, and no bills for such expenditures shall be paid without the signature of the Chairman of this Committee in approval. Said Committee are authorized, on behalf of this Board, to carry out the provisions of the statute of the Commonwealth for furnishing books to indigent children and others, and to present an estimate of Committee on Accounts.

the expenses of the Public Schools to the City Auditor on or before the first day of February annually.[1]

Mover of a motion, &c., to be notified of the time of its consideration.

SECT. 4. Whenever a motion, order, or resolution shall be referred to a Committee, the Chairman of the Committee shall cause the member offering the motion, order, or resolution, to be notified by the Secretary of the Board, or otherwise, of the time when the subject will be considered.

Committee on Schoolhouses.

SECT. 5. Whenever any application shall be made for the erection or alteration of a schoolhouse, such application shall be referred to the Committee on Schoolhouses, who shall consider the same, and shall consult with the District Committee who may have charge of the school or schools to be accommodated, and shall report to this Board, in writing, such recommendations in each case as they may deem expedient. It shall also be the duty of the Committee on Schoolhouses to exercise a general supervision over the warming and ventilation of the several schoolhouses throughout the year.

Warming and ventilation of schoolhouses.

Committee on Salaries.

SECT. 6. Whenever any proposition is submitted to this Board to extend the salary of any teacher beyond the time of actual service, or to change the regular salary of a teacher in any respect, or to pay for any extra service in teaching, *such* proposition shall not be acted upon before it has been referred to the Committee on Salaries, who shall report, in writing, such recommendations as they may deem expedient.

Committee on Text-Books.

SECT. 7. The Committee on Text-Books, when they think favorably of any application made by any author or publisher to introduce any new text-book into the Public Schools, shall give early notice thereof to the Board, and see that such author or publisher furnish every member of the Board with a copy of such text-book for examination, as a condition of its being presented to them for acceptance; and said Committee shall fully consider such application, examine thoroughly such text-book,

---

[1] The School Committee shall present to the Auditor, on or before the first day of February in each year, an estimate, in writing, of the expenses of the public schools for the next financial year, stating the amount required for salaries, for incidental expenses, and for the alteration, repair, and erection of schoolhouses. [City Ordinance, December 18, 1855, sect. 2.]

and at such time as they may be prepared, within three months from the date of the application, they shall make a written report to the Board, setting forth the reasons for or against the introduction of said text-book into the Public Schools. In the month of May, annually, this Committee shall examine the course of studies prescribed for the schools, and shall recommend to the Board, at the quarterly meeting in June, such improvements in the course of instruction, and such changes in the books used in the schools, as they may deem expedient.

SECT. 8. Whenever any new text-book is adopted by the Board, it shall be on the condition that the publisher will furnish copies to the pupils of the Public Schools at such reduction from the wholesale price as shall be agreed upon by this Board; and it shall be the duty of the Committee on Text-Books to see that this condition is fulfilled, and that said book comes into use at the commencement of the Public Schools after the August vacation, at which time only shall any new text-book be introduced. **Introduction of new books.**

SECT. 9. The Committee on Music shall exercise a general supervision over this department of Public Instruction in all the schools. They shall appoint, and nominate to the Board for confirmation, suitably qualified persons as Teachers of Music;[1] **Committee on Music.**

---

[1] *Ordered:* That, in addition to the teachers of music in the Grammar Schools, the Committee on Music be authorized to nominate to this Board for confirmation, a suitably qualified person as instructor in Music in the Primary Schools, with a salary not exceeding twelve hundred dollars per annum. (Passed June 21, 1864.)

At a meeting of the School Committee, Dec. 27, 1864, the following orders were passed: —

Ordered: That a Standing Committee of five on Gymnastics and Military Drill be hereafter appointed, whose duty it shall be to enforce the regulations upon this subject, and superintend this branch of instruction, making from time to time such recommendations to the General Committee as they shall find expedient.

Ordered: That said Committee be authorized forthwith to employ an Instructor in vocal and physical gymnastics, at a salary not exceeding fifteen hundred dollars per annum, whose duty it shall be to attend the schools at such times and for so much of the time as the Committee shall deem necessary, they shall make examinations of each Grammar School in music, at least once in six months, and submit a written report thereupon semi-annually at the quarterly meeting in March and in September.

Committee on Printing.

SECT. 10. The Committee on Printing shall exercise a general supervision in relation to all printing which may be required by the Board, or for any of the Schools under its charge; and no bill for printing, of any kind, shall be paid without the signature of the Chairman of this Committee, in approval. Said Committee shall submit to this Board, at the quarterly meeting in March, a detailed account of all expenditures for printing during the year preceding.

Committees on High Schools.

SECT. 11. The Committees on the Latin School, the English High School, and the Girls' High and Normal School in all matters relating to said schools and the appointment of teachers therein, shall respectively observe the same rules, and perform the same duties, so far applicable, as are hereinafter prescribed for the several District Committees in relation to the Grammar Schools under their charge; and at meetings for the transaction of business, five members shall constitute a quorum.

Organization of District Committees.

SECT. 12. The member first named on each District Committee shall call a meeting of said Committee within ten days after its appointment. It shall organize by the choice,

---

upon consultation with him and the District Committees, for the purpose of instructing in gymnastic exercises, both vocal and physical, and of securing the careful and regular performance of those exercises at such hours as may be convenient, provided that not less than twenty minutes per day shall be devoted to this purpose in any grammar school, and not less than thirty minutes in any primary school, in addition to the ordinary recess.

Ordered: That the said Committee, upon consultation with the District Committees, be also authorized to arrange the Grammar Schools containing male pupils into groups, so that the boys of sufficient size to drill with arms, and in number sufficient to form a military company, may be instructed together in military drill, by a suitable instructor, to be employed by the Committee; that these companies be united into a larger organization, as the Committee shall find expedient; and that suitable places and arms be provided by the Committee; the hours of drill not to exceed two per week, except voluntary drills out of school hours; and no expenditure, exceeding fifteen hundred dollars per annum, to be incurred for these purposes without the prior authority of the whole Board.

from among its own members, of a Chairman and Secretary, notice of whose election shall be immediately sent to the Secretary of the School Board. It shall keep a record of its proceedings, and all its official acts shall be done in meetings duly called, at not less than twenty-four hours' notice, and, when reported to the Board, shall be submitted in writing.

SECT. 13. Each District Committee shall have charge of the Grammar Schools and the Primary Schools in the District, and may arrange the studies and classify the pupils in the latter in such a manner as they may consider most advantageous to the schools. Within ten days after its appointment, each District Committee shall divide itself into a suitable number of Sub-Committees, for the Primary Schools in its District. Said Committee shall then divide the Primary Schools in the District into as many divisions as there may be Sub-Committees, and shall assign each division to a Sub-Committee, who shall have the special charge of the schools in such division; shall visit each of them as often as once in each month; shall examine them quarterly; and shall report, in writing, their standing and progress, to the Chairman of the District Committee, at least one week previous to each quarterly meeting of the Board. Each Sub-Committee shall refer all matters of importance pertaining to the schools under its care, to the District Committee, for consideration and action.

Duties of District Committees.

Classifications of pupils.

Care of Primary Schools.

SECT. 14. Whenever any District Committee shall deem an additional Primary School necessary for the proper accommodation of the children under their care, they shall state the facts in the case to the Board, in writing, which communication shall be referred to the Committee on Schoolhouses, who shall consider and report on the same before the Board shall take final action on the subject.

Additional Primary Schools.

SECT. 15. The District Committee shall examine the Grammar Schools in their respective Districts at least once in each quarter; and shall visit them not less than once each month, without giving previous notice to the instructors; and shall, at each quarterly meeting of the Board, make a report in writing, giving the results of their examinations and visits, together with

Quarterly examinations.

the results of the examination by the Sub-Committees of the several Primary Schools under their charge; also stating any occurrences affecting the standing and usefulness of the schools, and mentioning the condition of the schoolhouses and yards and out-buildings connected therewith. They shall also state in their reports whether the rule relating to the infliction of corporal punishment has been complied with; and the names of all children admitted to the schools under their charge who do not reside in the city, and the reasons for their admission.

Quarterly reports.

SECT. 16. At each quarterly meeting, the Chairman of each District Committee, or any member thereof who may be present, shall be called upon for a report on the condition of the schools in the District; and in case of omission to make it, the Board shall pass a vote, enjoining the delinquent Committee to proceed without delay to the performance of their duty, and shall adjourn to receive their report.

Medals and certificates.

SECT. 17. The District Committee shall determine on the scholars who are to receive the medals and certificates of merit in their respective schools, and return the names to the Secretary, at least four days previous to the annual exhibition. It shall also be their duty, on the day of exhibition, to present the medals and certificates to the pupils to whom they have been awarded. The number of medals and certificates of merit to be awarded in each school, shall be based upon the average number of pupils belonging to the school during the school year. Each school shall be entitled to one medal, and one of each of the certificates of merit, for every sixty scholars; and an additional medal may be awarded in any Grammar School in which a majority fraction occurs, if the District Committee deem it expedient. But, in any school where the number of scholars in the first class is comparatively small, the number of medals awarded shall be proportionably less; and it shall never exceed one third of the number of candidates examined, nor shall any pupil be promoted for the purpose of increasing the number of candidates. In any school where there are no scholars much advanced in improvement, no medal shall be awarded. General scholarship, and more especially good conduct, shall be taken into consideration in awarding the medals and certificates; and in order that a just assignment may be made, the District Committee shall critically examine the candidates, and inspect the school records of their standing.

Pupils to attend school in section where they reside.

SECT. 18. No pupil shall be admitted to or retained in any school, except that for the Section in which such pupil resides, without the written consent of the District Committee, both of the school to which the pupil belongs, and of that where he seeks to be admitted or retained.

Teacher of Sewing.

SECT. 19. Instruction shall be given in Sewing to all the pupils in the fourth class in each of the Grammar Schools for girls, except whenever in the judgment of the District Committee it will be for the interest of the school to omit such instruction, in which case the District Committee shall apply to this Board for authority to suspend the action of this rule in that school. The District Committee of each school in which such instruction shall be given shall nominate to this Board, for confirmation, some qualified person as Teacher of Sewing, who shall give to each pupil two lessons of not less than one hour each, every week.

Examination of teachers.

SECT. 20. Whenever any new teacher, except a master, is, in the opinion of the District Committee, needed for any school under their charge, said Committee shall, *before* making any appointment, examine the candidates in the manner required by law, and with special reference to the place which is then to be filled; and also as to their competency to teach the elements of articulation, of music and drawing; and in regard to teachers in the Grammar Schools, they shall consult with the master in whose school such teacher is to be appointed.[1] And the same course shall be pursued in all cases where it is proposed to trans-

Teachers advanced to another grade to be examined.

---

[1] The School Committee, unless the town at its annual meeting determines that the duty may be performed by the Prudential Committee, shall select and contract with the teachers of the public schools; shall require full and satisfactory evidence of the good moral character of all instructors who may be employed; and shall ascertain, by personal examination, their qualifications for teaching and capacity for the government of schools. (Gen. Stat. Ch. 38, § 23.)

fer or to advance a teacher from one grade of school to another. Teachers so appointed shall be nominated by the District Committees, to this Board, for confirmation, and they shall be considered entitled to the established salary from the time of their entering upon their duties. It shall be the duty of the Secretary to give immediate information of such appointment to the City Auditor. Reappointed incumbents in the service of this Board shall rank as new teachers, and begin with the salary of such teachers.

Reappointed teachers to be considered as new teachers.

Names of well qualified candidates at examinations to be preserved.

SECT. 21. When, at any examination for assistant teachers, a larger number of candidates are found qualified than is required to fill the existing vacancies, it shall be the duty of the Secretary of the District Committee making the examination, to keep a record of the names of such well-qualified candidates as the said Committee may direct, and to deposit such record with the Superintendent of Public Schools. This record shall give the names and addresses of the said candidates, and such information in regard to their qualifications, whether for Grammar or Primary Schools, as the said Committee may direct. And any District Committee may elect Assistants for the Grammar Schools, or Primary School Teachers, from the candidates so recommended, with or without a new examination, at the option of said Committee.

Canvassing the lists of teachers.

SECT. 22. In the month of May, annually, the Committee on the Latin School, the English High School, the Girls' High and Normal School, and each District Committee, in a meeting regularly called, shall canvass the list of teachers in their District, and, after consultation with the master, they shall decide upon the persons whom they will recommend for re-election, and said Committee shall, at the annual meeting in June for the election of teachers, nominate the persons thus approved, who shall be considered the regular candidates for their respective offices. And in case any Committee have decided not to nominate any teacher for re-election, they may, if a majority of said Committee deem it expedient, give notice of their intention, to said teacher, before the annual election.

Nomination of teachers for re-election.

SECT. 23. The District Committee shall give their advice to the instructors in any emergency; and take cognizance of any difficulty which may have occurred between the instructors and parents of pupils, or between the instructors themselves, relative to the government or instruction of their schools. An appeal, however, to the whole Board, is not hereby denied to any citizen or instructor. In addition to the specific duties of the District Committees, it shall be their duty, generally, to make any temporary arrangement which they may find necessary for their schools, or for the convenience of the instructors, provided that nothing shall be done contrary to the School Regulations.

District Committees shall give advice to instrutcors, &c.

District Committees may make tempoary arrangements.

SECT. 24. Each District Committee may transfer their own Primary School Teachers from one Primary School to another, and may change the location of their Primary Schools from one schoolroom to another, as they may think proper; but notice of any such transfer or change, and of the appointment of any new Primary School Teacher, shall, within one week after they are made, be sent to the Secretary of the Board, and the same shall be mentioned in the next quarterly report of the District Committee; and any teacher, of any grade, actually in the employ of the city, may be transferred by this Board, without re-examination, to any vacant place of the same grade in the city.

Transfer of Primary Schools and teachers.

Notice to be sent to Secretary of the Board.

Transfer of Teachers by the Board.

SECT. 25. The Committees on the Latin School, the English High School, the Girls' High and Normal School, and each District Committee, shall, during the month of July, make a thorough examination of their respective schools, and shall report at the quarterly meeting in September, the results of their examinations, together with such suggestions for the improvement of the schools as they may see fit to offer, and the statistics of each school in a tabular form, on the following points, viz: 1. The number of teachers; 2. The changes of teachers made during the year; 3. The number of different scholars registered; 4. The number of these received from other Public Schools of the city; 5. The number discharged; 6. The largest number present at any one time; 7. The largest average

Annual examinations.

attendance for any one month, and the name of the month; 8. The average attendance for the year; 9. The number and names of the medal scholars, and the recipients of the Lawrence prizes; 10. The number and ages of the candidates offered and admitted at the High Schools, from each of the Grammar Schools. These reports shall be referred to a Special Committee of the Board, who shall make from them such selections as they may think important for public information, and shall add thereto such suggestions and remarks as they shall deem expedient; and their report, which shall be presented at the quarterly meeting in December, when accepted by the Board, shall be printed for distribution among the citizens.

Annual reports.

Chapter 5. — *Election of Instructors of Public Schools.*

School year.

SECTION 1. The school year shall commence on the first Monday in September, and end on the day immediately preceding the first Monday in September.

Annual election of teachers.

SECT. 2. In the month of June, annually, the Board shall elect the instructors of the Public Schools, and fix their salaries[1] for the ensuing year. Said instructors shall rank as

---

The salaries of the instructors in the various schools have been established as follows, for the present school year, viz: —

The salary of the Masters of the Latin, the English High, and the Girls' High and Normal Schools, is $ 2,600 for the first year's service, with an increase of $ 100 for each additional year's service till the salary amounts to $ 3,000 per annum.

The salary of the Sub-Masters of the Latin and English High Schools, and of the Masters of the Grammar Schools is $ 1,800 for the first year, with an annual increase of $ 100 till it amounts to $ 2,200.

The salary of the Ushers of the Latin and English High Schools, and of the Sub-Masters of the Grammar Schools, is $ 1,400 for the first year, with an annual increase of $ 100 till it amounts to $ 1,800.

The salary of the Ushers of the Grammar Schools is $ 1,000 for the first year, with an annual increase of $ 100, till it amounts to 1,200.

The salary of the Head Assistant of the Girls' High and Normal School is $ 700 per annum, and the salary of the other Assistants in this School is $ 600 per annum.

The salary of the Teacher of the Normal Department of the Girls' High and Normal School is $ 800 per annum.

follows: 1st, Masters; 2d, Sub-Masters; 3d, Ushers; 4th, Head Assistants; 5th, Assistants; 6th, Primary School Teachers; 7th, Music Teachers; 8th, Sewing Teachers,

SECT. 3. The Masters of the several schools having been duly nominated by their respective District Committees, shall be elected by ballot, and thirty votes at least shall in all cases be necessary to a choice, and the other instructors shall be elected by confirmation on nomination of their respective Committees; but no teacher, except a Master, shall be elected by this Board, without having served on trial at least three months in the Boston schools. Mode of choosing instructors.

The salary of the Head Assistants in the Grammar Schools is $600 per annum; and the salary of the other Assistants in the Grammar Schools, and of the Teachers of the Primary Schools, is $400 for the first year, with an annual increase of $50 till it amounts to $550 per annum.

The salary of the Music Teachers in the Grammar Schools is $125 per annum for each school.

The salary of the Instructor in Vocal and Physical Gymnastics in the Grammar Schools is $1,500 per annum.

The salary of the Teacher of Music in the Primary Schools is $1,200 per annum.

The salaries of the Sewing Teachers are as follows, — and the teachers shall severally devote to instructing their pupils the time designated herein: —

The Sewing Teachers of the Adams, Lyman, and Wells Schools shall teach sewing ten hours each week, and shall severally receive $225 per annum.

The Sewing Teachers of the Franklin, Lawrence, Lincoln, Bigelow, and Chapman Schools shall teach sewing twelve hours each week, and shall severally receive $260 per annum.

The Sewing Teachers of the Hancock and Everett Schools shall teach sewing sixteen hours each week, and shall each receive $300 per annum.

The Sewing Teacher of the Winthrop School shall teach sewing twenty hours each week, and shall each receive $400 per annum.

The Sewing Teacher of the Bowditch School shall teach sewing twenty-three hours each week, and shall receive $450 per annum.

The salary of the Teacher of French in the Latin School is $500 per annum. The salary of the Teacher of French in the Girls High and Normal School is $500 per annum. The salary of the Teacher of German in the Girls' High and Normal School is $500 per annum. The salary of the Teacher of Drawing in the Girls' High and Normal School is $900 per annum. The salary of the Teacher of Drawing in the English High School is $500 per annum. The salary of the Teacher of Vocal Music in the Girls' High and Normal School is $450 per annum.

Election of a *new* master.

SECT. 4. Whenever a new Master is to be elected for any of the Public Schools, the Secretary shall give notice thereof in such newspapers, and for such length of time, as the Board may direct, specifying in such notice that all applications for the office must be made in writing, and lodged with the Secretary, together with any written evidence of qualifications which the candidate may wish to present, on or before a day named in such notice.

Same.

SECT. 5. In case the vacancy to be filled is in the Latin School, the English High School, or the Girls' High and Normal School, the Committees of those schools shall together constitute a committee for the examination of candidates. But in case of a vacancy in any of the Grammar Schools, the Examining Committee shall be composed of the District Committee of the school in which the vacancy exists, and of the members for the two wards numerically nearest to the ward in which said school is situated; and one third of the members of either of these committees shall constitute a quorum for doing business.

Same.

SECT. 6. The Examining Committee shall take from the Secretary's files all the applications and written evidence, and shall have personal interviews with the applicants, and make inquiries as to their qualifications, and, at a meeting appointed for the purpose, shall carefully examine the candidates in the manner required by law,[1] and always with reference to the office that is then to be filled. And none but said Committee, the members of this Board, the Superintendent of Public Schools, and the candidates under examination, shall be present.

Examining Committee's report.

SECT. 7. The Examining Committee shall report to the Board, at some subsequent meeting, the names of all the applicants who have been examined by them, together with such other facts and circumstances respecting the candidates, their recommendations and qualifications, as they may deem necessary for the information of the Board. They shall also designate in their report the names of two or more of the candidates whose

---

[1] See page 113.

examinations were most satisfactory, with the opinions of the Examining Committee on their qualifications severally, and the Board shall then proceed to a choice by ballot.

SECT. 8. The instructors elected at the annual meeting shall hold their offices for one school year, unless sooner removed by vote of the Board. **Instructors to hold their offices for one year.**

Chapter 6. — *Duties of the Secretary.*

SECTION 1. The Secretary shall have charge of the Records of the Board, and of all papers directed by the Board to be kept on its files; he shall keep a permanent record-book, in which all its votes, orders, and proceedings shall by him be recorded. **Records and files.**

SECT. 2. He shall notify all stated and special meetings; he shall notify the Chairman of every Committee appointed, stating the commission, and the names of the members associated with him; he shall notify the meetings of all Sub-Committees, when requested by the Chairman or by any two members thereof; he shall notify the instructors of their appointments, and shall give such other notices as the Board may require. **Notices to be given.**

SECT. 3. He shall prepare the Annual Report required by the statute of the Commonwealth, and he shall transmit the same, legally signed, to the Secretary of State, on or before the thirtieth day of April.[1] **Report to Secretary of State.**

SECT. 4. He shall transmit copies of all votes, resolutions, and documents which are to be sent to the members of the Board, to the various Committees, to the Teachers, or to other persons. **Votes to be transmitted.**

SECT. 5. He shall see that the Medals and Diplomas awarded to the successful candidates in the Public Schools are procured, properly inscribed, and sent to the appropriate schools at least one day preceding the Annual Exhibitions. **Medals to be provided.**

SECT. 6. He shall examine all bills for salaries, and the bills for all articles purchased by order of the Board, or by the **Examination of bills.**

---

[1] See General Statutes, chapter 40.

Committee on Accounts, and shall perform such other duties as the School Committee shall prescribe, or from time to time direct.

Chapter 7. — Duties of the Superintendent.

Election.

SECTION 1. The Superintendent of Public Schools shall be elected annually, by ballot, at the quarterly meeting of the Board in June, to enter upon the duties of his office on the first day of September next ensuing. At the same meeting the salary of the Superintendent shall be voted, and no alteration in the amount of said salary shall be made during the year for which he is elected.

Salary.

General duties.

SECT. 2. He shall devote himself to the study of the Public School System, and keep himself acquainted with the progress of instruction and discipline in other places, in order to suggest appropriate means for the advancement of the Public Schools in this city, and see that the regulations of the Board in regard to these schools are carried into full effect.

Visiting schools.

SECT. 3. He shall visit each school as often as his other duties will permit, that he may obtain, as far as practicable, a personal knowledge of the condition of all the schools and be able to suggest improvements and remedy defects in their management. Shall advise the teachers on the best methods of instruction and discipline, and, to illustrate these methods in respect to Primary Schools, he shall hold occasional meetings of the teachers of the schools, and have authority, for this purpose, to dismiss the Primary Schools at such times as he shall deem advisable, not exceeding one half day in each quarter. He has authority, also, to dismiss the Grammar Schools, not exceeding one half day in each half year, for the purpose of holding meetings of the teachers of these schools.

Meetings of Primary School teachers.

Meetings of Grammar School teachers.

State Scholarships.

SECT. 4. Whenever vacancies occur in the State scholarships to which this city is entitled, it shall be his duty to give public notice thereof, and he shall be authorized, in conjunction with the chairman of each of the High School Committees, to examine candidates for said vacancies, and report to this Board the names of those to be recommended, according to law,[1] to the Board of Education. He shall make investigations as to the number and the condition of the children of the city who are not receiving the benefits offered by the Public Schools, and shall endeavor to ascertain the reasons, and to suggest and apply the remedies.

Absentees from school.

SECT. 5. He shall render such aid and communicate such information to the various Committees as they may require of him, and shall assist them, when desired, in the quarterly examinations. He shall see that all school registers, books of records, circulars, blanks for monthly reports of teachers, and annual reports of District Committees are prepared after uniform patterns, and ready to be furnished when needed.

Assistance to committees.

SECT. 6. He shall consult with the different bodies who have control of the building and altering of schoolhouses, and shall communicate to them such information on the subject as he may possess; and he shall suggest such plans for building and altering schoolhouses as he may consider best for the health and convenience of the teachers and pupils, and most economical for the city; and he shall advise with those through whom, either directly or indirectly, the school appropriations are expended, that there may result more uniformity in their plans and more economy in their expenditures.

Building and altering of Schoolhouses.

School expenses.

SECT. 7. It shall be his duty to attend the meetings of the Board, except when the subject of his own election is under consideration, and, when called upon through the President, to express his opinion on any subject under discussion, or to communicate such information as may be in his power. At the quarterly meetings in March and September, he shall present to the Board a semi-annual Report, in print, giving an account of the schools he has visited, and of the other duties he has performed, together with such facts and suggestions relating to the condition of the schools, and the increase of their efficiency and usefulness, as he may deem advisable. He shall also embrace in his Report an abstract of the semi-annual returns of the

Attend meetings of Board.

Semi-annual report.

---

[1] General Statutes chapter 37, § 3.

Public Schools, and a schedule showing the number of teachers then employed in the schools; and these reports shall be referred to the Special Committee on the Annual Report of the School Board.

Record of names of applicants.

SECT. 8. He shall keep a record of the names, ages, and residences of persons who may desire to be considered as candidates for the office of Assistant or Primary School Teacher, with such remarks and suggestions respecting them as he may deem important for the information of Committees; which record shall be at all times open to the inspection of any member of this Board. And he shall perform such other duties as the School Committee shall prescribe, or from time to time direct.

Chapter 8. — *General Regulations of the Public Schools.*

Teachers to observe the school regulations.

SECTION. 1. All teachers in the Public Schools are *required* to make themselves familiar with these Regulations, and especially with the portion that relates to their own duties, and to the instruction and discipline of their respective schools, and to see that these are faithfully observed.

General duties of teachers.

SECT. 2. The instructors shall punctually observe the hours appointed for opening and dismissing the schools; and, during school hours, shall faithfully devote themselves to the public service. In all their intercourse with their scholars they shall strive to impress on their minds, both by precept and example, the great importance of continued efforts for improvement in morals, in manners and deportment, as well as in useful learning.

School hours.

SECT. 3. From the first Monday in May to the first Monday in September, the Grammar and Primary Schools shall commence their morning sessions at 8 o'clock, and close at 11 o'clock; and shall begin their afternoon sessions at 2 o'clock, and close at 5 o'clock. From the first Monday in September to the first Monday in May, they shall commence their morning sessions at 9 o'clock, and close at 12 o'clock; and shall begin their afternoon sessions at 2 o'clock, and shall close at 5 o'clock, except that from the third Monday in October to the first Monday in March, they may omit the afternoon recess and close at

4 o'clock. *Provided*, that nothing in this section shall be so construed as to prevent the teacher from the judicious exercise of the right to detain a pupil for a reasonable time after the regular hour for dismissing school, either for purposes of discipline, or to make up neglected lessons.

Teachers and pupils to be at school early.

SECT. 4. All the schoolrooms shall be opened, and the teachers be present, both morning and afternoon, *fifteen minutes* before the time fixed for the session to begin. The teachers shall require the scholars to be in their seats, and shall commence and close the exercises of the schools, punctually at the prescribed hours.

Opening the schools.

SECT. 5. The morning exercises of all the schools shall commence with the reading of a portion of the Scriptures, by the teacher, in each school; the reading to be followed by the Lord's Prayer, repeated by the teacher alone. The afternoon session shall close with appropriate singing.

Moral instruction.

SECT. 6. Good morals being of the first importance to the pupils, and essential to their highest progress in useful knowledge, instruction therein shall be daily given in each of the schools.[1] The pupils shall be carefully instructed to avoid idleness and profanity, falsehood and deceit, and every wicked and disgraceful practice, and to conduct themselves in an orderly and proper manner; and it shall be the duty of the instructors, so far as practicable, to exercise a general inspection over them in these regards, both in and out of school, and also while go-

---

[1] "It shall be the duty of the president, professors, and tutors of the University at Cambridge, and of the several colleges, and of all preceptors and teachers of academies, and all other instructors of youth, to exert their best endeavors to impress on the minds of children and youth committed to their care and instruction, the principles of piety, justice, and a sacred regard to truth, love to their country, humanity and universal benevolence, sobriety, industry and frugality, chastity, moderation, and temperance, and those other virtues which are the ornament of human society, and the basis upon which a republican constitution is founded; and it shall be the duty of such instructors to endeavor to lead their pupils, as their ages and capacities will admit, into a clear understanding of the tendency of the above-mentioned virtues to preserve and perfect a republican constitution, and secure the blessings of liberty, as well as to promote their future happiness and also to point out to them the evil tendency of the opposite vices." (Gen. Stat. chap. 38, § 10.)

ing to the same and returning home; and on all suitable occasions to inculcate upon them the principles of truth and virtue.

School register and records.

SECT. 7. The principal teacher in every school shall keep a register, in which shall be recorded the names, ages, dates of admission, and places of residence of the scholars. In addition to this register, other records shall be kept, in which shall be entered the daily absence of the scholars, and such notes of their class-exercises as may exhibit a view of their advancement and standing.

Blanks for schools.

SECT. 8. All school registers and other books for records, as well as all blanks for monthly reports, and circulars required in the several schools, shall be after uniform patterns, to be determined by the Superintendent of Public Schools, to whom all teachers are expected to apply whenever such articles are needed by them.

Masters to examine their schools.

SECT. 9. Each master shall make a careful examination of his school as often as he can consistently with proper attention to the pupils under his immediate charge.

Semi-annual returns.

SECT. 10. During the week preceding the quarterly meeting in March and in September, the principal teacher in each school shall make to the Superintendent of Public Schools semi-annual returns of the number of pupils belonging to the school, conformably to the blanks furnished for this purpose. They shall also include in their reports the names of those pupils belonging to their respective schools whose parents or guardians do not reside in the city, with the dates of their respective admissions.

Notices to be given to the Secretary.

SECT. 11. Each master shall, within one week after the appointment of a teacher, send to the secretary of this Board the full name of such teacher, with the precise date of his or her commencing service in his school; and if the person appointed has previously been in the service of the city as a teacher, he shall state where, when, and how long such service was rendered. In like manner he shall give notice when any teacher shall have relinquished service in his school.

Teachers visiting schools.

SECT. 12. The instructors may, for the purpose of observing the modes of discipline, and instruction, visit any of the

Public Schools in the city; but such visits shall not be made oftener than once a quarter, nor till provisions satisfactory to the Chairman of the District Committee or of the Sub-Committee has been made for the proper care of the pupils under their immediate charge.

Corporal punishment.

SECT. 13. All instructors shall aim at such discipline in their schools as would be exercised by a kind, judicious parent in his family; shall avoid corporal punishment in all cases where good order can be preserved by milder measures; and in no case shall resort be had to confinement in a closet or wardrobe, or to other cruel or unusual punishment, as a mode of discipline. It shall be the duty of the several masters and teachers in the public schools, at the close of each month, to make, in writing, to the Chairmen of their District Committees, a report of all cases in which corporal punishment has been inflicted; which report shall state the name of the pupil, the amount of punishment, and the reason for its infliction; and the Chairman of each District Committee shall, in his quarterly report, give the number of cases of corporal punishment during the previous quarter, and the average to each teacher of the District. Corporal punishment shall be inflicted only after the nature of the offence has been fully explained to the scholar, and shall be restricted to blows on the hand with a rattan, except in cases where a pupil refuses to submit to such punishment. Corporal punishment shall not be inflicted on a girl in a grammar school without the consent and approval of the master, which, in each individual case, must first be obtained.

Exclusion of a pupil.

SECT. 14. For violent or pointed opposition to authority in any particular instance, a principal teacher may exclude a child from school for the time being; and thereupon shall inform the parent or guardian of the measure, and shall apply to the District Committee for advice and direction. Whenever any scholar is absent from school, the teacher shall immediately ascertain the reason; and, if such absence be not occasioned by sickness or other sufficient cause, or is not satisfactorily explained, such pupil, with the consent of the Sub-Committee, may be suspended or discharged from the school, and a record of such proceeding shall be made.

Suspension and restoration of pupils.

SECT. 15. When the example of any pupil in school is very injurious, and in all cases where reformation appears hopeless, it shall be the duty of the principal teacher, with the approbation of the Committee on the Schools, to suspend such pupil from the school. But any child under this public censure, who shall have expressed to the teacher his regret for his folly or indiscretion, as openly and explicitly as the nature of the case may require, and shall have given evidence of amendment, shall, with the previous consent of said Committee, be reinstated in the privileges of the school.

Absence of pupils.

SECT. 16. Whenever a teacher has satisfactory evidence that a pupil has left school without the intention of returning, such pupil's name shall forthwith be stricken from the list; but any absence recorded against the name of the pupil before the teacher receives this notice shall be allowed to remain, and be regarded the same as any other absences. When a pupil is absent from school more than five consecutive school days, the name of such pupil shall be stricken from the list at the end of the five days; and the absences shall in all cases be recorded while the name remains on the list. The name of a pupil who is suspended from school by any rules of the School Board, shall be stricken from the list, and any pupil shall be considered as absent whose attendance at school shall not continue for at least one half of the regular school session of the half day. In noting the absences of pupils, the short vacations shall be disregarded, and pupils who are not present on the first half day of a term after either of those vacations, shall be marked as absent.

Instructors, in cases of difficulty, to apply to District Committees.

SECT. 17. In cases of difficulty in the discharge of their official duties, or when they may desire any temporary aid, the instructors shall apply to the District Committees of their respective schools for advice and assistance.

Absentees must pay their substitutes.

SECT. 18. Whenever any instructor shall be absent from school, and a temporary instructor rendered necessary, the amount required to pay said substitute shall be withdrawn from the salary of the absentee; unless upon a representation of the case, by petition, and a report on said petition from the Standing Committee on Salaries, the Board shall order an allowance to be made. And no substitute shall be employed in any of the Primary Schools for more than one day at a time, without the approbation of one or more of the Sub-Committee of the school; nor in any department of the Grammar Schools without the approbation of two or more of the District Committee, the Chairman being one of them. The compensation per day allowed for substitutes in the Primary Schools, and for Assistants in the Grammar Schools, shall be $ 1.25; for Assistants in the Girls' High and Normal School, $ 1.50; for Ushers in the Grammar Schools, $ 2.75; for Sub-Masters in those schools, and for Ushers in the Latin and English High Schools, $ 3.75; for Sub-Masters in the Latin and English High Schools, and for Masters in the Grammar Schools, $ 5.00; for Masters in the Latin, English High, and Girls' High and Normal Schools, $ 6.00; for each day, counting six school days in the week, during which such substitute shall be employed. The compensation of temporary teachers shall be the same as that of substitutes.

Temperature and ventilation.

SECT. 19. It shall be the duty of all the instructors, to give vigilant attention to the ventilation and temperature of their schoolrooms. A regular system of ventilation shall be practised, as well in winter as in summer, by which the air in the rooms shall be effectually changed at each recess, and at the end of each school session before the house shall be closed.

Examination of cellars and unoccupied rooms in season of fires.

SECT. 20. The Masters of the Grammar School shall examine, or cause some competent person connected with each school to examine, during the season of fires, the cellars and unoccupied rooms in their respective buildings; such examinations to be made during the first and every suceeeding hour of the forenoon and afternoon sessions, and the result made known to the master of the school.

Recesses.

SECT. 21. There shall be a recess of fifteen minutes for every pupil each half day, including the time occupied in going out and coming in, which shall take place as nearly as may be at the expiration of one half of each school session.

Physical exercise in schools.

SECT. 22. The masters, ushers, and teachers, in the Public Schools shall so arrange the daily course of exercise in their respective classes that every scholar shall have daily, in the forenoon and afternoon, some kind of physical or gymnastic exercise; this exercise to take place as nearly as practicable midway between the commencement of the session and recess, and between recess and the end of the session.

Care of school premises.

SECT. 23. The principal teachers of the several schools shall prescribe such rules for the use of the yards and out-buildings connected with the schoolhouses as shall insure their being kept in a neat and proper condition, and shall examine them as often as may be necessary for such purpose, and they shall be held responsible for any want of neatness or cleanliness on their premises; and when anything is out of order they must give immediate notice thereof to the Superintendent of Public Buildings.

Things not allowed.

SECT. 24. No instructor in the Public Schools shall be allowed to teach in any other public school than that to which he or she has been appointed, nor to keep a private school of any description whatever, nor to attend to the instruction of any private pupils before six o'clock, P. M., except on Wednesday and Saturday afternoons, nor to engage as editor of any newspaper, or of any religious or political periodical.

Same.

SECT. 25. The instructors shall not award medals or other prizes to the pupils under their charge; nor shall instructors become the recipients during term-time, and only from a graduating class at any other time, of any present of money, or other property, from the pupils. No subscription or contribution, for any purpose whatever, shall be introduced into any public school.

Presents.

Subscription or contribution.

No advertisement to be read to the pupils.

SECT. 26. No person whatever shall read to the pupils of any school, or post upon the walls of any school building, or fences of the same, any advertisement. Nor shall any agent or other person be permitted to enter any school for the purpose of exhibiting, either to teacher or pupils, any new book or article of apparatus.

No agent to exhibit articles in school.

SECT. 27. The books used and the studies pursued in all the Public Schools shall be such, and such only, as may be authorized by the Board; and the teachers shall not permit any books, tracts, or other publications to be distributed in their schools.

Authorized books and studies.

SECT. 28. No pupils shall be allowed to retain their connection with any of the Public Schools unless they are furnished with the books and utensils regularly required to be used in the respective classes.

Pupils must have the books and utensils required.

SECT. 29. In cases where children are in danger of being deprived of the advantages of education, by reason of inability to obtain books, through the poverty or negligence of parents or guardians, the Committee on Accounts are authorized, on behalf of the School Committee, to carry out the provisions of the Statute on this subject.[1] During the first week in April, annually, the principal teacher in each Grammar School, and the teacher of each Primary School, shall make to the Secretary of the Board, a return of the names of all scholars supplied with books at the expense of the city, the names of the books so furnished, together with the names of the parents, guardians, or masters of said pupils; and suitable blanks shall be provided for this purpose by the Secretary.

Books, &c., for indigent children.

SECT. 30. All children living within the limits of the city, who are not otherwise disqualified, and who are upwards of five years of age, shall be entitled to attend the public schools of

Children entitled to attend the public schools.

---

[1] "If any scholar is not furnished by his parent, master, or guardian, with the requisite books, he shall be supplied therewith by the School Committee at the expense of the town.

"The School Committee shall give notice, in writing, to the assessors of the town, of the names of the scholars supplied with books under the provisions of the preceding section, of the books so furnished, the prices thereof, and the names of the parents, masters, or guardians, who ought to have supplied the same. The assessors shall add the price of the books to the next annual tax of such parents, masters, or guardians; and the amount so added shall be levied, collected, and paid into the town treasury, in the same manner as the town taxes.

"If the assessors are of opinion that any parent, master, or guardian, is unable to pay the whole expense of the books so supplied on his account, they shall omit to add the price of such books, or shall only add a part thereof to his annual tax, according to their opinion of his ability to pay." [Gen. Stat. chap. 38, §§ 30, 31, 32.

the city; but no child whose residence is not in the city, or who has only a temporary residence in it for the purpose of attending the Public Schools, shall be received or retained in any school, except upon the consent previously obtained of the District Committee; and said District Committee may, in accordance with the provisions of the General Statutes, require the parent or guardian of such child, to pay a sum equal to the average cost per scholar of such school, for such period as said child may attend thereat.[1]

Same.

SECT. 31. No pupil shall be admitted to the privilege of one school who has been expelled from another, or while under suspension, unless by vote of the Board.

Certificate of vaccination.

SECT. 32. No pupil shall be admitted into any of the Public Schools without a certificate from a physician that he or she has been vaccinated, or otherwise secured against the smallpox; but this certificate shall not be required of pupils who go from one public school to another.

Cleanliness of pupils required.

SECT. 33. No child who comes to school without proper attention having been given to the *cleanliness* of his person and of his dress, or whose clothes are not properly repaired, shall be permitted to remain in school, but shall be sent home to be prepared for school in a proper manner.

Tardiness and absence of pupils.

SECT. 34. Tardiness shall be subject to such penalty as in each case the teacher may think proper. No pupil shall be allowed to be absent any part of the regular school hours for the purpose of receiving instruction, or taking lessons of any kind, elsewhere. Pupils detained at home must, on returning

---

[1] "All children within the Commonwealth may attend the public schools in the place in which they have their legal residence, subject to the regulations prescribed by law." [Gen. Stat. chap. 41, § 3.]

"With the consent of school committees first obtained, children between the ages of five and fifteen may attend schools in cities and towns other than those in which their parents or guardians reside; but whenever a child resides in a city or town different from that of the residence of the parent or guardian, for the sole purpose of attending school there, the parent or guardian of such child shall be liable to pay to such city or town, for tuition, a sum equal to the average expense per scholar for such school, for the period the child shall have so attended." [Gen. Stat. chap 41, § 7.]

to school, bring an excuse for such detention; and every pupil, wishing on any day to be dismissed before the close of the session, must assign satisfactory reasons therefor and obtain the consent of the teacher. Teachers having charge of pupils who are habitually truant shall report their names and residences, and the names of their parents or guardians, to the truant officers of the district.

Dismission of pupils before the close of the session.

Truancy.

SECT. 35. There shall be an annual exhibition of the Latin School on the Saturday, and of the English High School on the Monday, preceding the third Wednesday in July; and on the Tuesday following said Wednesday there shall be an exhibition of the several Grammar Schools; at which exhibitions the medals and diplomas shall be conferred upon the pupils. *Provided, however*, that the District Committees on the several Grammar Schools for *girls* may, if they deem it advisable, direct that such exhibition shall be on the Monday, instead of on the Tuesday, following said Wednesday. The hours for the exhibitions of the several schools shall be arranged by the President of the Board. The Exhibitions of the Grammar Schools shall be conducted in such manner as shall best present the actual condition of each school in the prominent branches of study, and shall not exceed two hours in length. On the first five school days of the week previous to the Exhibition, the parents and friends of the children shall be invited to witness the usual exercises of the school, and on the last day of that week the several Grammar Schools shall be closed. And in the afternoon of the day of the Annual Exhibitions of the Grammar Schools, the Annual School Festival shall be held, to which members of the School Committee, all the teachers in the public Schools, and the medal scholars of the current year shall be invited.

Annual exhibitions.

School festival.

SECT. 36. The following holidays and vacations shall be granted to the schools, viz: every Wednesday and Saturday afternoon, throughout the year; Christmas day, New Year's day, the Twenty-second of February, Good Friday, Fast day, May day, Artillery Election, and the Fourth of July; Thanksgiving week; the week immediately preceding the first Monday in March; one week commencing on the Monday preceding the

Holidays and vacations.

last Wednesday in May; and the remainder of the school year following their respective exhibitions; and to the Girls' High and Normal School from the Monday following the third Wednesday in July to the Saturday next preceding the second Monday in September. The Primary Schools shall be allowed the holidays aud vacations of the Grammar Schools, and also the day preceding and the day of the annual Exhibition of the Grammar Schools; and the President of the Board is authorized to suspend the schools *on such public occasions* as he may think proper, not exceeding three days in any one municipal year. In addition to these holidays the Latin and English High Schools shall be entitled to the two days of public exhibition at Harvard University. No other holidays shall be allowed except by special vote of the Board; and no school shall be suspended on any other occasion, except for special and important reasons relating to a particular school, and then only by express permission of the Sub-Committee.

Reading of Washington's Farewell Address.

SECT. 37. On the 21st of February, annually, the Masters of the High and Grammar School shall assemble their pupils, each in the hall of his schoolhouse, and read to them, or cause to be read to them, by one or more of their own number, extracts from Washington's Farewell Address to the People of the United States, combining therewith other patriotic exercises. And the regular exercises of the session shall be suspended so far as is necessary to give opportunity to this reading.

Chapter 9. — Regulations of the Primary Schools.

Admission of pupils to Primary Schools.

SECTION. 1. Every teacher shall admit to her school all applicants of suitable age and qualifications, residing nearest to the school under her charge, provided the number in her school will warrant the admission; and in all cases of doubt or difficulty in the discharge of this duty, she shall apply to her Sub-Committee for advice and direction.

Transfer of pupils.

SECT. 2. When any child shall apply to be admitted from another Primary School, the teacher shall require a certificate of transfer from the teacher of the former school; which certificate shall serve instead of a Certificate of Vaccination.

SECT. 3. The regular promotion of scholars to the Grammar Schools shall be made semi-annually, on the first Monday in March, and on the first Monday in September. But occasionally promotions may be made on Monday of any week, whenever the Sub-Committee of the Primary School and the Master of the Grammar School may deem it *necessary*. Promotion to Grammar Schools.

SECT. 4. One or more schools for the special instruction of children *over seven years of age*, and not qualified for the Grammar School, may be established in each District. The course of study shall be the same as in the Primary Schools; and it shall be in the power of each District Committee to introduce Writing, and the elements of Written Arithmetic. Any scholar over eight years of age, and not in the first or second class, may be removed from any Primary School to a school for special instruction, at the discretion of the Sub-Committee. Schools for special instruction.

SECT. 5. *The School on the Western Avenue* shall be connected with the Phillips School District. Children over eight years of age may be admitted into this school at the discretion of the Sub-Committee; and their studies shall conform to the regulations of the Grammar Schools. School on Western Avenue.

SECT. 6. The teachers shall attend to the physical education and comfort of the pupils under their care. When, from the state of the weather or other causes, the recesses in the open air shall be impracticable, the children may be exercised within the room, in accordance with the best judgment and ability of the teachers. In the schools which are kept in buildings occupied by Grammar Schools, the recesses shall be arranged by the masters so as not to interfere with the exercises of those schools. Proper care of the pupils in school. Recesses for Primary Schools in Grammar School buildings.

SECT. 7. The schools shall contain, as nearly as practicable, an equal number of pupils, the maximum number being fifty-six; and the pupils in each of the schools shall be arranged in six classes, unless otherwise ordered by the District Committee. Number of pupils to a school. Classes.

SECT. 8. Plain sewing may be introduced into any Primary School, at the discretion of the Sub-Committee, and singing shall form part of the opening and closing exercises of every Sewing.

Singing.

session; and such time be devoted to instruction in Music in each school as the Sub-Committee may deem expedient.

Order of studies; text-books.

SECT. 9. *The following Books and Studies shall be attended to in the respective classes. The* ORDER *of the exercises and lessons assigned to each class to be determined by the teacher; subject, however, to the direction of the Committee of the school.*

SIXTH CLASS.

Hillard's First Primary Reader to the 30th page; the words in columns to be spelled without book, and also words selected from the reading lessons.

Boston Primary School Tablets. Number Eleven, — the words and elementary sounds repeated after the teacher. Number One, — the name and sound of each letter, including the long and short sound of each vowel. Number Fifteen to be read and spelled by letters and by sound, and read by calling the words at sight. Number Sixteen to be read by spelling, and by calling words at sight, with oral lessons on the meaning of the sentences. Number Thirteen to be spelled by sounds. Numbers Nine and Ten to be used in reviewing the Alphabet, for variety of forms of letters. Number Five, — the pupil to name and point out the lines and plane figures. Number Two, — analyze the forms of the capitals, and tell what lines compose each.

Boston Primary School Slate, No. 1. — Print the small letters, and draw the straight lines and the rectilinear figures. The blackboard and tablets to be used in teaching the slate exercises.

Develop the idea of numbers to ten, by the use of objects. Count to one hundred on the numeral frame.

Repeating verses and maxims. Oral lessons on size, form, and color, illustrated by objects in the schoolroom; also upon common plants, and animals, illustrated by the objects themselves or by pictures.

Learning to read and spell from letter and word cards, at the option of the teacher.

Singing for five or ten minutes twice at least each day.

Physical exercises for five or ten minutes, twice at least each session.

FIFTH CLASS.

Hillard's First Primary Reader, as in the sixth class, completed.

My First School Book, for spelling to the 24th page, and for reading to the 70th page.

Boston Primary School Tablets. Review the exercises on Tablets prescribed for the sixth class. Number Nineteen, entire, and Number Twenty to L. Number Six, — name and point out the figures, and their parts. Number Eleven to be taught from the tablet. Number Fourteen, — syllables to be spelled by sound.

Boston Primary School Slate, No. 1. Review the slate exercises prescribed for the Sixth Class. Print the capital letters, also short words; draw the curvilinear figures.

Counting real objects, and counting with the numeral frame by twos to one hundred.

Repeating verses and maxims. Oral lessons on form, size, and color, and on plants, and animals. Singing and physical exercises as above.

FOURTH CLASS.

My First School Book, completed both as a reader and a speller.

Hillard's Second Primary Reader, to the 50th page; the words in columns to be spelled, and also words selected from the reading lessons. Spelling words by sounds.

Boston Primary School Tablets. Numbers Five and Six reviewed, with description or analysis of the lines and figures. Numbers Eleven, Thirteen, and Fourteen, reviewed. Numbers Twelve and Twenty to be learned. Numbers Seventeen and Eighteen, — names of punctuation marks.

Boston Primary School Slate, No. 1, — used daily. Copies in printing and drawing reviewed and completed. Printing four or five words daily. Writing Arabic figures.

Adding and subtracting numbers to twenty, illustrated by

objects and the numeral frame. Counting on the numeral frame by twos to one hundred, and by threes to fifty.

Repeating verses and maxims. Oral lessons on objects as above, with their parts, qualities, and uses. Singing and physical exercises as above.

THIRD CLASS.

Hillard's Second Primary Reader, completed; the words in columns to be spelled, and also words selected from the reading lessons. At each lesson in reading and spelling, words spelled by sounds. Conversations on the meaning of what is read.

Spelling and Thinking Combined, — to the thirty-fifth page. Spelling words by sounds. Questions on the meaning of words.

Boston Primary School Tablets. Numbers Five, Six, Eleven, Twelve, Thirteen, Fourteen, and Twenty, reviewed. Number Three. Number Eighteen, — use of punctuation marks commenced.

Boston Primary School Slate, No. 2. Write the small script letters and draw the plane figures. Exercises in writing and drawing to be illustrated by tablets and blackboard. Print a few words in capitals.

Eaton's Primary School Arithmetic begun. Miscellaneous questions in adding and subtracting small numbers. Practical questions involving similar combinations. The idea of multiplication devolving by the use of the numeral frame. Numbers to be combined, occasionally written on slates from dictation.

Repeating verses and maxims. Abbreviations. Oral lessons as above, and upon common objects, and the senses. Singing and physical exercises as above.

SECOND CLASS.

Hillard's Third Primary Reader, to the 100th page; the words in columns to be spelled, and also words selected from the reading lessons. Difficult words to be spelled by sounds. Conversations on the meaning of what is read.

Spelling and Thinking Combined, — to the seventy-fifth page.

Spelling words by sounds. Questions on the meaning of words.

Eaton's Primary Arithmetic, — addition, subtraction, and multiplication tables to be learned, and the practical questions under these rules to be attended to.

Boston Primary School Tablets. Numbers Three, Five, Six, Eleven, Twelve, and Eighteen, to be reviewed. Number Seven, — drawing and oral lessons on the objects represented. Number eighteen, — uses and definitions, of points and marks learned, and applied in reading lessons.

Boston Primary School Slate, No. 2. Writing capital and small letters, and drawing planes and solids, with illustrations from tablets and blackboard. Writing short words. Review abbreviations and Roman numerals.

Repeating verses and maxims. Oral lessons on objects, trades, and the most common phenomena of nature. Singing and physical exercises as above.

FIRST CLASS.

Hillard's Third Primary Reader, completed; with definitions, explanations, spelling, by letters and by sounds; also questions on punctuation, the use of capitals, and the marks indicating the pronunciation.

Spelling and Thinking Combined, completed. Spelling words by sounds. Questions on the meaning of words.

Eaton's Primary Arithmetic, completed. The tables of multiplication and division to 12×12 and 144÷12. Notation to 1,000. Counting by threes and fours, forwards to a hundred, and backwards, from a hundred to one. Practical questions to be attended to.

Boston Primary School Tablets. Review those used in the Second Class. Frequent drill on Number Twelve. Number eight, drawing and oral lessons on the objects represented.

Boston Primary School Slate, No. 2. Writing capitals and small letters, the pupil's name, and words from the spelling lessons, with particular care to imitate the letters on the frame. Drawing all the copies on the frame.

Repeating verses and maxims. Review abbreviations. Oral lessons on objects, trades, occupations, with exercise of observation by noting the properties and qualities of objects, comparing and classifying them, considering their uses, the countries from which they come, and their modes of production, preparation, or fabrication.

Singing and physical exercises as above.

SECT. 10. No scholars are to be promoted from one class to another till they are familiar with all the lessons of the class from which they are to be transferred, except for special reasons, satisfactory to the Sub-Committee.

Chapter 10. — *Regulations of Grammar Schools.*

SECTION 1. These schools form the second grade in the system of public instruction established in this city.

The following are their names, locations, and dates of establishment:—

List of Grammar Schools.

Name.	Location.	Sex.	Establishment.
1 — Eliot School	North Bennet Street	For Boys	1713
2 — Franklin School	Ringgold Street	" Girls	1785
3 — Mayhew School	Hawkins Street	" Boys	1803
4 — Boylston School	Fort Hill	" Boys	1819
5 — Bowdoin School	Myrtle Street	" Girls	1821
6 — Hancock School	Richmond Place	" Girls	1822
7 — Wells School	Blossom Street	" Girls	1833
8 — Winthrop School	Tremont Street	" Girls	1836
9 — Lyman School	East Boston	" Boys and Girls	1837
10 — Lawrence School	South Boston	" Boys and Girls	1844
11 — Brimmer School	Common Street	" Boys	1844
12 — Phillips School	Southac Street	" Boys	1844
13 — Dwight School	Springfield Street	" Boys	1844
14 — Quincy School	Tyler Street	" Boys	1847
15 — Bigelow School	South Boston	" Boys and Girls	1849
16 — Chapman School	East Boston	" Boys and Girls	1849
17 — Adams School	East Boston	" Boys and Girls	1856
18 — Lincoln School	South Boston	" Boys and Girls	1859
19 — Everett School	Northampton Street	" Girls	1860
20 — Bowditch School	South Street	" Girls	1861

In these schools are taught the common branches of an English Education.

Instructors in boys' schools.

SECT. 2. The schools for boys shall each be instructed by a master, a sub-master, an usher, a head assistant, and three or more female assistants.

The schools for girls shall each be instructed by a master, a head assistant for each story in the building, and three or more female assistants. In girls' schools.

The mixed schools (boys' and girls') shall each be instructed by a master, a sub-master, a head assistant for each story in the building, and three or more female assistants. In mixed schools.

Any existing exceptions to the foregoing organizations, authorized by special vote of the Board, shall remain until otherwise ordered.

SECT. 3. Each school shall be allowed a teacher for every fifty-six pupils on the register, and an additional female assistant may be appointed whenever there are thirty scholars above the employment for the teachers already in the school, if the District Committee deem it expedient; and whenever the number of pupils on the register shall be reduced to thirty less than such complement, one female assistant may be removed from such school, if the District Committee recommend it; *provided*, that, in determining the number of teachers to which any school may be entitled under this section, one head assistant shall not be counted. Number of pupils to a teacher.

SECT. 4. Any pupil may be admitted into the Grammar Schools who, on examination by the master or any of his assistants, shall be found able to read, at first sight, easy prose, to spell common words of one, two, or three syllables; to distinguish and name the marks of punctuation; to perform mentally such simple questions in Addition, Subtraction, and Division, as are found in Eaton's Primary Arithmetic; to answer readily to any proposed combination of the Multiplication Table in which neither factor exceeds ten; to read and write Arabic numbers containing three figures, and the Roman numerals as far as the sign of one hundred; and to enunciate, clearly and accurately, the elementary sounds of our language. And no pupil who does not possess these qualifications shall be admitted into any Grammar School, except by special permit of the District Committee. Qualifications for admission to the Grammar Schools.

SECT. 5. Within the two weeks preceding the first Monday in March, annually, the Master of each Grammar School shall visit each Primary which is expected to send pupils to his Examination of primary scholars for promotion to Grammar School.

schools; and he shall examine the first class in each of said schools, and shall give certificates of admission to the Grammar School to such as he may find qualified in accordance with the foregoing requirements. But in the month of July, annually, each teacher in the Primary Schools shall accompany her first class to such Grammar Schoolhouse in the vicinity as the master may designate, when he and his assistants shall examine the candidates for admission to the Grammar School, in presence of their instructors, and shall give certificates to those who are found to be properly qualified. If, however, the parent or guardian of any applicant not admitted on the examination of the master, is dissatisfied with his decision, such person may appeal to the District Committee for another examination of said applicant.

Certificates of admission.

Times of admitting pupils to Grammar Schools.

SECT. 6. Pupils admitted from the Primary Schools are expected to enter the Grammar Schools on the first Monday of March and of September; but all other applicants residing in the District, found on examination *qualified in all respects*, may enter the Grammar Schools, by applying to the master at the schoolhouse, on Monday morning of any week when the schools are in session. Pupils regularly transferred from one Grammar School to another, may be admitted at any time, on presenting their certificates of transfer, without an examination.

Out-of-school lessons.

SECT. 7. No lessons shall be assigned to girls to be studied out of school; and, in assigning out-of-school lessons to boys, the instructors shall not assign a longer lesson daily than a boy of good capacity can acquire by an hour's study; nor shall the lessons to be studied in school be so long as to require a scholar of ordinary capacity to study out of school in order to learn them; and no out-of-school lessons shall be assigned on Saturday.

Classes and sections.

SECT. 8. Each school or department of a school shall be divided into four classes. Each class shall consist of two or more divisions, each of which sections shall pursue the studies and use the text-books assigned to its class; but whenever it shall appear that a division of a lower class has, in any particular branch of study, made the attainments requisite for promotion to a higher class, at a period earlier than the regular time for general promotion, then such division may, at the discretion of the master, and with the approval of the Committee, enter upon the study of one of the text-books prescribed for the next higher class.

SECT. 9. The books and exercises of the several classes shall be as follows, viz: — Text-books.

Class 4. — No. 1. Worcester's Spelling Book. 2. Hillard's Fourth Reader. 3. Writing in each school, in such Writing Books as the District Committee may approve. 4. Drawing in Bartholomew's Drawing Books. 5. Eaton's Intellectual Arithmetic, with lessons in Written Arithmetic on the slate and blackboard. 6. Warren's Primary Geography. Same.

Class 3. — No. 1. Worcester's Spelling Book. 2. Hillard's Intermediate Reader. 3. Writing, as in Fourth Class. 4. Eaton's Intellectual Arithmetic, and Eaton's Common School Arithmetic, revised edition. 5. Drawing in Bartholomew's Drawing Books. 6. Warren's Primary Geography. 7. Kerl's Elementary English Grammar. Same.

Class 2. — No. 1. Spelling. 2. Hillard's Fifth Reader. 3. Writing, as in Fourth Class. 4. Eaton's Intellectual Arithmetic, and Eaton's Common School Arithmetic, revised edition. 5. Warren's Common School Geography, with exercises in Map Drawing, on the blackboard, and by pen and pencil. 6. Kerl's Elementary English Grammar, or Kerl's Comprehensive English Grammar. 7. Drawing in Bartholomew's Drawing Books. 8. Exercises in Composition, and, in the boys' schools, Declamation. 9. Swan's First Lessons in the History of the United States. Same.

Class 1. — No. 1. Spelling. — Adams's Spelling Book for advanced classes, *permitted*. 2. Reading in Hillard's Sixth Reader. 3. Writing as in Fourth Class. 4. Geography, as in Class Two. 5. Eaton's Intellectual Arithmetic, and Eaton's Common School Arithmetic, revised edition. 6. Grammar. 7. Exercises in Composition, and in the boys' schools, in Declamation. 8. Drawing in Bartholomew's Drawing Books. 9. Worcester's Dictionary. 10. Book- Text-books.

Keeping by single entry. 11. Worcester's History. 12. Hall's Manual of Morals, — a Monday morning lesson, with oral instruction. 13. Instruction in Natural Philosophy, using Hooker's Natural Philosophy, as a text-book, with the Philosophical Apparatus provided for the schools, shall be given at least to the first division of the First Class. 14. Instruction in Physical Geography, by occasional exercises; the treatise of Warren, or of Cartée, being used as a text-book. 15. Hooker's Primary Philosophy.

Permitted books.

SECT. 10. In teaching Arithmetic to the several classes, every teacher shall be at liberty to employ such books as he shall deem useful, for the purpose of affording illustration and examples; but such books shall not be used to the exclusion or neglect of the prescribed text-books; nor shall the pupils be required to furnish themselves with any book but the text-books.

Arithmetic.

SECT. 11. One treatise on Mental Arithmetic, and one treatise on Written Arithmetic, and no more, shall be used as text-books in the Grammar Schools.

Instruction in music.

SECT. 12. Two half-hours each week in the Grammar Schools shall be devoted to the study and practice of Vocal Music. Instruction shall be given to the First and Second Classes by the music teachers. Musical notation, the singing of the scale, and exercises in reading simple music shall be practised twice a week by the lower classes under the direction of the assistant teachers; and the pupils shall undergo examinations and receive credits for proficiency in music, as in the other studies pursued in the schools.

Examination in music.

Arrangement of the studies and recitations.

SECT. 13. It is recommended that in the arrangement of the studies and recitations in the Grammar Schools, those which most severely task the attention and effort of the pupils be, as far as possible, assigned for the forenoon.

Committees to superintend the organization of the first class.

SECT. 14. It shall be the duty of the Committee of each Grammar School, at the beginning of each school year, either at a special meeting called for this purpose, or through their chairman, previously authorized to act in their name, to superintend the organization of the first class, and to see that none are retained members thereof who ought to join the English High School, or the Girls' High and Normal School. No pupils to be retained who should join the High Schools.

Chapter 11. — *Regulations of the English High School.*

SECTION 1. This school is situated in Bedford Street. It was instituted in 1821, with the design of furnishing the young men of the city who are not intended for a collegiate course of studies, and who have enjoyed the usual advantages of the other Public Schools, with the means of completing a good English education, and fitting themselves for all the departments of commercial life. The prescribed course of studies is arranged for three years, and those who attend for that period and complete that course, are considered to have been graduated at the school. Those who wish to pursue further some of the higher departments of mathematics, and other branches, have the privilege of remaining another year at school. This institution is furnished with a valuable mathematical and philosophical apparatus, for the purpose of experiment and illustration. To this school apply the following regulations, in addition to those common to all the schools. English High School established, and its object.

SECT. 2. The instructors in this school shall be a master, two sub-masters, and as many ushers as shall allow one instructor to every thirty-five pupils, but no additional usher shall be allowed for a less number. The Sub-Committee may furnish the master with an assistant in his room whenever the number of pupils remaining in the school through the fourth year shall in their judgment make it necessary. The salary of said assistant shall not exceed the salary paid to an usher in this school during his first year of service. It shall be a necessary qualification in all these instructors that they have been educated at some respectable college, and that they be competent to instruct in the French language. Instructors.

SECT. 3. Candidates for admission to this school shall be examined once a year, on the Wednesday and Thursday next succeeding the exhibition of the Grammar Schools in July. Any boy then offering himself as a candidate for admission, shall present a certificate from his parent and guardian that he Time of examining candidates for admission.

has reached the age of twelve years, also a certificate of good moral character, and of presumed literary qualifications, from the master of the school which he has attended, and shall pass a satisfactory examination in the following studies, viz: Spelling, Reading, Writing, English Grammar, Arithmetic, Modern Geography, and the History of the United States.

Annual examination of candidates.

SECT. 4. It shall be the duty of the Committee on the English High School to be present at the annual examination of candidates for admission, but said examination shall be conducted by the instructors, from questions previously prepared, on all the branches, and subject to the approval of the Committee. The examination shall be strict; and a thorough knowledge of the required studies shall be indispensable to admission.

SECT. 5. On admission, pupils shall be arranged in divisions according to their respective degrees of proficiency. Individuals, however, shall be advanced according to their scholarship, and no faster; and no one shall remain a member of the school longer than four years.

Reviews.

SECT. 6. It shall be the duty of the master to examine each division as often as may be consistent with the attention due to those under his immediate instruction. Each class or section shall be occasionally reviewed in its appropriate studies, and once a quarter there shall be a general review of all the previous studies of that quarter.

School hours.

SECT. 7. The school shall hold one session daily. Commencing at 9 A. M. and closing at 2 P. M., except on Saturday, when the school shall close at 1 o'clock.

Course of studies and text-books.

SECT. 8. The course of study and instruction in this school shall be as follows:—

Class 3. Review of preparatory studies, using the text-books authorized in the Grammar Schools of the city. 2. Ancient Geography. 3. Worcester's General History. 4. Sherwin's Algebra. 5. French Language. 6. Drawing.

Same.

Class 2. 1. Sherwin's Algebra, continued. 2. French Language, continued. 3. Drawing, continued. 4. Legendre's Geometry. 5. Book-keeping. 6. Blair's Rhetoric. 7. Constitution of the United States. 8. Trigonometry, with its application to Surveying, Navigation, Mensuration, Astronomical Calculations, &c. 9. Paley's Evidences of Christianity, — a Monday morning lesson.

Class 1. Trigonometry, with its applications, &c., continued. 2. Paley's Evidences, continued, — a Monday morning lesson. 3. Drawing, continued. 4. Astronomy. 5. Natural Philosophy. 6. Moral Philosophy. 7. Political Economy. 8. Natural Theology. 9. Shaw's Lectures on English Literature. 10. French, continued, — or the Spanish Language may be commenced by such pupils as in the judgment of the master have acquired a competent knowledge of the French. Warren's Treatise on Physical Geography, or Cartée's Physical Geography and Atlas, is *permitted* to be used. **Same.**

For the pupils who remain at the school the fourth year, the course of studies shall be as follows : —

1. Astronomy. 2. Intellectual Philosophy. 3. Logic. 4. Spanish. 5. Geology. 6. Chemistry. 7. Mechanics, Engineering and the higher Mathematics, with some option. **Same.**

SECT. 9. The several classes shall also have exercises in English Composition and Declamation. The instructors shall pay particular attention to the penmanship of the pupils, and give constantly such instruction in Spelling, Reading, and English Grammar, as they may deem necessary to make the pupils familiar with these fundamental branches of a good education. **Same.**

SECT. 10. Each pupil who shall graduate from this school, having honorably completed its course of instruction to the satisfaction of the Principal and the Committee, shall be entitled to receive a suitable diploma on leaving school. **Diplomas to graduates.**

Chapter 12. — *Regulations of the Girls' High and Normal School.*

SECTION 1. This school is situated in Mason Street. It was instituted in 1852, with the design of furnishing to those pupils who have passed through the usual course of studies at the Grammar Schools for girls, and at other girls' schools in this city, an opportunity for a higher and more extended educa- **Establishment and object of the school.**

tion, and also to fit such of them as desire to become teachers. The following are the regulations of this school, in addition to those common to all the schools.

Instructors.

SECT. 2. The instructors shall be, a master, and as many assistants as may be found expedient; but the whole number of assistants shall not exceed the ratio of one for every thirty pupils.[1]

Admission of pupils.

SECT. 3. The examination of candidates for admission to the schools, shall take place annually, on the Wednesday and Thursday next succeeding the day of the annual exhibition of the Grammar Schools in July.

Same.

SECT. 4. Candidates for admission must be over fifteen, and not more than nineteen years of age. They must present certificates of recommendation from the teachers whose schools they last attended, and must pass a satisfactory examination in the following branches, viz: Spelling, Reading, Writing, Arithmetic, English Grammar, Geography, and History.

Same.

SECT. 5. The examination shall be conducted by the instructors of the school, both orally and from written questions previously prepared by them, and approved by the Committee of the school. It shall be the duty of the said Committee to be present and to assist at the examination, and the admission of candidates shall be subject to their approval.

Course of instruction.

SECT. 6. The course of studies and instruction in this school shall be as follows: —

---

[1] At a meeting of the School Committee held May 17, 1864, the following Orders were passed: —

1. ORDERED, That the Committee, on the Girls' High and Normal School be authorized to employ a special instructor in the Normal Department of that School, with a salary not exceeding $ 800 per annum.

2. ORDERED, That those members of the Senior Class in the Girls' High and Normal School who intend to become teachers, shall be required to attend the sessions of one or more of the Primary and Grammar Schools in the city, not less than four weeks during the year, in order to observe the methods of teaching, and to acquire practical knowledge of the instruction and government of school, by acting as teachers themselves; — it being understood that they are to be under the supervision and direction of the Chairman of the District Committee, and of the master of the school in which they are employed, and that they are to receive no remuneration.

Junior Class. Reading, Spelling, and Writing, continued. Arithmetic, Geography, and Grammar, reviewed. Physical Geography, Natural Philosophy, Analysis of Language and Structure of Sentences. Synonymes. Rhetoric. Exercises in English Composition. History. Latin, begun. Exercises in Drawing and in Vocal Music.

Middle Class. Natural Philosophy, continued. English Literature. Algebra. Moral Philosophy. Latin, continued. French, begun (instruction given by a native French teacher). Rhetoric, with exercises in Composition, continued. Physiology, with Lectures. General History. Exercises in Drawing and in Vocal Music. Reading standard English Works, with exercises in Criticism.

Senior Class. Latin and French continued. Geometry. General History. Intellectual Philosophy. Astronomy. Chemistry, with lectures. Exercises in Composition. Exercises in Drawing and in Vocal Music. Exercises in Criticism, comprising a careful examination of works of the best English authors. Instruction in the Theory and Practice of Teaching. Such instruction in Music shall be given to all the pupils as may qualify them to teach Vocal Music in our Public Schools.

School hours.

SECT. 7. The sessions of the schools shall begin at 9 o'clock, A. M. and close at 2 o'clock, P. M., except on Wednesday and Saturday, when the school shall close at 1 o'clock.

Visitations by parents and friends.

SECT. 8. Instead of a public exhibition in this school the parents and friends of the pupils shall be invited through the pupils to attend the regular exercises in the various rooms during the five days preceding the last school-day of the school year. And during such visitations the exercises of the school shall be conducted in the usual manner.

Pupils may remain three years.

Diploma.

SECT. 9. The plan of study shall be arranged for three years. Pupils who have attended for that period, and who have completed the course in a manner satisfactory to the teachers and the Committee on the school, shall be entitled to receive a diploma or certificate to that effect, on leaving the school.

Chapter 13. — *Regulations of the Latin Grammar School.*

SECTION. 1. This school, situated in Bedford Street, was instituted early in the 17th century.

Objects of the schools.

SECT. 2. The rudiments of the Latin and Greek languages are taught, and scholars are fitted for the most respectable colleges. Instruction is also given in Mathematics, Geography, History, Declamation, English Grammar, Composition, and in the French language.

The following Regulations, in addition to those common to all the schools, apply to this school.

Instructors.

SECT. 3. The instructors in this school shall be a master, a sub-master, and as many ushers as shall allow one instructor to every thirty-five pupils, and no additional usher shall be allowed for a less number.

Same.

SECT. 4. It shall be a necessary qualification for the instructors of this school, that they shall have been educated at a college of good standing.

Candidates for admission.

SECT. 5. Each candidate for admission shall have attained the age of ten years, and shall produce from the master of the school he last attended a certificate of good moral character. He shall be able to read English correctly and fluently, to spell all words of common occurrence, to write a running hand, understand Mental Arithmetic and the simple rules of Written Arithmetic, and be able to answer the most important questions in Geography, and shall have a sufficient knowledge of English Grammar to parse common sentences in prose. A knowledge of Latin Grammar shall be considered equivalent to that of English.

Time of examining candidates for admission.

SECT. 6. Boys shall be examined for admission to this school only once a year, viz: on the Friday and Saturday of the last week of the vacation succeeding the exhibition of the school in July.

Pupils may remain six years.

SECT. 7. The regular course of instruction shall continue six years, and no scholar shall enjoy the privileges of this school beyond that term, unless by written leave of the Committee.

But scholars may have the option of completing their course in five years or less time, if willing to make due exertions, and shall be advanced according to scholarship.

SECT. 8. The sessions of the school shall begin at 9 o'clock A. M. and close at 2 o'clock P. M. on every school-day throughout the year, except on Saturday, when the school shall close at 1 o'clock. School hours.

SECT. 9. The school shall be divided into classes and subdivisions, as the master, with the approbation of the Committee, may think advisable. Classes.

SECT. 10. The master shall examine the pupils under the care of the other teachers in the school as often as he can consistently with proper attention to those in his own charge.

SECT. 11. The books and exercises required in the course of instruction in this school, are the following: — Course of studies and text-books.

Class 6. Andrews and Stoddard's Latin Grammar. 2. English Grammar. 3. Reading English. 4. Spelling. 5. Mental Arithmetic. 6. Mitchell's Geographical Questions. 7. Declamation. 8. Penmanship. 9. Andrews's Latin Lessons. 10. Andrews's Latin Reader.

Class 5. 1, 2, 3, 4, 7, 8, continued. 11. Viri Romæ. 12. Written translations. 13. Colburn's Sequel. 14. Cornelius Nepos. 15. Arnold's Latin Prose Composition.

Class 4. 1, 2, 3, 4, 7, 8, 12, 13, 15, continued. 16. Sophocles's Greek Grammar. 17. Sophocles's Greek Lessons. 18. Cæsar's Commentaries. 19. Fasquelle's French Grammar. 20. Exercises in speaking and reading French with a native French Teacher.

Class 3. 1, 2, 3, 4, 7, 8, 12, 13, 15, 16, 19, 20, continued. 21. Ovid's Metamorphoses. 22. Arnold's Greek Prose Composition. 23. Felton's Greek Reader. 24. Sherwin's Algebra. 25. English Composition. 26. Le Grandpere. Text-books.

Class 2. 1, 2, 3, 4, 7, 8, 15, 16, 19, 21, 22, 23, 24, 25. continued. 27. Virgil. 28. Elements of History. 29. Translations from English into Latin. Same.

Class 1. 1, 7, 15, 16, 19, 20, 21, 22, 23, 25, 27, 28, 29, Same.

continued. 30. Geometry. 31. Cicero's Orations. 32. Composition of Latin Verses. 33. Composition in French. 34. Ancient History and Geography.

Same. The following books of reference may be used in pursuing the above studies: —

Leverett's Latin Lexicon, or Gardner's abridgment of the same.

Andrews's Latin Lexicon.

Liddell and Scott's Greek Lexicon, or Pickering's Greek Lexicon, last edition.

Worcester's School Dictionary.

Smith's Classical Dictionary.

Smith's Dictionary of Antiquities.

Baird's Classic Manual. Warren's Treatise on Physical Geography, or Cartée's Physical Geography and Atlas is *permitted* to be used.

Translations and keys forbidden. SECT. 12. No Translations, nor any Interpretation, Keys, or Orders of Construction, are allowed in the school.

Penmanship, reading, spelling, &c. SECT. 13. The instructors shall pay particular attention to the penmanship of the pupils, and give constantly such instruction in Spelling, Reading, and English Grammar, as they may deem necessary to make the pupils familiar with those fundamental branches of a good education.

Diploma. SECT. 14. Each pupil who shall honorably complete the course of studies prescribed for this school, to the satisfaction of the Principal and the Committee, shall be entitled to receive a suitable diploma or certificate to that effect at graduation.

SCHOOLHOUSES.

RULES.

.. Janitors to be appointed, their residence and compensation; entries, passages, and rooms to be swept.

2. Furniture and walls to be swept and dusted.

3. Windows and doors to be cleaned.

4. Fires to be made; use of fuel and ashes.

5. Opening and closing of houses; care of yards and walks.

6. Masters to supervise the Janitors and indorse their bills.

RULES.[1]

Ordered: That, the Superintendent of Public Buildings shall mploy such persons as he may deem competent, to have the are of Schoolhouses. Such persons shall reside in the city of Boston, and shall receive such compensation as the Committee n Public Buildings may determine upon. And persons so mployed shall comply with the following Appointment of janitors.

Rules.

1. The Entries, Stairways, and Passages to be swept daily; he Rooms every Wednesday and Saturday of each week; and he Cellars once a week, or as often as required to keep them n good order. Entries and rooms to be swept.

2. The School furniture is to be dusted as often as the Rooms are swept. The Windows, Blinds, Walls, and Ceilings of the rooms and entries are to be dusted as often as required to be kept in good order. Furniture, walls, &c., to be swept and dusted.

3. The Windows shall be cleaned twice in each year, viz: in the vacation in February and August, for which purpose the Janitor may employ a suitable person, at a price satisfactory to the Superintendent of Public Buildings. And it shall be the duty of the Janitor to see that they are properly cleaned. The Doors and all other painted surfaces, including Seats and Desks, whenever necessary, and the Ink-wells once in three months. Windows and doors to be cleaned.

[1] Rules and Regulations for the Care of Schoolhouses, as established by the Committee on Public Buildings. [See Laws and Ordinances, pp. 476 and 478.]

Fires to be made.

4. Fires, whenever necessary, are to be made in season to have the House properly warmed at the time for opening the School.

Use of fuel and ashes.

The fuel is to be economically used, the ashes to be thoroughly screened, and the screenings to be used on the fires. When stoves are used, fuel sufficient for the day must be carried to the several rooms.

Opening and closing of houses; yards and walks.

5. The House is to be opened and closed daily, Sundays excepted. The Yards, Walks, and Outhouses are to be kept clean and in good order.

The Rooms for Singing and Exhibitions are to be prepared for these exercises, and a general supervision of the Estate maintained during vacations.

Masters to supervise the janitors.

6. The Masters of each School are requested to see that the Janitors perform the above-named duties in a satisfactory manner, and the bills of the Janitor must be indorsed by the Master, which will certify that the foregoing Rules and Regulations have been complied with.

The Bills must be left at the Office of the Superintendent of Public Buildings for approval, on or before the twentieth of each month.

STREET WATERING.

RULES.

1. Applications for license.
2. Expense to be borne by abuttors.
3. Mode of watering to be fixed by Superintendent of Health.
4. License for one year only, and revocable at pleasure.
5. Time of watering to be fixed by Superintendent of Health.
6. Crossing stones not to be wet.

RULES.[1]

1. All applications for watering the streets of the city shall be referred to the Committee on Internal Health, who, if they agree that the application be granted, shall decide whether the street or streets applied for shall be watered with fresh or salt water, and the license shall expressly state which kind of water shall be used. Applications for license.

2. The *expense* of watering the streets is to be borne in all cases by the *abuttors*. Expense to be borne by abuttors.

3. The *mode* of watering the streets, and the *quantity of water* to be put upon the streets during each day, shall be determined upon by the Superintendent of Health. Mode of watering to be be fixed by Superintendent of Health.

4. The license shall be for the term of *one year only*, and shall be liable to be revoked at the pleasure of the Board of Aldermen. License for one year only; revocable at pleasure.

5. The time of *commencing* and *finishing* the duty of watering the streets, to be determined by the Superintendent of Health. Time of watering to be fixed by Superintendent of Internal Health.

6. In watering the streets, *especial care* must be taken to avoid wetting the *crossing stones* in each street. Crossing stones not to be wet.

---

[1] Rules prescribed by the Committee on Internal Health, by authority of the Board of Aldermen, given April 7, 1856.

TELEGRAPHIC FIRE ALARM.

REGULATIONS.

Constant watch kept; operators to alternate; sleep during watch forbidden.
Operators accountable for mistakes.
Account of alarms kept.
Where alarms are given; persons who have keys.
Manner of giving alarms.
Directions to those who hold signal keys.
Cautions.

REGULATIONS.[1]

Constant watch kept; operators to alternate; sleep during watch forbidden.

A constant watch is kept at the Office, Court Square, night and day, by the operators. Each operator serves two alternate terms of three hours each, as principal, and the same as assistant operator; so that twelve hours' service at the office, out of every twenty-four, is required from each operator. No operator is permitted to sleep during his watch, unless expressly relieved by some one else, and by consent of the Superintendent.

Operators accountable for mistakes.

Each operator is accountable to the Superintendent for any mistakes that may occur at the Office during his hours of duty.

Account of alarms kept.

An accurate account is kept of the time of giving each alarm, and of the Station from which it originates, and all other necessary information.

Where alarms are given; persons who have keys.

Alarms are transmitted to the Central Office, from the Signal Stations or Boxes, by turning a crank in the Box. The Police Officers, and one other person resident near each Station, have keys to the boxes.

The ringing of the bells and the tapping of the Boxes, *each* denotes the number of the Station from which the alarm origi-

---

[1] Regulations established by the Committee and Superintendent of Fire Alarms. [See Laws and Ordinances, pp. 225, 226.]

nated: thus, — one blow, a pause, three blows, another pause, and two blows (1 — 3 — 2) indicates that the alarm came from Box No. 132.

Manner of giving alarms.

Alarms are usually given in less than a minute from the time the crank is turned in any Box.

Directions to those who hold signal keys.

1. If a fire is discovered in your vicinity, go to the nearest Box.

2. Turn the crank *twenty-five times*, rather slowly at first, then quite fast at last. Wait at the box, and direct the firemen to the fire.

3. If you hear no reply at the Box, or on the bells, turn again. If still no reply, go to another Box.

4. The Police, upon hearing the bells, will spring their rattles and call the number of the Station.

Cautions.

1. Be sure your Box is locked before leaving it.

2. Never open the Box except in cases of fire.

3. Never let the key go out of your possession, unless called for by the Superintendent.

There are   Signal Stations distributed and located in conspicuous localities, all over the city.[1]

[1] The list of numbers and localities of the boxes is omitted for the reason that it is frequently changed; and the number of stations is constantly augmented, — the present number being about 75.

WATER BOARD.

RULES AND REGULATIONS.

Organization.
Meetings.
President.
Quorum.
Order of business.
Committees.
Rules and Reguluations.
Notification of meetings.
Bills and Accounts.
Subordinate officers.
Clerk, to keep books, &c.
Superintendent of Western Division; to have charge of, &c.
Superintendent of Eastern Division; to have charge of, &c.
City Engineer's duties.
Water Registrar's duties.

RULES AND REGULATIONS.[1]

Organization. The persons chosen by the City Council to constitute the Cochituate Water Board, shall meet on the first Monday in April in each year, and organize themselves by the choice of a President from their own number, and of a Clerk, and make such rules and regulations for their own government and in relation to all subordinate officers, as they may deem expedient.

Meetings. STATED meetings of the Board shall be held every other week, at such time as they may direct; special meetings shall be called by the President, and in an emergency, by any two members.

President. The President shall preside at all meetings of the Board, and in his absence a President *pro tem.* shall be chosen. He shall exercise a general supervision over all the Water Works, and the materials and property connected therewith, and over all subordinate officers and agents. Quorum. A majority of the Board shall constitute a quorum.

Order of business. The order of business shall be as follows: —

Reading of the Records.
Reports of Committees.
Examination of Claims.
Approval of Bills.
Motions and Resolutions.

---

[1] Rules and Regulations of the Cochituate Water Board, as adopted April, 1865. See Laws and Ordinances, p p 794–808.

The Committee on Accounts shall consist of the whole Board, and the following Committees consisting of three members each, shall be appointed by the President, and shall, subject to the direction of the Board, have the control and care of the departments to which they are appointed. **Committees.**

Committee on the Western Division.

Committee on the Eastern Division.

Committee on the Water Registrar's Department and Water Board Office.

Rules and regulations. All petitions and subjects presented to the Board, shall (unless they are prepared to act thereupon) be referred to a Committee, to report at the next regular meeting or at a special meeting called for the purpose.

When requested by a member of the Board the vote shall be taken by yeas and nays, and recorded by the Clerk.

These rules may be suspended by a majority of the members present, and they may be amended by a majority of the whole Board, notice having been given of the intention so to do, at the previous meeting.

Notification of meetings. All meetings shall be notified by the Clerk, by leaving a written or printed notification at the place of abode of the several members, unless otherwise ordered.

Bills and accounts. All bills and accounts against the city, authorized by this Board, after being approved by the Chairman of the Committee ordering the same, shall be entered by the Clerk in a monthly draft, which shall be presented to the Board previous to the 20th of each month, which, after being approved, shall be signed by the President, and delivered with the vouchers to the Auditor.

No bill or account shall be entered in the monthly draft, unless it be delivered to the Clerk on or before the 15th day of that month.

Subordinate officers. The following subordinate officers shall be appointed, and hold their offices during the pleasure of the Board, and receive such compensation as the Board may from time to time deem expedient.

A Clerk.

A Superintendent of the Western Division.

A Superintendent of the Eastern Division.

And such other Clerks and Assistants as may from time to time be necessary.

Clerk to keep books, &c.

The Clerk shall be chosen by ballot, and duly sworn to the faithful performance of the duties of his office. He shall give his whole time to the service of the Board, attend their meetings, and keep a record of their proceedings. The Books, Plans, and Documents, shall be kept at the office of the Board and be under his supervision.

It shall be his duty to keep Books, wherein shall be entered a full and accurate statement of all receipts and expenditures; receive all bills and accounts against the city, which are presented on or before the 15th day of each month, examine them in detail, and, when approved by the Committee or party who contracted them, enter them in the proper books, and present them with a schedule thereof, to the Board for approval; receive all applications for service pipes and for water to be let on or shut off, — and keep a record of the same specifying the time and reasons therefor; cause the water to be let on when the rates are paid, and when notified by the Registrar of non-payment, at once cause it to be shut off; report to the Board monthly the number of fines, cases of water cut off and of those let on; also all charges therefor, and for any other work performed under his direction; and perform such further services as may be required by the President or any Committee.

Superintendent of Western Division to have charge of, &c.

The Superintendent, under the direction of the President and the Committee on the Western Division, shall have the charge of Lake Cochituate, Brookline, and Chestnut Hill Reservoirs, Gate Houses and Pipe Chambers at Charles River, and of all the lands and property of the city in this division.

It shall be his special duty to attend to the protection of the above lands and property; the waste weirs at Dedman's Brook in Needham, Webber's Barn in Brookline, at Newton Centre and East Needham, to the prevention of all nuisances and trespasses upon all the said works or lands, or upon the waters of the Lake; keep the grounds and walks in good order, and forthwith report to the Committee and at the office, all cases of damage or casualty; make an accurate record of the water levels at the Lake every morning, specifying therein the depth of the water in the conduit, the height of the surface of the Lake above the conduit; the temperature of the water in the gate-house; of the air in the shade, and the height of the water on the 23-feet gauge below the outlet dam; also at the Brookline and Chestnut Hill Reservoirs, specifying therein the depth of the water above the bottom of the conduit in the Reservoirs, the depth in the gate-houses, the temperature of the water therein at eight feet below the surface, and of the air in the shade; ascertain the height of water at the Pipe Chambers at Charles River daily, every morning, above the bottom of the aqueduct, and report the same to the Board weekly, and to the City Engineer monthly; employ such assistants and laborers as may be required, first obtaining the consent and approval of the Committee on this Division; duly return to the Board on the first Mondays of January and July in each year, and as much oftener as they may require, a full report of the work and labor performed, and materials used, in his department, and annually on the first Monday of January, a correct statement of all the tools and other property in his possession belonging to the city, and perform such further services as may be required.

Superintendent of Eastern Division; to have charge of, &c.

The Superintendent under the direction of the President and the Committee on the Eastern Division, shall have the special charge of all the reservoirs, and of the public fountains in the city, and of all the iron mains and pipes in both Divisions; and it shall be his duty to protect them from all nuisances and trespasses, and attend to the protection of all other property in this Division belonging to the Water Works; keep an account of the pipes, machinery, and other property in the machine shop and yards; in case of accident to the mains or other pipes, forthwith repair them, distributing suitable notices before the stoppage of water, except in cases of emergency; give immediate notice at the office and to the Committee, of any accident which may happen to the mains, pipes, or anything connected therewith; put in such service pipes, and lay such mains and other pipes, as may from time to time be directed; repair any injuries to the streets or sewers caused by the Water Works; employ such assistants and laborers as may be required, first obtaining the consent and approval of the Committee; whenever any street, highway, or place, is liable to be obstructed, or rendered dangerous by the laying of pipes or making repairs, cause a sufficient fence to be erected, and light and guard the same; make a full report, quarterly to the Board, of the work and labor performed, and materials used in his department; measure the quantity of water in the reservoirs, take the temperature of the water in the Beacon Hill Reservoir, and of the air in the shade, every morning, noon and night, and keep a record and make a return thereof, to the Board weekly, and to the City Engineer monthly; duly return to the Board, on the first Monday of January in each year, and as much oftener as they may require, a correct statement of the quantity of pipes and other materials in the yards, and all the property belonging to the city which is under his care; and perform such further services as may be required.

City Engineer's duties.

It shall be the duty of the City Engineer to carefully inspect the Aqueduct and all other structures belonging to the Water Works in person, previous to making his Annual Report to the Board, and at such other times as they may require; make such surveys, plans, and estimates, connected with the works, as the Board may direct; when requested, give his opinion, in writing, of the best mode of constructing or repairing any portion of the works; keep in his office the returns of the Superintendents in relation to the water levels at the Lake, the reservoirs, and the pipe chambers at Charles River, and report them to the Board previous to the sixth day of January in each year.

Water Registrar's duties.

It shall be the duty of the Water Registrar, under the direction of the Board and the Committee on this department, to assess the water rates, according to the tariff established by the City Council; make out and distribute all bills for the same; exercise a constant supervision over the use of the water, and attend to the enforcement of all regulations relative thereto; keep suitable books, in which shall be entered the names of all persons who take water, the kind of building, the name and number of the street, the nature of the use, the number of taps, and the amount charged, which shall always be open to the inspection of the Board; make returns to the Clerk of the Board, of all places where the water is to be let on, and where to be shut off for non-payment, with full particulars as to the location of the premises; make monthly returns to the Board, of the receipts and expenditures of his department, and as much oftener as they may require, and employ such assistance as may be necessary in his department, first obtaining the approval of the Committee; and perform such other services as may be required.

He shall make no abatement of water rates after a bill has been rendered, nor apply any meter, or discontinue the use of any, without the approval of the President or the Committee.

SPECIAL ACTS.

BOSTON MILL CORPORATION.

ACTS.

1. Incorporating clause.
2. Property vested in corporation, and to be divided into 1,600 shares.
3. J. Peck authorized to call a proprietors' meeting.
4. Corporation allowed to hold other real estate than the Mill Pond.
5. Assessments may be levied, and shares of delinquents sold.
6. Mode of attachment of a share and execution.
7. Real estate of the corporation liable for its debts.
8. Proprietors authorized to divide their estate.
9. Powers may be delegated to President and Directors or a Committee.

ACTS.[1]

Incorporating clause. 1804, March 9.

SECTION 1. *Be it enacted by the Senate and House of Representatives, in General Court assembled, and by the authority of the same*, that John Peck, Benjamin Hichborn, and Mary Gilman, owners and proprietors of the water-mills, millpond, and land under the same, and estate adjoining to and belonging to the same, situate in Boston, in the County of Suffolk, commonly known by the name of the Millpond, together with their associates, and such as may hereafter associate with them and their successors and assigns, shall be a body politic, by the name of The Boston Mill Corporation; and by that name may sue and be sued, plead and be impleaded, defend and be defended, in any Courts of Record, or in any other place whatsoever; and shall and may do and suffer all matters, acts, and things which

[1] Act to Incorporate John Peck and others, by the name of the Boston Mill Corporation, passed March 9, 1804. Additional act (see § 8 and following) passed June 19, 1809. For "Historical References" to the Back Bay, etc., see Appendix to this volume.

bodies politic ought to do and suffer; and shall have power to make, have and use a common seal, and the same again at pleasure to break, alter, and renew; and also to ordain, establish, and put in execution such by-laws, ordinances, and regulations as to them shall appear necessary and convenient for the government of said corporation, and for the prudent management of their property and affairs; and for the breach of such by-laws, ordinances, and regulations may order fines and penalties, not exceeding thirteen dollars for every breach: *Provided*, That such by-laws, ordinances, and regulations shall not be repugnant to the laws of this Commonwealth.

Property vested in corporation, and to be divided into 1,600 shares. Ibid. § 2.

SECT. 2. *Be it further enacted*, That the stock, property, and estate now belonging to the said proprietors and their associates, shall be, and hereby are vested in the said corporation, and fully confirmed to them to every intent and purpose whatever; and shall be divided into sixteen hundred shares, which shall be divided among and held by the present proprietors, according to the proportion of interest which they now severally hold therein; and certificates of such shares, signed by the president, shall be issued to them accordingly, which shares shall be transferable by indorsement on the back of said certificates, and the property shall be vested in the vendee, when a record shall be made thereof by the clerk of said corporation, and new certificates shall be issued accordingly; and such shares shall in all respects be considered as personal estate.

J. Peck authorized to call a proprietors' meeting. Ibid. § 3.

SECT. 3. *Be it further enacted*, That John Peck aforesaid may call a meeting of the above-named proprietors, to be holden on the first Tuesday of April next, at some suitable place in Boston, by advertisement in the *Columbian Centinel*, or any other newspaper printed in Boston, ten days before said day; and at that and all other meetings, said proprietors may vote by themselves or proxy, always allowing to every proprietor one vote to each share: *Provided*, That no proprietor shall have more than forty votes: And said proprietors, by a majority of votes, shall choose a clerk and two or more directors, not exceeding five, from among the stockholders, by ballot, to continue in office one year, and until others are chosen, and no longer; and said directors shall meet as soon as may be after their election, and shall choose from their own number a president; and in case of vacancy by the death or resignation of such clerk, president, or director, such vacancy shall be filled by the directors already chosen and qualified.

Corporation allowed to hold other real estate than the Millpond. Ibid. § 4.

SECT. 4. *Be it further enacted*, That said corporation is hereby authorized to purchase and hold real estate, not exceeding in value thirty thousand dollars, more than they now hold; and their real estate may sell, exchange, and dispose of at pleasure; and the said president and directors shall convey the same, or the right, title, and interest of said corporation of, in, and to the same, whenever they shall be so directed by a major vote of the proprietors present or represented at any legal meeting notified for this purpose. And the said corporation generally shall have the power of managing and improving their mills and estate with the same facilities and in the same manner as other bodies corporate.

Assessments may be levied, and shares of delinquents sold. Ibid. § 5.

SECT. 5. *Be it further enacted*, That the president and directors may make such assessments on the shares of each and every member of this corporation as they may think proper and necessary for executing the purposes aforesaid; and in case such assessments are not paid in conformity to the rules and regulations for this purpose to be made and established by said corporation, may and shall have full power and authority to sell the share or shares of any of the proprietors who shall be delinquent in the payment of said assessments; and shall also, at such times as may be agreed on by said corporation, make such dividends of their rents, profits, and receipts as may arise thereon.

Mode of attachment of a share, and execution. Ibid. § 6.

SECT. 6. *Be it further enacted*, That the property of any individual member of this corporation, vested in the stock of the corporation, with the dividend or dividends due thereon, shall be liable to attachment and execution in manner following, viz: Whenever a proper officer, having a writ of attachment or execution in favor of any *bona fide* creditor, against any member, shall apply to the clerk, it shall be his duty to give him a certificate of the number of shares said member holds, and the amount of dividends due thereon; and whenever such share or shares shall be attached on *mesne process*, or taken in execution, in addition to a copy of such writ; or a summons to be left with the debtor, an attested copy thereof shall be left with the clerk of said corporation; and such share or shares may be sold on execution, after the same notification, and in the same manner as other personal property; and the officer making such sale, within five days thereafter, shall leave an attested copy of such execution, with his return thereon, with the clerk of said corporation, and the vendee shall become the absolute proprietor of such share or shares, with all the dividend or dividends due thereon.

Real estate of the corporation liable for its debts. Ibid. § 7.

SECT. 7. *Be it further enacted*, That the real estate of said corporation shall be liable for the debts of the corporation, and shall be liable to attachment and execution on any judgment against the corporation, in the same manner as other real estate; and the corporation shall have the right and equity of redeeming the same; and that nothing in this act contained shall be construed to affect the title of the said proprietors and their associates to said estate, or the claims of the town of Boston, or any corporation, to the same, or the claim or claims of any person or persons whatever.

Proprietors' authorized to divide their estate. 1809, June 17, § 1.

SECT. 8. *Be it further enacted*, That the Boston Mill Corporation shall be and hereby are authorized at any meeting to be called for that purpose, from time to time, to agree upon any mode for effecting a fair, equal, and convenient division or partition of their estate, or any part thereof, by lot, sale at auction among the proprietors, or otherwise, and upon such terms and principles as they may judge and determine to be expedient; and in case it shall so happen that the said estate, or such part thereof as may be ready for division, cannot conveniently be divided (in the opinion of said corporation) so as to accommodate each proprietor with a quantity of land, equal and in proportion to his interest, the said corporation shall have power to make all such rules and regulations, respecting credit to be given to those proprietors who become purchasers to a greater amount than their shares, and respecting the payment and indemnification of those who do not purchase to the amount of their shares, as they may judge expedient and for the interest of the corporation.

Powers may be delegated to president and directors or a committee. Ibid. § 2.

SECT. 9. All powers hereby given to said corporation, may be delegated to and exercised by their president and directors, or by any committee for that purpose specially to be appointed.

BOSTON AND ROXBURY MILL CORPORATION.

ACTS.

1. Persons incorporated; may hold real and personal estate.
2. May build a dam; boats may pass free of toll. Penalties and forfeitures. May lease and sell the right of using the waters.
3. May make a road. Toll free to the proprietors of marshes in Brookline.
4. Rights and privileges.
5. Board of Health authorized to cover flats with water.
6. May appoint a committee to estimate damage. Costs, &c.
7. Capital stock and number of shares.
8. Persons who may call a meeting.
9. May make assessments.
10, 11. When the corporation may receive tolls.
12. Dam may be widened.
13. Dam from Boston to South Boston.
14. Wharf may be extended to harbor lines.
15. Tolls on Western Avenue.
16. Acceptance of act required.

ACTS.[1]

Persons incorporated. 1814, 39, § 1.

SECTION 1. *Be it enacted by the Senate and House of Representatives, in General Court assembled, and by the authority of the same*, That Isaac P. Davis, Uriah Cotting, and William Brown, their associates, successors, and assigns, be, and they are hereby made a body politic and corporate, by the name of The Boston and Roxbury Mill Corporation; and by that name may sue and be sued, prosecute and be prosecuted to final judgment

---

[1] Act to establish the Boston and Roxbury Mill Corporation, 1814, Chap. 39. Additional acts (see § 10 and following), 1816, chap. 40; 1819, chap. 65; 1822, chap. 34; 1833, chap. 120; 1844, chap. 58; 1850, chap. 182. See also acts of 1861, chap. 201.

For agreements with the City of Boston, the Boston Water Power Company, and the Commonwealth, as to filling flats, etc., see "Agreements," Post. See also, in the Appendix, "Historical References" to the history of the Back Bay.

and execution. And said corporation shall have power to make and use a common seal, and the same to break and alter at pleasure, and may from time to time make by-laws for the regulation of the affairs of the corporation; *Provided*, That the same be not repugnant to the laws of the Commonwealth; may purchase and hold real and personal estates (not exceeding in value two millions of dollars), necessary to promote the objects of the corporation; and in general, may do and suffer all other acts and things, which bodies corporate may or ought to do and suffer.

Proviso.

May hold real and personal estate.

SECT. 2. *Be it further enacted*, That said corporation shall have power to build a dam from Charles Street, at the westerly end of Beacon Street in Boston, to the upland at Sewall's Point, so called, in Brookline, and as near as may be to the north side of tide-mill creek, which dam shall not be less than forty-two feet wide on the top, and made so as effectually to exclude the tide water, and to form a reservoir or empty basin of the space between said dam and Boston Neck; and said corporation shall have power to build a dam from Boston to South Boston, not northerly or easterly of South Boston bridge, with gates, sluiceways, and other things necessary to admit and detain the tide water between said dam and Boston Neck, at the height of common tides; and shall make in said dam, a good and sufficient lock, for the passage of rafts containing not less than ten thousand feet of timber or boards, of vessels and boats, burthen from ten to one hundred and fifty tons, and boats and barges of any dimensions, loaded with powder, to and from said basin, free of toll: *Provided*, That no vessel of less than fifty tons burthen, shall have a right to pass said lock, at any other time than at or near high water; all vessels, however, lying in said basin, paying to said corporation the customary dockage of the town of Boston, excepting where they shall lay at the wharves of any person, who in such case may charge and receive the same to their own account. And the said corporation may run a dam from Gravelly Point, in said Roxbury, to the dam first above-described, so as to inclose the tide water within tide-mill creek, and may connect the same with the full

May build a dam. Ibid. § 2.

Proviso.

basin on the east, by a canal, of at least one hundred feet wide, to be cut in some convenient place from said creek to the canal by Davis's works in said Roxbury, and may raise the banks of said canal and dike, the borders of the marshes on the easterly bank of said creek, so as to prevent the tide from flowing at any time into the empty basin, and boats and other things may pass and repass in said canal at all times free of toll. And if said corporation shall fail for the space of three years, from the passing of this act, to secure the tide waters as aforesaid, within said tide-mill creek, and to connect said creek to the said full basin on the east as is above described, then the legislature may compel the execution thereof upon such terms, and under such penalties and forfeitures, as it may think proper to impose. And the said corporation may cut any number of convenient race ways, from the full basin to the empty basin aforesaid, may maintain and keep up all their said works forever, and may lease or sell the right of using the water, and upon any terms, and in any manner they may think proper; and no person shall have a right to dispose of said water, without the consent of said corporation.

Boats may pass free of toll.

Penalties and forfeitures.

May lease and sell the right of using the waters.

SECT. 3. *Be it further enacted*, That the said corporation shall have power to make and finish the dam, in this act first mentioned, and connect the different parts thereof by bridges and causeways, so as to render the same a good and substantial road, suitable for the passing of men, loaded teams, carts, and carriages of all kinds, and shall open a road not more than eighty feet and not less than forty-two feet wide, from some point of said dam, where it crosses the marshes in Brookline, to the end of the Worcester Turnpike, near the Punch-bowl tavern, so called, in said Brookline, which road shall be made in a straight line, as nearly as can be done with convenience; and when the road on said dam shall be finished, railed at the sides, and furnished with lamps to the satisfaction of the selectmen of Boston, the said corporation may receive toll for passing over the same, at the same rate as is now granted to the Proprietors of the West Boston Bridge: *Provided*, That no toll shall be received as aforesaid, until said dam, and the dam

May make a road. Ibid. § 3.

Proviso. (See §§ 10 & 11.)

from Boston to South Boston, with the lock therein shall be completed, in a substantial manner, so as effectually to answer the purposes intended and set forth in the second section of this act. And if said corporation or some person under them, shall not, within five years from the passing of this act, establish mills, employing a power equal to turning twenty pair of common millstones, the legislature may suspend, as long as it shall think proper, the right of said corporation to take any toll as aforesaid. And the proprietors of the marshes in Brookline shall have the privilege of passing free of toll to and from their marshes, from and to the upland in Brookline, over said road or dam, and the said corporation shall make and maintain, at its own expense, a suitable number of sloping bridges, leading from the sides of said road and dam to the surface of the marsh land, and convenient to carry off the hay.

Toll free to the proprietors of marshes in Brookline.

SECT. 4. *Be it further enacted*, That the said corporation shall be entitled to all the advantages and benefits of the engagements of the town of Boston with the petitioners of this present act, as the same are expressed in the doings of said town at its meetings of the eleventh of June and twentieth of October last past; but shall have and enjoy the same, however, upon the same terms and conditions, and subject to all the restrictions, expressed in the report of said town committee, and accepted and recorded by the said town, at its meeting last above mentioned.

Rights and privileges. Ibid. § 4.

SECT. 5. *Be it further enacted*, That the Board of Health of the town of Boston, be, and hereby is authorized and empowered to cause the flats, on the westerly side of Boston, within said empty basin, or any portion of them, to be kept constantly covered with water, if, in the opinion of said Board, it shall be necessary to the health of the inhabitants of said town; and for that purpose to cause a dam of a suitable height, at their discretion, to be placed and kept at the sluice gate or gates in the principal dam of said empty basin, in order to retain the water therein, at the sole expense of said corporation.

Board of Health authorized to cover flats with water. Ibid. § 5.

SECT. 6. *Be it further enacted*, That any person or corporation, sustaining any damage by the building of said dams,

May appoint a committee to estimate damage. Ibid. § 6.

bridges, or causeways, or from cutting said canal or race ways, or from the exercise of any of the rights and powers, herein given to said corporation, may apply (if within one year from the time any such damage may have happened) to the Court of Common Pleas for the county in which the land lies, for a committee to be appointed to estimate the damage, and upon such application, the Court after thirty days' notice to said corporation to appear, and show cause why such committee should not be appointed, shall, if no good cause be shown to the contrary, appoint three or five disinterested freeholders within the same county, at the expense of said corporation, which committee being first duly sworn before some justice of the peace, to be nominated by said Court, and giving due notice to both parties to appear, if they see fit, for a hearing before them, shall proceed to the duties of their appointment; and they shall first inquire, whether any damage has been sustained from the causes aforesaid, and if any, they shall estimate the same, and where the damage is annual, they shall so declare the same in their report, and shall make return of their doings as soon as may be, into the said Court, and upon the acceptance of said report, judgment may be given thereon, with reasonable costs to the party prevailing: *Provided, however,* That either party, after the return of said report, may claim a trial by jury, and the Court shall thereupon stay judgment on said report; and upon such application for a jury, the Court shall issue a warrant to the sheriff of the same county, or if the sheriff shall be interested, then to some coroner, by name, who is not interested, directing him to summon a jury of twelve good and lawful men, which jury shall be sworn, and in all things shall proceed as is above directed, as to said committee, due notice to the parties being first given by the officer, of the time and place of their meeting; and their verdict shall be sealed up, and the officer shall return the same into Court, and judgment may be entered thereon. And if the party applying for a jury shall not obtain, in case it be the original applicant, an increase of damages, or in case it be the original respondent, a decrease of the damages awarded by the committee,

Proviso.

such party shall pay reasonable costs of such trial by jury, otherwise shall recover reasonable costs; and upon any judgment rendered upon the report of such committee on the verdict of such jury, the Court may issue its execution accordingly, and also from year to year where the damages awarded are annual, on motion of the party entitled thereto, and an action of debt may be maintained on such judgment; and if upon notice to said corporation as aforesaid, to show cause why such committee should not be appointed, said corporation shall appear and deny the applicant's title to the land damaged, or claim a title to do what is complained of, without the payment of damages, or for an agreed composition, the Court shall first order a trial of the issue at the bar of said Court, or if there be an issue in law, shall try it themselves; and in either case either party may appeal to the Supreme Judicial Court, as in other cases; and a certificate of the determination of the Supreme Judicial Court on such appeal, in favor of the original applicant, shall be filed in said Court of Common Pleas, before such committee shall be appointed; and where annual damages are awarded by said committee, or said jury, and judgment had accordingly, each party shall be entitled, after two years, to apply to said Court of Common Pleas, for an increase or decrease of said damages; and thereupon the same proceedings shall be had, as upon the original application. Costs, &c.

SECT. 7. *Be it further enacted*, That the stock and property of said corporation shall be divided into three thousand five hundred shares, certificates of which shall issue under the seal of the said corporation, and be signed by the President and Treasurer thereof, and said shares shall be deemed and taken to be personal estate, and may be transferred by deed acknowledged before some justice of the peace, and recorded by the clerk of said corporation in a book to be kept for that purpose; and the original subscription for at least fifteen hundred shares, shall be public, and continue open at least ten days, or until the whole shall be subscribed for, the time and place for which shall be regulated as hereafter provided. Capital stock and number of shares. Ibid. § 7.

Persons who may call a meeting. Ibid. § 8.

SECT. 8. *Be it further enacted*, That Isaac P. Davis, Uriah Cotting, and William Brown, or the major part of them, may call the first meeting of said corporation, by giving seasonable notice of the time and place for the same, in the *Columbian Centinel* and *Independent Chronicle*, printed in Boston; and at the said meeting there shall be appointed, by a majority of votes, a clerk, who shall be duly sworn to record the doings thereof; and also a committee of five persons, who shall direct the time and place for opening the public subscriptions for at least fifteen hundred shares as above mentioned, and shall appoint some person or persons to superintend the same; and shall also direct the manner in which the other shares may be subscribed for: *Provided*, That no person in any case, shall subscribe for more than fifty shares; and when two thousand shares shall be subscribed for, the said committee shall notify the subscribers to meet at some convenient time and place for the purpose of more fully organizing and arranging the affairs of said corporation, at which meeting every person shall be entitled to a number of votes equal to his number of shares; and the powers and duties of the President and other officers and servants of the corporation, together with the time and manner of choosing, and the number of the same, may be regulated by the by-laws of the corporation.

Proviso.

May make assessments. Ibid. § 9.

SECT. 9. *Be it further enacted*, That the said corporation or its officers, duly authorized, by its by-laws may make assessments upon the shares subscribed for, for the purpose of effecting the objects of the corporation, and for any other necessary purpose: *Provided, however*, That the whole amount of the assessments on each share shall not exceed the sum of one hundred dollars, after deducting the amount of any dividends previously declared thereon; and in case the amount of one hundred dollars, so assessed upon each share, will not supply the necessary funds, the corporation or its officers duly authorized, may raise the funds required by selling any shares not subscribed for, or by creating and selling any number of shares over and above the said three thousand five hundred. And if the proprietor of any share shall neglect or refuse to pay any

Proviso.

assessment for the term of thirty days from the time appointed therefor, the share or shares of such proprietor may be sold at public auction, notice of the time and place of such sale being given by the treasurer of said corporation, in some public newspaper, printed in Boston, three weeks at least previous to the time appointed therefor; and the proceeds of the sale shall be applied to the payment of the assessments due on the share or shares so sold, with incidental charges; and the surplus, if any, shall be paid by said treasurer to the former owner, or his legal representatives on demand; and such sale shall give a good and complete title to the purchaser of such share or shares, and he shall receive a new certificate therefor: *Provided, however*, That if before the actual sale of any such share or shares, the proprietor thereof will pay the assessments due thereon, with interest from the time they became due, and all necessary and reasonable charges, the sale shall not proceed. **Proviso.**

SECT. 10. *Be it further enacted*, That, whenever the dam from Beacon Street to Sewall's Point shall be completed according to the provisions of the act, entitled "An act to establish the Boston and Roxbury Mill Corporation," and whenever either of the other dams mentioned in said act shall be so far completed, as that mills can be established, employing a power equal to turning twenty pair of common millstones, and said corporation or its assigns shall have actually erected mills employing a power equal to ten pair of common millstones, the said corporation may receive the toll granted by said act: *Provided*, That nothing herein contained shall be construed to exempt them from any of the obligations, penalties, or forfeitures expressed in said act, except only in so far as relates to the said toll. **When the corporation may receive tolls.** 1816, 40, § 1. **Proviso.**

SECT. 11. *Be it further enacted*, That whenever the dam, now building by the Boston and Roxbury Mill Corporation, from Boston to Brookline, shall be made convenient for travelling thereon, the said corporation may receive the toll granted by the act, entitled "An act to establish the Boston and Roxbury Mill Corporation;" *Provided, however*, That the legislature may suspend the right of taking toll, at any time, before, **The same.** 1819, 65, § 1. **Proviso.**

and until the said corporation shall have so far completed one of the other dams, mentioned in the original act of incorporation, as that mills can be established, employing a power equal to turning twenty pair of common millstones; and said corporation, or its assigns, shall have actually erected mills, employing a power equal to turning ten pair of common millstones.

Dam may be widened. 1822, 34, § 1.

SECT. 12. *Be it further enacted*, That the Boston and Roxbury Mill Corporation be, and they hereby are authorized to widen their dam, leading from Boston to Sewall's Point, so called, in Brookline, by extending it one hundred feet on the northerly side thereof, upon the flats and tide-waters, where it can be done without interfering with the rights of individuals, or other corporations, for the purpose of forming landing-places, making wharves, erecting storehouses, and other necessary buildings: *provided*, that nothing herein contained shall authorize the widening of said dam, in any part thereof, more than one hundred yards to the northward and eastward of the present easternmost sluiceway.

Proviso.

Dam from Boston to South Boston. 833, 120, § 1.

SECT. 13. *Be it further enacted*, That unless the Boston and Roxbury Mill Corporation shall, on or before the first day of February, one thousand eight hundred and thirty-four, determine by legal vote, duly certified and filed in the office of the Secretary of State, to build, and actually commence building, a dam from Boston to South Boston, not northerly or easterly of Boston South Bridge, with gates, sluice ways, and other things necessary to admit and detain the tide waters between said dam and Boston Neck, at the height of common tides, with a good and sufficient lock, and in all respects as in the act establishing said corporation is provided; and also, unless said corporation shall fully complete the same within two years from the said first day of February one thousand eight hundred and thirty-four, in either case the right conferred on said corporation to build said dam shall cease and determine, and thereafter become forfeited and void: *Provided, however*, that any of the owners (other than the city of Boston) of land and flats above or southerly of said bridge may, at pleasure, fill up and improve any of their lands or flats without hindrance or molestation, un-

Proviso.

til said corporation shall actually commence building said dam: *and provided, also,* that nothing herein contained shall be deemed or taken to extend or confirm any rights or supposed rights of said corporation, nor in any way to impair the rights of those who have sustained or may sustain any damages in consequence of the exercise of any of the powers granted to said corporation.

Wharf may be extended to harbor lines. 1844, 58, § 1.

SECT. 14. *Be it further enacted,* That the Boston and Roxbury Mill Corporation, proprietors of a wharf in the westerly part of the city of Boston, lying at the westerly end of Beacon Street, and on the northerly side of said street and the Western Avenue, so called, and extending to, and bounding northerly on, the land now or formerly belonging to Jarvis Braman, are hereby authorized to extend and maintain their said wharf, into the harbor channel as far as the line established by an act entitled "an act concerning the harbor of Boston," passed on the seventeenth day of March, in the year one thousand eight hundred and forty, and by an act entitled "an act in addition to an act concerning the harbor of Boston," passed on the sixth day of March, in the year one thousand eight hundred and forty-one; and shall have the right and privilege of laying vessels at the end of said wharf, when extended, and of receiving dockage and wharfage therefor: *Provided,* that so much of said wharf as shall be erected under this act, north of a line drawn parallel to the north wall of said avenue, and two hundred feet distant therefrom, shall be built on piles; and that no building shall be placed on said wharf south of a line drawn parallel to the line of the north wall of said avenue, and twenty feet distant therefrom, and that this grant shall in no wise interfere with the legal rights of any person or persons whatever: *and provided, also,* that the authorities of the city of Boston shall have the right to extend Byron Street, so called, to the channel over the land so made, and to lay, continue, and maintain all necessary drains under the same.

Proviso.

Tolls on Western Avenue. 1850, 182, § 1.

SECT. 15. The Boston and Roxbury Mill Corporation shall have the right to demand and receive upon the Western Avenue, instead of the tolls heretofore established, the tolls now by law established upon the bridges of the Hancock Free Bridge Corporation : *provided*, that this act shall not extend the time allowed by their present obligations to the Commonwealth or any other party.

Acceptance of act required. Ibid. § 2.

SECT. 16. This act shall not take effect until it shall have been accepted by said corporation, at a meeting called for that purpose.

BOSTON WATER POWER COMPANY.

ACTS.

1. Persons incorporated. May hold water-power, and lands; and make flumes, &c., and dispose of them.
2. May hold real and personal estate. Call of first meeting.
3. Increase of capital authorized, to enable improvements to be made; rights of flowage to be relinquished; no nuisance to be created.
4. Legal rights of cities and other parties not to be affected.

ACTS.[1]

Persons incorporated. 1824, 26, § 1.

SECTION 1. *Be it enacted by the Senate and House of Representatives, in General Court assembled, and by the authority of the same*, That Thomas Bartlett, Horace Gray, and Nathan Parker, with their associates, successors and assigns, be and they hereby are incorporated, under the name of the Boston Water Power Company, and by that name may sue and be sued, have a common seal, and make by-laws and regulations not inconsistent with the constitution and laws of this Commonwealth, and may purchase and hold any quantity of the water power created by the establishment of the dams between Boston and Roxbury, or any lands contiguous to said dams, or within the

May hold water power and lands; and make flumes, &c., and dispose of them.

---

[1] Act to establish the Boston Water Power Company, 1824, chap. 26. Additional Resolve (see §§ 3 and 4), 1856, chap. 76. For agreements with the State, City, and Boston and Roxbury Mill Corporation, as to filling of flats, etc., see "Agreements," Post. See also, in Appendix to this Volume, the "Historical References" to the course of action in regard to the filling, and correlative matters.

limits of the basins connected therewith, or either of them, and may make flumes, canals, and race-ways, and may construct mill-wheels, factories, and other buildings and fixtures, at any convenient places within the limits aforesaid, and may dispose of the same, by lease or otherwise: *provided, however*, that the said company shall not make any such flume, canal or race-way, or construct any such mill-wheel, factory, or other building or fixture, through or upon the land belonging to any city, town, company or individual, without the consent of such owner in writing, to be recorded in the registry of deeds, in the county where the land may be: *and provided, also*, that nothing in this act shall be construed to extend the rights of the water power so to be purchased and held under the provisions of this act, beyond the rights of water power now possessed by the Boston and Roxbury Mill Corporation, by virtue of the acts establishing the same, or to alter or prejudice the rights of the city of Boston, or of any of the adjacent towns, as they now exist.

Provisos.

SECT. 2. *Be it further enacted*, That the said company may hold real estate and water power, not exceeding the value of three hundred thousand dollars, at the time of the purchase thereof, and personal estate not exceeding the value of one hundred thousand dollars. And the first meeting of said company may be called by any one of the persons herein named, by public notice, printed in any newspaper in the city of Boston, ten days at least before the time appointed for such meeting.

May hold real and personal estate.

Call of first meeting.
Ibid. § 2.

SECT. 3. *Resolved*, That to enable the Boston Water Company to fill up and make the avenues and other improvements, which they have contracted with the Commonwealth to make by their indenture, dated June ninth, eighteen hundred and fifty-four, they may increase their capital stock by the sum of two hundred and seventy-five thousand dollars: *Provided, however*, That the said company, by an acceptance of this Resolve,[1] shall be held to relinquish to any person or corporation who may become parties to the said indenture, or to any modification

Increase of capital authorized, to enable improvements to be made.
Resolve, 1856, 76, § 1.

---

[1] The resolve was duly accepted.

Rights of flowage to be relinquished.

thereof, made by virtue of the preceding resolve,[1] the right of flowage of said company in either basin of said Back Bay, so far as to allow every one of said persons or corporations to fill up their lands or flats, in conformity with such plan as the Committee, before mentioned, may devise, subject to the approval of the Governor and Council; and *provided*, further, that nothing herein mentioned shall authorize said company to create any nuisance on their said lands, and that said company shall be subject, as now, to the control of the Board of Health of the City of Boston, and also of the City of Roxbury, within their respective jurisdictions, according to the laws of the Commonwealth respecting nuisances.

No nuisance to be created.

Legal rights of cities and parties not to be affected. Ibid. § 2.

SECT. 4. *Resolved*, That the foregoing resolves shall not affect the legal rights of the City of Boston, the City of Roxbury, the town of Brookline, or of any other corporation or person, and they shall take effect from and after their passage.

---

[1] Preceding resolve provides for a committee of the legislature to modify contracts made by the commissioners on the Back Bay, &c.

BOSTON GAS LIGHT COMPANY.

1 Persons incorporated; powers and privileges; capital $ 75,000.
2. Directors, shares, and by-laws.
3. Right to sink pipes; Mayor and Aldermen may restrict.
4. Assessments.
5. First meeting.
6. $ 175,000 additional capital.
7. Powers and duties.
8. $ 250,000 additional capital.
9. May extend their pipes into other towns.
10. $ 500,000 additional capital.
11. $ 1,000,000 additional capital.

ACTS.[1]

SECTION 1. *Be it enacted, &c.*, That William Prescott, Alexander Parris, Bryant P. Tilden, Nathan Hale, John C. Gray, and all such persons as are, or shall be associated with them, and their successors, be, and they are hereby incorporated for the purpose of furnishing gas light in the city of Boston, by the name of the Boston Gas Light Company; and by that name may sue and prosecute, and be sued or prosecuted, to final judgment and execution, and do and suffer all other matters and things which bodies politic may, and ought to do or suffer; and may have and use a common seal, and the same break and alter, at their pleasure; and by their said corporate name, may purchase, take and hold real and personal estate, not exceeding in the whole value, seventy-five thousand dollars. Persons incorporated. 1822, 41, § 1. Powers and privileges. Capital $ 75,000.

SECT. 2. *Be it further enacted*, That the said corporation may elect so many directors and other officers, and divide their capital stock into such number of shares, and establish and put in execution such by-laws and regulations, as the members thereof may judge necessary; *provided*, the same are not repugnant to the laws and constitution of this Commonwealth. Directors, shares, and by-laws. Ibid. § 2.

[1] Act to incorporate the Boston Gas Light Company, 1822, chap. 41. Additional acts (see § 6 and following), 1836, chap. 17; 1837, chap. 74; 1852, 109; 1862, 99.

Right to sink pipes. Ibid. § 3.

SECT. 3. *Be it further enacted*, That the said corporation, with the consent of the mayor and aldermen of said city of Boston, shall have power and authority to open the ground in any part of the streets, lanes and highways, in said city, for the purpose of sinking and repairing such pipes and conductors as [*it*] may be necessary to sink for the purpose aforesaid. And that the said corporation, after opening the ground in the said streets, lanes or highways, shall be held to put the same again into repair, under the penalty of being prosecuted for a nuisance: *provided*, that the said mayor and aldermen, for the time being, shall at all times have the power to regulate, restrict and control the acts and doings of said corporation, which may, in any manner, affect the health, safety or convenience of the inhabitants of said city.

Mayor and Aldermen may restrict.

Assessments. Ibid. § 4.

SECT. 4. *Be it further enacted*, That said corporation shall have full power, from time to time, to make and assess such assessments and taxes, as they shall deem necessary, on the shares in said corporation; and on neglect or refusal to pay the same, to sell such shares at vendue, for the payment thereof, after advertising the same in two of the newspapers published in Boston, for the space of twenty days previous to the sale, paying the overplus, if any there be after the payment of such assessments and taxes, and of the charges of sale, to the owner of the share or shares so sold.

First meeting. Ibid. § 5.

SECT. 5. *Be it further enacted*, That the said William Prescott, or Alexander Parris, be, and they are hereby empowered to call the first meeting of the said corporation, by a notification in one of the newspapers of Boston, aforesaid, fourteen days previous to such meeting; and the said corporation, at such meeting, shall agree upon the mode of calling future meetings.

$175,000 additional capital. 1836, 17, § 1.

SECT. 6. *Be it further enacted*, That the Boston Gas Light Company are hereby authorized to increase their capital stock, by an amount not exceeding one hundred and seventy-five thousand dollars; and to purchase and hold real estate in the county of Suffolk, as part and parcel of their capital, not exceeding one half of their whole capital as provided in this act, and in the act to which this is in addition.

SECT. 7. The Boston Gas Light Company shall be subject to all the duties, restrictions, and liabilities, and shall have all the powers and privileges, set forth in the thirty-eighth and forty-fourth chapters of the Revised Statutes, passed on the fourth day of November, in the year one thousand eight hundred and thirty-five.

Powers and duties. Ibid. § 2.

SECT. 8. *Be it further enacted*: That the Boston Gas Light Company are hereby authorized to increase their capital stock, by an amount not exceeding two hundred and fifty thousand dollars, and to purchase and hold real estate in the county of Suffolk, as part and parcel of their capital not exceeding one half of their whole capital stock.

$250,000 additional capital. 1837, 74, § 1.

SECT. 9. The Boston Gas Light Company, with the consent of the selectmen of any town adjoining the city of Boston, may extend their pipes and conductors into such town; and for that purpose shall have power and authority to open the ground in any part of the streets, lanes, or highways of such town; and the said corporation, after opening the ground in any street, lane, or highway, for the purpose aforesaid, shall be held to put the same again into repair, under penalty of being prosecuted for a nuisance.

May extend their pipes into other towns. Ibid. § 2.

SECT. 10. The Boston Gas Light Company is hereby authorized to increase its capital stock by adding thereto a sum not exceeding five hundred thousand dollars, and to invest the same in real and personal estate as may be necessary and convenient for the purposes for which they were incorporated; *provided*, that no shares in said capital stock shall be issued for a less sum or amount, to be actually paid in on each, than the par value of the shares first issued.

$500,000 additional capital. 1852, 109.

SECT. 11. The Boston Gas Light Company is hereby authorized to increase its capital stock by adding thereto a sum not exceeding one million dollars, to be paid in at such times and in such amounts as the stockholders may from time to time authorize, and to invest the same in such real and personal estate as may be necessary and convenient for the purposes for which they were incorporated.

$1,000,000 additional capital. 1862, 99.

BOSTON WHARF COMPANY.

ACTS.

1. Persons incorporated; powers and duties.
2. May hold real and personal estate.
3. Capital stock $600,000; assessments, etc.
4. Right of voting.
5. Existing rights preserved.
6. May purchase and hold additional flats.
7. Capital reduced to $360,000; limitation of assessments.
8. Existing liabilities not affected.
9. Wharf in South Boston may be extended.
10, 11. Further extension authorized.
12, 13. Further extension authorized.
14. Capital stock increased $240,000.
15. May extend wharf; may receive dockage, etc.
16. Extensions to conform to plan.
17. Right of city to lay out streets.
18. Privileges limited.
19. Company to pay proportion of expense.
20. May extend wharf.
21. To pay proportion of expense of excavations.
22. Not to hold flats in front of other persons.
23. Reduction of value of shares.

ACTS.[1]

Persons incorporated. 1836, 259, § 1. Powers and duties.

SECTION 1. Cyrus Alger, Hall J. How, Josiah Dunham, their associates and successors, are hereby made a corporation by the name of "The Boston Wharf Company," with all the powers and privileges, and subject to all the duties, restrictions, and liabilities, set forth in the forty-fourth chapter of the Revised Statutes, passed on the fourth day of November, in the year one thousand eight hundred and thirty-five.

May hold real and personal estate. Ibid. § 2.

SECT. 2. The said corporation may take and hold all or any part of the land and flats, with their privileges and appurtenances, lying in South Boston, and whereof the said corporation shall legally acquire the property from the lawful owners of the same, that is to say, a parcel of land bounded and described as follows, to wit: beginning at a point about four hundred and

[1] Act to incorporate the Boston Wharf Company, 1836, chap. 209. Additional acts (see § 6 and following), 1837, chap. 70; 1838, chap. 118; 1845, chap. 239; 1850, chap. 246; 1852, chaps. 171, 278; 1854, chap. 218; 1855, chap. 455; 1863, chap. 209.

eventeen feet easterly of Turnpike Street, and bounding southerly on First Street, about eight hundred and twenty-two feet; asterly on land now or lately of the Glass Company, as far as rivate rights to said flats extend; and westerly on land now or ately of Winslow and others, as far as private rights to said ats extend; and the said corporation may receive dockage and wharfage for vessels laid at their wharves; and may, conformably to the provisions of such by-laws as shall from time to ime be established by them, make any conveyances of their orporate property, and lease, manage, and improve their said roperty as they shall deem expedient. And the said corporaion may also hold any personal property to an amount not xceeding one hundred thousand dollars.

SECT. 3. The said corporate property shall be divided into welve hundred shares of five hundred dollars each, and assessments may be made from time to time thereon, not exceeding he said sum of five hundred dollars on each share, and in case ny proprietor shall not pay such assessments as may be laid on is share or shares, the said corporation may cause the same to be sold by public auction, after fourteen days' notice in one or more daily newspapers published in the city of Boston, and he surplus, if any shall remain after paying the assessments, ogether with interest and incidental charges, shall, upon equest, be paid over to such proprietor, and the purchaser shall be entitled to a certificate of the share or shares so sold; *provided, always*, that all assessments on the shares shall be agreed to by at least two thirds in number of the votes of proprietors present, or represented in writing, at any meeting, of which meeting public notice in one or more daily newspapers published in said city of Boston shall be given seven days at east previously thereto.

Number of shares, assessments, etc. Ibid. § 3.

Proviso.

SECT. 4. Each share in the said corporation shall entitle the proprietor to one vote; *provided, however*, no proprietor shall be entitled to more votes than one fourth of the whole number of shares.

Right of voting. Ibid. § 4.

SECT. 5. Nothing herein contained shall be construed to authorize said corporation to obstruct or encroach upon the

Existing rights preserved. Ibid. § 5.

channel, or in any way to infringe or interfere with the rights of the Commonwealth in any flats in the harbor of Boston, or with the legal rights of any other person or persons.

Company may purchase and hold additional flats. 1837, 70.

SECT. 6. The Boston Wharf Company may, in addition to the flats described in the act to which this is in addition, purchase and hold other parcels of flats and land, not exceeding in value the sum of fifty thousand dollars, and not included within the limits described in the act aforesaid, for the purpose of obtaining therefrom, and for no other purpose whatever, the materials for filling and completing said wharf: *provided*, that nothing in this act shall in any way infringe or interfere with the rights of the Commonwealth in any flats in the harbor of Boston, or with the legal rights of any other person or corporation.

Proviso.

Capital reduced to $360,000. 1838, 118, § 1.

SECT. 7. The corporate property of the Boston Wharf Company shall be, and the same hereby is, reduced to the sum of three hundred and sixty thousand dollars; and the same shall be divided into three thousand six hundred shares of one hundred dollars each; and said shares may from time to time, be assessed to an amount, which, together with all assessments heretofore made on the corporate property of said company, shall not exceed the sum of one hundred dollars on each share; and the said assessments shall be collected in the manner provided for collecting assessments under the act to which this is in addition.

Limitation of assessments.

Existing liabilities not affected. Ibid. § 2.

SECT. 8. Nothing contained in this act shall be construed to affect, in any manner, the existing liabilities of the said company or the members thereof.

Wharf in South Boston may be extended. 1845, 239.

SECT. 9. The Boston Wharf Company are hereby authorized and empowered to extend and maintain their wharf in South Boston, in the direction in which it now runs, as follows, to wit: on the westerly side thereof, by the line established by an act concerning the harbor of Boston, passed on the seventeenth day of March, in the year one thousand eight hundred and thirty-seven, and running from the southerly angle of the above-mentioned commissioners' line, to a point in said line fourteen hundred feet northerly from the said angle; and thence easterly to the easterly line of their wharf continued; *provided*, that the said corporation shall not extend or maintain the extended part of their wharf over any creek or channel, and shall have the right to lay vessels at the sides and ends of said wharf, and receive wharfage and dockage therefor: *provided*, that the provisions of this act shall in no wise affect the legal rights of any persons or corporations whatever.

SECT. 10. The Boston Wharf Company are hereby authorized to extend and maintain their wharf in that part of Boston commonly called South Boston, in the direction in which it now runs, as follows, to wit: — on the westerly side thereof, by the line established by an act entitled "An Act concerning the harbor of Boston," passed on the seventeenth day of March, in the year one thousand eight hundred and forty, running from the southerly angle of the above-mentioned line to a point in said line, eleven hundred feet (instead of fourteen hundred feet, as is provided in the act to which this is in addition), northerly from said angle, and thence easterly to the easterly line of their wharf continued, the provision in said last-mentioned act, relating to a creek or channel, to the contrary notwithstanding; and said last-mentioned act, except as herein modified, is hereby confirmed. *Provided*, that this grant shall not be construed to extend to any land or flats of this Commonwealth lying in front of lands or flats other than those belonging to said company, or which would be comprehended by the true lines of such other lands or flats, extended northerly as far as the point to which said company are hereby authorized to construct their wharf: and *provided, also*, that this grant shall not impair the legal rights of any person.

Further extension authorized. 1850, 246, § 1.

Proviso.

Proviso.

SECT. 11. This act shall not take effect unless it shall be accepted by said company within sixty days from the day of its passage.

When to take effect. Ibid. § 2.

SECT. 12. The Boston Wharf Company is hereby authorized to extend and maintain its wharf in that part of Boston commonly called South Boston, as follows, to wit: on the westerly side thereof by the line established by an act entitled "An Act concerning the Harbor of Boston," passed on the

Further extension authorized. 1852, 171, § 1.

seventeenth day of March, one thousand eight hundred and forty, running from the southerly angle of the above-mentioned line to a point in said line fifteen hundred feet northerly from said angle; thence in a line in a southeasterly direction parallel to the line of the westerly part of the street called Broadway, to a point where it would intersect the most easterly line of their present wharf extended; meaning such easterly line as is referred to in an act entitled "An Act in addition to an act to authorize the Boston Wharf Company to extend their Wharf," passed in the year one thousand eight hundred and fifty, and it shall have the right to lay vessels at the end and sides of said wharf, and receive wharfage and dockage therefor: *provided*, that said company, before so extending its wharf, shall release to the Commonwealth all right and title which they may have acquired under former legislative acts to land or flats lying outside of said line, extending in a southeasterly direction from the point above named: *provided, also*, that this grant shall not be construed to extend to any land or flats of this Commonwealth lying in front of land or flats other than those belonging to said company, or which would be comprehended by the true lines of such other land or flats extended northerly as far as the point to which said company are hereby authorized to extend its wharf: and *provided, further*, that this grant shall not impair the legal rights of any person.

May receive wharfage, etc.

Proviso.

When to take effect. Ibid. § 2.

SECT. 13. This act shall not take effect unless it shall be accepted by said company within sixty days from the date of its passage.

$240,000 additional capital stock. 1852, 278.

SECT. 14. The Boston Wharf Company is hereby authorized to increase its capital stock by an amount not exceeding two hundred and forty thousand dollars, and may invest such increase in real and personal estate, necessary and convenient for the purposes for which it was incorporated: *provided*, that no shares in said capital stock shall be issued for a less sum or amount, to be paid in on each, than the par value of the shares as fixed by an act passed in the year one thousand eight hundred and thirty-eight, entitled "An Act in addition to an act to incorporate the Boston Wharf Company."

No shares to be issued at less than par value.

SECT. 15. The Boston Wharf Company is hereby authorized to extend and maintain its wharf in that part of Boston called South Boston, to the commissioners' line, of solid filling, established by an act entitled "An Act concerning the Harbor of Boston," passed May twenty-five, eighteen hundred and fifty-three, and shall have the right to lay vessels at the end and sides of said wharf, and receive wharfage and dockage therefor: *Provided, however*, That this grant shall not be construed to extend to any flats or land lying in front of the flats of any other persons, or which would be comprehended by the true lines of such flats continued to the commissioners' line; and *provided, also*, that this grant shall not impair the legal rights of any person or corporation whatever; and *provided, also*, that the said wharf shall be bounded on Fore Point Channel by the commissioners' line, established by an act entitled "An Act concerning the Harbor of Boston," passed on the seventeenth day of March, in the year of our Lord one thousand eight hundred and forty.

May extend wharf. 1854, 218, § 1. May receive dockage, etc. Provisos.

SECT. 16. The Boston Wharf Company, in making the extensions and improvements authorized by this act, shall conform to any plan which may be adopted by commissioners appointed under the authority of the present legislature, for the improvement of the South Boston Flats on the east side of Fore Point Channel.

To conform to plan, etc. Ibid. § 2.

SECT. 17. The City of Boston shall have the right to lay out such streets, with sewers under the same, as public convenience and necessity may require, on the territory over which the Boston Wharf Company is hereby authorized to construct their wharf: *Provided, however*, that all such streets shall be laid out within one year from the passage of this act.

Right of city to lay out streets. Ibid. § 3. Proviso.

SECT. 18. This act shall not authorize said company to hold any flats, which shall not be embraced between the true lines of its estate, legally extended, nor to interfere with nor to take compensation for any easement which the legislature have already granted to any railroad or other corporation in or over said flats.

Privileges limited. Ibid. § 4.

Company to pay proportion of expense. Ibid. § 5.

SECT. 19. The Boston Wharf Company shall pay their proportion of the expenses of making the excavations, set forth in the fifth section of the two hundred and fifty-fourth chapter of the acts of the year eighteen hundred and fifty; said proportion to be assessed by the commissioner appointed under said act.

May extend wharf. 1855, 455, § 1.

SECT. 20. The Boston Wharf Company are authorized to extend their wharf in South Boston from the line of private rights one hundred rods from high-water mark to the commissioners' line B, established by an act entitled "An Act concerning the Harbor of Boston," approved May twenty-fifth, eighteen hundred and fifty-three, and to maintain the same in the mode prescribed by law: *Provided, however*, that the width of their front, on the line B, shall be of the same width only as the width which may be decided by the supreme judicial court to be the legal width of the line of their legal rights on the aforesaid line one hundred rods from high-water mark; and *provided, also*, that the flats over which the company are hereby authorized to extend their wharf shall in no part thereof be of any greater width than the width of their legal rights on the aforesaid line one hundred rods from high-water mark. Said company are authorized to lay vessels at the westerly side, and at the end of their wharf, and to receive wharfage and dockage therefor. This act shall take effect from and after its passage.

Proviso.

Company to pay proportion of expenses. Ibid. § 2.

SECT. 21. The Boston Wharf Company shall pay their proportion of the expenses of making the excavations set forth in the fifth section of the two hundred and fifty-fourth chapter of the acts of the year eighteen hundred and fifty, said proportion to be assessed by the commissioner appointed under said act, and shall build such avenues or streets as the mayor and aldermen of the city of Boston may within five years direct, on property thus made, at their own expense.

Company not to hold certain land or flats. Ibid. § 3.

SECT. 22. This act shall not authorize said company to take and hold any land or flats lying in front of the land or flats of any other person or persons, or which shall not be embraced between the true lines of its estate, extended as they shall be defined by the supreme judicial court.

SECT. 23. The Boston Wharf Company is hereby authorized to reduce the par value of the shares of said corporation, in such manner, and upon such conditions, as three fourths of the stockholders of said company present and voting, at a meeting called for that purpose, shall determine: *provided, however*, that said par value shall not be reduced below twenty dollars, and that no assessment shall be laid upon the new shares. Reduction of par value of shares authorized. 1863, 209. Proviso.

SECT. 24. This act shall take effect upon its passage.

EASTERN AVENUE CORPORATION.

ACTS.

1. Corporators.
2. May build a solid structure.
3. May construct pile bridge; width in crossing commissioners' line; to be parallel with West Broadway in crossing flats; width in crossing channel.
4. May take land for street.
5. Avenue, &c.
6. Free of toll.
7. Corporation to give bond.
8. Act void, unless avenue is completed in five years.
9. Capital stock $ 150,000.
10. Corporation revived; corporators to organize within six months; avenue to be completed in five years, &c.
11. Westerly terminus changed; location of bridge changed.
12. Provision extended.
13. Construction of avenues; City of Boston authorized to grant aid.
14. Time for location extended.
15. City of Boston, powers to aid extended.
16. Franchise may be transferred to city; city to be relieved from bond; notice of transfer to be filed; commissioners on harbors and flats to approve mode of construction.
17. Powers of City Council in case of transfer; avenue may be laid out as highway.
18. City of Boston allowed till March 1, 1868, to construct avenue.
19. Conference with State Commissioners as to crossing flats of the Commonwealth.

ACTS.[1]

Corporators. 1852, 148, § 1.

SECTION 1. Robert Rantoul, jr., Samuel S. Perkins, Benjamin T. Reed, Samuel Leeds, Otis Rich, John P. Monks,

---

[1] Act to incorporate the Eastern Avenue Corporation, 1852, chap. 148; additional acts (see § 10 and following) 1859, chap. 251; 1860, chap. 71; 1861, chap. 79; 1862, chap. 163; 1865, chap. 55; and resolves 1865, chap. 72.

Joseph W. Ward, their associates and successors, are hereby made a corporation by the name of the Eastern Avenue Corporation, with all the powers and privileges, and subject to all the duties, liabilities, and restrictions, set forth in the forty-fourth chapter of the Revised Statutes.

May build a solid structure. Ibid. § 2.

SECT. 2. The said corporation is hereby authorized to construct and maintain an avenue, to be of solid structure, one hundred feet wide, for a street and sidewalks, commencing at L Street, being a point within the boundaries of the city institutions, in that part of Boston called South Boston, and running thence in a northwesterly direction one hundred rods from high-water mark, or to riparian line, so called; said avenue to be provided with proper draw or draws and sluiceways, which draw or draws or sluiceways it shall be in the power of the legislature to change and widen at the expense of the corporation or their successors.

May construct pile bridge. Ibid. § 3.

SECT. 3. The said corporation is also authorized and empowered to construct and maintain a pile bridge, not exceeding one hundred feet in width, with stone piers one hundred feet wide, and not less than four hundred feet apart, and with suitable draw or draws, which draw or draws it shall be in the power of the legislature to change and widen, at the expense of the corporation or their successors, commencing at the northwesterly end of the solid avenue described in the second section of this act, and running thence in a direct line to the foot of Summer Street, in the City of Boston: *Provided*, That none of the stone piers aforesaid shall be placed in Fore or Fore Point Channel. And *provided, also*, that the southerly side of said bridge, where it crosses the commissioners' line, on the easterly side of Fore Point Channel, shall be twenty-one hundred feet from the angle in said commisioners' line; and *provided, further*, that the portion of the said bridge or avenue, which crosses the flats, shall be parallel to West Broadway, in said South Boston; and *provided, further*, that said bridge where it crosses said channel shall not be more than sixty-six feet "in width."

Width in crossing commissioners' line.

In crossing flats, bridge to be parallel with West Broadway.

Width in crossing channel.

SECT. 4. The said corporation may purchase, or otherwise ake, any land necessary for the purpose of making a street fifty eet wide, from the westerly termination of the bridge aforesaid, uthorized by the third section of this act, to Summer Street; nd if they shall not be able to obtain such land by any agreenent with the owner or owners thereof, they shall pay therefor uch damages as shall be estimated and determined, in the nanner provided by the laws of this Commonwealth in the case f laying out and widening streets in the City of Boston; and ll damages to the estates of riparian proprietors, or owners, by he construction of any of the structures authorized by this act, hall be estimated and determined in the same manner. May take land for street. Ibid. § 4.

SECT. 5. The said avenue, bridge, street, draws, and luiceways, shall be constructed under the direction, and to the atisfaction of three commissioners, to be appointed by the govrnor and council, and to be paid by the said corporation; and he said corporation shall be held liable to keep the same in good repair, and to open the said draws and afford all proper ccommodations to vessels having occasion to pass the same by lay or by night. Avenue, etc. Ibid. § 5.

SECT. 6. The said bridge, street, and avenue shall be open or free travel for the use of the public, without toll or charge herefor. Free of toll. Ibid. § 6.

SECT. 7. Before commencing the structures contemplated n the second and third sections of this act, the said corporation hall give bond, with satisfactory sureties, to the attorney-genral of this Commonwealth, in the penal sum of fifty thousand lollars, that they shall be completed in all respects to the satsfaction of the commissioners aforesaid, and kept in good repair or public travel, and that the draw or draws shall be properly aised for all necessary demands of navigation, until such time s the said structures may be accepted by the City of Boston, vhich city shall be held to all the duties, liabilities, and retrictions, of the said corporation. And the said bonds shall lso be holden as security for the payment of all such damages o individuals as shall be estimated and determined in the nanner provided in the fourth section of this act. Corporation to give bond. Ibid. § 7.

Act void, unless, etc. Ibid. § 8.

SECT. 8. If said avenue, bridge, and street, shall not be completed within five years from the passage of this act, then the same shall be void.

Capital stock. No shares less than par value. Ibid. § 9.

SECT. 9. The capital stock of said corporation shall not exceed one hundred and fifty thousand dollars, and no shares shall be issued for a less sum, to be actually paid in on each, than the par value of the shares which shall be first issued.

Corporation revived. 1859, 251. Surviving corporators to organize within six months.

SECT. 10. The corporation created by chapter one hundred and forty-eight of the acts of eighteen hundred and fifty-two is hereby revived, and the parties named in said act, now surviving, are hereby authorized to call a meeting to organize said corporation anew, with all the powers conferred by said act: *Provided*, That said meeting be called, and said corporation be organized, within six months from the passage hereof; and

Avenue, etc., to be completed in five years. Damages.

provided, also, that the avenue, bridge, and street, named in said act, shall be completed within five years from the passage of this act; and *provided, also*, that the rights of parties to damages, occasioned by the laying out and construction of said avenue, bridge, and street, and the remedies therefor, and for securing the payment of the same, shall, in all respects, be the same as are by law provided in relation to damages occasioned by the laying out and constructing railroads.

Westerly terminus changed. 1860, 71. Location of bridge changed.

SECT. 11. So much of the act to incorporate the Eastern Avenue Corporation, passed on the twenty-fourth day of April, one thousand eight hundred and fifty-two, as requires their bridge and avenue to run in a direct line to the foot of Summer Street, is hereby repealed; and said corporation are hereby authorized so to change the location of their bridge and avenue, that it may run in a direct line either to Drake's Wharf or to Russia Wharf, opposite Congress Street, or to any point between said wharves: *Provided*, such new location shall be within the commissioners' lines, and the location shall be made by said corporation, and approved by the mayor and aldermen of the City of Boston, within one year from the passage of this act; and *provided, also*, that nothing contained in this act, shall in any way conflict with the provisions of the one hundred and third chapter of the Resolves of the year eighteen hundred and fifty-nine.

SECT. 12. The provisions of chapter twenty-one, of the acts of the year one thousand eight hundred and sixty, authorizing the Eastern Avenue Company to change their location, are hereby extended to January first, in the year eighteen hundred and sixty-two. Provisions of Act of 1860 extended. 1861, 79, § 1.

SECT. 13. So much of said avenue as shall be built within the commissioners' line, established May twenty-fifth, in the year one thousand eight hundred and fifty-three, for solid structure, may, with the consent of the mayor and aldermen of the city of Boston, be built solid; and said city of Boston is hereby authorized to grant aid to said corporation, in such manner, and upon such conditions, as the said city may deem expedient: *Provided*, said avenue shall be constructed with suitable draw or draws, and proper sluiceways, which draw or draws it shall be in the power of the legislature to change and widen, at the expense of the corporation, or their successors. Construction of avenue. Ibid. § 2. City of Boston authorized to grant aid. Proviso.

SECT. 14. The provisions of chapter seventy-one of the acts of the year eighteen hundred and sixty, authorizing the Eastern Avenue Corporation to change its location, are hereby extended to the first day of March, in the year eighteen hundred and sixty-three. Time for location extended. 1862, 163, § 1.

SECT. 15. The provisions of the second section of chapter seventy-nine of the acts of the year eighteen hundred and sixty-one, authorizing the city of Boston to grant aid to said corporation, in such manner and upon such conditions as the city may deem expedient, are hereby extended so that said city of Boston may render such aid by building said avenue or any part thereof, or otherwise. City of Boston, powers to aid extended. Ibid. § 2.

SECT. 16. The said Eastern Avenue Corporation may transfer its franchise and all its corporate rights to the city of Boston, and said city of Boston may accept the same; but no compensation shall be paid by said city for such transfer; and upon such transfer, the said city of Boston shall have all the powers and privileges, and be subject to all the duties, restrictions, and liabilities appertaining to the said Eastern Avenue Corporation, except that the said city of Boston shall not be required to give the bond mentioned in the seventh section of Corporation may transfer franchise to city. Ibid. § 3. City relieved from giving bond.

the one hundred and forty-eighth chapter of the acts of the year one thousand eight hundred and fifty-two. In case of such transfer to the city of Boston[1] of the franchises and corporate rights of said corporation, notice of such fact shall be given to the governor by the city of Boston, and in such case the time for location as extended by the first section of this act shall be further extended for two years; but said avenue shall be located with the approbation of, and be built according to specifications approved by, the commissioners appointed under the resolves in relation to the harbors and flats of the Commonwealth passed at the present session of the general court.

In case of transfer, notice to be filed with Governor.

Commissioners on harbors and flats to approve mode of construction.

Powers of City Council in case of transfer. Ibid. § 4.

SECT. 17. When the city of Boston shall have received the transfer provided for in the third section of this act, it may discharge all the duties incumbent on it, on account thereof, by the city council of the said city, or by any other agency which the said city council shall appoint; and when the avenue shall have been built, the board of aldermen of said city may lay out the same as a street or highway.

Aldermen may lay out as highway.

City of Boston allowed until March 1, '68. 1865, 55.

SECT. 18. The time allowed the city of Boston, as assignees of the franchise of the Eastern Avenue corporation, to construct the avenue across South Boston flats, is hereby extended to the first day of March, in the year eighteen hundred and sixty-eight.

Conference with State Commissioners as to crossing flats of this Commonwealth. Resolves 1865, 72.

SECT. 19. *Whereas*, The charter for the Eastern Avenue Corporation, now held by the city of Boston, contemplates the building of an avenue across flats belonging to the Commonwealth: *Resolved*, That the board of commissioners on harbors and flats be authorized to confer with the city government of Boston, or any committee thereof, concerning the building of said avenue, with power to give advice and such direction in the construction of such avenue as shall be consistent with the best interests of the Commonwealth and of the harbor of Boston.

---

[1] The city of Boston became the assignee of the Eastern Avenue Corporation, by order of the City Council, January 2, 1863.

SOUTH BAY COMPANY.

ACT.

1. Corporators; powers and duties.
2. May purchase and hold certain lands and marsh.
3. Capital Stock $ 100,000; no shares to be issued under par.
4. Not to infringe upon legal rights of Roxbury.
5. To take effect on passage.

ACT.[1]

SECTION 1. Uriel Crocker, Eben Jones, and Ellis Gray Loring, their associates and successors, are hereby made a corporation, by the name of the South Bay Company, with all the powers and privileges, and subject to all the duties, liabilities, and restrictions set forth in the forty-fourth chapter of the Revised Statutes. *Corporators. 1853, 344, § 1. Powers and duties.*

SECT. 2. Said corporation may purchase and hold the whole or any part of the land and marsh lying at or near the head of the Boston South Bay, between Dorchester Turnpike, the old road from Boston to Dorchester, Cottage Street, Norfolk Avenue, East Street, and tide water; not exceeding in the whole one hundred and fifty acres, and may grade and otherwise improve the same, and may sell said marsh and land or divide the same, or the proceeds thereof, among the stockholders, after paying all the debts of the corporation, and not otherwise. *May purchase and hold certain lands and marsh. Ibid. § 2.*

SECT. 3. The capital stock of said corporation shall not exceed one hundred thousand dollars; and no shares in the capital stock of said corporation shall be issued for a less amount, to be paid in on each, than the par value of the shares first issued. *Capital stock. Ibid. § 3. No shares to be issued under par.*

SECT. 4. Nothing contained in this act shall authorize said corporation to infringe upon the legal rights of drainage, or any other rights of the city of Roxbury, or of any other corporation *Not to infringe upon legal rights of Roxbury. Ibid. § 4.*

---

[1] Act to incorporate the South Bay Company, 1853, chap. 344.

or person whatever, or to make or extend any wharf, pier, or other structure whatever, into and over tide-water, not now authorized by law.

Ibid. § 5.

SECT. 5. This act shall take effect from and after its passage.

SOUTH COVE CORPORATION.

ACTS.

1. Persons incorporated; may hold real and personal estate to the amount of $1,100,000.
2. Real estate described which may be held.
3. Number of shares.
4. Real estate liable to attachment.
5. Directors and other officers.
6. Depots of railroads, streets, etc.
7. Water communication, how preserved.
8. General landing-place.
9. Assessments; sale of shares to pay.
10. First meeting; right of voting.
11. Drains and common sewers.
12. South Cove Company to be members, etc.
13. Laying out of streets, etc.
14. Duration of charter.
15. May extend their wharf.

ACTS.[1]

Persons incorporated. 1833, 17, § 1.

SECTION 1. *Be it enacted, &c.* That John Welles, Edward Tuckerman, Francis J. Oliver, Edward D. Clark, Henry H. Fuller, and Abraham A. Dame, their associates, successors, and assigns, be, and they are hereby constituted a body corporate, by the name of the South Cove Corporation, and by that name may sue and be sued, prosecute and be prosecuted to final judgment and execution. And said corporation shall have power to make and use a common seal, and the same to break, alter, and renew at pleasure; and may, from time to time, make, ordain, and establish all such by-laws, rules, and regulations as they shall deem expedient and useful to carry into effect the objects of this corporation: *Provided* the same be not repugnant to the constitution and laws of the Commonwealth.

Real and personal estate.

And said corporation may purchase and hold real estate, in fee simple or otherwise, to any amount not exceeding in value one million of dollars, and personal estate to any amount not ex-

[1] Act to incorporate the South Cove Corporation, 1833, chap. 17. Additional act (see § 15), 1850, chap. 208.

ceeding in value one hundred thousand dollars, necessary to promote the objects of the corporation; and, in general, may do and suffer all other acts and things which bodies corporate may and ought to do and suffer.

SECT. 2. *Be it further enacted*, That said corporation shall have power to purchase, hold, and possess any part or all the land, wharves, and flats, with the buildings and other improvements thereon standing, lying easterly of Front Street, southerly of Essex Street, and westerly of Sea Street in the city of Boston: *Provided*, said corporation shall legally acquire the same from the lawful proprietors thereof; and said corporation shall have power to grant, sell, and alien, in fee simple or otherwise, the said corporate property, or any part thereof; and to lease, mortgage, improve, or otherwise manage the same, in such manner as may be deemed most for the interest of said corporation, and by such forms of conveyance and contract, as shall by their by-laws be provided.

Real estate described which corporation may hold. Ibid. § 2.

SECT. 3. *Be it further enacted*, That the stock and property of said corporation shall be divided into not less than eight hundred nor more than twelve hundred shares, certificates of which shall be issued under the seal of the corporation, and be signed by the president and treasurer thereof, and said shares shall be deemed and taken to be personal estate, and may be transferred by an assignment on the back of the certificate, and recorded by the clerk of said corporation in a book to be kept for that purpose, and shall be liable to attachment on *mesne process*, and sale on execution, in the manner and according to the form of the statutes making provision for the attachment and sale of shares of debtors in incorporated companies.

Number of shares. Ibid. § 3.

SECT. 4. *Be it further enacted*, That the real estate and property of said corporation shall be liable to be attached on *mesne process*, and be set off and sold on execution against the corporation, in the same manner as the property or estate of individuals is by law subject to *mesne* or final process.

Real estate liable to attachment, &c. Ibid. § 4.

SECT. 5. *Be it further enacted*, That the immediate government and direction of the affairs of said corporation shall be vested in a board of not less than seven directors, who shall be

Directors and other officers. Ibid. § 5.

chosen by the members of this corporation, in the manner herein after provided, and shall hold their offices until others shall be duly elected to fill their places as directors; a majority of whom shall form a quorum for the transaction of business, and shall elect one of their own number to be president of the board, who shall also be president of the corporation; and they shall have authority also to choose a clerk, who shall be sworn to the faithful discharge of his duty, and a treasurer, who shall give bonds to the corporation, with sureties to the satisfaction of the directors, in a sum not less than forty thousand dollars, for the faithful discharge of his trust. And the president and directors aforesaid, for the time being, shall have and exercise, in the name and for the benefit of the corporation, all the powers granted in this act to said corporation, relative to the purchase, sale, and transfer of real estate.

Depots of railroads, streets, &c. Ibid. § 6.

SECT. 6. *Be it further enacted*, That the president and directors of said corporation, for the time being, shall have power, and they are hereby authorized to take such measures as they may deem expedient, to procure the location, upon the flats and lands aforesaid, of the railroads proceeding from Worcester and from Providence, to the city of Boston; and for that purpose may give, grant, sell, or otherwise convey to the Boston and Worcester Railroad Corporation, or the Boston and Providence Railroad Corporation, or both, such quantity of ground, lying between Sea Street and Front Street, as shall be necessary for depots, or terminations, of either or both of said railroads; and may enclose said flats with a sea wall, and fill up with mud and earth, and make solid ground for the purposes aforesaid, and may lay out and extend streets in any direction, from or near said depots or termini, to communicate with the existing streets in the vicinity, and may fill up and fully complete the same for public travel, and may fill up and make lots of building ground contiguous thereto, for the use and benefit of said corporation. And should said streets, in the course thereof, cross any land not embraced in the purchases of said corporation, and the same cannot be acquired by voluntary agreement, then, in that case, the owner or owners thereof shall be entitled to reasonable damage therefor, to be estimated and recovered of said corporation, in the manner provided by law for the recovery of damages happening by the laying out of highways. And, in consideration of the advantages to be derived from the location and final termination of said railroads, or either of them, upon the lands aforesaid, said corporation may give, in the nature of a bonus, to said railroad corporations, or either of them, such sums of money and parcels of land, together with such other facilities and advantages as may be found useful and profitable to said corporations. And said railroad corporations, or either of them, shall possess and enjoy all the benefit of such gifts, grants, sales, and other accommodations, made to them, or either of them, for the purposes aforesaid; and the right to possess and enjoy the same is hereby vested in said corporations; and all the engagements and agreements of said railroad corporations, or either of them, with said South Cove Corporation, in consideration of the gifts and grants aforesaid, shall, in like manner, be enjoyed by, and secured to said South Cove Corporation.

Water communication, how preserved. Ibid. § 7.

SECT. 7. *Be it further enacted*, That should it be found expedient, by reason of any defect in the titles to, or contracts made for any of said estates, or otherwise, to preserve a water communication through the sea wall or streets laid out and made as aforesaid, then, and in such case, said corporation shall leave an opening through such sea wall or streets near the free bridge, sufficiently capacious to preserve the usual flow of the tide waters in said cove, and the passage of vessels to said estates. And said corporation shall construct suitable and convenient draws over the same, which shall, in all respects, be well adapted to the public wants, and shall be holden to maintain and keep said draws in good repair, and shall raise and lower the same, at all times of day and night, for the accommodation of all persons passing through and over the same; and for any neglect so to do, said corporation shall be holden to pay reasonable damage, which may be recovered by an action on the case, before any tribunal competent to hear and determine the same.

General landing place. Ibid. § 8.

SECT. 8. *Be it further enacted,* That said corporation may locate and set apart such quantity of land, made as aforesaid, as may be necessary for a general landing-place, or place of deposit for wood, lumber, stone, and other bulky articles, which may be transported to or from the interior, on said railroads; and may charge and receive according to the accustomed rates of wharfage in the city of Boston, for the use and privilege of landing thereon.

Assessments. Ibid. § 9.

SECT. 9. *Be it further enacted,* That the directors of said corporation may make such equal assessments upon the shares aforesaid, from time to time, as they may deem expedient and necessary to effect the objects of the corporation, and may direct the same to be paid to the treasurer thereof, and if the proprietor of any share shall neglect or refuse to pay any assessment, for the space of thirty days from the time the same shall have been due, the directors may order the treasurer to sell said share or shares at public auction, to the highest bidder, after giving due notice thereof, and the same shall be transferred to the purchaser; and said delinquent proprietor shall be holden to pay said corporation the balance, if his share or shares shall sell for less than the amount assessed thereon, with the interest and cost of sale, and shall be entitled to the overplus, if his share or shares shall sell for more than the assessment due, with the interest and cost of sale: *Provided, however,* That no assessments shall be laid on any share in said corporation of a greater amount in the whole, than five hundred dollars on each share.

Sale of shares to pay assessments.

Proviso.

First meeting. Ibid. § 10.

SECT. 10. *Be it further enacted,* That either of the persons named in the first section of this act may call the first meeting of said corporation, by advertising said meeting three times previously, in any newspaper printed in Boston. And the corporation, at their first meeting, and afterwards annually, at such time as shall be established by the by-laws of said corporation, shall choose said board of directors by ballot; each proprietor being entitled to as many votes as he may hold shares in said corporation. Members may vote by proxy in writing.

Right of voting.

Drains and common sewers. Ibid. § 11.

SECT. 11. *Be it further enacted,* That said corporation shall be holden to extend and carry out all drains and common sewers which have their present termination in said cove, before they shall so fill up said cove as to obstruct and affect their use; and the same shall be done in such manner as shall be approved by the mayor and aldermen of the city of Boston. And if any other drains or common sewers shall from time to time hereafter be made by said mayor and aldermen into said cove, as far as it shall have been filled up at the time of making such other drains or common sewers, and the said corporation shall thereafter further proceed to fill up said cove beyond the termination of such other drains or common sewers, then the said corporation shall be further holden to extend and carry out from time to time, such other drains and common sewers before the said cove shall be farther filled up, so that the said filling up shall not obstruct and affect the use of such other drains and common sewers.

South Cove Company to be members, &c. Ibid. § 12.

SECT. 12. *Be it further enacted*, That all the members of a certain joint stock company, called "The South Cove Company," are hereby constituted and made members of this corporation, in conformity with certain principles and provisions, contained in an instrument creating and establishing said company, and bearing the signatures of its several members; and, as stockholders in said company, they shall severally be entitled to corresponding amounts of stock in this corporation, and shall be subject to all the provisions contained in said instrument, and the by-laws of this corporation relative to assessments and transfer of shares; and shall also remain subject to the provisions of said agreement in relation to certain covenants contained therein, with the Boston and Worcester Railroad Corporation.

Laying out of streets, &c. Ibid. § 13.

SECT. 13. *Be it further enacted*, That, before any street or streets which may be laid out and made by said corporation upon the lands and flats aforesaid, shall be extended across the lands of any individual or corporation, to communicate with any of the existing streets in that vicinity, said corporation shall deposit a plan with the mayor and aldermen of the city of Boston, upon which plan the location of any street or streets contemplated to be made and extended as aforesaid, shall be fully and particularly described. And said mayor and aldermen shall thereupon issue notice in such form and manner as they shall deem proper and expedient, that all persons interested may appear before them, at such time and place, as said mayor and aldermen shall appoint, to show cause, if any they have, why said corporation should not make or extend such street or streets, across the lands of such person or corporation, agreeably to the provisions contained in the sixth section of this act. And said mayor and aldermen, at the time and place appointed, as aforesaid, shall hear the parties, and determine upon the expediency of extending such street or streets in manner aforesaid. And if, upon such hearing, said mayor and aldermen shall be of opinion that the public necessity and convenience require the extension of such street or streets, they shall have power to authorize the extension thereof. And all streets so authorized shall be taken and deemed to be public highways.

Duration of charter. Ibid. § 14.

SECT. 14. *Be it further enacted,* That this act shall continue in force forty years from the passing thereof.

May extend their wharf. 1850, 208.

SECT. 15. The South Cove Corporation and the South Wharf Corporation are hereby authorized to extend the line of the flats and wharf owned by them respectively, on the west side of Sea Street, in the city of Boston, into the harbor channel, as far as the line established by the act entitled "An Act concerning the Harbor of Boston," passed on the seventeenth day of March, in the year one thousand eight hundred and forty, and to use and enjoy said flats according to their respective rights as settled between them: *provided, however,* that this grant shall not be construed to extend to any land or flats of this Commonwealth, lying in front of the land or flats of any other person or corporation, or which would be comprehended by the true lines of such land or flats continued to said commissioners' line: and *provided, also,* that no part of said flats below low-water mark shall be filled up, or made solid, and that any wharf or wharves erected thereon shall be built on piles, which piles shall not be nearer to each other than six feet in the direction of the stream, and eight feet in a transverse direction, and that this grant shall in no wise impair the legal rights of any person.

Proviso.

TREMONT IMPROVEMENT COMPANY.

ACTS.

1. Corporators; powers and duties.
2. May hold real estate in Boston and Roxbury.
3. May lay drains.
4. Capital stock $300,000.
5. Not to infringe on existing rights.
6. May acquire and convey additional land.
7. Captal stock increased $200,000.

ACTS.[1]

SECTION 1. John G. Tappan, Daniel Hammond, Lewis W. Tappan, George R. Sampson, John H. Cheever, Sidney B. Morse, Charles McBurney, and Samuel F. Morse, their associates and successors, are hereby made a corporation, by the name of the Tremont Improvement Company, with all the powers and privileges, and subject to all the duties, liabilities, and restrictions set forth in the forty-fourth chapter of the Revised Statutes. *Corporators. 1853, 364, § 1. Powers and duties.*

SECT. 2. Said corporation may purchase, hold, and convey the whole, or any part, of certain marsh and vacant lands situated partly in Boston and partly in Roxbury, not exceeding one hundred acres, and limited easterly by Lenox Street, in Boston; southerly by Washington Street, in Boston and Roxbury; westerly by Water Street, in Roxbury; northwesterly and northerly by Cabot Street, in Roxbury, and northerly by Tremont Street, in Roxbury and Boston; and may grade, drain, and otherwise improve said lands, and may divide the same, or the proceeds thereof, among the stockholders, after paying all the debts of the corporation, and not otherwise. *May hold real estate in Boston and Roxbury. Ibid. § 2.*

SECT. 3. Said corporation may, with the consent of the city of Boston and the Boston Water Power Company, make and maintain a drain or drains from the premises aforesaid, through Tremont and Northampton streets, or the lands of the Boston Water Power Company, to tide water. *May lay drains. Ibid. § 3.*

---

[1]Act to incorporate the Tremont Improvement Company, 1853, chap. 364. Additional act (see §§ 6 and 7), 1859, chap. 47.

Capital stock $300,000. Ibid. § 4.

SECT. 4. The capital stock of said corporation shall not exceed three hundred thousand dollars, and no shares in the capital stock shall be issued for a less sum or amount, to be paid in on each, than the par value of the shares first issued.

Not to infringe on existing rights. Ibid. § 5.

SECT. 5. Nothing contained in this act shall authorize said corporation to infringe upon the legal rights of drainage or any other rights of the city of Roxbury or the city of Boston, or of any person or corporation whatsoever.

May acquire and convey additional land. 1859, 47, § 1.

SECT. 6. The Tremont Improvement Company may purchase and convey any part of certain marsh and vacant lands situated partly in Roxbury and partly in Boston, on the northwesterly side of Tremont Street, and adjoining the land now owned by them: *provided, however*, the whole amount of land held by said company shall not exceed the number of acres to which they were originally limited by their act of incorporation; and may grade, drain, and improve said lands, and hold or divide the same, or the proceeds thereof, among the stockholders; with all the powers and privileges in regard to such lands, and subject to all the duties, liabilities, and restrictions granted to or imposed upon them by the act of incorporation.

Capital stock increased $200,000. Ibid. § 2.

SECT. 7. Said company are hereby authorized to increase their capital stock by adding thereto a sum not exceeding two hundred thousand dollars, and to invest such portion thereof in real and personal estate as may be necessary and convenient for the purposes for which they have been incorporated.

MASSACHUSETTS INSTITUTE OF TECHNOLOGY.

ACT.

1. Parties incorporated; purposes; powers.
2. May hold property to the amount of $200,000.
3. Reservation of land.
4. Right to occupy two thirds of said land on conditions; building to be erected, etc.
5. Society of Natural History may occupy one third of the reservation; to erect a building.
6. Buildings and grounds to be satisfactory to governor and council; rights forfeited when used for illegitimate objects.
7. Buildings not to cover but one third the area granted.
8. Lots fronting on the square to be reserved until the square is made sightly.
9. The square and surrounding lots to be appraised; if land sold do not realize the appraisement, Societies to pay deficit.
10. Act to be accepted.

ACT.[1]

SECTION 1. William B. Rogers, James M. Beebe, E. S. Tobey, S. H. Gookin, E. B. Bigelow, M. D. Ross, J. D. Philbrick, F. H. Storer, J. D. Runkle, C. H. Dalton, J. B. Francis, J. C. Hoadley, M. P. Wilder, C. L. Flint, Thomas Rice, John Chase, J. P. Robinson, F. W. Lincoln, Jr., Thomas Aspinwall, J. A. Dupee, E. C. Cabot, their associates and successors, are hereby made a body corporate by the name of the Massachusetts Institute of Technology, for the purpose of instituting and maintaining a society of arts, a museum of arts, and a school of industrial science, and aiding generally, by suitable means, the advancement, development, and practical application of science in connection with arts, agriculture, manufactures, and commerce; with all the powers and privileges, and subject to all the duties, restrictions, and liabilities, set forth in the sixty-eighth chapter of the General Statutes.

Parties incorporated. 1861, 183, § 1.

Purposes.

Powers.

[1] An act to incorporate the Massachusetts Institute of Technology, and to grant aid to said Institute and to the Boston Society of Natural History, 1861, chap. 183.

May hold property to the amount of $200,000. Ibid. § 2.

SECT. 2. Said corporation, for the purposes aforesaid, shall have authority to hold real and personal estate to an amount not exceeding two hundred thousand dollars.

Reservation of land. Ibid. § 3.

SECT. 3. One certain square of State land on the Back Bay, namely, the second square westwardly from the Public Garden, between Newbury and Boylston streets, according to the plan reported by the Commissioners on the Back Bay, February twenty-one, eighteen hundred and fifty-seven, shall be reserved from sale forever, and kept as an open space, or for the use of such educational institutions of science and art as are hereinafter provided for.

Right to occupy said land on conditions. Ibid. § 4.

SECT. 4. If at any time within one year after the passage of this act, the said Institute of Technology shall furnish satisfactory evidence to the governor and council that it is duly organized under the aforesaid charter, and has funds subscribed, or otherwise guaranteed, for the prosecution of its objects, to an amount at least of one hundred thousand dollars, it shall be entitled to a perpetual right to hold, occupy, and control, for the purposes herein before mentioned, the westerly portion of said second square, to the extent of two third parts thereof, free of rent or charge by the Commonwealth, subject, nevertheless, to the following stipulations, namely: persons from all parts of the Commonwealth shall be alike eligible as members of said institute, or as pupils for its instruction; and its museum or conservatory of arts, at all reasonable times, and under reasonable regulations, shall be open to the public; and within two years from the time when said land is placed at its disposal for occupation, filled and graded, said institute shall erect and complete a building suitable to its said purposes, appropriately enclose, adorn, and cultivate the open ground around said building, and shall thereafter keep said grounds and building in a sightly condition.

Building to be erected, etc.

Society of Natural History may occupy one third of the reservation to erect a building. Ibid. § 5.

SECT. 5. The Boston Society of Natural History shall be entitled to hold, occupy, and control, for the objects and purposes for which said society was incorporated, and which are more fully set forth in its constitution and by-laws, the easterly portion of said second square, to the extent of one third part thereof: *provided*, that the said society shall, within two years, from the time when said portion of land is placed at its disposal for occupation, filled and graded, erect a building suitable to said objects and purposes, and appropriately enclose, plant, and adorn the open ground around said building, and shall thereafter keep said grounds and building in a neat and ornamental condition.

SECT. 6. The rights and privileges given in the last two sections are granted, subject to these further conditions following, namely: All buildings whatsoever, which may be erected by either of the herein-named institutions, upon any portion of said second square, shall be designed and completed, the grounds surrounding said buildings enclosed, laid out and ornamented, and the said buildings and grounds kept and maintained in a manner satisfactory to the governor and council; and, in case either of the said institutions shall, after due notice given, neglect to comply with the requirements of this section, or fail to use its portion of said square, or at any time appropriate said portion, or any part thereof, to any purpose or use foreign to its legitimate objects, then the right of said delinquent institution to the use, occupation, or control of its portion of said square shall cease, and the Commonwealth, by its proper officers and agents, shall have the right forthwith to enter and take possession of the portion of land so forfeited.

Buildings and grounds to be satisfactory to governor and council. Ibid. § 6.

Rights forfeited when used for illegitimate objects.

SECT. 7. The above-named Societies shall not cover with their buildings more than one third of the area granted to them respectively.

Buildings not to cover but one third the area. Ibid. § 7.

SECT. 8. The commissioners on the Back Bay are hereby instructed to reserve from sale the lots fronting on said square, on Boylston, Clarendon, and Newbury streets, until said Societies shall, by enclosure and improvements, put said square in a sightly and attractive condition.

Lots fronting on the square to be reserved until, etc. Ibid. § 8.

SECT. 9. Upon the passage of this act, the governor, with the advice and consent of the council, shall appoint three disinterested persons, who shall appraise the value of all the lands specified in the third and eighth sections of this act, and make

The square and surrounding lands to be appraised. Ibid. § 9.

If lands sold do not realize the appraisement, societies to pay deficit.

a return of said appraisal to the governor and council; and if, when the lands mentioned in section eight shall have been sold, the proceeds of such sales shall not be equal to the whole amount of the appraisal above mentioned, then the societies named in this act shall pay the amount of such deficit into the treasury of the Commonwealth, for the school fund, in proportion to the area granted to them respectively.

Act to be accepted. Ibid. § 10.

SECT. 10. This act shall be null and void, unless its provisions shall be accepted within one year, by the Massachusetts Institute of Technology, and the Boston Society of Natural History,[1] so far as they apply to those societies respectively.

---

[1] The act was duly accepted by both societies.

AGREEMENTS.

CITY OF BOSTON, EDWARD TUCKERMAN AND OTHERS, AND THE BOSTON AND ROXBURY MILL CORPORATION.

AGREEMENT.

Parties.
Boundary lines fixed.
Mill Corporation to have certain portions of the basin.
City and other proprietors to have certain flats.
City and other parties to have right of drainage; and right to dig earth for filling.
Erection of buildings west of Charles Street restricted.
The Milldam may be laid out as a street.
Tide-water not to be let in higher than three feet above low water.
Further assurances to be made.
Executing clause.
Signatures.
Condition: if the Corporation shall build on land within 1,650 feet west of Charles Street, all land between Charles Street and the channel to revert to city.

AGREEMENT.[1]

Parties. 1826, Dec. 26.

Memorandum, of an agreement made this twenty-sixth day of December, A. D. 1826, by and between the city of Boston, by a Committee thereto duly authorized by votes of the City Council, copies of which are hereto annexed, of the first part; and Edward Tuckerman, Esq., and others, proprietors of flats and real estate on the easterly and southeasterly sides of the great or receiving basin, so called, of the Boston and Roxbury Mill Corporation of the second part; and the said Boston and Roxbury Mill Corporation by their Committee duly authorized by a vote, a copy whereof is likewise hereto annexed of the third part; each party and each individual of the second part for

[1] Agreement between the City of Boston, the Boston and Roxbury Mill Corporation, and Edward Tuckerman and others. Recorded with Suffolk Deeds, Liber 315, folio 278.

1826. themselves severally and respectively with each of the other parties.

Boundary lines fixed.

For the purpose of adjusting and settling all questions and controversies touching the claims and rights of the respective parties within and about the basin, and of fixing the boundary lines thereof, the parties aforesaid do severally and mutually agree each for themselves respectively with the others and with each of them, that the boundary line between the said city and the said proprietors and the said Boston and Roxbury Mill Corporation, respectively, shall be and hereby is settled as follows, that is to say: Beginning at a point on the dam, six hundred and fifty feet from Charles Street, thence running in a straight (being the first) line, southerly till it strikes the southwesterly line of Castle Street, continued into the basin at a point, twelve hundred feet from Washington Street, as marked upon a plan made by Mr. S. P. Fuller, thence running southwesterly in a straight (being the second) line, through or along land claimed by said proprietors or other individuals, passing through the boundary line between said city and Edward Tuckerman, Esq., at a point twelve hundred feet from Washington Street, and extending until it strikes a point in said city's land, two hundred feet distant from said boundary line last named; then turning and running westerly in a straight (being the third) line, by a cedar post to Northampton Street, as marked on said Fuller's plan; thence northerly along the easterly side of said Northampton Street to the boundary line between Boston and Roxbury.

B. and R. Mill Corporation to have certain portions of the basin.

And the said parties of the first and second parts do hereby severally agree with the said Boston and Roxbury Mill Corporation, in consideration of the several grants, covenants, and agreements of the said corporation hereinafter contained, that the said corporation shall have, hold, and enjoy all the right, title, and interest of every name and nature, which the said city or either of said proprietors of flats and real estate aforesaid, have or ever had in and to the land and space within said basin, lying westerly and northerly of the three lines first above described, and easterly of the line of Northampton Street above-named, excepting the right reserved to the Board of Health, by the act incorporating said Boston and Roxbury Mill Corporation. To have and to hold the above-granted premises with all their privileges and appurtenances to them the said Boston and Roxbury Mill Corporation, their successors and assigns to their own use and behoof forever, so that neither said city nor either or any of the said proprietors of flats and real estate, nor any person or persons claiming from, by, or under them or either of them shall claim or demand any right, title, use, property, or estate therein forever, excepting the exercise of the rights aforesaid of the said Board of Health and of those hereinafter granted. 1826.

City and other proprietors to have certain flats.

And in consideration of the premises, the said Boston and Roxbury Mill Corporation does hereby agree with the said parties of the first and second parts and each of them, that the said city and the said proprietors, parties hereto respectively, shall have, hold, and enjoy all the right, title, and interest whether of property or right of flowage and every other of what name or nature soever which said corporation has or ever had in and to the lands and flats claimed by the said city or the said proprietors, parties hereto respectively, lying between the three lines first described and the adjacent upland, and between said east side of Northampton Street, and the adjacent upland. To have and to hold the same, with all the privileges and appurtenances thereto belonging to them, the said city and the said proprietors separately and respectively according to their several rights and estates in and to the upland, to which the said flats are adjacent respectively, and to their several successors, heirs, and assigns, to their own use and behoof forever, so that neither the said corporation nor any person or persons claiming from, by, or under them shall have claim or demand any right, title, interest, or estate either of property or right of flowage therein forever.

City and other parties to have right of drainage.

And the said Boston and Roxbury Mill Corporation does hereby covenant, grant, and agree that the said parties of the first and second part, their respective successors, heirs, and assigns shall have and enjoy forever the right to dig, lay, and

1826. maintain all convenient and necessary sewers or drains from the upland to the channel or deep water within the basin according to law, and the common and usual practice for the time being within the city; and shall have and enjoy the right of digging and carrying away in common with said corporation and those whom they may license, mud and earth from the vacant flats within said basin; but this is not to be construed to give said parties of the first and second part any right to dig to a greater depth than the level of the sills of the sluiceways nor within one thousand feet of the main dam or cross dam west of the channel near Charles Street, nor east of said channel within two hundred feet of the main dam, nor for any other purpose than that of filling up and raising the said flats and land bordering upon said basin and belonging to the parties of the said first and second part, unless said corporation shall otherwise specially consent and agree.

Right to dig earth for filling.

Erection of buildings west of Charles Street restricted.

And the said corporation doth further covenant and agree with the said city that neither the said corporation or its assigns shall erect any building within said basin in front and west of the city's land on Charles Street, within the distance of one hundred rods from said street unless the said city or its assigns shall erect buildings upon their said land in front and west of said Charles Street; nor will said corporation or its assigns at any time erect any buildings within said basin, between said street and the channel immediately in front thereof, and west of said street, whether said city shall use its said land for building or not. But the erection by the city on their said land of gun-houses, schoolhouses, or other like buildings used exclusively for public purposes, and not for rent or profit, shall not authorize said corporation to build within a hundred rods of Charles Street, and whenever the said corporation shall build in said basin within one hundred rods of Charles Street, the city may build on the whole space which it owned before the signing of this contract, between Charles Street and the channel. And the city authorities, whenever they shall deem it expedient, may lay out as a free and common highway that part of the road or dam of the corporation which extends from Charles Street to the said chan-

The Milldam may be laid out as a street.

nel, and when it shall be so laid out, the corporation will place their toll-house westerly thereof. And the city may then fill up their land opposite to Charles Street so as to connect it with the adjacent dam, and to pass freely to and from the same. 1826.

And the said corporation agrees that they will not voluntarily let the tide-water into said basin higher than may be necessary for the common and ordinary use of the mill-power which they have or may have to the injury of any of the parties hereto. *Provided, however,* That no damages shall be claimed of said corporation, by any of the said parties, unless the water be thus voluntarily raised to a greater height than three feet above the level of low water in the said basin at neap tides. And the said corporation will furnish all reasonable facility not injurious to their own rights or interest, or those of their assigns for floating of scows employed in filling up the said lands of the other parties hereto as aforesaid.

Tide-water not to be let in higher than three feet above low water.

And the parties aforesaid do hereby mutually agree each for themselves respectively with the others, and with each of them, that they shall and will respectively make such other and further assurances as shall be necessary and proper to carry this agreement into effect according to the true intent and meaning thereof.

Further assurances to be made.

In witness whereof, the said committees and the said parties of the second part have set their hands to three several instruments of the same tenor and date, on the day and year first above written, and the said parties of the second part have also affixed their seals.

Executing clause.

Signed by a Committee of the City Council of Boston, and by a Committee of Boston and Roxbury Mill Corporation, and the attorneys for Edward Tuckerman and twelve other riparian owners.

Signatures.

It is the understanding of the Committee of the City Council, and one of the conditions of their signatures to this instrument, that in case the corporation shall build on the land west of the channel within sixteen hundred and fifty feet of Charles Street, all the land lying between Charles Street and the channel shall revert and belong to the city in fee-simple forever.

Condition: if corporation shall build on land within 1,650 feet west of Charles Street, all land between Charles Street and the channel to revert to the city.

CITY OF BOSTON, AND BOSTON AND ROXBURY MILL CORPORATION.

AGREEMENT.

Parties.
Boundary lines fixed.
Rights of property and flowage granted.
City to have the right to lay sewers.
Depth and locality of digging limited.
Buildings not to be erected within one hundred rods of Charles Street.
Except for public purposes.
City may lay out the dam as a highway.
Tide water not to be let in higher than necessary for mill power.

AGREEMENT.[1]

Parties. 1827, Feb. 1.

This Indenture, made this first day of February, in the year of our Lord one thousand eight hundred and twenty-seven, by and between the city of Boston of the one part, and the Boston and Roxbury Mill corporation of the other part. Witnesseth: That for the purpose of adjusting and settling all questions and controversies touching the claims and rights of the said parties, and each of them, within and about the receiving basin of said Corporation, and of fixing the boundary lines thereof, the said parties do hereby mutually covenant and agree that the boundary

Boundary lines fixed.

between the said city and the said corporation shall be, and it hereby is settled, as follows, that is to say: Beginning at a point on the Dam, six hundred and fifty feet from Charles Street; thence running in a straight line, being the first line, southerly, till it strikes the southwesterly line of Castle Street, continued into the Basin at a point twelve hundred feet from Washington Street, as marked upon a plan made by Mr. S. P. Fuller; thence running southwesterly in a straight line, being the second line, through or along land claimed by individuals, passing through the boundary line between said city and

[1] Recorded with Suffolk Deeds, Liber 314, folio 284.

Edward Tuckerman, Esquire, at a point twelve hundred feet from Washington Street, and extending on the same course until it strikes a point in said city's land two hundred feet distant from said boundary line last named; then turning and running westerly in a straight line (being the third line), by a cedar post, to Northampton Street, as marked on said Fuller's plan; thence northerly, along the easterly side of said Northampton Street, to the boundary line between Boston and Roxbury. And the said city, in consideration of the grants, covenants, and agreements of the said corporation, hereinafter contained, doth hereby give, grant, and convey to the said corporation all the right, title, and interest, of every name and nature, which the said city has, or ever had, in and to the land and space within said basin lying westerly and northerly of the three lines first above described, and easterly of the line of Northampton Street, above named, excepting the right reserved to the Board of Health, by the Act incorporating said Boston and Roxbury Mill Corporation. To have and hold the above-granted premises, with all their privileges and appurtenances, to them, the said Boston and Roxbury Mill Corporation, their successors and assigns, to their own use and behoof forever; and that neither the said city nor any person or persons claiming by, from, or under it, shall have, claim, or demand any right, title, use, property, or estate therein forever, excepting the exercise of the rights aforesaid of the said Board of Health, and of those hereinafter granted. And in consideration of the premises, the said Boston and Roxbury Mill Corporation do hereby give, grant, and convey to the said city, all the right, title, and interest, whether of property or right of flowage, and every other of what name or nature soever, which the said corporation have, or ever had, in and to the land and flats claimed by said city, lying between the three lines first described and the adjacent upland; and between said east side of Northampton Street and the adjacent upland. To have and to hold the same, together with all the privileges and appurtenances thereto belonging, to the said city, its successors and assigns, to their own use and behoof forever, so that neither the said corporation

1827.

Rights of property and flowag granted.

1827.

nor any person or persons claiming from, by, or under them, shall have, claim, or demand, any right, title, interest, or estate, either of property or right of flowage, therein forever. And the said corporation, in consideration of the premises, doth hereby, further covenant, grant, and agree to and with the said city, that the said city, its successors and assigns, shall have and enjoy forever the right to dig, lay, and maintain all convenient and necessary sewers or drains from the upland to the channel, or deep water within the basin, according to law and the common and usual practices for the time being within the city; and shall also have and enjoy the right of digging and carrying away, in common with said corporation, and those whom they may license, mud and earth from the vacant flats within said basin. Provided, however, that the said city or its assigns shall not dig to a greater depth than the level of the sills of the sluice ways, nor within one thousand feet of the main dam, or cross dam, west of the channel near Charles Street, nor on the east side of said channel, within two hundred feet of the main dam, nor for any other purpose than that of filling up and raising the flats and land bordering upon said basin, and belonging to said city, unless said corporation shall otherwise specially consent and agree. And the said corporation, in consideration of the premises, do further covenant and agree with the said city that neither the said corporation nor their assigns shall erect any building within said basin in front and west of the city's land on Charles Street, within the distance of one hundred rods from said street, unless the city or its assigns shall erect buildings upon their said land in front and west of said Charles Street; and that neither the said corporation nor their assigns shall, at any time, erect any buildings within said basin, between said street and the channel immediately in front thereof, and west of said street, whether said city shall use its said land for building or not. But the erection by the city on its said land of gun-houses, schoolhouses, or other like buildings, used exclusively for public purposes, and not for rent or profit, shall not authorize said corporation to build within a hundred rods of Charles Street; and whenever

City to have the right to lay sewers.

Depth and locality of digging limited.

Buildings not to be erected within 100 rods of Charles Street,

Except for public purposes.

the said corporation shall build in said basin within one hundred rods of Charles Street, then all the land in said basin, east of the following line, that is to say: a line beginning on the Mill-dam, six hundred and ninety feet from the westerly side of Charles Street, and running southerly in a straight course to a point on the line between Josiah Vose's land and the city's land, distant nine hundred and twenty-six feet three inches from the northerly corner of said Josiah Vose's house on Pleasant Street, measuring on the line of said Vose's land, as marked on the plan of said Fuller, shall revert to said city, and belong to its successors and assigns in fee simple forever, and the said corporation will convey or release to the city accordingly. And the said corporation, in consideration of the premises, do further covenant and agree that the city authorities, whenever they shall deem it expedient, may lay out, as a free and common highway, that part of the road or dam of the corporation which extends from Charles Street to the said channel; and when it shall be so laid out, the corporation will place their toll-house westerly thereof, and the city may then fill up their land opposite to Charles Street, so as to connect it with the adjacent dam, and to pass freely to and from the same. And the said corporation, in consideration of the premises, do further covenant and agree, that they will not voluntarily let the tide-water into said basin higher than may be necessary for the common and ordinary use of the mill power which they have, or may have, to the injury of the said city or its assigns. Provided, however, that no damages shall be claimed of said corporation by said city or its assigns, unless the water be thus voluntarily raised to a greater height than three feet above the level of low water in said basin at neap tides. And the said corporation will furnish all reasonable facilities not injurious to their own rights and interests, or those of their assigns, for floating of scows employed in filling up the lands and flats aforesaid of the said city.

1827.

City may lay out the dam as a highway.

Tide-water not to be let in higher than necessary for mill power.

Duly executed.

EPHRAIM MARSH AND OTHERS, AND THE BOSTON AND ROXBURY MILL CORPORATION.

AGREEMENT.
Parties.
Boundary lines fixed.
Rights of property and flowage granted.
First parties to have right of laying drains, but with limitation.
Corporation not to let in tide-water higher than necessary for mill power.

AGREEMENT.[1]

Parties. 1828, Sept. 30.

Memorandum of an agreement made this 30th day of September, in the year of our Lord one thousand eight hundred and twenty-eight, by and between Ephraim Marsh and others who have or may sign and seal this agreement, proprietors of flats and real estate on the easterly side of the great receiving basin, so-called, of the Boston and Roxbury Mill Corporation, of the first part, and of the said Boston and Roxbury Mill Corporation, by a committee of the Directors of said Corporation, duly authorized by votes of the Corporation and Directors hereto annexed, of the second part, each individual of the first part for himself severally and respectively with the other party. For the purpose of adjusting and settling all questions and controversies touching the claims and rights of the respective parties within and about the basin, and fixing the boundary lines thereof, the parties aforesaid do severally and mutually agree, each of the first part for himself respectively, and the said Corporation by their committee, of the second part, for the said Corporation, by and with the others, and with each of them, that the boundary line between the individuals who have or may sign and seal this instrument of the first part, and the

[1] Recorded with Suffolk Deeds, Liber 358, folio 217.

said Boston and Roxbury Mill Corporation of the second part, respectively, shall be and hereby is settled to be their boundary line, as follows, that is to say: A straight line, beginning at a cedar post on said dam, six hundred and fifty feet from Charles Street, established as a boundary line between lands of the City of Boston and said Boston and Roxbury Mill Corporation, and continued by a stone post at the bottom of the city's land upon Pleasant Street, to a stone post on Castle Street, it being the same line called the first line in an agreement fixing the boundary lines between lands of said Corporation and the City of Boston and others, which agreement bears date twenty-sixth day of December, A. D. 1826.[1] Said line shall be the boundary line between the lands of the individuals of the first part, and of said Boston and Roxbury Mill Corporation. And the said individuals of the first part do hereby severally agree with the said Boston and Roxbury Mill Corporation, in consideration of the several grants, covenants, and agreements of the said Corporation hereinafter contained, that the said Corporation, shall have, hold, and enjoy all the right, title, and interest of every name and nature which the said individuals, or either of them the proprietors of flats and real estate aforesaid, have or ever had in and to the land and space within said basin, lying westwardly of said boundary line. To have and to hold the above-granted premises with all the privileges and appurtenances to the same belonging to them, the said Boston and Roxbury Mill Corporation, their successors and assigns, to their own use and behoof forever. So that neither of said proprietors of flats and real estate of the first part, nor any person claiming from, by, or under them, or either of them, shall claim or demand any right, title, or property or estate therein forever. And in consideration of the premises, the said Boston and Roxbury Mill Corporation does hereby agree with the said individuals of the first part, and each of them, that the said individuals respectively, shall have, hold, and enjoy all the right, title, and interest, whether of property or right of flowage,

Boundary lines fixed.

Rights of property and flowage granted.

[1] See *ante*, p. 214.

and every other, of what name or nature soever, which the said Corporation has or ever had, in and to the lands and flats claimed by said individuals of the first part respectively, lying eastwardly of said line, and between said line and said individuals' adjacent upland. To have and to hold the same, with all the privileges and appurtenances thereto belonging to them separately and respectively, according to their several rights in and to the upland to which the said flats are adjacent respectively, and to their heirs and assigns, to their use and behoof forever, so that neither the said Corporation, nor any person or persons claiming from, by, or under them, shall have, claim, or demand any right, title, interest, or estate, either of property or right of flowage therein forever. And the said Boston and Roxbury Mill Corporation does hereby covenant, grant, and agree, that the said individuals of the first part, their heirs and assigns, shall have and enjoy forever the right to dig, lay, and maintain all convenient and necessary drains from said upland to the channel or deep water within the said basin according to law, and the common and usual practice for the time being within the City of Boston, and shall have and enjoy the right digging and carrying away, in common with said Corporation and those whom said Corporation has or may license, mud and earth from the vacant flats within said basin. But this is not to be construed to give said individuals of the first part, any right to dig to a greater depth than the level of the sills of the sluice-ways, nor within one thousand feet of the main dam or cross-dam west of the channel near Charles Street, nor east of said Channel within two hundred feet of the main dam, nor for any other purpose than that of filling up and raising said flats and lands bordering upon said basin and belonging to said individuals of the first part, unless said Corporation shall otherwise specially consent and agree. And the said Corporation agrees that they will not voluntarily let the tide-water into said basin higher than may be necessary for the common and ordinary use of the mill power which they have or may have to the injury of the parties hereto; provided, however, that no damages shall be claimed of said Corporation by any of said parties, unless the

First parties to have right of laying drains, but with limitation.

Corporation not to let in tide-water higher than is necessary for mill-power.

water be thus voluntarily raised to a greater height than three feet above the level of low water in said basin at neap tides. And the said Corporation will furnish all reasonable facility not injurious to their own rights or interests, or those of their assigns, for the floating of scows employed in filling up said lands, and of the other parties hereto as aforesaid. And the parties aforesaid do hereby mutually agree, each for themselves respectively, with the others, and with each of them, that they shall and will respectively make such other and further assurances as shall be necessary and proper to carry this agreement into effect, according to the true intent and meaning thereof.

Duly executed.[1]

---

[1] The signers were Ephraim Marsh, Lemuel Pope, Abrm. W. Fuller, Ralph Huntington, Henry Codman, *Trustee*, Catharine Codman, *Trustee*, Francis Codman, George Codman, Amos Lawrence, Abbott Lawrence, Nath. R. Cobb, Francis C. Lowell, Henry Purkitt, P. Mackintosh, Jr., and D. Mackintosh.

BOSTON AND ROXBURY MILL CORPORATION AND BOSTON WATER POWER COMPANY.

AGREEMENT.

Preamble.

Property and rights of B. and R. Mill Corporation southerly of the main dam and southwesterly of the road from Sewall's Point to the Punch Bowl tavern, conveyed to the Water Power Company; consideration, $ 175,000.

Strip of land reserved.

Rights of highway over the cross-dam reserved; rights of widening, repairs, &c. reserved.

B. and R. M. Corporation to maintain the main dam, except the sluices, &c.

Conveniences for travel not to be erected to interfere with the tolls on the dam.

Further assignments and assurances to be made.

Boston Water Power Co. agree to fulfil the duties and obligations of the B. and R. Mill Corporation.

AGREEMENT.[1]

Parties. 1832, May 9.

This Indenture, made this ninth day of May, A. D. eighteen hundred and thirty-two, by and between the Boston and Roxbury Mill Corporation of the one part, and the Boston Water Power Company of the other part, Witnesseth; Preamble. Whereas, the original act of Incorporation of the Boston and Roxbury Mill Corporation, and the subsequent acts in addition thereto, had in view the advancement of two great objects of public interest, the one to authorize and empower the Boston and Roxbury Mill Corporation to erect and maintain dams and roads for the purpose of a public highway, subject to tolls from travellers for the benefit of said Corporation, the other for the purpose of creating an extensive tide-water mill power, and as in furtherance of both these objects much money has been expended, property acquired, contracts made, and obligations incurred, and much still remains to be done, and as it is

[1] Recorded with Suffolk Deeds, Liber 360, folio 262.

the intention of the parties the better to promote the success of these two objects of public improvement, to separate them as far as can be conveniently done from each other, so that the Boston and Roxbury Mill Corporation shall retain all the property rights, privileges and immunities, and continue still liable to all contracts and obligations which appertain to the making and maintaining said dams and roads as highways for toll, together with all the land, rights, and privileges they now own on the northerly side of their main dam, and other things as specified below, and that said Boston Water Power Company should become the assigns of all the property rights, privileges, contracts and immunities, and should be bound by, and responsible for all contracts, conditions and obligations, and other matters connected with or arising from the creation and support of said tide-water mill power, or the lands and property hereafter assigned them, so as fully in all things touching the same, to stand in place and stead of said Boston and Roxbury Mill Corporation, subject to such modifications and exceptions as are hereafter expressed: Now, therefore, be it known, that the said Boston and Roxbury Mill Corporation, in consideration of one hundred and seventy-five thousand dollars to them paid by the said Boston Water Power Company, the receipt whereof is hereby acknowledged, and of their covenants and agreements hereinafter set forth have granted, sold, conveyed, assigned, set over, released, and quitclaimed, and by these presents do grant, sell, convey, assign, set over, release, and quitclaim, to said Boston Water Power Company all the right, title, interest, and estate corporeal and incorporeal in possession, remainder, reversion in fee or for years, or other estate which said Boston and Roxbury Mill Corporation have in and to all the land and real estate, dikes, dams, canals, raceways, and privileges and other matters belonging to the assigned premises within the towns of Boston, Dorchester, Roxbury, and Brookline, which lie southerly of the main dam of the assigns which runs from Charles Street in Boston to Sewall's Point in Brookline, and southwesterly of the road which runs from the end of said dam at Sewall's Point to the

Property and rights of B. and R. Mill Corporation southerly of main dam and southwesterly of the road from Sewall's Point to the Punch Bowl tavern conveyed to Water Power Co.; consideration, $ 175,000.

Punch Bowl Tavern in Brookline. Also, all the right, privileges, power and immunities granted at any time by the General Court to said assigns, to make and maintain within said limits, dams, dikes, canals, and other things necessary or convenient to create a mill power, to cut canals, to erect mills, cut raceways, and to support the same, to enclose or exclude the tide-water in the several basins and receivers, and of doing any other matter or thing touching in any way the creation of a tide-water mill power, and the use, enjoyment, sale or disposition of the same. Also, all similar or analogous rights, powers, privileges and immunities within said limits, derived to said assignors from any city, town, corporation, or individual. Also, all the agreements, covenants, debts, rents, dues or benefits contained or stipulated for said assignors in any leases, bargains, or other contracts heretofore made touching or concerning said mill power or the use of the water, or touching the lands and estates, their rights and privileges within said limits above assigned, with all the benefit and advantage, sums of money, forfeitures, or other things to be derived from them hereafter, with full power from said assignors to said assignees, their successors and assigns, in their own name if proper, or that of the assignors if necessary; the same to claim, demand, sue for and receive and recover, and all entrees for forfeiture and inspection, or other purpose, to make as the said assignors might do the whole for the exclusive benefit, use, and advantages, of said assignees, their successors and assigns forever; excepting, however, from the above assignment, and conveyance, and reserving to said assignors, their successors and assigns, the strip of land running from the northeasterly end of Gravelly Point into what was formerly known as Tide Mill Lane or Road, in Roxbury, and over which strip the present road in that direction now runs, with the right of making said road ten feet wider on each side, so, however, as not to injure any building now erected thereon; and the grantees and their assigns are always to have the right to make and repair mill-races and flumes under said road, incumbering the same as little as possible, and repairing the

Strip of land reserved.

injury they may do the said road. Also reserving to said assignors their successors and assigns an open way and road as a highway to and from their main dam, in and over the top of the cross-dam, so called, which connects said main dam with Gravelly Point, as the same is now used, in making and maintaining said road, however, to Roxbury, and widening the same sufficient space for the water to flow in the creeks over which bridges are or may be thrown, is to be left as heretofore, reserving, also, the right of way and use over and upon the adjoining water and land not built on for the purpose of repairing said road on said cross-dam, and for widening and repairing the said road over the said strip of land to Roxbury above reserved. The said assignors likewise, reserve the right of making said Punch Bowl road twenty feet wider in the whole or any part of its length on the southeasterly side, with the right of way and use in and over the adjoining land and water for that purpose, or repairing said road. To have and to hold the above conveyed and assigned premises, and according to the nature thereof to them, the said Boston Water Power Company, their successors and assigns, and to their own use and behoof forever in the same way and manner, in the same estate and subject, on the part of the assignees to the same conditions, limitations, covenants, obligations and duties of every kind, the payment of all damages and taxes included as the same, till the unsealing hereof were had and holden by the said assignors.

Right of highway over the cross-dam reserved; right of widening, repairs, &c., reserved.

1832, May 9.

And the said Boston and Roxbury Mill Corporation covenant that they will always, at their own charge and cost, support and maintain said main dam, except as to the gates sluices, &c., as hereafter mentioned, in good condition forever, so as effectually to retain the tide-water within the full basin, so called, and to exclude it from the empty or receiving basin, so called, as is now done; any damages to the property or rights of persons, corporation, or estates occasioned by excluding the tide-water as aforesaid to be borne and paid by said grantees. It is mutually understood and agreed, the Boston Water Power Company are at their own cost and charge for-

B. and R. M. Corp. to maintain the main dam, except the sluices, &c.

1832, May 9.

ever, to make and maintain all the sluices, gates, and other things necessary for the flowing of the water in or out of said basins, which are now, or according to the agrcement below, may hereafter be made in said dam, and the liberty and authority is hereby given them, their servants and agents, to work in and about said dam for the purposes aforesaid; and they are hereby also empowered to enlarge the sluices or gateways for supplying the full basin by making new gates in said dam anywhere between the present gates and Sewall's Point, provided that the whole width of all the filling sluices, including those now in use, shall not exceed three hundred feet, and provided also that they are not to be opened in any part of the dam by which injury would be done to any wharf house, or other building, or improvements which, previously to opening said gates and sluices, shall have been made on the north side of said dam by said assignors or their assigns, or where said assignors have sold any land or privileges north of said dam before the ensealing of these presents, unless the owner shall consent.

Conveniences for travel not to be erected to interfere with the toll on the dam.

And provided, also, and it is agreed, that said Boston Water Power Company shall by temporary bridges or other convenient modes, prevent any interruptions of the travel over said dam when building or repairing any of their said gates or sluices, or doing any other thing they have a right to do, and they are forever to support and maintain all such parts of said dam as are essentially necessary for the support of their gates and sluices, and repair all damages which they may do from time to time, in making, repairing, or working in and about said gates and sluices; and they are also to make and forever maintain, at their own expense, a tight, strong, and firm covering over all the gates and sluices made or to be made, and of the width of the dam and of a levee therewith, to support and accommodate the travel; but the top repairs of such covering required from time to time afterwards as a highway, are to be at the expense of the said Boston and Roxbury Mill Corporation.

And it is further mutually covenanted and agreed, that all

the houses or other buildings erected by said Boston Water Power Company or their assigns southerly of the south wall of said main dam, may have an open way, but at their own expense, to and from such building from and to the said dam, and from and to the road running from the main dam to Tide-Mill Lane, or road so called, in Roxbury; but for passing said dam or road the same toll is to be required as in other cases, but no house or other building is to be erected within twenty feet of the south wall of said dam, and the intermediate space of twenty feet is forever to be left open for a highway, as part of said dam, and for that purpose is to be either filled up or well and firmly arched or bridged, and so forever maintained by the said Boston Water Power Company, their successors and assigns, but the top repairs from time to time, to make the same convenient for a highway, are to be made by the grantors, and neither said grantors or their assigns are at any time to dig or carry away any earth or other material from any part of the empty basin within two hundred feet of the south wall of the main dam, except so far as may be necessary for drains and other conveniences usually attached to buildings. And in order to protect said grantors against the making and using ways and streets by which the payment of toll may be shunned or evaded, the said grantees for themselves, successors, and assigns, covenant that they will not build or erect, or permit any others to build or erect, within two thousand feet of said south wall, any bridges, road, or other thing convenient to travel across the channel, in which are placed the emptying sluices, nor across the large channel next westerly of where the city is now filling up its land between said channel and Charles Street; and if any such thing be done, then, in addition to their action at law, the said grantors, their agents or assigns, may remove the same and stop all passing and travel over the same, let the same be made by what person or authority, or by what means soever. 1832, May 9.

And the said Boston and Roxbury Mill Corporation do hereby covenant that they will, at all times hereafter, at the request of said assignees, make any further assignments and Further assignments and assurances to be made.

1832, May 9. assurances to them, their successors and assigns, and will execute to them all needful deeds of authority and power proper, necessary, or convenient to carry into full effect the intentions of the parties touching the premises, and do also agree that they will prosecute, and, if necessary, in their own name, but at the cost of the other party, the petition which was pending before the General Court at its last session, for an increase of capacity in the full basin by enclosing Charles River, and, if granted, will assign the right granted to said Boston Water Power Company.

Boston Water Power Co. agrees to fulfil the duties and obligations of the B. and R. M. Corp.

And the said Boston Water Power Company do hereby covenant with the said Boston and Roxbury Mill Corporation, that they will, in all respects whatever towards the Commonwealth, the city of Boston, and all persons or corporations whatever touching the assigned premises, stand in place and stead of said Boston and Roxbury Mill Corporation, and do assume and will be bound by all the covenants, conditions, limitations, obligations, and duties of every name and nature, damages and taxes included, by which said assignors are bound, or to which by law they are subject, touching the said premises, and will faithfully execute and perform the same, and will forever save them harmless, and indemnify them against any damages arising therefrom forever, excepting, however, all damages which Mr. Horace Gray may receive for breach before the date hereof of any covenant by said Boston and Roxbury Mill Corporation, are to be borne and paid by said Boston and Roxbury Mill Corporation.

Duly executed, etc.

BOSTON AND ROXBURY MILL CORPORATION, AND THE BOSTON WATER POWER CO.

AGREEMENT.
Parties: Lease of Flats to Water Power Company.
Term: 999 years.
Rent: $10 a year.
No permanent obstructions to be erected within 20 feet of the dam.
Water Power Company to pay the taxes.
To keep the sea-wall in order.

AGREEMENT.[1]

Now this Indenture witnesseth: That said Boston & Roxbury Mill Corporation doth hereby lease, let, and demise unto said Boston Water Power Company a certain parcel of flats, described as follows, to wit: Beginning at the northerly side of the Milldam of said Boston & Roxbury Mill Corporation, at a point distant about forty-seven feet from the westerly end of the stone sluice ways of the receiving basin, then running by said Dam four hundred and thirty-three feet to a point fifteen feet beyond the westerly abutment at the end of the old wooden sluiceways, then turning at right angles and running northwardly two hundred feet, then turning at right angles again and running eastwardly upon a line parallel to Milldam and distant two hundred feet therefrom, to a point opposite the point of beginning; then turning at right angles again, and running southwardly two hundred feet, upon a line meeting the Milldam at right angles, at the point of beginning. To hold for the term of nine hundred and ninety-nine years from the first day of July, in the year eighteen hundred and thirty-seven, the said lessees yielding and paying rent therefor the sum of ten dollars per annum for each and every year during said term,

Parties. Lease of flats to Water Power Company. 1837, July 1.

Term, 999 years.

Rent, $10 a year.

[1] Recorded with Suffolk Deeds, Liber 439, folio 269.

1837, July 1.

and after the same rate for any part of a year. Provided, however, and this lease is upon the following condition, to wit: that during the term of this lease no building, fence, or other permanent obstruction shall be erected on said land within twenty feet of the present north line of the Dam. And the said Boston Water Power Company, for itself and its assigns, doth hereby covenant with said Boston & Roxbury Mill Corporation and its assigns, that said Boston Water Power Company will, and its assigns shall, pay said rent annually on demand, on or after the first day of July in each year, during the term of this lease. That said Boston Water Power Company and its assigns will and shall from time to time, upon request by said Boston & Roxbury Mill Corporation and its assigns, pay them such sum or sums of money as shall be equal to the amount that shall be paid from time to time during the said term by the said Boston & Roxbury Mill Corporation, for the taxes and duties that shall be levied or assessed on the demised premises, or any erections or additions that may be made upon or to the same by the said lessees or their assigns for each year and part of a year during the term aforesaid. And further that the said Boston Water Power Company and its assigns will and shall, at the expiration of said term peaceably yield up all and singular the demised premises to said Boston & Roxbury Mill Corporation or its assigns. And said Boston Water Power Company, for itself and its assigns doth further covenant with said Boston & Roxbury Mill Corporation and its assigns that said Boston Water Power Company and its assigns will and shall, during the term of this lease keep and maintain the said sea-wall and solid structure between said wall and the Milldam and next northerly and adjoining said dam, which has been erected in compliance with the foregoing agreement, in such repair and condition as effectually to prevent the tide water from flowing through the same and undermining the Milldam roads. And provided further, that in case of the neglect or refusal of said Boston Water Power Company, after reasonable notice, to repair any damages which may be consequent upon the insufficiency or bad condition of the sea-wall or

No permanent obstruction to be erected within 20 feet of the dam.

Water Power Co. to pay axes.

To keep sea-wall in order.

solid structure aforesaid, or any wilful neglect or default in the performance of any of the other covenants on the part of said Boston Water Power Company above contained, or any breach of said condition, then, and in either of said cases, said Boston & Roxbury Mill Corporation, by its servants or agents, or its assigns, lawfully may immediately, or at any time thereafter, and whilst such neglect or default continues, without further notice or demand, enter into or upon the demised premises, or any part thereof, in the name of the whole, and repossess the same as of their former estate, and expel the lessors, or those claiming under them, and remove their effects, forcibly if necessary, without being taken or deemed guilty of any manner of trespass, and without prejudice to any remedies which might otherwise be used for arrears of rent or preceding breach of covenant. 1837, July 1.

Duly executed, etc.

EPHRAIM MARSH, FRANCIS C. LOWELL, AND THE BOSTON WATER POWER COMPANY.

AGREEMENT.
Parties.
Boundary lines fixed.
Mutual release of rights and interests.
First parties to have rights of drainage.
Tide-water, except for mill power, to be excluded.

AGREEMENT.[1]

This Indenture, made this twenty-fourth day of March, A. D. eighteen hundred and forty-one, by and between Ephraim Marsh, of the city of Boston, in the Commonwealth of Massachusetts, carpenter, and the several persons whose seals and names are hereto set and subscribed, of the first part, and the Boston Water Power Company, a Corporation established by law in said Commonwealth, of the second part, witnesseth: — Parties. 1841, March 24.

That, for the purpose of adjusting and settling all controversy and questions touching the claims and rights of the respective parties within and about the empty basin, and fixing

[1] Recorded wiih Suffolk deeds, Lib. 467, folio 65.

1841, March 24. the boundary lines thereof, the parties aforesaid do severally and mutually agree that the boundary lines between the lands and flats of the individuals who have become parties to this Indenture, and the said Boston Water Power Company, shall be, and hereby is, settled to be as follows, viz: A straight line, beginning at a cedar post on the Western Avenue, six hundred and fifty feet from Charles Street, and continued by a stone post at the most westerly bound of the land of the city of Boston, upon Pleasant Street, to a stone post on Castle Street, it being the same line called the first line in an agreement between the Boston and Roxbury Mill Corporation and said city of Boston and others, dated the 26th day of December, A. D. eighteen hundred and twenty-six.

Boundary lines fixed.

Mutual release of rights and interests.

And the said individuals of the first part do hereby severally agree with the said party of the second part, in consideration of the several grants, covenants, and agreements of said Boston Water Power Company hereinafter contained, that the said Corporation shall have, hold, and enjoy all the right, title, and interest of every name and nature which the said individuals, or either of them, the proprietors of flats and real estate bounding on said basin, have in and to the land and space within said basin lying westwardly of said boundary line, and do hereby grant, convey, release, and quitclaim the same to the said Boston Water Power Company and their successors and assigns. To have and to hold said lands, space, and flats westward of said boundary line, with the privileges and appurtenances to the same belonging to the said Boston Water Power Company, their successors, and assigns, forever.

And the said party of the second part, in consideration of the premises, does hereby agree with the said individuals, parties of the first part, and each of them, that the said individuals, parties of the first part, respectively, shall have, hold, and enjoy all the right, title, and interest, whether of property or right of flowage, and every other of what name or nature soever which the said Corporation has, or ever had, in and to the lands and flats claimed by said individuals of the first part respectively, eastwardly of said line, and between said line and said individuals' adjacent upland, and does hereby release and quitclaim all said Corporation's right over, upon, and to said lands so lying as aforesaid, eastwardly of said line to the said individuals, with all the privileges and appurtenances thereto belonging, according to their several rights in and to the upland adjacent to said granted premises, to hold the same to them and their heirs and assigns forever. 1841, March 24.

First parties to have rights of drainage.

And the said Boston Water Power Company does hereby covenant, grant, and agree that the said individuals of the first part shall have and enjoy forever, with their heirs and assigns forever, the right to dig for and lay and maintain all convenient and necessary drains from their said lands eastward of said line to the channel or deep water within the said basin according to law, and the common and usual practice for the time being within said city of Boston.

Tide water, except for mill power, to be excluded.

And the said Corporation agrees that they will not voluntarily let the tide-water into said basin higher than may be necessary for the common and ordinary use of the mill power which they have, or may have, to the injury of the parties hereto; provided, however, that no damages shall be claimed of said Corporation by any of said parties, unless the water be thus voluntarily raised to a greater height than three feet above the level of low water in said basin at neap tides. And the parties hereto do mutually covenant and agree, each for themselves respectively, with the others, that they shall and will make such other and further assurances as shall be necessary to carry this agreement into full effect, according to the true intent and meaning thereof.

In testimony whereof, the said Ephraim Marsh and the other persons, subscribers hereto, have hereunto set their respective hands and seals, and the said Boston Water Power Company have caused this Indenture to be executed, by being signed by Lemuel Pope, of said Boston, President of said Corporation, and the Corporate seal of said Company being hereto affixed on the day and year first above written.

Duly executed.[1]

---

[1] Signed by Lemuel Pope, President of the Water Power Company, on 24th March, and by Ephraim Marsh and Francis C. Lowell, on 23d April.

THE COMMONWEALTH AND THE BOSTON WATER-POWER COMPANY.

AGREEMENT.

Parties.

1. Commonwealth relinquishes to Water Power Company all claim to certain lands and flats, excepting avenues, etc. Avenues located.
2. Water Power Company relinquishes to the Commonwealth all claim to certain lands and flats.
3. Third parties release claims; Commonwealth releases channels, etc., to third parties.
4. Water Power Company grants the right of filling up the basin to third parties.
5. Commonwealth not to take more than one third of land for streets. Water Power to be undisturbed.
6. Water Power Company and third parties to fill up and drain according to Commissioners' plans.
7. Water Power Company to build avenue No. 1 and part of No. 2, according to direction of the Commissioners.
8. Water Power Company and third parties to complete avenues within a fixed time.
9. Commonwealth may enforce compliance with plans; and, if parties neglect, at their expense.
10. Water Power Company to keep sluiceways open.
11. Indenture to take effect upon signature; and then owners may become parties at discretion of Commissioners.
12. Improvements requiring coöperation of third parties may, if they neglect, be carried out at their expense.

AGREEMENT.[1]

Parties. 1854, June 9.

This Indenture of three parts, made and concluded this ninth day of June, A. D. 1854, by and between the Commonwealth of Massachusetts, acting by John A. Bolles, Giles H. Whitney, and William H. Swift, the Board of Commissioners of said Commonwealth, appointed under and in pursuance of the Resolves concerning Boston Harbor and the Back Bay, approved May 20, 1852, of the first part, the Boston Water Power Com-

[1] Indenture of June 9, 1854, between the Commonwealth, the Boston Water Power Co., and other parties, recorded with Suffolk Deeds, Liber , folio

pany of the second part, and all such other owners or claimants, individual or corporate, of lands or flats in the Back Bay as shall, by signing this Indenture, become parties hereto, of the third part, witnesseth as follows, to wit: — 1854. June 9.

Commonwealth relinquishes to Water Power Company certain lands and flats; excepting avenues, &c.

ARTICLE 1. That in consideration of the grants, releases, covenants, and agreements in this indenture contained and set forth, the said Commonwealth doth hereby release and forever quitclaim to said Boston Water Power Company, its successors and assigns, subject to the provisions of article third of this indenture, and subject, also, to all the avenues as public highways, and to all the railroads laid down on the plan hereto annexed, so long as the same shall continue, all the right, title, interest, and estate of said Commonwealth in and to all lands, channels, and flats situated in the empty basin, so called, in the Back Bay, lying below the riparian line and easterly of avenue number four, and southerly of a line drawn from avenue numbered four to Providence Street, parallel with avenue numbered two, and one hundred and fifty feet south thereof; and in and to all land, channels, and flats in said basin lying westerly of a line extending at right angles, from the Milldam parallel with avenue numbered six, to avenue numbered five, starting at a point on said dam distant eastwardly thirteen hundred and fifty-seven feet from the junction of the east line of the cross-dam continued with the south line of said Milldam continued, and lying northerly of avenue numbered five, and southerly of the said Milldam, and easterly of the cross-dam, and in and to the land, channels, and flats south of avenue numbered two, north of the Boston and Providence Railroad, and east of avenue numbered one; subject to the rights of way hereinafter described, said several avenues being the same so numbered on the plan hereto annexed: upon which plan are laid down six avenues, numbered one, two, three, four, five, and six, situated and described as follows, viz: —

Avenues located.

Avenue number one begins at the harbor line, on the northerly side of the Milldam, and, crossing the dam at right angles, runs, in the same course, southerly, of the width of eighty feet,

1854, June 9. to the Tremont Road: the point where the easterly line of the said avenue intersects the southerly wall of the dam, being, as measured on said wall, four hundred and ninety-one $\frac{54}{100}$ feet westerly of the western wall of the Public Garden.

Avenue number two begins at the westerly end of Boylston Street, and runs westerly, at right angles with avenue number one, of the width of eighty feet, to tide-mill road or the cross-dam on Gravelly Point: its southerly side being an extension in the course above described of the southerly line of Boylston Street.

Avenue number three begins on avenue number one at a point three thousand two hundred and thirty-eight $\frac{62}{100}$ feet southerly from the south wall of the Milldam, and runs westerly, of the width of eighty feet to the Dike.

Avenue number four, beginning at the harbor line, north of the Milldam, crosses the dam at right angles, and runs southerly, of the width of one hundred and twenty feet, parallel with avenue number one, to the Tremont Road; the point where its easterly line intersects the southerly wall of the dam, being two thousand one hundred and two $\frac{67}{100}$ feet westerly of the west line of avenue number one.

Avenue number five, beginning on the westerly line of said avenue number one, at a point five hundred and ninety-two $\frac{31}{100}$ feet distant southerly from the south wall of the Milldam, runs westerly, of the width of one hundred and twenty feet, parallel with avenue number two and the Milldam, to the cross-dam.

Avenue number six, beginning at the harbor line north of the Milldam, crosses the dam at right angles, its easterly line intersecting the south wall of the dam at a point thirteen hundred and fifty $\frac{84}{100}$ feet westerly of the west line of avenue number four, and runs southerly, of the width of one hundred feet, parallel with avenue number four, to the Tremont Road:—

To have and to hold said released premises unto the said Boston Water Power Company, its successors and assigns, to their own use and behoof forever.

Water Power Company relinquishes to

ARTICLE 2. That in consideration of the release aforesaid, the said Boston Water Power Company hereby releases and forever quitclaims to said Commonwealth and its assigns, all the right, title, interest, and estate of said Company, in and to all land, channels, and flats, in said empty basin lying below said riparian line, and southerly of the Milldam, excepting those lands which are by article first of this indenture released by said Commonwealth to said Company, so far as to allow the Commonwealth and its assigns, and each and every person or corporation who shall become a party to this indenture, and their several and respective heirs, executors, administrators, successors, and assigns, to fill up his or their lands and flats within said Back Bay, in conformity with the plan hereto annexed, and such further plans as said Commissioners, or their successors in office or authority, shall devise, adopt, and prescribe, and in accordance with the provisions of this indenture; and so far as to allow said Commissioners, and their said successors, to execute or cause to be executed, any lake, pond, reservoir, or other public improvement, which they may desire and design in pursuance of said resolves and of this indenture; and also all right, title, and interest in that tract of land bounded north by the Milldam, west by avenue numbered one, east by the Public Garden, and south by the southerly line of avenue numbered two; and also the right through any sluiceway in the dam, or any water-way that may be constructed through the dam or cross-dam under avenues numbered one, four, five and six, and through any sewer or drain constructed as hereinafter provided, to receive and discharge, at any and all times, the water needful for filling or emptying any such sewer or drain, or any of the lakes, ponds, reservoirs, or improvements aforesaid; and also the full and free right of way, in common with every other party hereto and their assigns, over and upon all spaces marked and laid down as avenues on the plan hereto annexed.

Commonwealth certain lands and flats.

1854, June 9.

To have and to hold said released premises to said Commonwealth and its assigns forever.

ARTICLE 3. That, for the considerations aforesaid, the said several persons and corporations, parties hereto of the third part, do hereby severally and respectively release and forever quitclaim to said Water Power Company, its successors and as-

Third parties release claims.

1854, June 9.

signs, one undivided half part of all such portions of land owned by said parties of the third part, respectively, as are situated below said riparian line, and within the limits of release from said Commonwealth to said Company, described in article first of this indenture, and to said Commonwealth and said Company respectively, and their respective successors and assigns, all such portions of land owned by said parties of the third part, respectively, as are situated above said riparian line, and east of avenue numbered four, and west of avenue numbered one, and north of avenue numbered three, and south of the Milldam, and lying within the several and respective lines of release described in articles first and second of this indenture; and also the right of way to said Commonwealth and its assigns, and to every other party hereto and his respective successors and assigns, over all avenues or streets laid down on the plan hereto annexed; for the purposes of this article the line marked red on the said annexed plan, being taken by all parties hereto to be the line of riparian proprietorship.

To have and to hold said released premises to said Commonwealth and its assigns, and to said other releasees and their respective heirs, executors, administrators, successors, and assigns forever.

Commonwealth releases certain channels, &c., to third parties.

And, for the considerations aforesaid, the said Commonwealth doth hereby release and forever quitclaim to the several and respective persons and corporations who may, as riparian owners of land and flats on the westerly side of the empty basin in the Back Bay, become parties hereto, by signing this indenture, all the right, title, interest, and estate of said Commonwealth in and to any and all channels, guzzles, and flats, in said empty basin lying south of avenue numbered five and west of avenue numbered four on said plan hereto annexed, and which would be included within and between the several and respective boundary lines of the said parties legally produced and extended to the avenues aforesaid; and doth also hereby release and forever quitclaim to the several and respective persons and corporations who may, as riparian owners of land or flats on the easterly side of said empty basin, become parties hereto in manner aforesaid, all the right, title, and interest of said Commonwealth in and to all guzzles, flats, and channels in said empty basin, east of avenue numbered one and south of avenue numbered two on said plan, which would be included within and between the several and respective boundary lines of said parties, produced and extended in their legal directions to said avenue numbered one: — 1854, June 9.

To have and to hold said released premises to said several and respective persons and corporations within their several and respective limits, and to their respective heirs, executors, administrators, successors, and assigns, forever.

Water Power Co. grants the right of filling up the basin to third parties.

ARTICLE 4. That, for the considerations aforesaid, the said Boston Water Power Company doth hereby grant, sell and assign to said Commonwealth and its assigns, and to each and every of the other persons and corporations party hereto, their heirs, executors, administrators, successors, and assigns, the right of flowage of said Company in either basin in said Back Bay, so far as to allow each and every one of said other parties, his heirs, executors, administrators, successors, and assigns, as fast as he or they may desire, to fill up his said land and flats in conformity with such plan or plans as said Commissioners, or their successors, may have devised or shall devise and adopt, and in accordance with the provisions of this indenture: *provided, however*, that no person or corporation claiming lands in said empty basin, below the riparian line, under title adverse to the Commonwealth, shall be allowed to fill up his said lands, as herein provided, until such person or corporation shall have become party hereto, or shall have agreed with said Commonwealth and said Company, to execute releases to said Commonwealth and said Company, as described in article third of this indenture, whenever and as soon as the judgment or decree of the Supreme Judicial Court, or the award of Referees chosen for that purpose, shall have determined that such claimant has any such right, title, or interest in said premises which can be released as herein provided. To have and to hold the same to said several and respective persons and corporations, their heirs, executors, administrators, successors, and assigns, forever.

Commonwealth not to take more than one third of land for streets.

1854, June 9.

ARTICLE 5. That, for the considerations aforesaid, the said Commonwealth doth hereby covenant and agree to and with each and every of the other persons and corporations, parties hereto, and their several and respective heirs, executors, administrators, successors, and assigns, that said plans, devised or to be devised, by said Commissioners and their successors, shall not require for streets or other public use more than one third part of the land and flats of either of said parties included within said plans, — reckoning as part of said third all avenues or portions of avenues to be, by said parties of the second and third parts, constructed in accordance with this indenture: and that, in order that the water power be not needlessly injured or diminished, all streets and avenues shall be so laid out and arranged by said Commissioners and their successors upon their said plans, as to allow the flow of water to and from the mills of said Boston Water Power Company and its lessees, under or across said streets and avenues, and over all such spaces in the Back Bay as are not, from time to time, actually filled up, or in process of being filled or set apart for any public improvement, conformably to the provisions of this indenture so far as may be consistent with the system of drainage that may, by said Commissioners or their successors, be established as hereinafter provided, and that the said Commissioners or their said successors will, within ninety days after the approval of this indenture by the Governor and Council, furnish so much of their plan as shall be applicable to that part of the lands of said corporation situated in the empty basin and lying south of the Boston and Providence Railroad, and east of the junction or crossing of said railroad and of the Boston and Worcester Railroad, and the portion of their plan applicable to the remainder of said corporation's lands in said basin within two years after the said approval.

Water power to be undisturbed.

Water Power Co. and third parties to fill up and drain according to Commissioners' plans.

ARTICLE 6. That, for the considerations aforesaid, the said Boston Water Power Company, for itself, its successors and assigns, and the said parties hereto of the third part, for themselves and their respective heirs, executors, administrators, successors, and assigns, do hereby severally and respectively covenant and agree, to and with said Commonwealth and its assigns, that they will, and their several and respective heirs, executors, administrators, successors, and assigns, shall fill up, lay out, and drain their respective lands already made, and all other their lands and flats within the Back Bay, or laid down upon or included within the Commissioners' said plans, conformably to such directions and plans, as to materials and height of filling, mode of drainage, location and arrangements of streets, squares, and other public areas, and as to the location and construction of sluices, culverts, bridges, and other public improvements, as may, under the said resolves and according to the provisions of this indenture, be prescribed by said Commissioners or their successors, and duly made known to said parties. 1854, June 9.

Water Power Co. to build Avenue No. 1 and part of No. 2, according to direction of the Commissioners.

ARTICLE 7. That, for the considerations aforesaid, the said Boston Water Power Company, for itself and its successors and assigns, doth hereby covenant and agree, to and with said Commonwealth and its assigns, that said Company will, and its successors and assigns shall, within such time as said Commissioners or their successors shall, in writing, direct and notify, complete, to the satisfaction of said Commissioners, under their direction, and according to their plan, all that portion of the avenue numbered one on the plan hereto annexed, and the sewers, drains, culverts, and bridges connected therewith, which extends from the line of said Company's land near the Tremont Road to avenue numbered two on said plan, and also the southerly half part of said avenue numbered two, from the end of Boylston Street to said avenue numbered one.

Water Power Co. and third parties to complete avenues, and within a fixed time.

ARTICLE 8. That, for the considerations aforesaid, the said Boston Water Power Company, for itself and its successors and assigns, and the several other persons and Corporations who shall become parties hereto, of the third part, for themselves and their several and respective heirs, executors, administrators, successors, and assigns, do hereby severally covenant and agree, to and with said Commonwealth and its assigns, that they will respectively, within the periods specified in this article, complete to the satisfaction of said Commissioners or their successors, at their own several and respective cost and charge,

1854, June 9.

all such portions of the following avenues, including all sewers and drains, sluices, culverts, and bridges appurtenant to said portions, as are, or may be, laid out wholly upon their several and respective lands and flats, or on or under said cross-dam, namely, avenue numbered two on the plan hereto annexed, within three years from the first day of May, A. D. 1854, avenues numbered three and four on said plan within five years, and avenues five and six on said plan within six years from said date, or within such longer time as said Commissioners or their said successors shall hereafter prescribe, and will and shall in like manner make any alteration of sluices, culverts, and bridges, in size, structure, or position, connected with either of said avenues, as may, in the judgment of said Commissioners, or their said successors, be needful for the flowage described in the fifth article of this indenture; and that they will and shall in like manner, within said several and respective periods, and at their several and respective cost and charge, severally complete one half part of all such portions of the aforesaid avenues, sewers and drains, sluices, culverts, and bridges, as bound or touch upon their said several estates: it being understood that full power is reserved by said Commissioners at any time, to vary either of said avenues within the line of the Commonwealth's land, or, by his consent, within the limits of any other party hereto.

Commonwealth may enforce compliance with plans; and if parties neglect, at their expense.

ARTICLE 9. That, for the considerations aforesaid, it is hereby covenanted and agreed by each and all of said persons and corporations, parties hereto of the second and third parts, for themselves severally and respectively, and their respective heirs, executors, administrators, successors and assigns, to and with said Commonwealth and its assigns, that said Commonwealth by said Commissioners, or by such other agents as may by law be thereto authorized, may, at any and all times hereafter, enforce a compliance with, and a full execution of, the said plans of said Commissioners and their successors, in regard to the filling up of the land and flats aforesaid, and laying out and construction of streets, squares, ponds, sluices, culverts, drains, sewers, bridges and other public improvements, in, upon, and over the lands and flats included in said plans, and for this purpose may enter upon the said lands and flats, and remove therefrom any building or other structure, or obstruction interfering with said plans; and that said Commissioners or their said successors in authority, after due notice to any of said parties who shall, in the judgment of such Commissioners or of their successors aforesaid, unreasonably delay or neglect to keep and perform the covenants and undertakings of this indenture, may proceed, in such manner as they may deem proper, and at the expense of the party so neglecting or delaying, to construct and complete any of the avenues laid out and numbered on the plan hereto annexed, together with any or all sluices, culverts, drains, sewers or bridges, forming parts of said Commissioners' said plans, according to the true intent and meaning of this indenture; and that the lands and flats of each of said parties of the second and third parts hereof within said plans, shall forever remain subject to the covenants of this indenture on the part of such party, his heirs, executors, administrators, successors and assigns, to be kept and performed. 1854, June 9.

Water Power Co. to keep sluiceways open.

ARTICLE 10. That, for the considerations aforesaid, the said Boston Water Power Company, for itself, and its successors and assigns, doth hereby covenant and agree, to and with said Commonwealth and its assigns, that until the whole of the lands and flats in the Back Bay are filled up and laid out as herein provided, or until said Water Power Company shall surrender its mill franchise, said corporation, its successors and assigns, will and shall, subject as now to the control of the board of health of the city of Boston, keep and maintain in good condition, the filling sluices of both basins in said Back Bay, and also the emptying sluices of the empty basin, and so regulate the flow of water into, through, and from said basins, as to prevent any nuisance or inconvenience to the public health or comfort, so far as the same may depend on the said flow of tide waters, and in such manner, also, as to secure, according to the said Commissioners' said plans, and to their satisfaction, an efficient system of sewerage and drainage, so far as the same

1854, June 9.

may depend upon the ebb, flow, and circulation of tides and tide waters.

Indenture to take effect upon signature.

ARTICLE 11. That for the considerations aforesaid, it is hereby mutually agreed by and between the actual parties hereto, that this indenture shall, in all its parts, take immediate and full effect upon each and all of said parties, their heirs, executors, administrators, successors and assigns, so far as the said party or his interests are concerned, upon the execution thereof, and shall not await or remain dependent upon the signing, sealing, acknowledgment, or delivery of said indenture by any other party; and that any person or corporation owning or claiming land in the Back Bay, may, at any time hereafter, at the discretion of said Commissioners or their said successors, but not otherwise, become parties hereto, and receive and enjoy the full benefit of the releases, covenants, and agreements herein contained and set forth, subject to all the duties and obligations herein created and imposed.

Other owners may become parties at discretion of Commissioners.

Improvements requiring co-operation of third parties may, if they neglect, be carried out at their expense.

ARTICLE 12. And for the considerations aforesaid, it is hereby mutually covenanted and agreed, that where any avenue laid out on the plan hereto annexed, or any culvert, sluiceway, sewer, drain or bridge, that may by said Commissioners or their successors, be prescribed as part and portion of said avenues, or any sewer or drain that may, by said Commissioners or their successors, be deemed needful for the system of drainage aforesaid, in pursuance of said resolves, and in conformity with the provisions of this indenture, requires for its completion the co-operation of two or more parties hereto of the second and third parts, because bounding upon or touching their estates; where the same are conterminous, either of said conterminous owners may give notice in writing, to the other or others so bound to co-operate, of his desire and intention to proceed in constructing and completing the same at joint expense and in ratable proportion, and if the party or parties so notified shall refuse or neglect to comply with said notice, the party giving such notice may proceed to construct and complete the whole of such public improvement upon the said conterminous property, and may and shall recover of the delinquent party or parties, his or their full, ratable and distributive share of the cost of such work, with interest upon such share at the rate of ten per cent per annum. 1854, June 9.

Duly executed.[1]

THE COMMONWEALTH AND THE BOSTON AND ROXBURY MILL CORPORATION.

AGREEMENT.

1. Parties: Commonwealth releases to the Boston and Roxbury Mill Corporation certain lands; reserving rights of drainage.
2. Boston and Roxbury Mill Corporation releases to Commonwealth the Milldam; excepting rights of way, toll, and flowage; and agrees to build a sea-wall along the northerly side to Brookline.
3. Boston and Roxbury Mill Corporation to drain certain lands, according to plans of Commissioners; to surrender franchise of toll in certain events; may arrange with any city or town for maintaining the dam, roads, and bridges.
4. Commonwealth may enforce this covenant at expense of the Boston and Roxbury Mill Corporation, if the latter neglect.

AGREEMENT.[2]

Parties. 1854, June 9.

This Indenture of two parts, made and concluded this ninth day of June, A. D. 1854, by and between the Commonwealth of Massachusetts, acting by John A. Bolles, Giles H. Whitney, and William H. Swift, the Board of Commissioners of said Commonwealth, appointed under and in pursuance of the Resolves concerning Boston Harbor and the Back Bay, approved May 20, 1852, of the first part, and the Boston and Roxbury Mill Corporation, a corporation created by the laws of said

---

[1] Signed by John A. Bolles, Giles H. Whitney, and W. H. Swift, Commissioners of the Commonwealth, and by John C. Gray, President of the Boston Water Power Company.

[2] Recorded with Suffolk Deeds, Liber , page

1854, June 9.

Commonwealth, of the second part, witnesseth as follows, viz: —

Commonwealth releases to B. & R. M. Corporation certain lands; reserving rights of drainage.

ARTICLE 1. That in consideration of the covenants and agreements hereinafter contained and set forth, the said Commonwealth doth hereby release and forever quitclaim to said Boston and Roxbury Mill Corporation, its successors and assigns, all the right, title, interest and estate of said Commonwealth, in and to that tract of land, two hundred feet in width, consisting of flats, channels, and land already made by said Corporation, lying next north of the original north wall of the Milldam, and within two hundred feet thereof, situated partly in Boston and partly in Brookline, and extending from ordinary high-water mark on the Boston to shore, ordinary high-water mark on the Brookline shore; saving and reserving to said Commonwealth, and its assigns, the right of drainage from the Back Bay into Charles River, through said released premises and the Milldam, across and under all avenues or streets laid out, or to be laid out, as hereinafter provided, and the right in common with said corporation and its assigns, to pass and repass, toll free, upon and over all avenues or streets laid out, or to be laid out, from north to south across said released premises and said dam, by said Commissioners or their successors, as hereinafter provided.

To have and to hold said released premises to said Boston and Roxbury Mill Corporation, its successors and assigns, forever.

B. & R. M. Corporation releases to Commonwealth the Milldam, excepting right of way, toll, and flowage, and agrees to build a sea-wall along the northerly side to Brookline.

ARTICLE 2. That in consideration of the foregoing release, the said Boston and Roxbury Mill Corporation doth hereby release and forever quitclaim to said Commonwealth and its assigns, all right, title, interest and estate, except the existing rights of way and toll, in and to the land upon and over which said Milldam was originally constructed, to be forever kept open as a public highway, together with all right not heretofore conveyed to the Boston Water Power Company, to flow any of the lands in the Back Bay, southerly of said Milldam; and doth hereby, for itself and its successors and assigns, covenant and agree, to and with said Commonwealth and its assigns, that said corporation will, and its successors and assigns shall, within such period of time as may be prescribed by said Commissioners or their successors in office or authority, in conjunction with the Governor for the time being of said Commonwealth, construct and complete a sea-wall in a manner, of materials, and to a height satisfactory to said Commissioners or their successors aforesaid, extending along the northerly line of said released premises, from the westerly end of the present sea-wall of said corporation, to ordinary high-water mark on said Brookline shore, with suitable sluices for the admission of water into the full basin, so called, in the Back Bay, and from the empty basin, so called, in said Back Bay, and will and shall forever keep said sea-wall from shore to shore and said sluices in good repair, and will and shall fill up with materials and in a manner satisfactory to said Commissioners or their said successors, the whole space inclosed or to be inclosed by said sea-wall, from shore to shore, as aforesaid, to the full height of the Milldam, as fast as may be deemed proper either by the major part of a committee consisting of said Commissioners or their said successors, and a like number of persons elected for that purpose on the part of said corporation, or by said Commissioners or their successors alone, if no such persons shall be so elected by said corporation; and will and shall, whenever requested by said Commissioners, or their said successors, fill up any portion of the space aforesaid, in manner aforesaid, which said Commissioners or their said successors may deem needful to be filled, to prevent leakage through said Milldam. 1854, June 9.

Article 3. That for the consideration last aforesaid, the said Boston and Roxbury Mill Corporation, for itself, its successors and assigns, doth hereby covenant and agree, to and with said Commonwealth and its assigns, that said corporation will, and its successors and assigns shall, lay out and drain all land by said corporation already made west of Otter Street, and all land hereafter by said corporation to be made, west of said street, in conformity with such plan as may by said Commissioners, or their said successors, be devised and prescribed: *provided* such plan, so far as it relates to land now made, shall be furnished within sixty days after the Governor and Council

B. & R. M. Corporation to drain certain lands according to plan of Commissioners.

1854, June 9.

shall have approved of this indenture, and so far as it relates to land hereafter to be made, shall be furnished within sixty days after any portion of said land, not less than one hundred feet in length, shall have been completed to the satisfaction of said Commissioners or their said successors, and shall not require for streets, or other public uses, more than one third part of said lands, including in said third part twenty feet to be added to the width of the highway over said dam; and will and shall, from time to time, remove the toll-house of said corporation, so as to keep the same westward of all dwelling-houses that may hereafter be built east of the junction of said dam with the cross-dam, during the continuance of the toll franchise of said corporation, and shall and will surrender said franchise of toll, together with all said corporation's present rights of way over the Milldam and cross-dam, and over all bridges and roads as said roads are now constructed, connected with, or leading to, either of said dams, whensoever either of the following events shall occur, viz: Whenever avenue number two on the plan hereto annexed, shall be extended and opened as a street for public travel to the cross-dam; or whenever a strip of land, not less than one hundred and fifty feet wide, shall be made and filled to the height of the Milldam, extending from Otter Street, on the north side of said dam, as far west as the point opposite the end of the cross-dam, or extending on the south side of said dam to a point on the Milldam thirteen hundred and fifty-seven feet east of the cross-dam; or at the expiration of ten years from the first day of May, A. D. 1853; it being understood, however, that said corporation has, and shall have liberty at any time, to surrender its toll franchise to said Commonwealth, or to enter into an arrangement, subject to the covenants herein contained, with any city or town within which any parts of the dam, cross-dam, bridges or roads aforesaid are situated, for the maintenance of such parts, and that said corporation shall remain bound, as now, until such arrangement or surrender, to keep said dams, roads and bridges in good repair: *provided, however*, that the toll franchise shall not terminate in consequence of the filling up of said land north of the dam,

To surrender franchise of toll in certain events.

May arrange with any city or town for maintaining the dam, roads, and bridges.

under the direction of said Commissioners, or their said successors, to prevent leakage through said dam, as herein before provided. 1854, June 9.

ARTICLE 4. That for the consideration aforesaid, the said Boston and Roxbury Mill Corporation, for itself, and its successors and assigns, doth hereby covenant and agree, to and with said Commonwealth, that said Commonwealth by said Commissioners, or by such other agents as may by law be thereto authorized, may, at any and all times hereafter, enforce a compliance with and an execution of the terms, conditions and covenants of this indenture in regard to the building of said sea-wall, the filling up and laying out and draining of all lands included within the same, and in regard to all other the premises, and for this purpose may enter upon any portion of the said lands, and remove therefrom any obstruction interfering with said Commissioners' said plans; and that said Commissioners or their said successors, after due notice to said corporation or its successors or assigns who shall, in the judgment of said Commissioners or their said successors, unreasonably delay or neglect to keep and perform said terms, conditions and covenants, may proceed, at the expense of said dilatory or negligent party, to build or repair such sea-wall, sluiceway, sewer, or drain, or to fill up such space and lay out and construct such street, or other public area, as under the covenants of this indenture should be built, laid out or constructed by said corporation, its successors or assigns, and that the said covenants shall run with the land released as aforesaid, until fulfilled, or until released by said Commonwealth.

Commonwealth may enforce this covenant at expense of B. & R. Corp. if the latter neglects.

Duly executed, etc.

THE COMMONWEALTH AND THE BOSTON WATER POWER COMPANY.

AGREEMENT.

Parties.

Preamble relating to agreement of June 28.

1. Commissioners allowed further time to complete plan.
2. Location of Avenue No. 1 changed.
3. Avenues Nos. 1 and 2 to be completed in two years.
4. Water Power Company to fill up and drain all its lands east of the Railroad junction.
5. Commonwealth releases to Water Power Company a certain parcel of land.

AGREEMENT.[1]

Parties. 1854, Sept. 26.

THIS INDENTURE of two parts, made and concluded this 26th day of September, A. D. 1854, by and between the Commonwealth of Massachusetts, acting by John A. Bolles, Giles H. Whitney, and William H. Swift, Commissioners of said Commonwealth, appointed under and in pursuance of the Resolves concerning Boston Harbor and the Back Bay, approved May 20, 1852, of the first part, and the Boston Water Power Company of the second part, witnesseth: —

Preamble relating to agreement of June 28.

That *whereas*, by an indenture of three parts between said Commonwealth, acting by said Commissioners of the first part, said Water Power Company of the second part, and all such other owners or claimants, individual or corporate, of lands or flats in the Back Bay, as should by signing become parties thereto of the third part, approved by the Governor and Council on the 28th day of June, A. D. 1854,[2] and now recorded in the several and respective Registries of Deeds for the Counties of Suffolk, Norfolk, and Middlesex, it was, on the part of said Boston Water Power Company covenanted and agreed to and with said Commonwealth, that said Company, its successors and assigns, would and should, within such time as said Commissioners, or their successors, should in writing direct and notify, complete to the satisfaction of said Commissioners and

---

[1] Recorded with Suffolk Deeds, Liber 719, Folio 26. [2] *Ante*, p. 234.

according to their plan all that portion of a certain avenue 1854, Sept. 26. marked as avenue numbered one on the plan annexed to said indenture of three parts, and also all sewers, drains, culverts, and bridges connected therewith, which extends from Tremont Road to the avenue numbered two on said plan, and also the southerly half part of said avenue numbered two from the end of Boylston Street to the said avenue numbered one;

And *whereas*, said Boston Water Power Company has given bond to said Commonwealth for the faithful performance of said covenant and of all other covenants and agreements in said indenture of three parts contained, on its part to be kept and performed, and has made, executed, acknowledged and delivered to said Commonwealth, a mortgage of all said corporation's real estate, as security for the performance of said covenants and agreements;

And *whereas*, by article eighth of said indenture of three parts, full power is reserved to and by said Commissioners at any time to vary said avenues within the line of the Commonwealth's land, or by his consent within the limits of any other party to said indenture;

And *whereas*, said Boston Water Power Company is desirous that said avenue numbered one shall be so varied and removed westward that its southerly end shall enter Tremont Road opposite Dover Street, and its northerly end intersect avenue numbered two in the manner shown upon the plan hereto annexed, and is willing and has agreed to construct and complete said avenue numbered one, varied and removed as aforesaid, within such time, not less than two years from the date hereof, as said Commissioners shall prescribe, and is also willing and has agreed, upon the consideration hereinafter expressed to construct and complete the whole of said avenue numbered two, westward from the end of Boylston Street, to the westerly side of avenue numbered one, as the same is varied and removed and laid down upon the plan hereto annexed;

And *whereas*, said Commissioners by article fifth of said indenture tripartite, are bound to furnish to said Water Power Company within ninety days after the approval of said indenture

1854, Sept. 26.

by the Governor and Council, so much of said Commissioners' plan for filling up, laying out and draining the Back Bay as may be applicable to the lands and flats of said Company situated in the empty basin and lying south of the Boston and Providence Railroad, and east of the junction of said road with the Boston and Worcester Railroad, which ninety days will expire on the 28th day of September, instant, and it has become desirable to extend said period and allow further time to said Commissioners, and a further period of one month, to wit, until the 28th day of October, A. D. 1854, has been agreed upon for the furnishing said portion of said Commissioners' plan,— it has therefore been covenanted and agreed by and between the said parties hereto, in manner and form set forth and expressed in the various articles following, to wit:—

Commissioners allowed further time to complete plan.

ARTICLE 1. For the considerations aforesaid, it is hereby covenanted and agreed by said Boston Water Power Company, to and with said Commonwealth, that said Commissioners, or their successors, may at any time within four months from the 28th day of June, 1854, furnish said corporation with that portion of said Commissioner's plan of filling up, laying out and draining the lands and flats of said corporation, which relates or applies to lands and flats lying south of said Boston and Providence Railroad, and east of the junction or crossing of the railroads aforesaid in said empty basin.

Location of Avenue No. 1 changed.

ARTICLE 2. For the considerations aforesaid, it is hereby covenanted and agreed by said Boston Water Power Company, to and with said Commonwealth, that avenue numbered one upon the plan annexed to the aforesaid indenture tripartite, may (without prejudice to any of the covenants and agreements in said indenture contained, or to the bond and mortgage herein before referred to) be so varied and altered by said Commissioners as to run from the Tremont Road towards the Milldam in the manner indicated by the plan hereto annexed.

Avenues 1 and 2 to be completed in two years.

ARTICLE 3. For the considerations aforesaid, it is hereby covenanted and agreed by said Water Power Company, its successors and assigns, to and with said Commonwealth and its assigns, that said Company, its successors and assigns, will and shall, within such time, not less than two years from the date hereof, as said Commissioners, or their successors, shall prescribe and require, construct and complete to the satisfaction of said Commissioners, all that portion of avenue numbered one on the plan hereto annexed which extends from Tremont Road to avenue numbered two on the annexed plan, and also the whole of that part of avenue numbered two on said plan annexed which extends from the end of Boylston Street, to the westerly side of said avenue numbered one on said annexed plan, so that each of said avenues shall be of the full width of eighty feet at the top thereof, and of such height and grade and with such sewers, drains, bridges and culverts, as may by said Commissioners, or their successors, be deemed needful; all of said work and materials to be to the satisfaction and acceptance of said Commissioners or their successors. 1854, Sept. 26.

Article 4. For the considerations aforesaid, it is hereby covenanted and agreed by said Boston Water Power Company, its successors and assigns, to and with said Commonwealth and its assigns, that said corporation, its successors and assigns will and shall fill up, lay out and drain all the lands and flats of said corporation east of said railroad junction according to such plan as the said Commissioners may furnish within said period of four months in conformity with said indenture tripartite and with these presents, including all such sewers, drains, bridges and culverts, as said Commissioners may deem needful and convenient.

Water Power Company to fill up and drain all its lands east of the R. R. junction.

Article 5. For the considerations aforesaid, it is hereby covenanted and agreed by said Commonwealth to and with said Boston Water Power Company, its successors and assigns, that upon the completion of the afore-described portions of avenues numbered one and two on the plan annexed, within the time that may by said Commissioners be prescribed as aforesaid, and to the satisfaction of said Commissioners or their successors, the said Commonwealth will release and convey to said corporation, its successors and assigns, all the right, title and

Commonwealth releases to Water Power Company a certain parcel of land.

1854, Sept. 26. interest now owned by said Commonwealth, in and to that parcel of lands and flats one hundred and fifty feet in width and about three hundred and forty feet in length, which lies south of and adjoining to avenue numbered two, and east of and adjoining to avenue numbered one on the plan annexed hereto, subject to the conditions, covenants, and agreements of said bond, mortgage, and indenture tripartite.

Duly executed.

THE COMMONWEALTH AND THE BOSTON WATER POWER COMPANY.

AGREEMENT.

Parties.

Preamble relating to previous agreements.

1. Streets to be filled to a certain height.
2. Parties to build streets at option; except that they must complete theirs when the Commonwealth completes its portion.
3. Commonwealth releases certain mortgaged property.
4. Water Power Company assents to use its streets for drainage on the same terms as are made by the Commonwealth.

AGREEMENT.[1]

Parties. 1856, July 11. THIS INDENTURE of two parts, made and concluded this 11th day of July, A. D. 1856, by and between the Commonwealth of Massachusetts, acting by its committee appointed under and in pursuance of the "Resolves in relation to lands in the Back Bay," approved May 30, A. D. 1856, of the first part, and the Boston Water Power Company, a corporation established by the laws of the Commonwealth, of the second part, witnesseth: —

---

[1] Recorded with Suffolk Deeds, Liber 719, p. 28.

Whereas, a certain indenture of three parts by and between the said Commonwealth, by its Commissioners, and the Boston Water Power Company and all such other owners and claimants, individual or corporate, of lands or flats in the Back Bay, as should, by signing, become parties thereto, was made on the 9th day of June, A. D. 1854, and was the same day executed by the Commonwealth, by its said Commissioners, and by the Boston Water Power Company, and has never been signed or executed by any other persons or corporations; [1] and *whereas*, a certain other indenture by and between the Commonwealth, by its said Commissioners, and the Boston Water Power Company, was made and executed on the 26th day of September, A. D. 1854; [2] and *whereas*, a certain mortgage was made and executed by the said Boston Water Power Company to the Commonwealth, on the said June 9, A. D. 1854, and is recorded in Suffolk Registry, book 665, page 151; and, *whereas*, by the Resolves first above mentioned, approved on the said May 30, A. D. 1856, the Committee therein mentioned are empowered, among other things, to "alter, reform, or amend all contracts, whether by deed or otherwise, heretofore made by the Commissioners on the Back Bay, subject to the approval of the Governor and Council, all parties to the same agreeing thereto."

Preamble relating to previous agreements.

1856, July 11.

And *whereas*, the said Committee, in behalf of the Commonwealth, and the said Boston Water Power Company, the only parties to said indentures above mentioned, after mutual consultation and conference, have agreed upon certain alterations and modifications of the contracts heretofore made by and between the Commonwealth and the said Boston Water Power Company.

Now, therefore, in consideration of the premises, and of one dollar paid by each to the other, it is hereby agreed to alter, reform, and amend all contracts heretofore made, whether by deed or otherwise, by and between the Commonwealth, and the said Boston Water Power Company, in the following respects, that is to say,

---

[1] *Ante*, p. 234. [2] *Ante*, p. 250.

Streets to be filled to a certain height.

1856, July 11.

First. The Commonwealth and the Boston Water Power Company and other persons or corporations, who may become parties to the indenture of June 9, A. D. 1854, shall fill the streets or avenues enumerated in said indenture of June 9, A. D. 1854, or laid out on the plan accompanying the Third Annual Report of the State Commissioners, dated February 16, A. D. 1855, or upon any plan that may be hereafter adopted by the State Commissioners, in accordance with the indenture, to the level of the Milldam as the same now is, and as much higher, not exceeding three feet (excepting where necessary to cross the railroad), as the State Commissioners, subject to the approval of the Governor and Council, may order: and the State Commissioners, with the President of the Water Power Company for the time being, subject to the approval of the Governor and Council, may order and determine that any street or avenue may be made at a less grade, if they deem such course to be expedient, and the remainder of the territory, not included in the streets, shall be filled to a point within five feet of the level of the Milldam.

Parties to build streets at option; except that they must complete them when the Commonwealth completes its portion.

Second. Neither the Commonwealth nor the Boston Water Power Company, nor any other person or corporation who may become a party to said indenture of June 9, shall be obliged to complete the avenues enumerated in said indenture, or laid out on the plan accompanying the Third Annual Report of the State Commissioners, dated February sixteenth, eighteen hundred and fifty-five, or upon any plan that may be hereafter adopted by the State Commissioners, in accordance with the indenture, until they may severally and respectively deem it expedient so to do; but the Water Power Company and any other person or corporation shall be held to complete any such avenue, in the manner agreed upon, and upon their own land, as soon as the Commonwealth or their assigns shall complete the same upon the territory released to it by said indenture, to the end that such avenue may be opened its entire length at the same time; and the State Commissioners shall notify the other parties when they desire such avenues to be completed. But in no case shall the parties be required to complete the same before the times mentioned in said indentures.

Third. The Commonwealth shall release from the mortgage given by the Boston Water Power Company on the said 9th of June, eighteen hundred and fifty-four, all the territory included in said mortgage, except that part of the same, bounded northerly by land of the Commonwealth, easterly by avenue number one, southerly by avenue G, easterly by avenue B, southerly by avenue numbered three, and westerly by avenue numbered four, containing by estimation two million feet; and the State Treasurer, with the consent of the Commissioners or any persons exercising their powers, and of the Governor and Council, may from time to time release portions of the territory last above mentioned, whenever they may deem it expedient so to do, and upon such terms and conditions as they may approve. And in consideration of the premises and of one dollar to it paid, the Commonwealth doth hereby remise, release, and forever quitclaim to the said Boston Water Power Company all the land and territory included in the said mortgage and not included in the boundaries above mentioned. To have and to hold the same to the said Company, its successors and assigns, forever.

Commonwealth releases certain mortgaged property. 1856, July 11.

Fourth. *Whereas*, the Committee propose to make certain arrangements with the cities of Boston and Roxbury in reference to drainage, the Boston Water Power Company consents and agrees that said cities may use the streets of said Company for such purpose, when graded and opened, upon the same terms and conditions which the Committee may impose upon said cities during the present year relative to the use of the same streets on the territory of the Commonwealth, and also of the avenue numbered two; and if, in making such arrangements, any question shall arise as to the terms to be imposed for a right of drainage by the city of Roxbury through K Street, the same shall be determined by three referees to be appointed, one by the Committee, one by the Boston Water Power Company, and one by the city of Roxbury.

Water Power Company assent to use of its streets for drainage on the same terms as are made by the Commonwe'lth.

Duly executed.

THE COMMONWEALTH OF MASSACHUSETTS, THE BOSTON WATER POWER COMPANY, AND THE CITY OF BOSTON.

AGREEMENT.

Parties.

Preamble relating to previous Indentures; Sewers agreed upon; described; city of Boston may lay other sewers and assess expense; the sewers here provided for to be in lieu of rights of drainage under Indentures with Tuckerman, &c.; restrictions against digging earth from the flats to be removed; Commonwealth and city jointly to build an eighty-foot street from Beacon Street to Boylston Street; city may enter certain sewers into these; and may build a sewer from Boylston or Providence Street to the main sewer; Commonwealth to convey lands to Water Power Company, notwithstanding conditions of Indenture of September 26, 1854.

1. Commonwealth to build a portion, described, of the main sewer.
2. Commonwealth grants to Water Power Company, the right to enter said sewer. Proviso.
3. Commonwealth to release to Water Power Company certain lands on completion of avenues one and two.
4. City may lay sewers in all the streets on the Commonwealth land and assess expense; and to build a sewer from Boylston or Providence Street to main sewer.
5. Commonwealth grants a certain piece of land to the city.
6. Commonwealth appropriates and agrees to fill up for an eighty-foot street, a strip of land adjoining.
7. Water Power Company agrees to build the sewer from Camden Street to the main sewer.
8. Water Power Company grants to the city the right to lay sewers in its streets, and assess expense.
9. City of Boston agrees to build a portion of the main sewer and to extend and keep the street in which it is to be built.
10. City grants to Water Power Company the right to enter said portion of the main sewer.
11. City releases rights to dig and lay drains in the Receiving Basin.
12. City releases restrictions, by previous Indentures, on certain lands, and grants the Commonwealth the right to build west of the land released to the city; and the city agrees to fill up its half of the eighty-foot street and to lay out said street.

AGREEMENT.[1]

THIS INDENTURE, of three parts, made and concluded this eleventh day of December, in the year of our Lord one thousand eight hundred and fifty-six, by and between the Commonwealth of Massachusetts, acting by its Committee appointed under and in pursuance of the resolves in relation to lands in the Back Bay, approved May 30, A. D. 1856, of the first part; the Boston Water Power Company, a corporation established by the laws of said Commonwealth, of the second part; and the city of Boston, acting by its Committee duly authorized, of the third part, witnesseth: — Parties. 1856, Dec. 11.

Whereas, the said Commonwealth, by Commissioners duly authorized, did enter into an indenture with the Boston and Roxbury Mill Corporation, which indenture is dated June 9, A. D. 1854, and recorded in Suffolk Registry of Deeds, Lib. 665, Fol. 149;[2] also into an Indenture with the Boston Water Power Company, dated on said June 9, A. D. 1854, and recorded with Suffolk Deeds, Lib. 665, Fol. 145[2]; and also into another indenture with said Water Power Company, dated September 26, A. D. 1854,[2] and recorded in Suffolk Registry of Deeds, which several indentures were duly approved by the Governor and Council. Preamble relating to previous indentures.

And *whereas*, by said indentures, provision is made for filling up the lands in the receiving basin of the Boston Water Power Company, belonging to said Company and to said Commonwealth, situated partly within the limits of the city of Boston, and partly within the limits of the city of Roxbury; and for laying out avenues, streets, and other public improvements mentioned in said indentures, conformably to the directions and

---

[1] This is what is known as the "Tripartite Indenture," under which the filling of the Back Bay was practically first begun. Recorded with Suffolk Deeds, Liber 719, page 30.

For an Indenture between the same parties, greatly modifying this, see *post*, p. 288.

[2] *Ante*, pp. 234, 245, 250.

1856, Dec. 11. plans therein contained, as to material and height of filling, mode of drainage, location, and arrangement of squares, streets, and other public areas, said Commissioners not to require for streets and other public uses more than one third part of the lands of flat of the parties thereto respectively; also, for the location and construction of sluices, culverts, bridges, and other public improvements, to be made under the resolves referred to in said Indentures, and as may be prescribed by said Commissioners on the Back Bay, or their successors, for a more full understanding of which provisions, reference is hereby had to said Indentures.

And *whereas*, by an Indenture, by and between the Commonwealth and said Water Power Company, dated July 11, A. D. 1856,[1] it is provided that all the streets and avenues enumerated in said Indenture of June 9, 1854, or laid out on the plan accompanying the Third Annual Report of the State Commissioners, dated February 16, 1855, or upon any plan that may be hereafter adopted by the State Commissioners, in accordance with the Indenture, are to be filled to the level of the Milldam, as the same now is, and as much higher, not exceeding three feet, (excepting where necessary to cross the railroad,) as the State Commissioners, subject to the approval of the Governor and Council, may order; "and the remainder of the territory, not included in the streets, shall be filled to a point within five feet of the level of the Milldam;" which last Indenture is hereby referred to for a more particular understanding of the provisions thereof, being recorded herewith.

And *whereas*, it is important for the interests of all parties hereto, that the system of draining the land in the Back Bay, and that part of the territory of the city of Boston contiguous thereto, and also a part of the city of Roxbury, should be the best that can be devised; and whereas, it has been agreed, by and between the parties hereto, that the following described main sewers shall be built in said Back Bay, to wit: one

Sewers agreed upon.

---

[1] *Ante*, p. 254.

large main sewer, beginning at Tremont Street in the city of Boston, and passing through the first street east of avenue numbered four on the said plan of the Back Bay lands, accompanying said Commissioners' Third Annual Report (which street is to be extended by the city of Boston to Tremont Street), to the first street south of the Milldam; thence through said last mentioned street to a point opposite to the most easterly discharging sluice of the receiving basin; thence to said sluiceway, and opening into Charles River through the same. Also, another main common sewer, from Camden Street to the aforesaid main sewer. The location of which main sewers, so far as the same is determined, is indicated on a copy of said plan of the State Commissioners, recorded with Suffolk Deeds, at the end of Lib. 709, to which reference is hereby made for the purpose of indicating said sewers, and the location of a street eighty feet wide hereinafter referred to, and for no other purpose. Said sewers to be not less than three feet in diameter, at Tremont and Camden streets, and not less than nine feet at said sluice. Said sewers to be built of such materials and at such grades as may be hereafter agreed upon by the Board of Aldermen of said city of Boston and the State Commissioners on the Back Bay, or whoever may represent them; and to be constructed as fast as the Board of Health of the city of Boston may deem necessary to prevent nuisances being created by the drains which may open into the basin; said two main sewers to be for the use and benefit of all the parties hereto, and to be built as hereinafter provided.

1856, Dec. 11.

Described.

City of Boston may lay other sewers and assess expense.

And *whereas*, it may be necessary for the authorities of the city of Boston to lay and maintain other sewers through some or all the streets and passageways laid out or to be laid out, within the limits of the city of Boston, by the Commissioners on the Back Bay; and whereas, it is herein provided that said city may use such streets or passageways for the purpose of such drains, and assess a just and equitable portion of the expense thereof upon the lots in said Back Bay which shall be benefited thereby, according to the rules established for the city sewers and the laws of the Commonwealth relating thereto at

1856, Dec. 11.

the time such drains shall be built, the amount of such assessments to be paid by the owners of such lots when the same shall be filled up as aforesaid and require drains, and in no case before; said sewers to be built in the passageways, in the rear of the lots, in preference to the streets, when the Board of Aldermen of said city shall think it expedient to do so, in conformity with the system of sewerage which may be adopted by the Commissioners on the Back Bay. Said sewers which may be so built by the city through any of said streets or passageways, and assessed upon the lots benefited thereby, shall supersede and be in lieu of the sewers which are mentioned in the Indentures between the Commonwealth and the said Water Power Company, for the same territory; but not for any other sewers that said Commissioners may deem necessary for draining any other portion of the land in the Back Bay, as provided by said Indentures. It being understood that said Water Power Company, and said Commonwealth, and their respective assigns, shall in no case be assessed or required to share the expense of more than one set of sewers or drains, for the drainage of the same territory.

The sewers here provided for to be in lieu of rights under indentures with Tuckerman and the Boston and Roxbury Mill Corporation.

And the sewers herein provided for are to be substituted, and in lieu of the rights of building and maintaining drains in said basin under the Indenture between Edward Tuckerman and others and the city of Boston of the one part, and the Boston and Roxbury Mill Corporation of the other part, dated December 26, A. D. 1826, recorded with Suffolk County Deeds, Lib. 315, Fol. 278,[1] and the Indenture between said city and said Mill Corporation, dated February 1, A. D. 1827, recorded with Suffolk Deeds, Lib. 315, Fol. 284,[2] and of any other rights which the city may have to lay and maintain drains in said basin, by virtue of any agreement or contract heretofore made.

Restrictions against digging earth from the flats removed.

And *whereas*, a portion of the land in said basin, now of the Commonwealth, formerly belonging to the Boston Water Power Company, was restricted by said Indentures of December

---

[1] *Ante*, p. 209. [2] *Ante*, p. 214.

26, 1826, and February 1, 1827, and the right of digging mud and earth from the vacant flats in a part of said basin was granted to said city of Boston under the restrictions contained therein; and it is agreed that said restrictions shall now be abolished, and a portion of the land so restricted be conveyed by the Commonwealth to said city, and that said city shall release to the Commonwealth said restrictions on the residue of said land, and also all rights that it may have to dig and convey away mud or earth from the lands and flats in said basin.

1856, Dec. 11.

And whereas, it is agreed that the Commonwealth and said city shall lay out and build a street eighty feet wide, from Beacon Street to Boylston Street, as indicated on the plan hereinbefore referred to, taking a strip of land forty feet wide from the land to be released to the city, and a strip forty feet wide from the remaining land of the Commonwealth; said street to be filled up, one half by the Commonwealth, and the other half by the city, as high as the level of the Milldam, and as much higher as the Board of Aldermen of said city, and the Commissioners on the Back Bay, or their successors, may deem expedient; and the residue of said restricted land to be filled up to the level specified in said Indenture dated July 11, A. D. 1856.

Commonwealth and city to jointly build an 80-foot street from Beacon Street to Boylston St.

And whereas, it is agreed by and between the parties hereto, that said city, at its own expense, may enter the sewers and drains which now are, or may hereafter be, laid within that part of said city lying northerly and westerly of the westerly side of Washington Street, from Roxbury line to Common Street, and westerly of Common and Tremont streets to Park Street, and westerly and southerly of Park and Beacon streets, into the above-mentioned common or main sewers.

City may enter certain sewers into these.

And whereas, it is agreed, by and between the parties hereto, that said city of Boston may extend to said main sewer a drain, either from Boylston Street or from Providence Street, through the lands belonging to the Commonwealth or the said Water Power Company, situated in the city of Roxbury, said drain to be built either in the avenue numbered two on the Commis-

City may build a sewer from Boylston or Providence St. to the main sewer.

1856, Dec. 11.

sioners' plan, or in the passageway in the rear of the lots on the southerly side of said avenue, and a just and equitable portion of the expense of such drain to be assessed upon the lots using the same, and the assessments to be collected in the manner heretofore provided for drains within the city of Boston.

And whereas, by said Indenture dated September 26, A. D. 1854, it was covenanted and agreed by said Commonwealth to and with said Water Power Company, its successors and assigns, that upon the completion of certain portions of avenues numbered one and two, as therein described, within the time that may, by the Commissioners on the Back Bay, be prescribed, and to the satisfaction of said Commissioners or their successors, the said Commonwealth will release and convey to said Corporation, its successors and assigns, all the right, title, and interest now owned by said Commonwealth in and to the parcel of land and flats, one hundred and fifty feet in width, and about three hundred and forty feet in length, which lies south of and adjoining to avenue numbered two, and east of and adjoining avenue numbered one, subject to the conditions therein expressed.

And whereas, by said agreement dated the 11th day of July, A. D. 1856, the time for building and completing said parts of said avenues, numbered one and two, have been extended beyond the time prescribed by said Commissioners for the completion of the same. And whereas, it is agreed that the Commonwealth shall convey to said Water Power Company the parcel of lands and flats above described, when the said portions of said avenues shall be completed, according to the provisions of said Indenture dated July 11, A. D. 1856, notwithstanding the provisions and conditions contained in said Indenture of September 26, 1854.

Commonwealth to convey lands to Water Power Company, notwithstanding conditions of indenture of Sept. 26, 1854.

ARTICLE 1. Now be it known, that the Commonwealth of Massachusetts, acting by its Committee as aforesaid, in consideration of the premises, and of the grants, releases, covenants, and agreements herein contained and set forth, doth hereby covenant and agree to and with the said city of Boston, and said Water Power Company, and their respective assigns, that said Commonwealth or its assigns shall and will build within a time, and of materials to be determined as hereinbefore set forth, all that part of the first-described main sewer extending from said Milldam to a point on said street first east from Avenue IV, twelve hundred feet southeasterly from the dividing line between the land of said Commonwealth and the land of said Water Power Company, and maintain, or cause to be maintained, that part thereof situated within the present limits of the city of Roxbury, until the same shall be included within the jurisdiction of said city of Boston. And said Commonwealth hereby covenants and agrees, for itself and its assigns, to and with the said city of Boston, that it and they will build the portion of said main sewer which said Commonwealth has herein covenanted to build, before it or they shall make use of any of the aforesaid premises in such way or manner as shall deprive the said city of Boston of the use of any of said city's drains or rights of drainage, as they now exist. Commonwealth to build a portion, described, of the main sewer.

ARTICLE 2. And for the considerations aforesaid, the said Commonwealth doth hereby give and grant unto the said Boston Water power Company and its assigns, free of all charge, the right to enter into said main sewer, to be built as aforesaid by said Commonwealth, the common sewer which is to be built by said Company, as hereinafter provided, in continuation of said main sewer; also, all other sewers and drains which may be required by the Commissioners on the Back Bay, to be built by said Company under the provisions of the Indenture heretofore referred to. Also, the right to permit drains to enter said sewer, to be built by said Company, to drain that part of the city of Roxbury situated between Washington Street and the Providence Railroad, and easterly of Water Street (but no other part of said city of Roxbury), upon such terms and conditions as the said Company may deem expedient. Provided, however, that no sewer or drain shall be allowed to enter into or use said main sewer, to drain any lands southerly of Camden Street, until the water from the brook that enters said territory in Roxbury, shall be carried into Stony Brook on the South Commonwealth grants to Water Power Comp'y the right to enter said sewer. Proviso.

Bay, or otherwise diverted so that it shall not enter said sewer; and provided, also, that the flow of the tide water shall be so far excluded from said territory southerly of Camden Street, as will prevent it from entering into said main sewer.

Commonwealth to release to W. P. Company certain lands on completion of Avenues 1 & 2.

ARTICLE 3. For the considerations aforesaid, the said Commonwealth hereby covenants and agrees to and with said Water Power Company, that upon the completion by the said Water Power Company of the said portions of said avenues numbered one and two, as provided in said Indenture of July 11, A. D. 1856, and to the satisfaction of the Commissioners on the Back Bay, or their successors, the said Commonwealth will release and convey to said Corporation, its successors and assigns, all the right, title, and interest now owned by the Commonwealth, in and to the parcel of land described in the fifth article of said Indenture of September 26, A. D. 1854.

City may lay sewers on all the streets on the Commonwealth's land, and assess expense; and to build a sewer from Boylston or Providence Street to the main sewer.

ARTICLE 4. And for the considerations aforesaid, the said Commonwealth hereby covenants and agrees to and with said city of Boston, that the city authorities shall have the right to lay and maintain sewers in all the streets and passageways which have been or shall be laid out over the land of said Commonwealth in the Back Bay about to be filled up, so far as the same at the time being shall be within the limits of said city, and may assess the expense of the same upon the lots benefited thereby, according to the rules established for the city sewers, and the laws of the Commonwealth relating thereto, at the time such sewers shall be built; the amount of such assessment to be paid by the owner of such lots, when the same shall be filled up as aforesaid and require drains, and in no case before. Provided, however, that said land of the Commonwealth shall in no case be assessed for the expense of more than one set of sewers and drains, for the drainage thereof. Said sewers to be built in the passageways in preference to the streets, as hereinbefore set forth. And said Commonwealth further grants to said city of Boston the right to enter into said main sewers to be built by the Commonwealth, all the sewers and drains which may be built by said city for the drainage of the land in the said basin, and the land contiguous thereto, but within the limits of said

Washington, Common, Tremont, Park, and Beacon streets, as hereinbefore set forth; also, the right to build the sewer from Providence or Boylston Street through the territory of the Commonwealth lying within the city of Roxbury, upon the terms and conditions hereinbefore set forth, and to enter the same into said main sewer.

Commonwealth grants a certain piece of land to the city.[1]

ARTICLE 5. And for the considerations aforesaid, the said Commonwealth doth hereby grant, remise, release, and convey to the said city of Boston, the piece of land hereinbefore referred to, bounded as follows, viz: Beginning on the southerly side of the Milldam or Beacon Street, at a point six hundred and thirty-six feet easterly from the easterly side of avenue numbered one, in the Back Bay, as now established by said Commissioners' plan; thence running southerly by a line parallel with said avenue "One," thirteen hundred and five feet, more or less, to Boylston Street, or avenue numbered two on said plan: thence by the northerly line of said avenue numbered two, to land belonging to said city of Boston; thence bounded easterly by land belonging to said city, called the "Public Garden," to Beacon Street; thence bounded northerly by said Beacon Street to the point of beginning.

To have and to hold the same to the said city of Boston, its successors and assigns forever, free from all restrictions or conditions, excepting as herein provided.

The Commonwealth appropriates and agrees to fill up, for an 80-foot street, a strip of land adjoining.

ARTICLE 6. And for the considerations aforesaid, the said Commonwealth further covenants and agrees to and with said city of Boston, that it will appropriate for the street eighty feet wide hereinbefore mentioned, a strip of land forty feet wide adjoining and westerly of the westerly line of the foregoing granted premises, in connection with a similar strip of land to be appropriated by the city on the easterly side of said line, which two pieces are to remain open for a public street or highway forever: and said Commonwealth covenants and agrees to fill up and build its half of said street, as hereinbefore set forth.

---

[1] A "heater-piece" between the Public Garden as then laid out, and the eighty foot Street provided, now known as Arlington Street.

Water Power Company agree to bring the sewer from Camden Street to the main sewer.

ARTICLE 7. And the said Boston Water Power Company, in consideration of the grants, covenants, and agreements in this Indenture contained and set forth, doth hereby covenant and agree, to and with said Commonwealth and said city of Boston, that said Company or its assigns shall and will build or cause to be built, within the time and in the manner to be determined as hereinbefore recited, all that common sewer hereinbefore described, extending from Camden Street to said main sewer, in such street through the land of said Company, as the said Commissioners on the Back Bay may locate the same. And said Company hereby covenants and agrees, for itself and its assigns, to and with the said city of Boston, that it and they will build the portion of said main sewer which said Company has herein covenanted to build, before it or they shall make use of any of the aforesaid premises in such way or manner as shall deprive the said city of Boston of the use of any of said city's drains or rights of drainage, as they now exist.

Water Power Company grants to the city the right to lay sewers in its streets and assess expenses.

ARTICLE 8. And for the considerations aforesaid, the said Water Power Company doth hereby grant and convey to said city of Boston the right to lay any sewers the city authorities may deem necessary, other than those which may be prescribed by said Commissioners on the Back Bay, through any of the streets or passageways (the latter to be preferred) in the limits of said Company's land, and enter the same into said main sewer extending from Camden Street, as aforesaid; and further the right to assess the expense thereof upon the land of said Company or its assigns benefited thereby, in the manner hereinbefore set forth. Provided, however, that such assessment shall not be collected by said city until such land is actually filled up as aforesaid and requires such sewers; and provided also that said Company and its assigns shall in no case be called upon to share the expense of building more than one set of sewers and drains within or for any portion of said Company's territory. Said sewers of said city to be only for the drainage of the portion of said city hereinbefore described, and lying within said Washington, Common, Tremont, Park, and Beacon streets.

ARTICLE 9. And in consideration of the grants, releases, covenants, and agreements in this Indenture contained, the said city of Boston hereby covenants and agrees to and with the Commonwealth and said Water Power Company, that the said city of Boston, or its assigns, shall and will, at its or their own sole expense, and without any assessment or claim upon other persons or corporations, build within the time and in the manner hereinbefore recited, all that part of the first-described main sewer which extends southerly through said street, the first easterly of avenue numbered "Four," from said point, twelve hundred feet southeasterly from the division line between the land of the Commonwealth and the land of said Water Power Company, to Tremont Street, and that said city will lay out and extend said street, of the width of sixty feet, from the land of said Water Power Company to said Tremont Street, as a public street or highway, and keep the same open forever.

City of Boston agrees to build a portion of the main sewer, and to extend and keep open the street in which it is to be built.

ARTICLE 10. And for the considerations aforesaid, the said city of Boston doth hereby grant to the said Water Power Company and its assigns, the right to enter their sewers and drains, free from all charge for so doing, into said portion of said main sewer to be built by said city, including any drainage of the portion of the city of Roxbury contemplated to be carried through said main sewer extending from Camden Street, but within the limits and in the manner hereinbefore set forth. And the said city of Boston further covenants and agrees that the said Commonwealth and the said Water Power Company, and their respective assigns, may enter sewers and drains into all other sewers which may be built by said city within said basin, upon the payment by them respectively of their proportional part of the expense of building the same, to be assessed in the manner and at the times hereinbefore set forth. And said city hereby covenants and agrees to and with said Commonwealth and said Water Power Company and their respective assigns, that the authorities of said city shall not collect such assessments until the land through which the sewers are built is actually filled up and requires drains, as hereinbefore recited.

City grants to Water Power Company the right to enter said portion of the main sewer.

City releases rights to dig and lay drains in the receiving basin.

ARTICLE 11. And for the considerations aforesaid, the said city of Boston doth hereby release, remise, and forever quit-claim, to the said Commonwealth and said Water Power Company and their successors and assigns, all the rights that said city has to dig, lay, and maintain drains in said receiving basin of said Company, and all right to dig and carry mud and earth from the vacant flats in said basin, as the same are given in said Indentures, dated December 26, A. D. 1826, and February 1, A. D. 1827.

City releases restrictions on lands by specified indentures; and grants the Commonwealth the right to build west of the land released to the city; and the city agrees to fill up its half of the 80-foot street, and to lay out said street.

ARTICLE 12. And for the considerations aforesaid the said city of Boston doth hereby release all the land and flats restricted by said Indentures of December 26, 1826, and February 1, 1827, from the restrictions contained therein, in regard to the erection of buildings, and doth hereby agree that the said Commonwealth and its assigns may erect buildings on any and all the lands belonging to said Commonwealth, lying westerly of the land hereinbefore released and conveyed by the Commonwealth to said city. And said city doth hereby covenant that it will warrant and defend so much of said Commonwealth's land as lies between said land so released to said city, and the old channel west of Charles Street, to said Commonwealth and its assigns, against the lawful claims and demands of said city, and of all persons claiming by, through or under said city, but against none other. And for the considerations aforesaid, the said city doth hereby agree to lay out, in conjunction with said Commonwealth, the said street of eighty feet in width, from Beacon to Boylston Street, and to fill up its half thereof, and the residue of said land herein released to said city to the level and in the manner hereinbefore set forth.

Duly executed.[1]

---

[1] This Indenture was signed, on behalf of the Commonwealth, by the Commissioners on the Back Bay, viz: John H. Shaw, John Batchelder, George M. Thatcher, Horatio G. K. Calef, Elijah B. Stoddard, Jonathan E. Morrill, Charles Hale, Stephen P. Fuller, E. C. Purdy, and Thomas B. Hall, (the approval of the Governor's Council being certified by the Secretary of the Commonwealth); by Thomas G. Carey, President of the Boston Water Power

THE COMMONWEALTH AND THE BOSTON WATER POWER COMPANY.

AGREEMENT.

Preamble, relating to the eighty-foot Street next the Public Garden, and avenue "five"; the latter to be widened; and to be divided up into roadway and walks, with trees, &c., houses to set back twenty feet; Water Power Company to fill up portions of the avenue; a railway to be laid for purposes of filling up only.

The Commonwealth agrees to lay out said avenue on its land, with the restrictions named.

The Commonwealth releases certain rights to the channel in the Receiving Basin.

The Water Power Company agrees to lay out its portion of said avenue, and fill up, &c; and impose the restrictions named.

AGREEMENT.[1]

This Indenture of two parts, made and concluded this twenty-seventh day of December, in the year of our Lord eighteen hundred fifty-six, by and between the Commonwealth of Massachusetts, acting by its committee appointed under and in pursuance of the Resolves in relation to lands in the Back Bay, approved May 30, A. D. 1856, of the first part, and the Boston Water Power Company, a corporation established by the laws of said Commonwealth, of the second part, witnesseth: — Parties. 1856, Dec. 27.

That *whereas*, said Commonwealth and the city of Boston have recently laid out a new street, eighty feet wide, between the "Public Garden," so called, of said city, and land of said Commonwealth, extending from the Milldam, or Beacon Street, to Boylston Street. Preamble relating to the 80-foot street next the Public Garden, and Avenue Five.

And *whereas*, by an Indenture between said Commonwealth and said Boston Water Power Company, dated June 9,

---

Company; and by a Committee of the City Council of the city of Boston, viz: Farnham Plummer, Pelham Bonney, Oliver Frost, Ezra Farnsworth, and John G. Webster, the approval of the Mayor being appended.

[1] Recorded with Suffolk Deeds, lib. 719, fol. 36.

1856, Dec. 27. A. D. 1854, and recorded with Suffolk Deeds, lib. 665, fol. 145, an avenue therein called avenue number "five," was laid out one hundred and twenty feet wide, extending over the receiving basin of said company parallel with the Milldam, from avenue number "one," described in said Indenture, to the "cross-dam."

Avenue Five to be widened.

And *whereas*, it is now agreed by and between the parties hereto, that instead of said avenue number "five," a wider and more extended avenue shall be laid out as follows: An avenue beginning on said new street, the point of intersection of the northerly line thereof with the westerly line of said new street, being five hundred fifty-two and a half feet southerly from the Milldam, or Beacon Street, thence extending westerly, of the clear width of two hundred feet, parallel with the Milldam, to the road leading from the westerly end of said Milldam to Roxbury and Brookline, called the "Punch Bowl" road. Said avenue to be filled up to the level of the Milldam.

And to be divided into roadway and walks with trees, &c.

And *whereas*, it is further agreed by and between the parties hereto, that not less than forty-four feet in width from each side of the foregoing described avenue shall be appropriated and used as and for open streets or highways, part to be roadway, and part sidewalk, and to remain forever open and unobstructed; and that the remainder of said avenue, not exceeding one hundred and twelve feet in width, shall be appropriated for a walk, the planting of trees, shrubbery, and grass, and otherwise ornamented, so as to exclude carriages, horses, and other vehicles and animals from the same, excepting where intersected by streets or avenues.

Houses to set back 20 feet.

And *whereas*, it is further agreed by and between the parties hereto, that buildings shall never be erected on the lots belonging to either party bounding on said avenue, any part of which buildings shall be within the distance of twenty feet from the front line of such lots: *provided, however*, that fences may be erected and maintained on the said front line of said lots, and steps and other usual projections from the fronts of said buildings may be made within said distance of twenty feet from said front line.

And *whereas*, it is further agreed by and between the parties hereto, that said Boston Water Power Company shall fill up sixty feet in width of the portion of said avenue situated easterly of the cross-dam, where said Company owns the land adjoining on one side only, and one hundred and twenty feet, where it owns the land adjoining on both sides thereof; said filling to be done on the same terms and conditions as now provided by the several indentures between said Commonwealth and said Company for the filling of said avenue number "five." It being understood that the residue of said portion of said avenue bounded by the land of said Company, and east of the cross-dam, may be filled by either of the parties hereto, or such parties as they may authorize, and neither party is bound to fill the same until they shall deem it expedient so to do.

Water Power Company to fill up portions of the avenue.

1856, Dec. 27.

And *whereas*, it is further agreed by and between the parties hereto, that the said Commonwealth, or the said Water Power Company, may build, or cause to be built, a railroad in said avenue hereinbefore described, over the lands in said avenue belonging to the respective parties, from said "Punch Bowl" road to the easterly boundary of the land belonging to said Commonwealth, for the purpose of bringing in earth and gravel, and materials for filling the lands of said Commonwealth and said Company, and for no other purpose: *provided*, that said railroad shall not be used for such transportation of earth and gravel in said avenue or any other street where the same shall be completed and buildings erected thereon, without the consent of both parties hereto.

A railroad may be laid for purposes of filling up only.

Now, in consideration of the premises, and of the grants, releases, covenants, and agreements in this indenture contained and set forth, the said Commonwealth doth hereby covenant and agree to and with the said Boston Water Power Company and its assigns, that the said Commonwealth will lay out, and it doth hereby lay out so much of said avenue herein described, of the width of two hundred feet, as passes through the land belonging to said Cmmonwealth; that neither said Commonwealth nor its assigns shall ever erect, or cause to be erected, any building on the lots bordering on said avenue within

Commonwealth agrees to lay out said avenue on its land with the restrictions named.

1856, Dec. 27.

twenty feet from the lines thereof on either side; and that said avenue shall be kept open and used for the purposes and in the manner hereinbefore mentioned and described, forever.

Commonwealth releases certain rights to the channel in the receiving basin.

And for the considerations aforesaid, the said Commonwealth doth hereby release, and forever quitclaim and convey to the said Boston Water Power Company, its successors, and assigns, all said Commonwealth's right, title, and interest in and to the channel in the receiving basin, which is situated westerly of the fourth avenue described in said indenture of June 9, 1854, and southeasterly of the Boston and Providence Railroad, reserving the right to lay out streets over the same on the terms and conditions provided by the several indentures between the Commonwealth and said Company for laying out streets in the Back Bay over the lands of said Company; and also, all the right, title, and interest of the said Commonwealth in and to the soil and freehold of the flats and channels in the full basin of said Company, reserving the aforesaid right of said avenue of two hundred feet in width, as herein described and provided.

Water Power Company agrees to lay out its portion of said avenue, and fill up, &c., and impose the restrictions named.

And in consideration of the grants, releases, covenants and agreements in this Indenture contained and set forth, the said Boston Water Power Company doth hereby covenant and agree to and with the said Commonwealth and its assigns, that said Company will lay out, and it doth hereby lay out, so much of said avenue herein described, of the width of two hundred feet, as passes through the land of said Company; that it will fill a portion of the same to the extent and in the manner hereinbefore referred to and set forth; that neither the said Company, nor its successors or assigns, shall ever erect, or cause to be erected, any building on the lots bordering on said avenue within twenty feet of the lines thereof on either side; and that said avenue shall be kept open and used for the purposes and in the manner hereinbefore mentioned and described, forever.

Duly executed.

THE COMMONWEALTH AND THE BOSTON AND ROXBURY MILL CORPORATION.

AGREEMENT.

Parties.

Preamble, relating to previous Indentures; boundaries of dams and roads defined; dams and roads to be free of toll after May 1, 1863; a parcel of land to be kept open as a public square, described.

The Mill Corporation releases its rights to dams, roads, &c. to the Commonw'h, subject to rights of way and franchise of toll.

A public square to be kept open.

The Mill Corporation releases to the Commonwealth all its rights south of Milldam, reserving the right to maintain a toll-house.

The Commonwealth releases to Mill Corporation, certain lands and flats.

The Mill Corporation to retain right of way and franchise of toll, according to Indenture of June 9, 1854.

AGREEMENT.[1]

Parties. 1856, Dec. 30.

THIS INDENTURE of two parts, made and concluded this thirtieth day of December, by and between the Commonwealth of Massachusetts, acting by its Committee appointed under and in pursuance of the Resolves in relation to the lands in the Back Bay, approved May 30, A. D. 1856, of the first part, and the Boston and Roxbury Mill Corporation, a corporation duly established by the laws of said Commonwealth, of the second part, witnesseth: —

Preamble relating to previous indentures.

That *whereas*, by an Indenture between the said Mill Corporation and the Boston Water Power Company, dated May 9, A. D. 1832,[1] duly recorded with the Deeds of Norfolk

[1] Recorded with Suffolk Deeds, liber 719, page 82.

1856, Dec. 30.

and Suffolk County, it is among other things provided, that "no house or other building is to be erected within twenty feet of the south wall of said dam," (meaning the main dam of said Mill Corporation,) "and the intermediate space of twenty feet is to be kept open for a highway," and also that the Boston Water Power Company, its successors and assigns, will not build or erect, or permit any others to build or erect, within two thousand feet of the said south wall of the said Milldam, any bridge, road or other thing convenient for travel across the channels in the Back Bay therein described.

And *whereas*, the said Mill Corporation has agreed to release the aforesaid restrictions to the said Commonwealth, with all their right, title and interest in and to the lands in the receiving and full basins, southerly of and adjoining said Milldam.

And *whereas*, by an Indenture made and concluded June 9, A. D. 1854,[2] between the parties hereto, duly recorded with said deeds of said counties of Norfolk and Suffolk, the said corporation did covenant and agree amongst other things, that said corporation shall and will surrender to the said Commonwealth its franchise of toll, together with its right of way over the Milldam and cross-dam, and over all bridges and roads, as said roads are now constructed, connected with or leading to either of said dams, whenever certain events therein mentioned shall occur; or at the expiration of ten years from the first day of May, A. D. 1853.

And *whereas*, it is now agreed by and between the parties hereto, that the limits and boundaries of the dams and roads referred to in said Indenture of June 9, A. D. 1854, shall be defined and established as follows, to wit: —

Boundaries of dams and roads defined.

That the southerly line of the Milldam shall be the southerly wall thereof, and the northerly line shall be a line parallel with, and twenty feet distant northerly from, the present northerly wall of said dam. That the lines of the cross-dam and the road leading therefrom shall be parallel with the centre line

---

[1] *Ante*, p. 222. [2] *Ante*, p. 245.

of said cross-dam and road, and thirty feet distant therefrom on both sides of the same, from the main dam to Stedman's Cove; and from thence to the westerly side of Stony Brook the easterly line shall be the present easterly line of said road, and the westerly line sixty feet westerly therefrom, all the aforesaid lines of said road on both sides to be extended straight at the angle at said cove until the same shall intersect; and from said Stony Brook to the land of Nahum Ward, the easterly line shall bound on the land conveyed by John Heath to Henry J. Oliver, and another; and the westerly line shall be the westerly side of said road as now used. That the lines of the Brookline branch or "Punch Bowl" road shall be parallel with and thirty feet distant on each side thereof from the centre line of said road as now built, and extending from said Milldam to Washington Street, in the town of Brookline. That the lines of the Brighton branch or road shall be parallel with and thirty feet distant on each side thereof from the centre line of said road as now built, and shall extend from the Milldam aforesaid to the road leading from Brighton to Cambridgeport, and also that a triangular piece of land near or at the junction of the said Brookline and Brighton branches, filled up by said corporation, also a triangular piece of land at the said road from Brighton to Cambridgeport, described as containing thirty-nine rods, more or less, in the deed from John English to said corporation, dated November 28, 1818, shall both be a part of said road or roads. That the lines of the road called the "Watertown Turnpike" shall be parallel with and thirty feet distant on each side thereof from the centre line of said road as now built, and shall extend from said Brighton road to the main road in the town of Watertown. 1856, Dec. 30.

And *whereas*, it is agreed by and between the parties hereto that said above-described dams and roads with the bridges connected therewith, shall forever be open as public highways, free from all toll, from and after the 1st day of May, A. D. 1863; and that said Mill Corporation shall now execute a formal surrender of said dams, roads and bridges unto said Commonwealth, subject to said corporation's rights, herein named, to

Dams and roads to be free of toll after May 1, 1863.

1856, Dec. 30.

maintain its toll franchise and right of way until the happening of certain events, or until May 1, 1863.

And *whereas*, it is agreed that all the residue of the lands belonging to said Boston and Roxbury Mill Corporation not included within either of the dams or roads above described, shall not be deemed or taken as a part of the said dams or roads to be surrendered to the said Commonwealth, according to the true intent and meaning of said Indenture of June 9, A. D. 1851.

A parcel of land to be kept open as a public square; described.

And *whereas* it is agreed by and between the parties hereto, that the following described parcel of land, wharf and flats, shall be laid out and kept open and unobstructed as a public square, for the use and benefit of the parties hereto and their assigns forever, to wit: a parcel bounded westerly by the westerly line of avenue number "Four," laid out through the receiving basin of the Boston Water Power Company, extended to the Commissioners' line of Boston harbor, southerly by the Milldam, two hundred and forty-five feet easterly by a line at right angles with said dam, and northerly by the Commissioners' line aforesaid, two hundred and forty-five feet: and that said corporation shall not build a sea-wall, or fill up the said flats between the discharging sluices in said Milldam, and said Commissioners' line, between the most easterly and the most westerly side of said sluices; and shall fill only so much of the residue of said square, as the Commissioners on the Back Bay, or their successors, may require to be filled. And it is further agreed by and between the parties hereto, that the said parcel of land, flats and wharf to be laid out and kept open, as aforesaid, as a public square, shall be deemed and taken as a part of the land which the said Indenture, dated June 9, A. D. 1854, authorizes the Commissioners on the Back Bay, or their successors, to require for streets or other public uses.

The Mill Corporation releases its rights to dams, roads, &c. to the Commonwealth, subject to rights of way and franchise of toll.

Now, in consideration of the covenants, agreements and releases herein set forth, the said Boston and Roxbury Mill Corporation doth hereby release, remise and forever quitclaim to the said Commonwealth and its assigns, all the right, title and interest of said corporation in and to the foregoing described dams and roads, with all its rights in and to the land, flats and channels, with the bridges as above defined and described, and appertaining in all or either of said dams or roads, situated in either of the cities of Boston or Roxbury, or either of the towns of Brookline, Brighton, or Watertown. It being expressly understood, however, that said Mill Corporation retains and expressly reserves all the rights which it now has by its charter, and under the provisions of said Indenture, dated June 9, A. D. 1854, relative to its right of way and franchise of toll, and rights necessary and convenient to the full enjoyment of said rights of way and franchise of toll in, upon and over the several dams, roads and bridges hereinbefore described, upon the same terms and conditions, and for the same time, as provided in said Indenture of June 9, A. D. 1854. To have and to hold the foregoing granted and released premises to the said Commonwealth and its assigns forever, subject, nevertheless, to the uses and reservations above referred to and described.

1856, Dec. 30.

A public square to be kept open.

And for the considerations aforesaid, the said parties hereto covenant and agree to and with each other that the aforesaid parcel of land, wharf and flats on the northerly side of said Milldam, and adjoining said sluiceways, shall forever remain open and unobstructed as a public square, and for the use and benefit of the parties hereto and their respective assigns as hereinbefore set forth.

The Mill Corporation releases to the Commonwealth all its rights south of the milldam, reserving the right to maintain a toll-house.

And for the considerations aforesaid the said Mill Corporation doth hereby grant, remise, release and forever quitclaim unto the said Commonwealth and its assigns all the said corporation's rights, title, interest and estates of every kind in, upon and over the lands, marsh, channels and flats in the two basins of the Back Bay in the cities of Boston and Roxbury, and the town of Brookline, adjoining and southerly of the southerly wall of the Milldam aforesaid, including in this release the restrictions hereinbefore mentioned as contained in said Indenture, dated May 9, 1832, between the said Mill Corporation and the Boston Water Power Company; reserving, however, to said corporation the right to keep and maintain its

1856, Dec. 30. toll-house during the continuance of its toll franchise, as hereinbefore named, at some convenient point south of said dam over the land of said Commonwealth, as mentioned in said above-named Indenture of June 9, 1854.

Commonwealth releases to Mill Corporation certain lands and flats.

And in consideration of the releases, covenants and agreements herein contained and set forth, the said Commonwealth doth hereby release and forever quitclaim to the said Boston and Roxbury Mill Corporation, and its assigns, all the land, marsh and flats now or heretofore belonging to said corporation, not included within the lines of said roads, dams and ways, hereinbefore described, excepting the following described piece of land and flats, to wit: Bounded easterly by a line twenty feet westerly of and parallel with the easterly line of avenue number "One," extended to the Harbor Commissioners' line; southerly by the Milldam; westerly by a line drawn at right angles with said dam from the westerly end of the northerly wall thereof; and northerly by said Commissioners' line: which land, so excepted, is to remain subject to the mortgage made by said Mill Corporation to said Commonwealth, and also to all the provisions and reservations contained in said Indenture, dated June 9, A. D. 1854. To have and to hold to said Mill Corporation and its assigns forever.

The Mill Corporation to retain right of way and franchise of toll according to indenture of June 9, 1854.

And for the considerations aforesaid, said Commonwealth covenants and agrees that said corporation may and shall have all the rights of way and franchise of toll which it now has under and by virtue of the several acts establishing the said Mill Corporation, and of said Indenture, dated June 9, A. D. 1854, for the time and on the terms and conditions therein contained.

Duly executed.

THE CITY OF ROXBURY AND THE BOSTON WATER POWER COMPANY.

AGREEMENT.

Parties.

1. City of Roxbury, for $2,000, releases to the Water Power Company, certain lands and flats.
2. City of Roxbury agrees to release certain other lands and flats upon completion of a certain sewer into Charles River; proviso, reserving rights of watercourses.
3. The Water Power Company releases all rights of flowage in the full basin.
4. The Water Power Company releases to the city of Roxbury, the right to lay a described drain.
5. The Water Power Company releases to the city of Roxbury the right to take up the gates of the full basin.

AGREEMENT.[1]

Parties, 1864, Dec. 28.

This Indenture of two parts, made and concluded this 28th day of December, in the year eighteen hundred and sixty-four, by and between the city of Roxbury, a Municipal Corporation duly established by law in the County of Norfolk, and Commonwealth of Massachusetts of the first part, and the Boston Water Power Company, a corporation duly established by law in said Commonwealth of the second part witnesseth as follows, to wit: —

City of Roxbury, for $2000, releases to Water Power Company certain lands and flats.

ARTICLE 1. That the said city of Roxbury in consideration of the sum of two thousand dollars to it paid by the said Boston Water Power Company, the receipt whereof is hereby acknowledged, and of the grants, releases, covenants and agreements hereinafter set forth, doth hereby release and forever quitclaim to the said Boston Water Power Company, and its successors, and assigns, all the estate, right, title and interest of the said city in and to the lands, channels, and flats lying below the riparian line in the empty basin so called in the Back Bay on the westerly side of the city of Boston described in and released

[1] Recorded with Suffolk Deeds, lib. 852, page 265.

1864, Dec. 28.

by the first article of a certain Indenture made the 9th day of June, A. D. 1854,[1] by and between the said Commonwealth of the first part, the said Boston Water Power Company of the second part, and such other owners or claimants of said land or flats in said Back Bay, as should by signing the same, become parties thereto, of the third part, approved by the Governor and Council on the 28th day of June, A. D. 1854, and now recorded in the respective registries of deeds within and for the several Counties of Norfolk, Suffolk, and Middlesex. To have and to hold the said released premises to the said Boston Water Power Company, and its successors and assigns, to its and their own use and behoof forever.

City of Roxbury agrees to release certain other lands and flats, upon completion of a certain sewer into Charles River.

ARTICLE 2. That for the considerations aforesaid, the said city of Roxbury, for itself and its successors doth hereby covenant and agree to and with the said Boston Water Power Company and its successors and assigns, that so soon as the said city shall have completed the sewer into Charles River, hereinafter described, the said city will release and forever quitclaim to the said Boston Water Power Company, and its successors and assigns, all the right, title, interest, and estate which the said city in and to all the lands, channels, and flats in the full basin, so called, in said Back Bay, and lying below the line of riparian ownership.

Proviso, reserving rights of watercourses.

Provided, however, that neither this covenant nor the contemplated release shall affect any right which said city or its successors may have in common with other owners of land, over or through which any watercourse passes to a safe, suitable, or proper outlet and channel for such watercourse or courses to tide water.

The Water Power Company releases all right of flowage in the full basin.

ARTICLE 3. That in consideration of the releases and covenants hereinbefore written, the said Boston Water Power Company, for itself and its successors, doth hereby relinquish, release, and abandon all the rights of flowage of said Company in the full basin, in said Back Bay, subject to said Company's contracts with the Commonwealth of Massachusetts, now duly recorded in the proper Registry or Registries of Deeds, and

[1] *Ante*, p. 234.

doth hereby covenant and agree to and with the said city of Roxbury and its successors, and assigns, that neither the said Boston Water Power Company nor its successors or assigns, shall ever hereafter claim or exercise, or attempt to exercise any such right of flowage forever, except as they may be required to do, by virtue of the said contract with the Commonwealth of Massachusetts. 1864, Dec. 28.

The Water Power Company releases to the city of Roxbury the right to lay a described sewer.

ART. 4. That for the considerations aforesaid, the said Boston Water Power Company doth hereby for itself and its successors, release and grant to the said city of Roxbury, and its successors and assigns, so far as it has the right so to do under the said contracts, with the Commonwealth of Massachusetts, the right to lay out, construct, and forever maintain, a drain or sewer in and through the lands which now belong or may hereafter belong to the said Boston Water Power Company, in the said full basin in the Back Bay, from the Roxbury line to low water-mark north of the Milldam in and through some street or streets, laid out or to be laid out by the said Boston Water Power Company east of the junction of Brookline Avenue, so called, with the Milldam and west of the eastern abutment of the sluiceway in the full basin, and running as directly as may be, and as nearly as may be at right angles with the said Milldam, which said drain or sewer may be of sufficient size and capacity, not exceeding forty feet in width, for the proper drainage of that territory, within the corporate limits of the said city of Roxbury which is now drained or in the course of the improvement and settlement of the said city, may require to be or may conveniently be drained through said full basin; and the said drain or sewer shall be the sole property of the said city of Roxbury and its successors and assigns, who shall have power to prescribe the mode of using the same and the terms upon which the right to enter and use the same by any other person or persons shall be granted; giving to said Boston Water Power Company the right to use and enter the same upon the same terms upon which like rights may be given to other persons. And it is further understood and agreed that the said city of Roxbury shall not require the payment of such

1864, Dec. 28. assessment as may be lawfully made upon the lands of the said Boston Water Power Company for or on account of the construction of said sewer, or any part thereof, until the land through which the said sewer shall be built shall be entirely built up and require drainage.

The Water Power Company releases to the city of Roxbury the right to take up the gates of the full basin.

ART. 5. That for the considerations aforesaid the said Boston Water Power Company doth hereby, for its successors, release and grant to the said city of Roxbury and its successors and assigns, so far as it has the right so to do under said contracts with the Commonwealth of Massachusetts, and also under its contracts with the Boston and Roxbury Mill Corporation, and subject thereto, the right at any time to remove the gates of the full basin aforesaid and to take up and remove any part or the whole of the substructure or foundation of the same, *provided* that such taking up and removal shall be done in a workmanlike manner and so as not to impair the strength of the said Milldam.

Duly executed.

CITY OF BOSTON AND J. E. AND N. BROWN.

AGREEMENT.

Parties.
Conveyance of certain lands to the city.
J. E. and N. Brown, to construct a bridge.
City of Boston to construct a drain through certain land.
Specifications of bridge.
Bridge to be conveyed to city, but not the land under it.
J. E. and N. Brown, to grade the land described.
Consideration, to be paid by city, $ 53,850.
City to set edgestones and pave gutters.

AGREEMENT.[1]

Parties. 1864, June.

This Indenture of two parts, made and concluded this day of June, in the year of our Lord one thousand eight hundred

---

[1] This Agreement was approved by the City Council, June 20, 1864, but never was executed by the parties. The stipulations, however, were carried

and sixty-four, by and between the city of Boston, of the first part, and Joseph E. Brown of Boston, in the County of Suffolk, and Nathan Brown of Roxbury, in the County of Norfolk, and both in the Commonwealth of Massachusetts, of the second part, witnesseth: — 1864, June.

Conveyance of certain lands to the city.

That, *whereas* the said parties of the second part have by their deed of even date with these presents conveyed to the said city of Boston certain lands in said deed fully described and shown on a plan made by Alexander Wadsworth, dated September 14, 1863, and to be therewith recorded, certain portions of which are to be laid out and used as a public street of said city; and *whereas* they have agreed with said city that they will, as soon as said city shall have laid the drain hereinafter provided for, and in conformity to the specifications herein contained, proceed to grade, and construct a bridge to connect the following-described parcels of said land, to wit: beginning at a point in Columbus Avenue, so called, three feet and seven inches southwestwardly from its point of coincidence with Grenville Place, so called, as shown on said plan; thence running southwardly by a line parallel with and distant three feet southwestwardly from the line called the first line on the plan of the Back Bay Lands, to land of the Boston and Worcester Railroad Company, and seventy-eight feet two and one half inches further in the same direction; thence westwardly by the line drawn on said plan forty-one feet three and one quarter inches; thence northwardly by a line parallel with and distant forty feet southwestwardly from the first-described line, to said Columbus Avenue; and thence northeastwardly by said avenue, to the point of beginning: the second of said parcels of land consisting of all that is included between the first and third courses of the foregoing description, extended, and between H Street, so called, and the southerly side of the land of said Boston and Worcester Railroad Company; now, therefore,

J. E. and N. Brown to construct a bridge.

---

out; the street, sewer, and bridge were built, and the consideration ($53,850) was paid by the city in May, 1865. The paper is here printed on account of its relation to the general topic of the Back Bay filling, etc.

City of Boston to construct a drain through certain land. 1864, June.

The said city of Boston hereby covenants and agrees forthwith to construct a drain throughout the entire length of said first-described parcel of land,[1] from the land of the Boston and Worcester Railroad Company to said Columbus Avenue.

Specifications of bridge.

The said parties of the second part hereby covenant and agree that, as soon as said drain shall have been laid as aforesaid, they will commence and with all reasonable despatch prosecute to completion the erection of a bridge to connect said two parcels of land and the grading of said land, in accordance with the following specifications, to wit: —

The said bridge shall extend from the southerly side of the first-described parcel of land to the northerly side of the parcel last described, across the land and tracks of the Boston and Worcester Railroad Company, and shall be of the uniform width of forty feet; said bridge shall be built of iron beams six inches deep, and iron trusses, Boles's Patent, according to plans of the same for the roadway thereof, now in the possession of said city; said roadway shall be planked with three-inch plank, which shall be covered with two-inch plank, and the sidewalks shall be planked with two-inch plank, all to be of good sound spruce, and properly nailed; the outside fences of the sidewalks shall be a light truss of wood, covered with sheathing on both sides, four feet in height above the sidewalk, with a suitable coping thereto of wood; the iron trusses shall be painted, and the fences shall all be painted with three coats of paint well sanded to imitate sandstone or granite; the piles and stone abutments of the bridge shall be similar and in all respects equal to those of the bridge on Berkeley Street erected by the Boston and Providence Railroad Company; and said bridge shall be seventeen feet in clear height above the tracks of the Boston and Worcester Railroad. And when said bridge shall be completed the said parties of the second part hereby covenant and agree that they will convey the same to the said city, but with no title to the land under it belonging to the Boston and Worcester Railroad Company.

Bridge to be conveyed to city, but not the land under it.

---

[1] Now Ferdinand Street.

And the said parties of the second part further covenant and gree that they will grade the land described in the last of the oregoing descriptions from the present grade of said H Street p to the top of said bridge by a gradual and regular ascent; hat they will grade the first-described parcel of land to a uniorm grade of eighteen feet throughout its entire length, excepting that the grading of the same from the northerly side of aid bridge shall be gradual and of easy descent to said grade of ighteen feet. The grading of said first-described land shall be upported by piling and planking on the easterly side thereof rom the northerly stone abutment of said bridge to said Columbus Avenue, and on the westerly side thereof from said butment to the land now owned by said parties of the second art, excepting where intersecting streets or ways are to enter pon said land, in which places the earth may slope down, provided the grade of eighteen feet be attained for the full width of forty feet. The said land shall be graded ready for the setting of edgestones and paving the gutters thereof: and all the said work shall be done to the satisfaction of said city.

J. E. and N. Brown to grade the land described. 1864, June.

In consideration whereof, the said city of Boston hereby covenants and agrees to pay to the said parties of the second part the sum of fifty-three thousand eight hundred and fifty dollars, from time to time as the work progresses, in such intalments as to it shall seem meet and proper; and when said work shall be completed, said city covenants and agrees to furnish and set edgestones and pave the gutters of the land before described.

Consideration to be paid by city: $ 53,850.

THE COMMONWEALTH OF MASSACHUSETTS, THE BOSTON WATER POWER COMPANY, AND THE CITY OF BOSTON.

AGREEMENT.

Parties.

Preamble, relating to Tripartite Indenture of 1856; and certain sewers therein agreed upon.

1. Release of obligations to build the main sewer.
2. The Commonwealth agrees to construct a sewer in Berkeley Street; described.
3. The Water Power Company to pay the city $50,000.
4. The city to continue the Berkeley Street sewer to the Worcester Railroad, and also to build sewers in Columbus Avenue.
5. Plan to be adopted; streets to correspond therewith.
6. The Water Power Company to convey certain lands to the city for an Institute of Fine Arts.
7. The Water Power Company to give the city the option of purchasing "Reserved" lots at fifty cents a foot.
8. The Commonwealth may make certain changes in its plans.
9. Indenture of December 11, 1856, to remain in force except as modified.

AGREEMENT.[1]

Parties. 1864, Dec. 31.

This Indenture, of three parts, made and concluded this 31st day of December, in the year of our Lord one thousand eight hundred and sixty-four, by and between the Commonwealth of Massachusetts, acting by its Commissioners on Public Lands, of the first part, the Boston Water Power Company, a corporation established by the laws of the said Commonwealth, of the second part, and the city of Boston, acting by its committee duly authorized, of the third part.

Preamble relating to Tripartite Indenture of 1856, and certain sewers therein agreed upon. 1864, Dec. 31.

Witnesseth, that, whereas by an Indenture of three parts, made and executed between the same parties, bearing date the 11th day of December, in the year of our Lord one thousand eight hundred and fifty-six,[2] provision is made for the building of two large main sewers, in the Back Bay Lands, so called, one beginning at Tremont Street, in the city of Boston, and passing through the first street of avenue numbered four on

---

[1] Recorded with Suffolk Deeds, liber 854, folio 241.

[2] This is known as the "New Tripartite Agreement." See *ante*, p. 258.

a plan of the Back Bay Lands referred to in said Indenture, to the first street south of the Milldam, thence through said last-mentioned street to a point opposite to the most easterly discharging sluice of the receiving basin; thence to the said sluiceway and opening into the same; and one from Camden Street to the aforesaid main sewer; the said sewers were to be not less than three feet in diameter at Tremont and Camden streets, and not less than nine feet at said sluice, and to be built by the three said several parties in parts as specified in the said Indenture; and whereas it is deemed expedient and for the interest of all the said parties, that the said sewers shall not be built, and that other means of draining shall be provided in lieu thereof; and whereas by the said Indenture certain provisions were made in regard to the laying out and making of streets or ways on the Back Bay Territory, so called, lying in the westerly part of the city of Boston, which it is deemed expedient to change in some respects. Now, therefore, it is agreed by the said parties as follows, viz: — 1864, Dec. 31.

First. Each of the said parties is hereby released and discharged from its obligation to build any part of the two aforesaid main sewers or of either of them. Release of obligations to build the main sewers.

Second. The said Commonwealth hereby covenants and agrees, in place of the sewer it has laid in Berkeley Street to construct in bricks and cement in a good, substantial, and workmanlike manner, equal in capacity to a sewer of six feet in diameter, a sewer from Charles River through Berkeley Street to the line of the Boston and Providence Railroad, and also a similar sewer of equal capacity from Charles River through Dedham Street to the line of the Commonwealth's land, and a continuation of the last-mentioned sewer, with a gradual and regular diminution in size, until it is reduced to a capacity equal to a sewer of three feet in diameter at its terminus, from the said line of the Commonwealth's land, across the land of the said Boston Water Power Company, a distance of three hundred feet towards the Boston and Worcester Railroad; and to furnish and set for each of the said sewers substantial tidal gates: and to do all the said work at a grade agreed upon, so The Commonwealth agrees to construct a sewer on Berkeley Street; described.

1864, Dec. 31.

as to accommodate existing lateral sewers, by and under the superintendence of an engineer employed by the city of Boston; and the said sewers shall thereafter become a part of the sewerage of the city of Boston; and until the streets through which they run are accepted by the said city as public highways, the said city shall have the right to enter upon the said streets for the purpose of repairing, cleaning, or relaying the said sewers. The Commonwealth shall, however, have the right under the direction of the Superintendent of Sewers in said city, to enter its other drains or sewers into the two said main sewers, to drain all its lands; but this right shall not extend to the assignees of the Commonwealth.

Water Power Company to pay the city $50,000.

Third. The said Boston Water Power Company hereby covenants and agrees to pay the said city of Boston the sum of fifty thousand dollars in consideration of the premises.

City to continue the Berkeley Street sewer to the Worcester Railroad, and also to build sewers in Columbus Avenue, etc.

Fourth. The said city of Boston covenants and agrees, that it will build a continuation of the sewer to be laid by the Commonwealth in Berkeley Street as aforesaid, with a reduced diameter, under the Boston and Providence Railroad, across the land of the said Boston Water Power Company to the Boston and Worcester Railroad; also a sewer of three feet in diameter at its commencement and six feet at its outlet, from some point on Camden Street north of Tremont Street, through Columbus Avenue, Avenue Third, Dedham Street, Montgomery Street, Union Park and Union Park Street, to the South Bay; and also a sewer of proper dimensions from the last-mentioned sewer and connecting therewith, through Montgomery and Clarendon streets, and other streets, if necessary, to the Boston and Worcester Railroad, or as near thereto as a sewer may be needed for domestic purposes. The lines of all said sewers are marked on the plan hereinafter referred to.

Plan to be adopted; streets to correspond therewith.

Fifth. The said parties of the first and second parts covenant and agree, and the said party of the third part assents, that a plan of the said territory, bearing even date herewith and signed by the three said several parties hereto, showing the contemplated streets on the said territory, shall be adopted in lieu of the plan which was heretofore agreed upon by the said parties, or any of them; and that all streets and ways which shall be made on so much of the said territory as belongs to the said parties of the first and second parts shall be according to the said plan adopted by this instrument. Provided, that nothing in this new plan shall interfere with the plan of lands belonging to the Commonwealth and adopted by the Commissioners on public lands, except as hereinafter provided, and except so far as is necessary to connect Huntington Avenue with Boylston Street.

1864, Dec. 31.

Sixth. The said party of the second part covenants and agrees to and with the said party of the third part; that it will convey to the said party of the third part, upon the execution of this instrument, a certain parcel of land in fee, which is delineated on the said plan hereby adopted and marked "Proposed Site for an Institute of fine arts;" and the conveyance shall include all the land so marked extending to the middle of each of the streets or ways by which the said land is bounded, as indicated on the said plan. The said conveyance shall, however, restrict the said party of the third part from using the said land or permitting it to be used for any purpose other than a public square or for a building to be devoted to the promotion of the fine arts.

Water Power Company to convey certain land to the city for an Institute of Fine Arts.

Seventh. The said party of the second part further covenants and agrees to and with the said party of the third part, that it will convey to the said party of the third part any or all of the parcels of land, after they shall have been filled to the established grade, which are designated on the said plan hereby adopted as "reserved," so far as the said parcels are within the limits of the lands of the said party of the second part, which the said party of the third part shall elect to purchase at the rate of fifty cents per square foot; and so often as either of the said parcels of land designated as "reserved" shall be filled as aforesaid, the said party of the second part shall give notice thereof to the said party of the third part, and the said party of the third part shall thereupon determine whether it will purchase such parcel as aforesaid.

Water Power Company to give the city the option of purchasing Reserved lots at fifty cents a foot.

Eighth. The said party of the first part may so alter the

Commonwealth

may make certain changes in its plans.

1864, Dec. 31.

plan heretofore adopted for laying out and selling the lands of the Commonwealth on the Back Bay as to reduce the width of the street next West of Dedham Street, and running parallel thereto from the Boston and Worcester Railroad to Beacon Street, from eighty feet to sixty feet in width, and may discontinue as a public square and sell for building purposes the land laid down as a public square on the said plan at the corner of the street next west of Dedham Street and Beacon Street, and may also discontinue and sell for building purposes the land laid down on the said plan as a street running from Marlborough Street to Beacon Street. And it shall be optional with the Commissioners on Public Lands, or those having their powers, at any time hereafter before making further sales on Dedham Street, to increase the width of said Dedham Street from the point where it connects with Huntington Avenue to Beacon Street to one hundred feet, to correspond with the laying out of said Huntington Avenue.

Indenture of Dec. 11, 1856, to remain in force except as modified.

Ninth. The aforesaid Indenture dated the 11th day of December, A. D. eighteen hundred and fifty-six, shall remain in full force, except in so far as the same is expressly changed or modified by this instrument; and all rights which have accrued to either of the said parties thereunder shall remain and continue as perfect as if this instrument had not been made.

Duly executed.[1]

---

[1] Signed by the Commissioners on Public Lands, for the Commonwealth; by Nathan Matthews, President of the Water Power Company, and by the Joint Special Commissioners on the Back Bay, for the city.

CITY OF BOSTON AND BOSTON AND WORCESTER RAILROAD CORPORATION.

AGREEMENT.
Boston and Worcester Railroad Corporation conveys to the city of Boston a described parcel of land, at the foot of Fayette Street; reserving rights of way and claims for damage by closing Fayette Street.

AGREEMENT.[1]

KNOW ALL MEN BY THESE PRESENTS;

That the Boston and Worcester Railroad Corporation, a Corporation duly established by law in the Commonwealth of Massachusetts, in consideration of five thousand two hundred and six and $\frac{50}{100}$ dollars paid by the city of Boston, a Corporation duly established by law in said Commonwealth, the receipt whereof is hereby acknowledged, do hereby convey, grant, remise, release, and forever quitclaim unto the said city of Boston, their successors and assigns, a certain piece of land situated within the city of Boston, and bounded and described as follows: — 1865, May 19.

Beginning at a point in the line dividing the land of the said Corporation from land of John Simmons and Joseph E. and Nathan Brown, which point is three feet distant westerly from the compromise line between land of said city of Boston and land of the Boston and Roxbury Mill Corporation, and from said point running westerly forty-one feet, three and one quarter inches by land of said Simmons and Browns, then running southerly eighty-three feet by a line parallel with, and forty-three feet distant westerly at right angles from said compromise line, to the southerly face of the stone abutment recently erected by said Browns; then running easterly by the south-

[1] Recorded with Suffolk Deeds, liber 859, folio 291.

1865, May 19. erly face of said stone abutment about forty-two feet to a point three feet distant from said compromise line, thence running northerly about twenty-one feet to the line of Fayette Street, continued by a line parallel with and three feet distant westerly from said compromise line, thence running easterly about three feet to said compromise line, by the southerly side of said Fayette Street continued, thence running northerly thirty-six feet by said compromise line to the northerly line of said Fayette Street, thence running westerly about three feet by the northerly line of said Fayette Street continued, thence running northerly about twenty-eight feet to the point of beginning by a line parallel with, and three feet distant from said compromise line, containing three thousand four hundred and seventy-one square feet. Reserving for said Boston and Worcester Railroad Corporation, their successors and assigns, servants and agents, a right of way as now used and enjoyed by them under the bridge, resting, in part, on said abutment, to pass and repass at any and all times, and for any and all purposes, on foot and with vehicles, and animals of any and all kinds, to, from, upon, and over Fayette Street, to and from any and all lands of said Corporation upon and over all and any part of a strip of land, parcel of the land before described and hereby released. Bounded southerly by the north stone abutment recently erected by said Browns, of the bridge by which Ferdinand Street passes over the railroad of said Corporation, northerly by a line parallel with said abutment, and forty-six feet therefrom, easterly by Fayette Street, and westerly by land of said Corporation, said city, by accepting, and in consideration of this deed, agrees to pay said grantors, their successors and assigns, full compensation for any and all loss, damage, or injury, if any to them actually caused by said city discontinuing, raising, or lowering said Fayette Street, or in any way interfering with the free and convenient access to use of, or passage over either the same or said way above reserved, agreeing, that unless, after the delivery of these presents, such change shall take place in the condition of the lands of the grantor Corporation abutting on the premises, or the mode of using the same, shall be so changed, that no damage, loss, or injury is in fact so caused, they would be entitled to compensation as aforesaid, and would be so entitled under existing circumstances. To have and to hold the above-released premises with all the privileges and appurtenances to the same belonging to the said city of Boston, their successors and assigns, to their use and behoof forever. And they, the said Boston and Worcester Railroad Corporation, for themselves and their successors, do covenant with the said city of Boston, their successors and assigns, that the premises are free from all incumbrances made or suffered by Boston and Worcester Railroad Corporation. And that they will, and their successors shall warrant and defend the same to the said city of Boston, their successors and assigns, forever, against the lawful claims and demands of all persons claiming by, through, or under said Boston and Worcester Railroad Corporation, but against none other. 1865, May 19.

Duly executed,[1] &c.

CITY OF BOSTON AND THE BOSTON AND WORCESTER RAILROAD COMPANY.

AGREEMENT.

Parties.

City conveys certain land to railroad; reserving right of way over; and grants to the railroad the right to widen its track; to grade the land for widening H Street, etc.; Boston and Worcester Railroad to build a new abutment for Tremont Street Bridge; city to build a portion of abutment; Boston and Worcester Railroad to maintain a stone wall on line of H Street; and gives certain land for street purposes; city to have right to carry over water-pipes; notice to be given of commencement of work.

AGREEMENT.

This Indenture of two parts by and between the city of Boston partly of the first part and the Boston and Worcester Railroad Corporation, a Corporation duly established by authority Parties. 1865, Dec. 21.

---

[1] On the 19th day of May, 1865.

1865, Dec. 21. of the Commonwealth of Massachusetts party of the second part witnesseth: —

That said parties each in consideration of the grants and agreements of the other herein contained, hereby respectively grant and agree as follows: —

City grants certain land to Boston and Worcester Railroad; reserving right of way over.

First. The said city of Boston doth hereby give, grant, bargain, sell, and convey, to the said Boston and Worcester Railroad Corporation, its successors and assigns, a strip of land on the southerly side of the railroad of said Corporation, where said railroad passes under Tremont Street in said city; twenty-two (22) feet wide, measuring from the northerly face of the present southerly abutment of the present bridge by which said street now passes over said railroad and of a length equal to the present width of said Tremont Street at this place. Reserving to said city the right to have said Tremont Street maintained and carried by a substantial bridge over said strip of land and the railroad of said party of the second part as and for a public highway within the limits, at the height and in the manner herein set forth and provided.

And grants to the railroad the right to widen its track.

And said city of Boston agrees that said party of the second part may widen its railroad under Tremont Street by taking and permanently holding said strip of land, may remove the southerly abutment of said bridge, and build a new abutment, the northerly face of which at its foot shall be not more than thirty-five (35) feet southerly from the centre of the space between the present tracks of said railroad.

City to grade the land for widening H Street, &c.

Said city of Boston agrees to fill up and grade the parcel of land hereinafter described, required to widen street H so called, between Ferdinand and Tremont streets, after said party of the second part shall have built the retaining wall as hereinafter provided, and to do all the filling, grading, and paving, made necessary by the widening of said Street H, or the rebuilding of the bridge and abutment herein agreed upon; and said city of Boston also agrees to build and forever maintain all structures necessary for carrying the Cochituate water pipes over the railroad of said Corporation. Said structures shall be without columns or piers, and shall be placed at the same height in the clear above the tracks of said railroad as the bridge which said party of the second part is to build as herein provided, shall be westerly of said bridge, and of such width only as the party of the first part shall deem necessary; but in no event to extend in width more than twelve (12) feet westerly of said bridge, nor shall any portion of said structures or of anything connected therewith, be placed below said height, where the same passes over the said strip of land or the location of said railroad.

1865, Dec. 21.

The said Boston and Worcester Railroad Corporation hereby agrees to remove the present southerly abutment of the bridge over its railroad at Tremont Street, and to build and forever maintain a new abutment, the northerly face of which at its foot shall not be more than thirty-five (35) feet southerly from the centre of the space between the present tracks of the said railroad; said abutment to commence at the easterly side of Tremont Street and to extend in a westerly direction thirteen and four-tenths feet beyond the westerly line of said street, said portion so extending to be built as hereinafter provided; to build and forever maintain a substantial iron bridge over its railroad and said strip of land of a width equal to the present width of Tremont Street the top surface of which when completed shall be at the level of twenty-two (22) feet above mean low water; said bridge to be so constructed as to have not more than two roadways, and to have suitable sidewalks ten (10) feet wide.

Boston and Worcester Railroad Company to build a new abutment for Tremont Street Bridge.

The said city of Boston agrees to build at its own expense that portion of the abutment which will extend thirteen and four-tenths ($13\frac{4}{10}$) feet west of Tremont Street, upon which will rest the structures necessary to carry the water pipes over the said railroad, and agrees with said party of the second part that said city will pay all damages sustained by any person by reason of raising either Tremont Street or the said bridge above the present grade or level of the said street or said present bridge respectively.

City to build a portion of abutment.

Said party of the second part agrees to build and forever maintain a good and substantial stone-wall between Ferdinand

Boston and Worcester Railroad to main-

tain a stone wall on line of H Street.

1865, Dec. 21.

Street and the northerly end of the new southerly abutment, above referred to, on the line of the widening of said Street H, and as high as the grade which has been established by said city, for said street H, at this locality.

Boston and Worcester Railroad gives certain lands for street purposes.

Said Boston and Worcester Railroad Corporation doth hereby give, grant, bargain, sell and convey to said city, a parcel of land situate in said city, bounded and described as follows, viz: southerly by the present line of said street H, there measuring seventy-three (73) and four tenths ($\frac{4}{10}$) feet; westerly by Ferdinand Street, sixteen and seventy-two one hundredths ($16\frac{72}{100}$) feet; northerly by the proposed line of widening of said Street H, eighty-seven and three tenths ($87\frac{3}{10}$) feet; northerly again by the same thirteen and four tenths ($13\frac{4}{10}$) feet (the last-described line being the line of said extension of the said abutment as aforesaid); and easterly by Tremont Street, to said present line of street H, about forty-eight and thirty-two one hundredths ($48\frac{32}{100}$) feet; containing two thousand six hundred and thirty-one (2,631) square feet more or less. Said parcel to be used only for the purposes of a public street of the city of Boston, and for the necessary structures for carrying the Cochituate water pipes over said railroad. Also a certain other parcel of land on the northerly side of said railroad required by said city for the northerly abutment of the structure necessary for carrying the Cochituate water pipes over said railroad, bounded as follows, viz: Beginning at a point where the westerly line of Tremont Street intersects the southerly face of the northerly abutment of the Tremont Street Bridge, thence running westerly by a line in the continuation of the southerly face of said abutment twenty and eighty-three one hundredths ($20\frac{83}{100}$) feet; thence turning at right angle and running northerly by land of said Corporation six (6) feet; thence northeasterly by land of said Corporation thirty-four and seventy-five one hundredths ($34\frac{75}{100}$) feet; thence easterly by the same, two and six tenths ($2\frac{6}{10}$) feet; thence southerly along the said westerly line of Tremont Street twenty-four (24) feet to the point of beginning. Containing three hundred and forty and six tenths ($340\frac{6}{10}$) square feet more or less; reserving to said Corporation the right to pass and to repass over such portions, or the whole of the parcel of land last described, and to make all such other uses thereof, as shall be compatible with the safety, security, and maintenance of the water pipes, but not to pass over the same in such manner, or to make any such use thereof, as shall be in the reasonable opinion of the Cochituate Water Board, not compatible with the safety, security, protection, and location of said water pipes. The said city of Boston agrees to build at its own expense, the abutment which is to stand on the last-described parcel of land. 1865, Dec. 21.

The above described and conveyed strip and parcels of land proposed widening of street H, and proposed location of abutment, are shown on a plan made by N. Henry Crafts, City Engineer, dated December 4, 1865, signed by the respective parties, and deposited in the office of the said City Engineer, and whereon said strip of land first mentioned, is marked A, said second mentioned parcel B, and said third mentioned parcel C.

Said Corporation also hereby grants to said city the right to build and forever maintain suitable structures for carrying said water pipes over its railroad, but only in the limits and manner aforesaid. City to have right to carry over water-pipes.

Each party agrees to give at least sixty days' notice in writing to the other, of its intention to commence the work to be done by such party as herein set forth, and so to prosecute the same as not to endanger the safety or security of said water pipes, or of the said railroad or its business, respectively. Notice to be given of commencement of work.

All the work as herein specified, is to be completed during the year A. D. eighteen hundred and sixty-six, unless otherwise mutually agreed upon by the said parties of the first and second part, by a written indorsement upon this instrument signed by the said parties.

Duly executed.

JACOB ULMAN AND OTHERS, AND THE BOSTON WATER POWER COMPANY.

AGREEMENT.

Boundary lines fixed.
Parties release to the Water Power Company all rights of property in the basin.
The Water Power Company guarantees the rights of parties to property and drainage east of the boundary line fixed.
The water Power Company guarantees right to dig drains to the channel.
Tide water not to be raised more than necessary for mill power.

AGREEMENT.[1]

Parties. 1839, Jan. 9.

This Indenture, bearing date this 9th day of January, Anno Domini 1839, made by and between the several persons whose names and seals are hereto set and subscribed of the first part, each for himself severally, and not one for any other, and the Boston Water Power Company, a Corporation established within and by the authority of the Commonwealth of Massachusetts of the second part, witnesseth: —

That for the purpose of adjusting and settling all controversy and questions touching the claims and rights of the respective parties within and about the basin, and fixing the boundary lines thereof, the parties aforesaid do severally and mutually agree, each of the first part, for himself respectively, and the said Corporation of the second part, by and with the others, and with each of them, that the boundary line between the lands and flats of the individuals who have become parties hereto of the first part, and the said Boston Water Power Company of the second part, respectively shall be, and hereby is settled to be their boundary line as follows: that is to say, a straight line beginning at a cedar post on said dam, six hundred and fifty feet from Charles Street, established as a boundary line between land of the city of Boston and the Boston and Roxbury Mill Corporation, and continued by a stone post

Boundary lines fixed.

[1] Recorded with Suffolk Deeds, liber 463, folio 217.

at the bottom of the land of the city upon Pleasant Street, to a stone post on Castle Street; it being the line called the first line in an agreement fixing the boundary lines between lands of said Corporation and the city of Boston, and others, which agreement bears date the 26th day of December, A. D. 1826; said line shall be the boundary line between the lands of the individuals of the first part, and of said Boston Water Power Company. And the said individuals of the first part do hereby severally agree with the said Boston Water Company, in consideration of the several grants, covenants, and agreements of the said Corporation hereinafter contained, that the said Corporation shall have, hold, and enjoy all the right, title, and interest of every name and nature which the said individuals or either of them, the proprietors of flats and real estate aforesaid, have or ever had in and to the land and space within said basin lying westwardly of said boundary line; and do hereby grant and convey the same accordingly. To have and to hold the above-granted premises, with all the privileges and appurtenances to the same belonging, to them the said Boston Water Power Company, their successors and assigns, to their own use and behoof forever: so that neither of said proprietors of flats and real estate of the first part, nor any person claiming from, by, or under them, or either of them, shall claim or demand any right, title, property therein forever. And in consideration of the premises, the said Boston Water Power Company does hereby agree with the said individuals of the first part, and each of them, that the said individuals respectively shall have, hold, and enjoy all the right, title, and interest, whether of property or right of flowage, and every other, of what name or nature soever, which the said Corporation has or ever had in and to the land and flats claimed by said individuals of the first part, respectively, lying eastwardly of said line, and between said line and said individuals' adjacent upland. To have and to hold the same, with all the privileges and appurtenances thereto belonging to them separately and respectively, according to their several rights in and to the upland to which the said flats are adjacent respectively, and to their heirs and as-

1839, Jan. 9.

Parties release to the Water Power Company all right of property in the basin.

The Water Power Company guarantees the right of parties to property and flowage east of the boundary line fixed.

1839, Jan, 9.

signs, to their use and behoof forever; so that neither the said Corporation, nor any person or persons claiming from, by, or under them shall have, claim, or demand any title, interest, or estate, either of property or right of flowage therein, forever.

Water Power Company guarantees right to dig drains to the channel.

And the said Boston Water Power Company does hereby covenant, grant, and agree that the said individuals of the first part, their heirs and assigns, shall have and enjoy forever the right to dig, lay, and maintain all convenient and necessary drains from said uplands to the channel or deep water within the said basin, according to law, and the common and usual practice for the time being within the city of Boston. And the said Corporation agrees that they will not voluntarily let the tide water into said basin higher than may be necessary for the common and ordinary use of the mill power which they have, or may have, to the injury of the parties hereto: *provided*, *however*, that no damages shall be claimed of said Corporation by any of said parties, unless the water be thus voluntarily raised to a greater height than three feet above the level of low water in said basin at neap tides. And the parties aforesaid do hereby mutually agree, each for themselves respectively, with the others, and each of them, that they shall and will respectively make such other and further assurances as shall be necessary and proper to carry this agreement into effect, according to the true intent and meaning thereof.

Duly executed.[1]

---

[1] Signed by the President of the Water Power Company, and by Jacob Ulman, James Newman, James Savage, and B. G. Trustees, George Hills, Joseph N. Howe, Isaac Parker, Isaac P. Townsend, and Jonathan Ireland.

THE CITY OF BOSTON AND THE BOSTON WATER POWER COMPANY.

AGREEMENT.

Parties.
Preamble relating to previous indentures.
The city of Boston releases the Water Power Company from restrictions as to building; other stipulations not impaired.
The Water Power Company to erect a certain class of buildings.
No damages to be claimed for laying out Boylston Street extended as a highway.
City of Boston to have right of drainage to the channel.

AGREEMENT.[1]

This Agreement, made this 19th day of December, in the year of our Lord 1855, by and between the city of Boston of the first part and the Boston Water Power Company of the second part witnesseth: — Parties, 1855, Dec. 19.

That whereas by a certain Indenture by and between the city of Boston and Edward Tuckerman and others, and the Boston and Roxbury Mill Corporation, dated December 26, 1826,[2] and by a certain other Indenture by and between the said city of Boston and the Boston and Roxbury Mill Corporation, on the 1st day of February, 1827,[3] it was, among other things, agreed, "that neither the said Corporation nor their assigns shall erect any building within said basin [therein mentioned] in front and west of the city's land on Charles Street, within the distance of one hundred rods from said street, unless the city or its assigns shall erect buildings upon their said land in front and west of said Charles Street; and that neither the said Corporation nor their assigns shall at any time erect any buildings within said basin between said street and the channel immediately in front thereof, and west of said street whether said city shall use its said lands for building or not." And whereas the Boston Water Power Company, which Corpora- Preamble relating to previous agreements.

---

[1] Recorded with Suffolk Deeds, liber 710, folio 11.
[2] *Ante* p. 209. [3] *Ante* p. 214.

1855, Dec. 19. tion has succeeded to the rights of the Boston and Roxbury Mill Corporation is desirious of improving its land on the southerly side of Boylston Street continued; and whereas there is a controversy as to their rights to erect buildings thereon; and whereas there is now no objection to the erection of buildings thereon, but on the contrary, such improvement of the territory is desirable, as increasing the taxable property of the city.

Now therefore know all men, that the city of Boston, in consideration of the premises, and one dollar paid by the said Boston Water Power Company, the receipt whereof is hereby acknowledged, does hereby remise and release and forever quitclaim to the said Water Power Company, its successors and assigns the stipulation and agreement recited in words and figures as aforesaid, so far, and so far only, as said agreement and stipulations restrict said Company, its successors and assigns, from building on the land of said Water Power Company south of the southerly line of said Boylston Street, as it now is, or as it may be when extended westerly in the same direction and between that line and the Providence Railroad track, and the said city makes no objections to the erection of buildings on such of the said Water Power Company's lands as are named in the portion of said Indenture recited as aforesaid, and are south of the southerly side of said Boylston Street extended as aforesaid, within the restrictions hereinafter named; but this release and agreement are not to affect or impair in any way or to any extent, any of the other stipulations, covenants or agreements, restrictions, or conditions, contained in said Indentures, nor the portions of same recited as aforesaid, in their application, if they do apply, to lands north, or northwesterly of the said southerly line of Boylston Street extended as aforesaid, or otherwise than as particularly specified above. And the said Boston Water Power Company in consideration of the premises, does hereby for itself its successors and assigns, covenant and agree with the said city of Boston, its successors and assigns, that all buildings erected on any portion of said lands situated within one hundred and twenty-five feet of Boylston Street, or the extension thereof as aforesaid, shall be of a good class not

City of Boston releases the Water Power Company from restrictions as to building.

Other stipulations not impaired.

The Water Power Company to erect a certain class of buildings.

1855, Dec. 19.

less than three stories in height, and built of no other materials than brick, stone or iron, and that none of them shall be used for white or blacksmiths' shops, carpenters' shops, or for foundry or manufacturing purposes for railroad depots or stations, or for any business which shall be offensive to the neighborhood for dwelling-houses; and in case any building shall be erected or used in violation of this covenant or restriction, the said city may enter on the said land and remove the said buildings so erected, without any claim or right of damages on the part of the said Water Power Company, its successors or assigns, after sixty days' notice of their intention thus to enter and remove: and these covenants and restrictions are to run with and attach to said lands. And it is further agreed that, in case the city of Boston, at any time hereafter, shall lay out and accept the said Boylston Street, extended according to the plan of house lots and other land offered for sale by the Boston Water Power Company, dated April 10, 1855, from the end of Boylston St. to the Roxbury line, or shall lay out and accept Providence Street, extended to said line, as delineated on said plan, which plan is herein referred to for the purpose of showing said streets, and for no other purpose; the said Boston Water Power Company, their successors, and assigns, shall make no claim for land damages therefor, and the said city shall have the usual and all proper and necessary rights of sewerage and draining through the said streets, and such other streets or avenues of said company and their successors and assigns as may be necessary to secure a proper and suitable outlet to the channel.

No damages to be claimed for laying out Boylston Street, extended as a highway.

City of Boston to have right of drainage to the channel.

COMMONWEALTH OF MASSACHUSETTS TO THE CITY OF BOSTON.

AGREEMENT.

The Commissioners on Public Lands agree to give the city of Boston a certain part of Boylston Street as a highway, with right of drainage, &c.

AGREEMENT.[1]

KNOW ALL MEN BY THESE PRESENTS:

1865, May 27. That the Commissioners on Public Lands of the Commonwealth of Massachusetts, acting under the authority conferred upon them by the 142d chapter of the acts of the year 1861, do hereby offer to the city of Boston, as and for a public street, all the right, title, and interest of the Commonwealth in and to that portion of Boylston Street which extends from Arlington to Berkeley streets as laid down on the plan accompanying the Fifth Annual Report of the Commissioners on the Back Bay, dated January 21, 1857, and recorded with Suffolk deeds, September 2, 1858, and also on the plan recorded with Suffolk deeds, Liber 788, folio 159, bounded as follows: —

The Commissioners on Public Lands agree to give the city of Boston a certain part of Boylston Street as a highway, with right of drainage, &c.

Northerly by abutting lots five hundred and ninety-six feet; westerly by Berkeley Street eighty feet; southerly by abutting lots five hundred and ninety-six feet; easterly by Arlington Street eighty feet. And upon the acceptance by said city of Boston of this offer, the said parcel of land shall become a public street, with all the rights of way, and of laying sewers for draining and pipes for the distribution of water and gas, and with all other rights and privileges which now do or hereafter may, by law, appertain to public streets in said city of Boston.

---

[1] Recorded with Suffolk Deeds, liber 863, folio 95.

THE BOSTON WATER COMPANY TO THE CITY OF BOSTON.

AGREEMENT.
The Water Power Company grants to the City of Boston certain land; to be used only for a public square, or building for the promotion of the Fine Arts.

AGREEMENT.[1]

KNOW ALL MEN BY THESE PRESENTS.

That the Boston Water Power Company, a Corporation duly established by the laws of the Commonwealth of Massachusetts, in pursuance of the provisions of a tripartite indenture made by and between the Commonwealth of Massachusetts of the first part, the said Boston Water Power Company of the second part, and the said city of Boston of the third part dated the 31st day of December, in the year 1864, and in consideration of one dollar paid by the said city of Boston to the said Boston Water Power Company, the receipt whereof is hereby acknowledged, doth hereby grant, bargain, sell, and convey to the said city of Boston and its assigns forever, a certain parcel of land situated on the Back Bay so called, in the city of Boston in the County of Suffolk and Commonwealth aforesaid, and bounded and described as follows, viz: —

1865, December.

The Water Power Company grants to the City of Boston certain land.

Northward by the centre line of St. James Street, there measuring three hundred and ten feet; westwardly by the centre line of Dartmouth Street (formerly called Dedham Street) three hundred and ninety-five feet; southwardly by the centref line of a street forty feet wide running parallel with and three hundred and fifty feet distant southwardly from said St. James Street; three hundred and ten feet, and eastwardly by the centre line of a street forty feet wide, running parallel with and two hundred and sixty feet distant eastwardly from said Dartmouth Street, three hundred and ninety-five feet; containing one hun-

[1] Recorded with Suffolk Deeds, liber 870, folio 216.

1865, Dec.

dred and twenty-two thousand four and fifty square feet, more or less, and being delineated on a plan made by N. Henry Crafts, City Engineer, dated December 16, 1865, and deposited in his office, and a duplicate whereof is recorded with Suffolk Deeds at the end of Liber 869. Said land is hereby conveyed with the restriction that so much thereof as is not included in the aforesaid streets, shall never be used by the grantee or its assigns for any purpose other than a public square or buildings to be used and devoted to the promotion of the Fine Arts. To have and hold the aforegranted premises with all the privileges and appurtenances thereto belonging to the said city of Boston, its successors and assigns, to its and their own use forever in fee simple. And the said Boston Water Power Company doth hereby covenant with the said city of Boston, its successors and assigns, that the said Boston Water Power Company is lawfully seized in fee of the aforegranted premises, that they are free from all incumbrances, that it hath good right to sell and convey the same to the said city of Boston, as aforesaid, and that it will warrant and defend the same to the said city of Boston, its successors and assigns forever, against the lawful claims and demands of all persons.

To be used only for a public square or building for the promotion of the Fine Arts.

TRUSTS.

T R U S T S.

FRANKLIN FUND,[1]

FOR THE ENCOURAGEMENT OF YOUNG MECHANICS.

Dr. Franklin, in his Will, gave the inhabitants of Boston, in 1791, One Thousand Pounds Sterling, which he directed to be loaned in sums of not more than £60 nor less than £15, to one applicant at 5 per cent. interest; to be repaid in annual instalments of 10 per cent. each. These loans are restricted to "Young Married Artificers, under the age of 25, who have faithfully served an apprenticeship in Boston, so as to obtain a certificate of good moral character, from at least two respectable citizens, who are willing to become their sureties in a bond for the repayment of the money."

The Doctor calculated (not anticipating any losses) that the One Thousand Pounds would increase in the course of one hundred years, to one hundred and thirty-one thousand pounds, ($582,000); and of this amount he would have the managers lay out 100,000 pounds in public works: and the remaining 31,000 pounds he would have continue on interest for another term of one hundred years, at the end of which time he calculated that the fund would be £4,610,000; of which £1,610,000 was to be at the disposition of the inhabitants of the Town of Boston, and the balance to the Government of the State.

Amount of one bond in the hands of Frederick U. Tracy, Esq., the Treasurer,[2] $96 00

---

[1] As it stood Dec. 31, 1865.

[2] The office of the Treasurer of this Fund, F. U. Tracy, Esq., is at the City Treasurer's office, City Hall. His account is examined every year by a Committee of the Board of Aldermen, appointed for that purpose.

Amount deposited with Massachusetts Hospital Life Insurance Co.,	$109,204 53
Amount deposited in Provident Institution for Savings,	451 91
Amount deposited in Suffolk Institution for Savings,	430 12
Amount 31st December, 1865,	$110,182 56
Amount 31st December, 1864,	102,156 73
Increase in 1865,	$8,025 83

FRANKLIN SCHOOL MEDAL FUND.

This is a legacy by Benjamin Franklin, in 1790, the interest on which, since 1792, has been invested in Silver Medals, and distributed at the Annual Examination, among the most deserving boys in the Writing and Grammar Departments.

One Certificate of city five per cent Stock, $1,000 00

LAWRENCE HIGH SCHOOL FUND.

This is a donation made by the late Hon. Abbott Lawrence, of Boston, in the year 1844, the interest on which is payable annually to the Sub-Committee of the English High School, for the time being; and is by them distributed in prizes for the best performances in various branches of Literature and Science in that Institution; and in such other Rewards to the Scholars in that School as the Committee shall recommend.

One Certificate of city five per cent Stock, $2,000 00

LAWRENCE LATIN SCHOOL FUND.

This is a donation made by the late Hon. Abbott Lawrence, in the year 1845, the interest on which is payable annually to the "Chairman of the sub-Committee of the

PUBLIC LATIN SCHOOL, for the time being," and is distributed in Prizes for the general encouragement of the Scholars in such a way as the Sub-Committee of that School shall consider advisable.

One certificate of city five per cent Stock, $ 2,000 00

LATIN SCHOOL PRIZE FUND.

This is a donation from a number of Gentlemen of Boston, in the year 1816, the interest of which is invested in Prizes which are annually distributed among the most deserving Scholars in the PUBLIC LATIN SCHOOL.

One Certificate of city five per cent Stock, $ 1,050 00

WEBB'S FRANKLIN SCHOOL FUND.

This is a legacy made in the year 1828, by RUFUS WEBB, ESQ., who was for a great many years a WRITING MASTER in one of our Public Schools.

The Income from this Fund is applied to the purchase of Books, &c., for the use of the Indigent Scholars in the WRITING DEPARTMENT OF THE FRANKLIN SCHOOL.

One Certificate of city five per cent Stock, for $ 1,000 00

SMITH FUND.

This is a legacy by ABIEL SMITH, ESQ., of Boston, (who died in 1815,) to the SELECTMEN of the TOWN OF BOSTON, for the time being.

The Income from this Fund is appropriated towards the expense of "the Free Instruction of COLORED CHILDREN in Reading, Writing, and Arithmetic."

One Certificate of city five per cent Stock, payable in the year 1880, for $ 4,000 000

Eleven shares Suffolk National Bank, Boston, par value, 1,100 00

Thirteen shares in the Boston and Providence Railroad Corporation, par value,	1,300 00
Four Shares Continental National Bank, par value,	400 00
Two United States $7\frac{3}{10}$ Bonds,	200 00
	$7,000 00

POOR WIDOWS' FUND.

This is a donation made by MRS. JOANNA BROOKER, and others, in 1810, to the Selectmen of Boston, for the time being.

The Income from this Fund is paid over in equal proportions, to the Aldermen of the city, and they distribute the same, at their discretion, for the relief of POOR WIDOWS AND SICK PEOPLE.

One Certificate of city six per cent Stock, for	$1,500,00
One Certificate of city six per cent Stock,	700 00
	$3,200 00

LIBRARY FUNDS.

BIGELOW FUND. — This is a donation made by HON. JOHN P. BIGELOW, in August, 1850, when Mayor of the city.

The income from this Fund is to be appropriated to the purchase of Books for the increase of the Library.

One Certificate of city six per cent Stock, for $1,000 00.

Payable to the Chairman of the Committee on the Public Library for the time being.

BATES FUND. — This is a donation made by JOSHUA BATES, ESQ., of London, in March, 1853.

One Certificate of city six per cent Stock, for $50,000 00.

"The Income only on this Fund is to be, in each and every year, expended in the purchase of such Books of permanent value and authority as may be found most needful and most useful."

Payable to the Mayor of the city for the time being.

PHILLIPS FUND. — This is a donation made by the HON. JONATHAN PHILLIPS, of Boston, in April, 1853.

One certificate of city six per cent Stock, for $ 10,000 00.

The interest on this Fund is to be used exclusively for the purchase of books for the said Library.

Also, a bequest by the same gentleman, in his will, dated 28 September, 1849.

One Certificate of city six per cent Stock, for $ 20,000 00.

The Interest on which is to be annually devoted to the maintenance of a free Public Library.

Both of these items are payable to the Mayor of the city for the time being.

Mr. Phillips died on the 29th July, 1860, at the age of 82, and this latter sum was realized by the city in April, 1861.

LAWRENCE FUND. — This is a Bequest by the late HON. ABBOTT LAWRENCE, of Boston.

One Certificate of city six per cent Stock, for $ 10,000.

The interest on this Fund is to be exclusively appropriated for the purchase of Books for the said Library, having a permanent value.

Payable to the Mayor of the city for the time being.

TOWNSEND FUND. — This is a note secured by mortgage on an estate in the town of West Roxbury, for $ 4,000.

It is a Donation from William Minot, and William Minot, Jr., Esqrs., executors of the will of Miss Mary P. Townsend, of Boston, at whose disposal she left a certain portion of her estate in trust, for such charitable and public institutions as they might think meritorious. Said executors accordingly selected the Public Library of the City of Boston, as one of such institutions, and attached the following condition to the legacy: "The income only shall in each and every year be expended in the purchase of Books for the use of the Library; each of which books shall have been published in some one edition at least five years at the time it may be so purchased."

Franklin Club Fund.

One Certificate of city six per cent Stock, for $1,000.

This is a Donation made in June, 1863, by a Literary Association of young men in Boston, who, at the dissolution of the Association authorized its Trustees, Thomas Minns, John J. French, and J. Franklin Reed, to dispose of the fund on hand in such manner as to them should seem judicious. They elected to bestow it on the Public Library, attaching to it the following conditions: "In trust, that the income, but the income only, shall, year by year, be expended in the purchase of books of permanent value for the use of the Free Public Library of the city, and, as far as practicable, of such a character as to be of special interest to young men." The Trustees expressed a preference for books relative to Government and Political Economy.

Besides the above, the following Donations have been made to the Public Library, and the amounts have been appropriated to the purchase of books, according to the intentions of the Donors, viz: —

The late Hon. Samuel Appleton,	$1,000 00
Mrs. Sally Inman Kast Shepard,	1,000 00
James Brown, Esq., late of Cambridge,	500 00
J. Ingersoll Bowditch, Esq.,	300 00
Nathaniel I. Bowditch, Esq.,	200 00
James Nightingale, Esq.,	100 00
	$3,100 00

RECAPITULATION OF LIBRARY-FUNDS.

Bigelow donation,	$1,000 00
Bates donation,	50,000 00
Phillips donation,	10,000 00
Phillips bequest,	20,000 00
Lawrence bequest,	10,000 00
Miss Townsend's bequest,	4,000 00
Franklin Club,	1,000 00
Invested Funds,	$96,000 00
Donations expended,	3,100 00
	$99,100 00

PHILLIPS STREET FUND.

This is a bequest from the HON. JONA. PHILLIPS, who died in July, 1860.

One Certificate of city six per cent Stock, payable to the Mayor of the city for the time being, for $ 20,000.

The interest on this fund "may be expended annually by the Board of Aldermen, subject to the approval of the Mayor, to adorn and embellish the Streets and Public Places of the city."

CITY HOSPITAL FUNDS.

THE GOODNOW FUND. — MR. ELISHA GOODNOW, of South Boston (Ward 12,) who died in the year 1851, and whose Will is dated 12 July, 1849, bequeathed to the city "all the rest and residue of his Estates, real and personal, not otherwise disposed of," — supposed to be some $ 25,000 in value,— for the purpose of establishing, in the Eleventh or Twelfth Wards of the city, a Hospital for the Sick. One half of said funds to be applied for the establishment and maintenance of free beds, which should always be at the disposal and under the control of the officers of the Government of said Hospital for the time being. Under this Will, the city came into possession of certain real estate situated on Cross Street, which has been disposed of, and has produced thus far the sum of $ 16,500, which has been invested in City of Boston six per cent Stock.

There is a lot of Land belonging to this Estate, situated on Third Street, South Boston, containing 6,683 feet, valued by the Assessors, in 1860, at $ 4,000. The New York Central Railroad passes through this lot, but no settlement for damages has ever been made with this corporation.

THE NICHOLS FUND. — MR. LAWRENCE NICHOLS, who died in September, 1862, made the following bequest to the city: "I give the city of Boston, towards the establishment and endowment of a City Hospital, in case such Hospital shall have been established at the time of my decease, the sum of

One Thousand Dollars." And in case such Hospital should not have been established by the city at the time of his decease, he directed the same amount to be deposited with the Massachusetts Hospital Life Insurance Company, and suffered to accumulate by the addition of interest, until such an hospital should be established.

The Executor of the Will, Wm. Perkins, Esq., has paid into the Treasury Nine Hundred and Thirty-seven Dollars and Twenty-five Cents ($ 937.25), being the amount devised, less the *Internal Revenue Tax* on the same, and $ 530.50 as one of the "*residuary legatees in the United States*," from the surplus remaining undisposed of. The $ 937.25, with the accumulated interest thereon, has been invested in a Certificate of city Stock for $ 1,000. The balance ($530.50,) remains in the hands of the city Treasurer.

RECAPITULATION CITY HOSPITAL FUNDS.

Goodnow Fund. — One Certificate city six per cent, payable to the Mayor for the time being,	$ 16,500 00
Nichols Fund. — One certificate six per cent Stock, payable to the Mayor for the time being,	1,000 00
Cash in city Treasury,	530 50
	$ 18,930 50

The Ordinance in relation to the City Hospital, R. O. Sec. 9, page 328, provides that said scrip shall be deposited with the Auditor, who shall receive the interest as the same shall become due thereon, and add to it the moneys which shall have been appropriated for the use of the Hospital.

FUNDS FOR THE POOR.[1]

The principal fund for the benefit of the poor, in the hands of the Overseers of the Poor, is the "Pemberton Fund." The

[1] For a full and detailed description of these funds, their history and present condition, see the "Manual of the Overseers of the Poor."

first donation received for this fund was from an anonymous person "A. B.," who gave, on the 16th of May, 1760, £66, 13s, 4d, "the principal never to be diminished; and the interest to be given to such persons of good character who by the Providence of God, have been reduced from affluent or good circumstances to penury or want." This was augmented the same year by a donation from John Scollay, of $222.22; in 1785, Margaret Blackador gave £26, 13s, 4d, for the same purposes; in 1761, Alice Quick gave an equal amount; in 1764, Anne Wheelwright made a donation of Ten Guineas, and in 1763 Mary Ireland made a legacy of similar terms to the donation of "A. B."

In 1772, the Overseers of the Poor were incorporated to take charge of these legacies and funds; and when in 1782, Benj. Pemberton died, making the Overseers of the Poor the residuary legatees of his estate, the several small legacies above mentioned were merged into the "Pemberton Fund." Several other small bequests have since been added to it.

Daniel Oliver bequeathed to the Overseers of the Poor, in 1782, a parcel of real estate, which was sold the next year, and the income of the proceeds is devoted to the teaching of poor children to read, and general charity.

David Jeffries, who had been Town Treasurer for 31 years, gave the town, in 1786, 200 acres of land. The proceeds constitute the Jeffries Fund.

In 1793, John Boylston founded what are now the Boylston Relief and Boylston Education Funds. He gave £1000, to be administered by Trustees, the income to be applied for the instruction of poor orphans; also £1000 for the support of the aged poor and orphans; and £500 additional upon the death of one of his legatees. In 1865, the Educational Fund amounted to $44,716.44, and the Relief Fund to $15,000.00.

In 1798, Jonathan Mason gave $1000, for the support of a chaplain for the Almshouse and Workhouse. This is the "Mason Fund."

In 1811, Samuel Dexter founded the Dexter Fund, by giving $350.00 for "supplying Firewood and coal to poor persons."

Thus were established the various funds which are now controlled by the Board of Overseers. On the second of July, 1866, the total amount was $182,548.49.

ORIGIN

OF THE

HOUSE OF INDUSTRY.

41

Origin of the House of Industry.

ORIGIN OF THE HOUSE OF INDUSTRY.

At a meeting of the freeholders and other inhabitants of the town of Boston, holden at Faneuil Hall, on Monday, March, 12, 1821, and adjourned to March 13, certain petitions on the subject of erecting a workhouse were read. Whereupon it was voted, that the subject be referred to a committee of thirteen, to be nominated from the chair; the said committee to consider the subject at large and report, and that the report be printed and distributed among the inhabitants; and the selectmen were requested to call a meeting to act on said report. The following gentlemen were nominated and appointed on the committee, viz: Hon. Josiah Quincy, Joseph Lovering, James Savage, Henry J. Oliver, Francis Welsh, Joseph May, Thomas Howe, William Thurston, Abraham Babcock, Samuel A. Wells, James T. Austin, Benjamin Rich, and Joseph Woodward, Esquires.

Boston Records, vol. 10, pp. 290, 296.

At a subsequent meeting, on Monday, May 7, 1821, the committee appointed on the 12th day of March, "on the subject of pauperism at large, and on the expediency of erecting a workhouse," within the said town, made a long report, in which they express themselves as unanimously of opinion, that the accommodations, provided for the poor at the almshouse in Boston, are not such as comport with the honor and interests of the town; and that, in aid of the present establishment, a workhouse, to be denominated a House of Industry, should be erected, with a sufficient quantity of land attached to it, &c.; and submitted the following votes, which were passed:

Ibid, pp. 305, 307.

Voted, That it is expedient to establish, forthwith, within this town, a House of Industry.

Voted, That a committee be appointed consisting of —— persons, with full authority to select a suitable place for the erection

Ibid, p. 326.

of a House of Industry, with an extent of land, attached to it, not less than fifty acres; and that the said committee be authorized to take any of the unappropriated lands, belonging to the town, for that purpose; or, in case they deem any other spot, or like extent of land, within the town, a better location for such an establishment than any the town now possesses, that they be authorized to purchase the same; and that the said committee be instructed to proceed forthwith to erect suitable buildings, and to form a system for the conduct of such institution; and to report their proceedings, in the premises, from time to time, to the town, as they may deem expedient.

Voted, That the committee appointed by the preceding vote, be authorized to draw on the town treasurer for such sum, or sums of money, as may from time to time be found necessary, for the carrying into effect the purposes therein expressed; provided always that the amount of said drafts shall never exceed twenty thousand dollars.

Voted, That the report this day made to the town on the subject of pauperism and a House of Industry, be referred to the committee appointed by the preceding votes, and that they be instructed to take into consideration the various subjects suggested in it, and particularly to inquire into the general state of the poor, within the town, and concerning the operations, effects, modes, and principles of extending relief to the poor, adopted by the various charitable institutions existing in it; and from time to time to report such measures in relation to the whole, or any, of the subjects aforesaid, as they may deem it expedient for the town to adopt.

Ibid, p. 334. Hon. Josiah Quincy, Joseph Lovering, James Savage, Henry J. Oliver, Francis Welsh, Ebenezer Francis, Thomas Howe, William Thurston, Abraham Babcock, Samuel A. Wells, James T. Austin, Benjamin Rich, and Joseph Woodward, Esquires, were nominated from the chair and appointed a committee, in conformity to the second vote.

Ibid, pp. 388, 410. At a meeting of the freeholders, &c., held by adjournment from September 25, 1821, on October 22, 1821, the chairman of the committee made a long report, stating that the committee had procured a tract of land at South Boston,[1] containing fifty-three acres, owned by Samuel Brown, Esq., and were proceeding with the work of erection; and that the establishment was then advancing to the third story. The thanks of the town were voted to the chairman and members of the committee, and the sum of $ 6,000 in addition to that previously voted, was placed at their disposal. Ibid, p. 430.

The committee made a further report March 28, 1822; and it was voted that the sum of $ 15,000 be put at their disposition. They were also instructed to prepare a system for the general conduct and management and discipline of said house, and of the land connected with it, and lay the same before the city authorities as soon as practicable after their organization. Ibid, pp. 462, 4.

May 3, 1822, the committee represented, that they apprehend, that the power of devising rules for the management and discipline of the institution is vested in the board of Overseers of the Poor, under the act of 8 and 9 George II., (1735); and the committee therefore postponed any action in relation to this duty, until the action of the city council; and they suggest either an application to the legislature, or a reference of the subject matter to the board of overseers. This report was read and committed to a joint committee. City Record vol. 1, p. 7.

May 7, 1822, the joint committee on the subject recommended a reference of the matter to the board of Overseers of the Poor and the committee for building the House of Industry conjointly; which report was read and accepted. Ibid. p. 12.

May 24, 1822, the board and committee made a report recommending an application to the legislature for an act, authorizing the establishment of a new board; which report was read and committed. Ibid, p. 30.

June 4, 1822, the committee reported a bill to be presented to the general court. Ibid, p. 36.

Sept. 16, 1822, the committee for building the House of Industry reported the house as substantially completed; and stated that a balance of expense of $ 5,406.71 remained, for which Ibid, p. 79.

---

[1] The House of Industry was removed from South Boston to Deer Island January 1, 1854. (See Records of the House of Industry, Vol. E.)

provision was yet to be made. The report was read and committed.

Ibid, p. 221. May 21, 1823, $8,000 was appropriated for completing the House of Industry, outbuildings, fences, and for the purpose of stock, furniture, &c., and for carrying the said House of Industry into effective operation, and the directors of the said House of Industry were authorized to draw their warrants on the city treasurer therefor from time to time, as occasion might require.

After the erection of the House of Industry, there appears to have been considerable difficulty between the directors of the institution, the city council and the Overseers of the Poor, respecting the rights and duties of the latter in relation to the poor. The following report and resolutions, drawn up by Mr. Quincy, the mayor, were accepted and adopted by the city council May 12, 1825.

Mr. Quincy's report. (Accepted by the city council May 12, 1825.)

"The committee of both branches of the city council, to whom was referred the application of the Overseers of the Poor, for the providing of a suitable house for the accommodation of the poor and distressed, and expressing their readiness to take the oversight, care, and government of such house, respectfully report:

"That such a house is already provided in this city, established by law, and placed under the oversight and care of the directors of the House of Industry, who are invested in this respect by the statutes of this commonwealth, with all the powers and authorities 'had and exercised by Overseers of the Poor,' that the state of this house under the wise and active management of those directors is, in every respect satisfactory; the poor of every class content; and the moral and physical condition of the inmates placed upon a new system, calculated to ameliorate both in as high a degree as, in the nature of things is possible under the wise arrangements of these directors, annually chosen by and responsible to the city council.

"While your committee are happy in being thus able to state the results and prospects of this institution, they are not less gratified, that the city council are able, consistent with the legally invested rights of the directors of that house, to avail themselves in relation to it of the general aid of the Overseers of the Poor, and at the same time to grant them all the practical and useful facilities, relative to providing for the poor, which from the tenor of their application they desire; and thus the general arrangements of the poor of the city enjoy the advantage of the intelligence and experience of the members of both the Overseers of the Poor and of the directors of the House of Industry.

"Their general views will be developed in the subjoined resolutions, which they respectfully report to the city council for its consideration and adoption.

"*Resolved*, (1) That the Overseers of the Poor be and they are hereby authorized and requested to grant permits for the admission of any person in their judgment entitled to receive the support of the city in the tenement of the city denominated the House of Industry at South Boston, in like manner as the directors of said house are authorized by law; and that the superintendent of said house be and he hereby is authorized and directed to receive and take charge of persons to whom such permits have been granted; and to provide for their relief, support, and employment in said house, according to the regulations, and under the superintendence of the directors of the House of Industry.

"*Resolved*, (2) That the Overseers of the Poor be and they hereby are authorized and requested, at their discretion, with, or without notice, to visit the establishment called the House of Industry at South Boston, to inquire into the condition, treatment and employment of the poor who may be inmates therein, and to make such representations and suggestions, from time to time, to the city council, in relation to their said condition, treatment, and employment, as their wisdom and experience may suggest.

"*Resolved*, (3) That the mayor and aldermen be and they hereby are authorized to provide a suitable vehicle for the conveyance to the House of Industry, of sick, decrepit persons, or those otherwise incapacitated from going of themselves to such house, and that the same be, at all times, subject to the order of the Overseers of the Poor, and of the directors of the House of Industry, for the purpose above specified."

Subsequently to the adoption of these resolutions, a committee of the city council, to whom was referred a communication from the Overseers of the Poor, reported that they had laid the whole subject before counsel learned in the law, Hon. William Prescott, Charles Jackson, and Daniel Webster, Esquires; and the committee reported the following resolves which were passed:

"*Resolved*, That the Overseers of the Poor be and they hereby are directed to cause all persons who, from the nature of the illness under which they labor, or of the accident which has befallen them, are incapable, without endangering life, to be removed from the place where they are, to be relieved and supported in such place, until they are capable so to be removed, and as soon as they are capable of being removed, the said overseers are directed to cause them forthwith to be removed for further relief and support to the House of Industry.

"*Resolved*, That the Overseers of the Poor be, and they hereby are directed, as it respects those householders and others, who in their opinion require partial relief, and who may be rendered more comfortable by a small supply at their own houses, than by being wholly supported in a poorhouse, to grant such partial relief and small supply of necessaries at their own houses.

"*Resolved*, That the Overseers of the Poor be, and they hereby are directed to see that all poor and indigent persons, having lawful settlement in the city of Boston, and standing in need of relief, other than those belonging to the classes specified in the two preceding resolves, to be suitably relieved, supported and employed in the House of Industry, according to the regulations and under the superintendence of the directors of said house."

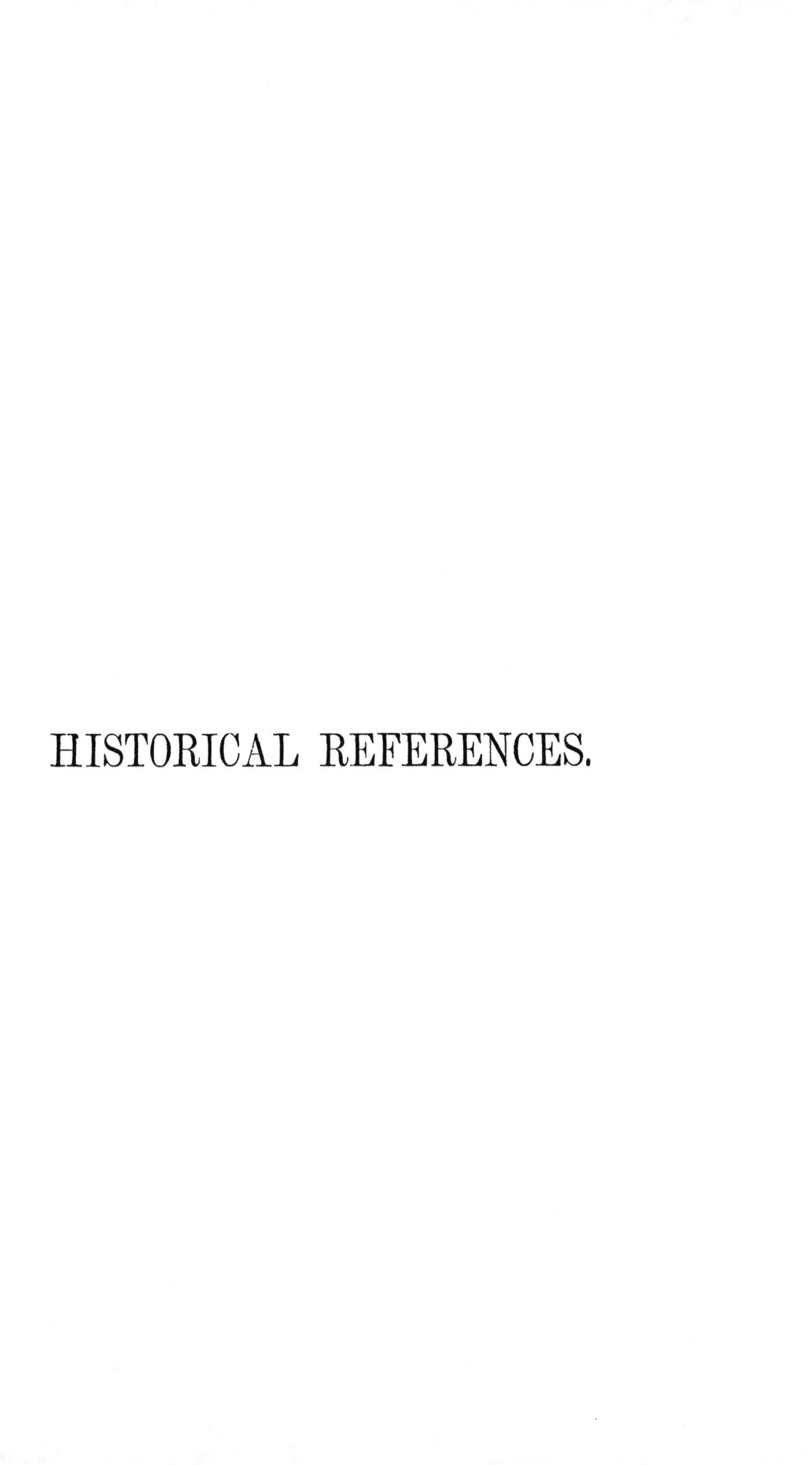

HISTORICAL REFERENCES.

HISTORICAL REFERENCES

TO THE LEGISLATION AND MUNICIPAL ACTION RESPECTING THE BACK BAY AND ADJACENT TERRITORY.[1]

Anno.
The "Colonial Ordinance," so called, of this date, was an 1641.
ancient law of Massachusetts, probably actually passed in 1647. 1647.
It is in the following words: "That in all creeks, coves, and other places about and upon salt water, where the sea ebbs and flows, the proprietor of the land adjoining shall have propriety to the low-water mark, where the sea does not ebb above a hundred rods, and not more wheresoever it ebbs further."

This law has never been changed, and all the riparian proprietors rely upon this law for their boundaries at low-water mark.

May 15. At town meeting this day the marsh lands at the 1770.
bottom of the Common were ordered to be leased.

July 30. Seven ropewalks at the great fire in Pearl and 1794.
Purchase streets, were burnt and destroyed, and great interest was made to remove the ropewalks from the middle of the town; and the town, in sympathy for the sufferers, on Sept. 1, voted to Isaac Davis and others the right of using the land at the bottom of the Common, on certain conditions, and six ropewalks were at that time erected there. They were all destroyed by fire (five being rebuilt again), Feb. 18, 1806.

Aug. 31. The selectmen of Boston executed a deed to 1796.
William and A. McNeil, two of the first grantees, for ropewalks. One of the conditions of said deed is, "that the inhabitants reserve the liberty and privilege, at any time here-

---

[1] Enlarged from the Appendix to the Report of the Joint Special Committee on the Back Bay streets, City Doc. 81 of 1863.

1796. after, to carry sluiceways or drains through the said land, in any direction towards the salt water."

1800. About this period Charles Street was laid out.

1813. June 11. A project of erecting a western avenue or mill-dam was brought before the town, and the inhabitants gave their assent to its execution.

Boston, Oct. 21. A Town Meeting was holden on Wednesday last, the Hon. Thomas Dawes, Moderator. The report of a Committee, consisting of the Selectmen and a citizen from each of the wards, on the petition of I. P. Davis and others, for liberty to build a Milldam and Turnpike Road, from the bottom of Beacon Street, and for other mill improvements, was taken up. The report went largely into the merits of the subject, and proposes that the Town do cede or grant to the corporation when organized, certain lands and flats, on condition that certain improvements are duly made before the year 1815. The report having been printed, and circulated for the information of the inhabitants, a very feeble opposition was made to it, and it was accepted by nearly an unanimous vote. The Committee also reported that agents be appointed by the Town, to attend the sittings of the Commissioners of the General Court, to whom the petition should be referred, to see that all the necessary conditions are inserted in the act of incorporation, and that the right of subscription of the inhabitants for a due proportion of shares be reserved to such persons as wish to engage in the undertaking; which was accepted, and the Hon. Thomas Dawes, Wm. Sullivan, Josiah Marshall, Chas. Davis, and Wm. Hammatt, Esqrs., were appointed the Agents.[1]

1814. June 14. A charter was granted to the Boston and Roxbury Mill Corporation,[2] giving them authority to build a dam from Charles Street, in Boston, to the upland at Sewell Point (so called), in Brookline.

1818. Jan. 9. Uriah Cotting, Esq. issued an address on the advantages of a western avenue and mill power to the city. Subscription papers were opened, and all the shares were taken

---

[1] Columbian Centinel, Oct. 23, 1813.

[2] See ante, p. 166.

in one day, and the next day were on sale at an advanced price. 1818.
Afterwards these shares greatly depreciated. Mr. Cotting did not live to see the completion of the avenue. Col. Loammi Baldwin took his place.

Four of the ropewalks were again destroyed by fire, at the 1819.
bottom of the Common.

July 2. The Western Avenue or Milldam was opened for 1821.
passengers, and a cavalcade of citizens, under the direction of Gen. Wm. H. Sumner, entered the town over the Dam, and was received on this side by the inhabitants of Boston.

This year the City of Boston was incorporated.

By a partition deed, Gravelly Point and the land and flats in 1822.
the Receiving Basin were conveyed to David Sears and others.

Jan. 17. An Act entitled "An Act to authorize the Bos- 1823.
ton and Roxbury Mill Corporation to widen their dam,"[1] was passed by the Legislature.

April 28. An agreement was made between Roxbury and Boston, establishing the line between them. Confirmed by the act of 1836, ch. 37.

Feb. 11. An act was passed, authorizing the Boston and 1824.
Roxbury Mill Corporation to fill their flats and tide waters to the extent of 200 feet more.[2]

The respective boundaries between the City of Boston and land of David Sears and others, were established by indenture.

Feb. 25. The City purchased all the rights of the proprietors of the ropewalks, in the land now known as the Public Garden.

This year, the Boston Water Power Company were incorporated,[3] in whom the interest within the basin is now vested (1850).

Dec. 26. An Indenture in three parts was entered into 1826
between the City of Boston, E. McKennon, the Boston and Roxbury Mill Corporation, and other proprietors of the flats,[4] and a line was agreed upon and established as the line of flowage, which is marked on several well-known plans as "the

---

[1] See ante p. 166. [2] See ante p. 166. [3] See ante p. 176. [4] See ante p. 209.

1826. line between the Boston & Roxbury Mill Corporation and the City of Boston and others."

1827. Feb. 1. An Indenture was made between the City of Boston and the Boston and Roxbury Mill Corporation,[1] confirming the indenture of Dec. 26, 1826, each party releasing certain rights to the other. This deed not only confirms the previous deed of 1826, but also gives to the City of Boston the entire control of erecting buildings on the Back Bay, the digging and laying of drains, &c.

1832. May 9. The Boston and Roxbury Mill Corporation, by an Indenture,[2] transferred to the Water Power Company a large part of their property, with certain exceptions and covenants.

This year the respective boundaries between the city of Roxbury and David Sears were established by Indentures.

1836. This year the respective boundaries of the City of Boston and Town of Roxbury in the empty basin or Back Bay were confirmed and established by an act of the Legislature.

All the original surveys from 1822 to 1836, as per plans of S. P. Fuller, show that the full basin contains 193 acres 2 qrs. 26 rods to high water, and the receiving basin 549 acres 1 qr. 5 rods to high water.

(By lines delineated by the Town of Boston in 1813, $466\frac{3}{4}$ acres; by line of flowage in 1826, in March, $493\frac{3}{4}$ acres; by line established December, 1226, $412\frac{1}{4}$ acres.)

837. Ephraim Marsh's petition to have the Sewer in Fayette Street repaired, was referred to a Committee. A Sewer was laid, and assessments made by the Supt. of Sewers were approved by the

1838. Board.

January. The City of Boston assigned to Horace Gray and Associates $20\frac{1}{2}$ acres of Back Bay land for a Public Garden on certain terms and conditions. The assignment was never accepted, and no action was ever had under it.

This year the B. & R. M. Corporation transferred another parcel of their flats to the Boston Water Power Company.

E. Marsh offered Fayette Street for acceptance. Petition of Denison for abatement of Sewer Assessment denied. An order was passed to pay E. Marsh for repairing the street.

---

[1] See ante p. 214. [2] See ante p. 222.

February 1. By an Act of Legislature, Horace Gray and 1839.
Associates were made a Corporation under the name of "Proprietors of the Botanic Garden in Boston." The Corporation was never completed.

E. Marsh renewed his application for the acceptance of Fayette 1842.
Street, and the Committee offered to accept if a bond was given to indemnify the City from grade damages; which was declined.

An Act of the General Court gave the right to the B. & R. 1843.
Mill Corporation to fill up and use 100 feet of flats north of the Milldam, to Sewell's Point in Brookline.[1]

The Commonwealth passed an Act, granting permission for 1844.
the B. & R. M. Corporation to extend a wharf at the foot of Beacon Street.[2]

E. Marsh again petitioned for the acceptance of Fayette Street. 1845.

Petitions for repair and acceptance of Fayette Street were pre- 1846.
sented by Mr. Marsh. The Board gave him leave to withdraw.

August 11. The Boston W. P. Company "released in fee" to the B. & Worcester R. R. Company a tract of land within the basin.

October 26. An order was passed by the City Council, granting the residue of the land between the Public Garden and the continuation of Boylston Street, to Horace Gray and Associates, on the same terms, &c. as the previous grant in 1838; but no use was made of the grant.

Fayette Street was accepted. 1848.

May 10. The General Court passed a Resolve appointing five Commissioners to consider and report respecting the rights and duties of the Commonwealth in the Harbor and Back Bay and respecting the filling up of the flats, &c.

September 4. The Commissioners met, and again met on 25th September, and held also eight subsequent meetings; all the interested parties appeared before them.

July 2. The Board of Mayor and Aldermen order a special 1849.
committee to report the best mode of drainage for that part of the City which drains into the Back Bay.

---

[1] See ante p. 166. [2] See ante p. 166.

1849. October 1. The Board ordered the report and plans to be accepted and adopted (according to plan of drainage presented by E. Lincoln, Jr.), and appointed a Committee with full powers to advertise and contract, limiting the amount to $ 50,000, the work not to be commenced before 1st May, 1850.

The Board of Mayor and Aldermen ordered the Report and plan of E. Lincoln, Jr. to be recommitted and submitted to E. S. Chesbrough and W. P. Parrott for their examination and opinion, and the Committee reported to adopt the plans of Messrs. Chesbrough and Parrott.[1]

1850. March. The State Commissioners made a Report giving a description of the Back Bay as cut off by the Milldam, and a statement of the rights and titles claimed by the various parties.

H. A. S. Dearborn, Mayor of Roxbury, sent a Remonstrance to the General Court against the action of the Water Power Company in filling up the flats, &c., &c.

May. Three Commissioners were appointed by the Legislature, under the Resolves of this date respecting the Back Bay Lands; and the Cities of Boston and Roxbury, B. & R. M. Corporation, the B. W. Power Company, and other parties, by their counsel, appeared before them November 13, 1850.

December 16. A letter was addressed by David Sears, Esq., to the Chairman of the Commission on the Back Bay, relating to an extension of the Public Garden, with a lake, &c.

1852. March 11. The State Commissioners in their Report make a full statement of the rights of all parties, with the titles claimed by Municipal and other Corporations, &c., in the Back Bay and flats; and an Act[2] was passed declaring the title of the Commonwealth to all the flats or lands within the two basins of the Back Bay below the riparian line, &c. Resolves[3] were also passed authorizing the appointment of three Commissioners to determine the rights of claimants of land below high-water mark to sell the lands of the Commonwealth, to devise plans for

[1] City Doc. 48, 1849.

[2] An Act to secure the title of the Commonwealth to flats or lands in the Back Bay in Boston Harbor, 1852, chap. 253.

[3] Resolves concerning Boston Harbor and the Back Bay, 1852, chap. 79.

filling and improving the same, diverting the flats from mill 1852.
purposes to land purposes.

The Commissioners of the State divided with the Boston 1854.
Water Power Company.[1] It was a part of the stipulations with the State that the tolls upon the Milldam should cease from and after May 1, 1863.

December. The Mayor was authorized to petition the Legislature for a grant in fee of a portion of the Back Bay, with certain privileges and conditions.

May. The State Commissioners addressed a communication 1855.
to the Mayor of Boston, calling his attention to the drains which they propose to have constructed through the lands on the Back Bay. This was laid before the City Council and sent to a Committee.

Resolves[2] were passed authorizing the State Commissioners to lay out and construct streets and sewers at the Back Bay, and authorizing the construction of railways upon the Back Bay to facilitate the filling. The title of the Commissioners was changed to the "Commissioners on the Back Bay."

February 25. David Sears, Esq., and the Riparian Proprie- 1856.
tors sent a memorial to the General Court, complaining of the nuisance caused by the Boston Water Power Company in cutting off the ebb and flow of the sea; and asking protection, &c.

A Joint Committee of the Legislature reported several Resolves relating to the filling up the Back Bay, grading streets, &c.

March. John S. Sleeper, Mayor of Roxbury, remonstrated against the passage of the "Resolves concerning the Back Bay."[2]

March. The heirs of Ephraim Harrington, Eben Francis, and the City of Boston, also remonstrated against passing the "Resolves concerning the Back Bay."

April 21. The Joint Committee reported "Resolves in relation to lands in Back Bay, &c.," in an amended form; and

---

[1] See ante p. 234. [2] Resolves in favor of giving additional powers to the Commissioners on Boston Harbor and the Back Bay, 1855, chap. 60.

1856. Resolves[1] were passed appointing a Joint Committee of the Legislature to sell the Back Bay lands, to modify contracts before made, &c.; also increasing the capital stock of the Water Power Co. to enable them to improve. An Act[2] was also passed directing the first proceeds of sales of Back Bay Lands, to the amount of $300,000, to be invested for the redemption of unfunded debt-scrip.

December. An Indenture was executed between the State, City, and Water Power Company,[3] the several parties releasing certain rights and privileges to each other.

1857. An Act[4] was passed confirming the Tripartite Indenture of 1856. Resolves[5] were passed authorizing the Commissioners to use not more than half the proceeds of sales for continuing the filling.

1858. In April, the first announcement was made that a scheme of building on the Back Bay was to be carried into execution, and efforts were made by George H. Snelling, Esq., and others, to prevent the accomplishment of this measure, on sanitary and economical grounds.

1859. An Act[6] was passed increasing the school fund and granting aid to several institutions of learning out of the proceeds of Back Bay land sales; but reserving a fund of $100,000 for the support of bridges and roads on the Back Bay.[7] An Act[8] was also passed changing the boundary line between Boston and Roxbury; requiring the Commissioners to fill up Arlington Street, and build the great sewer contemplated by the Tri-

---

[1] Resolves in relation to lands in the Back Bay, 1856, chap. 76.

[2] An Act making provision for the unfunded debt of the Commonwealth, 1856, chap. 235.

[3] See ante p. 258.

[4] An Act to confirm an Indenture concerning the Back Bay, 1857, chap. 169.

[5] Resolves concerning the Back Bay, 1857, chap. 70.

[6] An Act to increase the school fund, and to grant aid to the Museum of Comparative Zoology, Tufts', Williams', and Amherst Colleges, and the Wesleyan Academy at Wilbraham, out of the proceeds of the sales of Back Bay lands; 1859; chap. 154.

[7] This last provision was repealed by Acts of 1861, chap. 201.

[8] An Act in relation to the Back Bay and the Public Garden in the City of Boston; 1859; chap. 210.

partite Indenture, and authorizing the Governor of Massachusetts and the Mayor of Boston to appoint three Commissioners to determine what equivalent (in lands) the State should give the City for relinquishing its right to build on the strip of land between the Public Garden and Arlington Street. This act was submitted to the people (April 25, 1859) of Boston, and accepted; and the Commissioners awarded to the City two lots of land, then valued at about $40,000. Another Act[1] was passed requiring conveyances of land to be approved by the Governor and Council; and also providing that if chap. 210, Acts of 1859, should not have full effect, the rights of neither party should be prejudiced. Resolves[2] were passed giving the Land Agent, under the Governor and Council, control of all the Commonwealth's flats, except the Back Bay. 1859.

April. An Act was passed incorporating the Massachusetts Institute of Technology, and appropriating about 130,000 feet of land for the purposes of the Institute and the Boston Society of Natural History. 1861.

The following resolve[3] was passed:—

Resolved, That the Commissioners on Public Lands are hereby authorized and instructed to forthwith negotiate with the Boston Water Power Company and with the Riparian owners of territory lying west of the land of the Commonwealth and east of the Cross dam adjoining the full basin, so called, for an improvement of the lands of the said section, and of the lands of the Commonwealth contiguous thereto, by a reservation of a water space therein. And for the purposes of this Resolve the said Commissioners may alter and amend any Indenture or contract, with the consent of all parties to the same. Provided, however, that no such alteration and no Indenture or contract executed under this Resolve shall be binding upon this Commonwealth until all the provisions thereof shall be reported to and ratified by the next Legislature of the Commonwealth.

---

[1] An Act in relation to conveyances of lands or flats belonging to the Commonwealth.

[2] Resolves concerning flats and shores belonging to the Commonwealth; 1859; chap. 103.

[3] Chap. 201 Resolves of 1861.

1866. An Act[1] was passed giving the City of Boston authority to purchase or otherwise take the land and buildings on the territory between Boylston and Tremont streets and the Back Bay, with a view of raising the same, and improving the drainage; with a clause appointing Commissioners to determine whether the State or Water Power Co., were responsible in any degree for the existing defective drainage. This act was made subject to the acceptance of the Boston Water Power Company; and was by that Company rejected.

The Legislature confirmed the Tripartite Indenture of 1864.

---

[1] An Act for the better drainage of certain lands in the City of Boston, and for the preservation of the public health in said City; 1866; chap. 229.

A DIGEST

OF

DECISIONS OF MUNICIPAL INTEREST

OF THE

SUPREME JUDICIAL COURT

OF

MASSACHUSETTS.

1804–1865.

PREFACE.

This digest has been prepared in accordance with the suggestion of the committee under whose supervision the last edition of the Laws and Ordinances of Boston was published, that the supplementary volume proposed by them should contain "an explanatory list . . . of the cases decided in the Supreme Court upon points of municipal interest." Laws and Ordinances, (ed. of 1863,) page XIV.

All the published volumes of reports of the decisions of the Supreme Judicial Court of this state have been carefully examined in its preparation, from the first volume of Massachusetts Reports to the tenth volume of Allen's Reports, inclusive, and also the decisions which are to appear in the unpublished volumes (the twelfth, fifteenth, and sixteenth) of Gray's Reports. Some unpublished decisions in the hands of Mr. Allen are also cited. In citing unpublished decisions, those volumes of reports are referred to in which the cases will probably appear.

It has been thought best to omit from this digest decisions considered to have no direct or indirect application to the affairs of the city of Boston. Among these are cases concerning the form, service and return of warrants for town meetings, concerning the creation of and alterations in school districts, and concerning controversies between towns and county commissioners as to the construction of ways.

Some decisions considered to have been rendered obsolete by subsequent legislation have also been omitted. Among these are the unpublished cases concerning alien passengers in Boston, decided in 1860.

JAMES C. DAVIS.

BOSTON, June 1, 1866.

INDEX.

NOTE.—Titles which contain references to other titles only, are printed in italic capitals in this index.

PAGE.

ACTIONS 1

SET-OFF 4

TRUSTEE PROCESS 5

AMUSEMENTS 5

ANNEXATION AND DIVISION OF TOWNS 5

APPRENTICES 6

APPROPRIATIONS 6

OF THE REMEDY IN EQUITY IN CASES OF ILLEGAL APPROPRIATIONS . . . 9

ASSESSORS 9

BONDS 9

BOUNDARIES 10

BOUNTIES TO VOLUNTEERS 11

BRIDGES 11

BUILDINGS 11

BURIALS AND BURIAL-GROUNDS 11

CARRIAGES 11

LAW OF THE ROAD 12

FAST DRIVING 12

CHARTER 12

COLLECTORS 13

COMMON AND PUBLIC SQUARES 13

CONSTABLES 13

CONSTITUTIONAL LAW 13

CONTRACTS 14

DISTURBANCE OF PUBLIC MEETINGS 16

DOGS 17

DOMICIL 17

ELECTIONS 19

QUALIFICATIONS OF ELECTORS 20

OF THE REMEDY AGAINST OFFICERS FOR REFUSING VOTES, &C 20

PAGE.

ESTOPPEL 21

FANEUIL HALL MARKET 21

FAST DRIVING. See CARRIAGES.

FERRIES 22

FIELD DRIVERS; POUNDS AND IMPOUNDING OF CATTLE 22

FINANCE 25

FIRE 25

FISH 26

FLATS 26

GUNPOWDER 26

HEALTH 27

HOUSE OF CORRECTION AND JAILS 28

IMPOUNDING OF CATTLE. See FIELD DRIVERS, &c.

INDICTMENT 30

INFORMATION 30

JURIES 30

LAW OF THE ROAD. See CARRIAGES.

LICENSES 31

LORD'S DAY 31

MARKET-HOUSES 31

MILITIA 31

MILK 31

NUISANCES 32

OFFICERS 32

ORDINANCES AND BY-LAWS 35

OVERSEERS OF THE POOR 37

PAUPERS 38

I. WHAT CONSTITUTES A PAUPER, AND WHO CAN ACQUIRE A SETTLEMENT 38

II. SETTLEMENT OF PAUPERS; HOW ACQUIRED OR LOST 39

(*a*) By Approbation, and not being warned out 39

(*b*) By Derivation 40

(*c*) By living on a Freehold Estate, &c 42

(*d*) By having an Estate, &c., and being assessed therefor 43

(*e*) By serving as a Town Officer, or being an Ordained Minister 44

(*f*) By Incorporation or Division of Towns 44

(*g*) By Residence and paying Taxes 47

(*h*) How prevented by being relieved as a Pauper 49

(*i*) How lost, when once acquired 50

III. ACTIONS FOR SUPPORTING PAUPERS 50

(*a*) Against the Pauper's Kindred 50

(*b*) By Individuals against Towns 51

(*c*) By Towns against Individuals 53

(*d*) By Towns against Towns 53

(1) *When and for what the Action will lie; and of the Pleadings, Evidence, and Trial* 53

PAGE.

(2) *Of the Notice* 58

(3) *Estoppel* 60

IV. Removal of Paupers 61

V. Penalty for bringing a Pauper into a Town 61

VI. Lunatic Paupers and State Paupers 62

PENALTIES 63

POLICE 64

POUNDS. See Field Drivers, &c.

PRESCRIPTION 65

PUBLIC BUILDINGS 65

PUBLIC LANDS 65

RAILROADS 66

Street Railways 69

RECONSIDERATION 69

RECORDS 69

REPRESENTATIVES IN THE GENERAL COURT 70

REWARDS 70

RIOTS 71

SCHOOLS 71

SEALS 74

SET-OFF. See Actions.

SEWERS AND DRAINS 75

SMOKING IN THE STREETS 76

SPENDTHRIFTS 77

STABLES 77

STATE TREASURY 77

STEAM ENGINES 77

SWINE 77

TAXES 77

I. Persons and Property subject to Taxation 77

II. Where and to whom Polls and Property shall be assessed . 80

III. Manner and Validity of the Assessment 84

IV. Collection of Taxes 86

(*a*) Generally 86

(*b*) By Action at Law 87

(*c*) By Arrest 87

(*d*) By Distress and Sale; Lien on Land 88

V. Remedy for an Illegal Tax 91

(*a*) Whether by Action or Abatement 91

(*b*) Of the Action to recover back 92

(*c*) Of the Abatement 93

(*d*) Of Actions against Assessors and others 94

TREASURER 94

TRUSTEE PROCESS. See Actions.

TRUSTS 95

PAGE.

WATER 95

WAYS 96

I. PROCEEDINGS IN LAYING OUT AND ALTERING PUBLIC WAYS 96

(a) Application; and Adjudication as to whether the Public Safety and Convenience require the Laying out or Alteration 96

(b) Location or Laying out, and Altering; Prior Notice thereof; Agreements with Land owners 98

(c) Where Ways may be laid out 102

II. PUBLIC WAYS BY DEDICATION, BY PRESCRIPTION AND USE, AND BY NECESSITY 103

(a) By Dedication 103

(b) By Prescription and Use 104

(c) By Necessity 106

III. DISCONTINUING PUBLIC WAYS; DAMAGES THEREFOR 106

IV. PROCEEDINGS ON AN APPLICATION FOR A JURY 107

(a) Who are entitled to Damages; Waiver of Damages 107

(b) Application for a Jury, and Notice thereon 108

(c) Proceedings before Jury; their Powers and Duties 110

(d) Elements and Computation of Damages; Evidence thereof 110

(e) Verdict, and Judgment thereon 114

V. REPAIRING PUBLIC WAYS; POWERS AND DUTIES OF HIGHWAY SURVEYORS 115

VI. DEFECTS AND OBSTRUCTIONS IN WAYS 116

(a) Liability of Towns to an Action 116

(b) Where the Plaintiff's Negligence or other Causes concur 120

(c) Evidence, Trial, Damages 124

(d) Indictments against Towns 127

(e) Liability of Individuals for Obstructions; Civilly and Criminally . . 128

VII. RIGHTS OF THE PUBLIC AND OF LAND OWNERS IN THE SOIL OF PUBLIC WAYS 131

VIII. LIMITS AND BOUNDARIES OF WAYS; FENCES, &C. 132

IX. RAILROAD CROSSINGS; SIDEWALKS IN THE CITIES OF LOWELL AND CHARLESTOWN 133

X. OF THE REMEDIES FOR IRREGULARITIES IN LAYING OUT AND COMPLETING WAYS; AND OF SOME OTHER MATTERS 135

TABLE OF CASES 138

DIGEST.

ACTIONS.

1. When judgment is recovered against the inhabitants of a city, town, parish, or school district, execution may be levied upon the property of any inhabitant thereof, as each inhabitant must be considered a party to the suit. 5 Dane Ab. 158. *Riddle* v. *Proprietors of Locks and Canals*, 7 Mass. 187 (1810). *Brewer* v. *New Gloucester*, 14 Mass. 216 (1817). *Chase* v. *Merrimack Bank*, 19 Pick. 564 (1837). *Gaskill* v. *Dudley*, 6 Met. 546 (1843).

2. D. recovered judgment by default against a school district, in an action of contract, and levied his execution on the goods of G., an inhabitant of the district. G. sued D. in an action of trespass, for so levying on his goods. *Held*, that G. could not give evidence that D. ought not to have recovered judgment against the district, by reason of a breach by him of the contract declared on in his action. *Gaskill* v. *Dudley*, 6 Met. 546 (1843).

3. An incorporated city need not sue in the name of "the inhabitants of the city," but may sue by its name of incorporation. *Lowell* v. *Morse*, 1 Met. 473 (1840).

4. A suit by "the city of Lowell," (the corporate name of the plaintiffs,) on a bond given to the plaintiffs, may be maintained, although it appears that the plaintiffs were named in the bond "the inhabitants of the city of Lowell." *Ib.*

5. An action on a promise to the mayor and aldermen of a city to pay for a license for a theatrical exhibition, is rightly brought in the name of the city, the mayor and aldermen being merely agents of the city. *Boston* v. *Schaffer*, 9 Pick. 415 (1830).

6. On a bond made to the Commonwealth, "for the use of the town of N.," no action lies by the town, although the forfeitures belong to the town by statute. *Northampton* v. *Elwell*, 4 Gray, 81 (1855).

7. An action on the bond of a collector of taxes, brought by authority of the town treasurer, in the name of the town to whom it was made, may be maintained without proof of a formal vote of the town authorizing the action. *Blackstone* v. *Taft*, 4 Gray, 250 (1855).

8. An action sounding in tort may be maintained against a municipal corporation. *Thayer* v. *Boston*, 19 Pick. 511 (1837).

9. A municipal corporation may be liable in an action of the case, for an act which would warrant a like action against an individual, provided that such act is done by the authority of the corporation, or of a branch of its government invested with jurisdiction to act for the corporation upon the subject to which the particular act relates, or that after the act has been done, it has been ratified by the corporation by any similar act of its officers. *Ib.*

10. A city is not liable for an assault and battery committed by its police officers, even though it was done in an attempt to enforce an ordinance of the city. *Buttrick* v. *Lowell*, 1 Allen, 172 (1861).

11. The action of a city in authorizing and employing its solicitor to appear and defend an action brought against its police officers for an assault and battery committed by them, does not make the city liable to pay damages for the assault and battery. *Ib.*

12. A town is not liable for an injury sustained by reason of the negligence of a laborer employed by one of its highway surveyors, to aid him in performing the duties of his office. *Walcott* v. *Swampscott*, 1 Allen, 101 (1861).

13. An action of tort lies against a city in behalf of the owner of land through which its agents have unlawfully made a sewer. *Hildreth* v. *Lowell*, 11 Gray, 345 (1858).

14. A town is not liable for an arrest and imprisonment by its collector, for nonpayment of taxes, illegally included in his warrant, and since abated, although it afterwards pays the collector's fees for serving the warrant, and the charges of the imprisonment. *Perley* v. *Georgetown*, 7 Gray, 464 (1856).

15. If a tax title proves invalid, the purchaser at the collector's sale cannot maintain

an action against the town to recover back the money paid by him as the consideration of the purchase, and the expenses of defending his title. *Lynde* v. *Melrose*, 10 Allen, 49 (1865). But see St. 1862, c. 183, § 6.

16. A town, which has assumed the duties of school districts, is not liable for an injury sustained by a scholar attending the public school from a dangerous excavation in the schoolhouse yard, owing to the negligence of the town officers. *Bigelow* v. *Randolph*, 14 Gray, 541 (1860).

17. A police officer is not a servant of the city which appoints him, in any such sense as to take away his right of action against it for an injury sustained by reason of a defective highway. *Kimball* v. *Boston*, 1 Allen, 417 (1861).

18. If the expense of keeping a bridge in repair is imposed by statute upon several towns and a railroad company jointly, with a provision that the municipal authorities of one of the towns shall have the care and superintendence of it, and shall employ all services necessary in the care of it, no action lies against said town in favor of the railroad company, to recover for damages sustained by the latter in consequence of a defect in the bridge. *Malden & Melrose Railroad* v. *Charlestown*, 8 Allen, 245 (1864).

19. County commissioners, having laid out a highway through a town, and across two channels of a stream, ordered the town to make an embankment, several rods from the highway, which should turn all the waters of the stream into one of its channels, and prevent the necessity of making more than one bridge in the highway. The town passed no vote and did no act in the matter, but the selectmen caused the embankment to be made, and paid for making it by an order on the town treasurer. *Held*, that the town was not liable to an action by the owner of land which was flooded and injured in consequence of the making of the embankment. *Anthony* v. *Adams*, 1 Met. 284 (1840).

20. An action of tort will not lie against a city for obstructing a stream to the injury of a mill, by the erection of a bridge, if the bridge is suitably constructed so as to let the water pass off with reasonable freedom, at all times, except in case of extraordinary freshets not occurring annually. *Sprague* v. *Worcester*, 13 Gray, 193 (1859). See *Lawrence* v. *Fairhaven*, 5 Gray, 110; *Perry* v. *Worcester*, 6 Gray, 544; *Wheeler* v. *Worcester*, 10 Allen.

21. No action lies against a city for the injury occasioned to land bounding on a public street from the accumulation of water on the surface of the street, which the city has neglected to drain. *Flagg* v. *Worcester*, 13 Gray, 601 (1859).

22. The remedy of an owner of land for injury done to his land by the city by making an excavation in a public street, and thus turning the water accumulated thereon into a private drain running through his land, is by petition under the Rev. Sts. c. 25, § 6, (Gen. Sts. c. 44, § 19,) and not by action of tort. *Ib.*

23. No action lies against a city for a failure to keep a public sewer and cesspool in repair, whereby waste water accumulates and flows into the cellar of a neighboring house, which is not connected by a drain with the public sewer. *Barry* v. *Lowell*, 8 Allen, 127 (1864).

24. A citizen who furnished cattle to a public enemy, at the request of the selectmen and other citizens of the town, in compliance with the exactions of such enemy upon the town, and to prevent the execution of his threats of violence, acquired thereby no right of action against the town for his indemnity. *Haliburton* v. *Frankfort*, 14 Mass. 214 (1817).

25. An inhabitant of another state, who sustains an injury in consequence of a defect in a highway, may bring his action against the town or city bound to repair the same, in any county in the commonwealth. *Raymond* v. *Lowell*, 6 Cush. 524 (1850).

26. A town which voluntarily pays the fees of commissioners appointed by the legislature to establish the boundary line between it and another town, under a resolve of the legislature providing that such fees shall be paid by the towns, one half by each, cannot recover from the other town any part of the sum paid. *South Scituate* v. *Hanover*, 9 Gray, 420 (1857).

27. Money charged by a city for a wagoner's license, and paid with a full knowledge of the facts, will be deemed to have been paid voluntarily, though paid under protest, and cannot be recovered back. *Cook* v. *Boston*, 9 Allen, 393 (1864).

28. Selectmen of a town may discontinue a suit in equity brought by them to restrain a railroad corporation from unlawfully and dangerously running cars on their road; although a temporary injunction has been issued; and although some of the inhabitants of the town move to come in and prosecute the suit. *Mears* v. *Boston & N. Y. Central Railroad*, 5 Gray, 371 (1855).

29. Orders for money, made payable to bearer, drawn by the selectmen of a town and accepted by the town treasurer, without express authority of the town, will not render the town liable to an action in the name of any one other than the person to whom they were issued. *Smith* v. *Cheshire*, 13 Gray, 318 (1859).

30. A town treasurer is not liable in an action for money had and received, to a creditor

of the town, for merely neglecting to pay over money in his hands appropriated by the town to the payment of the claim of such creditor, and ordered to be so paid by the selectmen; but the remedy of the creditor is by an action against the town. *Weston* v. *Gibbs*, 23 Pick. 205 (1839).

31. In an action brought by a town against the town treasurer for money had and received by the defendant to the plaintiff's use, the evidence tended to show that the defendant had received certain sums as such treasurer, which had not been charged to him in his annual settlement, and that, therefore, a larger balance should have been credited to the town by him in his account. The defendant's answer put in issue any such liability. *Held*, that the whole account between the parties was necessarily opened, and that the defendant might show that certain taxes charged to him in the account had not been legally assessed, and that he could not legally collect them. *Adams* v. *Farnsworth*, 16 Gray, (1860.)

32. A town is not liable to an action by the state commissioner for the sale of liquors, for the price of liquors bought of such commissioner on credit by the town agent appointed under St. 1855, c. 215, § 5 (Gen. Sts. c. 86, § 17). *Mansfield* v. *Stoneham*, 15 Gray, (1860). But see now St. 1861, c. 136, § 2.

33. Where a statute requires a demand to be made in writing on the mayor and aldermen of a city thirty days before the commencement of a suit, an agreement in a case stated, that a demand was made on the city, will be understood to be such a demand as is required by the statute. *Jennison* v. *Roxbury*, 9 Gray, 32 (1857).

34. In action against a town to recover for work done under a contract in building a road, the plaintiff may recover under a general count the value of the work, provided it was done in good faith and is beneficial to the defendants, although the contract has not been fully performed. *Reed* v. *Scituate*, 5 Allen, 120 (1862).

35. A city, whose charter and ordinances provide that no contract shall be binding on the city, unless made by some authorized agent, and within some appropriation for the purpose, is not liable for legal services, beneficial to the city, performed by counsel retained by a majority of the members of the board of aldermen, without any official action of the city council or of either branch thereof; although the usage of the city has been to pay such bills, approved by a committee of either board, without any formal vote. *Butler* v. *Charlestown*, 7 Gray 12 (1856).

36. Where a drain was dug by a surveyor of highways, for the purpose of raising a legal question as to the bounds of a highway, and the town appointed a committee to defend an action brought against the surveyor therefor, and voted to defray the expenses incurred by the committee, it was held, that the town was bound by such vote, and that the committee were entitled to compensation and indemnity from the town, for their expenses and services. *Bancroft* v. *Lynnfield*, 18 Pick. 566 (1836).

37. It is competent for the inhabitants of a town to take upon themselves the expenses of a suit against their agent or servant, in which the interests of the town are directly involved. *Babbitt* v. *Savoy*, 3 Cush. 530 (1849).

38. A town having appointed a committee for an illegal purpose, with authority to defend all suits which might grow out of the same, and also voted that all costs, expenses, and trouble which the committee might incur in the premises, should be paid by the town; it was held, that the town were not liable for the services of the committee rendered in effecting the purpose of their appointment; but were liable for services performed by them in defending an action brought against the town on account thereof; *Drake* v. *Stoughton*, 6 Cush. 393 (1850); and were also liable for professional services rendered by counsel employed by the committee in defence of such a suit. *Cushing* v. *Stoughton*, Ib. 389.

39. The inhabitants of a school district, having passed a vote to build a schoolhouse, appointed a committee to select and purchase a lot of land for that purpose, and, upon a report of the committee, gave them instructions to purchase a particular lot; the committee accordingly purchased the lot so designated, and as the only condition upon which they could obtain a conveyance, gave the seller their individual note for the purchase money; a deed was then made to the committee and the other inhabitants of the district, in their corporate capacity, of the lot of land thus purchased; the district subsequently rescinded their votes relative to the building of the schoolhouse, and the committee afterwards paid the note which they had given for the land. In an action by the committee against the district, it was held, that the plaintiffs were entitled to recover the sum so paid by them, notwithstanding they had reason to suppose, before the purchase was made, that a meeting of the district would be held for the purpose of rescinding the votes under which the plaintiffs were authorized to proceed, and notwithstanding the rescinding of those votes, and the fact that the payment was made by the plaintiffs subsequently thereto. *Kingman* v. *North Bridgewater*, 2 Cush. 426 (1848).

40. A town is not bound by its corporate vote, to pay the expenses of a field driver in defending a suit brought for taking up and impounding cattle running at large contrary to law; such agreement not being within the

scope of a town's corporate powers. *Vincent* v. *Nantucket*, 12 Cush. 103 (1853).

41. On a vote of a town to indemnify their selectmen against any claim for damages and costs of a certain description which may be legally substantiated against them, the selectmen may maintain an action against the town to recover the amount of a judgment rendered against them for such damages and costs, and the fees of counsel and witnesses, and other expenses, incurred reasonably and in good faith in defending the action in which the judgment was recovered, without proving that the town had notice of the pendency of the action. *Hadsell* v. *Hancock*, 3 Gray, 526 (1855).

42. A vote of a town to indemnify its three selectmen against any claim for damages and costs of a certain description which may be legally substantiated against them or either of them, will support a joint action against the town by two of the selectmen, without joining the third, to recover the amount of a judgment for such damages and costs recovered in an action against the two, and paid by one of them, and also the reasonable expenses of defending the action, paid and incurred by the two separately. *Ib.*

43. An action of tort lies against a city to recover damages occasioned by the obstruction, owing to negligence on the part of the city, of a natural watercourse, through a culvert under a highway, although the plaintiff is the owner of the land on both sides of the highway. *Parker* v. *Lowell*, 11 Gray, 353 (1858).

44. In an action against a city for damages suffered by the obstruction of a culvert for a watercourse under a highway, the judge instructed the jury that the burden of proof was on the plaintiff to show that the injury sustained by him was attributable solely to the negligence of the defendants in omitting to remove the obstruction, and that in the absence of any proof of neglect or want of care by the plaintiff or a stranger, in any way contributing to the injury or to the obstruction in the culvert, if the defendants through negligence suffered the culvert to be obstructed, and the injury was caused by reason solely of said obstruction, the defendants would be liable. It was held, that the defendants had no ground of exception. *Ib.*

45. Inhabitants of a town are not competent to be appraisers of land upon the extent of an execution in favor of the town. *Boston* v. *Tileston*, 11 Mass. 468 (1814). But see Gen. Sts. c. 122, § 13.

46. If the defendants in an action brought in favor of a town have filed an affidavit of merits at the first term, the objection that the action was brought without the authority of the town cannot be taken after the expiration of that term, even though they have leave to file their answer in the vacation. *Walpole* v. *Gray*, 11 Allen, (1865).

47. A citizen of a town who enlisted in the military service of the United States after a vote of the town to pay a monthly sum to each citizen thereof who should so enlist had been terminated, under St. 1861, c. 222, § 2, by the lapse of ninety days, cannot maintain any action against the town to recover the bounty so voted. *Curtis* v. *Pembroke*, 11 Allen, (1865),

48. If prior to St. 1861, c. 222, a town has voted that a certain sum monthly should be paid to each citizen of the town who should enlist in the military service of the state, with the intention of serving in the army of the United States, if called upon, a citizen who so enlisted under that vote, may, under that statute, maintain an action against the town to recover such pay for a time not exceeding ninety days from his enlistment. *Grover* v. *Pembroke*, 11 Allen, (1865).

49. Receiving state aid will not prevent a soldier from recovering any sum to which he may be entitled under the votes of the town in which he enlisted. *Ib.*

50. A vote passed at a town meeting, appointing a committee "to settle the dispute" between the town and the plaintiff, was held not to take the plaintiff's demand out of the statute of limitations. *Fiske* v. *Needham*, 11 Mass. 452 (1814).

51. A vote of an authorized committee of a city, electing their clerk city engineer for a year from a subsequent day, duly recorded, and signed by him as their clerk, is sufficient to take his appointment out of the statute of frauds, although the amount of compensation is not named in the vote. *Chase* v. *Lowell*, 7 Gray, 33 (1856).

See ANNEXATION AND DIVISION OF TOWNS, 5; APPROPRIATIONS, 20-23; CONTRACTS; DOGS, 2; ELECTIONS, 25-32; FINANCE; FIRE; FISH, 6-8; GUNPOWDER; HEALTH, 14; HOUSES OF CORRECTION AND JAILS; OFFICERS; ORDINANCES; PAUPERS; PENALTIES; SCHOOLS, 24, 27, 33-37; SEWERS AND DRAINS; TAXES; TREASURER; WATER, 2-4; WAYS.

Set-off.

52. Where the official bond, given to a town by a collector of taxes and his sureties, is several as well as joint, and the collector brings an action against the town on a demand which is itself the subject of set-off, the defendants may set off their claim on such bond for money which the plaintiff has received on tax bills committed to him for collection, and which he has not accounted for nor paid over. *Donelson* v. *Colerain*, 4 Met. 430 (1842).

53. Taxes, being neither judgments nor contracts, are not the subject of set-off under

the provisions of the Rev. Sts. c. 96 (Gen. Sts. c. 130). *Peirce* v. *Boston*, 3 Met. 520 (1842). See *Commonwealth* v. *Phœnix Bank*, 11 Met. 135; *Appleton* v. *Hopkins*, 5 Gray, 533.

Trustee Process.

54. An order of a city council, upon laying out a street, that a certain sum be paid, as damages, to a party over whose land the street was laid out, does not constitute a debt due from the city, and therefore does not make the city liable as trustee of such party, under the provisions of statute regulating the trustee process. *Fellows* v. *Duncan*, 13 Met. 332 (1847).

55. Payment of money by a town to the prudential committee of a school district in the town, for the purpose of being paid over to an instructor of a school for his wages, does not make the committee liable in the trustee process as the instructor's trustee, nor discharge the town from its liability to the instructor. *Clark* v. *Great Barrington*, 11 Pick. 260 (1831).

56. A city officer, who is chosen for a year, subject to be removed from office at any time, at the will of the mayor and aldermen, and whose salary is payable quarterly, may legally make an assignment of a quarter's salary before the quarter expires. *Brackett* v. *Blake*, 7 Met. 335 (1844).

57. Future wages to be earned under an existing appointment as watchman of a city may be assigned, by an order addressed to the treasurer of the city; and such an order, given in the middle of a month, for "the amount on my month's wages, when due," means the wages of that month. *Macomber* v. *Doane*, 2 Allen, 541 (1861); and see Ib. 40.

58. A city cannot be charged as trustee of a teacher of a public school, paid by a quarterly salary, upon a process of foreign attachment served in the middle of a quarter. *Hadley* v. *Peabody*, 13 Gray, 200 (1859).

59. A county is not chargeable, in a trustee process, for compensation due to a juror and ordered to be paid from the county treasury. *Williams* v. *Boardman*, 9 Allen, 570 (1865).

AMUSEMENTS.

1. Under St. 1821, c. 110, authorizing the mayor and aldermen of Boston to license theatrical exhibitions, the license need not be in writing. *Boston* v. *Schaffer*, 9 Pick. 415 (1830).

2. Under the provision authorizing the mayor and aldermen to license theatrical exhibitions, "on such terms and conditions as to them may seem just and reasonable," they may exact money for the license. *Ib.*

3. An action on a promise to the mayor and aldermen to pay for a license, is rightly brought in the name of the city, the mayor and aldermen being merely agents of the city. *Ib.*

4. It is competent to the legislature to grant to a city or town power to exact the payment of money as one of the conditions of granting a license for theatrical exhibitions. *Ib.*

5. A school for the teaching of dancing does not require a license from the mayor and aldermen or selectmen, although admittance thereto is paid for on each evening. *Commonwealth* v. *Gee*, 6 Cush. 174 (1850).

ANNEXATION AND DIVISION OF TOWNS.

1. The act for the annexation of Charlestown to Boston, (St. 1854, c. 433,) is unconstitutional and wholly void; because it undertakes to erect the territory of Charlestown, until the next decennial census, into a representative district which is neither a town nor a city; and contains no adequate provisions to secure to the inhabitants of Charlestown their rights to elect representatives and senators in the general court, and representatives in congress. And the mayor and aldermen of Charlestown were therefore justified in refusing to certify to the secretary of the Commonwealth the result of the votes of the inhabitants of Charlestown accepting said act. *Warren* v. *Charlestown*, 2 Gray, 84 (1854).

2. Where a part of a town had been annexed to and made part of a parish in another town, without notice to such town or to the inhabitants of the part so annexed, and the same had been acquiesced in for nearly eighty years; it was held to be too late for this court to inquire into the constitutional authority of the legislature to make such annexation. *Cobb* v. *Kingman*, 15 Mass. 197 (1818).

3. When an act incorporating part of a town and constituting it a new town provides that all the debts due to or from the original town shall be divided between the two towns, in proportion to the state valuation, and that the poor, with which the original town was then chargeable, together with those then removed therefrom and afterwards returning for support, shall be divided in the same proportion, — the legal construction of such a provision is, that the debts are to be paid to or by the original town, who may be compelled by the new town to pay over to it its proportion of debts received, and may compel such new town to reimburse its proportion of debts paid; and that the charges of maintaining the poor, and not their persons, are to be divided, each town having a remedy against the other

for a reimbursement of any excess of such charges beyond its due proportion. *Brewster* v. *Harwich*, 4 Mass. 278 (1808).

4. Such a provision does not affect the settlement of any of the inhabitants of either of the towns. *Ib.*

5. Where a town was divided, and a part of it established as a new town, after the commencement of a suit in equity by such town against a railroad corporation, for a nuisance to a public highway, which, upon the division, fell within the limits of the new town, and the act for the division provided that such suit should be assumed, and might be prosecuted to final judgment, by the new town, at their expense and for their benefit, but in the name of the old town; it was held, that the division did not operate to vacate or otherwise affect the suit. *Springfield* v. *Connecticut River Railroad*, 4 Cush. 63 (1849).

6. The act incorporating a new town, created partly from the town of B., provided that it should be entitled to a proportion of all the property, rights and credits of B. It was held, that such new town was not therefore entitled to any part of a fund arising from the sale of land originally appropriated to the use of the ministry in the town of B. *Harrison* v. *Bridgeton*, 16 Mass. 16 (1819).

7. Where part of a town is set off from one county and annexed to a town in another county, by a statute which provides that "all taxes heretofore assessed shall be paid in the same manner as heretofore," and that the first town "shall be holden to make the same appropriations on the territory thus set off, for roads, the current year, as though this act had not passed;" a highway which the county commissioners of the first county, before the act of separation took effect, laid out and ordered to be built by the first town, must be completed by that town, and its completion may be enforced by said commissioners, if it be proved that the town made an appropriation and assessed a tax for the purpose before the act took effect; but not otherwise. *Norwich* v. *Hampden*, 4 Gray, 172 (1855).

8. St. 1853, c. 114, incorporating the town of Nahant from the city of Lynn, and providing that it should be entitled to receive of the city of Lynn its proportion of all the corporate property then owned by Lynn, did not transfer or vest in Nahant the title to any real estate owned by Lynn. It gave them the right to receive their proportion of the corporate property. But when their proportion was ascertained, a conveyance would be necessary to pass the title to real estate. *Simmons* v. *Nahant*, 3 Allen, 316 (1862).

See Paupers, 32, 52, 105-135, 237, 266; Taxes, 33, 47, 63.

APPRENTICES.

1. Under St. 1793, c. 59, § 4, (Gen. Sts. c. 111, §§ 4, 5,) which provides that in certain cases male children may be bound out as apprentices by the overseers of the poor "until they come to the age of twenty-one years," the overseers are not authorized to bind out a male child to serve as an apprentice until he shall be twenty years of age. *Reidell* v. *Congdon*, 16 Pick. 44 (1834).

2. The same statute requires that in indentures of apprenticeship by overseers of the poor, provision shall be made for instructing the male children "to read, write, and cipher" and "for such other instruction, benefit and allowance, either within or at the end of the term, as to the overseers may seem fit and reasonable." It was held, that an indenture, in which the master merely covenanted to give the apprentice "the privilege of all the town school usually taught in the town" was void. *Ib.*

3. An indenture of apprenticeship entered into by overseers of the poor, which does not contain a provision for the instruction of the minor in reading, &c. pursuant to the statutes, is void in regard to all the parties. *Butler* v. *Hubbard*, 5 Pick, 250 (1828).

4. The covenants in an indenture of apprenticeship that the apprentice shall serve, and that the master shall instruct him and provide for him, are independent; so that if the apprentice, by reason of incurable illness, becomes unable to learn his master's trade, or to perform the stipulated services, the master cannot of his own authority put an end to the contract. *Powers* v. *Ware*, 2 Pick. 451 (1825).

5. So if the apprentice steal his master's goods. *Ib.*

6. The selectmen of a town, who were *ex officio* overseers of the poor, no persons having been especially chosen overseers, bound out a child as an apprentice, by an indenture wherein they designated themselves simply as selectmen. It was held, that the indenture was valid; and an action brought upon it by overseers of the poor was sustained. *Powers* v. *Ware*, 2 Pick. 451 (1825).

7. Where the master cut out his signature from the indenture, by permission of one only of the selectmen, it was held, that he was not discharged of the contract. *Ib.*

APPROPRIATIONS.

1. It is doubtful whether a town can legally vote to pay for property furnished by a citizen to a public enemy, at the request of the selectmen, in compliance with the exactions of such enemy upon the town, and to prevent the ex-

ecution of his threats of violence. *Haliburton* v. *Frankfort*, 14 Mass. 214 (1817).

2. Towns have no authority, without special authority from the legislature, in time of war and danger of hostile invasion, to raise money to give additional wages to the militia and for other purposes of defence. *Stetson* v. *Kempton*, 13 Mass. 272 (1816).

3. A town have no authority to vote money for the purchase of uniforms for an artillery company; and will be restrained by injunction from paying the money, even after the officers of the company, upon the faith of an order drawn in their favor by the selectmen on the town treasurer, have purchased the uniforms and deposited them in the armory, to be there kept as the property of the town. *Claflin* v. *Hopkinton*, 4 Gray, 502 (1855).

4. If an expenditure of money was reasonably necessary and proper to enable towns to fill the quotas of troops allotted to them respectively in the late war, it was competent for the legislature to authorize the appropriation of money for that purpose, or to confirm and make valid the doings of towns in raising money for that object. *Fowler* v. *Danvers*, 8 Allen 80 (1864).

5. The legislature have power to authorize towns to raise money by taxation for the purpose of refunding sums which have been contributed by individuals into a common fund for the general purpose of filling quotas of troops under calls of the President of the United States during the recent war; but not for the purpose of refunding sums paid by individuals for substitutes. *Freeland* v. *Hastings*, 10 Allen, 570 (1865).

6. The building of a theatre, a circus, or any other place of mere amusement, at the expense of the town, could not be justified under the term "necessary town charges." Nor could the inhabitants be lawfully taxed for the purpose of raising a statue or monument, these being matters of taste and not of necessity; unless, in populous and wealthy towns, they should be thought suitable ornaments to buildings or squares, the raising and maintenance of which are within the duty and care of the governors or officers of such towns. PARKER, C. J., in *Stetson* v. *Kempton*, 13 Mass. 279 (1816).

7. Cities and towns in this commonwealth, by virtue of their general powers, have authority, in their corporate capacity, to build a market-house, to appropriate money therefor, and to assess the same upon the inhabitants. *Spaulding* v. *Lowell*, 23 Pick. 71 (1839).

8. Where a town built a market-house two stories high, and appropriated the lower story for a market, which was *bona fide* their principal and leading object in erecting the building, it was held, that the appropriation of the upper story to other subordinate purposes was not such an excess of authority as to render the erection of the building and the raising of money therefor illegal. *Ib.*

9. A town which acts also as a parish, may raise money to repair a meeting-house as a compensation for the use of it for municipal purposes, or to pay a sexton for ringing the bell for town meetings, but such design should appear in the vote; for *prima facie* money to repair a meeting-house, or for the pay of a sexton, is for parochial and not municipal purposes, and cannot be assessed on such inhabitants as are not members of the parish. *Woodbury* v. *Hamilton*, 6 Pick. 101 (1828).

10. Towns have no authority to expend money, or pledge their credit, to celebrate the anniversary of the surrender of Cornwallis. *Tash* v. *Adams*, 10 Cush. 252 (1852). But see St. 1861, c. 165.

11. A town has no authority to appropriate money for the celebration of the Fourth of July. *Hood* v. *Lynn*, 1 Allen, 103 (1861). *Gerry* v. *Stoneham*, Ib. 319. But see St. 1861, c. 165.

12. A town has authority to provide for the support of a public clock, and to assess the expense thereof upon the inhabitants of the town. *Willard* v. *Newburyport*, 12 Pick. 227 (1831).

13. A town voted to raise and appropriate a certain sum for purchasing a fire engine, provided that the same amount should be raised by private subscription within ninety days, the engine to be located by the selectmen. A subscription was obtained for the sum required, but on condition that the engine should be located in a particular place designated, and in consequence the assessors declined accepting it. Thereupon, with the consent of a portion of the subscribers, but without the knowledge of the others, the condition was erased; but one of the subscribers verbally guaranteed to the assessors the payment of the whole sum; and in this form the subscription was accepted, and the sum voted by the town was assessed. *Held*, that there was a substantial compliance with the proviso of the vote, and, therefore, that the assessment was authorized. *Torrey* v. *Milbury*, 21 Pick. 64 (1838).

14. A town is authorized to appropriate money for the repair of fire engines used for the purpose of extinguishing fires therein, whether they belong to the town or were purchased by private subscription. *Allen* v. *Taunton*, 19 Pick. 485 (1837).

15. A town has authority to appropriate money for the construction of reservoirs for water to supply fire engines. *Hardy* v. *Waltham*, 3 Met. 163 (1841).

16. A town has no authority, it seems, to erect an embankment or other separate work,

wholly detached from a road, for the purpose of facilitating the making, maintenance, or future repair of the road. *Anthony* v. *Adams*, 1 Met. 286 (1840).

17. A town has no authority to raise money to aid in the construction of a road which by law is to be made at the expense of the county, and consequently a tax laid by the town for the purpose of collecting the money is illegal and void. *Parsons* v. *Goshen*, 11 Pick. 396 (1831).

18. A town is authorized to indemnify its officers against any liability which they may incur in the *bona fide* discharge of their duties, although it turn out that they have exceeded their legal rights and authority. *Bancroft* v. *Lynnfield*, 18 Pick. 566 (1836).

19. A town may appropriate money to indemnify its school committee for expenses incurred in defending an action for an alleged libel contained in a report made by them in good faith, and in which judgment has been rendered in their favor. *Fuller* v. *Groton*, 11 Gray, 340 (1858).

20. In 1819 a town voted to raise a sum of money for state, county, and town taxes, and the same was assessed, collected, and paid in due proportions into the state, county, and town treasuries; but in consequence of irregularities in the assessors' proceedings, the assessment was held to be illegal, and the assessors, to prevent the bringing of actions against them by persons whose property had been distrained, refunded each a third part of the amount which had been collected by distress, and afterwards, in 1824, the town voted to raise a sum of money, and to direct the town treasurer to pay over, when it was collected, to the assessors, the amount which they had so refunded for the use of the town. It was held, that without such a vote the town could not have been compelled to indemnify the assessors. *Nelson* v. *Milford*, 7 Pick. 18 (1828).

21. *Held*, also, that this vote was a promise, founded, so far as regarded the town tax, on a valid consideration, and that it could not be rescinded by a subsequent vote. *Ib.*

22. *Held*, also, that in respect to the state and county taxes, this promise was without consideration. *Ib.*

23. *Held*, also, that the plaintiff, one of the assessors, might bring his action against the town to recover his third part embraced by the promise; but that his own tax, paid by him voluntarily, was not included in the promise, and could not be recovered back. *Ib.*

24. The power of towns to vote and grant money for the support of town schools is not restricted to the amount that is necessary to support the schools which the Rev. Sts. c. 23, §§ 1-5, and 60, (Gen. Sts. c. 38, §§ 1, 2, 14,) require them to support, under a penalty for refusal or neglect so to do; but they have power to vote and grant money for the support of other town schools, for instruction in other branches of knowledge which the revised statutes do not require to be taught in such schools. *Cushing* v. *Newburyport*, 10 Met. 508 (1845).

24 *a*. A town which had raised money for the support of all the schools required by law, and had supported them, also raised money to support, and did support, a female high school for the purpose of teaching book-keeping, algebra, geometry, history, rhetoric, mental, moral and natural philosophy, botany, the Latin and French languages, and other higher branches of knowledge than were taught in the grammar schools of the town. It was held, that this was a town school, within the meaning of the revised statutes, and that the money for its support was legally raised by tax. *Ib.*

25. A town which had received its portion of the surplus revenue of the United States, under St. 1837, c. 85, voted that the same should be lent equally to each and every inhabitant, that the notes of the individuals receiving the money should be taken therefor, payable when the state government should call for the money, and that sureties should not be required on such notes. *Held*, that such a disposition of the money would be a violation of the provision of the statute that towns shall apply their portions of such surplus revenue, or the interest thereof, to those public objects of expenditure, for which they might lawfully raise and appropriate money, and to no other purpose. *Simmons* v. *Hanover*, 23 Pick. 188 (1839).

26. Towns have no authority to raise money for the purpose of abating a particular class of taxes; and, therefore, had no right to appropriate the interest of the portion of the surplus revenue of the United States distributed to them under St. 1837, c. 85, for the payment of poll-taxes. *Cooley* v. *Granville*, 10 Cush. 56 (1852).

27. Certain surplus revenue of the United States having been distributed to the several states, and the share of this commonwealth thereof having been by St. 1837, c. 85, deposited with the towns, to be applied "to those public objects of expenditure for which they may now lawfully raise and appropriate money," a town was enjoined from loaning its portion of the same to its inhabitants individually, on their personal security. *Pope* v. *Halifax*, 12 Cush. 410 (1853).

28. A town has no authority to appropriate money for the payment of expenses incurred by individuals, prior to its corporate existence as a town, in procuring the passage of its charter. *Frost* v. *Belmont*, 6 Allen, 152 (1863).

29. A town is not responsible for the fidelity of its field drivers; and is not bound by its

corporate vote, to pay the expenses of a field driver in defending a suit brought for taking up and impounding cattle running at large contrary to law; such agreement not being within the scope of a town's corporate powers. *Vincent* v. *Nantucket*, 12 Cush. 103 (1852).

30. The St. of 1863, c. 38, does not legalize a vote of the inhabitants of a town to pay money to persons who had already enlisted in the service of the United States. *Fowler* v. *Danvers*, 8 Allen, 80 (1864).

See FINANCE; PUBLIC BUILDINGS, 1.

Of the Remedy in Equity in Cases of illegal Appropriations.

31. Under St. 1847, c. 37, (Gen. Sts. c. 18, § 79,) the supreme judicial court have jurisdiction in equity, upon a proper case being made, to compel the restoration of money, with interest thereon, to the treasury of a town, which has been taken therefrom and applied to illegal purposes by officers of the town, under a vote of a majority of the inhabitants thereof. *Frost* v. *Belmont*, 6 Allen, 152 (1863).

32. This court will not restrain by injunction the collection of a town tax "for contingent expenses," if it appears that the objects for which the money is wanted were stated orally at the meeting at which the vote to raise the money was passed; that no objection to the form of the vote was then made; that the objects for which it was raised were necessary expenditures of the town; that no appropriation of any part of the money to any unlawful purpose is intended; and that for many years the town has been in the habit of passing votes to raise money in that form. *Freeland* v. *Hastings*, 10 Allen, 570 (1865).

33. An injunction will not be granted to restrain the payment of money illegally voted by a town, if the petitioners have been guilty of gross laches, and knowingly have permitted others to incur liabilities in good faith, relying on such appropriation for reimbursement. *Tash* v. *Adams*, 10 Cush. 252 (1852).

34. A delay of ten months by inhabitants and tax payers of a town before bringing their bill to restrain the payment of money for expenses already incurred in draining a pond, under a vote of the town, is such laches as will forfeit their right to equitable relief. *Fuller* v. *Melrose*, 1 Allen, 166 (1861).

35. A town must be a party to a bill in equity to restrain its treasurer from paying out money voted for illegal purposes at legal meetings of the town. *Allen* v. *Turner*, 11 Gray, 436 (1858).

See *ante*, 3.

ASSESSORS.

See ELECTIONS, 32; ESTOPPEL; OFFICERS, 30-32; TAXES.

BONDS.

1. A town treasurer and collector is liable on his bond for not paying over money collected by him, although the same has been stolen from him without his fault. *Hancock* v. *Hazzard*, 12 Cush, 112 (1853).

2. A bond executed to a town by its collector of taxes, and placed in the hands of the town treasurer, may be enforced against the collector and his sureties, without proof of its approval by the selectmen, or of its delivery. *Wendell* v. *Fleming*, 8 Gray, 613 (1857).

3. Defects in the warrant and tax list committed to a collector of taxes constitute no defence to an action on his bond by a town, to recover money received by him for taxes, and not paid to the town. *Sandwich* v. *Fish*, 2 Gray, 298 (1854).

4. Where a town, yearly, for four successive years, charges a collector of taxes in account with the amount of taxes intrusted to him for collection, and with the balance of the previous year's account, and credits him with the money received from him, and with the balance carried to the next year's account, and no other appropriation of the sums paid by him is made by either party, they will be applied to the extinguishment of the earliest charges; and the balance of each year's account, except the last, being thus extinguished, the town may recover the final balance of him and his sureties in an action on his bond for the fourth year. *Ib.*

5. When the same person is collector of taxes for two successive years, and pays to the town the arrears of taxes collected on the tax list of the first year, with the money collected on the tax list of the second year — the town not knowing whence the money came — and fails to perform the condition of his official bond for the second year, his sureties on that bond, when sued for his default, are liable to the extent of the default, and are not entitled to deduct the amount so paid by him for the taxes of the first year. *Colerain* v. *Bell*, 9 Met. 499 (1845).

6. When a collector is removed from office within a year after the taxes are committed to him to collect, his sureties, if sued on his official bond, may give evidence, for the purpose of reducing damages, that the uncollected taxes of certain persons on his tax list could not be collected, by reason of their inability to pay. Otherwise, if the collector was not removed until after a year from the time when the taxes were committed to him. *Ib.*

7. When a collector of taxes is removed from office, he and his sureties are liable, on his official bond, for such part of the taxes committed to him as are lost by reason of his remissness, although the uncollected taxes have been committed to his successor, who

has also given bond for the faithful discharge of the duties of his office. *Ib.*

8. If a collector of taxes, who has given bond to the town treasurer, instead of to the town, carries money, collected by him for taxes, to the treasurer, and would pay it to him, if payment were required, and the treasurer thereupon agrees with him, without the consent or knowledge of his sureties on the bond, that he may keep the money for a time, and pay his own debts with it, and he does so, the sureties are thereby discharged from their liability for the money so retained. *Johnson* v. *Mills*, 10 Cush. 503 (1852).

9. Payments made by a collector of taxes in behalf of the town, and allowed to him by the town in account, cannot be again allowed him in an action by the town on his official bond. *Cheshire* v. *Howland*, 13 Gray, 321 (1859).

10. In an action by a town on the bond of its collector of taxes, amounts paid by the collector on negotiable orders drawn by the selectmen upon him cannot be credited to the defendants. *Ib.*

11. In such action interest is to be allowed upon the amount due from the time of a demand upon the collector. *Ib.*

12. A constable's bond in the city of Boston is properly made to the treasurer of the city, under the present statutes. *Tracy* v. *Goodwin*, 5 Allen, 409 (1862).

13. The condition of a constable's bond, which provides that "he shall faithfully perform all the duties of a constable in the service of all civil processes which may be committed to him," is not broken by his failure to pay to the plaintiff in a writ money intrusted to him for that purpose by the defendant therein, after completion of the service. *Boston* v. *Moore*, 3 Allen, 126 (1861).

14. The St. of 1814, c. 165, which provides that no action shall be brought on the bond of a constable given to the treasurer of the city of Boston for a breach of the condition thereof, until a judgment has first been recovered on account thereof against the constable, is unrepealed and in full force. *Calder* v. *Haynes*, 7 Allen, 387 (1863).

15. A bond, given to the selectmen of a town and their successors in office, for the faithful performance, by the principal obligor, of the duties of treasurer and collector of the town, is not a bond required by law, and no action can be maintained thereon in the name of the successors of the obligees. *Stevens* v. *Hay*, 6 Cush. 229 (1850).

16. A bond given by a town treasurer and collector of taxes, not to the town, as required by Rev. Sts. c. 15, § 80, (Gen. Sts. c. 18, § 72,) but to the selectmen of the town, is valid at common law; and the selectmen may maintain an action upon it for the benefit of the town. *Sweetser* v. *Hay*, 2 Gray, 49 (1854).

17. After a collector of taxes had given bond with sureties for the collection of a tax of $2,572.82, it was ascertained that the tax was erroneously assessed, the assessors having added more than five per cent. to the amount of the tax voted, and the tax was, therefore, reassessed and made to amount to the sum of $2,490.01, and, without the knowledge of the sureties, the condition of the bond was altered so as to stipulate for the faithful collection of the new tax. *Held*, that the sureties were thereby discharged from all liability under the bond. *Doane* v. *Eldridge*, 16 Gray, (1860).

18. A bond given by a county treasurer for the faithful discharge of the duties of his office, is intended to protect the public from defaults of the officer occurring during the year for which he was elected. *Bigelow* v. *Bridge*, 8 Mass. 274 (1811). See *Chelmsford Co.* v. *Demarest*, 7 Gray, 1; *Middlesex Manuf. Co.* v. *Lawrence*, 1 Allen, 339; *Lexington, &c. Railroad* v. *Elwell*, 8 Allen, 371.

See Actions, 4, 6, 7, 52; Seals, 2, 3.

BOUNDARIES.

1. The recent perambulation of a line between two adjoining towns by the selectmen, affords strong, but not conclusive evidence, that it is the true line. *Freeman* v. *Kenney*, 15 Pick. 44 (1833).

2. Perambulations of the boundaries of towns by the selectmen are no evidence against the Commonwealth of the title to flats within those towns. *Commonwealth* v. *Roxbury*, 9 Gray, 451 (1857).

3. Upon the division of Boston into wards, in 1822, a part of the boundary line of the fifth ward was described, in the return of the selectmen, as running by the river, which was a navigable arm of the sea. It was held, that the exterior boundary of said ward did not extend into the river, beyond low-water mark. *Trull* v. *Wheeler*, 19 Pick. 240 (1837).

4. A committee appointed to settle the boundary between two towns, in a report, which was accepted by both towns, defined a line by bounds, courses, and distances, and added, "Some deviations from the original or natural boundary and some exchanges of territory are involved; and consequently it is supposed that the sanction of the legislature will be necessary to render valid the arrangement agreed to." The legislature afterwards passed an act declaring that the lines thus defined "should constitute and be considered the boundary lines between the said towns, and the territory and jurisdiction on either side of said line as hereby established are accordingly confirmed to said towns respectively." *Held*, that neither the agreement of

the towns nor the act of the legislature affected the title of the Commonwealth to the seashore within one of the towns. *Commonwealth* v. *Roxbury*, 9 Gray, 451 (1857).

See ACTIONS, 26; WAYS, 144, 450–460.

BOUNTIES TO VOLUNTEERS.

See ACTIONS, 47–49; APPROPRIATIONS, 4, 5, 30; CONSTITUTIONAL LAW, 3; CONTRACTS, 25–29.

BRIDGES.

See ACTIONS, 18, 20; OFFICERS, 43; SEWERS AND DRAINS, 21; WAYS, 54–58, 63, 77, 93, 205, 206, 270, 277, 288, 332, 350, 386, 396, 501, 502.

BUILDINGS.

1. The enlarging and fitting up as a livery stable, in Boston, within one hundred and seventy feet of a church, of a dwelling-house which was built before the passing of St. of 1810, c. 124, is an "erecting" of a livery stable within the meaning of that statute, and, while the building is used and improved as a livery stable, renders the owner or keeper thereof liable to the penalties imposed by that act. The St. of 1810, c. 124, is not repealed by Rev. Sts. c. 58, § 4 (Gen. Sts. c. 88, § 31). *Hastings* v. *Aiken*, 1 Gray, 163 (1854).

2. The chief engineer of the fire department is a very proper person to commence a suit under St. 1835, c. 139, to insure obedience of the law regulating the erection of wooden buildings in the city of Boston. But such suit must be brought within one year from the erection of the building, or no penalty can be enforced against the person erecting the building, in such suit or in any subsequent prosecution under said statute. And the statute, begins to run, as to the penalty, from the time of the erection, and not from the time of the completion, of the building. *Barnicoat* v. *Folling*, 3 Gray, 134 (1854). (But wooden buildings erected in violation of the statute may be abated at any time as common nuisances by the mayor and aldermen. St. 1847, c. 132.)

3. Where a by-law of a city prohibits the moving of buildings through the public streets, without a license granted by the mayor and aldermen, the board of aldermen cannot delegate to the mayor alone the power to grant such licenses. *Day* v. *Green*, 4 Cush. 433 (1849).

4. The mayor of a city, who, under the authority of an order of the board of aldermen, which they had no power to pass, has granted a license for the moving of a building through the streets, is not estopped, in an action of trespass against him, for removing the building out of the street, where it has been left by the owner in the course of such removal, to set up the invalidity of the license. *Ib.*

See ORDINANCES, &c. 9; PUBLIC BUILDINGS.

BURIALS AND BURIAL-GROUNDS.

See HEALTH, 9–14, 16, 17.

CARRIAGES.

1. Under the provisions of the act of 1847, c. 224, (Gen. Sts. c. 19, § 14,) the mayor and aldermen of the city of Boston have authority to make regulations as to the use of omnibuses and stage-coaches, for the transportation of persons for hire from Roxbury to Boston, and from Boston to Roxbury, while passing over and using the public streets of Boston, if, in the opinion of the mayor and aldermen, from the character of such vehicles, as to size, numbers, or mode of use, they would otherwise endanger or greatly incommode the public generally, who have occasion to use such public streets; and such regulations may prescribe certain streets as the route of travel for the vehicles mentioned in the same, and may provide for their exclusion from certain other streets; provided such regulations are "necessary and expedient for the due regulation," within the city of Boston, of the omnibuses and other vehicles therein specified. *Commonwealth* v. *Stodder*, 2 Cush. 562 (1848).

2. But said act does not authorize the mayor and aldermen of Boston to require the payment of money to the city by persons resident in Roxbury, who may set up and drive omnibuses and stage-coaches from Roxbury to Boston and back, for the conveyance of persons for hire, as a tax or duty upon such vehicles, before using the same; or to pass an ordinance, requiring persons resident in other towns and cities, and setting up and driving omnibuses and other vehicles from such towns or cities to the city of Boston, and back to their respective stations in such other towns and cities, for the transportation of passengers for hire, to obtain a license therefor, (irrespective of the requirement of the payment of money for the same,) from such mayor and aldermen. *Ib.*

3. A by-law of the city of Boston, having provided, in one section, that no carriage should be allowed to stand in any street more than fifteen minutes; and in another, that at any theatre or place of public entertainment, where hackney carriages attend for passengers, the police authorities might give directions re-

specting the standing of such carriages, while waiting for their passengers; and the police authorities having prescribed certain regulations for the standing of carriages at the Boston Museum, and, among others, that a space of thirty-five feet in front of the door thereof should be kept open and unincumbered; it was held, that the driver of a hackney carriage, who had placed the same on the space aforesaid, and refused to remove therefrom, when directed so to do by the police authorities, for more than fifteen minutes, was guilty of an offence and liable to be prosecuted only under the last and not under the first-named section. *Commonwealth* v. *Robertson*, 5 Cush. 438 (1850).

4. Money charged by a city for a wagoner's license, and paid with full knowledge of the facts, will be deemed to have been paid voluntarily, though paid under protest, and cannot be recovered back. *Cook* v. *Boston*, 9 Allen, 393 (1864).

Law of the Road.

5. St. 1820, c. 65, (Gen. Sts. c. 77, § 1,) establishing the law of the road, applies to the streets in Boston. *Fales* v. *Dearborn*, 1 Pick. 345 (1823).

6. A person driving a vehicle across the street must see that he does not interfere with others in the proper exercise of their right of passing. *Ib.* See *Parker* v. *Adams*, 12 Met. 415.

7. The law of the road, Rev. Sts. c. 51, § 1, (Gen. Sts. c. 77, § 1,) extends to all places appropriated, *de jure* or *de facto*, to the purpose of passing with carriages, &c., whether they are so appropriated by public authority or by the general license of the owners thereof, expressed or implied; and such owners themselves, while using their land as a road, must conform to this law. *Commonwealth* v. *Gammons*, 23 Pick. 201 (1839).

8. By the "travelled part" of the road, in the statute, which requires persons meeting each other with carriages, &c. to turn to the right of the middle of such part, is meant that part which is usually wrought for travelling, and not any track which may happen to be made in the road by the passing of a vehicle. *Clark* v. *Commonwealth*, 4 Pick. 125 (1826).

9. But when that part of a road which is wrought for travelling is hidden by snow, and a path is beaten and travelled on the side of the wrought part, persons meeting on such beaten and travelled path are required to drive their vehicles to the right of the middle of such path. *Jaquith* v. *Richardson*, 8 Met. 213 (1844).

10. The statute requires travellers in carriages, who meet in a road, seasonably to drive their carriages to the right of the middle of the travelled part of the road; and they cannot avoid the penalty by seasonably turning to the right of the wrought part of the road, though they leave sufficient room for the travellers whom they meet to pass with convenience and safety, in the use of ordinary skill and care. *Commonwealth* v. *Allen*, 11 Met. 403 (1846).

11. In a complaint against a traveller for offending against this statute, it is not necessary to set forth a particular description of the road. *Ib.*

12. The law of the road does not apply to a case where one vehicle is passing along a street, and another is turning into the same street from a cross road or way intersecting it, but is applicable only where vehicles meet or pass each other in travelling in the same street. *Lovejoy* v. *Dolan*, 10 Cush. 495 (1852). *Garrigan* v. *Berry*, 12 Allen, (1866).

13. A master is not liable, under the Rev. Sts. c. 51, § 3, (Gen. Sts. c. 77, § 4,) for the damages sustained by any party by reason of the omission of his servant seasonably to drive the master's vehicle to the right of the middle of the travelled part of the road, when meeting another vehicle. *Goodhue* v. *Dix*, 2 Gray, 181 (1854).

14. Driving a sleigh without the bells required by statute does not make the driver liable, nor exempt the town from liability, for injuries caused by collision with his sleigh upon a defective highway, unless his neglect contributes in some degree to the accident. *Kidder* v. *Dunstable*, 11 Gray, 342 (1858).

Fast Driving.

15. The city of Boston have authority to make a by-law prohibiting persons having the charge of a wagon, cart, &c. from driving their horses on a trot or gallop in the streets of the city, such by-law not being in restraint of trade, but a reasonable regulation of it. *Commonwealth* v. *Worcester*, 3 Pick. 462 (1826). And see St. 1865, c. 31.

16. Although the object of such by-law be to prevent passengers in the streets from being endangered by fast driving, yet in a prosecution on the by-law it is not necessary to prove that any individual was actually endangered thereby. *Ib.*

17. Upon an indictment for a breach of such by-law, evidence of the defendant's general character as a careful driver is inadmissible. *Ib.*

18. So of evidence of permission from the mayor and aldermen of the city to drive faster than the by-law allows. *Ib.*

CHARTER.

The town of Boston became a city immediately after adopting St. 1821, c. 110, pursuant to § 31. *Commonwealth* v. *James*, 1 Pick. 375 (1823).

See Appropriations, 28; Ordinances, &c. 4; Overseers of the Poor, 1; Taxes, 185; Ways, 495.

COLLECTORS.

See Bonds; Elections, 8-10; Estoppel; Officers, 33, 34; Taxes.

COMMON AND PUBLIC SQUARES.

1. All the common lands fronting the college in Cambridge were, in 1769, granted to the town of Cambridge, to be used as a training-field, to lie undivided and to remain for that use forever, provided that if the town should dispose of, grant, or appropriate the same or any part thereof to any other use, the whole of the premises should revert to the grantors. By St. 1830, c. 6, certain inhabitants of Cambridge were empowered, at their own expense and under the direction of two commissioners to be appointed by the executive, to enclose such part or parts of these lands as the commissioners should determine, and to level the surface, plant trees, and lay out walks within the enclosure, with the approbation of the selectmen of Cambridge, leaving suitable avenues for foot passengers to enter or pass over it; the commissioners were authorized to make such alterations with respect to the direction of the roads by which the lands were traversed as they should see fit; the enclosure was to be forever appropriated to public use only, as a public park, promenade, and place for military parade; and provision was made for the punishment of any person who should injure or destroy the fences, &c. Said statute was held not to be unconstitutional, although there was no distinct adjudication by the legislature that the enclosure and improvement of the lands were of common convenience and necessity. *Wellington, Petitioner*, 16 Pick. 87 (1834).

2. Nor is it unconstitutional on the ground that no provision is made therein for compensation for damages done to private property; for if this were a valid objection to a statute affecting private property, it could have no force here, because the act refers to no property not already appropriated to public use. *Ib.*

3. Nor on the ground that no provision is made for the maintenance and repair of the roads laid out by the special commissioners around the enclosures, in lieu of those by which the land was originally traversed; for the roads so laid out being lawful highways, the town thereupon became liable to the duty of supporting them as such. *Ib.*

4. Nor on the ground that no provision is made for the preservation and support of the improvements when made. *Ib.*

5. Nor on the ground that the section of the act providing that the enclosure should be forever appropriated to public use only as a public park and place for military parade, encroaches upon the right of eminent domain inherent in the sovereign power of the state; for this right is not superseded by the act, the word "forever," in this connection, signifying, until the provision should be altered by competent authority. *Ib.*

6. The term "undivided," applied to this land in the grant, does not mean that the land shall not be divided into parcels, but that it shall not be set off in severalty to individual proprietors; and the enclosure of the land in three distinct parcels and the other improvements and appropriations contemplated by the St. 1830, c. 6, were held not to be inconsistent with the clause in the grant which provided that the land should be used as a training-field and should lie undivided, and that if it should be appropriated by the town to any other use, it should revert to the grantors; and, consequently, the consent of the town to the statute, and to the improvements made by virtue of it, could not operate a forfeiture of the land by the town. *Ib.*

7. Wherever the legislature has annexed the character of public use to any property, and such public use would be destroyed or interrupted by the laying out of a highway, the power of the county commissioners to lay out such highway is superseded. Thus St. 1830, c. 6, authorizing "the enclosing of a part of Cambridge common," superseded the power of the county commissioners to lay out a highway across such enclosure. *Ib.*

CONSTABLES.

See Bonds, 12-14; Dogs, 7, 8; Officers, 38, 39; Taxes, 114, 118, 166.

CONSTITUTIONAL LAW.

1. The legislature have authority to enact that the interest which an inhabitant of a city may have in a penalty for the breach of a by-law thereof shall not disqualify him to act as a judge or juror in a prosecution to recover such penalty. *Commonwealth* v. *Worcester*, 3 Pick. 462 (1826). See Gen. Sts. c. 122, § 13.

2. The property of a private individual may

be appropriated to public use in connection with measures of municipal regulation; but in such case compensation must be provided for, or the appropriation will be unconstitutional and void. *Baker* v. *Boston*, 12 Pick. 194 (1831).

3. The legislature of the Commonwealth have the constitutional power to levy a tax on all the inhabitants of the Commonwealth for the payment of bounties to soldiers, and the reimbursement of towns which have voluntarily advanced such bounties without previous legislative authority. *Lowell* v. *Oliver*, 8 Allen, 247. See *Freeland* v. *Hastings*, 10 Allen, 570.

See Amusements, 4; Annexation and Division of Towns, 1, 2; Appropriations, 4, 5; Common and Public Squares, 1—5; Elections, 1—6; Juries, 12; Ordinances, &c. 2—6; Paupers, 34; Penalties, 8; Representatives in the General Court; Sewers and Drains, 14; Ways, 499, 501.

CONTRACTS.

1. A town, in its corporate capacity, will not be bound, even by the express vote of a majority, to the performance of contracts or other legal duties not coming within the scope of the objects and purposes for which it is incorporated. Shaw, C. J., in *Anthony* v. *Adams*, 1 Met. 286 (1840).

2. A contract in this form: "We, the undersigned, a committee chosen by the town of A. to finish the basement of their town-house, do hereby agree to pay," &c., for the finishing of said basement, and signed and sealed by the committee as "committee for the town," is not the contract of the town, but of the individuals who sign it. *Fullam* v. *West Brookfield*, 9 Allen, 1 (1864.)

3. If a town authorize a committee to bind them by a contract, and the committee enter into a sealed contract, for the benefit of the town, which binds only themselves, the town, by subsequently revoking the authority of the committee and prohibiting and preventing the execution of the contract, do not render themselves liable in damages to the individual with whom the contract was made. *Ib.*

4. Where a contract was made in pursuance of a vote of a town, but before the contract was performed the vote was rescinded, it was held, that the person with whom the contract was made was not affected by the rescission, not having had notice thereof; and *quære*, whether notice would have made any difference. *Allen* v. *Taunton*, 19 Pick. 485 (1837).

5. Where a committee was chosen by a town to rebuild a bridge which the town was bound to maintain, it was held, that the members of such committee were not to be deemed public agents, but were subject to the same rules in regard to personal liability on their contracts made for that purpose, as other agents. *Simonds* v. *Heard*, 23 Pick. 120 (1839).

6. It was held, also, that such committee was authorized to make contracts with third persons for the construction of the bridge, binding the town to pay therefor, although the town had appropriated money for the purpose of rebuilding it, and empowered the committee to borrow, on the credit of the town, such sums as might be required. *Ib.*

7. Such committee having entered into a contract, not under seal, for the building of the bridge, in which after describing themselves as a committee of such town, "said committee" agreed to pay the contractor a certain sum when the work should be completed, it was held, that the members of the committee were personally responsible on such contract. *Ib.*

8. It seems, that in an action upon such contract, against the members of the committee personally, the acts and declarations of the contractor tending to show that credit was given by him to the town, are admissible in evidence. *Ib.*

9. A committee appointed by the vote of a town to "let out and superintend the making" of a new highway, which the town had been ordered by the county commissioners to make, contracted on behalf of the town with F. for the construction thereof; and F. proceeded to construct so much of the highway as he contended he was bound to do, and declined doing anything further. It was held, that the vote of the town conferred a special authority on the committee, which was completely executed by the making of such contract and superintending the construction of the highway; that if F. did not fulfil his contract, the power and duty devolved on the town to insist upon or waive its execution; that consequently it was not competent for the committee, without a new authority from the town, to enter into a new contract for the completion of what was left unfinished by F.; and that the town was not liable for money paid by the committee in pursuance of such new contract. *Keyes* v. *Westford*, 17 Pick. 273 (1835).

10. In the same case it appeared that the contract with F. provided for the construction of a better but more expensive road than was prescribed by the order of the county commissioners. It was held, that the reference to the order of the county commissioners limited the authority of the committee; that the contract with F. was in excess of their authority; and that the second contract, to complete the

road, was founded in a like excess of authority, and therefore imposed no obligation on the town. *Ib.*

11. An agreement for the purchase of land for a town, made by all the members of a committee duly authorized by the town to purchase it, and put in writing and signed by part of the committee, on behalf and at the verbal request of the committee, is the written agreement of the whole committee, and binding on the town. *Haven* v. *Lowell*, 5 Met. 35 (1842).

12. Where an agreement, made for the purchase of land for a town, by a committee of the town, is invalid, such agreement is ratified and confirmed by a subsequent vote of the town, authorizing the committee to complete the purchase of the land by them bargained and contracted for. *Ib.*

13. Where an individual made a contract in writing to build two drains for a city, in a thorough, skilful, and workmanlike manner, satisfactory to the committee of the board of aldermen having the same in charge; to execute the work under the general direction and superintendence of the committee; and to cause the work to be carried forward and finished with as much rapidity as could reasonably and beneficially be attained: it was held, that such general direction and superintendence were not limited to the quality of the materials, and the manner of doing the work, but also extended to the time of doing the same; as to which, the committee, acting with an honest and just regard to the interests of the city, and not arbitrarily, capriciously and unreasonably towards the other party, were exclusively authorized to judge. *Chapman* v. *Lowell*, 4 Cush. 378 (1849).

14. The inhabitants of a town having voted to build a town-house according to a plan and specifications agreed upon, and appointed a committee to contract for and superintend the erection of the same, "with power to make any slight alteration in the plan which should in their wisdom be deemed just and proper;" it was held, that whether the authority given to the committee to make such slight alterations would justify them in employing an architect to draw plans for the purpose, was a question for the jury. *Upjohn* v. *Taunton*, 6 Cush. 310 (1850).

15. A committee chosen by a town "to procure a master builder and superintend the building of a meeting-house for the town," with authority to borrow money if necessary, have power to make contracts for the building, where no special committee is appointed for that purpose. *Damon* v. *Granby*, 2 Pick. 345 (1824).

16. A town has power to increase the number of such committee after the contract is made, and if the new members are excluded from acting with the others by mistake or design of the chairman, the proceedings of such others will be irregular. *Ib.*

17. A major part of such committee are necessary to constitute a quorum, and the act of a majority of a quorum is the act of the committee. *Ib.*

18. Where a parish appointed a committee of three to build a meeting-house, a contract by one of the number was not binding on the parish. *Kupfer* v. *Augusta*, 12 Mass. 185 (1815).

19. If a person contracts with a town "to erect a meeting-house on a place to be designated by a committee," and a place is so designated, and the town afterwards disagrees to the designation and gives notice to the contractor, but not until he has made some of the window frames and carried materials to the ground pointed out, although this is a beginning to execute the contract, it is not a beginning to erect the meeting-house, and the town may disagree to the first designation at any time before the ground shall be prepared for erecting the frame of the house, they indemnifying the contractor for any extra labor and expense occasioned by their fluctuating proceedings. *Damon* v. *Granby*, 2 Pick. 345 (1824).

20. The contract of a committee of a town, under their own seals, cannot be declared on as the deed of the town, but it may be evidence of a contract made by the town. *Ib.*

21. A vote of a town appointing a committee to appropriate money for constructing a road which is by law to be made at the expense of the county, is an illegal and void act; and a contract for constructing it entered into by such committee in behalf of the town, will not be binding upon the town. *Parsons* v. *Goshen*, 11 Pick. 396 (1831).

22. Under St. 1786, c. 81, § 4, which provided that when the sum appropriated and assessed for the repair of the highways in the limits of any particular surveyor should be insufficient for that purpose, it should be lawful for him "with the consent of the selectmen" to make additional expenditures, to be repaid out of the town treasury, a ratification by the selectmen after the expenditures have been made, will bind the town to repay the surveyor. *Emerson* v. *Newbury*, 13 Pick. 377 (1832).

23. A contract made with the brother of a female pauper by a committee appointed by a town "to negotiate the case" of that pauper, and signed by the committee in their own names, the terms of which are that the brother shall pay the town a certain sum annually during the life of the pauper, and release all claim to a certain fund in the hands of another

relation for her support, and the town shall support her and save him harmless from all litigation with his brothers in relation to such support, which contract is afterwards acted upon by the brother and the town, is valid, and binds the town, though not expressly ratified by them. *Palmer* v. *Ferry*, 6 Gray, 420 (1856).

24. If the inhabitants of a town have authorized their treasurer to borrow a certain sum of money for a specific purpose, and to give his note as treasurer therefor, and he has exercised this authority, they are not liable upon a note given by him in their name for money subsequently borrowed by him and converted to his own use, although he assumed to be acting under the authority conferred upon him, and the lender supposed that he was doing so. *Lowell Savings Bank* v. *Winchester*, 8 Allen, 109 (1864). See *Benoit* v. *Conway*, 10 Allen, 528.

25. The St. of 1863, c. 38, ratifying contracts of towns to pay bounties to soldiers, does not operate to revive a contract which had become extinct under St. 1861, c. 222. *Grover* v. *Pembroke*, 11 Allen, (1865).

26. A town passed a vote "that all men belonging to the town, enlisting into the service of the United States, and who shall be accepted and mustered into the service of the same, shall receive a bounty from the town of one hundred and twenty-five dollars," and at the same meeting passed another vote "that, shall the full quota required of the town be enlisted and accepted as aforesaid, an additional sum of seventy-five dollars shall be paid each man thus enlisting, but should there be a failure in making up the full quota of nine months' men, then those enlisting and being accepted and mustered as aforesaid shall receive only the sum of one hundred and twenty-five dollars each." After the lapse of nearly four months the quota was not filled, and, a draft having been ordered, the town chose an agent, who filled the quota by recruits from abroad. *Held*, that an inhabitant of the town who enlisted under the above votes was entitled to only one hundred and twenty-five dollars. *Bishop* v. *Rochester*, 11 Allen, (1865).

27. If, prior to St. 1861, c. 222, a town had voted to pay to each volunteer soldier raised or being an inhabitant therein, and mustered into the service of the United States for the defence of the government, a certain sum per month, and also "that each volunteer soldier belonging to this town be allowed one dollar per day for each and every day he is drilled under proper authority," and an inhabitant in pursuance thereof signs a paper enrolling himself with others into a company of volunteer militia for five years, "with the full understanding that we are liable at any moment to be ordered into active service under the government of the United States," and is drilled for several days under proper authority, and shortly afterwards enlists in the military service of the United States, he may under that statute maintain an action against the town to recover such pay for a time not exceeding ninety days from his enlistment, and also for the time spent in drilling. *Jones* v. *Scituate*, 11 Allen, (1865).

28. An enlisted soldier can maintain no action against a town to recover money for a uniform, under a vote of the town appointing a committee "to expend for each enlisted soldier, a sum of money not exceeding ten dollars, for a uniform." *Ib.*

29. An enlisted soldier can maintain no action against a town to recover bounty money, under a vote of the town appropriating a certain monthly sum during a certain time, to each citizen who should enlist for the war, "to be paid in such manner and to such persons as the selectmen shall deem expedient." *Williams* v. *Plymouth*, 11 Allen, (1865).

30. A proposal was received from the plaintiff by the superintendent of public lands of Boston for the purchase for $600 of a tract of land belonging to the city. A sub-committee of the land commissioners subsequently reported favorably upon this proposal to the full board, who thereupon passed the following vote: "That we recommend on the part of the board of land commissioners the sale and transfer by quitclaim deed, for the sum of $600 cash, of all the right, title and interest the city of Boston may have in and to the lot," &c. to the plaintiff. This vote was sent to the mayor for his approval, and he approved the same about four months afterwards; but no further action was taken by the land commissioners. *Held*, that there was no contract between the plaintiff and the city which could be enforced in equity, and that the vote of the land commissioners did not import a contract, though approved by the mayor, but was only an authority to the proper officers to execute a deed, which was to constitute the contract when executed and delivered. *Dunham* v. *Boston*, 12 Allen, (1866).

See ACTIONS; FISH, 4, 6, 7; OFFICERS, 7, 9, 10, 14–16; ORDINANCES, &c. 9; PAUPERS, 197, 238; REWARDS; SCHOOLS, 33, 34; TAXES, 79; TREASURER; WAYS, 48–53.

DISTURBANCE OF PUBLIC MEETINGS.

1. Disorderly behavior in a town meeting is an indictable offence at common law.

Commonwealth v. *Hoxey*, 16 Mass. 385 (1820). And see Gen. Sts. c. 165, § 23.

2. As the law has not defined what shall be deemed an interruption and disturbance, it must be decided as a question of fact in each particular case. It must be wilful and designed, an act not done through accident or mistake. *Commonwealth* v. *Porter*, 1 Gray, 480 (1854).

3. The disturbance of a meeting of citizens assembled for the discussion of the subject of temperance is an offence punishable under St. 1849, c. 59 (Gen. Sts. c. 165, § 23). *Ib.*

DOGS.

1. Under Gen. Sts. c. 88, § 64, one who suffers loss by reason of the worrying, maiming or killing of his horse by dogs is, upon proof thereof, entitled to an order from the selectmen of the town wherein the damage is done, upon the treasurer of the town, for the amount of his loss, to be paid from the fund created by taxes on dogs according to the provisions of that statute; and if the selectmen refuse to draw such order, upon proof of the facts, a writ of *mandamus* will be granted, ordering them to do so. *Osborn* v *Lenox*, 2 Allen, 207 (1861).

2. No action lies against a town under St. 1859, c. 225, in favor of the owner of sheep who have been killed by dogs therein, to recover the value of the sheep. *Chenery* v. *Holden*, 16 Gray, (1860).

3. No liability is created by St. 1859, c. 225, on the part of towns, for the omission, neglect or refusal of the selectmen to perform the duties imposed on them by the provisions of that act, and none exists at common law. *Ib.*

4. A complaint on St. 1859, c. 225, § 9, charging the defendant with keeping a dog in violation of the provisions of that act, need not allege that he is the owner of the dog. *Jones* v. *Commonwealth*, 15 Gray, (1860).

5. A by-law of the city of Lowell, which provides generally that the owners of dogs shall not suffer them to go at large in the city or to escape from their master's premises, without being safely muzzled, is valid, and may be enforced against all persons who are inhabitants of Lowell. *Commonwealth* v. *Chase*, 6 Cush. 248 (1850).

6. A dog is "going at large" in a town, if he be loose and following the person who has charge of him, through the streets of the town, at such a distance that he cannot exercise a control over the dog, which will prevent his doing mischief. *Commonwealth* v. *Dow*, 10 Met. 382 (1845).

7. A dog at play with his owner's son upon his owner's land, is not "at large" within the meaning of Gen. Sts. c. 88, § 58; and a constable who under such circumstances calls him away and shoots him while he is upon his owner's land, and then enters upon such land and pursues him for the purpose of shooting him again, is liable in damages therefor. *McAneany* v. *Jewett*, 10 Allen, 151 (1865). But see Sts. 1864, c. 299, § 7; 1865, c. 197, § 4.

8. St. 1858, c. 139, does not authorize a person, in order to destroy a dog not registered, &c. to enter the owner's house without his leave. *Bishop* v. *Fahay*, 15 Gray, (1860).

9. A by-law of a town, made under Rev. Sts. c. 58, § 10, (Gen. Sts. c. 88, § 67,) concerning the licensing, regulating and restraining of dogs going at large within the town, will be construed to apply only to dogs owned or kept in the town, although in its terms it applies to "any person permitting his dog to go at large within the town;" and if it is otherwise valid, it may be enforced against the owner or keeper of a dog within the town. *Commonwealth* v. *Dow*, 10 Met. 382 (1845).

10. The same section in a by-law of a town imposed a penalty of $ 10 on any person permitting his dog to go at large in the town, unless the dog should be licensed to go at large, and should wear a collar with the name of the owner or keeper and the word "licensed" distinctly marked thereon; and the further penalty of $ 10, if said dog should wear a collar without a license. It was held, that although the latter part of the section might be repugnant to Rev. Sts. c. 58, § 12, (Sts. 1864, c. 299, § 1; 1865, c. 197, § 1,) and therefore void, yet that the former part was valid; and that the penalty thereby imposed was recoverable of a person who permitted his dog to go at large without being licensed. *Ib.*

11. The penalties imposed by the by-laws of the town of New Bedford in relation to dogs, may be recovered by complaint before the police court of that town. *Ib.*

12. Under Gen. Sts. c. 88, §§ 52, 55, 56, one who purchases an unlicensed dog after the 30th of April in any year is not subject to a penalty for the omission to cause him to be registered, numbered, described and licensed, until the 30th of April in the next year. *Commonwealth* v. *Brimblecom*, 4 Allen, 584 (1862). But see now St. 1864, c. 299, §§ 1, 2, 5.

DOMICIL.

1. Every person must have a domicil somewhere. *Abington* v. *North Bridgewater*, 23 Pick. 170 (1840).

2. A person can have only one domicil, for one purpose, at one and the same time. *Ib.*

3. Where the boundary line between the

towns of R. and N. B. passed through a dwelling-house so that the portion of the house which was in N. B. was sufficient in itself to constitute a habitation, while the portion in R. was not sufficient for that purpose, it was held, that a person, by occupying such house, acquired a domicil in N. B. *Ib.*

4. It seems, that if, in such case, the line had divided the house more equally, the fact that the occupant had habitually slept in that part which was in N. B. would be a preponderating circumstance to show that he was domiciled in that town, and, in the absence of other evidence, would be decisive of the question. *Ib.*

5. Where a dwelling-house is so divided by the boundary line between two towns, as to leave that portion of the house in which the occupant mainly and substantially performs those offices which constitute his home, (such as sleeping, sitting, eating and receiving visitors,) in one town, he is a citizen of that town, and has no right to elect to reside and be taxed for his personal property in the other town. *Chenery* v. *Waltham,* 8 Cush. 327 (1851).

6. Whether a person removing from one town to another intends to change his residence is a question of fact and not of law. *Fitchburg* v. *Winchendon,* 4 Cush. 190 (1849). See *Chicopee* v. *Whately,* 6 Allen, 508.

7. A domicil, being once fixed, will continue, notwithstanding the absence of the party, till a new domicil is acquired. *Jennison* v. *Hapgood,* 10 Pick. 77 (1827).

8. The intention to abandon a domicil, and actual residence at another place, if not accompanied with the intention of remaining there permanently, or at least for an indefinite time, will not produce a change of domicil. *Ib.*

9. It is difficult to give an exact definition of habitancy. In general terms, one may be designated as an inhabitant of that place which constitutes the principal seat of his residence, of his business, pursuits, connections, attachments, and of his political and municipal relations. It is manifest, therefore, that it embraces the fact of residence at a place, with the intent to regard it and make it one's home. The act and intent must concur, and the intent may be inferred from declarations and conduct. In a case of much doubt the mere declaration of the party, made in good faith, of his election to make one place, rather than another, his home, may be sufficient to turn the scale. But the question is one of fact for the jury, to be determined from all the circumstances of the case. SHAW, C. J., in *Lyman* v. *Fiske,* 17 Pick. 234 (1835).

10. If an inhabitant of a town removes to another town in this commonwealth, not intending to remain there permanently, but with the intention of not returning to his former home, and does not so return, he loses his domicil in the former town. *Mead* v. *Boxborough,* 11 Cush. 362 (1853).

11. The fact that such person was taxed in the town to which he has removed, is not competent evidence to show that he did not continue to be taxable in the town of his former residence. *Ib.*

12. A citizen of this commonwealth, removing with his family to another state, and retaining no dwelling-place in this commonwealth, though retaining his place of business here, and intending to retain his domicil here, and to return at some future indefinite period of time, has no domicil in this commonwealth. *Holmes* v. *Greene,* 7 Gray, 299 (1856).

13. A student of a college does not change his domicil by his occasional residence at the college. *Granby* v. *Amherst,* 7 Mass. 1 (1810).

14. A seafaring man, having lands occupied by himself, his servants or hired people, although frequently absent on long voyages, has always been considered as having his residence on his lands, and as not losing his domicil by following his profession. PARSONS, C. J. *Ib.* See also *Abington* v. *Boston,* 4 Mass. 312.

15. The domicil of a person *non compos mentis* and under guardianship, may be changed by the direction and with the consent of the guardian, express or implied. *Holyoke* v. *Haskins,* 5 Pick. 20 (1827).

16. A person *non compos,* born in the county of Suffolk, removed, upon the death of her father, into the county of Middlesex, where she lived in her brother's family many years, and until her death, being for the last years of her life under a guardian who provided for her support, whose residence was in Suffolk county. *Held,* that her domicil at the time of her death was in Middlesex county. *Ib.*

17. Evidence that the selectmen of a town decided that a person taxed there was an inhabitant, and put his name on the voting list, is not admissible for the purpose of showing that his domicil was in that town, without showing that they did it at his request. *Fisk* v. *Chester,* 8 Gray, 506 (1857).

18. In an action to try the question whether the plaintiff, who had left the country with his family, was liable afterwards to be taxed as an inhabitant of the place of his former residence, a letter from him to his agent in that place, expressing his intention to remain abroad permanently, is admissible in evidence, if written before he knew that a tax had been assessed upon him, though written after the

assessment. Otherwise, it seems, as to such letters written after he knew that he was taxed. *Thorndike* v. *Boston*, 1 Met. 242 (1840).

19. A man's declarations as to the place of his residence, and his designation thereof in his will, are competent evidence after his death, upon the question of his domicil, at a time shortly after the making of the declarations and of the will. *Wilson* v. *Terry*, 9 Allen, 214 (1864).

20. A citizen, having lived many years at Waltham in the county of Middlesex, purchased and furnished a house in Boston, and afterwards with his family continued to spend his summers at his house in Waltham, where he continued to pay his taxes, and spent his winters at his house in Boston, and died while so residing in Boston. It was held that he was an inhabitant of Waltham, and that his will might be admitted to probate in the county of Middlesex. *Harvard College* v. *Gore*, 5 Pick. 369 (1827).

21. A person having a family domiciled in a town in this commonwealth was occasionally absent in another town engaged in his duties as clerk of courts and making arrangements for the removal of his family, and subsequently removed his family to such other town. It was held that his domicil did not change until the removal of his family. *Williams* v. *Whiting*, 11 Mass. 424 (1814).

22. The mere facts, that a student, who has a domicil in one town, resides at a public institution in another town, for the sole purpose of obtaining an education, and that he has his means of support from another place, do not constitute a test of his right to vote and his liability to be taxed in the latter town. He obtains this right and incurs this liability only by a change of domicil; and the question, whether he has changed his domicil, is to be decided by all the circumstances of the case. *Opinion of the Justices*, 5 Met. 587 (1843).

23. The rule that a domicil once acquired is presumed to continue until a subsequent change is shown applies to questions as to the settlement of a pauper. *Chicopee* v. *Whately*, 6 Allen, 508 (1863).

See ELECTIONS, 17-19; PAUPERS, 157-159, 272; TAXES, 61-78, 136-138.

ELECTIONS.

1. A town having a right to send one or more representatives to the general court, can constitutionally and legally vote not to send a representative; and such vote will be binding on a minority of voters, dissenting therefrom, in such town. *Opinion of the Justices*, 15 Mass. 537 (1815).

2. If a representative in the general court is elected into the senate or the council the vacancy may be supplied by a new election by the town which he represented. *Opinion of the Justices*, 3 Pick. 517 (1826).

3. The constitution does not admit of an adjournment of the second meeting for the choice of representatives, which it provides may be held on the fourth Monday of November, (Amendments, Art. 15,) to a day beyond such fourth Monday. *Opinion of the Justices*, 23 Pick. 547 (1840).

4. The polls of aliens may, within the intent of the constitution, be ratable polls, when they are made liable by the legislature to be taxed. *Opinion of the Justices*, 7 Mass. 523 (1811). See Gen. Sts. c. 11, § 1.

5. Ratable polls of aliens may constitutionally be included in estimating the number of ratable polls, in order to determine the number of representatives any town may be entitled to elect. *Ib.*

6. Printed votes are written votes, within the meaning of the provision in the constitution that "every member of the house of representatives shall be chosen by written votes." *Henshaw* v. *Foster*, 9 Pick. 312 (1830). See Gen. Sts. c. 3, § 7, cl. 20.

7. *Mandamus* lies to county commissioners to compel them to certify that the petitioner for the writ had a majority of the votes for county treasurer, although another candidate has been by them declared to be county treasurer, and is in possession of the office. *Ellis* v. *Bristol*, 2 Gray, 370 (1854).

8. St. 1822, c. 104, § 2, requiring a collector of taxes to return to the selectmen annually, fifteen days before the first Monday in March, a list of persons from whom he shall have received payment of a state or county tax, intended that the return should not be made more than fifteen days before such Monday. *Claflin* v. *Cheney*, 4 Pick. 118 (1826). See now Gen. Sts. c. 6, § 3.

9. The St. of 1822, c. 104, (Gen. Sts. c. 6, § 3.) requiring each collector of taxes to return annually to the selectmen of his town lists of the persons from whom he shall have received payment of a state or county tax, intends that the list shall remain with the selectmen for their use, and not be taken away again by the collector. *Adams* v. *Moulton*, 7 Pick. 286 (1828).

10. It is not necessary that such list should be delivered to the selectmen at a meeting of the board; a delivery to one of them is sufficient. *Ib.*

11. It is competent for selectmen, though not their duty, to add the name of a legal voter to the voting list, after the voting commences; but they cannot, during such time, hold a regular meeting for the correction of the list. *Waite* v. *Woodward*, 10 Cush. 143 (1852).

12. Selectmen have authority, even after the opening of a town meeting, to strike from the list of voters the name of a person who is not a legal voter. *Humphrey* v. *Kingman*, 5 Met. 162 (1842).

13. It is a misdemeanor, at the common law, for a citizen who is a legal voter, at a town meeting, to give more than one vote for a municipal officer, at one time of balloting. *Commonwealth* v. *Silsbee*, 9 Mass. 417 (1812).

14. It is no objection to an election, that illegal votes were received, or legal votes rejected, unless the majority is thereby changed. *Blandford* v. *Gibbs*, 2 Cush. 39 (1848). *Christ Church* v. *Pope*, 8 Gray, 140 (1857).

15. It is not a valid objection to an election, that illegal votes were received, if they did not change the majority. *Sudbury* v. *Stearns*, 21 Pick. 148 (1838).

16. Several illegal voters having been permitted to vote at a parish meeting in the election of officers, many of the legal voters protested against the proceeding and withdrew without voting; but the persons declared to be elected having received the votes of a majority of the legal voters who remained and voted, it was held, that they were duly elected. *Ib.*

See Officers 22, 23; Representatives in the General Court.

Qualifications of Electors.

17. A person having his permanent home in one town, and being legally qualified to vote in such town at the election of public officers, is not disqualified by a temporary absence in another town, and having been there admitted to vote. *Lincoln* v. *Hapgood*, 11 Mass. 350 (1814).

18. The mere facts, that a student, who has a domicil in one town, resides at a public institution in another town, for the sole purpose of obtaining an education, and that he has his means of support from another place, do not constitute a test of his right to vote and his liability to be taxed in the latter town. He obtains this right and incurs this liability only by a change of domicil; and the question whether he has changed his domicil is to be decided by all the circumstances of the case. *Opinion of the Justices*, 5 Met. 587 (1843).

19. A student in the theological institution at Andover, being of age, and making that town his home, and having no residence elsewhere, is entitled to vote in that town. *Putnam* v. *Johnson*, 10 Mass. 488 (1813).

20. Payment of a state or county tax, within two years next preceding the election of governor, &c., by one who is in other respects a qualified voter, entitles him to vote at such election, although such tax was illegally assessed upon him. *Humphrey* v. *Kingman*, 5 Met. 162 (1842).

21. Though a tax which is assessed upon one person, is paid for him by another, without his previous authority, yet if he recognizes the act, and repays or promises to repay the amount, on the ground that such person acted as his agent, he thereby acquires the same right to vote as if he had paid the tax with his own hand. *Ib.*

22. Persons who have the requisite qualifications as to age and residence, but who have been, for two entire years, exempted from taxation by town assessors, either by being omitted to be assessed, or by abatement of the tax, as being unable by reason of age, infirmity or poverty to contribute towards the public charges, are not entitled to vote for governor, lieutenant-governor, senators and representatives, under the third article of the amendments to the constitution. *Opinion of the Justices*, 11 Pick. 538 (1832).

23. Persons who have the requisite qualifications as to residence, but who have been exempted from taxation, on account of their poverty, during the two years previous to the election at which they may claim a right to vote, are not entitled to vote for governor, lieutenant-governor, senators and representatives, under the third article of the amendments to the constitution. *Opinion of the Justices*, 5 Met. 591 (1844).

24. Persons who reside on lands purchased by or ceded to the United States for navy yards, forts and arsenals, where there is no other reservation of jurisdiction to the state than that of a right to serve civil and criminal process on such lands, do not acquire by residing on such lands any elective franchise as inhabitants of the towns in which the lands are situated. *Opinion of the Justices*, 1 Met. 580 (1841). *Commonwealth* v. *Clary*, 8 Mass. 77 (1811). See *Mitchell* v. *Tibbetts*, 17 Pick. 298.

See Domicil.

Of the Remedy against Officers for refusing Votes, &c.

25. An action lies against selectmen for refusing to receive the vote of a qualified elector, or for omitting to put his name on the list of voters, although not chargeable with malice. *Lincoln* v. *Hapgood*, 11 Mass. 350 (1814). *Blanchard* v. *Stearns*, 5 Met. 298 (1842). But see Gen. Sts. c. 6, § 11.

26. But in order to maintain such action, it must be shown that the plaintiff furnished the defendants with sufficient evidence of his having the legal qualifications of a voter, and requested them to insert his name on the list

of voters, before the defendants refused to receive his vote, or omitted to insert his name on such list. *Blanchard* v. *Stearns*, 5 Met. 298 (1842).

27. A voter who is challenged at the polls, cannot maintain an action against selectmen for refusing to receive his vote, if they do not act wilfully or maliciously, but under a mistake into which they are led by his conduct, which was likely to mislead them into a belief that he had abandoned his claim to a right to vote. *Humphrey* v. *Kingman*, 5 Met. 162 (1842).

28. The remedy of one whose name is erased from the voting list by the selectmen before the voting commences, and whose vote, when offered, is refused by them, is an action against them for erasing his name, and not an action for refusing his vote. *Harris* v. *Whitcomb*, 4 Gray, 433 (1855).

29. In an action against the selectmen of a town for refusing to receive the plaintiff's vote, it appeared that at the election in question a selectman, stationed in front of a table, upon which a box was placed for the reception of the votes, took the votes as they were presented, in his hand, and when the names of the voters were found on the check list, deposited the votes in the box; that when the plaintiff came to vote, the selectman offered to take the vote in his hand, as he had previously done in every instance, but the plaintiff demanded the box which was on the table, in order that he might deposit his vote therein himself; that the selectman declined complying with such demand, but reached towards him another box, which had been used on former occasions for the reception of votes, and that the plaintiff refused to put his vote therein. It was held, that the box so presented to the plaintiff was the ballot box, within the meaning of Rev. Sts. c. 4, § 4, which provide that no vote shall be received "unless deposited ('presented for deposit;' Gen. Sts. c. 7, § 12) in the ballot box by the owner in person;" and, consequently, that in the absence of any malicious design to deprive the plaintiff of his rights, this was not an unlawful refusal to receive his vote. *Gates* v. *Neal*, 23 Pick. 308 (1839).

30. No action lies against the selectmen of a town for refusing to put upon the list of voters therein the name, and rejecting the vote, of one who was not a legal voter, although the proof produced by him to them was sufficient to establish, *prima facie*, his right to vote; and they may prove at the trial that in fact he was not a legal voter. *Lombard* v. *Oliver*, 3 Allen, 1 (1861).

31. In an action against the selectmen of a town for refusing to put the plaintiff's name upon the list of voters, and rejecting his vote, the plaintiff may prove his own statements relating to his residence, made to the selectmen before offering his vote, not under oath, for the purpose of furnishing to them evidence of his having the legal qualifications of a voter; and he may testify to his own intention in leaving the town for a prolonged absence, previously to the time of the acts complained of. *Lombard* v. *Oliver*, 7 Allen, 155 (1863).

32. An action cannot be maintained against assessors by an individual who is liable to taxation, for their omission to tax him, whereby he loses his right to vote at an election, unless it be shown affirmatively that they omitted to tax him wilfully, purposely, or with design to deprive him of his vote; or unless they had actual knowledge of his liability to taxation, so plain and obvious that a sinister purpose and wilful omission to tax him, in pursuance of such purpose, may be reasonably inferred by a jury. *Griffin* v. *Rising*, 11 Met. 339 (1846).

ESTOPPEL.

A city is not estopped from claiming land which it owns, by the wrongful act of its assessors in taxing it to a person who had no title to or possession of the same, or by a collector's sale for non-payment of such tax. *Rossire* v. *Boston*, 4 Allen, 57 (1862).

See PAUPERS, 304-315.

FANEUIL HALL MARKET.

1. A by-law of the city of Boston, providing that no inhabitant of the city or of any town in the vicinity thereof, not offering for sale the produce of his own farm, &c., shall without permission of the clerk of Faneuil Hall Market, be suffered to occupy any stand for the purpose of vending commodities, in certain streets which by the by-law are a part of the market, was held to be a salutary police regulation, and not void as making a distinction between the inhabitants of the city and its vicinity and those of distant towns, nor as being uncertain, nor as being in restraint of trade. *Nightingale, Petitioner*, 11 Pick. 168 (1831). But see Sts. 1859, c. 211; 1860, c. 152.

2. The city government had an undoubted right to prohibit the occupation of a stand in the streets by any one, or by any one not having a license or permission for that purpose from the clerk of the market. WILDE, J. Ib. 171. But see Sts. 1859, c. 211; 1860, c. 152.

3. A by-law of the city of Boston, passed for the regulation of Faneuil Hall Market,

was valid, which provided that "no inhabitant of said city, nor any inhabitant of any town or city, whose dwelling-house is less than twenty miles distant from said market, shall, at any time, without the permission of the clerk of said market, occupy any stand therein, with cart, wagon, sleigh or otherwise, for the purpose of vending any articles within the limits of said market, unless he shall, before selling or offering to sell such articles, satisfy the said clerk, when requested, that all the said articles are the produce of his own farm, or of some farm not more than three miles distant from his dwelling-house." *Commonwealth* v. *Rice*, 9 Met. 253 (1845). But see Sts. 1859, c. 211; 1860, c. 152.

4. It is a violation of said by-law, for an inhabitant of Boston to occupy a stand within the limits of the market, and there offer for sale articles which are the property of a person residing more than twenty miles from the market, as the agent of such person, and by his direction, without satisfying the clerk of the market, when requested, that the articles are the produce of such inhabitant's own farm, or of some farm not more than three miles distant from his dwelling-house. *Ib.*

5. A stand may be occupied within the meaning of said by-law, by a person's having a box within the limits of the market, containing articles for sale, and offering them for sale. *Ib.*

6. Said by-law does not require that the clerk of the market, before entering a complaint for violation of the regulations of the market, should have the direction of the mayor and aldermen to make such complaint. *Ib.*

FERRIES.

1. Where a petition for a license to set up a ferry was presented to the mayor and aldermen of Boston, and, upon a hearing of the parties interested, the petition was granted, it was held, that these proceedings were of a judicial nature, and therefore might be removed to this court by *certiorari*. *Fay, Petitioner*, 15 Pick. 243 (1834).

2. But where, in a petition for a *certiorari*, such ferry was claimed by the proprietors of an ancient ferry as appurtenant thereto, it was held, that it was not competent for the court under this summary process, to try the conflicting titles of the parties to such franchise. *Ib.*

3. The court of sessions, previously to its abolition, was authorized to establish ferries over navigable rivers and arms of the sea. *Ib.*

4. Under St. 1821, c. 109, § 11, abolishing the court of sessions in the county of Suffolk, and transferring its authority, with certain exceptions, to the mayor and aldermen of Boston, the power of licensing ferries within the territorial limits of Boston was vested in the mayor and aldermen, it not being a power in which a trial by jury can be required, and so not within the exceptions. *Ib.*

5. If a ferry claimed by the city of Boston as owners, be leased by the city, through the agency of the mayor and aldermen, with covenants for the exclusive enjoyment of such franchise, such covenants will not restrain the mayor and aldermen from exercising the power vested in them by statute, to license another ferry over the same waters, if it be required by the public convenience and necessity; but if the city be the owner of an exclusive franchise in the ferry, the lessees would hold it notwithstanding any license to others. *Ib.*

6. Where a petition presented to the mayor and aldermen of Boston for a license to set up a ferry was referred to a committee, and a report was made in favor of licensing the petitioners, and subsequently a hearing of the persons interested was had before the whole board, and the petition was granted, it was held, that it was immaterial whether the report was agreed to by the committee or not. *Ib.*

7. Upon a petition for a writ of *certiorari* to quash the proceedings of the mayor and aldermen in licensing a ferry, it was held, that the court would not review the decision of the mayor and aldermen upon the question of public convenience and necessity, the regularity of their proceedings only being open to examination under such process. *Ib.*

8. On a petition for a *certiorari* to quash the proceedings of the mayor and aldermen of Boston in licensing a ferry "between Noddle's Island and other parts of the city of Boston," it was held, that the license was not void for its generality and uncertainty, in not defining more particularly the *termini* of the ferry. *Ib.*

9. It seems that a right of ferry may exist separately from the ownership of the soil at the *termini* of the ferry. *Ib.*

FIELD DRIVERS; POUNDS AND IMPOUNDING OF CATTLE.

1. A pound-keeper may lawfully impound beasts which have been distrained *damage feasant*, in a yard furnished and used by the town as a town pound, if the town have furnished and used no other place as a pound, although the inhabitants of the town have passed no vote concerning the same, and taken no action at any town meeting for the purpose of establishing it as a pound. *Anthony* v. *Anthony*, 6 Allen, 408 (1863).

2. A vote of a town to restrain cattle from going at large within the limits of the town, is binding on persons not inhabitants, whose cattle are found so going at large. *Gilmore* v. *Holt*, 4 Pick, 258 (1827).

3. Cattle in a highway, not actually under the efficient control of a keeper, are "going at large in the highways, and not under the care of a keeper," within the meaning of the Rev. Sts. c. 19, § 22, and may be taken up and impounded by a field driver; although they have been entrusted by their owner to a servant, with other cattle, to be driven to pasture, and have only left the drove a mile before reaching the pasture, and turned into a different road, also leading to the pasture, over which they have sometimes been driven, and there remain feeding, and the servant returns in less than an hour to the place where he lost them. *Bruce* v. *White*, 4 Gray, 345 (1855).

4. A field driver took up a pair of oxen, at large in the highway without a keeper, and drove them into his private yard, which was near by, and then went to the house of their owner, which was at a distance of a third of a mile, and notified him that if he did not take them they would be driven to the pound. The owner refusing to take care of them, the field driver thereupon drove them to the pound and impounded them. *Held*, that the cattle were lawfully impounded, although the statute requires that beasts taken up by a field driver "shall be forthwith impounded." *Dean* v. *Lindsey*, 16 Gray, (1860).

5. The act of a field driver is not necessarily unlawful, although in taking an animal to the pound he drives it first upon the owner's premises. *Parker* v. *Jones*, 1 Allen, 270 (1861).

6. The owner of lands adjoining a highway, who owns to the centre thereof, may depasture his land in the highway; but he is bound, like all other persons, to prevent his cattle from going at large therein, without being under the care of a keeper. *Ib.*

7. A person who finds cattle at large in the highway, not under the care of a keeper, and drives them along the highway until he finds a field driver, is not a keeper, within the meaning of the Rev. Sts. c. 19, § 22, (Gen. Sts. c. 25, § 21,) and the field driver may lawfully receive and impound them. *Bruce* v. *White*, 4 Gray, 345 (1855).

8. Under Rev. Sts. c. 19, § 22, (Gen. Sts. c. 25, § 21,) requiring field drivers to take up and impound, at any time, cattle going at large in the highway without a keeper, a field driver is authorized to impound cattle so going at large on Sunday, the action of debt to which the owner is subjected by the statute in such cases, being merely a cumulative remedy. *Wild* v. *Skinner*, 23 Pick. 251 (1840).

9. The field driver, in such case, is not bound, under Rev. Sts. c. 113, § 6, (Gen. Sts. c. 25, § 27,) to leave with the pound-keeper a memorandum stating the cause of impounding and the damage demanded, this being requisite only where the cattle have been impounded *damage feasant*. *Ib. Pickard* v. *Howe*, 12 Met. 198 (1846).

10. A pound-keeper, who receives and impounds beasts going at large, and refuses to deliver them to the owner, on demand, unless his fees and those of the field driver are paid, is not liable therefor in an action of replevin. *Folger* v. *Hinckley*, 5 Cush. 263 (1850).

11. An inhabitant of a town taking up cattle found going at large within the town contrary to a vote of the inhabitants, may impound them in his private close. *Gilmore* v. *Holt*, 4 Pick. 258 (1827).

12. A private person who distrains and impounds cattle *damage feasant*, but does not leave with the pound-keeper a written account of the damage sustained, in pursuance of St. 1788, c. 65, § 3, (Gen. Sts. c. 25, § 27,) becomes a trespasser *ab initio;* for a statute authority must be strictly pursued. *Bassit* v. *Glover*, 1 Dane Ab. 137 (1799). See *Sherman* v. *Braman*, 13 Met. 407.

13. A private individual who impounds a beast taken *damage feasant*, in a town pound, is not liable for any injury which such beast may receive from cattle confined in the same pound. *Brightman* v. *Grinnell*, 9 Pick. 14 (1829).

14. It is the duty of a party impounding cattle to feed and water them as often as is required according to the usage of the country and of good husbandry. Where therefore a field driver, in warm weather, took up milch cows unlawfully going at large in the highway, and drove them to a town pound, and there restrained them from 7 o'clock in the morning to 5 o'clock in the afternoon, without giving them food or water, it was held that he was a trespasser *ab initio*. *Adams* v. *Adams*, 13 Pick. 384 (1832).

15. An application for a warrant of appraisement under the statutes relating to the impounding of cattle, need not be in writing. *Gilmore* v. *Holt*, 4 Pick. 258 (1827).

16. Under the Rev. Sts. c. 113, §§ 11, 12, (Gen. Sts. c. 25, §§ 32, 33,) providing that where appraisers are appointed to determine the amonnt due from the owner of an impounded beast for damages, &c., and the sum found to be due by them is not forthwith paid, the person impounding may cause the beast to be sold by auction, first advertising the sale by posting up a notice thereof twenty-four hours beforehand, it was held, that where

a beast impounded by a field driver was sold twenty minutes before the expiration of twenty-four hours from the time when the appraisement was completed, the sale was invalid, and the field driver a trespasser *ab initio*, although more than twenty-four hours had elapsed from the time of posting up the advertisement; and that it was immaterial, in such case, whether any actual injury had been sustained by the owner of the beast in consequence of this neglect of duty on the part of the field driver or not. *Smith* v. *Gates*, 21 Pick. 55 (1838).

17. The statute intends that the owner of the beast impounded shall have an opportunity to pay the appraised damages and charges before the posting up of an advertisement for the sale of the beast. *Ib.*

18. When the owner of cattle, that are impounded by a field driver for going at large contrary to law, commences an action of replevin against the field driver within twenty-four hours after they are impounded, he waives the notice which the Rev. Sts. c. 113, § 8, (Gen. Sts. c. 25, § 29,) require the field driver to give him, and cannot rely, in support of his action, on the want of such notice. *Wild* v. *Skinner*, 23 Pick. 251 (1840). *Field* v. *Jacobs*, 12 Met. 118 (1846).

19. The notice which the person who impounds beasts is required by statute to give to the owner of them, within twenty-four hours, need not state the hour of the day when they were impounded. And proof that notice was left in the hands of one of the owner's family, at his dwelling-house, is sufficient to authorize a jury to find that it was left at his place of abode. The field driver's name may be signed to such notice by another person, if it be done at the field driver's request. *Pickard* v. *Howe*, 12 Met. 198 (1846).

20. In an action of replevin brought against a field driver by the owner of cattle impounded by him for going at large, the defendant may show in evidence not only that he gave the plaintiff the notice required by Rev. Sts. c. 113, § 8, but also that he posted notices according to the provisions of § 9 (Gen. Sts. c. 25, §§ 29, 30). But the plaintiff cannot give evidence that the cattle were not suitably provided for, or were ill treated in the pound. *Ib.*

21. A notice given by a field driver to the owner of cattle, that they are impounded for going at large on the public highway, is *prima facie* evidence that they were so at large, and puts on the owner the burden of proving the contrary. A turnpike is a public highway, within the meaning of the provision of statute which requires field drivers to take up and impound cattle going at large in the public highway. *Ib.*

22. A notice in writing, given by a field driver to the owner of beasts impounded for going at large in the highway, which states that the beasts "were running at large, and were trespassing upon the premises of other individuals," does not state a sufficient cause of impounding, as required by Rev. Sts. c. 113, § 8 (Gen. Sts. c. 25, § 29). *Sanderson* v. *Lawrence*, 2 Gray, 178 (1854).

23. A written notice, posted up and published in a newspaper by a field driver who has impounded beasts going at large in a public highway, which states that the beasts were "going at large, and without a keeper," sets forth a sufficient cause of impounding, under Rev. Sts. c. 113, § 9 (Gen. Sts. c. 25, § 30). *Cleverly* v. *Towle*, 3 Allen, 39 (1861).

24. A field driver who lawfully impounds sheep running at large contrary to law, and duly posts a notice thereof, is not liable to the owner of the beasts, as a trespasser *ab initio*, although he fails either to restore the sheep or to sell them according to law, through the default of the pound-keeper or other person, or from the insufficiency of the pound; the animals being lawfully in the pound-keeper's custody. *Coffin* v. *Vincent*, 12 Cush. 98 (1853).

25. Actual knowledge, by the owner of beasts impounded, of the impounding thereof, is not equivalent to the written notice required by the Rev. Sts. c. 113, § 8 (Gen. Sts. c. 25, § 29). *Coffin* v. *Field*, 7 Cush. 355 (1851).

26. The owner of beasts impounded does not waive the right to maintain trespass against the field drivers by whom the beasts were taken and impounded, on the ground of irregularities or omissions in their proceedings, by paying the fees of the field driver and pound-keeper; nor by declaring to a third person, after the commencement of the action, that he should require the defendants to prove that the place where they took the beasts was a public highway. *Ib.*

27. In an action against a field driver, who had impounded sheep for running at large contrary to law, an instruction to the jury, that, if they were satisfied that the notice of the impounding was posted up within twenty-four hours in some public place by the defendant, containing a description of the sheep and a statement of the time, place, and cause of impounding, they might find a verdict for the defendant, sufficiently imports that the burden of proof is upon the defendant to show that the notice posted up contained a statement of some particular specific cause, known to the law, for which the beasts were taken up; especially if more specific instructions on this point are not requested by the plaintiff at the trial. *Coffin* v. *Vincent*, 12 Cush. 98 (1853).

28. A field driver took up a horse going at large in the highway without a keeper, and drove him, without unnecessary delay, to the

pound-keeper's house, and there left him in the barn, directing the pound-keeper's wife to tell her husband, on his return, to put the horse in the pound, which the pound-keeper, on his return, did, but the next day took the horse out of the pound and put him back in his barn, without the field driver's knowledge or consent. It was held, that the owner of the horse could not maintain replevin against the field driver. *Byron* v. *Crippen*, 4 Gray, 312 (1855).

29. In an action for taking and carrying away certain sheep, a portion of which had been impounded by the defendants as field drivers, the plaintiff is not restricted to damages for the sheep impounded, by reason of an agreement made between the parties that, "to avoid another suit, the plaintiff may offer evidence of the manner of driving the sheep, and the improper and injurious treatment of them after impounding." *Folger* v. *Fields*, 12 Cush. 93 (1853).

30. The action of replevin, given by Rev. Sts. c. 113, § 17, (Gen. Sts. c. 143, § 1,) to one whose beasts are unlawfully restrained or impounded, does not exclude all other remedies at common law; trespass will still lie. *Coffin* v. *Field*, 7 Cush. 355 (1851).

31. A cow which was found *damage feasant* upon a mowing field, was driven by the owner of the field into the road, and there delivered into the custody of a field driver, who drove her to his barn and there confined her, the owner of the field assisting him, and notifying him that he claimed remuneration for the damage done. It was held, that this was a legal impounding, under St. 1788, c. 65, § 3 (Gen. Sts. c. 25, § 26). *Pierce* v. *Josselyn*, 17 Pick. 415 (1835).

32. After a cow legally impounded had been rescued, the owner of the cow met the persons by whom she had been released, while they were engaged in driving her towards his house, and, with full knowledge of the facts, aided them in so driving her. It was held, that he was liable under St. 1788, c. 65, § 6, (Gen. Sts. c. 25, § 36,) for a breach of the pound. *Ib.*

33. Upon an indictment for pound-breach, the illegality of the distress cannot be shown in the defence. *Commonwealth* v. *Beale*, 5 Pick. 514 (1827). See *Melody* v. *Reab*, 4 Mass. 471 (1808); Gen. Sts. c. 25, § 37.

34. If one take cattle from the lawful custody of a field driver, when he is driving them to the pound, this is a rescue, although they are never out of view of the field driver, and are finally yielded to him and impounded. *Vinton* v. *Vinton*, 17 Mass. 342 (1821).

See *Merrick* v. *Work*, 10 Allen, 544.

See APPROPRIATIONS, 29.

FINANCE.

1. Votes by the inhabitants of a town instructing their treasurer "to consolidate the town debt for ten years, provided the money can be obtained at five and a half per cent.," and authorizing him "to borrow such sums as shall be necessary for the use of the town, under the direction of the selectmen," and also "to borrow twenty-five thousand dollars of the Mount Vernon Bank, at five and one half per cent. interest, and that the same be appropriated under the direction of the selectmen to the liquidation of the present town debt," do not authorize the treasurer to employ a broker in their behalf to negotiate the loan, or render them liable to pay for the services of a broker employed by him to borrow the money for them. *Butterfield* v. *Melrose*, 6 Allen, 187 (1863).

2. A *mandamus* will not be granted on the petition of the selectmen of a town (especially if not expressly authorized by vote of the town) to compel the town treasurer to pay the amount of an order drawn by them upon him in payment of a debt of the town. *Lexington* v. *Mulliken*, 7 Gray, 280 (1856).

See APPROPRIATIONS; TREASURER.

FIRE.

1. The provision in the Rev. Sts. c. 18, § 7, (Gen. Sts. c. 24, § 5,) that when the pulling down of a building, by the direction of firewards, shall be the means of stopping a fire, the owner of such building shall be entitled to recover reasonable compensation therefor from the town, does not apply to a building which is pulled down by such order, after it is so far burnt, that it is impossible to save it from destruction by fire. *Taylor* v. *Plymouth*, 8 Met. 462 (1844).

2. Independently of the statute, the pulling down of a building in a city or compact town, in time of fire, is justified upon the great doctrine of public safety, when it is necessary. But the town is responsible by force of the statute only, and such responsibility is limited to the cases specially contemplated. SHAW, C. J. *Ib.*

3. Three general directors appointed by the firewards of Nantucket having by law "the general direction of all the operations at fires" could not lawfully authorize one of their number to exercise, in urgent cases, the power of the whole board. *Coffin* v. *Nantucket*, 5 Cush. 269 (1850).

4. A person who has no legal title to a house, but merely a parol contract for a deed when he shall have paid the purchase money, is not an "owner" thereof, before the full

amount is paid, so as to allow him to maintain an action, under Rev. Sts. c. 18, § 7, (Gen. Sts. c. 24, § 5,) against a town, for the destruction of such house in order to prevent the further spreading of a fire. *Ruggles* v. *Nantucket*, 11 Cush. 433 (1853).

5. To maintain such action the owner must show affirmatively and clearly that the destruction of his house was ordered by three firewards, and not merely that they agreed generally that some houses should be demolished, and that the plaintiff's house was selected by one of them. *Ib.*

6. Under Gen. Sts. c. 24, § 5, one fireward has no more authority, acting alone, than any other person, to direct the destruction of a house to prevent the spreading of a conflagration, although it may be impossible for the other firewards, or the other officers named in the statute, to get to the place where the occasion for action upon the subject arises. *Parsons* v. *Pettingell*, 11 Allen, (1866)

7. If a fireward, without authority of law or the owner's consent, destroys property in order to prevent the spreading of a conflagration, he is liable to the owner for such property of the owner as might have been saved if the fireward had not interfered, and for no more. In case of an extensive conflagration, property may be so situated in respect to the fire, although not actually on fire, as materially to affect its value. *Ib.*

8. The St. of 1817, c. 171, § 10, which imposes a penalty on "any person who shall smoke, or have in his possession, any lighted pipe or cigar, in any street, lane or passageway" in Boston, applies to all open ways, used as such, although they may not be legally established as public ways. *Commonwealth* v. *Thompson*, 12 Met. 231 (1847).

See Appropriations, 14, 15; Rewards.

FISH.

1. A town has not, by the principles of the common law, a right of property in a fishery within its limits. *Randolph* v. *Braintree*, 4 Mass. 315 (1808).

2. Towns adjoining on, or extending across, a navigable river, may own the soil of the flats or even of the channel, if a grant has been obtained from the government; but the property in the fish and also in the tide waters is in the public. *Coolidge* v. *Williams*, 4 Mass. 140 (1808).

3. But by the common law, towns may appropriate the fish, if not appropriated by the legislature. If no appropriation be made of the fish, any citizen may take them, so that he does not trespass upon the land of others. Where two towns adjoin a river, the citizens of each may take the fish swimming in the tide waters. *Ib.*

4. A town in its corporate capacity, has no authority to transfer the right of taking oysters within its limits, and any contract made by a town for that purpose, is void. *Dill* v. *Wareham*, 7 Met. 438 (1844).

5. The Commonwealth, in a grant of a tract of land, granted also the privilege of taking fish, to be held in common among the grantees and other settlers. Afterwards the inhabitants on the land granted, having become a town, were authorized by law to appoint a committee to regulate the fishery within the town, and a penalty was imposed on any person, except such committee or those authorized by them, who should take any fish. It was held, that an owner of land adjoining the river was subject to the penalty, although he and those under whom he claimed, had used to take fish there before the grant of the Commonwealth. *Nickerson* v. *Brackett*, 10 Mass. 212 (1813).

6. Three adjoining towns on a river were authorized by statute to sell the right and regulate the times, &c. of taking fish within those towns. Two of the towns, for a valuable consideration, released to the third the right to the fishery in that town. It was held, that the third town might lawfully dispose of the fishery within its limits, and maintain an action, separately from the other two towns, against the hirer, for the agreed price. *Watertown* v. *White*, 13 Mass. 477 (1816).

7. A town sold to C. a privilege of fishing in a river, with the condition that they would not sell any further privilege; they did however afterwards sell another privilege to D. It was held, that the town could not maintain an action against C. for the purchase money, although the sale to D. was void, and although C. joined D. in carrying on the fishery under D.'s license. *Taunton* v. *Caswell*, 4 Pick. 275 (1826).

8. In an action by a town to recover the price of a right of fishing, sold by them under the authority derived from a statute, it is not necessary to set forth in the declaration their authority to make the sale. *Ib.*

FLATS.

See Boundaries, 2, 4; Fish, 2; Information; Taxes, 17; Ways, 62.

GUNPOWDER.

1. The board of engineers of the fire department of the city of Boston, to whose use the penalties incurred by violation of Sts.

1833, c. 151, and 1837, c. 99, (regulating the storage,&c. of gunpowder in Boston,) are made to enure,(except when any one of them shall be examined as a witness in the prosecution,) cannot authorize any person to sue for those penalties. *Colburn* v. *Swett*, 1 Met. 232 (1840).

2. It seems, that the only mode of enforcing the penalties imposed by those statutes, is by indictment, or suit in the name of the Commonwealth. *Ib.*

HEALTH.

1. Under Gen. Sts. c. 26, § 52, the selectmen of a town, acting as a board of health, may by a general order forbid the exercise of an offensive trade or employment therein, without first giving notice to those who at the time are engaged in carrying on the same. *Belcher* v. *Farrar*, 8 Allen, 325 (1864).

2. The party erecting or continuing a public nuisance may be prosecuted by indictment; and a part of the judgment may be, that it be prostrated and removed. SHAW, C. J., in *Eames* v. *New England Worsted Co.* 11 Met. 572 (1846).

3. In order to amount to a nuisance, it is not necessary that there should be a corruption of the atmosphere such as to be dangerous to health; it is sufficient that the effluvia are offensive to the senses and render habitations uncomfortable. SHAW, C. J. *Ib.*

4. It is not only the right but the duty of the city government of Boston, so far as they may be able, to remove any nuisance which may endanger the health of the citizens. *Baker* v. *Boston*, 12 Pick. 184 (1831).

5. And they have necessarily the power of deciding in what manner this shall be done, and their decision is conclusive, unless they transcend the powers conferred on them by the city charter. *Ib.*

6. Police regulations to direct the use of private property so as to prevent its being pernicious to the citizens at large, are not void, although they may in some measure interfere with private rights without providing for compensation. *Ib.*

7. The property of a private individual may be appropriated to public use in connection with measures of municipal regulation; but in such case, compensation must be provided for, or the appropriation will be unconstitutional and void. *Ib.*

8. Carrying on an offensive trade for twenty years in a place remote from buildings and public roads does not entitle the owner to continue it in the same place after houses have been built and roads laid out in the neighborhood, to the occupants of and travellers upon which it is a nuisance. *Commonwealth* v. *Upton*, 6 Gray, 473 (1856).

9. Since the statute of 1849, c. 211, § 7, (Gen. Sts. c. 26, § 50,) which provides that "all fines and forfeitures incurred under the general laws, or the special laws applicable to any town or city, or the ordinances, by-laws and regulations of any town or city, relating to health, shall enure to the use of such town or city, and may be recovered by complaint, in the name of the treasurer," such fines and forfeitures are recoverable only by complaint in the name of the treasurer of the city or town and in no other manner. *Commonwealth* v. *Fahey*, 5 Cush. 408 (1850). (Under Gen. Sts. c. 19, § 15, either the city treasurer or the chief of police may prosecute for such fines and forfeitures.)

10. The ordinances and by-laws of the city of Boston concerning burying-grounds and the burying of the dead, are regulations relating to health within St. 1849, c. 211, § 7. (Gen. Sts. c. 26, § 50). *Ib.*

11. The St. of 1832, c. 150, entitled "an act in addition to an act authorizing the town of Charlestown to establish a board of health," authorized the selectmen of Charlestown to appoint and locate the places where the dead may be buried in that town, to establish the police of the burying-grounds, to make regulations for funerals and the interment of the dead, to appoint all necessary officers to carry the same into effect, and to prescribe penalties for the violation of such regulations. The fourth section of a by-law made by the selectmen provided that no person should without leave in writing signed by a majority of the selectmen, bring into the town any dead body, or convey through any of the streets any dead body so brought into the town; or bury any dead body so brought into the town on any part of his own premises or elsewhere within the town. It was held, that the first part of this section of the by-law being unauthorized by the statute and void, (which was conceded,) the whole of the section was consequently void. *Austin* v. *Murray*, 16 Pick. 121 (1834).

12. It was held, also, that the latter part of the section was not a regulation but a prohibition, and therefore void; and if it were not a prohibition, yet that except when applied to a populous part of the town it was unreasonable and on that account void. *Ib.*

13. The third section of the by-law ordains that no person shall exercise the office of funeral undertaker within the limits of the town, unless he shall have been first appointed and licensed by the selectmen It was held, that this section did not apply to a person who without a license buried dead bodies brought into the town contrary to the fourth section; or if it was intended more effectually to enforce the prohibition in the fourth sec-

tion, and was to be taken in connection with that section, then it was void. *Ib.*

14. A tax payer in a town cannot maintain an action against the town for his proportion of the expenses of the burial of persons not paupers, paid by the town out of the money raised by town taxes. *Withington* v. *Harvard*, 8 Cush. 66 (1851).

15. A by-law of the city of Boston, prohibiting any person not duly licensed therefor by the mayor and aldermen, from removing house dirt and offal from the city, was held not to be in restraint of trade, but to be a valid by-law, and binding upon a stranger coming into the city. *Vandine, Petitioner*, 6 Pick. 187 (1828).

16. It was criminal to dig up and remove a dead body, at common law. *Commonwealth* v. *Cooley*, 10 Pick. 36 (1830).

17. The removal of a dead body is not an offence within the meaning of St. of 1830, c. 57, (Gen. Sts. c. 165, § 37,) unless done with the intent to use or dispose of the body for the purpose of dissection, and in an indictment under that statute such an intent must be averred. *Commonwealth* v. *Slack*, 19 Pick. 304 (1837).

18. Where a town incurs expenses, under the provisions of St. 1837, c. 244, § 1, (Gen. Sts. c. 26, § 16,) on account of paupers having a legal settlement in another town, the former is bound to give reasonable notice to the latter, before commencing an action for such expenses, and the selectmen of the respective towns are proper officers to give and receive such notice. *Springfield* v. *Worcester*, 2 Cush. 52 (1848).

19. On the 5th of May, 1846, a poor person, having a legal settlement in W., fell ill of the smallpox in S., and was there relieved, in pursuance of the provisions of St. 1837, c. 244, § 1, (Gen. Sts. c. 26, § 16,) and the selectmen of S., on the 25th of the same month, gave notice of the pauper's sickness and of the expenses incurred on his account, to the selectmen of W.; it was held, that such notice was reasonable and sufficient. *Ib.*

20. If the selectmen of a town, acting as a board of health, have brought a bill in equity to restrain the exercise of an offensive trade or employment which they have prohibited, under Gen. Sts. c. 26, § 52, this court have power to allow an amendment thereof, by substituting the inhabitants of the town as plaintiffs, after the term of office of the selectmen has ceased. *Winthrop* v. *Farrar*, 11 Allen, (1865).

21. An order by the selectmen of a town, acting as a board of health, forbidding the exercise of an offensive trade or employment therein, need not be served by an officer. *Ib.*

22. If the selectmen of a town, acting as a board of health, after passing a general order, under Gen. Sts. c. 26, § 52, forbidding the exercise of an offensive trade or employment therein, without first giving notice to those who at the time were engaged in carrying on the same, and after giving notice of the passage of such order to a person so employed, subsequently, and before the expiration of the three days allowed by § 56 for an appeal therefrom, gave notice to such person of the presentation of a petition to them, praying for the passage of a similar order upon him, appointing a time and place for a hearing, with the intention of preventing him from availing himself of his right of appeal from the order which they have already passed, and he is thereby so prevented, and thereby loses his right of appeal, this court will not enforce the order of the board of health by a process in equity. And if the selectmen have done this without an intention to mislead him, or to deprive him of his right of appeal, but he and his counsel have been actually mistaken in regard to his right of appeal from the order, and he has lost his appeal by reason of this mistake, and the consequences to him will be serious, this court in its discretion may and will refuse to enforce the order. *Ib.*

HOUSES OF CORRECTION AND JAILS.

See Sts. 1864, c. 270; 1866, c. 117.

1. Upon an appeal by a jailer to the court of common pleas under St. 1846, c. 11, § 3, (Gen. Sts. c. 178, § 23,) from a decision of the county commissioners fixing his compensation, the amount to be allowed him is within the discretion of that court, and not subject to revision or exceptions. *Adams* v. *Hampden*, 13 Gray, 439 (1859).

2. Where county commissioners have fixed the salary of a jailer and keeper of a house of correction, under St. 1859, c. 249, § 2, (Gen. Sts. c. 178, § 22,) and such jailer and keeper, deeming the salary so fixed inadequate, has petitioned the superior court under St. 1859, c. 249, § 3, (Gen. Sts. c. 178, § 23,) to fix his salary, this court will not, during the pendency of such petition, grant a writ of *mandamus* requiring the salary fixed by the county commissioners to be paid to such jailer and keeper out of the county treasury. *Adams* v. *Hampden*, 16 Gray, (1860).

3. The St. of 1787, c. 54, § 1, was peremptory on the court of sessions in each county to erect or provide a house of correction, and *mandamus* lay from this court to compel them to do it. *Commonwealth* v. *Hampden*, 2 Pick. 414 (1824). See Gen. Sts. c. 178, § 6.

4. The repeal of the law which directed that the surplus proceeds of the labor of convicts in houses of correction should be paid to them on their discharge, took away the authority to pay the proceeds of labor done before the repeal to those who were not discharged until after the repeal. *Williams* v. *Middlesex*, 4 Met. 76 (1842).

5. When an insane person, who is not able to pay for his own support, is confined in a house of correction, the town in which he has a settlement is liable for his support in such house, under St. 1836, c. 223, (Gen. Sts. c. 74, § 6,) if he have no parent, master or kindred, liable by law to support him. *Watson* v. *Charlestown*, 5 Met. 54 (1842).

6. Where an alien woman, having a nursing infant, which stood in need of immediate relief, was committed to a jail or house of correction, it was held, that such infant was not within the provisions of any of the statutes providing for the support of convicts and persons confined on criminal prosecutions. *Watson* v. *Cambridge*, 18 Pick. 470 (1836).

7. If the town in which the house of correction is situated, after due notice and request by the master thereof, refuse to assume the support of such infant, the master may recover from the town the expenses incurred by him on account of such infant, for clothing, medicine, &c., but not for any articles of food and nourishment furnished to the mother in consequence of her having an infant at the breast, different from, and in addition to, what he was required to furnish to other inmates of the house of correction. *Ib.*

8. Persons committed to a house of correction under St. 1787, c. 54, as rogues, common vagabonds, common beggars, or other idle, disorderly or lewd persons, are there maintained, not as paupers, but as criminals, and previously to the passing of St. 1826, c. 142, the keeper of such house, in order to recover of the towns where such persons have their settlements, the expenses incurred for their support, must have made a demand in writing in accordance with the requirements of St. 1802, c. 22, § 2. *Boston* v. *Westford*, 12 Pick. 16 (1831).

9. The master of a house of correction, under Sts. 1802, c. 22, § 2, and 1826, c. 142, after his accounts had been allowed and certified by the court of sessions, might maintain an action for the compensation allowed by such court, for keeping, supporting, and employing any person duly committed to the house, against the town in which such person was legally settled, if he had no estate and no kindred liable by law to support him. *Wade* v. *Salem*, 7 Pick. 333 (1828).

10. The neglect of the court of sessions to establish rules to govern the persons committed, to provide materials for their employment, and to keep accounts thereof, as required by St. 1802, c. 22, was no defence to an action by the master of a house of correction against a town. *Ib.*

11. Where the accounts of the master of a house of correction had been allowed by the court of sessions, and one of the towns charged in them appeared by counsel and contested their allowance, the only notice to the town of the claim having been given at the court; it was held, in an action by the master against the town, to recover the compensation allowed by the court of sessions, that the want of notice to the town afforded no defence to the action; but that the record of the court of sessions was not conclusive as to the liability of the town, which could make in the action any defence to which it might be legally entitled. *Ib.*

12. Under the Rev. Sts. c. 143, §§ 15, 16, (Gen. Sts. c. 178, §§ 57–59,) which provide that the expense of supporting a pauper in the house of correction "may be recovered of the town wherein he shall have his lawful settlement," the town in which he has a settlement at the time when such expense is incurred, is liable therefor, although he gains a settlement in another town before the account of such expense is audited and certified by the overseers of such house. *Boston* v. *Amesbury*, 4 Met. 278 (1842).

13. The persons and corporations that are made conditionally liable by the said statutes, for the support of persons committed to a house of correction, cannot be held to pay for such support, unless the account thereof be audited and certified by the overseers of such house, within the time prescribed by those statutes. *Ib.*

14. Where a pauper was confined in a house of correction, from December, 1836 to April, 1837, and the account of the expense of his support was not audited and certified by the overseers until January, 1839, it was held, that the town in which he had his settlement was not liable for such support. *Ib.*

15. The St. 1834, c. 151, § 10, (Gen. Sts. c. 178, §§ 57–59,) provides that whenever any sum shall be due for the care and expense of supporting any person committed to a house of correction, it may be recovered of such person, &c., or of the town wherein he is lawfully settled, if such person, town, &c. shall neglect to pay such sum for the space of fourteen days after the same shall have been demanded in writing of him or them respectively, or of one of the selectmen, &c. It was held, that the word "demand" does not mean a personal presentation of the account for immediate payment, and that a letter from the master to the selectmen of the town would be sufficient to answer

the requisitions of the statute. *Robbins* v. *Weston*, 20 Pick. 112 (1838).

16. The demand upon the selectmen of the town may be made by a person specially authorized by the master to make the same and to receive the money, but in such case the selectmen, being public agents, are entitled to be furnished, at the time of the demand, with the evidence of the authority of the agent. *Ib.*

17. Where, in an action instituted under Sts. 1824, c. 28, § 3; 1834, c. 151, § 10; and Rev. Sts. c. 143, § 16, to recover expenses incurred for the support of a prisoner in the house of correction in Boston, it appeared that the demand of payment, which is a prerequisite to the institution of such an action, was made by a person deriving his authority neither from the city nor from the master of the house of correction, but solely from the overseers of the house of correction, it was held, that such demand was insufficient. *Boston* v. *Weston*, 22 Pick. 211 (1839). See Gen. Sts. c. 178, §§ 57–59.

18. A town in which a convict, who is committed to a house of correction, has a settlement, is not liable, by any statute, to pay the expense of supporting him in such house, unless he be committed by virtue of the fifth or sixth section of c. 143 of the revised statutes (Gen. Sts. c. 161, § 21; c. 165, § 28). *Boston* v. *Dedham*, 8 Met. 513 (1844).

19. When a debtor imprisoned on mesne process claims support as a pauper, and his creditor, upon being required by the jailer to advance the money necessary for the support of the prisoner or to give security for his support, neglects to do so for twenty-four hours after demand, it is the duty of the jailer to discharge the prisoner forthwith. *Worcester* v. *Schlessinger*, 16 Gray, (1860).

20. An action to recover for expenses incurred in the support of a debtor imprisoned on mesne process in a county jail, cannot be maintained by the county against the creditor, if the creditor has not been notified that the debtor claims support as a pauper, or if the creditor, having been required to advance the money necessary for his support, or give security for his support, neglects to do so. *Ib.*

21. A prisoner confined in a house of correction under sentence of court, and while there put into solitary confinement for refractory conduct, in accordance with rules established for such cases, cannot maintain an action against the master thereof for neglect to provide for him sufficient food, clothing and fires, if he is kept in one of the usual cells, and there is no evidence of express malice, or of such gross negligence as to authorize the inference of malice. *Williams* v. *Adams*, 3 Allen, 171 (1861).

See Paupers, 7.

IMPOUNDING OF CATTLE.

See Field Drivers, &c.

INDICTMENT.

1. Where, pending an indictment against a town, the name of the town was altered by the legislature, the court refused to quash the indictment for that cause. *Commonwealth* v. *Phillipsburg*, 10 Mass. 78 (1813).

2. A town may be indicted as "the town of D.," and need not be described as "the inhabitants of the town of D." *Commonwealth* v. *Dedham*, 16 Mass. 141 (1819).

See Juries, 10; Ways, 14, 23, 38, 60, 391–396, 400, 417–429.

INFORMATION.

An information on Rev. Sts. c. 108, (Gen. Sts. c. 141,) against a town, does not admit its title in fee in flats sought to be recovered, by describing them as situated in that town. *Commonwealth* v. *Roxbury*, 9 Gray, 451 (1857).

JURIES.

1. Quakers are capable of serving as grand jurors. *Commonwealth* v. *Smith*, 9 Mass. 107 (1812).

2. A verdict will not be set aside on the ground that one of the jurors was more than sixty-five years old, and that this fact was not known to the party objecting before the verdict was returned; for persons of that age are not absolutely disqualified from serving as jurors by Rev. Sts. c. 95, § 2, (Gen. Sts. c. 132, § 2,) but are only exempted from serving at their own election, and made liable to exception, by either party, when the jury is empanelled. *Munroe* v. *Brigham*, 19 Pick. 368 (1837).

3. Attorneys at law, though retired from practice, are exempted from serving as jurors. *Swett's case*, 20 Pick. 1 (1838).

4. One having served as a juror in the courts of the United States within three years is not liable to be returned as a juror in the state courts. *Swan's case*, 16 Mass. 220 (1819).

5. A person is not liable to serve as a traverse juror who has served as a grand juror within three years, although it is a little more than three years since he was drawn as such. *Brown's case*, 8 Pick. 504 (1829).

6. Service on a sheriff's jury within three years is not the service contemplated in the statute, and does not exempt a person from serving as grand or traverse juror in a court. *Brewer* v. *Tyringham*, 14 Pick. 196 (1833).

7. A member of the legislature is entitled to be excused from serving on a jury while the legislature is in session. *Commonwealth* v. *Walton*, 17 Pick. 403 (1835). Gen. Sts. c. 132, § 2.

8. A minister of the Methodist Episcopal Church, who belongs to the "local connection," and whose duty it is to preach when called upon to churches within a convenient distance from his residence, is a "settled minister" within the meaning of the statute exempting certain persons from serving as jurors. (Gen. Sts. c. 132, § 2.) *Commonwealth* v. *Buzzell*, 16 Pick. 153 (1834).

9. A list of persons to serve as jurors was prepared and laid before a town by its selectmen. The town voted that said list be not accepted, and also voted to elect a list by nomination. Thereupon several persons, part of whom were on the list prepared by the selectmen, and part not on that list, were nominated and declared chosen. *Held*, that these persons were legally elected as jurors. *Page* v. *Danvers*, 7 Met. 326 (1843).

10. It is no sufficient exception to an indictment for an offence, to which the law annexes a fine for the use of the town where the offence is committed, that the foreman of the grand jury who found the indictment is a taxable inhabitant of such town. *Commonwealth* v. *Ryan*, 5 Mass. 90 (1809). See Gen. Sts. c. 122, § 13; c. 132, § 30.

11. The legislature have authority to enact that the interest which an inhabitant of a city may have in a penalty for the breach of a by-law thereof, shall not disqualify him to act as a juror in a prosecution to recover such penalty. *Commonwealth* v. *Worcester*, 3 Pick. 462 (1826). See Gen. Sts. c. 122, § 13; c. 132, § 30.

12. Rev. Sts. c. 95, § 28, (Gen. Sts c. 132, § 30,) which provides that "in indictments and penal actions for the recovery of any sum of money or other thing forfeited, it shall not be a cause of challenge to any juror that he is liable to pay taxes in any county or town which may be benefited by such recovery," is no violation of art. 29 of the Declaration of Rights, securing to every citizen "the right to be tried by judges as free, impartial, and independent as the lot of humanity will admit." *Commonwealth* v. *Reed*, 1 Gray, 472 (1854). See also Gen. Sts. c. 122, § 13.

See Actions, 59; Ways, 156–169, 214–227.

LAW OF THE ROAD.

See Carriages, 5–14.

LICENSES.

See Actions, 27; Amusements; Buildings, 3, 4; Carriages, 2; Ferries; Ordinances, &c. 9.

LORD'S DAY.

See Field Drivers, &c. 8, 9; Ways, 242, 264, 281, 389, 390.

MARKET-HOUSES.

See Appropriations, 7, 8; Faneuil Hall Market.

MILITIA.

See Appropriations, 2, 3; Contracts, 27; Riots.

MILK.

1. A complaint by H. F., inspector of milk in the city of Boston, alleging that the defendant, being a dealer in milk, and being recorded as a dealer in milk in the books of said H. F., sold adulterated milk, in violation of the provisions of Gen Sts. c. 49, § 151, does not sufficiently allege that he was recorded in the books of the inspector as a dealer in milk. *Commonwealth* v. *O'Donnell*, 1 Allen, 593 (1861). See now St. 1864, c. 122, § 4.

2. A complaint for selling adulterated milk in violation of the provisions of Gen. Sts. c. 49, § 151, which, after alleging the official character of the inspector, and that he kept an office and books as required by the statute, charges that the defendant, being a dealer in milk, and being recorded as a dealer in milk "in the books of said inspector," did sell, &c., does not sufficiently show that he was recorded in any such books as the statute requires the inspector to keep. *Commonwealth* v. *McCarron*, 2 Allen, 157 (1861). See now St. 1860, c. 122, § 4.

3. An indictment which alleges that the defendant "did unlawfully keep, offer for sale and sell" adulterated milk, charges but one offence. *Commonwealth* v. *Nichols*, 10 Allen, 199 (1865).

4. In support of such indictment, one who in a great many instances has used a lactometer for the purpose of testing the quality and purity of milk, may testify to the result of an experiment made by him with the same lactometer upon the milk in question, although no evidence is offered as to the character of the instrument. *Ib.*

5. A person may be convicted of selling

adulterated milk, under St. 1864, c. 122, § 4, although he did not know it to be adulterated; and an averment in the indictment that he had such knowledge may be rejected as surplusage. *Commonwealth* v. *Farren*, 9 Allen, 489 (1864). *Commonwealth* v. *Waite*, 11 Allen, (1865).

6. It is not necessary in such an indictment to aver that the milk was cow's milk. *Ib.*

7. An indictment alleging a sale of adulterated milk to a woman is not defeated by proof that she was married, and was acting as agent for her husband, if the seller had no notice, express or implied, of these facts. *Commonwealth* v. *Farren*, 9 Allen, 489 (1864).

8. An indictment under St. 1864, c. 122, § 4, which charges that the defendant sold a certain quantity of "adulterated milk, to which a large quantity, that is to say, four quarts, of water had been added," is not bad for duplicity. *Ib.*

9. No action lies to recover the price of milk sold by the can, at wholesale, in cans not sealed according to St. 1859, c. 206, § 4, (Gen. Sts. c. 49, § 150,) although the state sealer refused to seal them for the statute price. *Miller* v. *Post*, 1 Allen, 434 (1861).

10. St. 1864, c. 122, § 4, is not unconstitutional, although it authorizes the conviction of a person who had sold adulterated milk, not knowing it to be adulterated. It is the province of the legislature to decide what provisions are reasonable on the subject. *Commonwealth* v. *Waite*, 11 Allen, (1865).

11. On the trial of an indictment for selling adulterated milk, the certificate of an analyzer as to the quality of the milk sold by the defendant was admitted in evidence against the defendant's objection. The analyzer then personally testified to the same facts stated in the certificate. It was held, that the testimony of the analyzer destroyed all objections to the admissibility of his certificate. *Ib.*

NUISANCES.

See Health; Railroads, 17, 18, 22; Sewers and Drains, 18; Steam Engines; Ways, 55, 74, 397–429, 438.

OFFICERS.

1. As a general rule, a municipal corporation is not responsible for the unauthorized and unlawful acts of its officers, though done *colore officii;* it must further appear that the officers were expressly authorized by the corporation to do the acts, or that they were done *bona fide* in pursuance of a general authority to act for the corporation on the subject to which they relate, or that they were adopted and ratified by the corporation. *Thayer* v. *Boston*, 19 Pick. 511 (1837).

2. A town is authorized to indemnify its officers against any liability which they may incur in the *bona fide* discharge of their duties, although it turn out that they have exceeded their legal rights and authority. *Bancroft* v. *Lynnfield*, 18 Pick. 566 (1836).

3. Towns have the power to bind themselves by a vote to indemnify their officers and agents against liabilities incurred in the *bona fide* discharge of their duties. And the officers or agents are not required to give the town notice of the pendency of suits against them on such liabilities, in order to recover of the town their reasonable costs and expenses incurred in good faith in defending such suits. *Hadsell* v. *Hancock*, 3 Gray, 526 (1855).

4. If, after a vote by a town not to defend an action brought against it, the selectmen nevertheless make a defence, they are bound to indemnify the town against the costs of the defence. *Emerson* v. *Newbury*, 13 Pick. 377 (1832).

5. Town officers must be inhabitants of the town in which they are chosen, and they cease to be officers when they cease to be inhabitants. *Barre* v. *Greenwich*, 1 Pick. 129 (1822). See Gen. Sts. c. 18, § 41.

6. In St. 1785, c. 75, § 4, (Gen. Sts. c. 18, § 43,) respecting vacancies in town offices, the word "removal" means a removal from town. *Ib.*

7. The appointment by a city council, for a definite time, of a city officer entitled to compensation for his services, if accepted by him, constitutes a contract between him and the city, which cannot be changed by a subsequent ordinance of the city and vote of the city council, without his consent. *Chase* v. *Lowell*, 7 Gray, 33 (1856).

8. The mayor of a city, whose charter provides that he "shall be the chief executive officer of the city;" that "it shall be his duty to be vigilant in causing the laws and regulations of the city to be enforced;" and that "the executive power of said city generally and the administration of the police shall be vested in and may be exercised by the mayor and aldermen as fully as if the same were herein specially enumerated," may lawfully remove an awning erected in violation of an ordinance of the city, after a vote of the board of aldermen authorizing and instructing him "to proceed forthwith to remove all wood awnings now standing in said city in violation of law," although a street commissioner has been appointed, with the powers and duties of a surveyor of highways. *Pedrick* v. *Bailey*, 12 Gray, 161 (1858).

9. The mayor of a city has no authority by virtue of his office to employ counsel in behalf of the city, unless such authority is expressly conferred upon him by the city charter or ordinances. *Fletcher* v. *Lowell*, 15 Gray, (1860).

10. Upon a petition for a jury to assess damages against a city for laying out a bridge as a highway, the city council voted that it be "referred to the mayor, with power to employ such counsel as may be deemed expedient." *Held*, that this vote did not authorize the mayor to employ counsel to obtain the passage through the legislature of an act relating to the bridge, which might diminish the petitioner's claim for damages against the city. *Ib.*

11. If, under a charter authorizing the same, a city ordinance is passed which prohibits the obstruction of any street for the purpose of building, "without first obtaining a written license from the mayor and aldermen, or some person authorized by them," and complying with such reasonable conditions as they may impose, the mayor alone has no authority to grant a license to obstruct a street for the purpose of building, or to impose conditions therefor; and an agreement, made in consideration of such license from the mayor alone, to indemnify the city against damages that may arise in consequence thereof, is without consideration and void. *Lowell* v. *Simpson*, 10 Allen, 88 (1865).

12. Where a by-law of a city prohibits the moving of buildings through the public streets, without a license granted by the mayor and aldermen, the board of aldermen cannot delegate to the mayor alone the power to grant such licenses. *Day* v. *Green*, 4 Cush. 433 (1849).

13. The mayor of a city, who, under the authority of an order of the board of aldermen, which they had no power to pass, has granted a license for the moving of a building through the streets, is not estopped, in an action of trespass against him, for removing the building out of the street, where it has been left by the owner in the course of such removal, to set up the invalidity of the license. *Ib.*

14. Where a town appointed three persons, who were not inhabitants, to designate a place for building a meeting-house, it was held, that a designation by two only was insufficient, they being agents or commissioners and not technically a committee; but that if they had all concurred, the town might nevertheless reject a designation made by them. *Damon* v. *Granby*, 2 Pick. 345 (1824).

15. Where, upon the question whether a town would make the necessary repairs upon a town clock, a vote was passed to refer the matter to the selectmen, it was held, that the selectmen were authorized to determine not only whether the clock should be repaired, but also what repairs should be made, and that they were not restricted to inconsiderable repairs, such as had previously from time to time been made. *Willard* v. *Newburyport*, 12 Pick. 227 (1831).

16. Selectmen have no authority, by virtue of their office merely, to make a contract in behalf of a town for the hiring of a building for the purpose of holding town meetings in it. *Goff* v. *Rehoboth*, 12 Met. 26 (1846).

17. An information in the nature of a *quo warranto* does not lie against an officer elected for one year only, because it would be impossible to decide the question before the expiration of the term, when the mischief complained of would have ceased *Commonwealth* v. *Athearn*, 3 Mass. 285 (1807).

18. Where a minister of a town or parish is seised of any lands in the right of the town or parish, during a vacancy in the office the town or parish is entitled to the custody of the same, and may enter and take the profits until there be a successor. *Brunswick* v. *Dunning*, 7 Mass. 445 (1811).

19. A surveyor of highways sustaining damage from a defect in the highway within his district, which arises from his own neglect, has no remedy against the town for such damage. *Wood* v. *Waterville*, 5 Mass. 294 (1809).

20. A truant officer, appointed under Gen. Sts. c. 42, § 5, does not hold over after the expiration of his year, although no other has been appointed in his place. *Huse* v. *Lowell*, 10 Allen, 149 (1865).

21. It is no justification of a slander published of a town officer, relative to his official conduct and while in the exercise of his office, that the slanderer was a legal voter in the town, and so one of the constituents of such officer. *Dodds* v. *Henry*, 9 Mass. 262 (1812).

22. Where a selectman, acting in his official capacity, at a town meeting, during an election, said in good faith, and in the belief that the words were true, "B. (the plaintiff) has put in two votes," it was held, that an action of slander could not be maintained for the words so spoken. *Bradley* v. *Heath*, 12 Pick. 163 (1831).

23. It was also held, in an action against such selectman for speaking such words, that he might prove, under the general issue, the occasion of uttering the words, and that the plaintiff's own conduct was such as induced him to believe the imputation was true. *Ib.*

24. The assessors of a town having made an application to the town to reimburse them for expenses incurred in an action brought against them for having made false answers under oath in a former action brought against

them as assessors, and such application being under consideration at a meeting of the town, a tax payer who states in the course of debate upon the application that the defendants have perjured themselves, is not liable to an action for slander for making such statement, in the absence of malice, and may testify, in an action brought against him for speaking such words, concerning his motives in speaking them, his belief in their truth, and as to the absence of malice or ill will towards the plaintiff. *Smith* v. *Higgins*, 16 Gray, (1860).

25. Where the oath of office is administered to a town officer in open town meeting, by a justice of the peace, in presence of the town clerk, the clerk's record of the fact is competent evidence of the fact of the administration of the oath. *Briggs* v. *Murdock*, 13 Pick. 305 (1832).

26. The clerk of a city or town is the proper certifying officer to authenticate copies of the votes, ordinances, and by-laws thereof; and such copies so authenticated are admissible in evidence, when purporting to be duly attested, without any verification of the clerk's signature. *Commonwealth* v. *Chase*, 6 Cush. 248 (1850).

27. One who was formerly a town clerk, but is no longer in the office, cannot amend a town record made by him when town clerk. *Hartwell* v. *Littleton*, 13 Pick. 229 (1833).

28. It is competent for a town clerk to amend a record made by him when in office under a former election, such amendment being consistent with truth. *Welles* v. *Battelle*, 11 Mass. 477 (1814).

29. If the clerk of a school district wrongfully certifies to the assessors of the town that at a legal meeting of the district it was voted to raise a sum of money, and the assessors thereupon assess the same, a person arrested for not paying the tax cannot maintain an action against the clerk, the injury being but a remote consequence of his act. *Taft* v. *Metcalf*, 11 Pick. 456 (1831). See *Allen* v. *Metcalf*, 17 Pick. 208.

30. Where the defendants in an action justified as assessors, and showed by the records of the town that they were duly elected at a town meeting legally warned, it was held, that they were not bound to go behind the records and show that the meeting was in fact legally warned. *Thayer* v. *Stearns*, 1 Pick. 109 (1822). See *Gilmore* v. *Holt*, 4 Pick. 258.

31. Where a town votes that its assessors shall be allowed a certain gross sum for their services during the year, they are not entitled by the Rev. Sts. c. 7, § 45, to one dollar a day, (one dollar and fifty cents a day; Gen. Sts. c. 11, § 52,) in addition to the sum thus voted. *Moody* v. *Newburyport*, 3 Met. 431 (1841).

32. Assessors are entitled to the statute compensation of one dollar a day, (one dollar and fifty cents a day; Gen. Sts. c. 11, § 52,) for every day they are employed as such, although it exceeds the sum which the town may have voted as their compensation. And if the sum thus voted exceeds the statute compensation, they are entitled to such sum; but they are not entitled to such sum and also to the statute compensation, unless it appears from the terms of the vote of the town that the sum voted was intended to be in addition to said statute compensation. *Ib.*

33. The provision of statute, that when any person, committed to jail for non-payment of taxes, shall be discharged by taking the poor debtors' oath, " the collector shall be liable to pay the tax, with the charges of imprisonment, unless he shall have committed the party within one year after the tax was committed to him to collect," (Gen. Sts. c. 12, § 16,) does not render the collector liable to pay for the support of the person so committed, while in jail. *Townsend* v. *Walcutt*, 3 Met. 152 (1841).

34. A collector of city taxes is " a public officer" within the first section of the United States bankrupt act of 1841; and a debt which he owes the city in consequence of a defalcation in his office of collector, is a fiduciary debt. *Morse* v. *Lowell*, 7 Met. 152 (1843).

35. A committee appointed by a town to audit the accounts of the overseers of the poor, and to demand and receive from them the books of account belonging to the town, held by the overseers in their official capacity, have no such property in the books as will authorize them to apply in their own names for a *mandamus* to compel the surrender of the books. *Bates* v. *Plymouth*, 14 Gray, 163 (1859).

36. A city officer, who is chosen for a year, subject to be removed from office at any time, at the will of the mayor and aldermen, and whose salary is payable quarterly, may legally make an assignment of a quarter's salary before the quarter expires. *Brackett* v. *Blake*, 7 Met. 335 (1844).

37. Future wages to be earned under an existing appointment as watchman of a city may be assigned, by an order addressed to the treasurer of the city; and such an order, given in the middle of a month, "for the amount on my month's wages, when due," means the wages of that month. *Macomber* v. *Doane*, 2 Allen, 541 (1861); and see Ib. 40.

38. A constable's return of his service of an order of notice issued by a city council under an ordinance of the city is competent ev-

idence, supported by his testimony that he has no doubt of its truth, although he has no recollection of the fact of service. *Hildreth* v. *Lowell*, 11 Gray, 345 (1858).

39. Marshals appointed under a city ordinance which directs that they shall also be appointed constables, and that marshals shall pay over to the city the fees received by them in criminal cases or in the service of the city, and shall have salaries in full for all their services, are liable for such fees received by them as constables. *Worcester* v. *Walker*, 9 Gray, 78 (1857).

40. A city ordinance giving to police officers a fixed salary, and requiring them to pay over to the city the fees received by them as witnesses, or for penalties in criminal cases, or for service of any criminal process, or for any services in behalf of the city, is not contrary to public policy. *Ib.*

41. A *mandamus* will not be granted on the petition of the selectmen of a town, (especially if not expressly authorized by a vote of the town,) to compel the town treasurer to pay the amount of an order drawn by them upon him in payment of a debt of the town. *Lexington* v. *Mulliken*, 7 Gray, 280 (1856).

42. Under the city ordinances of Lowell, prescribing the duties of the city solicitor, he is entitled to recover against the city for services rendered by virtue of his office, without special employment, as assistant counsel, in the preparation and trial of a case of flowing land in which the city was one of numerous complainants, and for services in drafting exceptions and reports of cases; but not for examining records, and making a report of the business of his office to the city council. *Caverly* v. *Lowell*, 1 Allen, 289 (1861).

43. A city, whose officers, in repairing a bridge over a river, though acting in the honest exercise of their discretion, narrow the space for the passage of the water, so as in times of freshet to set it back upon a mill, are liable for the injury thus occasioned, in an action of tort, even if the owner of the mill was a member of the committee of the city council on whose report the alteration was made. *Perry* v. *Worcester*, 6 Gray, 544 (1856).

See Actions; Appropriations, 19–23, 29; Bonds; Contracts; Dogs, 3; Estoppel; Finance; Fire, 3, 5–7; Gunpowder; Ordinances, &c. 3; Paupers, 99–102, 273, 274, 328; Police; Railroads, 10; Records, 5; Rewards, 3–5, 8, 10, 11; Riots; Schools; Spendthrifts; Taxes; Treasurer; Ways.

ORDINANCES AND BY-LAWS.

1. Whether a by-law be reasonable or not is for the court to determine, and evidence to the jury on that question is inadmissible. *Commonwealth* v. *Worcester*, 3 Pick. 462 (1826).

2. The provision of statute that in prosecutions on the by-laws of Boston it shall not be necessary to set forth the by-law at large in the complaint, is not unconstitutional as conferring an exclusive privilege. (Gen. Sts. c. 171, § 16.) *Ib.*

3. The mayor and aldermen of Boston have no power to suspend a by-law of the city, nor to authorize a violation of it. *Ib.*

4. St. of 1817, c. 50, providing that prosecutions on the by-laws of Boston may be in the name of the Commonwealth, is not repealed by the act by which the town of Boston was incorporated as a city. *Ib.* Nor is it unconstitutional, notwithstanding that in prosecutions in that form the defendant is not allowed costs on acquittal. *Ib.* *Goddard, Petitioner*, 16 Pick. 504 (1835).

5. A by-law of a city is binding upon strangers coming within the territorial limits of the city. *Vandine, Petitioner*, 6 Pick. 187 (1828). And see Gen. Sts. c. 18, § 15.

6. It is no objection to a statute directing as to the manner of prosecuting offences against ordinances of the city of Boston, that its operation is confined to that city. *Commonwealth* v. *Worcester*, 3 Pick. 462 (1826).

7. A complaint for a breach of a by-law of Boston, concluding "against the form of the by-laws, &c. in such case made and provided," is not sufficient without concluding also "against the form of the statute," &c. *Commonwealth* v. *Gay*, 5 Pick. 44 (1827). But see Gen. Sts. c. 172, § 19.

8. Cities and towns had power, even before the St. of 1857, c. 82, (Gen. Sts. c. 45, § 10,) to make by-laws to prohibit permitting cattle to go at large or stop to feed on any highway. *Commonwealth* v. *Bean*, 14 Gray, 52 (1859).

9. If, under a charter authorizing the same, a city ordinance is passed which prohibits the obstruction of any street for the purpose of building, "without first obtaining a written license from the mayor and aldermen, or some person authorized by them," and complying with such reasonable conditions as they may impose, the mayor alone has no authority to grant a license to obstruct a street for the purpose of building, or to impose conditions therefor; and an agreement, made in consideration of such license from the mayor alone, to indemnify the city against damages that may arise in consequence thereof, is without consideration and void. *Lowell* v. *Simpson*, 10 Allen, 88 (1865).

10. An ordinance of a city, providing that no person shall maintain an awning before his door, without the consent of the mayor and aldermen, is reasonable; and an awning erected without such consent is an unlawful

obstruction. *Pedrick* v. *Bailey*, 12 Gray, 161 (1858).

11. A by-law of a city requiring the owners or occupants of houses bordering on streets to clear the snow from the sidewalks adjoining their respective houses and lands, is not strictly speaking a by-law levying a tax; and inasmuch as the burden created by it is imposed on a numerous class, and upon all persons equally who come within the description of such class, and as they commonly derive a peculiar benefit from the duty required, and are peculiarly able to perform it with the promptness which the good of the community demands, the by-law is not partial and unequal within the sense of the provision in the constitution, that assessments, rates, and taxes, imposed and levied on the inhabitants of the Commonwealth shall be proportional and reasonable; but such by-law is reasonable. *Goddard, Petitioner*, 16 Pick. 504 (1835). And see now Gen. Sts. c. 45, § 9.

12. Such a by-law is not invalid on account of a part of the city peculiarly situated being expressly exempted from its operation. *Ib.*

13. The making and regulation of streets in the city of Boston is provided for exclusively by special statutes; consequently, a by-law of Boston, containing a provision for removing snow in the streets, differing from the provision in the general statute of 1786, c. 81, concerning the laying out and regulation of highways, is not repugnant to this statute. *Ib.*

14. The selectmen of Charlestown were authorized by St. 1832, c. 150, to appoint and locate the places where the dead may be buried in that town, to establish the police of the burying-grounds, to make regulations for funerals and the interment of the dead, to appoint all necessary officers to carry the same into effect, and to prescribe penalties for the violation of such regulations. The fourth section of a by-law made by the selectmen ordained that no person should, without leave in writing signed by a majority of the selectmen, bring into the town any dead body, or convey through any of the streets any dead body so brought into the town; or bury any dead body so brought into the town, on any part of his own premises or elsewhere within the town. It was held, that the first part of this section of the by-law being unauthorized by the statute and void, (which was conceded,) the whole of the section was consequently void. *Austin* v. *Murray*, 16 Pick. 121 (1834).

15. It was held, also, that the latter part of the section was not a regulation but a prohibition, and therefore void; and if it were not a prohibition, yet that, except when applied to a populous part of the town, it was unreasonable and on that account void. *Ib.*

16. The third section of the by-law ordains that no person shall exercise the office of funeral undertaker within the limits of the town, unless he shall have been first appointed and licensed by the selectmen. It was held, that this section did not apply to a person who, without a license, buried dead bodies brought into the town contrary to the fourth section; or if it was intended more effectually to enforce the prohibition in the fourth section, and was to be taken in connection with that section, then it was void. *Ib.*

17. A by-law of a town, forbidding the sale therein by any person, without a license, of "strong beer, ale, or any other intoxicating liquor, in a less quantity than twenty-eight gallons, and that delivered and carried away all at one time," is invalid. *Commonwealth* v. *Turner*, 1 Cush. 493 (1848).

18. A city ordinance, providing that no person shall permit any swine under his care to go upon any sidewalk in the city, or otherwise occupy, obstruct, injure or incumber any such sidewalk, so as to interfere with the convenient use of the same by all passengers, is within an authority conferred by the charter to make all such salutary and needful by-laws as towns by the laws of the Commonwealth have power to make. *Commonwealth* v. *Curtis*, 9 Allen, 266 (1864).

19. It is the duty of a person who voluntarily drives swine through the streets of a city in which such an ordinance has been passed, to prevent them at all hazards from doing the acts therein mentioned; and if he fails to do so, he may be convicted of a violation of the ordinance. *Ib.*

20. A complaint for the violation of such ordinance, which alleges that the defendant, on a day named, "unlawfully did permit a large number of swine, to wit, thirty swine, under the care of him the said defendant, to go upon and injure the sidewalks on certain public streets in the city of C., to wit, the sidewalks in Harvard Square and North Avenue," contains a sufficient averment that the sidewalks named are a part of a highway; and is not bad for duplicity on the ground that it charges more than one offence; nor on the ground that the offence is alleged to have been committed on more than one street, if it appears that Harvard Square and North Avenue were one continuous street. *Ib.*

21. In support of such a complaint, evidence may be introduced of different acts of different swine, in going upon and injuring different parts of the sidewalks. *Ib.*

22. Under a city ordinance which prohibits permitting any cattle to go at large or "stop to feed" on any highway, a complaint which avers that the defendant suffered two cows "to stop and feed" on certain highways, is

bad, even after verdict. *Commonwealth* v. *Bean*, 14 Gray, 52 (1859).

23. Where a by-law of a city prohibits the moving of buildings through the public street without a license granted by the mayor and aldermen, the board of aldermen cannot delegate to the mayor alone the power to grant such licenses. *Day* v. *Green*, 4 Cush. 433 (1849).

24. A city ordinance giving to police officers a fixed salary, and requiring them to pay over to the city the fees received by them as witnesses, or for penalties in criminal cases, or for service of any criminal process, or for any services in behalf of the city, is not contrary to public policy. *Worcester* v. *Walker*, 9 Gray, 78 (1857).

25. A city ordinance having provided that, previous to an assessment of the expenses of building a sidewalk on the abutters, the city auditor should give notice in writing to each person reported to him as liable to be assessed, of his intention to make an assessment, appointing a time and place at which all persons might appear and be heard in relation to the assessment; it was held, that the giving of such notice was a condition precedent to the validity of the assessment, which was not complied with by notifying all the abutters, except one, of the time and place at which they might be heard, and afterwards notifying the remaining abutter of a different time and place, at which he might be heard. *Lowell* v. *Wentworth*, 6 Cush. 221 (1850).

26. A city ordinance prohibiting the sale of any timber brought into the city for sale, without a survey, does not apply to timber delivered there to be used for a specific purpose under a special contract made elsewhere. *Briggs* v. *A Life Boat*, 7 Allen, 287 (1863).

See Carriages, 1-3, 15-18; Constitutional Law, 1; Dogs, 5, 9-11; Faneuil Hall Market; Health, 9-13, 15; Officers, 7-10, 38, 39, 42; Penalties; Sewers and Drains, 8-13, 15; Taxes, 185; Water, 6; Ways, 40, 288, 293, 294, 412, 471-474.

OVERSEERS OF THE POOR.

1. In the year 1772 the overseers of the poor of Boston were incorporated by the legislature. The act of 1822, changing the town of Boston to a city, continued this corporation, and did not dissolve or suspend it. *Boston* v. *Sears*, 22 Pick. 122 (1839).

2. It was held, also, that the overseers of the poor of Boston were by their incorporation constituted an aggregate corporation, with perpetual and continued succession; that a grant to them of real estate would have carried a fee without being to their successors; and that, in a writ of right, they could count only on their own seisin within thirty years next before the commencement of the action. *Ib.*

3. Where overseers of the poor, upon the decease of a pauper, take possession of his effects, pursuant to St. 1817, c. 136, § 6, (Gen. Sts. c. 70, § 21,) and administration is not taken out within thirty days from his decease, they may sell so much of the property as shall be necessary to repay the expenses incurred for such pauper, notwithstanding the appointment of an administrator before the sale takes place. *Haynes* v. *Wells*, 6 Pick. 462 (1828).

4. In an action by the administrator of a pauper against the overseers, to recover the value of articles fairly sold by auction pursuant to that statute, and purchased by one of the overseers himself, the sale was held to be valid. *Ib.*

5. A pauper having a settlement in a town in this commonwealth, cannot lawfully be carried by the overseers, against his will, to a place without the Commonwealth, to be there supported. *Westfield* v. *Southwick*, 17 Pick. 68 (1835).

6. If the municipal authorities of a town have provided supplies for distribution among those out of the almshouse who need relief, upon orders of the overseers of the poor, and have given notice thereof to the overseers, the latter have no authority to contract debts in behalf of the town for the support of the poor; and one who, having knowledge of the facts, furnishes supplies to persons settled in such town upon orders of the overseers, cannot maintain an action against the town to recover for the same. *Ireland* v. *Newburyport*, 8 Allen, 73 (1864).

7. The admission of overseers of the poor, in a binding-out indenture, that a certain pauper is chargeable to their town, and their acts in paying bills to other towns for his support, are not admissible in evidence against the town in a litigation growing out of subsequent acts, for the purpose of showing that he and his descendants have their settlement therein. In performing these duties, they act as public officers, and not as agents of the town. *New Bedford* v. *Taunton*, 9 Allen, 207 (1864). And see Paupers, 273.

8. A committee appointed by a town to audit the accounts of the overseers of the poor, and to demand and receive from them the books of account belonging to the town, held by the overseers in their official capacity, have no such property in the books as will authorize them to apply in their own names for a *mandamus* to compel the surrender of the books. *Bates* v. *Plymouth*, 14 Gray, 163 (1859).

See Apprentices; Paupers.

PAUPERS.

I. What constitutes a Pauper, and who can acquire a Settlement.

II. Settlement of Paupers; How acquired or lost.

(*a*) By Approbation, and not being warned out.
(*b*) By Derivation.
(*c*) By living on a Freehold Estate, &c.
(*d*) By having an Estate, &c., and being assessed therefor.
(*e*) By serving as a Town Officer, or being an Ordained Minister.
(*f*) By Incorporation or Division of Towns.
(*g*) By Residence and paying Taxes.
(*h*) How prevented by being relieved as a Pauper.
(*i*) How lost, when once acquired.

III. Actions for supporting Paupers.

(*a*) Against the Pauper's Kindred.
(*b*) By Individuals against Towns.
(*c*) By Towns against Individuals.
(*d*) By Towns against Towns.

(1) *When and for what the Action will lie; and of the Pleadings, Evidence, and Trial.*
(2) *Of the Notice.*
(3) *Estoppel.*

IV. Removal of Paupers.

V. Penalty for bringing a Pauper into a Town.

VI. Lunatic Paupers and State Paupers.

I. What constitutes a Pauper, and who can acquire a Settlement.

1. The word "pauper" has long been understood to designate persons receiving aid and assistance from the public, for themselves or their families, under the provisions made by law for the support and maintenance of the poor. *Opinion of the Justices*, 11 Pick. 540 (1832).

2. Where a person who had been supported by his town as a pauper, had bodily health and strength, though of small mental capacity, and was able to earn more than enough to support himself, and had found an employer, it was held, that he was no longer a pauper; and consequently, where the town made a contract with the plaintiffs, that they should take care of all the paupers belonging to the town, and be entitled to their services, it was held, that they were not entitled to the services of the person above described. *Wilson* v. *Brooks*, 14 Pick. 341 (1833).

3. In an action between two towns to recover the amount of expenses incurred by the plaintiff town in relieving a person whose settlement was in the defendant town, the fact that such person might by going a short distance have obtained of his debtor as much money as was expended for his relief, was held not to be conclusive evidence that he was not a pauper. *Sturbridge* v. *Holland*, 11 Pick. 459 (1831). See *Paris* v. *Hiram*, 12 Mass. 262; *Groveland* v. *Medford*, 1 Allen, 23 (*post*, 268).

4. A revolutionary pensioner, who was very old and infirm, and had no property other than his wearing apparel and his pension, which was $ 96 a year, was held to be a pauper in the case of *Fiske* v. *Lincoln*, 19 Pick. 473 (1837).

5. Persons who reside on lands purchased by or ceded to the United States for navy yards, forts, and arsenals, where there is no other reservation of jurisdiction to the state than that of a right to serve civil and criminal process on such lands, do not gain a settlement in the towns in which the lands are situated, for themselves or their children, by residence for any length of time on such lands. *Opinion of the Justices*, 1 Met. 580 (1841).

6. Indians, residing within the limits of a town, and being under the guardianship of persons appointed by the government, have no legal settlement in such town. *Andover* v. *Canton*, 13 Mass. 547 (1816).

7. Persons confined as convicts in houses of correction are supported as paupers. *Wood* v. *Burlington*, 1 Met. 493 (1840). See *Opinion of the Justices*, 1 Met. 572.

8. A pauper cannot gain a settlement in his own right in the same town in which he derives a settlement from his father. *Salem* v. *Ipswich*, 10 Cush. 517 (1852).

9. A British soldier was made a prisoner of war by our army in 1777, and was never exchanged, but, not being confined, voluntarily continued his residence in this commonwealth until 1824. It was held, that he was a citizen, and capable of gaining a settlement in this commonwealth. *Cummington* v. *Springfield*, 2 Pick. 394 (1824).

10. So of one born in England, who deserted from the British army under General Burgoyne during the Revolution, and who had resided in this commonwealth from that time until 1824. *Phipps's case*, 2 Pick. 394, note (1824).

11. Every person is a pauper who receives relief at the public expense, and such as is provided by law for persons standing in need of immediate relief. Shaw, C. J., in *Charlestown* v. *Groveland*, 15 Gray, (1860), cited 6 Allen, 587.

12. Where a bond has been given by one individual to another for the support of a poor person, and the indemnity of the obligee,

who was chargeable for such support, the town of the pauper's lawful settlement is not thereby discharged from the obligation to maintain such pauper. *Watson* v. *Cambridge*, 15 Mass. 286 (1818).

II. Settlement of Paupers; How acquired or lost.

See Sts. 1865, c. 230; 1866, c. 288.

(a) By Approbation, and not being warned out.

Sts. 1692, c. 15; 1701, c. 13; 1767, c. 3; 1789, c. 14. Gen. Sts. c. 69, § 1, cl. 8.

13. A warning of a pauper "and his family" under Prov. St. 4 W. & M. c. 13, § 9, is sufficient to prevent the wife and children of the pauper from gaining a settlement. *Shirley* v. *Watertown*, 3 Mass. 322 (1807).

14. If a person, before the Prov. St. of 7 Geo. III. c. 3, had been duly warned to depart from a town, so as to prevent his acquiring a settlement in such town, and after the warning, removed from the town without an intention of returning, continuing absent long enough to gain a new settlement, and afterwards came back and dwelt in the town he had been warned to leave, he must have been again warned within a year from his return, or he would have gained a settlement. *Chelsea* v. *Malden*, 4 Mass. 131 (1808).

15. A warning under the Prov. St. of 4 W. & M. c. 13, to avoid the gaining of a settlement by a pauper, was without effect unless, either in the warrant or the return thereof, the length of time was stated that the party warned had resided in the town. *Hamilton* v. *Ipswich*, 10 Mass. 506 (1813).

16. A warrant which merely stated that the pauper had "lately come to reside" in the town, did not specify with sufficient distinctness the length of time that he had resided there. *Middleborough* v. *Plympton*, 19 Pick. 489 (1837).

17. A warning was held not to be proved by a record of the court of sessions, stating that "the selectmen of U. were allowed to enter their caution against C., whom they refuse to admit as an inhabitant, he having been duly warned, as by a warrant, &c. and return thereon, on file, appears," although it was shown that the warrant and return were lost; such act of the court of sessions being merely ministerial. *Sutton* v. *Uxbridge*, 2 Pick. 436 (1824).

18. Whether such record would have been sufficient evidence, if it had set forth particularly the necessary facts, *quære*. *Ib.*

19. If, in order to show that a person was prevented from gaining a settlement in a town by being warned to leave within one year after he came to reside there, pursuant to Prov. Sts. 4. W. & M c. 13, and 12 & 13 Will. III. c. 10, it be proved merely that such a warrant was issued, served, and returned, it cannot be presumed, in the absence of all other evidence on the subject, that the return on such warrant certified that he was warned within one year after he came to reside in such town. *Franklin* v. *Dedham*, 18 Pick. 544 (1836).

20. Where a stranger was received and entertained by an inhabitant of a town, previous to April 10, 1767, and his residence there was designedly concealed, so that the town officers had no opportunity to warn him to depart, it was held, that he did not gain a settlement. *Newbury* v. *Harvard*, 6 Pick. 1 (1827).

21. A vote of a town between 1767 and 1789, by which J. S. and others were "constituted" one of the school districts of the town, is no evidence of such approbation by the town of his dwelling there as was required by the Prov. St. of 7 Geo. III. c. 3, to give him a settlement in the town. *Amherst* v. *Shelburne*, 13 Gray, 341 (1859).

22. Between the years 1767 and 1789 there was no mode of acquiring a new settlement, but by approbation of the inhabitants of the town into which the person might remove. Parker, C. J., in *Andover* v. *Canton*, 13 Mass. 550 (1816).

23. Under Prov. St. 7 Geo. III. c. 3, § 4, a person coming into a town to reside could not gain a settlement by an *implied* "approbation by the town of his dwelling there." Thus the acceptance by a town of a list of jurymen, as revised by the selectmen, which contained the name of a person who had come into such town to reside, is not such an "approbation" as is required by that statute. *Orange* v. *Sudbury*, 10 Pick. 22 (1830).

24. According to the statute of 1751, for correcting the calendar, a person born on April 4, 1745, old style, would not come of age until April 15, 1766, new style; consequently, he could not gain a settlement in a town by a year's residence without being warned out, there being less than a year between the time of his coming of age and the 10th day of April, 1767, after which day (by Prov. St. 7 Geo. III.) a settlement could not be gained by mere residence without being warned out. *Danvers* v. *Boston*, 10 Pick. 513 (1830).

25. After the provincial act of 7 Geo. III. c. 3, and before St. 1789, c. 14, no settlement by a residence without being warned out could be gained except by the approbation of the town at a general meeting. *Granby* v. *Amherst*, 7 Mass. 1 (1810).

26. The provisions of St. 4 W. & M. c. 13, and St. 1789, c. 14, which required the warning of persons out of a town, to prevent their acquiring a settlement, did not apply to minors, although illegitimate. *Somerset* v. *Dighton*, 12 Mass. 383 (1815).

27. A male pauper, being married while under age, was not thereby so emancipated as to acquire a settlement by a year's residence without being warned out, under Sts. 4 W. & M. c. 13, and 12 & 13 Will. III. c. 10. *Taunton* v. *Plymouth*, 15 Mass. 203 (1818).

28. A child born to one who had been warned to depart the town, under St. 4 W. & M. c. 13, gained a settlement in such town by a year's residence, after coming of age, without being warned to depart. *Berkley* v. *Somerset*, 16 Mass. 454 (1820).

29. Where one, before the 10th of April, 1767, had hired a house, but before the removal of his family into it had gone abroad, and in his absence his family removed into it, and were not warned to depart within twelve months from such removal, he gained a settlement in the town in which such house was situated. *Hardwick* v. *Raynham*, 14 Mass. 362 (1817).

(b) By Derivation.

Sts. 1789, c. 14; 1793, c. 34. Rev. Sts. c. 45. Gen. Sts. c. 69.

Married Women.

30. A marriage of a man having a legal settlement within the Commonwealth gives such settlement to the wife, whether the marriage was solemnized within or without the Commonwealth. *Dalton* v. *Bernardston*, 9 Mass. 201 (1812).

31. A female does not change the place of her lawful settlement by going through the form of a marriage with a person *non compos mentis*. *Middleborough* v. *Rochester*, 12 Mass. 363 (1815).

32. A man and a woman having their settlements in the same town, intermarried, and the town being afterwards divided into two towns, it was held, that the wife took the settlement of her husband in one of the two towns, although but for the marriage her settlement would have been in the other. *North Bridgewater* v. *East Bridgewater*, 13 Pick. 303 (1833).

33. In an action to recover expenses incurred in support of a pauper, against a town in which his settlement is sought to be established by reason of a marriage, it cannot be shown in defence that the marriage was invalid by reason of the insanity of one of the parties. *Goshen* v. *Richmond*, 4 Allen, 458 (1862).

34. The legislature had power to pass St. 1845, c. 222, (Gen. Sts. c. 107, § 2,) providing that the validity of a marriage shall not be questioned in the trial of a collateral issue, on account of the insanity or idiocy of either party. That statute applies to marriages existing at the time of its passage. *Ib.*

Legitimate Children.

35. The children of a woman who marries a pauper follow his settlement. *Goshen* v. *Richmond*, 4 Allen, 458 (1862).

36. Upon a father's gaining a new settlement, a child who is of age, voluntarily living with him, does not thereby gain such new settlement. *Springfield* v. *Wilbraham*, 4 Mass. 493 (1808).

37. A woman of twenty-one years of age and upwards does not follow or have the settlement of her father, which is acquired by him in a town in this commonwealth after she reaches that age; although she continues to be a member of his family, and he then, for the first time, acquires a settlement in this commonwealth. *Shirley* v. *Lancaster*, 6 Allen, 31 (1863).

38. The widowed mother of a female pauper became possessed of an estate sufficient to confer a settlement from three years' possession; but, before the three years had passed, the daughter was married to an alien; and, although she continued to reside in her mother's family until after the expiration of the three years, it was held, that she derived no settlement from her mother. *Charlestown* v. *Boston*, 13 Mass. 469 (1816).

39. The settlement of one who is *non compos mentis*, and has not estate sufficient to give him a settlement in virtue thereof, follows and changes with the settlement of his father, as well after his coming of age as before. *Upton* v. *Northbridge*, 15 Mass. 237 (1818).

40. But it is otherwise if he becomes *non compos mentis* after he becomes of age. *Buckland* v. *Charlemont*, 3 Pick. 173 (1825).

41. And incipient insanity does not incapacitate one from gaining a settlement of his own. *Ib.*

42. Legitimate children cannot derive a settlement from their mother, unless their father has no settlement within the Commonwealth. *Amherst* v. *Shelburne*, 13 Gray, 341 (1859).

43. A legitimate child having a settlement by its father cannot acquire the settlement of its mother. *Scituate* v. *Hanover*, 7 Pick. 140 (1828).

44. A minor child, having the settlement of its deceased father, does not lose it and acquire the settlement of its mother, on her gaining a new settlement by a second mar-

riage. *Walpole* v. *Marblehead*, 8 Cush. 528 (1851).

45. A husband, having a settlement in this state, after a divorce *a vinculo* for adultery committed by him, removed to another state, where he married and had children, while his former wife was still living. It was held, that such marriage being permitted by the laws of that state, the children were legitimate, and that they had their father's settlement. *West Cambridge* v. *Lexington*, 1 Pick. 506 (1823).

46. Minor children, having the settlement of their mother, do not, at the common law, acquire a new settlement gained by her marriage, although they remove with her to the place of such new settlement. *Freetown* v. *Taunton*, 16 Mass. 52 (1819). But see Gen. Sts. c. 69, § 1, cl. 2.

47. Legitimate children under age, having the settlement of their mother, acquire the new settlement which she gains by another marriage. *Plymouth* v. *Freetown*, 1 Pick. 197 (1822).

48. Where a minor, deriving his settlement from his mother, resided in another state, employed in learning a trade, and the mother acquired a new settlement in this commonwealth by a second marriage, before he came of age, it was held, that his settlement followed that of his mother. *Great Barrington* v. *Tyringham*, 18 Pick. 264 (1836).

49. It seems, that the circumstance that the minor was not bound as an apprentice by indenture, is not material in such case. *Ib.*

50. The settlement of a widow, acquired by her after the death of her husband, is communicated to her infant children. *Dedham* v. *Natick*, 16 Mass. 135 (1819).

Illegitimate Children.

51. Under St. 1789, c. 14, § 3, the settlement of an illegitimate child followed that of his mother, and changed with it. *Petersham* v. *Dana*, 12 Mass. 428 (1815).

52. A man and a woman having their settlements in the same town intermarried, and the town being afterwards divided into two towns, it was held, that the wife took the settlement of her husband in one of the two towns, although but for the marriage her settlement would have been in the other; and that the settlement of her illegitimate child, born before the marriage and before St. 1793, c. 34, which had acquired no settlement in its own right, changed with and followed the settlement of its mother. *North Bridgewater* v. *East Bridgewater*, 13 Pick. 303 (1833).

53. But under St. 1793, c. 34, § 2, (Gen. Sts. c. 69, § 1,) cl. 3, an illegitimate child has the settlement of its mother at the time of its birth, and retains it until it gains a new settlement by some act of its own. Its settlement does not change with that of its mother. *Boylston* v. *Princeton*, 13 Mass. 381 (1816).

54. Under the provincial act of 7 Geo. III. c. 3, illegitimate children acquired no settlement by birth, but had the settlement of their mother. *Newton* v. *Braintree*, 14 Mass. 382 (1817).

55. An illegitimate child, born after April 10, 1767, and before the passage of St. 1789, c. 14, has the settlement of his mother at the time of his birth, if she then had any. *Blackstone* v. *Seekonk*, 8 Cush. 75 (1851).

56. If the parents of illegitimate children intermarry, and the father acknowledges the children as his, they are, by St. 1853, c. 253, (Gen. Sts. c. 91, § 4,) made legitimate to all intents and purposes, and thereupon take the settlement of the father. *Monson* v. *Palmer*, 8 Allen, 551 (1864).

Slaves.

57. Until the ratification of the constitution of this commonwealth, in 1780, the settlement of a slave always followed that of his master, and he could not acquire a settlement in his own right. *Winchendon* v. *Hatfield*, 4 Mass. 123 (1808). *Dighton* v. *Freetown*, Ib. 539. *Stockbridge* v. *West Stockbridge*, 12 Mass. 399 (1815). *Edgartown* v. *Tisbury*, 10 Cush. 410 (1852).

58. Slaves were not within the provincial statutes relating to the warning of persons in order to prevent their gaining a settlement, or relating to the gaining a settlement by residence. *Winchendon* v. *Hatfield*, 4 Mass. 123 (1808).

59. But when manumitted, they could acquire a settlement in their own right. *Ib.*

60. After manumission, a slave retained the settlement of his master until another was gained. *Dighton* v. *Freetown*, 4 Mass. 539 (1808).

61. A slave, as the personal property of his master, became upon his master's decease the property of his master's executor or administrator, and acquired the settlement of such executor, &c. *Ib.*

62. But if one purchased the use of a slave from his owner, the slave did not acquire the settlement of the hirer, although he lived ten years in his service. *Stockbridge* v. *West Stockbridge*, 12 Mass. 399 (1815).

63. Children born free of slave parents derived no settlement either from their parents or the masters of their parents. *Andover* v. *Canton*, 13 Mass. 547 (1816). *Lanesborough* v. *Westfield*, 16 Mass. 74 (1819).

64. Where, before the revolution, the possession of a slave had been transferred to a grandchild of the owner, the declarations of the parties to such transfer at the time were held to be part of the *res gestæ*, and so admis-

sible evidence in a suit respecting the slave. *Milford* v. *Bellingham*, 16 Mass. 108 (1819).

65. Although the mother of a child born in Massachusetts in 1772 was then a slave, and her settlement followed that of her master, yet the child was born free, and derived no settlement from her mother. A slave could not communicate a settlement. *Edgartown* v. *Tisbury*, 10 Cush. 408 (1852).

(c) **By living on a Freehold Estate, &c.**

Sts. 1789, c. 14; 1793, c. 34; 1821, c. 94. Rev. Sts. c. 45, § 1; Gen. Sts. c. 69, § 1, Fourth clause.

66. A citizen of the United States, living three years in any town within this state, on land conveyed to him by a warranty deed, gains a settlement in such town, although his grantor had in fact no title to the land. *Boylston* v. *Clinton*, 1 Gray, 619 (1854).

67. It is not necessary to prove that the deed was recorded, under which land was held, in order to establish a settlement under Sts. 1789, c. 14, § 1, and 1793, c. 34. *Belchertown* v. *Dudley*, 6 Allen, 477 (1863).

68. One may gain a settlement by reason of an estate of which he appears by record and possession to be the lawful owner, although his title may be defeasible. *Conway* v. *Deerfield*, 11 Mass. 327 (1814).

69. In order to gain a settlement in a town by having an estate of freehold or inheritance therein, it is sufficient if the person is seised by an apparently good title, and no present right of entry is outstanding in any other person. *Brewster* v. *Dennis*, 21 Pick. 233 (1838).

70. Thus, where one having bargained verbally for a piece of land and paid therefor, entered upon and occupied it for twenty years, without having ever received a deed or any other writing respecting it from the original owner; it was held, that, at the expiration of that period of time, he had gained an estate of freehold within the meaning of the statute. *Ib.*

71. A person does not gain a settlement by living upon land three years successively as the tenant of one who has a life estate therein; although such person is entitled to come into possession of the land on the termination of such life estate. The statutes refer to such an estate as a person has a right to occupy, and not to an estate in expectancy, where there is a preceding estate of freehold in some other person. *Ipswich* v. *Topsfield*, 5 Met. 350 (1842).

72. It was held, under St. 1789, c. 14, that one might gain a settlement by virtue of being seised of a freehold estate in right of his wife. *Windham* v. *Portland*, 4 Mass. 384 (1808).

73. One who has an estate as tenant by the curtesy initiate in land held by his wife to her sole and separate use, under St. 1845, c. 208, does not gain a settlement by living thereon three years successively. *Leverett* v. *Deerfield*, 6 Allen, 431 (1863).

74. A husband who for three years successively occupies land assigned to his wife as dower, obtains a settlement by virtue thereof. *Canton* v. *Dorchester*, 8 Cush. 525 (1851). But see *Leverett* v. *Deerfield*, 6 Allen, 431.

75. A person under guardianship as a spendthrift gained a settlement by living three years successively on an estate of inheritance or freehold, purchased with his money and conveyed by deed to him, although it was purchased by his guardian without the sanction of the probate court. *Hopkinton* v. *Upton*, 3 Met. 165 (1841).

76. An estate of freehold or inheritance in trust may give a settlement to the *cestui que trust*. *Orleans* v. *Chatham*, 2 Pick. 29 (1823). *Scituate* v. *Hanover*, 16 Pick. 222 (1834). *Randolph* v. *Norton*, 16 Gray, (1860).

77. A person occupying an estate in a town for three years, having a bond for a deed thereof, with permission granted in said bond to take the rents and profits to his own use, gains a settlement, by reason thereof, in such town. *Randolph* v. *Norton*, 16 Gray, (1860).

78. The occupation of an estate of freehold by the grantor, after a conveyance thereof which is fraudulent and void as against creditors, is not sufficient to give him a settlement, although he has a bond for reconveyance from the grantee. *Canton* v. *Dorchester*, 8 Cush. 525 (1851).

79. A mortgagor, occupying the mortgaged estate by leave of a lessee for years of the mortgagee, who has entered for condition broken, has no estate of inheritance or freehold in the premises, and cannot, by such occupation, acquire a settlement in the fourth method. *Oakham* v. *Rutland*, 4 Cush. 172 (1849).

80. A settlement may be acquired by owning an estate of freehold or inheritance, and residing thereon for three years successively, although the land be under mortgage, during the whole time, for its full value. *Mount Washington* v. *Clarksburgh*, 19 Pick. 294 (1837).

81. A settlement may be acquired in a town by a residence in a part thereof which is within the actual jurisdiction of the Commonwealth, although within the rightful jurisdiction of another state, which afterwards obtains the actual jurisdiction, on the establishment of the boundary line. *Somerset* v. *Rehoboth*, 6 Cush. 320 (1850).

82. A settlement in a town is not acquired by living undisturbed thirteen years in a

house built by mistake upon the land of another, adjacent to land of the builder, under Rev. Sts. c. 45, (Gen. Sts. c. 69,) § 1, cl. 4, which provide that a settlement may be gained in a town by having an estate of inheritance or freehold therein, and living on the same three years successively. *Wellfleet* v. *Truro*, 5 Allen, 137 (1862).

83. A person does not acquire a settlement in a town under Rev. Sts. c. 45, (Gen. Sts. c. 69,) § 1, cl. 4, by living therein undisturbed for three years in a house built by mistake upon the land of another, adjacent to his own land, and having outbuildings upon his own land. *Wellfleet* v. *Truro*, 9 Allen, 137 (1864).

84. In gaining a settlement by taking the profits for three years of an estate in dower, the time in which they are taken between the assignment of the dower by commissioners, and the ratification thereof by the judge of probate, is to be reckoned as a part of the three years. *Mansfield* v. *Pembroke*, 5 Pick. 449 (1827).

85. When a person having an estate in freehold leased the land for a year in satisfaction of an execution, he was considered, with reference to the gaining of a settlement, as taking the rents and profits during the year. *Ib.*

86. In order to give a citizen of the United States, twenty-one years of age, a settlement under St. 1793, c. 34, § 2, cl. 4, by having a freehold "of the clear yearly income of three pounds, and taking the rents and profits thereof three years successively," it is not necessary that he should have actually taken and received that sum yearly free of all charges. *Pelham* v. *Middleborough*, 4 Gray, 57 (1855).

87. If one who had an estate yielding an income of the requisite amount to give him a settlement, mortgaged the estate to secure a sum, the interest of which, being deducted from the annual income, reduced the income below the required amount, he could gain no settlement, under St. 1793, c. 34, § 2, cl. 4, by reason of the estate. *Groton* v. *Boxborough*, 6 Mass. 50 (1809). *Conway* v. *Deerfield*, 11 Mass. 327 (1814).

88. To gain a settlement in the fourth method described in St. 1793, c. 34, § 2, a citizen must dwell in the town the same three years that he held therein an estate of the prescribed value. *Boston* v. *Wells*, 14 Mass. 384 (1817).

(d) By having an Estate, &c., and being assessed therefor.

St. 1793, c. 34, § 2; Rev. Sts. c. 45, § 1; Gen. Sts. c. 69, § 1, Fifth clause.

89. A person cannot gain a settlement in a town under the fifth mode in St. 1793, c. 34, (Rev. Sts. c. 45, § 1; Gen. Sts. c. 69, § 1,) unless for five successive years his estate shall have been introduced into the valuation of estates made by the assessors, and shall have been valued, the principal at £ 60, (now $ 200,) or the interest at £ 3 12*s*., (now $ 12,) and he shall have been actually assessed for the same; it not being sufficient that he has had estate liable to taxation in the town, and was able to pay taxes, for that period of time. *Monson* v. *Chester*, 22 Pick. 385 (1839).

90. The several requisites prescribed for gaining a settlement in the fifth mode are indispensable, and if either of them is omitted, it is fatal to the acquirement of a settlement. MORTON, J. Ib. 390.

91. A settlement is gained in the fifth mode prescribed in the statute by possession of an estate valued at two hundred dollars, and being assessed for the same five years successively, whether the taxes so assessed be paid or not. *Westbrook* v. *Gorham*, 15 Mass. 160 (1818).

92. One holding an estate of the requisite value under a lease for four years, and afterwards a year by sufferance, and being assessed therefor for the five years, does not thereby acquire a settlement. *Templeton* v. *Sterling*, 15 Mass. 253 (1818).

93. The provision that a person shall gain a settlement in a town by "having an estate, the principal of which shall be set at $200, or the income at $12, in the valuation of estates, and being assessed for the same for the space of five years successively," applies to personal estate as well as to real. *Boston* v. *Dedham*, 4 Met. 178 (1842).

94. A citizen cannot acquire a settlement in the town in which he dwells and has his home, by having an estate therein of the required value, as tenant at sufferance or tenant at will, and being assessed therefor for five successive years. *Southbridge* v. *Warren*, 11 Cush. 292 (1853). *Dover* v. *Brighton*, 2 Gray, 482 (1854).

95. The person must reside in the town the whole of the five years for which he is assessed; in other words, he must reside there five full years, commencing on the first of May. *Southborough* v. *Marlborough*, 24 Pick. 166 (1833).

96. Proof that a citizen, in the town in which he dwelt and had his home, occupied and was assessed five successive years for real estate of sufficient value, not owned by him, but of which he had a lease by indenture for one of those years, is not sufficient evidence of his having acquired a settlement in that town, in the fifth mode in St. 1793, c. 34, and Rev. Sts. c. 45, (Gen. Sts. c. 69,) to exempt another town in which he had previously had his settlement, from liability for his support. *Dover* v. *Brighton*, 2 Gray, 482 (1854).

97. Proof that a citizen, in the town in

which he dwelt and had his home, was assessed five successive years for estate, real and personal, of which he was "possessed on the first day of May," the income of which was set by the assessors at not less than twelve dollars, and that he had an estate in fee in said real estate during the last two of said years, does not raise a presumption that he had so much as an estate for years in the real estate during any of the other years, and is not therefore such evidence of his having acquired a settlement in that town, under St. 1793, c. 34, § 2, or Rev. Sts. c. 45, (Gen. Sts. c. 69,) § 1, cl. 5, as will exempt another town, in which his father had a settlement, from liability for his support. *Boylston* v. *Groton*, 4 Gray, 282 (1855).

98. When it is shown, in a suit against a town for the support of a pauper, that his personal property was set, in the valuation of the estates of the town, at the required sum, and that he was assessed for the same for five successive years, such town cannot avail itself of the objection that there was not, in the valuation, any such schedule or description of the property as is directed by statute. *Boston* v. *Dedham*, 4 Met. 178 (1842).

(e) By serving as a Town Officer, or being an Ordained Minister.

St. 1793, c. 34, § 2; Rev. Sts. c. 45, § 1; Gen. Sts. c. 69, § 1, Sixth and Seventh clauses.

99. To gain a settlement in the sixth mode in St. 1793, c. 34, (Gen. Sts. c. 69,) a person must dwell in a town the whole year in which he serves as a town officer. *Barre* v. *Greenwich*, 1 Pick. 129 (1822).

100. If a person chosen into the office of constable is compulsorily removed from the town within the year, as by being committed to prison in another town, so that he is not able to discharge the duties of his office, he gains no settlement by virtue of such choice. *Paris* v. *Hiram*, 12 Mass. 262 (1815).

101. The year intended by the statute in that case is a municipal year, or from one election to another. *Ib.*

102. A collector of taxes for a school district is a collector of taxes for the purpose of gaining a settlement in a town. *Belgrade* v. *Sidney*, 15 Mass. 523 (1819).

103. Where a minister, who has been regularly ordained in one town, is afterwards settled in another, as a pastor, with the full character, rights and duties of a pastor, but without any new ordination or ceremony of induction, he will by such settlement as a minister, acquire a settlement as a pauper in the latter town; and it is immaterial whether or not he was settled under an engagement for a limited time, as for a year. *Bellingham* v. *West Boylston*, 4 Cush. 553 (1849).

104. By the present usages of the Baptist denomination, a minister can only be settled by the concurrent act of the church and society. The act of the society, however, need not appear by a formal recorded vote; but if the church has formally voted to settle the minister, the concurrence of the society may be shown by records recognizing him as filling that place, coupled with proof that he actually performed the duties thereof. *Leicester* v. *Fitchburg*, 7 Allen, 90 (1863).

(f) By Incorporation or Division of Towns.

St. 1793, c. 34, § 2; Rev. Sts. c. 45, § 1; Gen. Sts. c. 69, § 1, Ninth and Tenth clauses.

105. When an old town is divided into two towns, all the inhabitants at the time of the incorporation having settlements there become settled in the towns, respectively, within the limits of which they lived at the time of the incorporation. *West Springfield* v. *Granville*, 4 Mass. 486 (1808). *Westport* v. *Dartmouth*, 10 Mass. 342 (1813).

106. An inhabitant of a town, living in a part of it which, by an act of incorporation, is formed into a new town, and not having a settlement in the old town, gains none by such incorporation. *West Springfield* v. *Granville*, 4 Mass. 486 (1808).

107. When part of an existing town is detached and annexed to another existing town, the inhabitants of such part, having a settlement in the town from which they are detached, acquire by such annexation a settlement in the town to which they are annexed. *Groton* v. *Shirley*, 7 Mass. 156 (1810).

108. Where a part of a town was incorporated as a new town, a pauper having a previous settlement in the old town, and whose place of residence at the time of the incorporation could not be ascertained, was held to be chargeable to the old town. *Westport* v. *Dartmouth*, 10 Mass. 341 (1813).

109. Before St. 1793, c. 34, (Gen. Sts. c. 69,) when a new town was formed of part of an existing one, the settlement of persons absent at the time of the incorporation of the new town continued in the old town, though their former dwelling was in that part of which such new town was formed. *Windham* v. *Portland*, 4 Mass. 384 (1808). *Bath* v. *Bowdoin*, Ib. 452.

110. When an unincorporated place is made a town by incorporation, the inhabitants gain a settlement therein, and of course lose any former settlement they may have had. *Bath* v. *Bowdoin*, 4 Mass. 452 (1808). *Buckfield* v. *Gorham*, 6 Mass. 445 (1810).

111. Before the passage of St. 1793, c. 34, (Gen. Sts. c. 69,) a citizen who dwelt and had

his home in an unincorporated place, when it was incorporated into a district or town, gained a legal settlement in the district or town, by force of the act of incorporation; that statute having merely affirmed, in this particular, a preëxisting rule of law. *Sutton* v. *Orange*, 6 Met. 484 (1843).

112. Where parts of different towns, together with unincorporated territory, are incorporated into a district, a citizen dwelling and having his home in such unincorporated territory, gains a legal settlement in such district, by force of the act of incorporation, in the same manner as if such district had been wholly composed of territory previously unincorporated. *Ib.*

113. A pauper whose settlement in a town was acquired in a part which was afterwards incorporated into a new town, but whose home at the time of the division was in the other part, was held not to have a settlement in the new town. *Sutton* v. *Dana*, 4 Pick. 117 (1826).

114. Incorporating a district into a town made no alteration in regard to the settlement of persons residing in the territory. *Walpole* v. *Hopkinton*, 4 Pick. 357 (1826).

115. Under St. 1794, c. 34, (Gen. Sts. c. 69,) upon the division of a town, a person having a legal settlement therein, but not residing therein at the time of such division, acquired a settlement in that town in which his last dwelling-place in the original town happened to fall upon such division. *Lexington* v. *Burlington*, 19 Pick. 426 (1837).

116. But where a special statute set off an individual, with his family and real estate, from one town, and annexed them to another, it was held, that the settlement in the former town of another person, not then residing therein, but whose last residence therein was upon the land set off, was not transferred to the town to which such land was annexed. *Ib.*

117. Where a new town, A., was incorporated out of part of an old town, B., and the act of incorporation provided that A. should pay to B. a sum of money as a consideration for being exempted from any expense on account of paupers belonging to B. previous to the incorporation, except such as might thereafter be returned as paupers from some other town, who were born in or formerly were inhabitants of that part of B. which constituted A.; it was held, that the paupers returned to B. not born in A. for whose support A. must pay, were those who, when they removed to other towns, removed from the part of B. forming A., and not such as might have once lived in that part of B., not having been born there, but before they dwelt in another town, removed to and lived in the other part of B., and removed thence to other towns. *Salem* v. *Hamilton*, 4 Mass. 676 (1808).

118. A pauper had a derivative settlement in a part of the town of A. which was annexed to the town of B.; but being of age, and out of the Commonwealth, at the time of such annexation, his settlement continued in A. Afterwards the town of C. was incorporated, and contained within its limits the tract of land in right of which the settlement was held. In the act incorporating C., it was provided that persons who had gained a settlement in the part of B. which by the act was made a part of C., and who should thereafter need support, should be supported by C. This latter town was held liable for the support of the pauper. *Great Barrington* v. *Lancaster*, 14 Mass. 253 (1817).

119. One cannot affect his settlement by removing from one part to another part of the same town. Therefore, where, upon the incorporation of a new town from parts of several old ones, it was provided by the act of incorporation that the new town should be held to support such paupers as had gained a settlement in any of those parts of the old towns which formed the new one; it was held, that the new town was not liable for the support of paupers who derived their settlement from an ancestor who lived in a part of one of the old towns forming the new one, but who had before acquired a settlement by residence in another part of the same old town. *Princeton* v. *West Boylston*, 15 Mass. 257 (1818).

120. The act incorporating the town of A. from part of the town of B., provided that A. should receive and support four tenths of the poor persons then chargeable to B. D. S., one of the said poor persons, whose settlement in B. was not derived from his residence on that part of its territory which was formed into A., was, with his wife and children, assigned to and received and supported by A., in accordance with an agreement made between the two towns pursuant to said act. It was held, that D. S. did not thereby acquire a settlement in A.; and that his children, born after the agreement, were not chargeable to that town. *West Boylston* v. *Boylston*, 15 Mass. 261 (1818).

121. Where a new town was created of parts of several towns, and it was provided that the new town should support all such persons as before had been, then were, or thereafter might be, inhabitants of those parts of the former towns then incorporated into such new town, and were or might become chargeable, and who had not a settlement elsewhere; it was held, that the new town was not chargeable with the support of paupers who, at the time of the incorporation, were supported by one of the old towns upon the territory forming part of the new town,

but whose settlement was derived from owning and occupying real estate in another part of the old town. *Southbridge* v. *Charlton*, 15 Mass. 248 (1818).

122. The agreement of towns cannot affect the settlement of their inhabitants. Therefore, where a part of a town was about to be incorporated into a new town, and it was agreed that those who should afterwards become chargeable as paupers, should be supported by the town from whose territory they derived their settlement, it was held, that the old town was still liable to others for the support of one whose settlement was derived from the territory composing the new town, but who was not an inhabitant at the time of the incorporation. *Westborough* v. *Franklin*, 15 Mass. 254 (1818).

123. On the separation of East Sudbury from Sudbury, an agreement was made between the two towns "that all paupers who had gained a settlement in the old town before the division should be supported in the town in which they gained their habitancy." It was held, that a pauper who was born within the limits of East Sudbury had not acquired a new settlement by changing his residence within the town to the territory which remained in the old town on the separation. *Sudbury* v. *East Sudbury*, cited 15 Mass. 260 (1815).

124. By an act incorporating a town from part of an old one, it was provided that the two towns should bear their proportionable part of the expense of supporting the poor that were at that time relieved by the elder town. Afterwards the two towns made an agreement that if any person should thereafter be returned as a pauper, having a right to a support from the elder town, the new town should be bound to support him, if his last residence had been in that territory which constituted the new town. It was held, that the agreement was not binding on the new town, and it was not obliged to support a pauper so situated. *Norton* v. *Mansfield*, 16 Mass. 48 (1819).

125. In an act incorporating a town, which provided that certain remonstrants against the incorporation, who lived within the limits of the new town, should remain with their families to the old town, upon their leaving their names in the secretary's office within two years, it was held, that the privilege thus granted was personal to the remonstrants, and did not remain to their descendants. *Dillingham* v. *Burgis*, 16 Mass. 58 (1819).

126. A new town was formed of parts of several old towns. Sundry inhabitants within the limits of the new town were, with their estates and the heirs and assigns of such estates, to remain to the towns to which they had before belonged; but were authorized at their pleasure afterwards to transfer themselves and their estates to the new town. A., an inhabitant thus situated, sold his estate to B., and removed elsewhere. B. afterwards availed himself of the privilege, and became with the estate he had so purchased, a part of the new town. It was held, that the settlement of A. was not thereby affected. *Lancaster* v. *Sutton*, 16 Mass. 112 (1819).

127. A person having a settlement on the part of Bridgewater which remains Bridgewater, removed into the part which is now East Bridgewater, and would have gained a settlement there by owning a freehold, if that part had then been a separate town. It was held, that his settlement was still in Bridgewater, under St. 1823, c. 31, incorporating East Bridgewater, which provides that all persons who may hereafter become chargeable as paupers to Bridgewater or East Bridgewater, shall be considered as belonging to that town on the territory of which they had their settlement at the time of passing the act. *East Bridgewater* v. *Bridgewater*, 2 Pick. 572 (1824). See *Bridgewater* v. *West Bridgewater*, 9 Pick. 55.

128. By St. 1819, c. 147, by which a part of the town of P. was incorporated as a new town by the name of H., it is enacted that "the poor now supported by the town of P., and all such who may hereafter be returned for support in virtue of having acquired a settlement in said town, shall be supported in the town of P. or H., as they shall have acquired their settlement within the territorial limits of either town as described in this act." It was held, that this provision did not apply to a person not then a pauper, who had then acquired a settlement in the territory set off as the town of P., but whose dwelling-place was within the territory set off as the town of H., but that such person, upon the incorporation of H., acquired a settlement in that town. *Hanson* v. *Pembroke*, 16 Pick. 197 (1834).

129. An act incorporating a part of a town into a separate town, provided that any person who might have gained an habitancy within the part thus incorporated, and who should thereafter need to be supported as a poor person, should be supported by the new town. *Held*, that a pauper who had gained a settlement on that part of the territory which continued to be the old town, but had removed into the other part before it was incorporated as the new town, retained his settlement in the old town. *New Braintree* v. *Boylston*, 24 Pick. 164 (1833).

130. Parts of different towns formed into a new town, with a provision that the new town should support all the poor who had their legal settlement in either of the towns

from which it was formed, and who had removed therefrom, and whose dwelling-place or home was, before such removal, within the limits of the new town. *Held*, that this provision did not include those poor who had removed from the limits of the new town into another part of the same old town, and from thence into another town; but included those only whose *last* dwelling-place or home, previous to such removal, was within the limits of the new town. *Sutton* v. *Dana*, 1 Met. 383 (1840).

131. Parts of different towns were formed into a district, by an act of incorporation which contained a provision that the inhabitants of the district should "provide for the support of all the poor who were inhabitants within the district before the passing of the act, and shall be brought back for maintenance hereafter." *Held*, that the act was limited to those individuals who were before inhabitants within the district, and might be brought back, and did not include their descendants. *Harvard* v. *Boxborough*, 4 Met. 570 (1842).

132. St. 1842, c. 5, annexing parts of two other towns to the town of Dana, having provided that if persons who had theretofore gained a legal settlement in said annexed territory, should come to want and stand in need of relief and support, they should be relieved and supported by said town of Dana, in the same manner as if they had gained a settlement in that town; it was held, that the town of Dana was bound to support, from the time the statute was passed, the persons who had gained or derived, in the way mentioned in said section, a legal settlement in said annexed territory, and who might stand in need of relief since the statute was passed, though they had come to want and been relieved as paupers before it was passed. *Dana* v. *Hardwick*, 10 Met. 208 (1845).

133. The third section of St. 1811, c. 133, for dividing the town of Rehoboth, and establishing the town of Seekonk, which provided that one half of the paupers for which the town of Rehoboth was chargeable, including such as had removed therefrom, if lawfully returned there for support, should be delivered over to the overseers of the poor of the new town, to be there supported, did not change, as to the settlement of the paupers referred to in such act, the general law relating to the settlement of the inhabitants of a town, upon a division thereof. *Westborough* v. *Rehoboth*, 4 Cush. 185 (1849).

134. The incorporation of the town of Essex from a part of the town of Ipswich, does not exempt the latter town from the support of a pauper who had a settlement in Ipswich at that time, and resided in that part of the town which continued to be Ipswich. *Salem* v. *Ipswich*, 10 Cush. 517 (1852).

135. Under St. 1850, c. 62, which divides the town of Bradford, and incorporates a portion thereof into the new town of Groveland, and which provides that "the paupers now supported by the town of Bradford, and all such as may hereafter require support, in virtue of having acquired a settlement in said town, shall be supported by the town within the territorial limits of which they may have acquired a settlement," the inhabitants of Groveland are bound to support all paupers who have a settlement within the territorial limits of that town, whether such settlement is derivative, or has been acquired by their own act. *North Andover* v. *Groveland*, 1 Allen, 75 (1861).

See Annexation and Division of Towns, 3, 4.

(g) By Residence and paying Taxes.

St. 1793, c. 34, § 2; Rev. Sts. c. 45, § 1; Gen. Sts. c. 69, § 1, Twelfth clause.

136. A citizen, having taxable property, and being able to pay the taxes assessed upon him, gains a settlement in a town by dwelling there for ten years together, and half that time paying state and town taxes, although he is omitted in the county tax. *Wrentham* v. *Attleborough*, 5 Mass. 430 (1809).

136*a*. In order to gain a settlement under the twelfth clause, a person must have resided in the town ten years together, and if he has been absent for three months during the term, with the intention not to return, he does not gain a settlement. *Billerica* v. *Chelmsford*, 10 Mass. 394 (1813).

137. One residing in a town more than ten years, paying taxes for more than five of them for a small piece of land, which the owner of it permitted him to occupy at a small rent for one year, and which he continued to occupy for the other years without any express contract, being too poor to pay the rent in full, was held to have acquired a settlement in the town. *Sudbury* v. *Stow*, 13 Mass. 462 (1816).

138. A person having removed to this state from Vermont, resided in a town in this state for ten years, and paid taxes there during more than five of those years. It was held, that he acquired a settlement in such town, although he left his wife and children upon his farm in Vermont, and occasionally visited them there, and once remained there with them five or six months, during the ten years. *Cambridge* v. *Charlestown*, 13 Mass. 501 (1816).

139. The payment of highway taxes for

five years, by labor, with the requisite residence of ten years, gave a settlement under St. 1793, c. 34, no other taxes being assessed upon the person during those years. *Andover* v. *Chelmsford*, 16 Mass. 236 (1819).

140. A citizen dwelling in a town ten years, and having taxable property five of those years, does not gain a settlement in the twelfth mode mentioned in St. 1793, c. 34, (Gen. Sts. c. 69,) if the assessors, for a sufficient reason, omit to tax him. *Reading* v. *Tewksbury*, 2 Pick. 535 (1824).

141. Where a person lived in a town nine years and four months, and then absconded and never returned, but his wife remained there eight months longer, it was held, that he had not resided there ten years actually or constructively, and so had not gained a settlement in the twelfth mode in St. 1793, c. 34. *Athol* v. *Watertown*, 7 Pick. 42 (1828).

142. Labor performed by an individual in repairing highways to the amount of a highway tax irregularly and informally assessed upon him, would have no effect towards giving him a settlement. *Southampton* v. *Easthampton*, 8 Pick. 380 (1829).

143. Where the assessors assessed more than five per cent. over and above the sum committed to them to assess, it was held, that the tax was not "duly assessed," within the meaning of the statute relative to gaining a settlement. *Charlemont* v. *Conway*, 8 Pick. 408 (1829).

144. But the town cannot set up this defect, to defeat a settlement, where so long a time has elapsed since the payment of the tax that no claim for reimbursement could be sustained. *Ib.*

145. On the question between two towns whether a pauper has acquired a settlement in one of them by a residence there of ten years and payment of all taxes for any five years within that period, the fact that a highway tax assessed on him one year was not included in his tax bill of the ensuing year, raises a presumption that it was paid; but this presumption may be rebutted by evidence to the contrary. *Attleborough* v. *Middleborough*, 10 Pick. 378 (1830).

146. The burden of proof as to the fact of payment of such highway tax is upon the party alleging that a settlement was acquired in the mode above mentioned. *Ib.*

147. In order to gain a settlement in a town under the twelfth mode prescribed by St. 1793, c. 34, § 2, (Gen. Sts. c. 69, § 1,) a person must pay all the taxes duly assessed upon him for five out of the ten years of his residence in such town; and it is not sufficient if he pays a part only of such taxes, and is discharged from the payment of the residue by a vote of the town. *Shrewsbury* v. *Salem*, 19 Pick. 389 (1837).

148. The mere neglect of the officers of a town to enforce the payment of a tax which might by due diligence have been collected, will not have the same operation as an actual payment, towards giving the person assessed a settlement in the twelfth mode prescribed by St. 1793, c. 34, § 2, (Gen. Sts. c. 69, § 1,) viz: residing in a town ten years together and paying taxes five of them. *Robbins* v. *Townsend*, 20 Pick. 345 (1838).

149. A person, although he has no settlement within the Commonwealth, does not acquire a settlement in a town by residing there ten years together, and paying taxes for five of those years, if he receives aid as a pauper, from such town, before the expiration of the ten years. *West Newbury* v. *Bradford*, 3 Met. 428 (1841). And see *post*, 160–171.

150. Or if he is supplied by the town in which he has a settlement, with money to aid him in supporting his helpless children. *Taunton* v. *Middleborough*, 12 Met. 35 (1846).

151. A person does not acquire a settlement by residing in a town for ten years together and paying all taxes assessed upon him for five years within that time, if during that time the town has paid for his support while confined in its workhouse, on conviction for a criminal offence. *Worcester* v. *Auburn*, 4 Allen, 574 (1862). See *post*, 160–171.

152. A person does not gain a settlement by residing in a town for ten years together, and possessing real and personal estate, if the assessors omit to tax him; though such omission is not on account of his infirmity or poverty, or by mistake, but in order to prevent his acquiring a settlement; evidence, therefore, that a person, who has resided in a town ten years together, possessed such estate, and that the assessors thus omitted to tax him, is not admissible in proof of his having gained a settlement in such a town. *Berlin* v. *Bolton*, 10 Met. 115 (1845).

153. In an action brought by one town against another for the support of a pauper and his family, evidence that the pauper left his former home and came to the defendant town with the intention of removing his family there as soon as practicable, that he boarded and worked there for ten years, and paid taxes there five years of the ten, and that, a year after he came, his family removed there, and continued to reside with him for the rest of the ten years, after which they all removed to the plaintiff town, is sufficient to warrant a finding by the jury that the pauper had gained a settlement for himself and family in the defendant town. *Fitchburg* v. *Winchendon*, 4 Cush. 190 (1849).

154. In order to prove a settlement in the

twelfth mode provided by statute, by a residence and the payment of taxes in the town where the settlement was alleged to be, an original document preserved amongst the records of the town, and purporting to be an assessment of taxes for the year 1798, was produced in evidence, from which it appeared that taxes to the amount of $3.03 were assessed in that year upon the individual in question for his poll and estate; and it also appeared in evidence that the entry of these taxes on the bill of assessment had been erased by having a line drawn through it, and that the collector for the year 1798 had been allowed a credit with the treasurer of the town for a discount of said taxes; it was held, that whether the production of the bill of assessment raised any presumption of the payment of the taxes so assessed or not, the circumstances stated above were competent evidence to prove that the taxes in question were not in fact paid. *Boston* v. *Weymouth*, 4 Cush. 538 (1849).

155. The assessment of a tax on real estate to the occupant, and the payment of the same by him, not as of his own estate, but in right of another, are a sufficient assessment and payment of a tax, within the twelfth mode provided by statute, for acquiring a settlement as a pauper in the town where the occupant resides. *Randolph* v. *Easton*, 4 Cush. 557 (1849).

156. Insanity, incurring after a person has become an inhabitant of a town, will not prevent his acquiring a settlement by living therein ten years consecutively. *Chicopee* v. *Whately*, 6 Allen, 508 (1863).

157. The rule that a domicil once acquired is presumed to continue until a subsequent change is shown, applies to cases of settlement. *Ib.*

158. Absence from a town, without a definite purpose at all events to return to it as a home, will not interrupt the residence requisite to a settlement under the twelfth clause, until a new domicil is acquired elsewhere. *Worcester* v. *Wilbraham*, 13 Gray, 586 (1859).

159. A citizen of this state resided in Lenox with his family from May, 1823, till the summer of 1828, when he left Lenox for a temporary purpose and remained absent, without any intention of changing his residence, until the latter part of May, 1829, when he returned, and thereafter resided in Lenox until May, 1838, paying taxes assessed upon him therein yearly from 1831 to 1838. His wife and children had been left by him in Lenox during his absence, but before his return removed therefrom without his consent or knowledge. *Held*, that he gained a settlement in Lenox in the twelfth mode. *Lee* v. *Lenox*, 16 Gray, (1860).

(h) How prevented by being relieved as a Pauper.

160. A person does not acquire a settlement in a town by residing therein for ten years and paying taxes during five of those years, if before the expiration of the ten years he became poor, and was relieved by the overseers of the poor of the town of his former settlement. *East Sudbury* v. *Waltham*, 13 Mass. 460 (1816).

161. A person does not acquire a legal settlement by residing in a town ten years together and paying taxes for any five of those ten years, if within that time he is committed to jail, and while there applies for and receives relief as a pauper from the jailer. *East Sudbury* v. *Sudbury*, 12 Pick. 1 (1831).

162. Where one resided in a town for ten years together, and paid all taxes assessed upon him for five of those years, it was held, that he acquired a settlement therein, notwithstanding his wife was, at the same time, receiving support as a pauper from another town in which she resided, it not appearing that she was so supported at his request or with his knowledge, or that he was ever applied to for payment of the expenses thereof, or that he was unable to pay them. *Berkeley* v. *Taunton*, 19 Pick. 480 (1837).

163. A person will not acquire a settlement by living three years successively on land in which he has an estate of freehold or inheritance, if in the course of that period he receive relief as a pauper. *Brewster* v. *Dennis*, 21 Pick. 233 (1838). *Oakham* v. *Sutton*, 13 Met. 192 (1847).

164. A person could not acquire a settlement in a town by a residence of ten years therein and paying taxes five years of the ten, if during that time he applied to the overseers of the town for aid, and they supplied his wants, although he afterwards paid for the supplies, and although he had no settlement in the Commonwealth. *West Newbury* v. *Bradford*, 3 Met. 428 (1841), overruling on this point *Mount Washington* v. *Clarksburgh*, 19 Pick. 294 (1837).

165. A parent does not gain a settlement in a town by residing therein ten years together, and paying all taxes assessed on him for five of those years, if, during such residence, he is supplied by the town in which he has a settlement, with money to aid him in supporting his helpless children. *Taunton* v. *Middleborough*, 12 Met. 35 (1846).

166. A person who has a settlement within the Commonwealth does not acquire a new settlement by residing in a town ten years together, and paying taxes for five of those years, if his wife is committed to a state lunatic hospital upon his complaint or by his consent, and receives aid from the Common-

wealth as a state pauper, before the expiration of the ten years. *Charlestown* v. *Groveland*, 15 Gray, (1860).

167. A citizen of the United States, not having a settlement within the Commonwealth, does not gain a settlement in a town by having a freehold estate therein, and living on such estate three years successively, if before the expiration of the three years his wife is committed to a state lunatic hospital, and is there supported by the Commonwealth as a pauper, although he did not request or consent to her commitment, if he knew of such commitment. *Woodward* v. *Worcester*, 15 Gray, (1860).

168. Support granted to a person as a pauper by the overseers of the poor of the town in which he has a settlement, will prevent his acquiring a settlement in another town in which he resides, although the act of the overseers, in granting such support, be not ratified by the town of whose poor they are overseers. *Oakham* v. *Sutton*, 13 Met. 192 (1847).

169. A man does not obtain a settlement, under Rev. Sts. c. 45, (Gen. Sts. c. 69,) § 1, cl. 4, in a town where he owns a freehold, if before he has lived therein for three years successively he is committed to a state lunatic hospital and there supported as a pauper; although his family continue to reside on his land for the residue of the three years. *Choate* v. *Rochester*, 13 Gray, 92 (1859).

170. A person does not acquire a settlement by residing in a town for ten years together and paying all taxes assessed upon him for five years within that time, if during that time the town has paid for his support while confined in its workhouse, on conviction for a criminal offence. *Worcester* v. *Auburn*, 4 Allen, 574 (1862).

171. It is the reception of needed support or aid, furnished by the public, which prevents a person from gaining a settlement, although that support may not ultimately be at the expense of the public. *Ib.*

(i) **How lost when once acquired.**

172. A settlement gained in another state does not annul a previous settlement in a town within this state. *Canton* v. *Bentley*, 11 Mass. 441 (1814). *Wilbraham* v. *Sturbridge*, 6 Cush. 61 (1850).

173. A wife does not lose her settlement, derived from her husband, by means of a divorce, except for a cause which shows the marriage to have been void. *Dalton* v. *Bernardston*, 9 Mass. 201 (1812). See *Middleborough* v. *Rochester*, 12 Mass. 363.

174. A settlement is not lost until another is gained within the state; therefore, where a pauper, having a settlement derived from his father, removed into New Hampshire, and there had a son born, who afterwards came into this state and had children, it was held, that these children had a settlement in this state, derived from their great-grandfather. *Townsend* v. *Billerica*, 10 Mass. 411 (1813).

175. A person does not lose or gain a settlement by reason of his changing his domicil from one place to another in the same town. *Dalton* v. *Hinsdale*, 6 Mass. 501 (1810). *Princeton* v. *West Boylston*, 15 Mass. 260 (1818).

176. A person having a settlement in a town in Massachusetts, but living in Maine at the time of its separation from Massachusetts, did not by the separation lose her former settlement. *Middleborough* v. *Clark*, 2 Pick. 28 (1823).

177. Since the repeal of St. 1789, c. 14, by St. 1793, c. 34, a settlement in any town in this commonwealth is not lost by the acquisition of a settlement in another state, while the St. of 1789 was in force. *Wilbraham* v. *Sturbridge*, 6 Cush. 61 (1850).

178. The rule that a domicil once acquired is presumed to continue until a subsequent change is shown, applies to cases of settlement. *Chicopee* v. *Whately*, 6 Allen, 508 (1863).

III. Actions for supporting Paupers.

(a) **Against the Pauper's Kindred.**

St. 1793, c. 59. Rev. Sts. c. 46. Gen. Sts. c. 70.

179. The kindred of a pauper cannot be called upon to contribute to his support except by the overseers of the poor of the town of his legal settlement or by others of his kindred. *Salem* v. *Andover*, 3 Mass. 436 (1807).

180. The only remedy for a town other than that wherein he is settled, which has provided for a pauper, is by an action against the town where he has his settlement. *Ib.*

181. The terms "such poor person," and "such pauper" in Rev. Sts. c. 46, §§ 5, 6, (Gen. Sts. c. 70, §§ 4, 5,) include all poor and indigent persons, standing in need of relief. *Hutchings* v. *Thompson*, 10 Cush. 238 (1852).

182. The kindred by affinity of any poor person cannot maintain a complaint under Rev. Sts. c. 46, § 6, (Gen. Sts. c. 70, § 5,) against the father of such poor person, for the expenses of his relief and support. The term "any kindred" extends only to kindred by consanguinity. *Farr* v. *Flood*, 11 Cush. 24 (1853).

183. The word "kindred" includes only blood relations. A husband is not of kin to his wife, nor she to him. *Brookfield* v. *Allen*, 6 Allen, 586 (1863).

184. Upon a complaint to compel kindred

of a poor person to contribute towards his support, the superior court have power, under Gen. Sts. c. 70, § 11, to award costs, and no appeal lies from their decision. *South Reading* v. *Hutchinson*, 10 Allen, 68 (1865).

(b) **By Individuals against Towns.**

Sts. 1793, c. 59; 1826, c. 142; 1834, c. 151. Rev. Sts. c. 46. Gen. Sts. c. 70, § 16.

185. Under St. 1793, c. 59, § 13, an action against the town of a pauper's legal settlement, for supplies furnished the pauper, could not be sustained unless the plaintiff was an inhabitant of such town. *Mitchell* v. *Cornville*, 12 Mass. 332 (1815). But the provisions of this statute were changed by Rev. Sts. c. 46, § 18 (Gen. Sts. c. 70, § 16). *Underwood* v. *Scituate*, 7 Met. 214 (1843).

186. A surgeon, who has performed a difficult and necessary operation on a pauper, not resident in the town of his settlement, without the request of the overseers of the poor of such town, has no right of action therefor against such town. *Miller* v. *Somerset*, 14 Mass. 396 (1817).

187. Nor can a surgeon recover for such services from the town where the pauper resided, the services having been performed without notice and request made to the overseers of the poor of such town. *Kittredge* v. *Newbury*, 14 Mass. 448 (1817).

188. Where an inhabitant of a town incurs an expense for the relief of a pauper, for which the town is liable after notice and request to the overseers of such town, such notice and request need not be in writing. *Watson* v. *Cambridge*, 15 Mass. 286 (1818).

189. An action against the town for the reimbursement of such expense is not limited to two years after the notice. *Ib.*

190. Under St. 1793, c. 59, a town in which a prison was situated was liable to the jailer for the support of a pauper confined in prison for debt, whether he had a legal settlement in any other place or not, after due application to the overseers. *Cargill* v. *Wiscasset*, 2 Mass. 547 (1807). *Doggett* v. *Dedham*, Ib. 564 (1805).

191. So where the pauper was confined for not obeying the order of the court in providing for the maintenance of a bastard child, of which he had been adjudged to be the father. *Sayward* v. *Alfred*, 5 Mass. 244 (1809).

192. Otherwise, where the pauper had been committed to prison for a crime against the Commonwealth. *Adams* v. *Wiscasset*, 5 Mass. 328 (1809).

193. Under Sts. 1802, c. 22, § 2, and 1826, c. 142, the master of a house of correction, after his accounts had been allowed and certified by the court of sessions, might maintain an action for the amount allowed by that court for the support of a pauper duly committed to the house, against the town of the pauper's settlement, and want of notice to the town of the claim afforded no defence to the action. *Wade* v. *Salem*, 7 Pick. 333 (1828).

194. The expense incurred on account of an infant nursing at the breast of a woman committed to a house of correction may be recovered of the town where the house of correction is situated, after notice and request, but not the expense of extra articles of food furnished to the mother, because of her having an infant at the breast. *Watson* v. *Cambridge*, 18 Pick. 470 (1836).

195. Under St. 1834, c. 151, § 10, authorizing keepers of houses of correction to bring actions in certain cases for the support of convicts against the towns of the convicts' settlement, a personal presentation of an account was held not to be necessary, but a letter from the keeper or some one authorized by him, to the selectmen of the town, making a demand, was sufficient. Evidence of the authority of the agent should be furnished to the selectmen at the time of the demand. *Robbins* v. *Weston*, 20 Pick. 112 (1838).

196. But a demand made under the authority solely of the overseers of the house of correction in Boston, was held to be insufficient, although afterwards ratified by the board of aldermen. *Boston* v. *Weston*, 22 Pick. 211 (1839).

197. If a person agrees with a town to board a pauper for a year at the rate of a dollar a week, and the pauper dies within the year, so that the contract cannot be fulfilled, such person is entitled to recover, on an implied promise, for the part of the contract actually performed, but he cannot recover for the whole year. *Willington* v. *West Boylston*, 4 Pick. 101 (1826).

198. If a pauper is ill treated or insufficiently provided for by an individual who has agreed with the town to support him, another individual will not have a right to support him without notice to the town, so that it may reform the abuse or make other provision for the pauper. *Worden* v. *Leyden*, 10 Pick. 24 (1830).

199 The plaintiff, being the guardian of a person whose legal settlement was in the town of L., and who was incapable of labor, and had no property except a small pension, informed the overseers of the poor of the town of two successive years that he was running a risk, as he was obliged to become responsible for the board of his ward, and that when he received the pension it took about one half of it to pay arrearages due for the board, and that the town must take the risk. The ward died, when all the property belonging to him had been exhausted and further expenses had been

necessarily incurred by the guardian. It was held, that the ward was in need of relief, and that the plaintiff was entitled to recover of the town for the expenses incurred by him for the ward subsequently to notice and request. *Fiske* v. *Lincoln*, 19 Pick. 473 (1837).

200. As the relation of guardian and ward subsisted between the plaintiff and the pauper, the objection that the plaintiff was not obliged to relieve the pauper because the latter was not living with him but with another inhabitant of the town, was held to be inapplicable. *Ib.*

201. Where the plaintiff made a contract with the father of a female child to take her into his family, and for her services to maintain her in sickness and in health during the pleasure of the parties, and afterwards, when she had become ill, gave notice of the fact to the overseers of the poor, and requested assistance from the town for her support, it was held, that as he had not given the father notice of his wish to put an end to the contract, it continued in force, and he had no right of action against the town for supporting the child. *Peters* v. *Westborough*, 20 Pick. 506 (1838).

202. Since the Rev. Sts. c. 46, § 18, a person, though not an inhabitant of the town where a pauper falls into distress, may recover of such town any expense necessarily incurred by him for the relief of the pauper in said town, after notice and request made to the overseers of the poor of the town, and their neglect to provide for the pauper. *Underwood* v. *Scituate*, 7 Met. 214 (1843).

203. A physician, an inhabitant of the town of H., immediately after attending upon a person in the town of S., to whom he had been called, and who had received a wound, and was proper subject of relief by that town, gave notice to one of the overseers of the poor of said town, that said person needed and would need surgical assistance, but did not wish to be considered a pauper. He also requested said overseer to inform him whether the town of S. would pay him for the services which he had rendered and which it would be necessary to render. The overseers of the poor of S. took no order on this notice and request, and neglected to make any provision for said person. *Held*, that this notice and request were sufficient to entitle the physician to recover from the town of S. compensation for his services in attending upon said person until he was cured. *Ib.*

204. The provision in the Rev. Sts. c. 46, § 18, (Gen. Sts. c. 70, § 16,) that "every town shall be held to pay any expense which shall be necessarily incurred, for the relief of a pauper, by any person who is not liable by law for his support, after notice and request made to the overseers of the said town, and until provision shall be made by them," applies only to expense incurred in the support of a pauper found or residing in the town. *Smith* v. *Coleraine*, 9 Met. 492 (1845).

205. A. agreed with the town of C. to support two of its paupers, for one year, for a certain sum, and removed them into an adjoining town, where they were supported during the year at his charge in the family of their son-in-law. At the end of the year the town agreed with B. to support its paupers for one year at a certain sum. The said two paupers afterwards remained in the adjoining town, in the family of their son-in-law, who was requested by A. to support them, at his charge, until they should be removed to the town of C. A. also gave notice to the overseers of the town of C. that said paupers were on his hands, and requested the overseers to provide for them. No provision was made for said paupers by the overseers, and they were supported by their son-in-law at A.'s charge. *Held*, that the town of C. was not bound to pay to A. the expense incurred by him after the first year, for the relief of these paupers. *Ib.*

206. In an action against a town, by one of the inhabitants thereof, to recover for the support of a pauper therein, the plaintiff cannot prevail, unless he has given to the overseers of the poor of the town the notice required by statute, and it is not enough to show that the overseers had actual knowledge that the pauper was at the plaintiff's house and supported by him. *Walker* v. *Southbridge*, 4 Cush. 199 (1849).

207. The notice and request to overseers of the poor, after which a town is made liable by the statute to an individual for expense incurred by him in the support of a pauper, are conditions precedent to such liability. Such request must be an intelligible call on the overseers to take charge of the pauper at the expense of the town, and must be made by the individual himself claiming to recover, or by his agent or messenger. *Williams* v. *Braintree*, 6 Cush. 399 (1850).

208. Where the plaintiff had been rendering assistance gratuitously in the family of her married daughter for some weeks, as nurse and housekeeper, and continued her services there after all the members of the family had become ill of the small pox, and stood in need of relief as paupers, but requested another person "to call on the overseers of the poor for more help, or a person to take care of said paupers instead of herself, for she could not stand it any longer;" in an action against the town to recover for services subsequently rendered, it was left to the jury as a question of fact, to find whether the plaintiff intended, by such message, to give notice to the overseers that she should thereafter render her

services on the credit of the town, or only that the famliy needed further assistance in addition to her services, which she should continne to render without compensation. It was held, that the plaintiff had no ground of exception to this ruling. *Ib.*

209. Where a state pauper, for whose support provision is made in one town, voluntarily and without any cause of complaint, leaves the place of such support and goes into another town where he is not in any need of immediate relief, and is there supported by an individual, the latter acquires no cause of action thereby against the last-mentioned town. *Shearer* v. *Shelburne*, 10 Cush. 3 (1852).

210. If the municipal authorities of a town have provided supplies for distribution among those out of the almshouse who need relief, upon orders of the overseers of the poor, and have given notice thereof to the overseers, the latter have no authority to contract debts in behalf of the town for the support of the poor; and one who, having knowledge of the facts, furnishes supplies to persons settled in such town, upon orders of the overseers, cannot maintain an action against the town to recover for the same. But if he furnishes supplies upon such orders to persons settled elsewhere, he may recover from the town the amount actually received by it, on account of such supplies, from the towns which were liable to support the persons who were relieved thereby. *Ireland* v. *Newburyport*, 8 Allen, 73 (1864).

211. Under Gen. Sts. c. 70, § 16, an individual cannot recover of the town where a pauper has his settlement for necessary relief furnished to the pauper in another town, although the former town has made provision, which proves inadequate, for the pauper's support in the latter town. *Hawes* v. *Hanson*, 9 Allen, 134 (1864).

See Houses of Correction and Jails.

(c) By Towns against Individuals.

St. 1817, c. 186, § 5.

212. Prior to St. 1817, c. 186, a pauper was not liable to an action by the town wherein he had his lawful settlement, for any moneys paid for his relief as a pauper. *Deer Isle* v. *Eaton*, 12 Mass 327 (1815). *Medford* v. *Learned*, 16 Mass. 215 (1819).

213. St. 1817, c. 186, was repealed when the revised statutes took effect, and since the passage of the revised statutes a person relieved as a pauper, whether he has or has not property, is not liable to an action by the town to recover compensation for such relief. *Groveland* v. *Medford*, 1 Allen, 23 (1861).

214. The only claim a town now has upon the property of a person supported as a pauper is to take it after his death, if he was at the time of his death actually chargeable to the town. *Ib.* See Gen. Sts. c. 70, § 21; *Haynes* v. *Welles*, 6 Pick. 462.

215. One who, being in need of immediate relief and support, has received the same from the town of his lawful settlement, is not, in the absence of fraud, liable to an action by the town therefor, although he was possessed of property at the time. *Stow* v. *Sawyer*, 3 Allen, 515 (1862).

216. If the overseers of the poor relieve the wants of a wife whose husband has a legal settlement in another town, an action lies at the common law for the town whose overseers furnished the relief, against the husband, notwithstanding the statute remedy against the town of his settlement. *Hanover* v. *Turner*, 14 Mass. 227 (1817). See *Brookfield* v. *Allen*, 6 Allen, 585.

217. A town may maintain an action against an individual for supplies furnished to his wife and children, if they stood in need of support as paupers, but not otherwise. *New Bedford* v. *Chace*, 5 Gray, 28 (1855).

218. A town, which supports a wife neglected by her husband and standing in need of relief, may recover of the husband the amount necessary for her support as a pauper, but not for further supplies suitable to her condition in life, but not necessary for a pauper. *Monson* v. *Williams*, 6 Gray, 416 (1856).

219. A contract made with the brother of a female pauper by a committee appointed by a town "to negotiate the case" of that pauper, and signed by the committee in their own names, the terms of which are, that the brother shall pay the town a certain sum annually during the life of the pauper, and release all claim to a certain fund in the hands of another relation for her support, and the town shall support her and save him harmless from all litigation with his brothers in relation to such support, which contract is afterwards acted upon by the brother and the town, is valid, and binds the town, though not expressly ratified by them. *Palmer* v. *Ferry*, 6 Gray, 420 (1856).

(d) By Towns against Towns.

(1) *When and for what the Action will lie; and of the Pleadings, Evidence and Trial.*

220. A town which voluntarily maintains a pauper having a settlement in another town, cannot recover compensation therefor of such other town, except by virtue of provisions of statute, or on an express promise. *Dalton* v. *Hinsdale*, 6 Mass. 501 (1810).

221. In an action by one town against another, under St. 1793, c. 59, § 9, the declaration must aver the settlement of the

pauper, and notice to the defendant town within three months from the commencement of the expense. *Salem* v. *Andover*, 3 Mass. 436 (1807). *Wrentham* v. *Attleborough*, 5 Mass. 434 (1809).

222. Such action will not lie if notice has not been given to the defendant town until more than three months after the supplies have ceased to be furnished; but whether this limitation extends to the expenses of the removal or burial of the pauper, *quære*. *Bath* v. *Freeport*, 5 Mass. 325 (1809).

223. Where notice was given of a pauper's becoming chargeable in March, 1811, and again in October, 1812, and an action was commenced in May, 1813, the defendant town was held liable only for the expenses incurred during three months preceding the last notice. *Townsend* v. *Billerica*, 10 Mass. 411 (1813). See 23 Pick. 158.

224. No action lies in behalf of another town against the town of a pauper's settlement for any expenses incurred more than two years before the commencement of the action. *Readfield* v. *Dresden*, 12 Mass. 316 (1815).

225. The notice to the town of a pauper's settlement respecting supplies furnished to the pauper by another town must have been given within two years before the commencement of an action by the latter town against the former to recover for such supplies, in order to maintain such action, no judgment having been recovered in any former action concerning the pauper's settlement between the same parties. *Needham* v. *Newton*, 12 Mass. 452 (1815).

226. Expenses incurred in the support of a pauper, although within three months prior to giving the notice required by the statute, cannot be recovered if they arose more than two years before the commencement of the action. *Harwich* v. *Hallowell*, 14 Mass. 184 (1817).

227. Although the same plaintiffs have, in a former action, recovered from the same defendants expenses incurred for the support of the same pauper. And the notice given before the former action does not make a new notice unnecessary. *Hallowell* v. *Harwich*, 14 Mass. 186 (1817). See 23 Pick. 159.

228. The limitation of two years, within which the action must be brought, should be computed from the delivery of the notice, and not from its date. *Uxbridge* v. *Seekonk*, 10 Pick. 150 (1830).

229. In an action by a town for the support of a pauper, a charge for the expense and trouble of the overseers in providing for the abode and support of the pauper cannot be recovered. *Conway* v. *Deerfield*, 11 Mass. 327 (1814).

230. A town which has supported paupers properly chargeable to another town ought to be fully indemnified for all the expense properly incurred, but not for an extravagant sum, paid without notice to such other town. *Southbridge* v. *Charlton*, 15 Mass. 248 (1818). But see Gen. Sts. c. 70, § 14.

231. To entitle a town which has supported a pauper belonging to another town, to recover an indemnification, it is not necessary that the pauper be actually resident in the town at the time of giving notice to the town in which he has his legal settlement. It is sufficient that he was then supported at the expense of the town so giving the notice. *Marlborough* v. *Rutland*, 11 Mass. 483 (1814). See 12 Pick. 6; 1 Gray, 515.

232. When a pauper falls into distress in a place other than that of his settlement, he is to be relieved; and it does not lie with the town of his settlement to object, in an action against them for his support, that he was able, but unwilling, to provide for himself. *Paris* v. *Hiram*, 12 Mass. 262 (1815).

233. Where an inhabitant of the town of A., after a refusal by the overseers, had himself supported a pauper having his lawful settlement in B., and afterwards recovered satisfaction therefor of the town of A., it was held, that A. could not maintain an action against B., although such satisfaction was recovered within two years, the original expense having been incurred more than two years before the commencement of the action. *Readfield* v. *Dresden*, 12 Mass. 316 (1815).

234. Where an individual in a town gave notice to the overseers of the poor that he was supporting a pauper, and that he should look to the town for his pay, and the overseers thereupon gave notice to the town where the pauper had his settlement, that he had become chargeable, it was held, that the first town, though they had not paid such individual, might maintain an action against the other town for the support of the pauper. *Westfield* v. *Southwick*, 17 Pick. 68 (1835).

235. If a town relieves, as a pauper, a person imprisoned in a jail therein, it is no defence to an action to recover compensation therefor against the town of the pauper's settlement, that the pauper was unlawfully committed to the jail. *Taunton* v. *Westport*, 12 Mass. 355 (1815).

236. A town is not liable to another town for the support of an alien married to a woman having a legal settlement in the defendant town. *Cambridge* v. *Charlestown*, 13 Mass. 501 (1816).

237. By an act incorporating a town from part of an old one, it was provided that the two towns should bear their proportionate part of supporting the poor, which were at that time relieved by the elder town. Afterwards the two towns made an agreement that if any person should thereafter be returned as a pauper, having a right to a support from the elder

town, the new town should be bound to support him, if his last residence had been in that territory which constituted the new town. It was held, that the agreement was not binding on the new town, and that it was not bound to support a pauper thus situated. *Norton* v. *Mansfield*, 16 Mass. 48 (1819).

238. Notwithstanding the proviso in St. 1793, c. 59, § 9, (Gen. Sts. c. 70, § 12,) an action will lie against a town after two years, upon a verbal express promise of the overseers of the poor to pay the expenses incurred in supporting a pauper legally chargeable to the town; such a promise being barred only by the general statute of limitations. *Belfast* v. *Leominster*, 1 Pick. 123 (1822).

239. The obligation imposed on a town by statute to support paupers is a good consideration for an express promise. *Ib.*

240. A pauper, for whose support provision was made in the town of W., in which she had a settlement, went into the adjoining town of N. S., and there expenses were incurred for her support, although the pauper herself, the person with whom she there resided, and the inhabitants of N. S., all knew that a place was provided for her in W., to which she was able to walk without difficulty. *Held*, that N. S. could not recover of W. for these expenses. *New Salem* v. *Wendell*, 2 Pick. 341 (1824).

241. Upon a question whether a deceased person had a settlement, his declaration that he had no deed, but a writing to give him a deed, of certain land, was admitted to rebut the presumption arising from long possession by himself and his grantee, that he was seised of an estate in freehold. *West Cambridge* v. *Lexington*, 2 Pick. 536 (1824).

242. Where a pauper, after an action brought by one town against another to recover expenses incurred in his support, continues chargeable to the plaintiffs, to sustain an action for the new expenses, brought pending the first, a new notice is required. *Walpole* v. *Hopkinton*, 4 Pick. 358 (1827).

243. Whether a town can at any time set up their own illegal proceedings or those of their officers, in the assessment of a tax, after the tax has been paid, to defeat a settlement gained thereby, *quære*. But where so long a time had elapsed since the payment of the tax that no claim for reimbursement could be sustained, it was held, that they could not. *Charlemont* v. *Conway*, 8 Pick. 408 (1830).

244. Where the assessors assessed more than five per cent. over and above the sum committed to them to assess, it was held, that the tax was not duly assessed, within the meaning of St. 1793, c. 34, relative to gaining a settlement (Gen. Sts. c. 69, § 1, cl. 12). *Ib.*

245. In an action brought by the town of W. against the town of O. for expenses incurred in the support of a pauper, on the question whether the pauper derived a settlement in O. from his grandfather through his father, it was held, that copies of a deed executed by the grandfather in 1754, in which he was described as being of O., and of his last will, made in 1758, in which he was described as "now resident in O.," were admissible evidence to prove that the grandfather gained a settlement in O. under Prov. St. 12 & 13 Will. III. c. 10. *Ward* v. *Oxford*, 8 Pick. 476 (1829).

264. *Held*, also, that evidence proving that the grandfather, for a long time before 1754, had a settlement in the town of S., and that afterwards, for years previous to 1784, the father of the pauper was supported as a pauper by S., was admissible to rebut the presumption arising from the description of the grandfather in the will and deed. *Ib.*

247. In an action between two towns to recover the amount of expenses incurred by the plaintiff town in relieving a person whose settlement was in the defendant town, the fact that such person might, by going a short distance, have obtained of his debtor as much money as was expended for his relief, was held not to be conclusive evidence that he was not a pauper. *Sturbridge* v. *Holland*, 11 Pick. 459 (1831).

248. But if he was not a pauper, evidence is admissible to show that he was in distress, under such circumstances as to require immediate aid from the plaintiffs. *Ib.*

249. Where a pauper whose legal settlement was in the town of S. was relieved by the overseers of the poor of the town of C., and upon notice the expenses were reimbursed by the overseers of the poor of the town of E. S., upon the supposition that his legal settlement was in E. S., it was held, that the town of E. S. could not maintain an action for repayment against the town of S. *East Sudbury* v. *Sudbury*, 12 Pick. 1 (1831).

250. Under St. 1793, c. 59, § 9, (Gen. Sts. c. 70, § 12,) whereby a town furnishing support to a pauper may be entitled under certain circumstances to recover against the town in which the pauper has his settlement, for expenses incurred within a period of three months before, and two years after, notice of the pauper's having become chargeable, it is immaterial whether the support has been continuous or only occasional. *Attleborough* v. *Mansfield*, 15 Pick. 19 (1833).

251. In an action by one town against another to recover expenses incurred in the support of a pauper, it was held, that a notification addressed to the pauper by an inhabitant of a third town, warning him to attend a dis-

trict school meeting therein, was competent for the purpose of proving that the pauper resided at that time in such third town, it being testified by such inhabitant that he delivered the notification to the pauper. *West Boylston* v. *Sterling*, 17 Pick. 126 (1835).

252. In an action between two towns, it appeared that paupers having their settlement in the defendant town received support and medical attendance in the plaintiff town, and within thirty days after notice of that fact from the plaintiffs, the defendants made a contract with a person living in the plaintiff town, at whose house the paupers were, to keep them at the defendants' expense, and made provision for medical attendance; which the defendants made known immediately to one of the overseers and one of the selectmen of the plaintiff town, and offered to settle with them for the relief already furnished; whereupon the overseer and selectman made out a bill, charging the defendants at the rate of one dollar a week for each of the paupers, and an item for the funeral expenses of one of them, and the overseer receipted it and received the amount of it from the defendants. The paupers not being afterwards removed by the defendants before the expiration of the thirty days, the plaintiffs brought an action to recover the full amount of the expenses incurred by them; but it was held, that the settlement made by the parties was a bar to the plaintiffs' claim. *Medway* v. *Milford*, 21 Pick. 349 (1838).

253. On the question of a pauper's settlement, which depended on the settlement of an ancestor acquired by his dwelling in a house on or near the boundary line between two towns, which house was pulled down a long time ago, it was held, that the declarations of aged persons, since deceased, who lived in its vicinity, made while it was occupied by the ancestor, were admissible to show the position of the house in relation to the dividing line between the two towns. *Abington* v. *North Bridgewater*, 23 Pick. 170 (1840).

254. In an action by one town against another for the support of a pauper, who was the illegitimate son of a married woman, the plaintiff town having proved her settlement to have been originally in the defendant town, it was held, that the burden of proof was on the defendant town, to show that the husband had a settlement in some other town in the Commonwealth, and so that her settlement was changed by her marriage, and not on the plaintiffs to prove that the husband either had his settlement in the defendant town or had no settlement in the Commonwealth. (PUTNAM, J. dissenting.) *Randolph* v. *Easton*, 23 Pick. 242 (1840).

255. Where it is shown, in a suit against a town for the support of a pauper, that his personal property was set, in the valuation of the estates of the town, at the sum mentioned in St. 1793, c. 34, and Rev. Sts. c. 45, (Gen. Sts. c. 69, § 1, cl. 5,) and that he was assessed for the same for five successive years, such town cannot avail itself of the objection that there was not in the valuation any schedule or description of the property as directed by statute. *Boston* v. *Dedham*, 4 Met. 178 (1842).

256. Under the Rev. Sts. c. 143, §§ 15, 16, (Gen. Sts. c. 178, §§ 57, 58,) which provide that the expense of supporting a pauper in a house of correction "may be recovered of the town wherein he shall have his lawful settlement," the town in which he has a settlement when such expense is incurred, is liable therefor, although he gains a settlement in another town before such expense is audited and certified by the overseers of such house. *Boston* v. *Amesbury*, 4 Met. 278 (1842).

257. The persons and corporations that are made conditionally liable by Rev. Sts. c. 143, §§ 15, 16, (Gen. Sts. c. 178, §§ 57, 58,) for the support of persons committed to a house of correction, cannot be held to pay for such support, unless the account thereof be audited and certified by the overseers of such house within the time prescribed by those statutes. *Ib.*

258. Where a pauper was confined in a house of correction from December, 1836 to April, 1837, and the account of the expense of his support was not audited and certified by the overseers until January, 1839, it was held, that the town in which he had his settlement was not liable for such support. *Ib.*

259. A town in which a convict who is committed to a house of correction, has a settlement, is not liable by any statute to pay the expense of supporting him in such house, unless he be committed by virtue of the fifth or sixth section of c. 143 of the revised stattutes (Gen. Sts. c. 161, § 21; c. 165, § 28). *Boston* v. *Dedham*, 8 Met. 513 (1844).

260. When a town, on receiving notice that one of its paupers is supported in another town, replies to the notice by denying that his settlement is in the town, and neither removes him nor makes any provision for his support, it is liable, without any new notice, for the expenses incurred by the other town for his support, after the notice as well as before, until suit brought. *Topsfield* v. *Middleton*, 8 Met. 564 (1844).

261. The town of D., on receiving notice from the town of P., that certain paupers, whose settlement P. alleged to be in D., were supported in P., immediately paid the expense that had been incurred by P. for their support, removed part of the paupers to D., and made

provision for the support of the others in P. for the term of about forty days. Within two months from the time of receiving said notice from P., the overseers of the poor of D. replied to that notice, denying that D. was liable to support said paupers, and refusing to pay P. for any further support of them. *Held*, that the town of P. could not maintain an action against the town of D. for the subsequent support of said paupers, without first giving D. a new notice. *Palmer* v. *Dana*, 9 Met. 587 (1845).

262. In an action against a town to recover for the support of a pauper whose settlement was once in that town, the burden of proving that he afterwards acquired a settlement in another town, is on the defendants. *Oakham* v. *Sutton*, 13 Met. 192 (1847).

263. In an action for the support of a pauper, whose settlement is proved to have once been in the town defending, the burden of proving that he has since acquired a new settlement by residing for the space of ten years together in another town, is upon the defendant town. *Worcester* v. *Wilbraham*, 13 Gray, 586 (1859).

264. Grants of land are admissible in evidence as circumstances tending to show that the grantee, at their respective dates, dwelt in that part of the town in which the land was. *Hingham* v. *South Scituate*, 7 Gray, 229 (1856).

265. In an indenture of partition of lands in 1744 among the heirs of one deceased in 1742, a description of one parcel as "fifty-nine acres of land lying in S., being part of the homestead of the said deceased," is no evidence of his having had a dwelling in S. in 1695. *Ib.*

266. A description, in a town record, of land laid out in 1696, as "adjoining to the fence of C.'s home pasture," is admissible against a town subsequently created out of part of that town, to prove that C. then dwelt in that part of the town in which the land was. *Ib.*

267. By St. 1853, c. 338, § 3, dividing the town of Middleborough, and incorporating a part of it into a new town called Lakeville, it is provided that the said towns "shall hereafter be respectively liable for the support of all such persons, who now are relieved, or hereafter may be relieved, as paupers, whose settlement was gained by, or derived from a residence within their respective limits." In an action against the town of Middleborough to recover for expenses incurred in the support of a pauper, it was held, that the burden of proof was on the plaintiff to show that the pauper gained a settlement in Middleborough from a residence within its present limits; and that it was not sufficient to show that the pauper had a settlement in the old town of Middleborough, without proving that such settlement was not gained by a residence within the limits of Lakeville. *New Bedford* v. *Middleborough*, 16 Gray, (1860). And see *Hingham* v. *South Scituate*, 7 Gray, 230, 231.

268. The town of a pauper's settlement is not liable to another town in which the pauper becomes furiously insane and falls into distress, for the expenses of his removal to an asylum for the insane in another state, and for his support and medical attendance there, even though a removal to some asylum be necessary to the comfort and relief of the pauper, and as a matter of economy and humanity. *Deerfield* v. *Greenfield*, 1 Gray, 514 (1854).

269. Under Rev. Sts. c. 46, § 13, (Gen. Sts. c. 70, § 12,) a town which has furnished relief to a person found therein and standing in need of immediate relief may recover the expenses thereof from the town of his settlement, although sufficient provision may have been made for his general support by his father's will. *Groveland* v. *Medford*, 1 Allen, 23 (1861).

270. A town which has paid money for the support of a criminal in its workhouse cannot maintain an action to recover the same from the town where he had his settlement. *Worcester* v. *Auburn*, 4 Allen, 574 (1862).

271. In an action to recover for expenses incurred in support of a pauper, against a town in which his settlement is sought to be established by reason of a marriage existing before the passage of St. 1845, c. 222, (Gen. Sts. c. 107, § 2,) it cannot be shown in defence that the marriage was invalid by reason of the insanity of one of the parties. *Goshen* v. *Richmond*, 4 Allen, 458 (1862).

272. If a person whose settlement is in dispute is proved to have removed from one town to another, a new trial will not be granted on account of the admission of evidence, for the purpose of proving his domicil in the latter town, that he came to the latter town and said that he had sold out at the former town, and had come down and wanted to go to work; provided no special request was made for an instruction to the jury that his declaration was not of itself competent evidence of the fact of his selling out in the former town. *Monson* v. *Palmer*, 8 Allen, 551 (1864).

273. The admission of an overseer of the poor, in giving directions for a pauper's relief to one who has the care of the town's poor, that the pauper has a settlement in the town, derived from an ancestor, is not competent evidence against the town in an action subsequently brought against it by another town for another cause, in which the settlement of another pauper, which depends upon the settle-

ment of that ancestor, is in controversy. *Dartmouth* v. *Lakeville*, 7 Allen, 284 (1863).

274. The admission of overseers of the poor, in a binding-out indenture, that a certain pauper is chargeable to their town, and their acts in paying bills to other towns for his support, are not admissible in evidence against the town in a litigation growing out of subsequent acts, for the purpose of showing that he and his descendants have their settlement therein. In performing these duties, they act as public officers, and not as agents of the town. *New Bedford* v. *Taunton*, 9 Allen, 207 (1864).

See Houses of Correction and Jails.

(2) *Of the Notice.*

275. Notice from one town to another, to obtain the removal of a pauper or a reimbursement of the expenses of a pauper's support, is sufficient, if it be given to one of the overseers of the town on which the claim is made; but it must be in writing, and signed by a major part of the overseers of the town giving the notice, or perhaps by an agent duly authorized by the town. *Dalton* v. *Hinsdale*, 6 Mass. 501 (1810).

276. A notice was held to be sufficient which stated that the pauper had her settlement in the defendant town; that she was, at the time of the notice, resident in the plaintiff town; that she required support, and that it had been afforded to her by the plaintiff's overseers; and that the same was charged to the defendant town; and requested her removal. *Quincy* v. *Braintree*, 5 Mass. 86 (1809).

277. It is unnecessary that the notice should state the facts which would show a legal settlement of the pauper in the defendant town, or the manner in which the settlement was obtained. *Ib.* *Northfield* v. *Taunton*, 4 Met. 437 (1842).

278. A notice to a town to be charged with the support of a pauper, signed by one overseer of the poor, by order of all the overseers, is sufficient. *Westminster* v. *Bernardston*, 8 Mass. 104 (1811). And see 4 Mass. 275.

279. Under the Rev. Sts. c. 46, § 19, (Gen. Sts. c. 70, § 17,) a notification, signed by "J. D., chairman of the board of overseers of the poor" of a town, and sent to the overseers of the poor of another town, requesting them to remove a pauper, is sufficient, if otherwise in due form. *Northfield* v. *Taunton*, 4 Met. 433 (1842).

280. Although a notification, given by overseers of the poor, stating that A. and his wife and four children have become chargeable, &c., is defective, if A. have more than four children in his family, yet if such notification be answered, without objection to its generality, that objection is thereby waived. *Ib.* *Commonwealth* v. *Dracut*, 8 Gray, 455 (1857).

281. A notice from the overseers of one town to those of another that "the family of J. S." has become chargeable, was held to be too general; but the answer of the other town denying the settlement, but taking no exception to the deficiency of the notice, it was held, that the objection was waived. *Embden* v. *Augusta*, 12 Mass. 307 (1815).

282. A town sent a notice to another town that "A. B. and his family" had become chargeable, and had their lawful settlement in such other town. An answer was returned that A. B. had no such settlement, no objection being taken to the sufficiency of the notice as to the family. It was held, that such objection was waived. *Shutesbury* v. *Oxford*, 16 Mass. 102 (1819).

283. All objections to the sufficiency of a notice to charge a town with the support of a pauper are waived by returning an answer simply denying all liability on the ground that the pauper has no settlement in the town. *Paris* v. *Hiram*, 12 Mass. 267 (1815). *Commonwealth* v. *Dracut*, 8 Gray, 455 (1857).

284. The overseers of the poor of O. sent the following notice to those of S.: "A. E. and wife and three children, who have their legal settlement in your town, is now chargeable to this town. This is therefore to notify you to remove said paupers," &c. The overseers of S. answered, "We acknowledge the receipt of your letter, &c., stating that A. E. is in your town on expense, &c. We are satisfied that he has not gained a settlement in our town. We therefore shall not pay any expense for his support." It was held, that the notice was sufficiently certain as to all the paupers; but if insufficient, that the objection was waived by the answer. *Orange* v. *Sudbury*, 10 Pick. 22 (1830).

285. A notice by the overseers of the town of A. to those of the town of B. that expenses had been incurred for the support of "O. S., widow of G. S., who was an inhabitant of B." was held to be sufficient, and the meaning of these words was held to be, that the widow was an inhabitant of B. *Uxbridge* v. *Seekonk*, 10 Pick. 150 (1830).

286. Notice to the town of a pauper's settlement that such pauper has become chargeable in another town, is not notice that his wife and children have also become chargeable. *Andover* v *Canton*, 13 Mass. 547 (1816).

287. A letter from the overseers of the poor of one town to those of another, to obtain a reimbursement of the expenses of supporting a pauper, was received and answered. A mistake in this letter was corrected in a second letter, which was received but not answered, referring to the first. It was held, that the second, which by itself was an insufficient notice, might be taken in con-

nection with the first, so as to constitute a sufficient notice from the time when the second was received. *Shelburne* v. *Rochester*, 1 Pick. 470 (1823).

288. A notice respecting a pauper whose Christian name was Sally, calling her "Sarah or Sally," was held to be sufficient. *Ib.*

289. A notice that "E. S. and her three children" have become chargeable, she having four, was held to be too general as to the children, but sufficient as to E. S. *Walpole* v. *Hopkinton*, 4 Pick. 358 (1827)

290. P. Baxter, a pauper, known in the town of L. by the name of P. La Barron, was called, in a notice from that town to the town of N., P. Labern, and the overseers of the poor of N., after ascertaining what person was intended, returned an answer that P. Labern had not a settlement in N. *Held*, that the notice was insufficient. *Lanesborough* v. *New Ashford*, 5 Pick. 190 (1827).

291. A notice by overseers of the poor that expenses had been incurred for the support of "the child of Miss H. W., the daughter of T. W., who are inhabitants of the town of W.," was held to be sufficient to sustain an action against such town. *Ware* v. *Williamstown*, 8 Pick. 388 (1829).

292. In an action by one town against another, to recover expenses incurred in the support of a pauper, a notice signed by A. and B. as selectmen, they being overseers of the poor by virtue of their office of selectmen, was held sufficient. *Ashby* v. *Lunenburg*, 8 Pick. 563 (1830).

293. A written notification as follows, "To the overseers of the poor of the city of N.— Gentlemen — Mrs. A. B. and three children, whose legal settlement is in your city, but now residing in L., being in needy circumstances, has applied to this board for relief, which we have granted and charged to your city, and shall continue so to do until you remove or otherwise provide for their support. In behalf of the overseers of the poor of the city of L. —— C. D. Secretary," is sufficient, under Gen. Sts. c. 70, § 17. *Lynn* v. *Newburyport*, 5 Allen, 545 (1863).

294. Where notice was given in March, 1811, of a pauper's becoming chargeable, and again in October, 1812, and an action was commenced in May, 1813, the defendant town was held liable only for the expenses incurred within three months before the last notice. *Townsend* v. *Billerica*, 10 Mass. 411 (1813).

295. A notice by the overseers of the poor of one town to those of another that a person has become chargeable as a pauper, given within three months after the expenses were paid, but not within three months after they were incurred, is insufficient. *East Sudbury* v. *Sudbury*, 12 Pick. 1 (1831).

296. A notice sent by mail, the postage being unpaid, was held not to be sufficient; although it reached the post office of the defendant town, and was there refused. *Groton* v. *Lancaster*, 16 Mass. 110 (1819).

297. Where a notice to overseers was delivered to and received by one of them while attending to his duties as a member of the legislature, at a distance from his town, the delivery was held sufficient. *Walpole* v. *Hopkinton*, 4 Pick. 358 (1827).

298. When, in consequence of notice to the overseers of the town of a pauper's settlement, they provide for him; if the pauper afterwards receives aid from the same town which gave the notice, a new notice is necessary in order to charge the town of his settlement. *Sidney* v. *Augusta*, 12 Mass. 316 (1815).

299. Where a pauper, after an action brought by one town against another, to recover expenses incurred in his support, continues chargeable to the plaintiffs, to sustain an action for the new expenses, brought pending the first, a new notice is required. *Walpole* v. *Hopkinton*, 4 Pick. 358 (1827).

300. If the town furnishing the supplies sue for them, it cannot again, without a new notice, recover for any expenses incurred after the commencement of the first action. *Hallowell* v. *Harwich*, 14 Mass. 186 (1817).

301. The town of D., on receiving notice from the town of P., that certain paupers, whose settlement P. alleged to be in D., were supported in P., immediately paid the expense that had been incurred by P. for their support, removed part of the paupers to D., and made provision for the support of the others in P. for the term of about forty days. Within two months from the time of receiving said notice from P., the overseers of the poor of D. replied thereto, denying that D. was liable to support said paupers, and refusing to pay P. for any further support of them. It was held, that P. could not maintain an action against D. for the subsequent support of said paupers, without first giving D. a new notice. *Palmer* v. *Dana*, 9 Met. 587 (1845).

302. Where a town incurs expenses, under St. 1837, c 244, § 1, (Gen. Sts. c. 26, § 16,) on account of paupers having a legal settlement in another town, the former is bound to give reasonable notice to the latter before commencing an action for such expenses, and the selectmen of the respective towns are proper officers to give and receive such notice. *Springfield* v. *Worcester*, 2 Cush. 52 (1848).

303. On the 5th of May 1846, a poor person having a legal settlement in W., fell ill of the small pox in S., and was there relieved in pursuance of the provisions of St. 1837, c. 244, § 1, (Gen. Sts. c. 26, § 16,) and the selectmen of S. on the 25th of the same month gave no-

tice of the pauper's sickness and of the expenses incurred on his account to the selectmen of W.; it was held, that such notice was reasonable and sufficient. *Ib.*

See Houses of Correction and Jails.

(3) *Estoppel.*

304. If a town is duly notified under St. 1793, c. 59, § 12, (Gen. Sts. c. 70, § 17,) and requested to remove a pauper, and if its overseers have neglected for two months after the notice and request to make any objection thereto or to remove the pauper, the town is barred from contesting with the town giving the notice the settlement of the pauper. *Topsham* v. *Harpswell*, 1 Mass. 518 (1805). And from showing that the pauper was of sufficient ability to support himself. *Freeport* v. *Edgecumbe*, Ib. 459.

305. Even although the pauper may have in fact no settlement in any town within the Commonwealth. *Westminster* v. *Bernardston*, 8 Mass. 104 (1811).

306. A town which voluntarily pays the expenses incurred by another town for the support of a pauper, on notice and without objection, is not thereby estopped from denying the settlement of the pauper in an action brought by the same town to recover for subsequent expenses incurred for the pauper. *Leicester* v. *Rehoboth*, 4 Mass. 180 (1808). *Bridgewater* v. *Dartmouth*, Ib. 273. *Needham* v. *Newton*, 12 Mass. 454 (1815).

307. A voluntary payment by a town of a demand for the support of a pauper, after suit brought, does not estop the town to contest the settlement of such pauper's mother in another suit brought by the same plaintiffs to recover for her support. *Edgartown* v. *Tisbury*, 10 Cush. 408 (1852).

308. A notice from one town to another, claiming reimbursement for the expense of supporting a pauper, given pending an action for the recovery of such expense, or after its final decision, although unanswered, operates no estoppel on the town notified, to deny the settlement of the pauper with them. *Newton* v. *Randolph*, 16 Mass. 426 (1820).

309. If the town notified returns within two months a written answer, signed by one of its selectmen, who is also overseer of the poor, denying the settlement of the pauper, it is not estopped from afterwards disputing the settlement. *Bridgewater* v. *Dartmouth*, 4 Mass. 273 (1808).

310. Where, in an action against the town of A., for expenses incurred by the town of B. in the support of a pauper, it appeared that the pauper's settlement was not in A., but that the defendants were estopped from denying the settlement, and a verdict was given against them; the court refused to set aside the verdict for the purpose of permitting the defendants to pay the money found due by the verdict, and thus prevent a judgment, which would bar them upon the question of settlement, as to any after expenses. *Greene* v. *Monmouth*, 7 Mass. 467 (1811).

311. It is not a bar to an action by the town of A. against the town of B. to recover the expenses of supporting a pauper, that the plaintiffs had given notice to the town of C. and claimed payment of the same sums; and such notice not being answered according to the statute, had recovered judgment therefor against the town of C. *Braintree* v. *Hingham*, 17 Mass. 432 (1821).

312. Where the town of E., upon receiving a notice that a person had become chargeable in another town as a pauper, replied thereto denying its liability for his support, but no action was commenced thereon, and before the expiration of two years a second notice was received in relation to the same pauper, to which no reply was made within two months, it was held, that the town of E. was not estopped, by its neglect to make an earlier reply, from contesting the settlement of the pauper, in an action against it founded upon the second notice. *Marshpee* v. *Edgartown*, 23 Pick. 156 (1839).

313. An erroneous statement, made by the overseers of the poor of the town of A., in a notification sent by them to the town of B., respecting the means by which a pauper therein mentioned acquired a settlement in B., does not estop the town of A., in a suit against the town of B., to recover for the support of such pauper, to show that he acquired a settlement in B. by different means from those which were stated in the notification, unless that statement was made with a design to mislead. *Northfield* v. *Taunton*, 4 Met. 433 (1842).

314. If a notification be sent by the overseers of the poor of a town which has incurred expense for the relief of a pauper found therein, to the overseers of the poor of the town where his settlement is supposed to be, requesting his removal, the answer, by Gen. Sts. c. 70, § 18, must be signed by some one of the overseers; and, if it is not so signed, their town will be barred from contesting the question of his settlement, although the pauper is not actually removed there; and the answer will not be sufficient, if signed merely by another person with whom the town has contracted for the support of its paupers for that year. *Petersham* v. *Coleraine*, 9 Allen, 91 (1864).

315. Overseers to whom such an answer is sent do not waive the defect by sending a reply to the overseers of the other town, under

the belief that the answer came from one of them, or by subsequently sending a new notification to them for the removal of the same pauper. *Ib.*

IV. Removal of Paupers.

316. Under St. 1793, c. 59, § 10, a pauper is not removable unless actually chargeable, or likely to become so, from one or the other of the causes mentioned in the statute. *Walpole* v. *West Cambridge*, 8 Mass. 276 (1811).

317. In a complaint, and also in an adjudication, for the removal of a pauper under that statute, it was necessary to state the cause of the likelihood of his becoming chargeable. *Ib.*

318. The alleged pauper should be summoned to appear at the examination before the magistrate But the pauper only can avail himself of an omission to summon him, and neither of the towns contesting his settlement can take advantage of such omission. *Shirley* v. *Lunenburg*, 11 Mass. 379 (1814).

319. An adjudication that a person is "the proper poor" of a town is equivalent to an adjudication that he has his lawful settlement in such town. *Ib.*

320. Under St. 1821, c. 94, § 3, (Gen. Sts. c. 70, § 14,) the removal of the pauper is a condition precedent, which must be strictly performed; so that where a pauper, while her town was making preparations for her removal, removed of her own accord, it was held, that the town was liable for the reasonable expenses incurred for her support, although they exceeded one dollar a week. *Ware* v. *Wilbraham*, 4 Pick. 45 (1826).

321. The actual removal of a pauper by the town in which he has a settlement, within thirty days after legal notice of relief being furnished to him by another town, is a condition precedent, which must be strictly performed, in order to exempt the former town (under St. 1821, c. 94; Gen. Sts. c. 70, § 14) from a greater expense than one dollar per week; so that where such town, having, within the thirty days, prepared to remove the pauper, but, finding him too ill to be removed with safety, provided for his further relief and support in the place where he then was, by a contract with an individual, it was held, that the other town was nevertheless entitled to recover the whole amount of its expenses reasonably incurred on account of the pauper. *Seekonk* v. *Attleborough*, 7 Pick. 155 (1828).

322. A pauper having a settlement in a town in this commonwealth, cannot lawfully be carried by the overseers of the poor, against his will, to a place without the Commonwealth, to be there supported. *Westfield* v. *Southwick*, 17 Pick. 68 (1835). See *Deerfield* v. *Greenfield*, 1 Gray, 514.

323. The provision in the Rev. Sts. c. 46, § 15, (Gen. Sts. c. 70, § 14,) that "when any person shall be supported by a town, other than that in which he has his settlement, the town that is liable for his support shall not, in any case, be required to pay therefor more than at the rate of one dollar a week, provided the town that is liable for the support of the pauper shall cause him to be removed, within thirty days from the time of receiving legal notice that such support has been furnished," does not apply to the case of the removal of a pauper after his decease, though before his burial. *Webster* v. *Uxbridge*, 13 Met. 198 (1847).

324. In computing the thirty days within which a town liable for the support of a pauper, is required by Rev. Sts. c. 46, § 15, (Gen. Sts. c. 70, § 14,) to remove him from the town in which he has received support, in order to exempt the former from liability therefor at a greater rate than one dollar a week, the day on which notice is received that the support has been furnished is to be excluded. *Seekonk* *Rehoboth*, 8 Cush. 371 (1851).

V. Penalty for bringing a Pauper into a Town.

325. The offence intended to be punished by St 1793, c. 59, § 15, was that of bringing a poor person into a town, with intent to leave him there, a charge and burden upon such town; and one cannot be held liable under that statute unless such intent is shown. *Greenfield* v. *Cushman*, 16 Mass. 393 (1820). *Deerfield* v. *Delano*, 1 Pick. 465 (1823).

326. An overseer of the poor does not incur the penalty by endeavoring to avoid a charge upon his town by aiding a pauper on his journey to a town in another state, although an agent of such overseer, deviating from his instructions, leaves the pauper in an adjoining town with a view to subject that town to expense. *Deerfield* v. *Delano*, 1 Pick. 465 (1823).

327. One does not incur the penalty by bringing a pauper from another state to a town in this state in which he has a settlement. *Canton* v. *Bentley*, 11 Mass. 441 (1814). *Middleborough* v. *Clark*, 2 Pick. 28 (1823).

328. In an action by the town of S. to recover a penalty for bringing into and leaving in the town a poor and indigent female, she not being lawfully settled therein, with intent to charge the town with her support, (Gen. Sts. c. 70, § 20,) the defendant justified under an order from the overseers of the poor of the town of C., which recited that her lawful settlement was in S. and that she was actually a charge to C., and directed him, as constable, to remove her to S. It was held, that it was

not necessary that the order should recite such acts and proceedings on the part of the overseers as would warrant them in issuing the order, and that the defendant was not bound to go behind the order and show that the overseers had complied with the requisitions of the law. *Sturbridge* v. *Winslow*, 21 Pick. 83 (1838).

329. It seems, that an action for the penalty in such case should be brought in the name of the Commonwealth. *Ib.*

VI. Lunatic Paupers and State Paupers.

Lunatic Paupers.

330. After the passage of St. 1834, c. 150, the treasurer of a state lunatic hospital could not maintain an action under St. 1797, c. 62, § 3, or St. 1832, c. 163, § 4, against the town from which the pauper was committed to the hospital, for his support therein previous to the passage of St. 1834, c. 150. *Foster* v. *Worcester*, 16 Pick. 71 (1834).

331. Where an insane person, who is not able to pay for his own support, is confined in a house of correction, under St. 1836, c. 223, (Gen. Sts. c 74,) the town in which he has a settlement is liable for his support in such house, if he have no parent, master, or kindred, liable by law to maintain him. *Watson* v. *Charlestown*, 5 Met. 54 (1842). See Gen. Sts. c. 74, § 6.

332. Under St. 1834, c. 150, (Gen. Sts. c. 73,) requiring the town in which a pauper lunatic resides at the time of his commitment to a state lunatic hospital to pay the expense of supporting him while there, and giving to such town a remedy over against the town in which such lunatic has a legal settlement, notice of the expense incurred, given by the former town to the latter within three months after the hospital had demanded payment, was held to be seasonable notice to render the latter town liable to the former, if any notice is necessary, the commitment having been made by a judge of probate. *Worcester* v. *Milford*, 18 Pick. 379 (1836).

332 *a*. A town whose overseers of the poor send a lunatic pauper to a state lunatic hospital without any adjudication by any court or magistrate, may nevertheless recover their payments for his support, of the town of his legal settlement, under St. 1841, c. 77 (Gen. Sts. c. 73, § 25). Such a sending is a "commitment" of the pauper within the meaning of that statute. *Cummington* v. *Wareham*, 9 Cush. 585 (1852).

333. In an action for such expenses, by the town committing such lunatic pauper, against the town of his settlement, no recovery can be had for expenses incurred more than two years previous to the commencement of the action, or more than three months previous to notice to the defendant town. *Ib.*

334. The town of a pauper's settlement is not liable to another town, in which the pauper becomes furiously insane and falls into distress, for the expenses of his removal to an asylum for the insane in another state, and for his support and medical attendance there, even though a removal to some asylum be necessary for the comfort and relief of the pauper, and as a matter of economy and humanity. *Deerfield* v. *Greenfield*, 1 Gray, 514 (1854).

335. The whole amount paid to the treasurer of a state lunatic hospital by the town in which a lunatic pauper, having a settlement within the Commonweath, resided at the time of his commitment, for his expenses at the hospital within six years before such payment, may be recovered of the town of his settlement, by giving notice thereof within three months, and commencing an action within two years, after such payment; although part of the amount had once been paid by the Commonwealth to the hospital, on the supposition that the lunatic had no settlement within the Commonwealth, and since re-allowed by the hospital to the Commonwealth. *Andover* v. *Easthampton*, 5 Gray, 390 (1855). *Worcester* v. *Sterling*, Ib 393, note.

336. If money paid by the Commonwealth for the support of a lunatic at a state lunatic hospital, on the mistaken supposition that he had no settlement within the Commonwealth, is retained by the Commonwealth, on discovery of the mistake, out of money due to the hospital, the treasurer of the hospital may recover from the town in which the lunatic resided at the time of his commitment, unless the defendants prove that he had no settlement in the Commonwealth, for such support during the six years previous to the commencement of the action, and for that only. *Jennison* v. *Roxbury*, 9 Gray, 32 (1857).

337. The amount paid by a town for the support at a state lunatic hospital of an insane pauper committed by the judge of probate may be recovered from the town of the pauper's settlement, within two years after the payment, although more than two years after notice. *Amherst* v. *Shelburne*, 11 Gray, 107 (1858).

338. Notice by one town to another of a claim made by the treasurer of a state lunatic hospital for the past and future support of a pauper, is sufficient to support an action for the past expenses, (though not actually paid until more than three months after,) but not for expenses of the support of the pauper after such notice. *Ib.*

339. In an action by the treasurer of a state lunatic hospital against a town, to recover the

expenses of the support of a lunatic pauper, a general verdict and judgment for the defendant in a similar action between the same parties, to which the defendant answered, among other defences, that the pauper had no settlement within the Commonwealth, is conclusive evidence that the pauper had no such settlement during the period of furnishing the supplies sued for in the former action, if that question was submitted to the jury in that case. *Jennison* v. *West Springfield*, 13 Gray, 544 (1859).

340. If a married woman has been committed as a lunatic to a state lunatic hospital, by order of a judge of probate, the town of her settlement may maintain an action against her husband to recover sums which it has been obliged to pay for her support there, although he is in destitute circumstances. *Brookfield* v. *Allen*, 6 Allen, 585 (1863).

State Paupers.

341. A town is not bound to support an alien married to a woman having her legal settlement in such town. The town furnishing relief to such alien is entitled to be reimbursed by the Commonwealth. *Cambridge* v. *Charlestown*, 13 Mass. 501 (1816). See Gen. Sts. c. 71, §§ 43, 44; Sts. 1861, c. 94; 1866, c. 234.

342. A town has undoubtedly a right to the services of a state pauper residing therein, to aid in his support. *Wilson* v. *Church*, 1 Pick. 26 (1822). *Commonwealth* v. *Cambridge*, 20 Pick. 272 (1838).

343. The provision in St. 1823, c. 21, (Rev. Sts. c. 46, § 30,) that no male person over the age of twelve years and under the age of sixty years, while of competent health to labor, should be entitled to support as a state pauper, was designed to prohibit the support of persons at the public expense, who were of competent health and capacity to support themselves. It was not intended to apply to such as, though able to perform some labor, yet were not able to perform enough for their entire support. *Commonwealth* v. *Cambridge*, 20 Pick. 267 (1838).

344. Under Sts. 1830, c. 120, (Rev. Sts. c. 46, §§ 31, 32,) if the earnings collectively of all the state paupers supported by a town, during any year, together with the stated allowance made by the Commonwealth for each of them, did not exceed the expenses collectively of supporting them all during the year, the town was entitled to the whole of such earnings and allowances. *Ib.*

345. In a suit by the Commonwealth against a town, to recover back money overpaid for the support of state paupers, the accounts of the agent of the town respecting those paupers, although examined by a committee, who reported that they were correct, and whose vote was accepted by a vote of the town, are not conclusive evidence against the defendants, but may be shown to have been erroneous. *Commonwealth* v. *Cambridge*, 4 Met. 35 (1842).

346. A town, in stating an account with the Commonwealth as to the support of state paupers, is bound to credit the value of the paupers' labor only, and not any share of the profits, if there be any, which the town derives from their labor. *Ib.*

347. Where a state pauper, for whose support provision is made in one town, voluntarily and without any cause of complaint, leaves the place of such support and goes into another town where he is not in any need of immediate relief, and is there supported by an individual, the latter acquires no cause of action thereby against the last-mentioned town, under Rev. Sts. c. 46, § 18 (Gen. Sts. c. 70, § 16). *Shearer* v. *Shelburne*, 10 Cush. 3 (1852).

348. The Commonwealth cannot recover of the town of a pauper's settlement, under St. 1855, c. 445, § 4, (Gen. Sts. c. 71, § 49,) the expenses of supporting the pauper at a state almshouse more than three months next before notice thereof to the town. *Commonwealth* v. *Dracut*, 8 Gray, 455 (1857).

349. St. 1855, c. 445, (Gen. Sts. c. 71, § 49,) giving a remedy to the Commonwealth against towns for the support of "any pauper who shall become an inmate of the state almshouses," includes the support, since the statute took effect, of paupers who became inmates of one of the state almshouses before its passage. *Ib.*

350. No action could be maintained under St. 1846, c. 88, for the support of state paupers committed to a workhouse, until the county commissioners had settled and allowed the accounts of the keeper of such workhouse. *South Danvers* v. *Essex*, 1 Allen, 25 (1861).

PENALTIES.

1. An action of debt *qui tam* for a penalty may be brought against several joint offenders. *Boutelle* v. *Nourse*, 4 Mass. 431 (1808). *Burnham* v. *Webster*, 5 Mass. 266 (1809).

2. In informations on penal statutes, for forfeitures incurred by malfeasance, against several, some of the defendants may be convicted of the whole or of part of the offence charged, although others of the defendants are acquitted. Parsons, C. J., in *Hill* v. *Davis*, 4 Mass. 140 (1808).

3. In a *qui tam* action for the penalty inflicted by St. 1788, c. 65, for a rescous of cattle distrained, the defendant might show in evidence the illegality of the distress.

Melody v. *Read*, 4 Mass. 471 (1808). But see *Commonwealth* v. *Beale*, 5 Pick. 514; Gen. Sts. c. 25, § 37.

4. Where a statute gives a *qui tam* action for a penalty, several persons cannot join together in the suit as informers. *Vinton* v. *Welsh*, 9 Pick. 87 (1829).

5. Where a statute inflicts a penalty, partly to the use of the Commonwealth, and partly to the use of an informer, the Commonwealth may sue for the whole, no informer having commenced a *qui tam* action therefor. *Howard* v. *Commonwealth*, 13 Mass. 221 (1816).

6. An action may be sustained in this commonwealth upon a judgment recovered in a *qui tam* action in another state. *Healy* v. *Root*, 11 Pick. 389 (1831).

7. Where an act not before subject to punishment is declared penal, or is subjected to any specific penalty or forfeiture, by a statute, and a mode is pointed out in which it shall be prosecuted, that mode alone can be pursued. *Commonwealth* v. *Howes*, 15 Pick. 231 (1834).

8. A statute providing that prosecutions for violations of the by-laws of a city may be in the name of the Commonwealth, is not unconstitutional, notwithstanding that in prosecutions in that form the defendant is not allowed costs on acquittal. *Goddard, Petitioner*, 16 Pick. 504 (1835).

9. A statute gave a penalty, to be recovered by a *qui tam* action, one half to the use of the prosecutor, and the other half to the use of the town. A person having brought such an action, afterwards compromised it by receiving a sum of money of the defendant and having the action entered "neither party" on the docket. It was held, that the town could not maintain an action against the plaintiff in the *qui tam* suit to recover a part of the money received by him. *Raynham* v. *Rounseville*, 9 Pick 44 (1830).

10. The settlement of the *qui tam* action, being made without the leave of the court, is no bar to another action for the same penalty. *Ib.*

11. In an action commenced by a city treasurer against one who has fraudulently transferred shares in a corporation in order to avoid taxation, to recover the penalty imposed by St. 1843, c. 93, § 3, (Gen. Sts. c. 68, § 23,) "one half for the use of the city, and the other half for the use of the person furnishing the necessary evidence in the case," a nonsuit may be entered by agreement of the plaintiff and the defendant, against the objection of the person who furnished the evidence. *Wheeler* v. *Goulding*, 13 Gray, 539 (1859). See St. 1864, c. 201, § 6.

12. As a general rule, a common informer cannot maintain an action for a penalty, unless power is given to him for that purpose by statute. *Colburn* v. *Swett*, 1 Met. 232 (1840).

13. The board of engineers of the fire department of the city of Boston, to whose use the penalties incurred by violation of Sts. 1833, c. 151, and 1837, c. 99, (regulating the storage, &c., of gunpowder in Boston,) are made to enure, (except when any one of them shall be examined as a witness in the prosecution,) cannot authorize any person to sue for those penalties. *Ib.*

14. Since St. 1837, c. 99, and the repeal of the fourth section of St. 1833, c. 151, it seems, that the only mode of enforcing the penalties imposed by those statutes, is by indictment, or suit in the name of the Commonwealth. *Ib.*

15. Formerly in an action *qui tam* the declaration must conclude with "*contra formam statuti*," or something equivalent, and it was not sufficient to say that an action had accrued to the plaintiff "by force of laws and acts aforesaid." *Haskell* v. *Moody*, 9 Pick. 162 (1829).

16. But since St. 1852, c. 312, (Gen. Sts. c. 129,) it is unnecessary to allege that the offences were committed against the form of the statute. *Levy* v. *Gowdy*, 2 Allen, 320 (1861).

17. The penalty incurred by a sale of coal in violation of St. 1855, c. 188, § 2, (Gen. Sts. c. 49, § 189,) may be recovered in an action of tort. In such action it is not necessary to allege that the action is brought by the plaintiff as well for the town in which the sale was made as for himself, or to allege or prove that there was at the time of the sale a sworn weigher of coal therein. *Ib.* See *Libby* v. *Downey*, 5 Allen, 300; Sts. 1863, c. 171; 1865, c. 191.

18. An informer may sue in his own name for a penalty imposed by statute, to be recovered "one half to the use of the said town, and the other half to any person who shall prosecute therefor;" and need not aver that the prosecution was authorized by the town. *Nye* v. *Lamphere*, 2 Gray, 295 (1854).

19. A penalty for a violation of a legal by-law of a town against obstructing its streets, although payable into the town treasury, may be recovered by complaint before a justice of the peace residing in the town. *Hall* v. *Kent*, 11 Gray, 467 (1858).

See Health, 9, 10; Juries, 10-12.

POLICE.

1. A police officer of the city of Boston, who arrests an intoxicated person, while guilty of disorderly conduct, and releases him on his promise to go directly home, may law-

fully retake him, on his going into a bar-room before he is out of the officer's sight. *Commonwealth* v. *Hastings*, 9 Met. 259 (1845).

2. L. was appointed by the mayor and aldermen of Boston, under St. 1838, c. 123, "a police officer (at the National Theatre) with the power of a constable, except the power of serving civil process." *Held*, that if L's power was limited to a part of the city, yet that it was not limited to the space within the walls of the theatre, but extended to the environs, so far as the special vigilance of an officer might be required to keep the peace and preserve order among persons frequenting the theatre, or carrying others to and from it, or supplying refreshments; and also to all shops, stalls and stands, kept in the vicinity, for the purpose of supplying refreshments. *Ib.*

3. The law does not require that a police officer for the city of Boston, appointed pursuant to St. 1838, c. 123, should be sworn to the faithful discharge of the duties of his office; and therefore a person indicted for assaulting such police officer, and obstructing him in the discharge of the duties of his office, cannot defend by showing that he had never been sworn. *Commonwealth* v. *Dugan*, 12 Met. 233 (1847).

4. An appointment of a police officer by the selectmen of a town, "to continue in said office till the next annual town meeting," is a valid appointment during their pleasure, under St. 1851, c. 162, (Gen. Sts. c. 18, § 38,) authorizing selectmen to appoint police officers, who shall hold their office during the pleasure of the selectmen by whom they are appointed. *Commonwealth* v. *Higgins*, 4 Gray, 34 (1855).

5. A police officer arresting a person without a warrant, under St. 1855, c. 215, § 23, for being intoxicated in a public street, is not liable criminally for an assault, if he has reasonable cause to believe such person to be intoxicated, although he is not in fact intoxicated. *Commonwealth* v. *Presby*, 14 Gray, 65 (1859). See Gen. Sts. c. 86, § 40; *Commonwealth* v. *O'Connor*, 7 Allen, 584, 585.

6. A city ordinance giving to police officers a fixed salary, and requiring them to pay over to the city the fees received by them as witnesses, or for penalties in criminal cases, or for the service of any criminal process, or for any services in behalf of the city, is not contrary to public policy. *Worcester* v. *Walker*, 9 Gray, 78 (1857).

See Actions, 10, 11, 17; Rewards, 3; Ways, 285.

POUNDS.

See Field Drivers, &c.

PRESCRIPTION.

See Public Lands, 5, 6; Sewers and Drains, 7; Ways, 86–101.

PUBLIC BUILDINGS.

1. A town may erect a town-house of sufficient capacity for all the business which it may have occasion to do in such a building, and may in its erection make suitable provision for its prospective wants; and if the building contains rooms not wanted for the time being for municipal business, the town may let them temporarily, or allow them to be used gratuitously. And the condition of a deed of land to the inhabitants of a town, which provides that the same "shall not be used for any other purpose than as a place for a town-house for said inhabitants," is not broken by the erection thereon of a town-house with a hall in the second story, which has been used for miscellaneous purposes, and rooms upon the sides of the entrance, which have been let and used for shops, and other purposes not connected with municipal business, and the construction and use for several years of a lock-up under the building. *French* v. *Quincy*, 3 Allen, 9 (1861).

2. When the additions and improvements upon a court house and jail, necessary for the convenience and accommodation of all courts, officers and persons whose duty requires them to resort there, and for the preservation of the records and public papers of the county, would exceed in expense the amount which the county commissioners are authorized by law to expend, it is their duty to submit to the legislature a statement of the amount required, with evidence of the exigency for such improvements. *District Attorney* v. *Bristol*, 14 Gray, 138 (1859).

PUBLIC LANDS.

1. The inhabitants of a town may take lands by gift or devise, and hold them in their corporate capacity. *Worcester* v. *Eaton*, 13 Mass. 371 (1816).

2. Towns have authority to alienate their lands by vote without a deed. *Springfield* v. *Miller*, 12 Mass. 415 (1815).

3. A grant of lands by vote of a town is by our laws good without a seal. *Adams* v. *Frothingham*, 3 Mass. 352 (1807). *Springfield* v. *Miller*, 12 Mass. 415 (1815). *Damon* v. *Granby*, 2 Pick. 351 (1824). *Thomas* v. *Marshfield*, 10 Pick. 364 (1830). It is not necessary, in order to sustain such grant, to show any consideration for the grant. *Thomas* v. *Marshfield, ubi supra.*

4. Towns adjoining on, or extending across a navigable river, may own the soil of the flats or even of the channel, if a grant has been obtained from the government. *Coolidge* v. *Williams*, 4 Mass. 140 (1808).

5. The use of land on the sea shore by the individual inhabitants of a town, as a landing-place, does not tend to show a possession by the town in its corporate capacity, but, on the contrary, is adverse to the claim of such a possession. *Green* v. *Chelsea*, 24 Pick. 71 (1836).

6. An averment of a lost grant from the owner of a beach to the inhabitants of a town, in their corporate capacity, to the use of all the inhabitants thereof, to take sea-weed for manuring their lands, is not supported by evidence that individual inhabitants of the town had been accustomed, from a very early period of time, to take sea-weed from such beach for that purpose. *Sale* v. *Pratt*, 19 Pick. 191 (1837).

7. A grant of one hundred acres of land, to be "left common for the use of the town for building stones," constituted a grant of the quarry to the town, not for their use in a corporate capacity, but for the use and benefit of all those who were or might become inhabitants thereof. *Green* v. *Putnam*, 8 Cush. 21 (1851).

8. A city is not estopped to claim land which it owns, by the wrongful act of its assessors in taxing it to a person who had no title to or possession of the same, or by a collector's sale for non-payment of such tax. *Rossire* v. *Boston*, 4 Allen, 57 (1862).

9. A proposal was received from the plaintiff by the superintendent of public lands of Boston for the purchase for $600 of a tract of land belonging to the city. A sub-committee of the land commissioners subsequently reported favorably upon this proposal to the full board, who thereupon passed the following vote: "That we recommend on the part of the board of land commissioners the sale and transfer by quitclaim deed, for the sum of $600 cash, of all the right, title and interest the city of Boston may have in and to the lot," &c. to the plaintiff. This vote was sent to the mayor for his approval, and he approved the same four months afterwards, but no further action was taken by the land commissioners. *Held*, that there was no contract between the plaintiff and the city which could be enforced in equity, and that the vote of the land commissioners did not import a contract, though approved by the mayor, but was only an authority to the proper officers to execute a deed, which was to constitute the contract when executed and delivered. *Dunham* v. *Boston*, 12 Allen, (1866).

10. It seems, that under the colony laws a town by its establishment became the owner of the common lands within its assigned limits, in all cases where there was not a separate body of proprietors to whom such lands were granted. Hoar, J., in *West Roxbury* v. *Stoddard*, 7 Allen, 169 (1863).

See Annexation and Division of Towns, 8.

RAILROADS.

1. Under Rev. Sts. c. 39, § 67, (Gen. Sts. c. 63, § 48,) providing that every railroad corporation "may raise or lower any turnpike or way for the purpose of having their railroad pass over or under the same," a railroad corporation may raise a turnpike road for the purpose of constructing the railroad across it upon the same level. *Newburyport Turnpike* v. *Eastern Railroad*, 23 Pick. 326 (1839).

2. A railroad corporation was authorized by a statute passed March 17, 1841, (St. 1841, c. 108,) to extend its road across H Street, which was a section of the Middlesex Turnpike. The same statute subjected the corporation to all the duties, liabilities and provisions contained in Rev. Sts. c. 39, and other statutes relating to railroad corporations, and also required that said extended railroad should cross H Street under a bridge. By a statute passed March 13, 1841, the Middlesex Turnpike Corporation was dissolved, and the surrender of its charter accepted, to take effect on and after June 1, 1841. In September, 1842 the county commissioners laid out and established H Street as a public highway, and ordered the towns of C. and S., in which that part thereof over which the railroad had been extended, was situate, to erect a bridge over the track of the railroad across H Street. It was held, that the railroad corporation was bound by St. 1841, c. 108, and Rev. Sts. c. 39, to erect and maintain said bridge, and that the towns of C. and S. were entitled to a writ of *mandamus* requiring the corporation so to do. *Cambridge* v. *Charlestown Branch Railroad*, 7 Met. 70 (1843).

3. A bridge with lateral embankments, erected by a railroad corporation for the purpose of raising a highway and carrying it over their road, is as much a part of the structure authorized by their charter, as the railroad itself; and any person injured by the erection of such bridge and embankments, is entitled to recover his damages thereby occasioned, in the manner provided by the Rev. Sts. c. 39, § 56 (Gen. Sts. c. 63, § 21). *Parker* v. *Boston & Maine Railroad*, 3 Cush. 107 (1849).

4. In order to authorize a railroad corporation, under the provisions of the Rev. Sts. c. 39, §§ 67, 68, to raise or lower any way, it is not necessary that a previous agreement there-

for should be made with the selectmen of the town in which such way is situated, or that there should be a previous determination of the county commissioners as to whether any and what alteration should be made. The railroad corporation are first to give notice to the selectmen of their intention to raise or lower the way in question: the selectmen are then within thirty days to notify the corporation of the alterations, if any, which they require. If the selectmen and the corporation shall not agree what alterations are necessary, application may be made by either to the county commissioners, to determine the same; and if the selectmen give no notice to the corporation as to what alterations they require, the presumption is that they require none, but leave the whole matter to the corporation. *Ib.* See now Gen. Sts. c. 63, §§ 47, 48; St. 1865, c. 239.

5. In order to entitle the abutters on a highway which has been raised or lowered by a railroad corporation, under the provisions of the Rev. Sts. c. 39, §§ 67, 68, to recover the damages therefor to which they may be entitled, it is not necessary that the selectmen of the town should have authorized or directed such alteration to be made. *Ib.*

6. The remedy for an injury to an adjoining estate occasioned by the alteration of a highway, for the purpose of raising or lowering the same, by a railroad corporation, is not by an action against the town, but by a proceeding against the corporation for damages, under Rev. Sts. c. 39, § 56 (Gen. Sts. c. 63, § 21). *Ib.*

7. A bill in equity, to compel a railroad corporation to raise or lower a highway, in compliance with an order of county commissioners, may be brought by the town or city within which such highway is situated; although the case is one in which the mayor and aldermen, or selectmen, may, under St. 1842, c. 22, (Gen. Sts. c. 63, §§ 53, 54,) on the neglect or refusal of the corporation to carry the decision of the commissioners into effect, proceed to do the work, and maintain an action against the corporation to recover the cost thereof. *Roxbury* v. *Boston & Providence Railroad*, 6 Cush. 424 (1850).

8. The bill in equity provided by St. 1849, c. 222, § 5, (Gen. Sts. c. 63, § 63,) for enforcing the orders of county commissioners respecting the manner of constructing a railroad where it crosses a public highway, can be maintained only by the mayor and aldermen of the city, or the selectmen of the town, within which the way is situated, and not by any individual inhabitant of such city or town, although he is owner in fee simple of the land over which the way is located. *Brainard* v. *Connecticut River Railroad*, 7 Cush. 506 (1851).

9. County commissioners, in the exercise of the power conferred upon them by St. 1842, c. 22, (Gen. Sts. c. 63, §§ 53, 54,) relative to the raising or lowering of a turnpike, highway or town way, are to make a specific order, and not an order in the alternative. *Roxbury* v. *Boston & Providence Railroad*, 6 Cush. 424 (1850).

10. The selectmen of a town, or mayor and aldermen of a city, in all their proceedings under St. 1842, c. 22, (Gen. Sts. c. 63, §§ 53, 54,) act in their official capacity for such town or city, and as their agents. *Ib.*

11. A town is not responsible for a defect or want of repair in a bridge, whereby a public highway crosses a railroad, the proprietors of which are bound by law to keep the bridge in repair. *Sawyer* v. *Northfield*, 7 Cush. 490 (1851).

12. A railroad corporation, which proceeds under Rev. Sts. c. 39, § 67, (Gen. Sts. c. 63, § 48,) after notice to the mayor and aldermen of a city and on terms agreed upon between the corporation and the mayor and aldermen, to raise a street, that its railroad may pass under the same, acts by virtue of its independent corporate powers, and not as the agent or servant of the city; and such corporation is primarily liable, to third parties, for damages thereby caused to their estates. *Gardiner* v. *Boston & Worcester Railroad*, 9 Cush. 1 (1851).

13. A bond of indemnity taken by the city, and the appointment of a superintendent to take care of the public interests in the execution of this work during its progress, are prudent measures, which do not change the character of the work, or the general liability of the company. *Ib.*

14. If a railroad company unreasonably neglect to comply with the order of county commissioners allowing the company, upon their petition under St. 1846, c. 271, (St. 1865, c. 239,) to cross a highway upon a level, the only remedy is for the penalty given by section fourth of that statute, or by a proceeding in equity under St. 1849, c. 222, § 5 (Gen. Sts. c. 63, § 63). The commissioners cannot assess damages, or issue a warrant for a jury, in such a case. *Vermont & Massachusetts Railroad* v. *Franklin*, 10 Cush. 12 (1852).

15. The legislature may grant authority, either by express words or necessary implication, to construct a railroad on and along an existing public highway. *Springfield* v. *Connecticut River Railroad*, 4 Cush. 63 (1849).

16. Where a railroad corporation, under a general grant of power, lay out and construct their road over and along a public highway, the town within which such highway is situated, may proceed in equity against the

corporation in the supreme judicial court, under its general jurisdiction in matters of nuisance, in order to ascertain whether such laying out and construction are or are not within the power granted to the corporation; and it is immaterial, in this respect, whether the way in question be a highway, properly so called, or a town way. *Ib.*

17. A railroad, constructed over a highway in such a manner as to obstruct public travel, is liable to indictment as a nuisance, notwithstanding St. 1849, c. 222, § 4,(Gen Sts. c. 63, § 62,) conferring on county commissioners "the original jurisdiction of all questions touching obstructions to turnpikes, highways or town ways, caused by the construction or operation of railroads." *Commonwealth* v. *Nashua & Lowell Railroad*, 2 Gray, 54 (1854). *Commonwealth* v. *Vermont & Massachusetts Railroad*, 4 Gray, 22 (1855).

18. Where selectmen, besides requiring other alterations to be made by a railroad corporation in a way over which their railroad passed, pursuant to Rev. Sts. c. 39, § 67, (Gen. Sts c. 63, § 48; St. 1865, c. 239,) ordered a draw to be made in the railroad for the accommodation of public travel on the way, it was held, that the railroad corporation, having built their road without such a draw, so as to obstruct public travel, were liable to indictment for a nuisance. *Ib.*

19. An order of county commissioners, passed on the petition of the mayor and aldermen of a city, or selectmen of a town, under St. 1842, c. 22, (Gen. Sts. c. 63, §§ 53, 54,) which determines that the raising of a highway at a place named, where it is crossed by a railroad on a level, so as to pass over the railroad, is necessary for the security of the public, without defining the height above the railroad to which the highway shall be raised, the grade of the ascent, the mode and material of the structure, or the time within which it shall be made, is too indefinite to be specifically enforced by this court in equity under St. 1849, c. 222, § 5 (Gen. Sts. c. 63, § 63). *Roxbury* v. *Boston & Providence Railroad*, 2 Gray, 460 (1854).

20. A railroad corporation were authorized by the county commissioners to raise a highway at a certain grade so as to cross their road on a level, and raised the road accordingly, but at a steeper grade. The commissioners subsequently, on the application of the towns between which the highway lay, modified their former order by postponing the time within which it should be complied with, and assessed damages to the towns. It was held, that the part of the second order which assessed damages was unauthorized, and that the whole order was therefore void, and would not justify the corporation in not complying with the first order. *Commonwealth* v. *Vermont & Massachusetts Railroad*, 4 Gray, 22 (1855).

21. Under Rev. Sts. c. 39, § 69, town or city authorities had no power to lay out a highway across a railroad, on a level therewith; and a railroad company is not estopped from objecting to the exercise of such power by an agreement made by it with former owners of the land, which contained a stipulation for a right of way, to be used by such owners and their assigns, at the place where the highway was afterwards laid out. *Boston & Maine Railroad* v. *Lawrence*, 2 Allen, 107 (1861). See now Gen. Sts. c. 63, §§ 57 *& seq.*

22. A railroad laid out over and along a highway in such a manner as to obstruct it, without express statute authority or necessary implication, is liable to indictment as a nuisance. *Commonwealth* v. *Old Colony & Fall River Railroad*, 14 Gray, 93 (1859).

23. A railroad corporation, which has duly located its road across a public highway, and acquired a right to construct it there at a certain grade, without any restriction as to the number of tracks or the place where they should be laid, is authorized to lay and maintain as many tracks as are essential to the convenient transaction of its business; and for that purpose may make any necessary alteration in the surface of the highway. *Commonwealth* v. *Hartford & New Haven Railroad*, 14 Gray, 379 (1860).

24. An order of the mayor and aldermen of the city of Boston, passed on a petition of the owner of land taken by a railroad corporation for the construction of their road, for the assessment of his damages, "that this board will proceed no further in the premises, and that the respondents be hence discharged and go thereof without day," is a final adjudication that the petitioner has sustained no damage, and warrants him in applying to have his damages assessed by a jury. *Smith* v. *Boston*, 1 Gray, 72 (1854).

25. A *mandamus* will not lie to compel the mayor and aldermen of the city of Boston to revise their decision upon the merits of the claim of an owner of land for damages sustained by the construction of a railroad. *Ib.*

26. An open and travelled street in a city, though not located by the municipal authorities, is a "travelled place," within the meaning of St. 1849, c. 222, § 2, (Gen. Sts. c. 63, §§ 85, 86,) which provide for the erection of sign-boards and gates at crossings. *Whittaker* v. *Boston & Maine Railroad*, 7 Gray, 98 (1856). See St. 1865, c. 239.

26*a*. A city is not liable in an action at law for an injury to a private person by the obstruction of the flow of the water of a stream, caused by a bridge constructed by a railroad corporation, under the authority of its charter; or by a bridge constructed by the city, if the bridge when built was sufficient to allow the free flow of the water as the stream then was, or with such changes as were likely to be produced by natural causes alone, although it has proved insufficient for this purpose, with such changes as have been produced by the exercise by a railroad corporation of its chartered rights, or by the wrongful acts of individuals. *Wheeler* v. *Worcester*, 10 Allen, 591 (1865).

See Actions, 28; Taxes, 15, 17, 222; Ways, 207, 268-272, 277, 305, 397-399, 413, 414, 424, 425, 461-469.

Street Railways.

27. A franchise to construct, maintain and use a street railway over a highway, authorizes the grantees to drive their cars upon their track at the rate of speed usual for vehicles drawn by horses for the carriage of passengers, so far as this right can be enjoyed without preventing other vehicles on the highway from moving at their usual rate of speed. *Commonwealth* v. *Temple,* 14 Gray, 69 (1859).

28. The driver of a heavily loaded wagon on a highway, having one wheel in the track of a street railway established by authority of the legislature, and moving at the usual rate of speed of such wagons, but at a slower rate than street railway cars usually move, is bound to turn off from the track at the request of the conductor of a car owned by the proprietors of the railway, if there is room to do so, although it is usual and much easier to drive such wagons with one wheel upon the railway track. *Ib.*

29. A provision in the charter of a street railway company that, at any time after the expiration of ten years from the opening of any part of the road for use, a city may purchase of the corporation so much of the corporate property as lies within its own limits, at a specified price, does not give to the city any such interest or right as to enable it to maintain a bill in equity to restrain the corporation from raising passenger fares upon their road, in violation of conditions expressly assented to by the corporation, and imposed upon them by the mayor and aldermen of the city when granting to them the power to locate and build a new line of their railway through additional streets, if they are guilty of no fraudulent intent to destroy or depreciate the value of the corporate property; although the value of their franchise and property will be thereby diminished, and the portion of their railway constructed under such authority will perhaps be exposed to forfeiture. Nor can the mayor and aldermen of the city maintain such bill. *Cambridge* v. *Cambridge Railroad,* 10 Allen, 50 (1865).

30. The power of making regulations concerning the removal of snow from the tracks of street railways is given by law exclusively to the mayor and aldermen of the cities and the selectmen of the towns in which such tracks are located; and in the exercise of this power they may prohibit the removal of snow by the railway company at any and all times and places, when in their judgment the public interests may require it. *Union Railway* v. *Cambridge,* 11 Allen, (1866). See St. 1864, c. 229, § 16.

31. It is no objection to an order of the mayor and aldermen regulating the removal of snow from the track of a street railway, that it requires and permits such removal by the railway company only when it is allowed and in a manner to be designated by the superintendent of streets or other officer having charge of the condition or repair of streets. *Ib.*

See Taxes, 7.

RECONSIDERATION.

By the reconsideration of a vote, by a town meeting, at an adjournment of the same meeting by which it was passed, and before it has been acted on, such vote becomes revoked and ceases to have any effect, as if it had never been passed. *Withington* v. *Harvard,* 8 Cush. 66 (1851).

See Appropriations, 21; Contracts, 4; Officers, 7; Taxes, 204; Trusts, 2.

RECORDS.

1. An ancient book of records of the town of Boston, entitled the Book of Possessions, which, although not regularly authenticated, has been preserved among the records of the town, was held (there being nothing to impeach its verity) competent and sufficient evidence to establish the ancient titles under allotments from the town. *Rust* v. *Boston Mill Corp.* 6 Pick. 158 (1828).

2. An ancient book, kept among the records of a town, purporting to be the "selectmen's book of accounts with the treasury of the town," is admissible in evidence of the facts therein stated; and where the selectmen were at the same time assessors, an entry, in such book, of a credit, by an order in favor of the collector, for a discount of a particular individual's tax, was held to be evidence of an abatement of the tax of such individual. *Boston* v. *Weymouth,* 4 Cush. 538 (1849).

3. It is competent for a town clerk to amend a record made by him when in office under a former election, such amendment being consistent with truth. *Welles* v. *Battelle*, 11 Mass. 477 (1814). See 2 Allen, 594, 595.

4. One who was formerly a town clerk, but is no longer in the office, cannot amend a town record made by him when town clerk. *Hartwell* v. *Littleton*, 13 Pick. 229 (1833).

5. One chosen town clerk is competent to make a record of his own election and qualification. *Briggs* v. *Murdock*, 13 Pick. 305 (1832).

See OFFICERS, 25, 30; TAXES, 116, 118, 231.

REPRESENTATIVES IN THE GENERAL COURT.

Under the twenty-first article of amendment of the constitution of Massachusetts, the mayor and aldermen of Boston are empowered to apportion the number of representatives assigned to Suffolk county among the representative districts formed by them, under said article, as well as to form the districts; and their doings and returns in the premises are conclusive, and cannot be revised by the house of representatives in judging of the returns of elections and qualifications of its members. *Opinion of the Justices*, 10 Gray, 613 (1858).

See ELECTIONS, 1-6; JURIES, 7.

REWARDS.

1. The city of Boston having offered a reward for the detection and conviction of any person who might be guilty of feloniously setting fire to any building in said city; and the plaintiffs claiming the reward, on the ground of the detection and conviction of a person for wilfully and maliciously setting fire to and burning, in the daytime, a building, formerly used and occupied as a carpenter's shop, but then in the process of being altered and made into a dwelling-house, and not yet finished; it was held, that the court could not infer, from this description, that the burning was felonious. *Mead* v. *Boston*, 3 Cush. 404 (1849).

2. In an action to recover a reward for the detection and conviction of any person who may be guilty of a certain crime, the record of conviction is not conclusive evidence of the guilt of the person convicted, but it may be shown in defence that he should not have been convicted. *Ib.*

3. A watchman of the city of Boston, who while in the discharge of his duty as such, discovers a person setting fire to a building, and prosecutes him to conviction, is not entitled to claim a reward offered by the city government for the detection and conviction of an incendiary. *Pool* v. *Boston*, 5 Cush. 219 (1849). See *Davies* v. *Burns*, 5 Allen, 349.

4. The mayor and aldermen of the city of Boston passed an order, "that a reward of $ 500 be offered to any person who shall give information so that any person shall be convicted of setting fire to any building, for the purpose of burning the same." An advertisement was inserted in the city newspapers which were published on the next morning after said order was passed, reciting that sundry houses and other buildings had been recently set on fire, and offering a reward of $ 500 to any person "who shall give information so that any perpetrator of these outrages shall be convicted." This advertisement purported to be "by order of the mayor and aldermen," and was signed by the city clerk. *Held*, that the advertisement must be taken to be the official act of the mayor and aldermen. *Held*, also, that the order and the advertisement were to be construed together, as parts of the same transaction, and that by the true construction thereof, the reward was offered for information that would lead to the detection of offences previously committed, and not of offences thereafter committed. *Freeman* v. *Boston*, 5 Met. 56 (1842).

5. In an action against a town to recover a reward offered by its selectmen, it is not sufficient to allege that the selectmen made the offer of reward, without alleging that they did it in behalf of the town. *Codding* v. *Mansfield*, 7 Gray, 272 (1856).

6. On an offer of reward "to any person who will give information to the subscribers that will lead to the detection and conviction of the person who set fire to the dwelling-house of J.S.," a declaration which alleges that the plaintiff arrested such a person, and gave information thereof to the defendants, whereupon such proceedings were had that the prisoner was convicted, is insufficient. *Ib.*

7. An offer of reward for "the apprehension and conviction of any person who shall set fire to any building within the city of Roxbury" is not void for ambiguity; and entitles a person to the reward, who gives information to the police officers of the city, upon which an incendiary is arrested, and which has a tendency to procure ultimate conviction, and without which a conviction would not have been had, if the incendiary had not, while under arrest, confessed his guilt; although such person is not called as a witness on the trial, and does no act after the arrest, and the confession is given in evidence on the trial, and perhaps is the ground of the conviction.

Crawshaw v. *Roxbury*, 7 Gray, 374 (1856). See *Besse* v. *Dyer*, 9 Allen, 151.

8. An offer of reward, made by the mayor in behalf of a city, and subsequently ratified by the city council, is binding on the city, although not so ratified until after the performance of the service for which the reward is claimed. *Ib.*

9. The mayor of the city of Boston caused an advertisement to be published, for about a week, in the daily papers of the city, stating that there had been a frequent and successful repetition of incendiary attempts, and offering a reward, to be paid by the city, for the apprehension and conviction of any person engaged in these attempts. *Held*, that this was not to be regarded as an unlimited offer, continuing till it should be formally withdrawn, but as limited to a reasonable time; and that it ceased to be an offer after the lapse of three years and eight months. *Loring* v. *Boston*, 7 Met. 409 (1844).

10. The city council may bind the city by an offer of reward of a greater amount than that which the mayor and aldermen are authorized by statute to offer. *Crawshaw* v. *Roxbury*, 7 Gray, 374 (1856). See Gen. Sts. c. 170, § 7; St. 1866, c. 9.

11. Selectmen of a town have no authority to bind the town by an offer of a reward for the apprehension and conviction of a person who has not been charged with a crime by a complaint or indictment. *Day* v. *Otis*, 8 Allen, 477 (1864). But see now St. 1866, c. 9.

RIOTS.

1. To disturb another in the enjoyment of a lawful right is a trespass; and if this is done by numbers unlawfully combined, the same act is a riot. *Commonwealth* v. *Runnels*, 10 Mass. 520 (1813).

2. A riot must be committed by three persons at least, and the offence cannot exist without acting in concert and unlawful combination. *Commonwealth* v. *Porter*, 1 Gray, 480 (1854). *Commonwealth* v. *Berry*, 5 Gray, 93 (1855).

3. In order to constitute a riot, rout or unlawful assembly, there must be an unlawful assembling together; although the assembly may not have been unlawful on the first coming together of the parties, but becomes so by their engaging in a common cause, to be accomplished with violence and in a tumultuous manner. *Commonwealth* v. *Gibney*, 2 Allen, 152 (1861).

4. The determination of the mayor of a city that a riot or mob is threatened, is conclusive that the exigency existed, required by St. 1840, c. 92, § 27, (St. 1866, c. 219, § 141,) to authorize him to call out the volunteer militia to aid the civil authority in enforcing the laws. *Ela* v. *Smith*, 5 Gray, 121 (1855).

5. The volunteer militia, when called out by the mayor of a city under St. 1840, c. 92, § 27, (St. 1866, c. 219, § 141,) on the ground that a mob or riot is threatened, may, before such riot or mob has actually taken place, be ordered by the mayor to repair to a particular place, and there perform any specific duty, such as clearing the streets, which in his judgment is necessary to prevent the threatened mob or riot. *Ib.*

6. Officers of militia, called out by a civil magistrate to aid the civil authority in enforcing the laws, cannot be entrusted with discretionary power as to the measures to be adopted; but can only direct the details of the mode of executing specific orders received from the civil magistrate. *Ib.*

7. The power to call out the militia to prevent a threatened riot is not affected by the anticipated cause of the riot being the enforcement of an unconstitutional law. *Ib.*

8. Civil magistrates and military officers, giving unlawful orders to militia called out to aid the civil authority in enforcing the laws, are liable for acts done by the militia within the fair scope of the orders, but not for acts unauthorized by them. *Ib.*

9. Although the constitution provides that "the military power shall always be held in an exact subordination to the civil authority, and be governed by it," it is does not follow from this that the military force is to be taken wholly out of the control of its proper officers. They are to direct its movements in the execution of the orders given by the civil officers, and to manage the details in which a specific service or duty is to be performed. But the service or duty must be first prescribed and designated by the civil authority. BIGELOW, J., in *Ela* v. *Smith*, 5 Gray, 140 (1855).

SCHOOLS.

1. Persons who reside on lands purchased by or ceded to the United States for navy yards, forts or arsenals, where there is no other reservation of jurisdiction to the state than that of a right to serve civil and criminal process on such lands, are not entitled to the benefits of the common schools for their children in the towns in which the lands are situated. *Opinion of the Justices*, 1 Met. 580 (1841).

2. An indictment against a town for not providing a schoolmaster, which did not conclude "against the form of the statutes," &c., was held to be insufficient even after the defendant had pleaded *nolo contendere*. *Com-*

monwealth v. *Northampton*, 2 Mass. 116 (1806). But see now Gen. Sts. c. 172, § 19.

3. No person could be lawfully employed as a town schoolmaster, so as to protect the town from prosecution under St. 1789, c. 19, unless he first produced the certificates or evidence of his qualifications, required by that statute. *Commonwealth* v. *Dedham*, 16 Mass. 141 (1819).

4. To constitute a grammar school within the meaning of that statute, it must be duly regulated as to the admission of scholars; and the master must be engaged to keep a school of that description. *Ib.*

5. The grammar school required by St.1789, c. 19, to be maintained by every town having two hundred families or householders, must be kept for the use and benefit of all the inhabitants of the town. *Ib.*

6.*An indictment under Rev. Sts. c. 23, § 5, for neglecting to maintain a high school, need not negative a compliance with the subsequent St. 1850, c. 274. *Commonwealth* v. *Sheffield*, 11 Cush. 178 (1853).

7. If such indictment aver a neglect to maintain such school for three successive years, and a general verdict of guilty is returned, judgment will be arrested, as no certain penalty can be inflicted thereon under Rev. Sts. c. 23, § 60 (Gen. Sts. c. 38, § 14). *Ib.*

8. The prudential committee of a school district, in hiring a teacher for the district school, act as the agents of the town, and the teacher's remedy for his wages is an action against the town, and not against the district. *Clark* v. *Great Barrington*, 11 Pick. 259 (1831).

9. Payment of money by the town to the prudential committee, for the purpose of being paid over to the teacher, does not make the committee liable in the trustee process as the teacher's trustee, nor discharge the town from its liability to the teacher. *Ib.*

10. A majority of a prudential committee of a school district may lawfully do official acts, especially after a refusal of the minority to meet with them. *Kingsbury* v. *Quincy*, 12 Met. 99 (1846.)

11. A school district, by vote, instructed its prudential committee "to prosecute for trespasses that have been, or in future may be, committed, by breaking into the school-houses of the district," and the committee employed an attorney to commence several actions of trespass, which he commenced and prosecuted accordingly; and he afterwards sued the district for his fees and disbursements in those actions. It was held, that the district was bound by the acts of the committee, and that the attorney was entitled to recover, although the said vote of the district was not in pursuance of any article in the warrant for the meeting at which it was passed. *Ib.*

12. The prudential committee-man of a school district, chosen by the district, pursuant to a vote of the town, is not liable to the district for money received by him out of the treasury of the town, which had been raised by the town and appropriated by it to the support of the school in such district, and placed to the credit of the district on the town treasurer's books. *Belchertown* v. *Randall*, 7 Cush. 478 (1851).

13. The prudential committee of a school district, duly chosen in March, and authorized to contract with teachers, cannot interfere with a teacher engaged by the general school committee of the preceding year, under St. 1846, c. 223, § 1, for the entire winter term; and if they close, against a teacher so engaged, the school-house in which he is accustomed to keep his school, such general school committee may forcibly break open the school-house, and reinstate the teacher. *Natick* v. *Morse*, 8 Cush. 191 (1851).

14. Selectmen who, on the failure of a school district to agree where to place their school-house, have determined the location thereof, pursuant to Rev. Sts. c. 23, § 30, and St. 1848, c. 237, § 1, (Gen. Sts. c. 38, § 38,) cannot proceed to lay out the land and assess damages to the owner, without seven days' notice to him in writing; nor, it seems, until he has refused to sell the land or demanded an unreasonable price. *Norton* v. *Copeland*, 2 Gray, 414 (1854).

15. It seems, that the owner of land taken for a school-house lot under St. 1848, c. 237, (Gen. Sts. c. 38, § 38,) "in the same way and manner as is provided for laying out town ways," has no such right to remove trees or fences as the owner of land taken for a town way has. *Ib.*

16. It seems, that the receipt, by the owner of land taken for a school-house lot, of the damages awarded him by the selectmen pursuant to St. 1848, c. 237, § 1, (Gen. Sts. c. 38, § 38,) estops him to object to the regularity of their proceedings in taking the lot. *Ib.*

17. A building committee of the selectmen of a town which had not been divided into territorial school districts, selected a lot of land for a school-house, and, on the refusal of H., the owner, to sell it, applied to the selectmen to call a meeting of the town. At such a meeting, called "to see if the town will authorize the selectmen to select at their discretion a school-house lot," it was voted, "that the selectmen be and they are hereby authorized to select at their discretion a school-house lot and lay out the same, from the land of H. heretofore selected by the town." *Held*,

that this was not a sufficient designation of land by the town to authorize the selectmen to select out of it a school-house lot, under St. 1848, c. 237 (Gen. Sts. c. 38, § 38). *Harris* v. *Marblehead*, 10 Gray, 40 (1857).

18. It seems, that a notice that the selectmen, in accordance with a vote of the town, will on a certain day lay out and assess damages for the taking of a lot of land, but not stating that it is for a school-house, is insufficient. *Ib.*

19. A town which, against the owner's will, illegally takes a lot of land for a school-house lot, and erects a school-house thereon, cannot be allowed anything for betterments, under Rev. Sts. c. 101, §§ 19, 20 (Gen. Sts. c. 134, §§ 18, 19). *Ib.*

20. The tender of the appraised value of land selected and laid out as a school-house lot, if the owner lives out of the Commonwealth, may be made to a person who is left by him in possession of the land, and who, for some purposes, is his agent. *Gibbons* v. *East Granville*, 4 Allen, 508 (1862).

21. A will contained the following provisions: "I give, bequeath and devise unto a part of the inhabitants of the town of B. and unto a part of those persons who may become inhabitants of the said town of B., to wit, all that are now or may become inhabitants of said town of B., excepting" nine persons named, "and their descendants," a certain sum of money, "upon the following conditions, to wit, said town of B. is to loan said sum and secure the payment of the principal and interest by a mortgage or mortgages upon real estate; the principal is to be kept as a permanent fund; the interest is to be expended yearly after two years from my decease in the support of one school, to be kept near the centre of said B., in which such academical instruction shall be given as said town shall decide to be most useful;" "said school is to be free to all persons who are now or may become inhabitants of the town of B., excepting such persons as do not conform to proper rules and regulations that shall be established in said school by said town, and such persons as said town shall determine to be of an unsuitable age, and the aforesaid" nine persons "and their descendants, who are excluded from attending said school for the term of one hundred years; and after the expiration of said term of one hundred years the school is to be free to all the inhabitants of said town of B. who comply with the rules of said school." "Said town of B. is to be paid by my executors the aforenamed sum within two years from my decease, with interest on the same from the day of my decease." "Whenever the town of B. shall fail to fulfil the above conditions the said" sum of money "shall become the property of my legal heirs." "I also give, bequeath and devise unto the same aforenamed inhabitants of the town of B. to whom I bequeath" the money, certain land described, upon condition that "said land is to be used for the purpose of erecting a school-house upon it for the use of the school aforenamed, and to become the property of my heirs whenever said land shall be used for any other purpose, after the expiration of two years from my decease." It was held, that these provisions constituted a valid legacy and devise to the town in its corporate capacity, for the support of a public school for the benefit of all the inhabitants; and that the condition excluding certain persons and their descendants from the school, being repugnant to the nature of the grant, and contrary to law and public policy, was inoperative and void. *Nourse* v. *Merriam*, 8 Cush. 11 (1851).

22. The power of towns to vote and grant money for the support of town schools is not restricted to the amount that is necessary to support the schools which the Rev. Sts. c. 23, §§ 1-5, and 60, (Gen. Sts. c. 38, §§ 1, 2, 14,) require them to support under a penalty for refusal or neglect to do so; but they have power to vote and grant money for the support of other town schools, for instruction in branches of knowledge which the revised statutes do not require to be taught in such schools. *Cushing* v. *Newburyport*, 10 Met. 508 (1845).

23. A town which had raised money for the support of all the schools required by law, and had supported them, also raised money to support, and did support, a female high school for the purpose of teaching book-keeping, algebra, geometry, history, rhetoric, mental, moral and natural philosophy, botany, the Latin and French languages, and other higher branches of knowledge than were taught in the grammar schools of the town. It was held, that this was a town school, within the meaning of the revised statutes, and that the money for its support was legally raised by tax. *Ib.*

24. The teacher of a town school is not liable to any action by a parent, for refusing to instruct his children. *Spear* v. *Cummings*, 23 Pick. 224 (1839). See Gen. Sts. c. 41, § 11.

25. Under the clause in St. 1826, c. 143, (Gen. Sts. c. 38, § 29,) which provides that "the school committee of each town shall procure class books, at the expense of the town and to be paid for out of the town treasury," the committee may either get the books on the credit of the town, or buy them themselves and thereby make themselves creditors of the town. *Hartwell* v. *Littleton*, 13 Pick. 229 (1833).

26. The requisition of the statute, that the

school committee shall give notice of the place where such books may be obtained, is substantially complied with, if the books are placed in the hands of the schoolmasters, with notice to the schools that they may be obtained of the masters. *Ib.*

27. A report of the condition of the town schools, made and published as required by law, by the superintending school committee, is not libellous by reason of charging the prudential committee of one of the districts with employing a teacher and putting her in charge of a public school, in violation of law, and with taking possession of the school-house and excluding by force the general school committee and the teachers employed by them, if it does not impute corrupt motives. *Shattuck* v. *Allen*, 4 Gray, 540 (1855).

28. Under Gen. Sts. c. 38, §§ 23, 24, the authority and duty of the school committee of a town are not confined to ascertaining by examination the literary qualifications of teachers, and their capacity for the government of schools; but they are the sole judges of their qualifications in all respects to teach and govern the school for which they are selected. *Uxbridge* v. *Mowry*, 9 Allen, 94 (1864).

29. The general school committee of the city of Boston had power, in 1849, under the constitution and the laws of this commonwealth, then in force, to make provision for the instruction of colored children in separate schools established exclusively for them, and to prohibit their attendance upon the other schools. *Roberts* v. *Boston*, 5 Cush. 198 (1849). But see now Gen. Sts. c. 41, § 9.

30. The general school committee of a city or town have power, under the laws of this commonwealth, in order to maintain the purity and discipline of the public schools, to exclude therefrom a child whom they deem to be of a licentious and immoral character, although such character is not manifested by any acts of licentiousness or immorality within the school. *Sherman* v. *Charlestown*, 8 Cush. 160 (1851).

31. The power conferred on school committees by St. 1838, c. 105, § 2, (Gen. Sts. c. 38, § 23,) to "select and contract with the teachers for the town and district schools," includes the power to fix the compensation to be paid them, and to bind the town to pay the same. *Batchelder* v. *Salem*, 4 Cush. 599 (1849).

32. The school committee of Boston have the right to dismiss teachers employed by them, whenever in their judgment the public good requires it, and are the exclusive judges, in each case, of the propriety of such dismissal. *Knowles* v. *Boston*, 12 Gray, 339 (1859).

33. If one who has been authorized by the school committee of a city to take charge of an evening school, employs a person to render needful assistance in preserving order outside of the door while the school is in session, the city is liable to pay a reasonable compensation to such person, although the committee have never acted as a body upon this particular matter; and in such case, evidence is incompetent to show that in former years the school was under the sole control of the committee, or that the committee had rejected the claim for compensation. *Huse* v. *Lowell*, 10 Allen, 149 (1865).

34. It is no defence to an action against a school district, to recover the rent of a school-room hired by the prudential committee of the district, that the school was partly supported by private contributions, and so was continued longer than it otherwise would have been, or that the teachers were not legally employed or duly qualified for their situations, or that there was no legal appropriation or distribution by the town of the funds raised for the support of schools. *Allen* v. *Westport*, 15 Pick. 35 (1833).

35. The school committee of a town have no such property in the school registers required by law to be kept, as will enable them to maintain an action for the taking of the same out of their possession. *Perkins* v. *Weston*, 3 Cush. 549 (1849).

36. A teacher of a district school cannot recover payment for his services, until he has filled up and completed the register of the school kept by him, in compliance with the requirement of St. 1849, c. 209 (Gen. Sts. c. 40, §§ 5, 13); and the school committee of the town have no power to waive a performance of this duty by him. *Jewell* v. *Abington*, 2 Allen, 592 (1861).

37. A teacher in one of the public schools of the city of Boston, who is elected annually, and whose salary is payable quarterly, if dismissed in the middle of a quarter by the school committee, although for no misconduct on her part, cannot recover salary for the subsequent part of the quarter. *Knowles* v. *Boston*, 12 Gray, 339 (1859).

38. A truant officer, appointed under Gen. Sts. c. 42, § 5, does not hold over after the expiration of his year, although no other has been appointed in his place. *Huse* v. *Lowell*, 10 Allen, 149 (1865).

See Actions, 55, 58; Appropriations, 19.

SEALS.

1. It is not necessary that municipal corporations should act under seal, in order to

bind themselves, or obligate others to them. A vote of the body is sufficient for this purpose. PARKER, C. J., in *Rumford* v. *Wood*, 13 Mass. 199 (1816).

2. A *fac simile* of the seal of a corporation printed upon blank forms of obligations prepared to be executed by the corporation, at the same time when the blank is printed and by the same agency, is not a seal, at common law, nor will such forms, when executed by the corporation, be contracts under seal, although the language of them calls for a seal. *Bates* v. *Boston & N. Y. Central Railroad*, 10 Allen, 251 (1865).

3. The St. of 1855, c. 223, (Gen. Sts. c. 3, § 7, cl. 15,) providing that the mere impression of the seal of a corporation upon any legal instrument executed by such corporation shall thenceforth be valid, is not retrospective in its operation. *Ib.*

See *Commonwealth* v. *Griffith*, 2 Pick. 11; *Bradford* v. *Randall*, 5 Pick. 496; *Mill Dam Foundery* v. *Hovey*, 21 Pick. 417; *Tasker* v. *Bartlett*, 5 Cush. 359; PUBLIC LANDS, 3; TAXES, 122.

SET-OFF.

See ACTIONS, 52, 53.

SEWERS AND DRAINS.

1. A city or town is not responsible in damages for the inconvenience and loss of business occasioned to the abutters on a street by opening an old common sewer in the street for the purpose of enlarging and repairing it. *Brooks* v. *Boston*, 19 Pick. 178 (1837).

2. An action of tort lies against a city in behalf of the owner of land through which its agents have unlawfully made a sewer. *Hildreth* v. *Lowell*, 11 Gray, 345 (1858).

3. No action lies against a city for the injury occasioned to land bounding on a public street from the accumulation of water on the surface of the street, which the city has neglected to drain. *Flagg* v. *Worcester*, 13 Gray, 601 (1859).

4. No action lies against a city for a failure to keep a public sewer and cesspool in repair, whereby waste water accumulates and flows into the cellar of a neighboring house, which is not connected by a drain with the public sewer. *Barry* v. *Lowell*, 8 Allen, 127 (1864).

5. A canal corporation may maintain an action of tort against a city, for laying down sewers and drains through lands purchased by the corporation for the use of their canal, and emptying into the canal; although the city is authorized by its charter "to cause drains and common sewers to be laid down through streets and private lands;" and although the canal was constructed in the channel of an ancient watercourse. *Proprietors of Locks & Canals* v. *Lowell*, 7 Gray, 233 (1856).

6. In an action of tort against a city for breaking and entering the plaintiff's close, the defendant, under an answer alleging that the city council voted to lay out and did lay out a sewer, according to law, through the close in question, on the petition of the owners of the close, with notice to the abutters and before the plaintiff was owner of the close, may introduce as a justification the proceedings of the city council in laying out the sewer. *Hildreth* v. *Lowell*, 11 Gray, 345 (1858).

7. A right to empty a town drain upon the land of an individual cannot be acquired by twenty years' use, unless the drain be one and the same, and the use thereof uninterrupted during that number of years. If the drain, during those years, be enlarged, deepened and raised in its course and termination, the town cannot acquire such right, as against the owner of the land, by using the drain less than twenty years after it is thus enlarged and altered. *Cotton* v. *Pocasset Manuf. Co.* 13 Met. 429 (1847).

8. A by-law of the city of Boston, requiring that every person who enters his particular drain into a common sewer of the city shall be held to pay to the city such sum as is his just proportion of the expense of making such common sewer, having reference always to the last valuation of such person in the assessors' books previous to the expenditure, is void for inequality and unreasonableness. *Boston* v. *Shaw*, 1 Met. 130 (1840).

9. A city cannot maintain an action of contract on a *quantum meruit* against one who enters his particular drain into such common sewer, and upon whom no assessment has been laid for its cost. *Ib.*

10. A by-law of the city of Boston, providing that the expense of constructing a common sewer, after deducting the portion to be paid by the city, shall be assessed upon the persons and estates deriving benefit therefrom, either by the entry of their particular drains therein, or by any more remote means, apportioning the assessment according to the value of the lands thus benefited, independently of any buildings or improvements thereon, is valid. And it is no objection to the validity of an assessment, made pursuant to such by-law, that the greater part of one lot assessed is lower than the bottom of the sewer. *Downer* v. *Boston*, 7 Cush. 277 (1851).

11. The statute of 1841, c. 115, (Gen. Sts. c. 48,) in relation to sewers and drains, is a valid statute; and the by-laws of the city of

Boston, in relation to sewers and drains, passed June 14, 1841, and March 7, 1844, (Laws and Ordinances, 658-661,) are in conformity with that statute, and valid; and owners of vacant lots on a street in which a common sewer has been laid in pursuance of such by-laws, are properly assessed for their proportion of the cost thereof, as well as owners of lots built upon. *Wright* v. *Boston*, 9 Cush. 233 (1852).

12. An order of the mayor and aldermen of Boston, directing a main drain to be laid, upon a petition setting forth that the safety and convenience of the city require such a drain, is a sufficient adjudication of the necessity thereof under the city by-laws. *Ib.*

13. A city ordinance, which requires the city council, before laying out a drain across private property, to "give notice in writing to the several owners" of the property, appointing a time and place for hearing all parties interested, and to post two or more copies of such notice at public places in the city, is complied with by serving notice upon all known owners personally or at their usual places of abode, and publicly posting two copies thereof, and therein describing the premises as a passage way, without adding that they are private property. *Hildreth* v. *Lowell*, 11 Gray, 345 (1858).

14. A statute authorizing the city council of a city to "cause drains and common sewers to be laid down through any street or private lands, paying the owners thereof such damage as they may sustain thereby," is constitutional and valid. *Ib.*

15. Under an ordinance of a city, requiring the committee of the city council, upon laying out a drain through private land, to report the names of all the owners of such land, with the amount of damages allowed to each, a report of the names of all those owning land abutting on the sewer, without mentioning any damages, is a sufficient award that no one is entitled to damages. *Ib.*

16. County commissioners have no authority to issue a warrant for a jury to assess damages for land taken for a common sewer, under St. 1859, c. 137, (concerning sewers and drains in the city of Cambridge,) after the expiration of six months from the decision to take the land; although the owner of the land had no notice of their decision until after the expiration of the six months. *Cambridge* v. *Middlesex*, 6 Allen, 134 (1863).

17. The exclusive control of the construction of common sewers in the city of Boston is vested in the board of aldermen; and the city is not liable for any injury or inconvenience occasioned to private persons by their location or construction, according to the order of that board. *Child* v. *Boston*, 4 Allen, 41 (1862).

18. When constructed, they become the property of the city, and the duty of keeping them in order devolves upon the city; and the city is responsible for negligently suffering them to occasion a nuisance to the estates of the citizens whose private drains enter into them, if the nuisance does not result from their original plan of construction, and could be avoided by keeping them in proper condition. *Ib.*

19. When a sewer was ordered to be constructed with a waste weir discharging into the empty basin of the Back Bay, and was built according to the order, it was the duty of the city, when the flats between the upland and the channel of the basin were filled up and made solid land, to extend the drain through the land thus made, so as to keep an open place of discharge into the basin, the city having the right thus to extend it; and if, by their negligently omitting to do so, after notice, injury is occasioned to the estates of private persons by the overflow of the sewer, the city is answerable in damages. *Ib.*

20. An indenture conveying to the city of Boston the right forever "to dig, lay and maintain all convenient and necessary sewers and drains from the upland to the channel or deep water within the basin [in the Back Bay] according to law and the common and usual practice for the time being within the city," must be construed to apply, not only to the wants of the city as a private owner of lands in the neighborhood, but also to the sewers for general use which it might be their duty, in their municipal capacity, to construct and maintain. *Ib.*

21. A city is not liable in an action at law for an injury to a private person by the obstruction of the flow of the water of a stream, caused by an increase of the surface wash from the streets into the same, if such increase is only the natural result of the growth of the city; or by the emptyings of the sewers into the same, if these are no greater than would otherwise have been carried in by surface washing, and are not sufficient to exert any appreciable effect on such person; or by a bridge constructed by the city, if the bridge when built was sufficient to allow the free flow of the water as the stream then was, or with such changes as were likely to be produced by natural causes alone, although it has proved insufficient for this purpose, with such changes as have been produced by the exercise by a railroad corporation of its chartered rights, or by the wrongful acts of individuals. *Wheeler* v. *Worcester*, 10 Allen, 591 (1865).

SMOKING IN THE STREETS.

See Fire, 8.

SPENDTHRIFTS.

1. The purpose for which the selectmen of a town are empowered to apply to the judge of probate for the appointment of a guardian to a spendthrift, is to restrain the spendthrift from a course of vicious excesses, by taking from him the means of indulging in them, and thus to save both himself and his family from distress and ruin, as well as to save the town from expense for their support; where, therefore, the selectmen, having filed a complaint for the appointment of a guardian, relinquished the proceedings solely in consideration of a bond and mortgage, given to them by the spendthrift, with condition to indemnify the town from expense on account of himself and his family, it was held, that if there was good ground for the complaint, they had abandoned a public duty imposed upon them by law, and if the complaint was not well founded, they had used a public power, given for other purposes, to compel the giving of a particular security to the town, and that in either case the bond and mortgage were void. *Norton* v. *Leonard*, 12 Pick. 152 (1831).

2. A judge of probate may appoint a guardian to a spendthrift upon the complaint of the selectmen of the town where the spendthrift is domiciled, although the spendthrift has his legal settlement in a town in a different county from that in which such appointment is made. *Stacey* v. *Benson*, 18 Pick. 496 (1836). And see Gen. Sts. c. 109, § 9.

3. The selectmen of a town, having been appointed guardians of a spendthrift, under a statute authorizing the judge of probate to appoint the selectmen or "other suitable persons," do not cease to be such guardians on the expiration of the period for which they were elected to the office of selectmen. *Russell* v. *Coffin*, 8 Pick. 142 (1829).

See PAUPERS, 75.

STABLES.

See BUILDINGS, 1.

STATE TREASURY.

Under Gen. Sts. c. 15, § 32, the governor may instruct the state treasurer to withhold the payment of a portion of a sum of money due to a city or town, after he has, with the advice of the council, executed and delivered to the treasurer a warrant for the payment thereof, if such city or town illegally withholds money due to the Commonwealth. *Lowell* v. *Oliver*, 8 Allen, 247 (1864).

STEAM ENGINES.

A steam engine erected in a building situated on State Street in Boston, under a license from the board of aldermen, and with the safety plug required by law, is not a nuisance; and the landlord is not liable to third persons for any injury resulting to them from its maintenance or use by the tenant. *Saltonstall* v. *Banker*, 8 Gray, 195 (1857). See *Call* v. *Allen*, 1 Allen, 137.

SWINE.

See ORDINANCES, &c. 18–21.

TAXES.

I. PERSONS AND PROPERTY SUBJECT TO TAXATION.

II. WHERE AND TO WHOM POLLS AND PROPERTY SHALL BE ASSESSED.

III. MANNER AND VALIDITY OF THE ASSESSMENT.

IV. COLLECTION OF TAXES.

(*a*) Generally.
(*b*) By Action at Law.
(*c*) By Arrest.
(*d*) By Distress and Sale; Lien on Land.

V. REMEDY FOR AN ILLEGAL TAX.

(*a*) Whether by Action or Abatement.
(*b*) Of the Action to recover back.
(*c*) Of the Abatement.
(*d*) Of Actions against Assessors and others.

I. PERSONS AND PROPERTY SUBJECT TO TAXATION.

1. The polls of aliens are liable to taxation. *Opinion of the Justices*, 7 Mass. 523 (1811). And see Gen. Sts. c. 11, § 1.

2. The property of minors, personal as well as real, is liable to be assessed in the public taxes. *Payson* v. *Tufts*, 13 Mass. 493 (1816). *Baldwin* v. *Fitchburg*, 8 Pick. 494 (1829).

3. Non-resident owners of real estate may be taxed therefor, although the real estate is in the actual occupation of tenants at will. *Newburyport Turnpike* v. *Upton*, 12 Mass. 575 (1815).

4. Persons who reside on lands purchased by or ceded to the United States for navy yards, forts or arsenals, where there is no other reservation of jurisdiction to the state

than that of a right to serve civil and criminal process on such lands, are not liable to be assessed for their polls or estates to state, county, or town taxes, in the towns in which the lands are situated. *Opinion of the Justices*, 1 Met. 580 (1841). See *Commonwealth* v. *Clary*, 8 Mass. 72.

5. A manufacturing corporation is not liable to be taxed for its personal property in the town where the manufactory is established. Otherwise, as to its real property. *Salem Iron Co.* v. *Danvers*, 10 Mass. 514 (1813). *Amesbury Woollen Co.* v. *Amesbury*, 17 Mass. 461 (1821). See *Goodell Manuf. Co.* v. *Trask*. 11 Pick. 514.

6. Manufacturing corporations are not taxable for their personal property, except for their machinery. *Boston & Sandwich Glass Co.* v. *Boston*, 4 Met. 181 (1842). *Dunnell Manuf. Co.* v. *Pawtucket*, 7 Gray, 277 (1856).

7. An incorporated street railroad company is not taxable for horses or other personal property used in and necessary for the prosecution of its business. *Middlesex Railroad* v. *Charlestown*, 8 Allen, 330 (1864).

8. A testator bequeathed to his daughter, who was married, "the interest of $ 50,000" from the time of his decease, "during her natural life; and at her decease, the principal to be equally divided among her children or the survivors of them at her decease." The executors, who were also residuary legatees, having given bonds for the payment of debts and legacies, deposited, of their own motion, the sum of $ 50,000 in the Massachusetts Hospital Life Insurance office, subject to a contract providing that the insurance company should, during the life of the daughter, pay to her annually the same rate of interest thereon as they should receive on the other property in their possession; that at intervals of every five years during the life of the daughter, the executor should have the right to withdraw the sum so deposited, and the company should also have the right to pay off the same, and that the company should, after her decease, pay the principal sum and all interest due thereon to the executors, to be distributed according to the provisions of the will. The executors returned no inventory, and rendered no account at the probate office. It was held, that the executors were not liable to be taxed on account of the sum so deposited, it not coming under the head either of "moneys at interest more than they paid interest for," or of "debts due to them more than they were indebted for," in the provisions of the tax acts. *Gray* v. *Boston*, 15 Pick. 376 (1834).

9. A testator gave to his daughter, a married woman, "the interest of $ 50,000," from the time of his decease, "during her natural life, at her decease the principal to be equally divided among her children;" and his executors, being residuary devisees and legatees, gave bond to the judge of probate for the payment of all the debts and legacies. It was held, that under this bequest there was no "capital or principal sum" owned legally or equitably by, or held in trust or otherwise for, the daughter, and that consequently she was not liable to taxation under St. 1828, c. 143, § 2, which provided "that persons entitled to the income of any personal property held by others in trust for them, shall be liable to be taxed for the capital or principal sum in the town where such persons reside." *Swett* v. *Boston*, 18 Pick. 123 (1836).

10. An investment of $ 50,000, made by the executors, without the consent of the daughter, in trust to pay her the income, was held to have no effect upon her rights in regard to taxation under that statute. *Ib.*

11. Under St. 1830, c. 151, subjecting to taxation "shares or property in any incorporated company for a bridge or a turnpike road," a citizen of this state is liable to be taxed for his stock in a turnpike company of another state. *Great Barrington* v. *Berkshire*, 16 Pick. 572 (1835). See Gen. Sts. c. 11, § 4.

11 *a*. Inhabitants of this state who own stock in corporations established in other states are taxable for such stock at its full value, and no deduction is to be made on account of taxation to which such corporations are subject in the states where they are established. *Dwight* v. *Boston*, 12 Allen, (1866).

12. Water power for mill purposes, not used, being merely a capacity of land for a certain mode of improvement, cannot be taxed independently of the land. *Boston Manuf. Co.* v. *Newton*, 22 Pick. 22 (1839).

13. A corporation owning canals and land under and adjoining them, and gate-houses, feeders and other property used for raising and making available a water power, and whose business it is to furnish water power to its stockholders, who are taxed for the value thereof, in connection with their own mills, is taxable for the value of its property over and above the amounts so taxed to its stockholders on account of the water power furnished to them; although such value is derived merely from the surplus supply of water power which it is able to furnish to others during a portion of the year. *Lowell* v. *Middlesex*, 6 Allen, 131 (1863).

14. Under the Rev. Sts. c. 7, § 5, cl. 5, exempting houses of religious worship from taxation, such distinct tenements only are exempted as are used for religious worship and purposes connected therewith; and not tenements,

though under the same roof, which are used for purposes wholly secular. *Proprietors of Meeting-house, &c.* v. *Lowell*, 1 Met. 538 (1840). And see Gen. Sts. c. 11, § 5, cl. 7; St. 1865, c. 206.

15. The Western Railroad Corporation are not liable to be taxed for the land, not exceeding five rods in width, over which they were authorized to lay out their road, nor for buildings and structures thereon erected by them, if such buildings and structures are reasonably incident to the support of the road or to its proper and convenient use for the carriage of passengers and property — such as houses for the reception of passengers, engine-houses, car-houses and depots for the convenient reception, preservation and delivery of merchandise carried on the road. *Worcester* v. *Western Railroad*, 4 Met. 564 (1842). See *Charlestown* v. *Middlesex*, 1 Allen, 199.

16. The Boston Water Power Company are not taxable for their income, which is annually divided among the individual stockholders. *Boston Water Power Co.* v. *Boston*, 9 Met. 199 (1845).

17. The flats lying between the channels of Charles and Miller's rivers, outside of the location of the Boston and Maine Railroad Extension Company, and filled up by the said company, pursuant to the authority given by St. 1845, c. 224, § 1, for the location of engine-houses and wood-houses, and other purposes for the use of their road, and used, when so filled up, exclusively for such purposes, are not exempt from taxation. *Boston & Maine Railroad* v. *Cambridge*, 8 Cush. 237 (1851).

18. Land purchased in fee or otherwise taken by a city, by authority of the legislature, for the purpose of supplying the city with pure water, and used for that purpose only, is justly taken in the exercise of the right of eminent domain, and is therefore not liable to taxation. *Wayland* v. *Middlesex*, 4 Gray, 500 (1855).

19. Mutual fire insurance companies are not liable to taxation for personal estate invested in their corporate names and held by them for the purposes of their incorporation. *Worcester Ins. Co.* v. *Worcester*, 7 Cush. 600 (1851).

20. The real estate of a bank, including its banking house, is liable to taxation in the town where such estate lies. *Tremont Bank* v. *Boston*, 1 Cush. 142 (1848).

21. A bank cannot legally be taxed for railroad stock pledged to it as collateral security for a debt. *Waltham Bank* v. *Waltham*, 10 Met. 334 (1845). *Tremont Bank* v. *Boston*, 1 Cush. 142 (1848).

22. Savings banks are not taxable for bank stock in which they have invested money received on deposit. *Worcester Savings Inst.* v. *Worcester*, 10 Cush. 128 (1852).

23. A clerk in a post office, who is appointed by the deputy postmaster, and his appointment approved by the postmaster general, is taxable for the income derived from his employment as such clerk. *Melcher* v. *Boston*, 9 Met. 73 (1845).

24. The president and fellows of Harvard College having built a dwelling-house on land of the corporation within the college yard, and leased the same to one of their professors, to be occupied by him as a residence for himself and his family at an annual rent; it was held, that this was not an occupation of the real estate of the college by one of its officers, within the exemption from taxation provided by the Rev. Sts. c. 7, § 5, cl. 2 (Gen. Sts. c. 11, § 5, cl. 3); otherwise, if the building had been erected for one of the professors or officers, and had been occupied by him, with the permission of the college, without his having any estate therein, or paying any rent therefor. *Pierce* v. *Cambridge*, 2 Cush. 611 (1849).

25. The provisions of Rev. Sts. c. 7, § 10, (Gen. Sts. c. 11, § 12,) cl. 5, relating to the manner of assessing taxes upon personal property held in trust, apply to property in the hands of a receiver appointed by the circuit court of the United States to hold and invest the same, and to pay over the income thereof to another person, until the further order of the court. *Bates* v. *Boston*, 5 Cush. 93 (1849).

26. A., residing in another state, owned a building in Lawrence, in this state, standing by consent on the land of another person. The building was taxed to A. in Lawrence, as real estate belonging to a non-resident, but was subsequently sold by the tax collector as personal property. *Held*, that the sale was void. *Flanders* v. *Cross*, 10 Cush, 514 (1852).

27. Under the Rev. Sts. c. 7, an unmarried woman, an inhabitant of this state, is not taxable here for the principal or income of shares in corporations held in trust by trustees residing in another state, to pay the income to her. *Dorr* v. *Boston*, 6 Gray, 131 (1856). But see Gen. Sts. c. 11, § 12, cl. 5.

28. A corporation incorporated by the laws of another state, and authorized by a statute of Massachusetts to hold real estate here, is taxable for stock employed in manufactures in a town in this state where it carries on its business. *Blackstone Manuf. Co.* v. *Blackstone*, 13 Gray, 488 (1859).

29. The personal estate of an unmarried woman is liable to taxation in this commonwealth, although by the constitution women are not allowed to vote. *Wheeler* v. *Wall*, 6 Allen, 558 (1863).

30. Bonds issued under special legislative authority, by a state or city, for aiding in the construction of railroads, are public stocks, and taxable as such, under Gen. Sts. c. 11, § 4. *Hall* v. *Middlesex*, 10 Allen, 100 (1865).

31. A gas light company is not a public corporation in such a sense as to be exempt from taxation for its real estate and machinery in the town in which such real estate and machinery are situated. *Commonwealth* v. *Lowell Gas Light Co.* 12 Allen, (1866).

32. The mains, supply pipes and meters of a gas light company are "machinery" within the meaning of Gen. Sts. c. 11, § 12, cl. 2, and are taxable as such in the town where they are situated. *Ib.*

II. Where and to whom Polls and Property shall be assessed.

Where to be Assessed.

33. Where part of a town was incorporated into a new town, in accordance with a vote of the old town which provided that certain ministerial lands of the old town lying within the limits of the new town should not be taxed for town charges in the new town; it was held, that such lands were exempt from taxation for town charges in the new town, especially after the new town had omitted for one hundred and forty years to tax these lands. *Capen* v. *Glover*, 4 Mass. 305 (1808).

34. No man can be holden to pay for his poll, or for the same estate, any state or town tax but in one town during the same year. Parsons C. J., in *Richards* v. *Dagget*, 4 Mass. 539 (1808).

35. A manufacturing corporation is taxable for its real property in the town where it lies; but not for its personal property used in and about its manufactory. *Salem Iron Co.* v. *Danvers*, 10 Mass. 514 (1813). *Amesbury Woollen Co.* v. *Amesbury*, 17 Mass. 461 (1821).

36. A person liable to be taxed in one town for his poll and personal estate cannot legally be assessed for the same in another town; and if so assessed, even with his own consent, still he cannot be compelled to pay the tax. *Preston* v. *Boston*, 12 Pick. 7 (1831).

37. Where a dam extended across a river, the thread of which was the dividing line between two towns, and the water power created thereby was applied exclusively to drive mills situated in one of the towns, it was held, that the water power was not subject to taxation in the other town. *Boston Manuf. Co.* v. *Newton*, 22 Pick. 22 (1839).

38. One living in the town of A., and hiring a store in the town of B., in which he deposited a cargo of salt for sale, and also owning and fitting vessels in B., is liable to be taxed therefor in B. But for his income derived from business as an underwriter transacted in B., he is taxable in the town of A. *Little* v. *Greenleaf*, 7 Mass. 236 (1810). See *Gray* v. *Kettell*, 12 Mass. 160.

39. The owner of goods, wares and merchandise, living in one town, and doing business in another, where he has a privilege in a counting-room and has goods stored, but does not otherwise hire or occupy any store, shop or wharf, is not liable to taxation for such goods in the town where he so does his business. *Huckins* v. *Boston*, 4 Cush. 543 (1849).

40. A firm doing business in Boston as booksellers and publishers are not liable to taxes in Cambridge by reason of their keeping deposited in Cambridge some materials used in their business, and having some of their printing and binding done for them there by other firms. *Little* v. *Cambridge*, 9 Cush. 298 (1852).

41. The plaintiff, residing in Barre, hired a store in Boston every year, from December 1st to March 1st, and kept a stock of goods there for sale during that period, but had no establishment there on the first of May. *Held*, that the stock was not taxable in Boston. *Field* v. *Boston*, 10 Cush. 65 (1852).

42. Stock in trade of a partnership, employed in manufacturing or in any of the mechanic arts in a town in which the firm have not their principal place of business, but in which they hire or occupy a manufactory, shop, store or wharf, may be taxed in that town as one "other than where the owners reside," under Rev. Sts. c. 7, § 10, cl. 1, and § 13, and St. 1839, c. 139, § 1, (Gen. Sts. c. 11, § 12, cl. 1,) although one of the partners resides in that town. *Lee* v. *Templeton*, 6 Gray, 579 (1856).

43. To constitute an occupation, within the meaning of Rev. Sts. c. 7, § 10, cl. 1, and St. 1839, c. 139, § 1, (Gen. Sts. c. 11, § 12, cl. 1,) of a manufactory, shop, store or wharf, there must be an actual possession, use and efficient control of it — such an occupation as one who owns or hires would ordinarily have. *Ib.*

44. Merchants, sending goods to a manufactory not owned or hired by them, in a town in which they do not reside, to be passed through one of the processes of manufacturing by one who contracts to put the goods through that process, and who, in order to secure a continuance of their custom, permits them to sort and count the goods there before finishing, and to pack them there afterwards, do not thereby "occupy" the manufactory, within the meaning of Rev. Sts. c. 7, § 10, cl. 1, and St. 1839, c. 139, § 1, (Gen. Sts. c. 11, § 12, cl. 1,) so as to be liable to taxation for such goods in the town where the manufactory is situated. *Ib.*

45. Under St. 1839, c. 139, stocks in trade and stock employed in manufacturing in a town within the state other than where the owner resides, is taxable in such town, if the owner hire or occupy a manufactory therein, although the owner is an inhabitant of another state. *Leonard* v. *New Bedford*, 16 Gray, (1860). And see now Gen. Sts. c. 11, § 12, cl. 1.

46. Under the Rev. Sts. c. 7, § 13, and St. 1839, c. 139, § 2, ships belonging to a partnership and employed in its business are to be taxed to the partners jointly in the town where their business is carried on, and not separately at their places of residence. *Peabody* v. *Essex*, 10 Gray, 97 (1857). But see now Gen. Sts. c. 11, § 16.

47. A person is liable to be taxed in the town where he resides on the first day of May, although he and his estate may be set off to another town by a special statute, before the assessment is completed and the tax bill delivered to the collector. *Harman* v. *New Marlborough*, 9 Cush. 525 (1852).

48. Under Rev. Sts. c. 7, § 10, cl. 7, the personal estate of a deceased person is taxable in the town where he last dwelt, until his executors or administrators give notice to the assessors thereof that it has been distributed and paid over to the persons interested therein. *Hardy* v. *Yarmouth*, 6 Allen, 277 (1863). And see Gen. Sts. c. 11, § 12, cl. 7.

49. The personal estate of a deceased person, which is taxable in the town where he last dwelt, under Rev. Sts. c. 7, § 10, (Gen. Sts. c. 11, § 12,) cl. 7, is not taxable in any other town. *Ib.*

50. If the trustees of trust property which is taxable to them as the owners thereof, under Rev. Sts. c. 7, § 9, reside in different towns, the property should be apportioned among them, for the purpose of taxation, and the share of each taxed in the town where he resides. *Ib.* See Gen. Sts. c. 11, § 12, cl. 5.

51. Returning a list of trust property to the assessors of a town in which it is not taxable does not authorize its taxation therein. *Ib.*

To whom to be Assessed.

52. A tax on land belonging to a company, in the occupation of their agent, who is one of the company, may be set to such agent by his name; nor will it vitiate such tax that there is added to his name the title of agent of said company. *Welles* v. *Battelle*, 11 Mass. 477 (1814).

53. Non-resident owners of real estate may be taxed therefor, although the real estate is in the actual occupation of tenants at will. *Newburyport Turnpike* v. *Upton*, 12 Mass. 575 (1815).

54. The real and personal property of minors should be assessed to their guardians personally. *Payson* v. *Tufts*, 13 Mass. 493 (1816). *Baldwin* v. *Fitchburg*, 8 Pick. 494 (1829). And see Gen. Sts. c. 11, § 12, cl. 4.

55. A tax cannot be legally assessed upon a person after his decease; but the assessment should be upon his estate in the hands of his heir, administrator, or whoever else may be in possession of the same. *Cook* v. *Leland*, 5 Pick. 236 (1827). See Gen. Sts. c. 11, § 12, cl. 7; *Hardy* v. *Yarmouth*, 6 Allen, 277 (*ante*, 48).

56. In December, 1845, O. S. died, leaving a will, in which A. S. was named as executor, by whom the will was presented for probate; but the validity thereof being controverted, A. S., in December, 1846, was appointed special administrator; and the validity of the will being established in August, 1847, A. S. was appointed executor under the same: The assessors of the town of H., in which the deceased last dwelt, having assessed a tax to A. S., in May, 1864, for the estate of O. S. in his hands as executor, it was held, that under the peculiar circumstances of the case, the same was rightly assessed. *Smith* v. *Northampton Bank*, 4 Cush. 1 (1849).

57. Before the revised statutes, (Gen. Sts. c. 11, § 13,) a ministerial fund in the hands of incorporated trustees, the interest of which was to be paid by them to the treasurer of the parish for the minister, was rightfully assessed to the trustees. *Gloucester* v. *Gloucester*, 19 Pick. 542 (1837).

58. The poll tax of minors who are in the service of a manufacturing corporation, and receiving salaries, cannot be legally assessed to said corporation. *Boston & Sandwich Glass Co.* v. *Boston*, 4 Met. 181 (1842).

59. The provision of Rev. Sts. c. 7, § 10, cl. 5, that all personal property held in trust, the income of which is to be paid to any married woman residing within the state, shall be assessed to the husband of such married woman in the town of which he is an inhabitant, applies to property in the hands of a receiver of the circuit court of the United States, appointed by that court to hold and invest the same, and to pay over the income thereof to such married woman until the further order of the court. *Bates* v. *Boston*, 5 Cush. 93 (1849). See Gen. Sts. c. 11, § 12.

60. Property held in trust by the "Trustees of the Greene Foundation," a chartered corporation, to apply the income to the support of an assistant minister of Trinity Church, in Boston, is taxable to the corporation in Boston, although the assistant minister, who is entitled to receive the income, resides in Brookline. *Trustees of the Greene Foundation* v. *Boston*, 12 Cush. 54 (1853).

As to Domicil.

61. A citizen of Boston, who had been at school in the city of Edinburgh when a boy, and formed a predilection for that place as a residence, and had expressed a determination to reside there, if he ever should have the means of so doing, removed with his family to that city in 1836, declaring at the time of his departure that he intended to reside abroad, and that if he should return to the United States he should not live in Boston. He resided in Edinburgh and the vicinity as a housekeeper, taking a lease of an estate for a term of years, and endeavored to engage an American to enter his family for two years, as an instructor of his children. Before he left Boston he made a contract for the sale of his mansion house and furniture there, but shortly afterwards procured said contract to be annulled, (assigning as his reason therefor that, in case of his death in Europe, his wife might wish to return to Boston,) and let his house and furniture to a tenant. *Held*, that he had changed his domicil, and was not liable to taxation as an inhabitant of Boston in 1837. *Thorndike* v. *Boston*, 1 Met. 242 (1840).

62. A native inhabitant of Boston, intending to reside in France with his family, departed for that country in June, 1836, and was followed by his family about three months afterwards. His dwelling-house and furniture were leased for a year, and he hired a house in Paris for a year. At the time of his departure, he intended to return and resume his residence in Boston, but had not fixed on any time for his return. He returned in about sixteen months, and his family in about nine months afterwards. *Held*, that he continued to be an inhabitant of Boston, and that he was rightly taxed there, during his absence, upon his poll and personal property. *Sears* v. *Boston*, 1 Met. 250 (1840).

63. Where a dwelling-house is so divided by the boundary line between two towns as to leave that portion of the house in which the occupant mainly and substantially performs those offices which characterize his home, (such as sleeping, eating, sitting and receiving visitors,) in one town, he is a citizen of that town, and has no right to elect to reside and be taxed for his personal property in the other town. *Chenery* v. *Waltham*, 8 Cush. 327 (1851).

64. O., a native of Boston, removed to New York in 1828, where he resided until 1840, at which time he returned to Boston, and continued an inmate of his father's family until 1848, when his father died. He then took rooms at a hotel, and remained in Boston, employed as executor of his father's will, until April 5, 1849. During this whole period he frequently expressed an intention of leaving Boston and removing to Europe or New York. On April 5, 1849, he went to New York, intending to sail for Europe, and either to fix his residence in Paris or return to New York. He did not sail from New York, but returned to Boston on May 7th, and sailed from that city June 6, 1849. In June, 1850, he returned and established his residence at Newport. *Held*, that he was an inhabitant of Boston on May 1, 1849, for the purpose of taxation. *Otis* v. *Boston*, 12 Cush. 44 (1853).

65. C. owned dwelling-houses in Boston, in Brookline, and in Beverly. He usually resided in Brookline about seven months of each year, from some time in April to November, (except a few weeks in midsummer, spent at his house in Beverly,) when he closed that house and removed to Boston until the following April. In April, 1850, the usual preparations were made for him to close the house in Boston and remove to Brookline, but from illness he was not able to go personally until some time in May. On the 28th of April he informed the assessors of Brookline of the cause of his detention in Boston, and that he desired to continue a citizen of Brookline, and taxable there, where for many years he had been taxed and had exercised all municipal rights and privileges. *Held*, that although actually in Boston on May 1, 1850, he was not rightfully taxed there upon his poll and personal estate. *Cabot* v. *Boston*, 12 Cush. 52 (1853).

66. A person is not taxable as having a residence in the city of Boston, who habitually resides, for seven months of the year, in his own house in another town, where he has for twenty years been taxed for his poll and personal property, and voted and exercised the rights of citizenship, although he spends five months of each year, including the winter months, in a house owned by him in Boston. *Lee* v. *Boston*, 2 Gray, 484 (1854).

67. An inhabitant of P., being out of health, gave up business there, and removed to F., with the intention of remaining there through the summer and returning to P. in the autumn, to reside and do business there. The next autumn his health was restored, but, not finding satisfactory business in P., he remained in F. until the following March, when he entered into business elsewhere, and intended, as soon as he could make arrangements, to remove to C. to reside, and made a contract for the removal of his furniture to C. as soon as possible, and on the first of May put it on board a vessel, and a few days after personally removed to C. *Held*, that he was rightly taxed in F. on said first of May. *Carnoe* v. *Freetown*, 9 Gray, 357 (1857).

68. A man who was born and resided in child-

hood in Vermont, afterwards lived in New York for five years next preceding his coming of age, then spent some months at his former home in Vermont in search of employment, and afterwards, for the same purpose, went to St. Louis and obtained employment as a clerk, but under no contract for any fixed length of time, and there became engaged to marry a woman residing at Roxbury, and came to Massachusetts in March to fulfil his engagement, without intending to make Roxbury his residence, hired a house in Brookline, at a rent beginning on the 1st of April, and put into it servants and furniture, and his own and his betrothed wife's movable property. They were married at Roxbury on the 9th of April, and immediately took a wedding tour, with no intention of returning to Roxbury, and on the 2d of May returned to the house in Brookline and resided there. *Held*, that his domicil was in Brookline on the first of May. *Williams* v. *Roxbury*, 12 Gray, 21 (1858).

69. A. formerly lived in Boston, and afterwards went to New Orleans, where he took up his residence, went into business, and became permanently fixed as a merchant, and has had no other place of business since. He married at the South, had children, came to Boston with them, intending to return, bought a house, commenced housekeeping, and sent his children to the public schools. He was in the habit of coming to Boston every summer, and remaining there and in the vicinity for a few months. He left his family in Boston for the benefit of his children's health, for two years, returned himself to his business at New Orleans, always styled himself as of New Orleans, exercised the rights and performed the duties of a citizen there, and in no other place, and intended that his domicil should be there. *Held*, that the supreme judicial court ought not to set aside a verdict which found, upon proof of the above facts, that his domicil was in New Orleans. *Cochrane* v. *Boston*, 4 Allen, 177 (1862).

70. If a minor leaves the domicil of his origin with the consent of his guardian, and lives for two consecutive years exclusively in another town, considering it as his home, with no definite intent on the part of his guardian to cause him to return, he acquires a new domicil in the latter place, and his property is properly taxable there. *Kirkland* v. *Whately*, 4 Allen, 462 (1862).

71. A person is legally taxable for personal property in the town of which he is an inhabitant when the tax is assessed; but his election to pay such tax in one town rather than in another, is only one circumstance bearing upon the question of his actual habitancy, and must be taken in connection with the other circumstances of the case, in order to determine where he is legally liable. *Lyman* v *Fiske*, 17 Pick. 231 (1835).

72. Whether a person removing from one town to another intends to change his residence, is a question of fact, and not of law. *Fitchburg* v. *Winchendon*, 4 Cush. 190 (1849).

73. If an inhabitant of a town removes to another town in this commonwealth, not intending to remain there permanently, but with the intention of not returning to his former home, and does not so return, he loses his domicil in the former town. *Mead* v. *Boxborough*, 11 Cush. 362 (1853).

74. The fact that a person was taxed in the town to which he has removed, is not competent evidence to show that he did not continue to be taxable in the town of his former residence. *Ib.*

75. An inhabitant of this commonwealth, who removes from the town of his residence, with the intention of never residing there again, and of removing to another state, is still, so long as he remains in this commonwealth, liable to taxation in that town, until he acquires another domicil. *Bulkley* v. *Williamstown*, 3 Gray, 493 (1855).

76. An inhabitant of the town of Rochester in this commonwealth removed out of the state on April 10, 1858, with the intention not to return or have his home in that town, and to make his future abode and home in Motthaven, in the state of New York. But before he took up his abode in Motthaven, he stopped at the abode of his son-in-law in the city of New York until and including May 1, 1858, and shortly afterwards went to Motthaven, where he subsequently resided. *Held*, that he was not an inhabitant of Rochester on May 1, 1858, nor taxable therein for his personal estate. *Briggs* v. *Rochester*, 16 Gray, (1860).

77. The words in Rev. Sts. c. 7, § 9, "where he shall be an inhabitant on the first day of May," are to be construed as meaning "where he shall have his home" on that day. *Ib.*

78. A man's declarations as to the place of his residence, and his designation thereof in his will, are competent evidence after his death, upon the question of his domicil, at a time shortly after the making of the declarations and of the will. *Wilson* v. *Terry*, 9 Allen, 214 (1864).

78 *a*. After proof of a man's declarations of his intention to leave a town, evidence is competent, upon the question of his domicil, that he was not there, except occasionally and for short visits, afterwards. *Wilson* v. *Terry*, 11 Allen, (1865).

78 *b*. If on a question of domicil instructions were given to the jury in the form of general propositions, which, when taken together, correctly express the law of the case and

contain all necessary explanations and qualifications, a new trial will not be granted for the reason that a single passage, taken abstractly, may have been erroneous. *Adams* v. *Nantucket*, 11 Allen, (1865).

See Domicil.

III. Manner and Validity of the Assessment.

79. An agreement between neighboring towns, not to tax in one the lands of the inhabitants of the other in their own occupation, is invalid. *Dillingham* v. *Snow*, 5 Mass. 547 (1809).

80. Assessors are not compellable to assess an illegal tax. They may exercise their judgment on the subjects for which the money appears to be voted; and they may refuse to cause the collection to be enforced, if they deem the tax illegal. Parker, C. J., in *Stetson* v. *Kempton*, 13 Mass. 282 (1816).

81. If a tax is illegally assessed, it need not be lost. The tax may be re-assessed, or the town may renew their vote to raise the money. Parker, C. J., in *Libby* v. *Burnham*, 15 Mass. 148 (1818).

82. In assessing improved lands, it is not necessary in invoices or tax lists to specify the number of acres; it is sufficient if the value of the land is stated. *Welles* v. *Battelle*, 11 Mass. 477 (1814).

83. Taxes must be assessed upon a valuation made for the year in which they are assessed, and cannot be assessed upon the valuation of the preceding year. *Nason* v. *Whitney*, 1 Pick. 140 (1822).

84. It is essential to the validity of an assessment of taxes that the valuation on which it is based, or a copy of it, should be deposited in the assessors' office. *Thayer* v. *Stearns*, 1 Pick. 482 (1823). See *Blossom* v. *Cannon*, 14 Mass. 177; Gen. Sts. c. 11, § 33.

85. The assessment of half a poll tax upon an individual is, it seems, illegal. *Southampton* v. *Easthampton*, 8 Pick. 380 (1829).

86. Assessors cannot lawfully add more than five per cent. to the amount of any tax which they are authorized to assess. *Libby* v. *Burnham*, 15 Mass. 144 (1818). *Charlemont* v. *Conway*, 8 Pick. 408 (1829). Gen. Sts. c. 11, § 32.

87. Under a vote to raise the sum of $250, assessors have no authority to assess a tax of $285.01. *Joyner* v. *Egremont*, 3 Cush. 567 (1849).

88. The circumstance that in the assessment of a tax, some individuals are assessed who are not liable to the tax, does not vitiate the assessment as respects those who are liable; and a second assessment made for the purpose of rectifying the error is illegal and void. *Inglee* v. *Bosworth*, 5 Pick. 498 (1827).

89. If assessors omit, through error of judgment or mistake of law, to assess a tax on an individual, the omission does not invalidate the assessment in regard to other persons. *Williams* v. *Lunenburg*, 21 Pick. 75 (1838).

90. A tax is not rendered void by the omission of the assessors to tax all the property of an individual which ought to be taxed. *Watson* v. *Princeton*, 4 Met. 599 (1842). See *George* v. *Mendon*, 6 Met. 497.

91. Where one is taxed and pays more than his due proportion of a town tax, in consequence of the omission of the assessors to tax other persons their due proportion, he cannot maintain an action against the town for money had and received, to recover back any part of the tax so paid. *Watson* v. *Princeton*, 4 Met. 599 (1842). *George* v. *Mendon*, 6 Met. 497 (1843).

92. Under St. 1823, c. 133, a tax was valid, although the assessors' list of assessments, and the rate lists committed to the collector, contained no separate column for income. *Blackburn* v. *Walpole*, 9 Pick. 97 (1829).

93. The provision of statute requiring that notice respecting an abatement to those who pay their taxes promptly, shall be posted up in public places, is merely directory to the assessors, and the plaintiff in an action of trespass against a collector for taking his goods in levying his tax, cannot avail himself of a failure in this respect, as an objection to the validity of the assessment. *Sprague* v. *Bailey*, 19 Pick. 436 (1837).

94. Nor can the plaintiff in such an action avail himself of the omission of the assessors to follow precisely the form of valuation prescribed by the statute. *Ib.*

95. A town voted to raise a certain sum for the support of schools and another sum for contingent expenses; and in assessing these sums, together with the county tax, the assessors made one list of the school tax and another of the county tax and the sum voted for contingent expenses, and on the first list the sum assessed exceeded the sum voted for schools by more than five per cent., but the excess on both lists together was less than five per cent. on the whole amount to be raised by taxation. It was held, that the assessment was valid. *Alvord* v. *Collin*, 20 Pick. 418 (1838).

96. An assessment by the assessors of a town, in pursuance of a legislative grant and apportionment of a state tax, would be valid, although made by the assessors without any warrant from the state treasurer. *Ib.*

97. So an assessment of a county tax, duly

granted and apportioned among the several towns in the county, would be valid, although made by the assessors without any warrant from the county treasurer. *Ib.*

98. Where in the assessment of a tax on unimproved land of a non-resident proprietor, the land, by mistake, was set in the list against the name of the previous owner, but was otherwise properly and sufficiently described, the tax was held to have been legally assessed. *Ib.*

99. A building owned by one person and standing by consent upon the land of another, should be assessed to the owner as personal and not as real estate. *Flanders* v. *Cross*, 10 Cush. 514 (1852).

100. The provision in Rev. Sts. c. 8, § 5, (Gen. Sts. c. 12, § 6,) that "if, in the assessors' lists, or in their warrant and list committed to the collectors, there shall be any error in the name of any person taxed, the tax assessed to him may, notwithstanding such error, be collected of the person intended to be taxed, provided he is taxable, and can be identified by the assessors," applies to the case of a person whose surname only is inserted in the list of the valuation and in the tax list committed to the collector. *Tyler* v. *Hardwick*, 6 Met. 470 (1843). See *Trustees, &c.* v. *Boston*, 12 Cush. 56; *Sargent* v. *Bean*, 7 Gray, 125.

101. Where the assessors' list of valuation and assessment of polls and estates did not exhibit in distinct columns the "true value of real estate" and the "reduced value," as required by the revised statutes, but contained a column of the "value," (and the like as to personal estate,) it was held, that the irregularity did not render the valuation and assessment void. *Torrey* v. *Millbury*, 21 Pick. 64 (1838). See Gen. Sts. c. 11, § 34.

102. A town voted to raise and appropriate a certain sum for purchasing a fire engine, provided the same amount should be raised by private subscription within ninety days, the engine to be located by the selectmen. A subscription was obtained for the sum required, but on condition that the engine should be located in a particular place designated, and in consequence the assessors declined accepting it. Thereupon, with the consent of a portion of the subscribers, but without the knowledge of the others, the condition was erased; but one of the subscribers verbally guaranteed to the assessors that the whole sum should be paid; and in this form the subscription was accepted, and the sum voted by the town was assessed. It was held, that there was a substantial compliance with the proviso of the vote, and, therefore, that the assessment was authorized. *Ib.*

103. Where a town chooses three assessors, two of whom are sworn, and the third does not refuse to accept the trust, but omits to take the oath of office, and when called upon by the other two declines to act, and the town does not choose another in his stead, the other two have authority to assess taxes. *George* v. *Mendon*, 6 Met. 497 (1843).

104. If one of three assessors, after due notice, refuses to attend and act in assessing a tax, the other two may proceed without him. *Williams* v. *Lunenburg*, 21 Pick. 75 (1838).

105. The list of estates, real and personal, which the inhabitants of towns are required to present to the assessors, before an assessment of taxes is made, is not intended to contain a statement of the estimated value of the property; and if the list contains a statement of the value, such statement is not, by Rev. Sts. c. 7, § 22, (Gen. Sts. c. 11, § 25,) conclusive on the assessors; but they are to exercise their own judgment in estimating the value of the property. *Newburyport* v. *Essex*, 12 Met. 211 (1846).

106. Assessors have no power to waive the bringing in of such list. *Winnisimmet Co.* v. *Chelsea*, 6 Cush. 477 (1850).

107. Such list must be brought in before the tax is assessed. *Porter* v. *Norfolk*, 5 Gray, 365 (1855).

108. Under Rev. Sts. c. 7, § 27, (Gen. Sts. c. 11, § 31,) the omission to assess upon the polls one sixth part of the state tax renders the whole assessment illegal. *Goodrich* v. *Lunenburg*, 9 Gray, 38 (1857). *Gerry* v. *Stoneham*, 1 Allen, 319 (1861). But see now Gen. Sts. c. 11, § 54.

109. An inhabitant of a town is not entitled to recover back the amount of a tax paid by him therein, although, (1.) The record of the choice of assessors, by whom the tax was assessed, as originally made, did not show that they were chosen by ballot, if they were in fact so chosen, and the record has been amended; (2.) The whole amount assessed in the town was less than the whole sum voted to be raised, by a sum exactly equivalent to the amount voted for bridges, if there was also a vote at the same meeting to repair the bridges by a labor tax; (3.) A vote was passed to make a discount on such taxes on property as should be paid within a specified time, but no discount on poll taxes, and a direction to this effect was inserted in the warrant to the collector; (4.) The valuation list was not deposited with the chairman of the assessors until the day before the tax list was committed to the collector; (5.) The valuation list contained no specification of particulars, under the several classes of property assessed, but only a general estimate of the value of each class, if the plaintiff did not furnish to the

assessors a list of his property. *Tobey* v. *Wareham*, 2 Allen, 594 (1861).

110. This court cannot say that a city or town may be excused from levying a tax according to the requirement of St. 1863, c. 218, on the ground that an insufficient time was allowed for the assessment and collection thereof, although the warrant for the tax was not received from the state treasurer until the ordinary taxes of such city or town had been assessed and committed to its treasurer for collection. *Lowell* v. *Oliver*, 8 Allen, 247 (1864).

111. Assessors of taxes are not bound by a list of property brought in for assessment and sworn to, if it appears from an examination of the person who brings it in that it is not true. *Hall* v. *Middlesex*, 10 Allen, 100 (1865).

112. Towns may raise money at a meeting duly called after the annual meeting; and if at the annual meeting they have voted to raise so much money as to require the assessment of the full sum allowed by law to be assessed upon polls in any one year, a tax subsequently voted must be assessed only upon property. *Freeland* v. *Hastings*, 10 Allen, 570 (1865).

112 *a*. Sales of the stock of a manufacturing corporation do not furnish the only test of the value of their real estate and machinery for the purpose of taxation, although the corporation owns no other property than this real estate and machinery, and owes no debts. The market value of shares of stock in such corporation is liable to be controlled by circumstances which do not affect the value of its real estate and machinery as a whole. *Chicopee* v. *Hampden*, 16 Gray, (1860).

112 *b*. Stock in corporations established in other states is to be assessed to stockholders in this state at its full value, and no deduction is to be made on account of taxation to which such corporations are subject in the states where they are established. *Dwight* v. *Boston*, 12 Allen, (1866).

See Appropriations.

IV. Collection of Taxes.

(a) Generally.

113. A collector of taxes is competent to collect taxes granted and agreed on before his appointment to office. *Colburn* v. *Ellis*, 7 Mass. 89 (1810).

114. Constables are *ex officio* collectors of taxes, when none others are appointed. *Colman* v. *Anderson*, 10 Mass. 105 (1813). Gen. Sts. c. 18, § 71.

115. A selectman and assessor of a town may legally be chosen collector of taxes also. *Howard* v. *Proctor*, 7 Gray, 128 (1856).

116. A collector of taxes may be sworn at any time before entering upon the duties of his office; and his oath need not be matter of record, but may be proved by parol. *Ib.*

117. A collector of taxes is not obliged to return his warrant to the assessors. *Ib.*

118. A town record, showing a vote "to let out the collection of the taxes at auction immediately to the lowest bidder whom the town will accept," the bidding off of the collection of taxes, and a choice of the lowest bidder to be collector for the ensuing year, shows a sufficient authority to the person elected to collect the taxes; especially if he has previously been chosen constable. *Ib.*

119. Where a person was chosen collector of taxes "by bidding off the office at vendue," by which "he was to collect the taxes of the town for five per cent.," the election was sustained; but if the terms of the vendue had been that the person who would collect the taxes for the lowest compensation, should at all events, without regard to his fitness or qualifications, be the collector, it seems, that the election would have been illegal and void. *Alvord* v. *Collin*, 20 Pick. 418 (1838).

120. A deputy collector appointed under Rev. Sts c. 15, § 60, (Gen. Sts. c. 18, § 57,) by a collector who is also town treasurer, may execute a warrant for the collection of taxes, though he be appointed deputy before the warrant was issued, and though the warrant be directed to the collector only. *Aldrich* v. *Aldrich*, 8 Met. 102 (1844).

121. If the facts under which a town treasurer was to issue his warrant of distress, under St. 1785, c. 46, against a collector, for neglecting to collect and pay over taxes committed to him for collection, were properly certified to him, he had no discretion, but was obliged to issue his warrant. *Waldron* v. *Lee*, 5 Pick. 323 (1827). See now Gen. Sts. c. 12, § 51.

122. An assessors' warrant made out and signed by the assessors, with one seal affixed while they were together, and concluding with "given under our hands," without adding "and seals," was held to be valid. *Bradford* v. *Randall*, 5 Pick. 496 (1827). See now Gen. Sts. c. 11, § 39.

123. A warrant to a collector of taxes, signed by only a majority of the assessors, is valid. *Sprague* v. *Bailey*, 19 Pick. 436 (1837).

124. The provision in the "act to amend the revised statutes,"(Rev. Sts.page 804; Gen.Sts. c. 12, § 16,) that when any person committed to jail for non-payment of taxes, shall be discharged by taking the poor debtors' oath, "the collector shall be liable to pay the tax, with the charges of imprisonment, unless he shall have arrested and committed the party within one year after the tax was committed to him to collect," does not render the col-

lector liable to pay for the support of the person so committed, while in jail. *Townsend* v. *Walcutt*, 3 Met. 152 (1841).

125. Taxes, being neither judgments nor contracts, are not subject to be set off in an action by a tax payer against the city entitled to his tax. *Peirce* v. *Boston*, 3 Met. 520 (1842). See *Commonwealth* v. *Phœnix Bank*, 11 Met. 135; *Appleton* v. *Hopkins*, 5 Gray, 533.

126. The provision in Rev. Sts. c. 8, § 5, (Gen. Sts. c. 12, § 6,) that "if, in the assessors' lists, or their warrant and list committed to the collectors, there shall be any error in the name of any person taxed, the tax assessed to him may, notwithstanding such error, be collected of the person intended to be taxed, provided he is taxable, and can be identified by the assessors," applies to the case of a person whose surname only is inserted in the list of valuation and in the tax list committed to the collector. *Tyler* v. *Hardwick*, 6 Met. 470 (1843).

127. A tax warrant is not void by reason of containing an assessment of real and personal estate to two owners jointly, if it does not appear that the real estate was held by them as partners. *Howard* v. *Proctor*, 7 Gray, 128 (1856).

128. Nor by reason of containing an assessment of two poll taxes to two tenants in common of land; nor by reason of assessing a number of poll taxes to one person. *Ib.*

129. A tax warrant, good upon its face, protects the collector acting under it, notwithstanding any irregularity in the meetings at which, or the votes by which, the taxes were assessed. *Ib.*

130. A warrant to a collector of taxes, which directs him to collect the amount of a highway tax "in money or receipts from the surveyor of highways," is unauthorized by law. *Cheshire* v. *Howland*, 13 Gray, 321 (1859).

131. A collector of taxes is not responsible to the town for not collecting taxes under a warrant illegal on its face. *Ib.* See *Adams* v. *Farnsworth*, 16 Gray, .

132. When a person, after the assessment of a tax upon him, removes out of the precinct of the collector without paying his tax, and the collector issues a warrant, under St. 1842, c. 34, (Gen. Sts. c. 12, § 18,) to the sheriff of the county or his deputy, for the collection of such tax, the warrant must set forth the fact that the person taxed has removed out of the precinct of the collector without paying his tax, or it is invalid. *Williamstown* v. *Willis*, 16 Gray, (1860). But see *Cheever* v. *Merritt*, 5 Allen, 563 (*post*, 186).

133. But in such case if in fact the person taxed has removed out of the precinct of the collector without paying his tax, and a warrant has been issued to a deputy sheriff for its collection which omits to set forth the fact of such removal, and the deputy sheriff collects the tax upon such warrant, the sheriff is liable to the town for the default of his deputy in not paying over said tax to the town. *Ib.*

(b) By Action at Law.

134. A collector of taxes cannot maintain an action to recover them in any case besides those in which an action is given to him by the Rev. Sts. c. 8, § 15 (Gen. Sts. c. 12, §§ 19, 20). *Crapo* v. *Stetson*, 8 Met. 393 (1844).

135. A collector of taxes, in an action under St. 1789, c. 4, (Gen. Sts. c. 12, § 19,) cannot recover interest on the amount of the taxes demanded in the action. *Danforth* v. *Williams*, 9 Mass. 324 (1812).

136. If a person, after the assessment of a tax upon him, leave the precinct of the collector, with the intention of returning at the expiration of six months, this is a removal, within the meaning of Rev. Sts. c. 8, §§ 14, 15, (Gen. Sts. c. 12, §§ 18, 19,) which provide that if any person, after being assessed, remove out of the precinct of the collector without paying the tax, the collector may, in his own name, maintain an action therefor, in like manner as for his own debt. *Houghton* v. *Davenport*, 23 Pick. 235 (1839).

137. In an action brought by the collector of taxes for the town of Groton to recover a tax assessed upon the defendant for the year 1839, it being admitted that shortly before the tax was assessed the defendant was an inhabitant of Groton; it was held, that the burden was on the defendant to prove that he had, before the first of May, 1839, changed his domicil. *Kilburn* v. *Bennett*, 3 Met. 199 (1841).

138. When a person who is sued by a town collector for the recovery of a tax, defends on the ground that he was not an inhabitant of the town where he was taxed, at the time when the tax was assessed, but had removed therefrom, and this defence fails, he may then defend on the ground that he has not removed from the town since the tax was assessed. *Crapo* v. *Stetson*, 8 Met. 393 (1844).

139. A mortgagee of land, who has taken possession thereof for the purpose of foreclosure since the enactment of the General Statutes, is liable to an action, under Gen. Sts. c. 12, § 40, by the collector of taxes, for the unpaid taxes thereon. *Andrews* v. *Worcester Ins. Co.* 5 Allen, 65 (1862).

(c) By Arrest.

140. Under St. 1785, c. 70, § 7, taxes on the unimproved lands of non-resident proprietors or on improved lands of proprietors liv-

ing without the state, were not a personal charge, but a lien upon the land only, and the proprietors could not lawfully be arrested for non-payment of such taxes. *Rising* v. *Granger*, 1 Mass. 47 (1804).

141. A warrant for the collection of taxes, properly issued to a collector by a board of assessors, is "a lawful warrant issued by a court of competent jurisdiction," within the meaning of St. 1837, c. 221, § 1, (Gen. Sts. c. 144, § 42,) and a person who is arrested upon such warrant by the proper officer, for non-payment of taxes, is not entitled, as of right, to the writ of personal replevin, and to be thereby delivered. *Aldrich* v. *Aldrich*, 8 Met. 102 (1844).

142. A warrant issued by assessors for the collection of a tax, justified the arrest by the collector of a party on whom a tax was assessed, although he might have received a certificate of discharge under the United States bankrupt act of 1841. The question whether such certificate released the party from the tax could not be tried in an action against the collector. *Ib.*

143. A collector of taxes, under a warrant from the assessors in which the time for the completion of the collection of the taxes therein mentioned is specified, may arrest a person for the non-payment of his tax, after the expiration of the time limited in the warrant for the collection and payment of the tax. *Bassett* v. *Porter*, 4 Cush. 487 (1849).

144. The St. of 1855, c. 444, abolishing imprisonment for debt, does not apply to a warrant of distress for non-payment of taxes. *Appleton* v. *Hopkins*, 5 Gray, 530 (1855).

145. A non-resident owner of real estate may be arrested for non-payment of taxes thereon, after due demand upon him, and failure of the officer upon diligent search to find any goods belonging to him or on the estate. *Snow* v. *Clark*, 9 Gray, 190 (1857).

145 *a*. An officer, who returns upon a warrant for the collection of a tax assessed upon real estate to a non-resident owner thereof, that "having made diligent search for goods of" the said owner "and for goods upon the said real estate, whereon to levy this warrant," he arrested the said owner, does not make himself liable as a trespasser, by not more distinctly stating that he was unable to find such goods. *Ib.*

146. A collector of taxes has no right, under the Rev. Sts. c. 8, § 11, (Gen. Sts. c. 12, § 13,) to take the body for non-payment of taxes, if sufficient property is shown to him upon which to levy; although fourteen days have elapsed since a demand of payment. *Lothrop* v. *Ide*, 13 Gray, 93 (1859).

147. The return of a collector of taxes upon his warrant is only *prima facie* evidence in his favor, in an action against him for an unlawful arrest. *Ib.*

148. In the service of a warrant of distress for the collection of a tax, the collector cannot lawfully arrest the body of a tax debtor, unless he is unable to find property whereon to levy it, and by means of which payment of the tax may be secured. *Hall* v. *Hall*, 3 Allen, 5 (1861).

149. One who is unlawfully arrested and committed to prison on a warrant of distress for the collection of a tax, may show, as competent evidence on the question of damages, in an action to recover for the illegal arrest and imprisonment, the manner in which he lived while detained in prison, if he was subjected only to the ordinary inconveniences of persons lawfully detained there. *Ib.*

See Actions, 14.

(d) By Distress and Sale ; Lien on Land.

150. A collector of taxes can sell a distress taken by him only under statute authority, as he derives no authority to sell from the common law. *Caldwell* v. *Eaton*, 5 Mass. 403 (1809). *Crapo* v. *Stetson*, 8 Met. 393 (1844).

151. If goods distrained for non-payment of taxes be sold by the collector after the expiration of the time limited by statute for making such sale, the delay renders the collector a trespasser *ab initio*; and he is liable to an action by the owner for the conversion of the goods, although no demand thereof be made before the commencement of the action, the tortious taking of personal property being a conversion. *Pierce* v. *Benjamin*, 14 Pick. 356 (1833). See Gen. Sts. c. 12, § 8.

152. In such action it appeared that the collector applied the proceeds of the sale in part payment of the tax, and that the owner subsequently paid him the residue and required a receipt for the whole amount of the tax in order that he might settle with his landlord. It was held, that this was not a waiver of the right to bring the action. *Ib.*

153. In such action it was held, that the measure of damages was the value of the goods, deducting the amount applied by the collector to the payment of the tax. *Ib.*

154. The provision in the tax act of 1824, (Gen. Sts. c. 12, § 22,) that "whenever any tax shall be assessed on any real estate liable to taxation, said tax shall be a lien on said estate," extends to county and city taxes as well as to state taxes. *Hayden* v. *Foster*, 13 Pick. 492 (1833).

155. Where separate and distinct real estates belong to the same owner, they are to be considered as distinct subjects of taxation, and must be separately valued and assessed; and each estate is subject to a lien for the payment of that portion only of the owner's

tax which shall be assessed on each particular estate. *Ib.* See *Howe* v. *Boston*, 7 Cush. 276.

156. Where, at a sale of goods for the non-payment of taxes, the collector of taxes became himself the purchaser, it was held, that such sale was voidable, at the election of the owner of the goods. *Pierce* v. *Benjamin*, 14 Pick. 356 (1833).

157. It seems, that in such case the owner, in order to maintain an action for the conversion of the goods, must elect to annul the sale before the commencement of the action. *Ib.*

158. Where in the advertisement of a sale of unimproved lands of non-resident proprietors for the payment of taxes, a parcel of land was set against the name of the previous owner, through ignorance of its having been conveyed, but the amount of the tax, the time and place of sale, the town in which the land lay, the number of the lot, and the quantity of the land were expressed, it was held, that the notice of sale was sufficient. *Alvord* v. *Collin*, 20 Pick. 418 (1838).

159. Where a witness, upon being shown a writing certifying that a notice of a sale was posted up in his inn, testified that the signature was in his handwriting, and that he had no doubt the certificate stated the truth, though he did not recollect the fact; it was held, that the posting up of the notice was duly proved. *Ib.*

160. Where the only defect in a warrant issued by assessors to a collector of taxes is an omission to direct him to sell distrained goods within seven days, he is justified by such warrant in distraining goods and selling them within seven days according to law. *King* v. *Whitcomb*, 1 Met. 328 (1840).

161. A demand by a collector of payment of a tax assessed on a non-resident, who has no agent or attorney within the Commonwealth, is sufficient to justify a subsequent seizure and sale of his goods, if such demand be made at his last and usual place of abode in the town where he is taxed. *Ib.*

162. A distress for the non-payment of a tax cannot be made after the death of the person on whom the tax is assessed. *Wilson* v. *Shearer*, 9 Met. 504 (1845).

163. Though a warrant to a collector erroneously direct him, for want of goods and chattels, whereon to make distress, for the space of twelve days after demanding payment, (instead of fourteen days, as directed by the Rev. Sts. c. 8, § 11; Gen. Sts. c. 12, § 13,) to take the body, &c., yet if the warrant be in other respects sufficient, this error therein will not vitiate it, so as to render illegal a distress made by virtue of it, if, in making the distress, the warrant be executed according to law. *Barnard* v. *Graves*, 13 Met. 85 (1847).

164. Under the Rev. Sts. c. 8, § 8, (Gen. Sts. c. 12, § 8,) a collector of taxes, who distrains goods, may post a notification of the sale thereof before the expiration of four days after the seizure. *Ib.*

165. The return made by a collector on his warrant, of his doings in making a distress for taxes, is so far an official act as to be *prima facie* evidence in his favor, on the trial of an action against him for making the distress. And a demand by him of payment of a tax before he made distress for it, may be shown by his return. The return must be taken to be true, until it is impeached; and if it is impeached merely by showing facts which would justify the collector equally well with those stated in his return, he may rely on such facts to sustain his justification. *Ib.*

166. A collector's notification of the sale of a horse, distrained for non-payment of a tax by the owner, need not mention the owner's name, nor describe the horse, nor state the amount of the tax; nor is such notification vitiated by the collector's adding to his signature the word "constable" instead of collector, he being in fact constable as well as collector. *Ib.*

167. A warrant to collect taxes, issued by assessors to a collector, does not authorize him to collect a tax by distress, unless it is accompanied with a tax list; but it is not necessary that the tax list should be annexed to the warrant. *Ib.*

168. The third section of St. 1848, c. 166, requiring that the advertisement of the time and place of sale of real estate taken for taxes shall "in addition to the provisions contained in Rev. Sts. c. 8, § 25, contain a substantially accurate description of the rights, lots or divisions of the real estate to be sold," is only explanatory of the statute referred to, under which a description, though not expressly required, was necessary, by which the owner might know what rights, lots or divisions were to be sold. *Farnum* v. *Buffum*, 4 Cush. 260 (1849). See Gen. Sts. c. 12, § 29.

169. Where, in an advertisement of the time and place of sale of real estate taken for taxes, estates were described in these terms: "M. B. house and land," and "L. E. house, barn and one hundred and fifteen acres of land," L. E. being a tenant of M. B., but H. M. having at the time taken possession of the estates under a mortgage from M. B. to him; it was held, that H. M. was the owner, and that his name not being stated in the advertisement, there was no sufficient description within the Rev. Sts. c. 8, § 25, providing that where the name of the owner is not known to the collector, the advertisement shall state the amount of the taxes on the several rights, lots or divisions of the real estate to be sold. *Ib.*

170. In proving the posting of a notice by the collector of the time and place of sale of real estate taken for taxes, in some convenient and public place within his precinct, three weeks before the time of sale, as required by Rev. Sts. c. 8, § 27, the time when such notice was posted must be fixed with certainty, and its contents must be sufficiently shown, in order to identify it with the notice required to be published by § 24 of the same chapter. *Ib.* See Gen. Sts. c. 12, §§ 28-30.

171. Where the advertisement and notice of sale of real estate for non-payment of a tax of three dollars and thirty cents, state the amount of the tax to be four dollars and twelve cents, the sale is void. *Alexander* v. *Pitts*, 7 Cush. 503 (1851).

172. A., residing in another state, owned a building in Lawrence, in this state, standing by consent on land of another person. The building was taxed to A. in Lawrence, as real estate belonging to a non-resident, but was subsequently sold by the tax collector as personal property. *Held*, that the sale was void. *Flanders* v. *Cross*, 10 Cush. 514 (1852).

173. The purchaser who enters on premises sold for non-payment of an illegal tax, is liable in trespass to the real owner. *Ib.*

174. Where bank shares are seized and sold by a collector of taxes, in the manner provided by St. 1846, c. 195, (Gen. Sts. c. 12, §§ 10, 11.) on a warrant from assessors having jurisdiction of the subject matter, and *prima facie* a lawful authority to issue such warrant, and there is nothing on the face of the proceedings to indicate any want of jurisdiction or any error or defect therein, the cashier of the bank is authorized (if not required) to issue a new certificate of such shares to the purchaser, who will thereupon become entitled to accruing dividends, whether the tax, for the payment of which the shares are sold, be rightly assessed or not. *Smith* v. *Northampton Bank*, 4 Cush. 1 (1849). See *post*, 207.

175. A sale of bank shares for non-payment of town taxes assessed upon their owner, must be made within seven days after the seizure, or the sale is void, and passes no title to the purchaser. *Noyes* v. *Haverhill*, 11 Cush. 338 (1853). Gen. Sts. c. 12, §§ 8-11.

176. If the return of the tax warrant shows that such sale was made twenty days after seizure, the bank are not bound to issue a certificate of the shares to the purchaser, for the owner's title is not devested. *Ib.*

177. Under chapters 7 and 8 of the revised statutes, a tax on real estate, assessed to the mortgagor in possession, constituted a lien on the whole estate; and a sale of the estate, for non-payment of the tax, passed to the purchaser not only the equity of redemtion, but also the rights of the mortgagee. *Parker* v. *Baxter*, 2 Gray, 185 (1854). See Gen. Sts. c. 12, §§ 35, 36.

178. A sale and conveyance of land by a collector of taxes for non-payment of taxes assessed thereon to William S. H., but intended by the assessors to be assessed to Charles S. H., under a warrant in which the first name of the owner, as originally written, has been erased by the collector, and the name of Charles inserted, with the addition of the words, " or owner unknown," and after notices of sale in which Henry S. H. is mentioned as the owner, is not sufficient evidence of title against one who has been in possession of the land ten years. *Sargent* v. *Bean*, 7 Gray, 125 (1856).

179. A collector of taxes is not obliged to return his warrant to the assessors; he may make a distress after the first of January next succeeding his election; he may include, in the legal costs of a sale of property for the non-payment of a tax, a commission or percentage on the amount of the tax, for his own compensation. *Howard* v. *Proctor*, 7 Gray, 128 (1856).

180. A collector of taxes, holding two tax warrants, may make one sale of property for non-payment of the whole amount of taxes due under both. *Ib.*

181. If any demand is required before distraining for non-payment of taxes, a demand for payment of taxes assessed on two jointly may be made on them on different days. *Ib.*

182. A tax warrant, good upon its face, protects the collector acting under it, notwithstanding any irregularity in the meetings at which or the votes by which the taxes were assessed. *Ib.*

183. The owner of land advertised for sale for non-payment of taxes, but not yet sold, on tendering the amount due for taxes thereon, cannot be required to pay to the collector fees for a levy upon the land, or for travel to make a return to the state and county treasurers, or for a commission on the tax. *Converse* v. *Jennings*, 13 Gray, 77 (1859).

184. A tax title under Rev. Sts. c. 8, §§ 28, 29, (Gen. Sts. c. 12, § 33,) is not valid unless it appears by the collector's deed or otherwise that the land was so divided that no greater portion thereof was sold than was necessary to satisfy the tax and intervening charges, or that it could not be conveniently divided to that extent. *Crowell* v. *Goodwin*, 3 Allen, 535 (1862).

185. If the charter of a city provides that the city council may establish provisions for the collection of taxes, in addition to those prescribed by the laws of the Commonwealth, a city ordinance is valid which directs the collector, before proceeding to collect taxes by

distress, to issue a summons to delinquent persons assessed, and authorizes him to collect twenty cents therefor; and a warrant of distress issued by the collector of such city, under St. 1842, c. 34, (Gen. Sts. c. 12, § 18,) is not void by reason of requiring the collection of twenty cents for such summons. *Cheever* v. *Merritt*, 5 Allen, 563 (1863).

186. If a person after the assessment of a tax upon him, has removed out of the precinct of the collector without paying his tax, the collector's warrant of distress to the sheriff of the county or constable of the town where he may be found, under St. 1842, c. 34, (Gen. Sts. c. 12, § 18,) need not recite the facts which authorize the collector to issue it. *Ib.* But see *Williamstown* v. *Willis*, 16 Gray, (*ante*, 132).

187. A collector's deed of real estate, sold by him for taxes, is invalid, under the statutes of this commonwealth, if it does not state that the taxes were not paid within fourteen days after demand. *Harrington* v. *Worcester*, 6 Allen, 576 (1863).

188. If a tax title proves invalid, the purchaser at the collector's sale cannot maintain an action against the town to recover back the money paid by him as the consideration of the purchase, and the expenses of defending his title. *Lynde* v. *Melrose*, 10 Allen, 49 (1865). But see St. 1862, c. 183, § 6.

See Estoppel; *post*, 199, 201, 207.

V. Remedy for an Illegal Tax.

(a) Whether by Action or Abatement.

189. Where one who has personal property liable to taxation is overrated by the assessors, by their including in the valuation property of which he is not the owner, or that for which he is not liable to be taxed, his only remedy is by an application for an abatement, pursuant to the statute, and he cannot maintain any action at law to recover back the tax, if paid. *Little* v. *Greenleaf*, 7 Mass. 236 (1810). *Osborn* v. *Danvers*, 6 Pick. 98 (1828). And see *Wright* v. *Boston*, 9 Cush. 233. See 8 Allen, 333.

190. So where a person, who is liable to be taxed in a city or a town for any real estate, is overtaxed by the assessors, whether the excess is caused by too high a valuation of real estate for which he is liable to be assessed, or by including in the valuation estates for which he is not liable, his only remedy is by application to the assessors for an abatement. *Howe* v. *Boston*, 7 Cush. 273 (1851).

191. If a person owning real estate in a town in which he does not reside, is assessed by the assessors of such town for his poll and personal property as well as for his real estate, his remedy against the illegal tax on his poll and personal property is not merely by an appeal as for over taxation, but in case he is compelled to pay the same, he may recover back the money in an action against the town. *Preston* v. *Boston*, 12 Pick. 7 (1831).

192. The Boston Water Power Company were taxed, on separate valuations, for their mill, and for land owned by them in fee, which was used solely for the flowing of water from their mill. *Held*, that if the mill and land might have been valued and assessed together, as one estate, and if the taxes, as assessed, were too large, yet that they were not void, and therefore, if paid, could not be recovered back by action; but that the remedy was by application to the proper authority for an abatement. *Boston Water Power Co.* v. *Boston*, 9 Met. 199 (1845).

193. If the husband of a woman for whom personal property is held in trust, is possessed of personal property for which he is liable to be taxed, and is improperly taxed for a larger amount than he otherwise would be, on account of such property in trust, his only remedy is by an application to the assessors for an abatement. *Bates* v. *Boston*, 5 Cush. 93 (1849).

194. One who is liable to be taxed in a city or town for real and personal property cannot maintain assumpsit against the city or town to recover back any part of a tax assessed upon and paid by him, on the ground that the assessors, in their valuation list, assessed certain lots of land separately which should have been assessed together, and assessed other lots as one estate, which should have been assessed separately; nor on the ground that one item in the valuation list included personal property held by him in his own right and also personal property held by him as guardian for a person residing in another town, in which such property was legally taxed. *Lincoln* v. *Worcester*, 8 Cush. 55 (1851).

195. One who is taxed in the city where he is an inhabitant, for his own personal estate; and is also taxed, in a separate tax bill, by one valuation, for personal and real estate held by him "as trustee and guardian of" three persons named, of one of whom, who is a minor, he is guardian, and taxable as such; cannot maintain an action against the city to recover back the tax so assessed on the property held by him as trustee for the two others named, though they are of age and inhabitants of the Commonwealth. *Bourne* v. *Boston*, 2 Gray, 494 (1854).

196. An inhabitant of this state, who has no personal property or taxable income, may maintain an action against the city of his residence to recover back a tax unlawfully assessed to him on personal property in other

states held in trust for him. *Dorr* v. *Boston*, 6 Gray, 131 (1856).

197. Whether partners, taxed by one entire assessment, in a town in which they have no place of business, for stock in trade employed there in a manufactory occupied by them, and for other personal property, can, if the tax on the other personal property is illegal, recover back by action the whole tax, or at least that part of it, *quære*. *Lee* v. *Templeton*, 6 Gray, 579 (1856).

(b) **Of the Action to recover back.**

198. If part of a tax is valid and part void, only the part which is void can be recovered back by the person assessed. *Torrey* v. *Millbury*, 21 Pick. 64 (1838). And see Gen. Sts. c. 11, § 54; c. 12, § 56.

199. Where a person refused to pay a tax valid in part and void in part, and it was collected by distress, it was held, in an action in which he recovered back the void part, that he was not entitled to recover back the costs of the distress, the warrant having been rightfully issued for the valid part of the tax. *Ib.*

200. When taxes, illegally assessed and paid under protest, are recovered back by action, the plaintiff is entitled to interest thereon from the time of payment. When such taxes, so recovered, were paid upon compulsion, without protest, the plaintiff is entitled to interest thereon from the time of demanding repayment; or from the date of the writ, when no previous demand is made. *Boston & Sandwich Glass Co.* v. *Boston*, 4 Met. 181 (1842).

201. A person of whom a tax, illegally assessed, has been collected by distress, can recover of the town, in an action for money had and received, only the amount of the tax, with interest thereon from the time of the sale, and not the surplus value of the property sold, nor the costs of distress. *Dow* v. *Sudbury*, 5 Met. 73 (1842). *Shaw* v. *Becket*, 7 Cush. 442 (1851).

202. Assessors may recover of a town, on an express promise, the amount of an illegal town tax which was irregularly assessed by them and collected and paid to the town, and which, on account of such irregularity, the assessors were compelled to pay to the persons taxed. *Nelson* v. *Milford*, 7 Pick. 18 (1828).

203. But without an express promise by the town such action would not lie; nor would it lie upon such promise for state or county taxes. *Ib.*

204. A town voted to let an inhabitant, who sent his children to school in another town, "draw his proportion of school money;" and reconsidered this vote before the money was paid. It was held, that such inhabitant could not maintain assumpsit against the town for the amount of the taxes assessed upon and paid by him for the support of the schools. *Withington* v. *Harvard*, 8 Cush. 66 (1851).

205. A tax payer cannot maintain an action against the town for his proportion of the expenses of the burial of persons not paupers, paid by the town out of the money raised by town taxes. *Ib.*

206. It is no ground for retaining a tax illegally assessed by a school district against an inhabitant, who has paid the same, that the sum so received of him was only his due proportion of the amount necessary to discharge the debts of the district, and for payment of which the district might have legally raised a sufficient sum. *Joyner* v. *Egremont*, 3 Cush. 567 (1849).

207. If bank shares have been seized for non-payment of taxes due from their owner, and disposed of by the collector by a sale which was illegal and void, the owner cannot maintain assumpsit against the town to recover the proceeds of the sale, although they have been paid into the town treasury. Such proceeds belong to the purchaser of the shares, as he obtained no title to the shares under the collector's sale. *Noyes* v. *Haverhill*, 11 Cush. 338 (1853).

208. A manufacturing corporation, who are taxed in the town where their real estate is situated and their machinery employed, for such real estate and machinery, and also for their stock in trade and other personal property, and pay the whole tax, may maintain an action against the town to recover back the latter portion of the tax; and are not estopped to maintain such an action, by having, before the assessment of the tax, sent in to the assessors a statement of their taxable property, including all these items, if the assessors did not assess upon that valuation, and knew that they were a corporation. *Dunnell Manuf. Co.* v. *Pawtucket*, 7 Gray, 277 (1856).

209. A person who has paid his tax within the time prescribed by the town, and thus obtained a discount thereon, cannot maintain an action against the town to recover back the amount, upon the ground that the tax was illegal by reason of too small a portion of the state tax having been assessed on polls; even if he paid under protest. *Lee* v. *Templeton*, 13 Gray, 476 (1859).

210. A vote by the inhabitants of a town to appropriate money to celebrate the Fourth of July, and to raise for town expenses a sum which includes such appropriation, renders an assessment illegal which is based thereon; and a plaintiff is not estopped from maintaining an action to recover back money paid for

a tax so assessed, by proof that, after the vote thus to appropriate money, he, as selectman, presented to the town an estimate of the probable town expenses for the year, which included that sum. *Gerry* v. *Stoneham*, 1 Allen, 319 (1861). See St. 1861, c. 165.

211. The St. of 1859, c. 118, § 4, (Gen. Sts. c. 11, § 54,) which provides that "whenever, by any erroneous or illegal assessment or apportionment of taxation, any party is assessed more or less than his due and legal proportion, such tax and assessment shall be void only to the extent of the illegal excess of taxation, whenever such exists; and no party shall recover in any suit or process based upon such error or illegality greater damages than the amount of such excess," does not apply to an action pending at the time of its passage. *Ib.*

212. No action lies to recover back a tax paid before process had been issued for its collection, although the tax was illegal. *Barrett* v. *Cambridge*, 10 Allen, 48 (1865).

212 *a.* Evidence of the usage of assessors for many years in making certain deductions in assessing a certain class of taxes, is insufficient to control the legal interpretation of a provision of statute concerning taxation. *Dwight* v. *Boston*, 12 Allen, (1866).

See *Watson* v. *Princeton*, 4 Met. 599 (*ante*, 91); *Tobey* v. *Wareham*, 2 Allen, 594 (*ante*, 109); *Lincoln* v. *Worcester*, 8 Cush. 55 (*ante*, 194); *Lee* v. *Templeton*, 6 Gray, 579 (*ante*, 197); Appropriations, 23.

(c) Of the Abatement.

213. The judgment of the county commissioners upon a complaint for the abatement of a tax is a judicial act, and consequently a *mandamus* does not lie to compel them to revise such a decision. *Gibbs* v. *Hampden*, 19 Pick. 298 (1837).

214. If in such a case they err in matters of law, a writ of *certiorari* is the proper remedy. *Ib.* *Lincoln* v. *Worcester*, 8 Cush. 61 (1851). *Newburyport* v. *Essex*, 12 Met. 211 (1846).

215. The statute requirement that the owner of taxable property must carry in a list of his estate to the assessors, in order to entitle him to an abatement, is not complied with by an exhibition to the assessors of a plan of his real estate, or by referring them, orally, to a former list carried in by him two years before; nor is the fact that the assessors are satisfied without a list equivalent to the bringing in of one. *Winnisimmet Co.* v. *Chelsea*, 6 Cush. 477 (1850).

216. It is no good cause for an omission to carry in a list of taxable property to the assessors that the party assessed is a corporation; or that the estate taxed is owned in part by non-resident proprietors. If an omission by assessors to give notice to the inhabitants to bring in lists of their estates will excuse tax payers from bringing them in, (and the court do not decide that such omission will have that effect,) the burden of proving such want of notice is on the tax payer. *Ib.*

217. The list required by St. 1853, c. 319, like that required by Rev. Sts. c. 7, §§ 19, 40, (Gen. Sts. c. 11, §§ 22, 46,) in order to entitle an individual to apply for an abatement of his tax, must be brought to the assessors before the tax is assessed. *Porter* v. *Norfolk*, 5 Gray, 365 (1855).

218. It cannot be filed after an appeal from the assessors to the county commissioners. *Otis Co.* v. *Ware*, 8 Gray, 509 (1857).

219. The omission by a tax payer to bring in to the assessors a list of his property verified by oath, within the time prescribed by statute, is no ground for dismissing a petition to the county commissioners for the abatement of a tax, if the assessors expressly assented to the delay, and a list verified by oath was brought in before the filing of the petition for abatement. *Lowell* v. *Middlesex*, 3 Allen, 546 (1862).

220. But assessors have no power to waive the bringing in of the list. *Winnisimmet Co.* v. *Chelsea*, 6 Cush. 477 (1850).

221. The statutes providing that no abatement shall be made of the taxes assessed upon any individual until he shall have filed with the assessors a sworn list of his estate, applies to corporations. *Otis Co.* v. *Ware*, 8 Gray, 509 (1857).

222. A railroad company gave in a tax list as follows: "To the assessors of the city of C. The F. R.R. Co. submit and bring in the following list of all the estate of said Co. in said C. subject to taxation, being all the real estate of said Co. in said C. except that embraced and contained in the location of said Co.'s railroad, made and filed according to law, that is to say, three hundred and forty-eight thousand and three hundred and ten square feet of land and wharf with the buildings thereon — the same lying between Prison Point, so called, and Warren Avenue, valued at $350,000. F. R.R. Co., by M. D. B., Treasurer. Then personally appeared M. D. B., Treasurer, and made oath that the above statement by him subscribed was true. T. G., Assessor." It was held, that this was a sufficient tax list under St. 1853, c. 319, § 3 (Gen. Sts. c. 11, § 46). *Charlestown* v. *Middlesex*, 1 Allen, 199 (1861).

223. Upon a petition for an abatement of taxes, on the ground of an over valuation of property, county commissioners have no power to increase the taxes upon the same or other property of the petitioner. *Lowell* v. *Middlesex*, 3 Allen, 546 (1862).

224. Nor have they authority, upon such petition, to allow costs to the petitioner. *Ib.*

225. Under a petition for an abatement of taxes, county commissioners have no authority to allow costs to either party. *Lowell* v. *Middlesex*, 6 Allen, 131 (1863).

226. Under a petition for an abatement of taxes, county commissioners have no authority to allow to the petitioner interest upon the amount abated, which had been paid by him under protest. *Lowell* v. *Middlesex*, 3 Allen, 550 (1862).

227. Assessors have no power to abate a tax after their term of office has expired. *Cheshire* v. *Howland*, 13 Gray, 321 (1859).

(d) **Of Actions against Assessors and others.**

228. The assessors of a town are not responsible to a person assessed for any unintentional error committed by them in the assessment of a tax. *Ingraham* v. *Doggett*, 5 Pick. 451 (1828). And see Gen. Sts. c. 11, § 51.

229. Where a poll tax is assessed upon a person in a town of which he is not an inhabitant, and is collected by distress, the assessors are responsible for such assessment, the St. 1823, c. 138, § 5, exempting them from responsibility, not being applicable to such case; and it is not a defence that the residence of the person taxed was included within the boundaries of such town as perambulated. *Freeman* v. *Kenney*, 15 Pick. 44 (1833). See Gen. Sts. c. 11, § 51.

230. Assessors of a town, conducting themselves with fidelity and integrity in assessing a tax, in pursuance of a vote duly certified to them, are not responsible in any form of action, since Rev. Sts. c. 7, § 44, (Gen. Sts. c. 11, § 51,) for accidentally assessing a person not an inhabitant of the town and not liable to be taxed. *Baker* v. *Allen*, 21 Pick. 382 (1838).

231. In an action against assessors for causing the plaintiff to be arrested for non-payment of a tax, if the town records no not show that the defendants were duly sworn as assessors, evidence is admissible to prove the fact. *Pease* v. *Smith*, 24 Pick. 122 (1834).

232. The provision of Rev. Sts. c. 7, § 44, (Gen. Sts. c. 11, § 51,) exempting assessors from all responsibility, excepting "only for the want of integrity and fidelity on their own part," does not extend to the assessment of a school district tax, where the district has no legal existence. *Bassett* v. *Porter*, 4 Cush. 487 (1849). *Dickinson* v. *Billings*, 4 Gray, 42 (1855).

233. If the clerk of a school district wrongfully certifies to the assessors of the town that at a legal meeting of the district it was voted to raise a sum of money, and the assessors thereupon assess the same, a person arrested for not paying the tax cannot maintain trespass against the clerk, the injury being but a remote consequence of his act. *Taft* v. *Metcalf*, 11 Pick. 456 (1831).

234. A collector of taxes, acting under a warrant from the assessors, is not responsible to the party on whom he levies a tax, for the regularity of the town meeting, or the validity of the votes at the meeting at which the tax is granted. *Sprague* v. *Bailey*, 19 Pick. 436 (1837).

235. The return of a collector of taxes upon his warrant is only *prima facie* evidence in his favor, in an action against him for an unlawful arrest. *Lothrop* v. *Ide*, 13 Gray, 93 (1859).

236. When a tax warrant is good on its face and sufficient in form, and the assessors have jurisdiction of the subject, a collector is not liable for its due execution. *Hays* v. *Drake*, 6 Gray, 387 (1856).

237. But a warrant bad on its face affords no protection to the collector. *Eames* v. *Johnson*, 4 Allen, 382 (1862).

238. Under Rev. Sts. c. 25, § 12, if a highway tax is not worked out or paid during the year in which it is assessed, it must be placed in the next assessment of a town tax upon the delinquent, and not afterwards; and if it is placed in a subsequent assessment, and the tax list and warrant show upon their face the year in which it was originally assessed, and the tax is collected by seizure and sale of property, an action therefor lies against the collector, and such assessors as directed the proceedings of the collector. *Ib.*

TREASURER.

1. If the inhabitants of a town have authorized their treasurer to borrow a certain sum of money for a specific purpose, and to give his note as treasurer therefor, and he has exercised this authority, they are not liable upon a note given by him in their name for money subsequently borrowed by him and converted to his own use, although he assumed to be acting under the authority conferred upon him, and the lender supposed he was doing so. *Lowell Savings Bank* v. *Winchester*, 8 Allen, 109 (1864).

2. If the inhabitants of a town have by vote authorized their treasurer to borrow money for the adjustment of a state tax for the reimbursement of bounties to volunteers, and the tax has been adjusted without the necessity of borrowing money, his authority to borrow money under that vote thereupon ceases. *Benoit* v. *Conway*, 10 Allen, 528 (1865).

3. If a town treasurer without authority borrows money on the credit of the town, and

gives his note as treasurer, and mingles the money with his own private funds, by depositing the same to his own credit in a bank where he keeps an account in his own name, and uses the whole fund indiscriminately for the payment of his own debts and the debts of the town, so that the borrowed money cannot be specifically traced as having been applied in payment of the debts of the town, the lender cannot maintain an action against the town for money had and received. *Ib.*

4. Authority in a town treasurer to borrow money on the credit of the town cannot be established by proof of a long continued practice of the treasurer to borrow money and give and pay notes therefor, without any votes of the town, and at the end of each year to report to the town a list of the amounts borrowed and of the notes given and paid, and of the acceptance of such reports by the town; there being no such report of the borrowing of the money in controversy. *Ib.*

See Actions, 7, 29-31; Appropriations, 35; Bonds; Finance; Taxes, 120, 121.

TRUSTEE PROCESS.

See Actions, 54-59.

TRUSTS.

1. A city, in its corporate capacity, may act as trustee of a fund left by will, with a provision that the income thereof shall be expended in the purchase of fuel, "to be given, or sold at low prices, as may be deemed best by the trustees, to such worthy and industrious persons as are not supported in whole or in part at the public expense, but who may need some aid in addition to their own labor to enable them to sustain themselves and their families during the inclement season of the year; such aid to be afforded in the most private manner possible, and the names of the recipients to be withheld from the public." *Webb* v. *Neal*, 5 Allen, 575 (1863).

2. A testatrix by her will gave all her real and personal estate, after payment of debts and funeral expenses, to a town, for the purpose of establishing, for the use and benefit of all the inhabitants of the town, a free public library, and, if the funds should prove sufficient, a free public reading-room, to be under the control of trustees to be chosen by the inhabitants from time to time, which trustees were directed to sell certain of the real estate and empowered in their own names to convey the same, and were also directed to convert the personal estate into money and pay her debts and funeral expenses, and to appropriate the residue to the purposes above named by erecting a building, buying books and setting apart a fund for the future purchase of books and the establishment of a reading-room; and she provided that the town should forever pay all the incidental expenses of managing and insuring the library and building. The town at first voted to accept these provisions, and chose trustees accordingly; but afterwards reconsidered this vote, and voted to decline to accept the same. It was held, 1. That the will gave the estate to the town in fee. 2. That it was the duty of an administrator with the will annexed to collect the personal assets and pay the debts and funeral expenses of the testatrix, and that the direction to the trustees to do these things was inoperative and void. 3. That the trustees were vested with a power coupled with a trust, which entitled them to seek the instructions of this court as to the proper discharge of their duty. 4. That under Gen. Sts. c. 100, trustees for charitable trusts need not give bonds. 5. That the trusts created by this will were charitable trusts, although a burden was annexed to the acceptance thereof by the town. 6. That the town had power to accept the same; and after doing so cannot renounce the same. 7. That the town, by accepting these provisions, could not bind itself to expend more money than is allowed by Gen. Sts. c. 33, § 9, for that purpose. 8. That the charitable trusts will not be defeated nor the estate forfeited by a failure on the part of the town to pay the expenses put upon them by the will. *Drury* v. *Natick*, 10 Allen, 169 (1865).

See Public Buildings, 1; Schools, 21.

WATER.

1. The city of Boston did not, by St. 1846, c. 167, acquire the fee of land taken for the construction of the aqueduct from Long Pond, but only such an easement therein as is necessary for the purposes of the water works. *Harback* v. *Boston*, 10 Cush. 295 (1852).

2. The owner of land taken under St. 1846, c. 167, for supplying the city of Boston with pure water, may maintain a petition for damages under the sixth section of the statute, as soon as his land is actually entered upon and taken, and before a description of the land, signed by the mayor of the city, is filed in the registry of deeds, as required by the first section. *Moore* v. *Boston*, 8 Cush. 274 (1851).

3. If the owner of land taken under St. 1846, c. 167, dies before filing his petition, the right of action survives to his executor or administrator. *Ib.*

4. The only remedy for damages to land necessarily caused in the construction of the aqueduct from Long Pond to Boston, under St. 1846, c. 167, was by petition to the court of common pleas under § 6 of that statute, although such injury was to land not finally taken for the location of the aqueduct, but only adjacent thereto. *Tower* v. *Boston*, 10 Cush. 235 (1852).

5. Land purchased in fee or otherwise taken by a city, by authority of the legislature, for the purpose of supplying the city with pure water, and used for that purpose only, is justly taken in the exercise of the right of eminent domain, and is therefore not liable to taxation. *Wayland* v. *Middlesex*, 4 Gray, 500 (1855).

6. An assessment for a quarter of a year, made by the water registrar under the direction of the water board of Boston, at the rate of two cents for each one hundred gallons of water used in a hotel in Boston, the daily consumption of which, as measured by a water-meter placed therein, under the provisions of the city ordinance, exceeds 10,000 gallons a day, is legal; although water-meters have been put into only a portion of the hotels in Boston, and although the assessment, if made according to the provisions of the city ordinance applicable to hotels into which no water-meters have been put, would have amounted to only about one fourth as much. *Parker* v. *Boston*, 1 Allen, 361 (1861).

WAYS.

I. Proceedings in Laying out and Altering Public Ways.

(*a*) Application; and Adjudication as to whether the Public Safety and Convenience require the Laying out or Alteration.

(*b*) Location or Laying out, and Altering; Prior Notice thereof; Agreements with Land Owners.

(*c*) Where Ways may be laid out.

II. Public Ways by Dedication, by Prescription and Use, and by Necessity.

(*a*) By Dedication.

(*b*) By Prescription and Use.

(*c*) By Necessity.

III. Discontinuing Public Ways; Damages therefor.

IV. Proceedings on an Application for a Jury.

(*a*) Who are entitled to Damages; Waiver of Damages.

(*b*) Application for a Jury, and Notice thereon.

(*c*) Proceedings before Jury; their Powers and Duties.

(*d*) Elements and Computation of Damages; Evidence thereof.

(*e*) Verdict, and Judgment thereon.

V. Repairing Public Ways; Powers and Duties of Highway Surveyors.

VI. Defects and Obstructions in Ways.

(*a*) Liability of Towns to an Action.

(*b*) Where the Plaintiff's Negligence or other Causes concur.

(*c*) Evidence, Trial, Damages.

(*d*) Indictments against Towns.

(*e*) Liability of Individuals for Obstructions; Civilly and Criminally.

VII. Rights of the Public and of Land Owners in the Soil of Public Ways.

VIII. Limits and Boundaries of Ways; Fences, &c.

IX. Railroad Crossings; Sidewalks in the Cities of Lowell and Charlestown.

X. Of the Remedies for Irregularities in Laying out and Completing Ways; and of some other Matters.

I. Proceedings in Laying out and Altering Public Ways.

(a) Application; and Adjudication as to whether the Public Safety and Convenience require the Laying out or Alteration.

See St. 1866, c. 174.

1. A city council, in acting under a city charter which gives to them exclusive authority to lay out, alter or discontinue any street or way, the *termini* of which are entirely within the city, and makes no provision as to the manner in which the authority thus conferred shall be exercised, must conform to and be governed by the regulations prescribed in the General Statutes in relation to the same subject; and has no jurisdiction of an application to locate anew a road, or to ascertain the correct location thereof, and erect the necessary bounds, unless the same is signed in the manner required by Gen. Sts. c. 43, § 12, or § 87. *Barnes* v. *Springfield*, 4 Allen, 488 (1862). But see Gen. Sts. c. 43, § 78.

2. A petition for a highway from a particular place "to a point near the dwelling-house of A.," on a certain road, is not so indefinite in the description of the *terminus* as to require that the proceedings of county

commissioners, laying out a highway upon the same, should be quashed. *Westport* v. *Bristol*, 9 Allen, 203 (1864).

3. The power vested in the mayor and aldermen of Boston as to laying out or altering streets "whenever in their opinion the safety or convenience of the inhabitants shall require it," is judicial, and a *certiorari* lies to remove their proceedings. *Parks* v. *Boston*, 8 Pick. 218 (1829). *Stone* v. *Boston*, 2 Met. 220 (1841). *Dwight* v. *Springfield*, 4 Gray, 107 (1855).

4. Where such mayor and aldermen shall adjudge that the laying out or altering of a street is required by public safety and convenience, their having taken a bond from an individual to contribute towards the expense, will not vitiate their proceedings, provided the bond was not made the basis of their proceedings, and the adjudication was not colorably for the use of the city but really for the benefit of the individual. *Parks* v. *Boston*, 8 Pick. 218 (1829).

5. Where the common convenience or necessity is not sufficient to warrant the laying out of a highway wholly at the expense of a town, the court of sessions, under St. 1786. c. 67, § 4, could not adjudge it to be of common convenience or necessity in consideration of a bond having been filed by an individual to relieve the town of part of the expense. *Commonwealth* v. *Sawin*, 2 Pick. 547 (1824). But see *Parks* v. *Boston*, 8 Pick. 218; *Crockett* v. *Boston*, 5 Cush. 182 (*post*, 50).

6. It seems, that an adjudication "that the public convenience and necessity require that the road prayed for should be located in part," without designating the *termini*, is invalid, and will not support a location, though made in due form, over part of the route prayed for. *Danvers* v. *Essex*, 2 Met. 185 (1840).

7. The question whether an adjudication as to a highway or town way, made by county commissioners at the time of their view or at a special meeting, is to be regarded as final, or as subject to confirmation or reversal at a subsequent regular meeting, is to be determined by their intention, as manifested by their records. *New Marlborough* v. *Berkshire*, 9 Met. 423 (1845).

8. It seems, that an adjudication of county commissioners that public convenience requires a road to be laid out, may be rescinded by them at any time before the location of the road. *Thorpe* v. *Worcester*, 9 Gray, 57 (1857).

9. On a petition to county commissioners to rescind an adjudication that public necessity requires the construction of a road, no special notice to the original petitioners for the road is necessary, if the road has been located in part as prayed for by them; but service of copies of the petition to rescind on the town clerks of the towns in which the road is situated and the posting of copies of the petition in two public places in each of said towns is sufficient. *Ib.*

10. A vote of a town that the selectmen shall lay out a particular town way is unauthorized and improper, it being the intention of the statute that the selectmen shall exercise their own discretion upon the subject. *Kean* v. *Stetson*, 5 Pick. 492 (1828).

11. The circumstance that a county commissioner is a taxable inhabitant of a town through which a contemplated road is to pass, does not constitute such an interest as will disqualify him to act as a county commissioner in the proceedings relative to the laying out and making the road. *Wilbraham* v. *Hampden*, 11 Pick. 322 (1831).

12. The circumstance that a son and a brother of a county commissioner have joined with others in a petition that a road may be laid out, does not disqualify him to act on the question of the common convenience and necessity of the road, it not appearing that the son or brother has any other than a public interest in the subject of the petition. *Ib.*

13. A county commissioner is not disqualified to act in the laying out of a road by reason of his being a taxable owner of real estate in the town in which the road, or a part of it, is prayed for. *Danvers* v. *Essex*, 2 Met. 185 (1840).

14. By St. 1803, c. 111, annexing South Boston to Boston, the selectmen of Boston were authorized "to lay out such streets and lanes" in South Boston, as in their judgment would be for the common benefit of the proprietors of the land, and of the town of Boston, provided "that the town of Boston shall not be obliged to complete the streets laid out by their selectmen pursuant to this act, sooner than they may deem it expedient so to do." At a meeting of the selectmen of Boston, on Feb. 27, 1805, a street was laid out in pursuance of such statute. On Nov. 7, 1831, the mayor and aldermen (successors to the selectmen of Boston) passed an order that such street "should be made passable," "provided that a sum not exceeding $500 be expended during the current year." It was held, that such order of the mayor and aldermen was a declaration of the expediency of completing the way for public use; that the city were thereupon bound to complete it within a reasonable time; that the question of reasonable time was a question of law, to be determined by the circumstances of the case; and that the city was liable to an indictment for not keeping such street in repair. *Commonwealth* v. *Boston*, 16 Pick. 442 (1835).

(b) Location or Laying out, and Altering; Prior Notice thereof; Agreements with Land Owners.

See St. 1866, c. 174.

15. The mayor and aldermen of Boston cannot legally lay out a street without first giving to all persons interested, notice of their intention to do so. *Stone* v. *Boston*, 2 Met. 220 (1841).

16. Where the mayor and aldermen laid out a street over land belonging to minors, without giving any previous notice, and without making any estimate of the amount of damage thereby sustained by the owners, and more than a year elapsed before either of the owners became of age; a writ of *certiorari* was ordered on a petition filed by one of the owners at the first term after he came of age, although notice had been given to the tenant in possession to remove the buildings from the land, and he had communicated that notice to the guardian of said minors within a year after the street was thus laid out. *Ib.*

17. Where public notice of a meeting of the county commissioners for the purpose of locating a highway and assessing the damages was duly given, it was held, that it was sufficient as against the heirs of a person over whose land the highway was laid out, although such person died four days before the meeting, out of the Commonwealth, and none of his heirs resided, at that time, within the Commonwealth, or had actual notice. *Taylor* v. *Hampden*, 18 Pick. 309 (1836).

18. Where parties interested in the alteration of a street or highway, had actual notice of the proceedings, and attended and were heard concerning them, and have acquiesced therein for many years, a writ of *certiorari* to remove those proceedings will not be granted merely because it does not appear that they had the official notice prescribed by law; nor because one of them was *non compos mentis*, and had no guardian. *Hancock* v. *Boston*, 1 Met. 122 (1840).

19. Where commissioners, after notice to persons interested, viewed the route for a highway, and adjourned to a certain time and place for the purpose of locating the way and assessing the damages to individuals, it was held, that it was not necessary to give a new notice of the time and place so appointed. *Commonwealth* v. *Berkshire*, 8 Pick. 343 (1829). *Westport* v. *Bristol*, 9 Allen, 203 (1864).

20. When the parties interested are duly notified of the time and place of a meeting of commissioners, no new notice to them is necessary of the time and place of an adjourned meeting; of which they are bound to take notice. *New Salem, Petitioners*, 6 Pick. 470 (1828).

21. Parties who appear before commissioners cannot object to the proceedings on the ground of their not having had reasonable notice, unless they make the objection at the time of the hearing. *Ib.*

22. A city that has taken land and actually constructed a highway over it, cannot object that no notice was given of the purpose to locate the way; or that the names of the owners of the land were not stated in the laying out. *Haskell* v. *Bristol*, 9 Gray, 341 (1857).

23. Although the proceedings in laying out a way by selectmen, and the acceptance thereof by the town, may be avoided by the owner of the land over which the way passes, on the ground that he had no notice of the selectmen's proceedings; yet they cannot be avoided, on that ground, by a subsequent occupant of the land, who does not claim title under such owner. Hence such occupant cannot, on that ground, successfully defend an indictment against him for a nuisance within the limits of said way. *Commonwealth* v. *Weiher*, 3 Met. 445 (1841).

24. Neither the language of the statutes nor the principles of justice require that persons over whose land a town way is laid out should have any separate notice of the time and place appointed by the selectmen for a hearing on an assessment of damages, if they are notified of the time and place appointed by the selectmen for laying out the way. The laying out of the way and the estimation of damages are to be at the same meeting. *Higginson* v. *Nahant*, 11 Allen, (1866).

25. Taking land for a way which is already used as such, takes all things placed, fixed or existing upon it adapted to its use as a public way, such as gravel, stone or wood paving, plank-ways, flag-stones, bridges, culverts, guard or lamp-posts, and all works erected or connected with it for use, or rendering its use more safe and beneficial as a way. *Central Bridge* v. *Lowell*, 15 Gray, (1860).

26. Viewing premises and staking out a road over the same by selectmen of a town, do not constitute an incumbrance thereon; until a location is filed and accepted. *Shute* v. *Barnes*, 2 Allen, 598 (1861).

27. The selectmen of a town have no authority to lay out a private way "to be used only during the time of sleighing." *Holcomb* v. *Moore*, 4 Allen, 529 (1862).

28. It is no objection to the legality of a town way, laid out by the selectmen of a town, and accepted by the town with an observance of all the forms prescribed by statute, that the motive and purpose of the selectmen in laying it out was to provide access, not for the town merely, but for the public, to points or places in the land over which the way passes, es-

teemed by them as pleasing natural scenery. *Higginson* v. *Nahant*, 11 Allen, (1866).

29. A town voted to accept a road which had been laid out by the selectmen, "provided the expense do not exceed five hundred dollars." *Held*, that this was a sufficient acceptance of the road; and the cost not having exceeded that sum, the town was bound to keep the road in repair. *Jones* v. *Andover*, 9 Pick. 146 (1829).

30. It seems, that there is no objection to a town's having a town way made, part of the expense of which is paid by individuals. *Ib.*

31. Since St. 1827, c. 77, upon a petition for a new highway, the county commissioners may lay out a way which is only a part of that prayed for. *Princeton* v. *Worcester*, 17 Pick. 154 (1835).

32. It is no ground for issuing a *certiorari* to quash the location of a highway, that it omits to state the name of one person whose land is taken therefor, or to describe his land as of a person unknown. *Eaton* v. *Middlesex*, 7 Gray, 109 (1856).

33. Where the precise direction of a street in Boston, as laid out and recorded, was uncertain, the laying out was held to be void. *Hinckley* v. *Hastings*, 2 Pick. 162 (1824).

34. Where upon a petition for the alteration of a county road, or the location of a new road between two other county roads, commissioners laid out a new road between the *termini*, it was held, that their describing the new road as an alteration did not vitiate their proceedings. *Commonwealth* v. *Berkshire*, 8 Pick. 343 (1829).

35. The proceedings of county commissioners in laying out a highway were quashed, where the original petition for the way was defective in not expressing with sufficient exactness the *termini* of the proposed way, and where it appeared that the road as laid out was not within the road prayed for. *Pembroke* v. *Plymouth*, 12 Cush. 351 (1853).

36. An order of the mayor and aldermen of a city, for the laying out and establishing of a highway, having described the same as "delineated on a plan now before this board," it was held, that the laying out was sufficiently certain; that the limits of the highway might be proved by reference to the plan; and that parol evidence was admissible to show that a plan produced from the custody of the city clerk was the plan before the board when the order for laying out was made. *Stone* v. *Cambridge*, 6 Cush. 270 (1850).

37. On a petition to county commissioners to lay out a highway "over and along" an existing bridge, which was thirty-two feet wide, the commissioners have power to lay out the way fifty feet wide, if they think the public convenience requires it; and although they merely adjudge, in the first instance, that the way prayed for is required by common convenience and necessity, yet it is no departure from this order, if they subsequently locate the way wider than the bridge described. *Commonwealth* v. *Boston & Lowell Railroad*, 12 Cush. 254 (1853).

38. So if they adjudge that the way should be laid out fifty feet wide, it is not repugnant to this order to determine subsequently that only thirty-two feet in width should be made convenient for use at that time; and although the whole width of the way as laid out be not finished for travel, an obstruction erected on the part unfinished is a nuisance, for which an indictment will lie. *Ib.*

39. Selectmen laid out a town way over the land of A., and awarded him damages, to be paid by B. before the road should be opened. The town voted to accept the report of the selectmen, on condition that B. should "build the road and pay all expenses of the same, and defend the town against all prosecutions." The damages awarded to A. were tendered to him before his land was entered upon. *Held*, that the way was legally established, and therefore, that A. could not maintain an action against those who entered upon his said land for the purpose of constructing the road. *Harrington* v. *Harrington*, 1 Met. 404 (1840).

40. By an ordinance of the city of Lowell, a report of a committee of the city council, in favor of laying out a street, after it is made to the council, "shall remain in the city clerk's office seven days at least, before said council proceed to act thereon." A report of such committee, in favor of laying out a street, was made to the council June 27, 1840, and remained in the city clerk's office till July 8, 1840, when it was recommitted to the same committee, who made no further report. In the board of aldermen, the report, which had been recommitted, came up from the common council October 17, 1840, accompanied by a resolution to lay out the street; and on November 10, 1840, said resolutions passed both branches of the common council. *Held*, that the street was legally laid out conformably to said ordinance. *Lowell* v. *Hadley*, 8 Met. 180 (1844).

41. After an order of notice had been issued by the committee on streets of a city council, on a petition for an extension of a street, another petition praying for such extension, and also that the whole street from its beginning might be laid out and accepted as a highway, was referred to the same committee, who reported in favor of laying out the whole street by one description which did not distinguish the extension from the other part of the

street, and the city council laid out the street accordingly. *Held*, that the city council had no authority, on these proceedings, to lay out any part of the street except the extension prayed for in the first petition; and that the whole laying out was therefore void. *Dwight* v. *Springfield*, 4 Gray, 107 (1855).

42. The record of the laying out of streets in South Boston, made by the selectmen of Boston, pursuant to the directions of St. 1803, c. 111, is thus: "The selectmen have determined and agreed to lay out the streets through the whole of said tract, now called South Boston, according to the plan drawn by M. W., surveyor;" "the streets agreed upon and laid out are described as follows": among the streets so described were three "to the northward of Broadway, and parallel thereto, all of them fifty feet wide; the street on the northern shore in Boston Harbor to be called First Street," and to be two hundred and fifty feet distant from the second. First Street was laid out according to this description from the easterly part of South Boston as far westwardly as the width of the land between Broadway and the northern shore would allow. *Held*, that a section of a street, drawn on the plan of M.W. along the northern shore, though only forty feet wide, and only one hundred and eighty feet distant from the second street, and though neither it nor the corresponding part of the second street was parallel to Broadway, conformed to the description in the record sufficiently to authorize the mayor and aldermen of Boston to complete it. *Henshaw* v. *Hunting*, 1 Gray, 203 (1854).

43. The possession and fencing, for more than twenty years, by one holding no conveyance thereof, of land in South Boston, over which a street was laid out by the selectmen under St. 1803, c. 111, but which has not been ordered to be completed, is not such an adverse possession as to affect the right of the mayor and aldermen of Boston to complete the street. *Ib.*

44. By St. 1803, c. 111, annexing to Boston that part of Dorchester now known as South Boston, the selectmen of Boston were authorized to lay out such streets in South Boston as in their judgment would be for the common benefit of the proprietors of the land, and of the town of Boston; provided that no compensation should be allowed the proprietors for such streets.as should be laid out within twelve months from the passing of the act; and provided also that the town of Boston should not be obliged to complete the streets so laid out sooner than they might deem it expedient. In pursuance of this authority the selectmen, within the twelve months, laid out various streets over the entire territory of South Boston, and among others a very long street, named Second Street, which subsequently became distinguished into two parts, namely, Second Street East, and Second Street West, of Dorchester Street. The mayor and aldermen, in 1831, adopted an order that Second Street, west of Dorchester Street, should be made passable, and subsequently passed orders, in 1834 and 1836, appointing committees to "cause Second Street at South Boston to be repaired and put in good order," and "to be properly graded and gravelled;" in pursuance of which, that part of Second Street known as Second Street West had been completed and used as a highway; but no part of Second Street East, though it was occasionally used as a highway, had ever been ordered to be completed and made passable, unless included in the above orders. In an action against the city of Boston to recover damages for an injury occasioned by a defect in Second Street East, it was held, that in order to render the defendants liable, it was not sufficient to prove that the way complained of had been so travelled and used as to become a highway *de facto;* it must appear, not only that such way had been laid out, but that the mayor and aldermen, by an official act, had determined upon its completion, that is, when it should be graded, fitted for travel and opened for use; and that the orders above mentioned related only to Second Street West. *Bowman* v. *Boston*, 5 Cush. 1 (1849).

45. Under the proceedings of the selectmen of Boston on February 27, 1805, in laying out streets in South Boston, considered in connection with the plan of Mather Withington referred to in the record of those proceedings, the street called Fifth Street does not extend westwardly from H Street to G Street. *Glover* v. *Boston*, 14 Gray, 282 (1859).

46. A petition for the alteration of a highway which had been laid out fifty feet wide, prayed that it might be narrowed by taking ten feet from the easterly side, leaving the boundary line on that side along the wall of a building which the petitioner had erected there, in ignorance of the laying out of the highway. A committee appointed for that purpose reported that they had altered the highway according to the prayer of the petition, by setting off ten feet from the easterly side of the highway, leaving the highway forty feet wide, and bounded on the westerly side according to the original laying out, and on the easterly side by the building of the petitioner. This report was accepted. *Held*, that this was not a new laying out of the highway so as to take in more land upon the westerly side of it, although the westerly boundary, as it then stood, was a little less than thirty-nine feet from the building of the peti-

tioner. *Cutter* v. *Cambridge*, 6 Allen, 20 (1863).

47. The mayor and aldermen of a city, upon a petition for the assessment of damages by the raising of a street in front of the petitioner's house, accepted the report of a committee recommending that no damages should be allowed to the petitioner, but that the street should be lowered in front of the land, "so that said house shall stand relatively to the street as it did before the alteration now complained of, providing any action in the case is necessary." Three months afterwards, the mayor and aldermen, upon a request of the petitioner to act on his petition, voted to meet at the premises to view them, but took no further action in the matter. *Held*, that the acceptance of the report was a judgment against the petitioner's claim for damages; and that this judgment was not waived or modified by the subsequent action of the board. *Goddard* v. *Worcester*, 9 Gray, 88 (1857).

Agreements with Land Owners.

48. The abutters on a street in Boston entered into an agreement with a committee of the selectmen for the widening of the street, mutually promising each other to submit to the award of certain arbitrators concerning what each should pay or receive on account of the premises, according to the damage or benefit they should respectively receive. An action brought by the inhabitants of Boston upon the agreement was sustained against one of the abutters for the sum he was awarded to pay, although the said widening had not been recorded; and although the money was awarded to be paid to the other abutters and not to the inhabitants; and although a part of the money was to be paid to an abutter who was not a party to the agreement. *Boston* v. *Brazer*, 11 Mass. 447 (1814).

49. In March, 1833, a memorial was presented to the mayor and aldermen of Boston by several proprietors of lands, including the complainants, representing that the public convenience required that a street should be laid out over their lands, and that to promote this improvement they would for themselves individually relinquish their interest in the land for the street, provided the street should be opened during the year 1833, agreeably to a particular plan. In April, the mayor and aldermen passed a vote, that a certain sum of money be appropriated to defray the expenses of laying out a street according to the plan, to be paid when the street should be made and fitted for paving, to such person or persons as the memorialists should designate, and to be in full for all the expenses, as well as for all damages to be incurred on the part of the city in laying out and making the street. In June, the complainants addressed a letter to the other memorialists and sent a copy to the mayor, explaining their proposition to be an offer to relinquish all claim of damages for their land, but not their claim of incidental damages for removing and repairing their buildings. In October, the mayor and aldermen passed an order laying out the street according to the plan, and the street was finished during the year. Soon after the passing of this order the complainants protested against the making of the street without a previous agreement in relation to indemnity, and gave notice that they should hold the city responsible for all damages. It was held, that the proposition of the memorialists was a continuing offer during the year, if not revoked or rejected; that the vote of April was not a rejection, but a distinct proposition on the part of the city; that the offer of the memorialists was several in its nature, and until accepted or rejected by the city, each proprietor of land had a right to revoke or modify his offer, independently of the others; and that by laying out the street the city, in legal effect, accepted the complainants' offer as modified by their letter of explanation, and it then became a contract, binding upon both parties; and thereby the city became entitled to the land, and the complainants became entitled to incidental damages for removing and repairing their buildings. *Foster* v. *Boston*, 22 Pick. 33 (1839).

50. The board of aldermen of the city of Boston having referred it to a committee to consider a plan for widening Bromfield Street, and the committee having agreed upon a report of a plan for that purpose, an offer was made to the board, by one of the proprietors of land abutting on Bromfield Street, that if the city would establish a prospective line for widening said street, according to the report of the committee, and would take from a certain estate, and the proprietors of certain other estates would give, sufficient land from said estates, respectively, for the purpose, such proprietor would give free of charge the necessary amount of land which might be required for the purpose from his estate. It was held, that if such offer was accepted in a reasonable time, and the condition complied with, the contract thereby formed was not invalid by reason of its supposed interference with the duty of the mayor and aldermen, in deciding upon the public necessity and convenience of the way proposed; but would estop such proprietor from claiming damages for his land, if taken therefor, and for the obstruction of his adjoining land, during the laying out of the street; that it was not necessary that the mayor and aldermen should

accept the proposal in direct terms or by a formal vote; but that it was sufficient if they took seasonable measures to secure the actual fulfilment of the conditions of the offer, by making the necessary orders for carrying the proposed widening into effect, and by actually accomplishing the same; and that a year and four months was not an unreasonable time for this purpose. *Crockett* v. *Boston*, 5 Cush. 182 (1849).

51. The city of Boston agreed with certain individuals that, if the former would widen the street to a certain width, the latter would pay a portion of the expense thereof; and widened the street accordingly, but allowed the second story of a building on such street to project beyond and over the line of the lower story, the highway having in all other respects been made of the stipulated width. *Held*, that the right of the city to recover of such individuals the amount of their subscriptions was not defeated by reason of such projection. *Boston* v. *Simmons*, 9 Cush. 373 (1852).

52. A street was laid out in 1804, with an agreement by the owners of land taken therefor, not to claim compensation, and that the street need not be completed until it was deemed expedient to do so. In 1831 the proper authorities voted that the order of 1804, laying out said street, "be carried into execution, so far as the same remains unfinished," and some work was done under that vote. *Held*, that the street was thereby "completed" within the meaning of the original laying out, and was from that time so far an existing way that damages could be recovered, under Rev. Sts. c. 25, § 6, (Gen. Sts. c. 43, § 62,) for lowering the grade thereof in 1850, notwithstanding the agreement of 1804 not to claim compensation for the land. *Fernald* v. *Boston*, 12 Cush. 574 (1853).

53. In raising the grade of streets, a city government act as public officers, and not as agents of the city; and their agreement as to the amount of damages to be paid an owner of real estate injured by such change of grade does not of itself give to him an absolute right of action against the city to recover the same; but they may afterwards require him, as a condition of his receiving the money, to prove his title to the satisfaction of the city solicitor, and to execute a discharge. *Griggs* v. *Foote*, 4 Allen, 195 (1862).

See *ante*, 4, 5, 30, 39; *post*, 176, 428.

(c) Where Ways may be laid out.

54. The court of sessions had no authority to lay out a highway over a navigable river, so as to obstruct the river by a bridge. *Commonwealth* v. *Coombs*, 2 Mass. 489 (1807).

55. The court of sessions had no authority to locate a road across a navigable river, and a bridge erected in pursuance of such location is an obstruction which any citizen, having occasion to use the river for the passage of his vessel, might lawfully remove as a public nuisance, although a bridge had been maintained at the same place more than fifty years. *Arundel* v. *M'Culloch*, 10 Mass. 70 (1813).

56. If a highway is located over watercourses, either natural or artificial, the public cannot shut them up, but may make the road over them by the aid of bridges. *Perley* v. *Chandler*, 6 Mass. 453 (1810).

57. An inlet of the sea which is navigable to any useful purpose is public property. It was held, that an order of the court of sessions for laying out a road across such inlet was void. *Commonwealth* v. *Charlestown*, 1 Pick. 180 (1822).

58. Where the legislature authorized the building of a bridge across a navigable stream, "either solid or on piles, leaving sufficient passages for the water," as certain commissioners might deem necessary, and a bridge was built, by direction of those commissioners, two thirds of the length of which was solid, and the other third, over the channel and deeper parts of the stream, was on piles; and scows, gondolas, and boats and vessels without masts, empty or loaded, could and did advantageously pass and repass under said bridge; it was held, that the stream had not ceased to be navigable, and that the county commissioners had no authority to lay out a highway over it. *Charlestown* v. *Middlesex*, 3 Met. 202 (1841).

59. Selectmen have no authority to lay out a landing-place or town way between high-water mark and the channel of a navigable river. *Kean* v. *Stetson*, 5 Pick. 492 (1828).

60. A road located on the dividing line between two towns, so that one half of it is in each town through its whole course, was held to be legally established; and one of the towns was properly indicted for neglecting to keep it in repair. *Commonwealth* v. *Stockbridge*, 13 Mass. 294 (1816).

61. Wherever the legislature has annexed the character of public use to any property, and such public use would be destroyed or interrupted by the laying out of a highway, the power of the county commissioners to lay out such highway is superseded. Thus, St. 1830, c. 6, authorizing "the enclosing of a part of Cambridge common," superseded the power of the county commissioners to lay out a highway across such enclosure. *Wellington, Petitioner*, 16 Pick. 87 (1834).

62. A highway may be located, without special authority of the legislature, over flats, lying between high and low water mark,

which have been lawfully filled up by the proprietor of the adjoining upland. *Henshaw* v. *Hunting*, 1 Gray, 203 (1854).

63. A franchise to build and maintain a bridge may be taken for a highway, whenever the legislature deem that the public exigencies require it, reasonable compensation being made; and the legislature may authorize a city to take a toll bridge, and lay it out as a town way, paying damages to the proprietors. *Central Bridge* v. *Lowell*, 4 Gray, 474 (1855). *Central Bridge* v. *Lowell*, 15 Gray, (1860).

64. County commissioners have no jurisdiction to locate a highway upon a beach which forms one side of a harbor, and which, though not within the ebb and flow of ordinary tides, unaided by storm or wind, is almost invariably covered by spring tides, and part of which is often useful to vessels drifting from their anchorage in the harbor. And a writ of *certiorari* will be granted to quash such a location, if it would probably, although not necessarily, injure the harbor for the purpose of navigation, or interfere with public measures for its protection and improvement. *Marblehead* v. *Essex*, 5 Gray, 451 (1855).

65. Under Gen. Sts. c. 63, § 59, the mayor and aldermen of a city, or selectmen of a town, have no authority to lay out a way across any portion of the land, not exceeding five rods in width, which has been taken by a railroad corporation for their railroad, unless permission so to do has been granted by the county commissioners. *Commonwealth* v. *Haverhill*, 7 Allen, 523 (1863).

II. Public Ways by Dedication, by Prescription and Use, and by Necessity.

(a) By Dedication.

66. Dedication is the gift of land by the owner for a way, and an acceptance of the gift by the public, either by some express act of acceptance or by strong implication. Shaw, C. J., in *Hemphill* v. *Boston*, 8 Cush. 196 (1851).

67. A dedication is negatived by the fact that gates were established and kept up across the way by the proprietors of the land. Parker, C. J., in *Commonwealth* v. *Newbury*, 2 Pick. 57 (1823).

68. In England there may be a dedication of a way, that is, by throwing open a piece of land and permitting the public to use it as a way, without putting up a bar or the like to denote that the owner retains his rights over it. But it is not known that in this commonwealth a way has ever been made by dedication. Lincoln, J., in *Hinckley* v. *Hastings*, 2 Pick. 164 (1824).

69. He who gives his land to the public may prescribe the terms and limitations on which he gives it; and if it be accepted at all, it must be accepted with the limitations, qualifications and restrictions prescribed. *Hemphill* v. *Boston*, 8 Cush. 195 (1851).

70. A way may be acquired by dedication or user. Twenty years' use of land will raise a presumption that it has been dedicated by the owner to the public for a way, and forty years' use of the land as a way will give the public a right of way over it. *Valentine* v. *Boston*, 22 Pick. 75 (1839). See *Williams* v. *Cummington*, 18 Pick. 312.

71. A highway may be established in this commonwealth by a dedication on the part of the owner of the soil, and an assent thereto on the part of the public. But *quære*, whether the assent of the public is necessary to an effectual dedication, and if necessary, in what manner is it to be given or withheld. *Hobbs* v. *Lowell*, 19 Pick. 405 (1837).

72. It seems, that in this commonwealth, and especially since St. 1846, c. 203, (Gen. Sts. c. 43, § 82,) no public way can be established by dedication merely, and without the assent, express or implied, of the city or town which will be bound by law to keep the same in repair. *Bowers* v. *Suffolk Manuf. Co.* 4 Cush. 332 (1849).

73. Where a county road was stopped up by an impassable canal, fences and dwelling-houses, and an owner of adjoining land opened a road over his land in the general direction of the old road, passing the canal by a bridge and joining the old road at each extremity, and travel was wholly diverted into the new road, and had continued therein for six years, and the selectmen put up a guide-post at the corner of the new road directing persons to travel thereon to the town to which the old road had led; it was held, that the town had expressed its assent to the dedication of the road, and accepted it. *Hobbs* v. *Lowell*, 19 Pick. 405 (1837).

74. Where acts are done by the owners of land, which manifest an intention on their part to dedicate it to the public as a highway, acts of appropriating money or labor to the making or repair of such way, by the town or city within which it is situated, manifest an intention on the part of such city or town to accept the dedication, and render the place so dedicated a complete highway, the obstruction of which is a public nuisance. *Wright* v. *Tukey*, 3 Cush. 290 (1849).

75. The dedication of a highway to the public is to be proved by showing the acts and accompanying declarations of the owners of the land alleged to be dedicated. *Ib.*

76. One who has sold and conveyed land, and, at the same time, taken a reconveyance

to himself by way of mortgage, which is afterwards foreclosed, is to be deemed the owner so far as relates to a dedication thereof to the public as a highway, notwithstanding such conveyance. *Ib.*

77. The building of a bridge by a town on a public highway is *ipso facto* a dedication of the bridge to the public. *Springfield* v. *Hampden*, 10 Pick. 67 (1830).

78. The proceedings of a town, however irregular, in the laying out of a highway, may be admissible in evidence to show the commencement of the way, in order to rebut a presumption of a dedication; or as a ground for the presumption of a grant, or a confirmation of the way as actually used, by the owner of the land; or to enable the jury to determine whether the way is a public or a town way. *Avery* v. *Stewart*, 1 Cush. 496 (1848).

79. The proprietors of certain real estate in the city of Lowell laid out and constructed a street through the same, in the manner in which roads are usually built, with a carriage way in the centre, of the ordinary width, after which the street was and continued to be used by the public, without obstruction or objection. They afterwards conveyed a portion of the land, including a part of that over which the street was laid out, to the defendants, with a provision in the deed that the street should be forever maintained as a road, for the common use of the parties to the conveyance, their successors and assigns, the grantees severally keeping in repair those parts which passed over their respective estates. The proprietors subsequently conveyed to the plaintiff a lot of land bounding on the street and so described, with all the privileges and appurtenances thereto belonging; and then sold at auction all their remaining lands on said street, together with other lands, declaring in the printed conditions of sale that all the streets mentioned therein (including the street in question) should be reserved and kept open for the benefit of the abutters; but that any of them which were not graded might be altered or discontinued, with the consent of the abutters thereon; and the city afterwards laid out that part of the street on which the plaintiff's lot was bounded, as a public highway. It was held, that no intention on the part of the proprietors to dedicate the street in question to public use could be inferred from these facts, and that the plaintiff had a right of way in that part of the street not laid out by the city, for an obstruction of which by the defendants he might maintain an action on the case. *Bowers* v. *Suffolk Manuf. Co.* 4 Cush. 332 (1849).

80. Where the owners of land in a city open and dedicate it to public use, as a footway, placing a fence across it which allows foot passengers to pass, but is dangerous to horses and carriages, the city, whether they have accepted the way or not, are not liable for an injury occasioned by the fence to a horse and carriage, though driven with ordinary care and skill. *Hemphill* v. *Boston*, 8 Cush. 195 (1851).

81. St. 1846, c. 203, (Gen. Sts. c. 43, § 82,) limiting the liability of towns for damages from defects in ways opened and dedicated to the public use, but not duly laid out and established, applies only to ways over land dedicated by its owner to the use of the public as a way, and does not, as to other ways, repeal the Rev. Sts. c. 25, § 26, making the actual repair of a way by a town conclusive evidence of its location. *Hayden* v. *Attleborough*, 7 Gray, 338 (1856).

82. A conveyance of land adjoining land of the grantor, and bounded on the same street, "with a right of way in the street to a street" on the other side of the grantor's land, and a covenant that the street on which the land is bounded shall be of a certain width as far as the granted land extends, is no evidence of an agreement of the grantor to dedicate to the public a strip necessary to make the street of the same width throughout its length. *Brown* v. *Worcester*, 13 Gray, 31 (1859).

83. Evidence that a grantor, at the time of making conveyances of lands bounded upon a street, said to his grantees that he should not throw out a strip of his own land into the street then, but should "eventually throw it out all the way," does not show a dedication of the land to the public. *Ib.*

84. No way or street can be made a public way merely by throwing it open to the public, or permitting the public to use it, without the assent of the public authorities and its acceptance as a street by them; and this assent and acceptance, since St. 1846, c. 203, (Gen. Sts. c. 43, § 82,) can only be given by laying out the street according to the ordinary mode prescribed by law. Hoar, J., in *Morse* v. *Stocker*, 1 Allen, 154 (1861).

85. A way constructed and kept in repair by a private corporation upon its own land for its own use and convenience and the use and convenience of tenants occupying its houses on both sides thereof, opening into a public street, having a sign "Private way" upon the corner, but left open to public travel for more than twenty years without interruption, is not thereby dedicated to the public; nor does it become a public way by prescription. *Durgin* v. *Lowell*, 3 Allen, 398 (1862).

(b) By Prescription and Use.

86. The existence of a highway may be

proved by immemorial usage. *Folger* v. *Worth*, 19 Pick. 108 (1837).

87. A way is sufficiently shown to be a highway, by proof that it has been known and used as a highway for forty years, and during that time has been repaired by the town in which it is situated. *Reed* v. *Northfield*, 13 Pick. 94 (1832).

88. It seems, that a town way may be proved by prescription, or by the presumption arising from use and enjoyment. *Stedman* v. *Southbridge*, 17 Pick. 162 (1835).

89. The proper laying out of a town way, in distinction from a public highway, may be presumed by a jury from long user and occasional repairs, with other circumstances tending to show that the way was originally laid out as such way. *Commonwealth* v. *Belding*, 13 Met. 10 (1847).

90. A plea of a highway from time immemorial is supported by proof of the existence of the way for sixty years, there being no evidence showing its commencement. *Odiorne* v. *Wade*, 5 Pick. 421 (1827).

91. Evidence of a usage for all persons to pass over a common will not support a plea that the land is a public highway. *Emerson* v. *Wiley*, 7 Pick. 68 (1828).

92. Where a highway is established by user merely over a tract of land of the usual width of a highway, the right of the public is not limited to the travelled path; but such user is evidence of a right in the public to use the whole tract as a highway by widening the travelled path or otherwise, as the increased travel and the exigencies of the public may require. *Sprague* v. *Waite*, 17 Pick. 309 (1836).

93. The erection and support of a bridge by a town, and the use of it by the public for thirty-eight years, are sufficient proof of its existence as a highway. *Williams* v. *Cummington*, 18 Pick. 312 (1836).

94. In the case of a highway established by user, the jury may be authorized by the circumstances to find that its limits extend beyond the travelled path. *Hannum* v. *Belchertown*, 19 Pick. 311 (1837).

95. If a private way exists over a person's land, he is liable to an action for stopping the way, but not for suffering it to be out of repair, unless he is bound by covenant or by prescriptive obligation to keep it in repair. Jackson, J., in *Doane* v. *Badger*, 12 Mass. 69 (1815).

95 *a*. The way must be kept in repair by the owner of the easement, and not by the owner of the land over which it passes. Morton, J., in *Jones* v. *Percival*, 5 Pick. 487 (1827).

96. A quay in the city of Boston, on which the warehouses of the defendant and others fronted to the south, had been used for more than sixty years for all the usual purposes of a street, but there was no record of its having been laid out as a street. The mayor and aldermen then duly laid out and recorded a street, and afterwards staked out a line in continuation of the north side of it, passing in front of and at some distance from the warehouses, and paved a space on the south of such line, of the same width with the street so laid out, and treated it in all respects like the streets in said city, but it was never laid out and recorded as a street; and the city, claiming the fee in the land between the line so staked out and the defendant's warehouse, sold this land to the defendant, and the defendant built a new warehouse thereon up to such line. It was held, that these facts were sufficient to prove a highway by prescription over the quay, and that they were not sufficient to prove that such highway had been legally discontinued over the land on which the defendant erected his new warehouse. *Stetson* v. *Faxon*, 19 Pick. 147 (1837).

97. The owner of land abutting on a street in the city of Boston laid out as a town way, set his building back from the line of the street, thus leaving an open strip of land, which was used by the public as a part of the street for more than forty years. It was held, that the public or the city had acquired a right of way over this strip, so that upon a new street being laid out over it by the city, the owner of the soil was not entitled to damages. *Valentine* v. *Boston*, 22 Pick. 75 (1839).

98. Evidence of general, uninterrupted, public use of a road as a highway for twenty years is sufficient to charge a town with liability to keep it in repair, notwithstanding St. 1846, c. 203, (Gen. Sts. c. 43, § 82,) providing that no way by dedication shall be made chargeable upon a town unless accepted. *Jennings* v. *Tisbury*, 5 Gray, 73 (1855). See *Holt* v. *Sargent*, 15 Gray, .

99. Evidence that a way was built and kept in repair by a private corporation for more than twenty years before St. 1846, c. 203, (Gen. Sts. c. 43, § 82,) took effect, open to the public and frequently travelled, is sufficient to prove that it was a public highway. *Taylor* v. *Boston Water Power Co.* 12 Gray, 415 (1859).

100. As a general principle, the right acquired by the public in a way by user is commensurate with the way actually used. *Pickering* v. *Shearer*, 11 Gray, 153 (1858).

101. A highway may be proved by prescription, even at or near a place where a particular way is shown by a record to have been established. *Commonwealth* v. *Old Colony & Fall River Railroad*, 14 Gray, 93 (1859).

See *ante*, 85.

(c) **By Necessity.**

102. A traveller on a highway rendered impassable by a sudden and recent obstruction, may pass over the adjoining fields, so far as may be necessary to avoid the obstruction, doing no unnecessary damage, without being guilty of a trespass. *Campbell* v. *Race*, 7 Cush. 408 (1851).

III. DISCONTINUING PUBLIC WAYS; DAMAGES THEREFOR.

See St. 1866, c. 174.

103. A town has power to discontinue a town way. *Commonwealth* v. *Tucker*, 2 Pick. 44 (1823).

104. The general court may have a right to discontinue a public highway. PARSONS, C. J., in *Wales* v. *Stetson*, 2 Mass. 146 (1806).

105. It is a sufficient ground for the discontinuance of a highway, that it has become useless. *Commonwealth* v. *Roxbury*, 8 Mass. 457 (1812).

106. Where a highway is once legally discontinued, it ceases to be chargeable to the town, unless it is laid out anew, although the reason for its discontinuance may have ceased. *Commonwealth* v. *Western*, 1 Pick. 136 (1822).

107. A public landing-place is not a way, and a town has no power to discontinue it. *Commonwealth* v. *Tucker*, 2 Pick. 44 (1823).

108. The location of a street, once made by the mayor and aldermen of Boston, cannot be waived by them except by a legal discontinuance of the way. *Loring* v. *Boston*, 12 Gray, 209 (1858).

109. In pursuance of authority from the legislature, a canal was located in such a manner as to include a county road, and was partly made. It was held, that the road had been discontinued, and consequently that the town was not responsible to a person injured by reason of its being out of repair. *Tinker* v. *Russell*, 14 Pick. 279 (1832).

110. Upon a petition for a new highway from M. to R., a highway was laid out over a portion of an old highway from S. to M. This was held not to operate as a discontinuance of the old highway over any land not embraced within the limits of the new highway. *Sprague* v. *Waite*, 17 Pick. 309 (1836).

111. In a vote to discontinue a town way, a description of it, as "leading from W. G.'s to the pond," is sufficient. *Avery* v. *Stewart*, 1 Cush. 496 (1848).

112. It seems, that a laying out of a highway, in terms, as an alteration of a former way, discontinues the old way between the ends of the new one. But in the absence of any record of the laying out of either way, evidence of the construction and subsequent repair of the new way by public authority does not necessarily presuppose the discontinuance of the old one. *Johnson* v. *Wyman*, 9 Gray, 186 (1857).

113. Where a party had due notice of the time and place of the meeting of county commissioners to view a road which they had been desired to discontinue, and might have appeared before them, and opposed the discontinuance, but did not; it was held, after he, and all others who were interested, had acquiesced, for nearly five years, in the discontinuance, that a writ of *certiorari* should not issue, on his petition, to remove the record of the proceedings of the commissioners in discontinuing the road, although those proceedings were not perfectly regular. *Holden* v. *Berkshire*, 7 Met. 561 (1844).

114. At a town meeting, the town, under an article to see if they would discontinue a town way, voted "to leave it to the discretion of the selectmen;" and at a meeting subsequently called "to see if they would accept the doings of the selectmen in discontinuing the road," the selectmen reported that the way should be discontinued, and the town accepted their report. *Held*, that the way was legally discontinued. *Niles* v. *Patch*, 13 Gray, 254 (1859).

115. Where county commissioners upon a petition praying that a new piece of road may be made, or the existing road altered and shortened, and such parts of the existing road, if any, as may be rendered unnecessary may be discontinued, laid out a new piece of road from one point in the existing road to another, and passed an order discontinuing so much of the existing road as was rendered unnecessary by the new location: *Held*, that that part of the road then existing for which the new location was a substitute, was discontinued. *Goodwin* v. *Marblehead*, 1 Allen, 37 (1861).

116. Establishing an alteration in a way, upon a petition praying that it may be widened and straightened, is in law a discontinuance of those portions of the way which do not come within the newly assigned limits; and no special order of discontinuance is necessary. *Bowley* v. *Walker*, 8 Allen, 21 (1864).

117. Although a highway is discontinued before it is opened or worked, or any contract is made to work it, yet a party who sustains damages by such discontinuance, is entitled to recover those damages. *Hallock* v. *Franklin*, 2 Met. 558 (1841). But see now Gen. Sts. c. 43, § 14.

118. The discontinuance of part of a street in a city, by order of the mayor and aldermen, whereby the value of lands abutting on other parts of the street, and on the neighboring streets, is lessened, is not a ground of action

against the city by the owner of such lands, if they are still accessible by other public streets. *Smith* v. *Boston*, 7 Cush. 254 (1851).

119. The discontinuance of a highway gives no right to recover damages to the owner of land not abutting on the way discontinued, and accessible by other ways. *Castle* v. *Berkshire*, 11 Gray, 26 (1858).

120. Upon the question whether a public way has been discontinued, evidence is admissible of its obstruction from time to time during a series of years by successive owners or occupiers of the soil, by whatever right or title they were possessed of the premises. *Holt* v. *Sargent*, 15 Gray, (1860).

121. In 1826, the commissioners of highways adjudged that "an alteration in the road from the Central Bridge to P." was of common convenience and necessity, and their record described the road by courses and distances in part over lands of certain persons named and in part "over old road." In 1827, on a petition for an alteration in the highway located in 1826, but not now worked, they adjudged the alteration to be of common convenience and necessity, and described it by lines and boundaries in part "over road as formerly laid out in" 1826, "and said commissioners adjudge that all that part of the road by them located in 1826," between certain points described, "be and the same is hereby discontinued." In 1853 and 1854, upon a petition to define the boundaries of this road and locate it anew, the county commissioners described a new location very exactly by metes and bounds. It was held, that evidence of these proceedings, with evidence that the old way had not been travelled upon since 1826, excepting that up to 1839 it was used by persons crossing the river in winter upon the ice, and since then by persons driving cattle to drink, showed a discontinuance of the old way. *Bennett* v. *Clemence*, 6 Allen, 10 (1863).

122. For the purpose of proving that an existing way has not been discontinued by the substitution of a new way therefor, evidence is competent to prove the existence of a public landing, to which the way furnishes a necessary access, or can reasonably be considered as appurtenant. *Ib.*

123. County commissioners have no authority to discontinue a public landing; and the alteration of a way by the substitution of a new one therefor has not the effect to discontinue the old way, if such old way is necessary to furnish access to a public landing, or can reasonably be considered as appurtenant thereto. *Ib.*

See *ante*, 96; *post*, 154.

IV. Proceedings on an Application for a Jury.

(a) Who are Entitled to Damages; Waiver of Damages.

124. A possessory title to land, over which a highway is located, is sufficient to entitle the party in possession, who is aggrieved by the doings of county commissioners in locating the highway, to have a jury to determine the matter of his complaint. *State Lunatic Hospital* v. *Worcester*, 1 Met. 437 (1840).

125. Possession of land for nine years, under a claim of title in fee, is *prima facie* sufficient to support a petition for damages thereto, sustained by reason of the discontinuance of a highway. *Hawkins* v. *Berkshire*, 2 Allen, 254 (1861).

126. Before the Rev. Sts. one tenant in common of land over which the commissioners have laid out a highway, could not apply for a jury, without the joinder of his co-tenants. *Merrill* v. *Berkshire*, 11 Pick. 269 (1831). But since the Rev. Sts. c. 24, § 48, (Gen. Sts. c. 43, § 53,) he can. *Dwight* v. *Hampden*, 7 Cush. 533 (1851).

127. Where part of a lot of land under lease is taken by the mayor and aldermen of Boston for the purpose of widening a street, the lease is not thereby extinguished; nor is the lessee discharged from his liability to pay the reserved rent during the remainder of the term. But the lessor and lessee are each entitled to recover compensation for the damage so sustained by them respectively. *Parks* v. *Boston*, 15 Pick. 198 (1834).

128. The estate of a tenant who holds a house under a lease for years, which contains this clause: "It is also agreed that if the lessor shall sell the said house, or that the city shall cut off said premises, that the said tenant shall consent thereto, and that the said tenant shall do all repairs at his expense," is determined, if the city cuts off the premises; and the tenant can recover no damages of the city for the injury done thereby. *Munigle* v. *Boston*, 3 Allen, 230 (1861).

129. If, after county commissioners have laid out a highway and assessed the damages sustained by the owner of land over which it is laid out, such owner removes his fences and rebuilds them on the line of the highway so laid out, he does not thereby deprive himself of his right to a jury to re-assess the damages. *Endicott, Petitioner*, 24 Pick. 339 (1834).

130. S., an owner of land over which a highway was laid out, agreed with the county commissioners "to release all claims for damages consequent on laying out the same, except some damage for removing fence."

Held, that S. had not, by this agreement, bound himself to accept such damages for removing his fence as the commissioners might, in their discretion, allow him; but that he was entitled to have them estimated by a jury. *Sturtevant* v. *Plymouth*, 12 Met. 7 (1846).

131. In a petition for damages caused by raising and grading a highway, the petitioner is not estopped by his waiver of damages caused by the deposit of gravel from a sidewalk built along the highway by the surveyor who raised the way. *Mitchell* v. *Bridgewater*, 10 Cush. 411 (1852).

132. Damages arising from the taking of land for a highway may be released by a parol agreement made before the county commissioners and entered on their records. *Fuller* v. *Plymouth*, 15 Pick. 81 (1833).

133. An agreement made between one of several tenants in common and the county commissioners in relation to the location of a highway over the land held in common, or the assessment of damages, is not binding on the co-tenants. *Merrill* v. *Berkshire*, 11 Pick. 269 (1831).

134. When a town way is laid out by county commissioners over land which A. has conveyed to B. by deed not recorded, and B. does not make known to the commissioners his title and claim for damages, although he has an opportunity so to do, and they award damages to A. and not to B., a writ of *certiorari* will not be issued, on the petition of B., for the purpose of quashing the commissioners' proceedings. *Brown* v. *Essex*, 12 Met. 208 (1846).

135. Where county commissioners, on the location of a highway, awarded no damages to a land owner, because, in their judgment, the benefit resulting to him from the highway was equivalent to the damage which he thereby sustained; and, such land owner's claim for damages being afterwards brought before a sheriff's jury, the commissioners there took the ground that the petitioner had waived his right to damages; it was held, that this was not inconsistent with the former ground, and that both bore directly upon the real question in issue, namely, whether such land owner was entitled to damages. *White* v. *Norfolk*, 2 Cush. 361 (1848).

136. If, at the time of the adjudication by county commissioners that the location of a highway, petitioned to be laid out by them, is of common convenience and necessity, an owner of land over which the same passes waives all claim to damages, he will be bound thereby, and cannot afterwards, at the location of such highway, retract his waiver and claim damages. *Ib.*

137. A provision in the location of a highway by county commissioners, that the owner of a house, part of which comes within the location, "is to have the privilege to have his house remain as it is, and not be required to remove it until he, his heirs or assigns, have occasion to rebuild or remove it," does not prevent him from claiming damages for the expense of removing it, if rendered expedient by the location, or from claiming damages for injuries occasioned to it by such location. *Brown* v. *Worcester*, 13 Gray, 31 (1859).

138. The burden of proving a waiver of damages by one whose land has been taken for a highway is on the party alleging the waiver. *Ib.*

See *ante*, 52.

(b) Application for a Jury, and Notice thereon.

139. Under the Rev. Sts. c. 24, § 55, a petition for a jury to assess damages for land taken to widen a street in Boston must be filed within a year after the vote of the mayor and aldermen for laying out the street. *Loring* v. *Boston*, 12 Gray, 209 (1858). And see Gen. Sts. c. 43, § 79.

140. A complaint to the court of common pleas, setting forth that the complainant's land had been taken by the city of Boston to widen a street, and praying for a jury to assess his damages, must be brought within twelve months from the time when the land was so taken. *Goddard* v. *Boston*, 20 Pick. 407 (1838).

141. An application under Rev. Sts. c. 24, §§ 68, 76, (Gen. Sts. c. 43, § 73,) for a jury to assess damages occasioned by taking land for a town way must be made within one year from the laying out of the way, and not merely within one year from the assessment of damages by the selectmen or mayor and aldermen. *Russell* v. *New Bedford*, 5 Gray, 31 (1855).

142. Under Rev. Sts. c. 25, § 6, a petition for a jury to assess damages caused by changing the grade of a street in a city may be filed at any time within a year after the refusal of the mayor and aldermen to give damages, although the mayor and aldermen do not act upon the petition to them for more than six months after the completion of the alterations complained of. *Erskine* v. *Boston*, 14 Gray, 216 (1859). See Gen. Sts. c. 44, §§ 19, 20.

143. Such petition must be filed within a year after the adjudication of the mayor and aldermen upon the petition to them, even if work has been done upon the street after the adjudication. *Revere* v. *Boston*, 14 Gray, 218 (1859). See Gen. Sts. c. 44, §§ 19, 20.

144. Any party aggrieved by the action of county commissioners in locating a road anew, for the purpose of establishing the boundary lines thereof, under Rev. Sts. c. 24, § 9, (Gen. Sts. c. 43, § 12,) is entitled to a

jury to determine his damages, in the same manner as on an original laying out of such road. *Hadley* v. *Middlesex*, 11 Cush. 394 (1853). See *Barnes* v. *Springfield*, 4 Allen, 488.

145. When county commissioners, on laying out a highway or ordering specific repairs therein, make no return of damages sustained by a party, this is equivalent to a return that he has sustained no damage; and the party, if aggrieved, must apply for a jury within the same time as if the commissioners had expressly returned that he had sustained no damage. *Monagle* v. *Bristol*, 8 Cush. 360 (1851).

146. Under the Rev. Sts. c. 25, § 6, the owner of land adjoining a highway or town way was not entitled to damages for injuries to his estate sustained by raising or lowering such way, until the act of raising or lowering it was done. In the city of Lowell, the application for damages, in such case, must be first made to the mayor and aldermen, as a board separate from the city council; and until their determination is made on such application, the county commissioners have no authority to issue a warrant for a jury to estimate such damages. *Brown* v. *Lowell*, 8 Met. 172 (1844).

147. The board of aldermen of a city upon petition laid out and accepted as a highway a new road, and the road was constructed as laid out, with some alterations made by agreement with abutters. More than a year afterwards, without any new petition being filed, the board of aldermen ordered the superintendent of streets to make an additional return following the line of the road as constructed, and the board of aldermen passed an order accepting that road as a highway. *Held*, that a petition for a jury to assess damages, by an owner of land not affected by the alterations, should have been presented within a year from the original laying out. *Haskell* v. *Bristol*, 9 Gray, 341 (1857).

148. The provision in St. 1842, c. 86, (Gen. Sts. c. 43, § 14,) that no person claiming damage for the laying out of a highway shall "have a right to demand the same until the land over which the highway is located shall have been entered upon, and possession taken, for the purpose of constructing said highway," does not prohibit a person over whose land a way is laid out by county commissioners, and who is aggrieved by their estimate of his damage, from having the damage assessed by a jury before his land is entered upon, and possession thereof taken for the purpose of constructing the way. *Harding* v. *Medway*, 10 Met. 465 (1845). See *post*, 496-498.

149. The location and acceptance of a road by the board of aldermen of a city, and an assessment of damages in favor of a land owner by a jury, and acceptance of their verdict, are not sufficient to entitle the land owner to recover the damages so assessed, if the road was not in fact constructed, nor the land in fact entered upon for the purpose of opening the street, and the order for its construction was afterwards revoked. *New Bedford* v. *Bristol*, 9 Gray, 346 (1857).

150. Exceptions to the form of a petition to county commissioners, praying for a warrant for a jury to assess land damages, cannot be taken after the warrant has issued and a verdict has been returned for the petitioner. *Thayer* v. *Worcester*, 10 Cush. 151 (1852).

151. When a warrant for a jury to assess damages occasioned by taking land for a town way is issued without any order of notice, the objection that the application for a jury was not made within the time limited by law, may be first made upon the return of the warrant, and before the empanelling of the jury; and if overruled by the presiding officer, is ground for setting aside the verdict, when returned to the court of common pleas. *Russell* v. *New Bedford*, 5 Gray, 31 (1855).

152. What is seasonable notice to appear before a jury summoned to estimate damages caused by laying out a way, depends on the circumstances of each case. *Barre Turnpike* v. *Appleton*, 2 Pick. 430 (1824).

153. Where a turnpike corporation appeared before such a jury and objected to the want of due notice, but declined being allowed further time, and proceeded on the trial, it was held to be a waiver of the insufficiency of the notice. *Ib.*

154. It is not necessary in a petition for damages to land sustained by reason of the discontinuance of a highway, that one who is in possession of the same, claiming title thereto in fee as trustee, should describe himself as trustee in his petition. *Hawkins* v. *Berkshire*, 2 Allen, 254 (1861).

155. If a petition, addressed to "the Board of Mayor and Aldermen and Common Council of the city of Worcester," and praying for an assessment of damages to an estate in the city of Worcester, caused by altering the grade of an adjoining highway, has been acted on by the mayor and aldermen, and damages refused, and thereupon on application to the county commissioners a warrant has been issued for a jury to determine the damages, and a trial had before them, and their verdict set aside, it is too late for the city, on an application for a new warrant for a jury, to object to the irregularity in the address of the original petition. *Worcester* v. *Keith*, 5 Allen, 17 (1862).

(c) Proceedings before Jury; their Powers and Duties.

156. Where a jury empanelled to determine a question relating to the location of a highway were unable to agree, it was held, that the town was entitled to have the question determined by another jury. *Mendon* v. *Worcester*, 10 Pick. 235 (1831).

157. In a proceding against a city or town to assess damages occasioned to adjoining land by the raising or lowering of a highway, a person who, though not residing in the city or town, has a claim against the respondents of a like character to that in controversy, and feels himself aggrieved and injured by the alteration in question, is not competent to sit on the jury. *Flagg* v. *Worcester*, 8 Cush. 69 (1851).

158. Where a jury empanelled in the court of common pleas to assess the damages sustained by the owner of land taken in Boston to widen a street, under St. 1821, c. 109, § 8, have viewed the land, the jurors may exercise their own judgment and knowledge of like subjects in estimating the damages, but it seems, that if a juror has knowledge of any fact bearing upon the case, he must disclose and testify to it in court. *Parks* v. *Boston*, 15 Pick. 198 (1834).

159. A bill of exceptions lies to the instructions and rulings of the court upon such trial. *Ib.*

160. A petition for the assessment of damages occasioned by the taking of land to widen a highway, and a petition for a jury to revise the damages to the same land, assessed by selectmen, for altering the grade of the way, may be submitted together to one jury. *Dickenson* v. *Fitchburg*, 13 Gray, 546 (1859).

161. A jury, summoned to assess the damages occasioned by the laying out or altering of a highway, are authorized by Rev. Sts. c. 24, § 33, (Gen. Sts. c. 43, § 39,) to extend the time allowed by the county commissioners for the owner of the land to take off the fences, trees, &c.; although the petition and warrant are for a jury to assess damages only. *Dwight* v. *Springfield*, 6 Gray, 442 (1856).

162. A jury has authority, under Rev. Sts. c. 24, § 13, (Gen. Sts. c. 43, §§ 19, 20,) to make alterations in a highway that has been located anew by county commissioners. *State Lunatic Hospital* v. *Worcester*, 1 Met. 437 (1840).

163. Under the Rev. Sts. c. 24, § 13, (Gen. Sts. c. 43, § 20,) authorizing a jury to make any alterations that may be prayed for, between the *termini* of a highway laid out by county commissioners, a jury has no authority to make an entire new line of way from one *terminus* to the other. *Gloucester* v. *Essex*, 3 Met. 375 (1841).

164. Under the authority given to a jury by the Rev. Sts. c. 24, §§ 13, 76, (Gen. Sts. c. 43, §§ 20, 73,) to make any alterations that may be prayed for between the *termini* of a town way laid out by selectmen, the jury may, on petition of a party over whose land the way is located, move the location of a portion of the way, beginning at one *terminus* thereof, a rod to one side of the location by the selectmen. *Hayward* v. *North Bridgewater*, 5 Gray, 65 (1855).

165. It is the province of the county commissioners to determine the general course and terminations of a highway, and the jury may make only such minor alterations as in their opinion may improve the highway or render it less burdensome to individuals or corporations affected by it. *Merrill* v. *Berkshire*, 11 Pick. 269 (1831). Gen. Sts. c. 43, § 20.

166. The jury cannot lawfully decide that there shall be no road, when the county commissioners have determined that common convenience requires that there should be one. *Ib.*

167. They are bound by the judgment of the county commissioners as to whether the road is of common convenience and necessity, and cannot alter it. *Lanesborough* v. *Berkshire*, 22 Pick. 278 (1839). Gen. Sts. c. 43, § 20.

168. The jury have no authority to lay out the way over the land of any person except the petitioners for the jury; it is therefore not necessary that their verdict should name the owners of the land over which the way is established. *Merrill* v. *Berkshire*, 11 Pick. 269 (1831). *Gloucester* v. *Essex*, 3 Met. 375 (1841).

169. If a petition for a jury to revise the judgment of county commissioners in laying out a highway asks for various specific alterations in the highway as ordered by them, some of which a jury have power to make, and others not, a warrant for a jury should issue, and upon the trial the presiding judge should decide, upon the facts as they then appear, whether any specific alteration which is asked for is within their power. *Westport* v. *Bristol*, 9 Allen, 203 (1864).

(d) Elements and Computation of Damages; Evidence thereof.

See St. 1866, c. 174.

170. In estimating the damage sustained by the laying out of a highway, the value of the land taken, the expense of fencing against the road, and the damage done to the remaining land of the owner, are to be allowed; and from this is to be deducted the benefit of the road, if any, to the owner of the land. *Commonwealth* v. *Coombs*, 2 Mass. 492 (1807). *Commonwealth* v. *Norfolk*, 5 Mass. 437 (1809). Gen. Sts. c. 43, § 16.

171. The benefit which the owner of the land derives from the laying out a way over it may exceed the value of the land covered by the way. In such case he is entitled to no damages. *Commonwealth* v. *Middlesex*, 9 Mass. 388 (1812).

172. If the laying out of a highway subjects the owner to the inconvenience of opening a watercourse at his own expense, this may be estimated among other causes of damage. *Perley* v. *Chandler*, 6 Mass. 458 (1810).

173. In estimating the value of land taken for a highway, its value to build permanent brick and stone buildings upon in the future is to be considered. *Dickenson* v. *Fitchburg*, 13 Gray, 546 (1859).

174. The value of land taken for a highway is to be assessed according to its value at the time of the taking, having regard however to the uses to which it may probably be applied. *Ib.*

175. In estimating the damages occasioned by taking land for a highway, no benefit is to be set off which is received by the petitioner in common with other abutters on the same street, no part of whose land is taken. *Ib.*

176. An agreement made between one of several tenants in common and the county commissioners, as to the assessment of damages on the location of a highway over the land held in common, is not binding on the co-tenants. *Merrill* v. *Berkshire*, 11 Pick. 269 (1831).

177. Where land is taken by the mayor and aldermen of Boston for the purpose of widening a street, it is to be estimated in the assessment of damages, at its value at the time of the taking, and not at its value at the time of the trial. *Parks* v. *Boston*, 15 Pick. 198 (1834).

178. Where the jury have viewed the land, the jurors may exercise their own judgment and knowledge of like subjects, in estimating the damages; but it seems, that if a juror has knowledge of any particular fact bearing upon the case, he should disclose and testify to it, in court. *Ib.*

179. Where the lessee of a store in Boston was prohibited, under certain penalties, by the terms of the lease, from making any alterations in the store without the consent of the lessor, and, subsequently to the execution of the lease, the street was widened by the city authorities, it was held, that the city was not responsible to the lessee for any damage occasioned by a delay on the part of the lessor to give his consent to the alterations rendered necessary by the widening of the street. *Brooks* v. *Boston*, 19 Pick. 174 (1837).

180. Upon a complaint for damages in such case by the lessee against the city, evidence that his sales were less during the time when the street as widened was being fitted for use, than in the corresponding season of the next year after the alteration had been completed, is not admissible, unless it is connected with other evidence tending to show that the diminution of business was in fact occasioned by the operation of widening the street. *Ib.*

181. A city or town is not responsible in damages for the inconvenience and loss of business occasioned to the abutters on a street by incumbrances and obstructions placed in the street for the purpose of repairing it, or by opening a common sewer in the street. *Ib.*

182. The complainant took a lease of a store in the city of Boston, for three years, covenanting to pay the rent and to leave the premises in good repair at the end of the term, and the lessor reserving a right to enter and make improvements. The front part of the land was taken and the front wall of the building was cut off by the city, for the purpose of widening the street. It was held, that the lessee, in the first instance, and if he declined, the lessor, had a right to build a new wall on the new line fixed for the street, and the expense of it was a proper item of claim for damages against the city. *Patterson* v. *Boston*, 20 Pick. 159 (1838).

183. Whether the lessee built such wall himself, or paid the lessor for building it, does not affect his claim against the city, unless the lessor built it on his own account and received remuneration from the city; in which case he was not entitled to recover the amount from the lessee, and the city is not to be charged a second time for the same damage. *Ib.*

184. The damage sustained by the lessee in being deprived of the use of his store, for which he is entitled to recover of the city, is to be computed for such time as would be reasonably necessary to remove his goods and make the repairs and move back again; and the loss of the value of the store to him for that period, and not the rent and taxes specifically, is the measure of the indemnity to which he is entitled. *Ib.*

185. The lessee is also to be remunerated for the diminished value of the premises for the residue of the term, caused by the taking of part of the premises, he continuing to pay rent and taxes at the same rate. *Ib.*

186. It seems, that he is not entitled to damages for loss of custom, occasioned by his being obliged to occupy a less advantageous place of business while the repairs are making. *Ib.*

187. Soon after the commencement of a lease for three years of a warehouse or store in Boston, in which lease the lessee covenanted to pay the rent during the term, and to

leave the premises in good repair, the city took the front part of the land on which the building stood, and cut down the front wall, for the purpose of widening the street. The building remained in this condition about two years, when the lessor took it down and erected a new store on the same site, but diminished by the strip of land taken by the city. Before the wall was taken down, the lessee removed into another store, and remained there until the new one was erected, when he removed back into the new one. In a complaint by the lessee against the city for damages, it was held, that the plaintiff was entitled to recover the expenses of removing his goods from and back to his original place of business, and for the loss of earnings for the few days occupied in such removals, and a reasonable sum for the rent of another store for so long a time as would reasonably have been required for putting up a new front wall; (or, if he had suspended his business, that he might have recovered for the loss of earnings during a reasonable time for rebuilding the wall;) that he had a right forthwith to rebuild the wall, carrying it up to the roof, and if he had done so, inasmuch as he could not have compelled a contribution from the lessor, he would have been entitled to recover the whole cost from the city; but that as he did not in fact put up the wall, but left the lessor to make his full claim for damages on the city, he could recover only such proportion of the estimated expense as his interest (regard being had to the portion of the store occupied by him and the time his lease had to run) bore to the value of the whole estate. *Patterson* v. *Boston*, 23 Pick. 425 (1839). See *Foster* v. *Boston*, 22 Pick. 39, 40.

188. An estimate, not on oath, of damages that would be sustained by a party over whose land a railroad was afterwards laid out, made by a committee of a town, while a petition of the town for a change of the route of the railroad was before the legislature, and merely stating those damages as the least the party would take, is not admissible in evidence to a jury empanelled to appraise damages caused by laying out the railroad over the land, although such estimate was made at the request of an agent of the railroad company. *Webber* v. *Eastern Railroad*, 2 Met. 147 (1840).

189. At a hearing before a sheriff's jury to assess damages caused by laying out a highway, the opinion of competent witnesses as to the comparative value of the land before and after the laying out, is competent evidence, its weight and value being determined by the jury. *Dwight* v. *Hampden*, 11 Cush. 201 (1853).

190. In estimating the benefit to a land owner from the laying out of a highway, the jury are not to inquire merely how much the estate would be benefited by selling for building lots, as if that must be the future use of the property, but may consider how much the estate would be benefited, using it as men of ordinary prudence, economy, and wisdom would use it. *Ib.*

191. Steps projecting from the door of a house, over land taken for a highway, are obstructions to the highway, and must be removed by the owner of the land, and are to be included in the assessment of the damages occasioned by such taking of his land; and so of eave spouts and bay windows, if they interfere with the public use of the entire limits of the highway. *Hyde* v. *Middlesex*, 2 Gray, 267 (1854).

192. The owner of land, who has built a house on a part thereof over which there is a right of way, may recover, as part of the damages occasioned by the subsequent taking of the land for a highway, the value of the right to have the house remain on the land until its removal be required by the owner of the right of way. *Tufts* v. *Charlestown*, 4 Gray, 537 (1855).

193. Upon the taking, for a highway, of part of land held by a parish for the site of a meeting-house and its appurtenances, the parish may recover damages for the diminution in value of the land for the purpose to which it was devoted, if it does not appear that they have any other right to the land, but cannot recover damages for the anticipated annoyance to worshippers in the meeting-house, resulting from the use of the highway on the Lord's day by noisy and dissolute persons, riding for pleasure. *Woburn* v. *Middlesex*, 7 Gray, 106 (1856).

194. The true rule of damages in most cases of this nature, is the diminution of the absolute value of the land owner's property by the laying out of the highway, and not the diminution of its value for the specific use to which he had devoted it. METCALF. J. *Ib.*

195. A jury empanelled to assess damages caused by altering a highway were instructed that they were to set off any benefit occasioned by the alteration; that this benefit must be some direct, peculiar and special benefit derived by this estate, and not the general benefit, acquired by all the estates adjacent, of having a wider street; that if the alteration by cutting off some of the petitioner's estate left a smaller estate with a longer front, which was of more value in the market, this was a benefit which should be allowed; but unless the petitioner's estate derived some benefit not received in common by all the other estates on that street between the two nearest cross streets, the benefit was not to be deducted. *Held*, that the respondents had no ground of exception. *Farwell* v. *Cambridge*, 11 Gray, 413 (1858).

196. When a town way has been laid out so that it is above the level of the adjoining land, a petitioner for damages to adjoining land may prove the cost of filling up which has become necessary in order to pass from his land to the way. *Plympton* v. *Woburn*, 11 Gray, 415 (1858).

197. Evidence that land taken for a highway has since been laid out as a sidewalk is inadmissible in reduction of the owner's damages. But evidence that when it was taken it was probable that it would be improved in that way is admissible. *Dickenson* v. *Fitchburg*, 13 Gray, 546 (1859).

198. It seems, that the surrender of a lease to the lessor, after the land has been taken for a highway, with a release of the lessee's claim to damages, is admissible in evidence on the assessment of the damages. *Ib.*

199. Evidence that a witness, not shown to be an expert, "offered the petitioners one dollar a foot for a portion of the land in question," is incompetent. *Ib.*

200. A witness who has testified to his opinion of the value of the land, may be asked on his examination in chief, the facts and reasons on which his opinion is founded. *Ib.*

201. The petitioner, if an expert, may testify to his opinion of the value of the land.

202. A special county commissioner, who as such has assessed damages in other cases for land taken for highways, is competent to give his opinion of the effect of taking for a highway part of certain land which he has often seen. *Ib.*

203. At a hearing for the assessment of damages occasioned by the location of a highway, a witness, called to testify to the value of land taken on one side of the highway, may be asked on cross-examination concerning the value of land upon the opposite side of the way, although the jury have not had their attention called to land upon that side. *Brown* v. *Worcester*, 13 Gray, 31 (1859).

204. On a petition under Rev. Sts. c. 24, § 55, (Gen. Sts. c. 43, § 79,) for damages for taking for a street certain land described by metes and bounds, damages may be recovered for an injury thereby resulting to adjoining land of the petitioner. *First Church in Boston* v. *Boston*, 14 Gray, 214 (1859).

205. A bridge, which had been built by a bridge corporation under a charter which authorized them to take tolls thereon for seventy years, unless the bridge should be sooner redeemed for the public under certain specified conditions, was laid out by a city as a highway. Upon a trial for the assessment by a jury of the damages sustained by the corporation by such laying out, the jury were instructed that they might take into consideration the petitioners' right of property in the bridge as a structure belonging to them, independently of their franchise, at the actual value of such a structure. *Held*, that the instruction was erroneous. *Central Bridge* v. *Lowell*, 15 Gray, (1860).

206. It was held, further, that the whole beneficial interest of the corporation consisted in their right to take the specified tolls until the grant should revert, or be redeemed according to the reservations therein made, and that the damages to be awarded to the petitioners should be a just and reasonable compensation for the appropriation to public use of this qualified and redeemable franchise. *Ib.*

207. In estimating the damages sustained by a railroad company by the laying out of a highway across their railroad, the jury have no right to take into consideration any supposed future benefit to them from a probable increase of business in consequence of the establishment of the new highway; and evidence of payments of money by them for accidents at their several crossings, and of the comparative profit of the local and other travel over their railroad, is inadmissible. *Boston & Maine Railroad* v. *Middlesex*, 1 Allen, 324 (1861).

208. If a petitioner for damages to land sustained by reason of the discontinuance of a highway relies upon title by deed and by possession, and evidence is offered of his possession thereof, and the only evidence of title by deed is of two deeds, one of which conveyed a part of the land in question to two other persons described as trustees of the United Society of Shakers, and the other conveyed the residue to the petitioner and another person as trustees of the same society, and these deeds are allowed to go to the jury as proper evidence, with instructions that they may decide upon the deeds and from the whole evidence, whether the petitioner is entitled to damages, a verdict for the petitioner assessing damages cannot be sustained. *Hawkins* v. *Berkshire*, 2 Allen, 254 (1861).

209. In assessing damages for taking a portion of an estate for widening a street, no allowance should be made for an increased injury to the residue of the estate from a supposed easement of light and air, claimed by an adjoining proprietor, unless its existence is proved or admitted by the petitioner. *Paine* v. *Boston*, 4 Allen, 168 (1862).

210. Evidence of actual sales of other similar land in the vicinity is competent, to aid in determining the value of land taken for widening a street. And if evidence of sales of other land on the same street, and within one hundred and seventy-six feet, is rejected on the sole ground that it is too remote, this is a sufficient reason for granting a new trial. *Ib.*

211. On the trial of a petition for the assessment of damages for land taken for a public way, evidence of the opinion of witnesses as to the value of land must be confined to the land in controversy. *Rand* v. *Newton*, 6 Allen, 38 (1863).

212. A petitioner for damages to land by reason of the widening of a street may be asked in cross-examination if he has not expressed opinions as to the effect of the alteration upon the value of the estates upon the street; and he will not be entitled to a new trial, after a verdict against him, because, in the same connection, other questions designed to aid in eliciting his real opinion upon this point were allowed to be put to him, especially if it does not appear what answers were given to them, although the questions taken by themselves alone might be irrelevant. *Fowler* v. *Middlesex*, 6 Allen, 92 (1863).

213. The value of the land in controversy may be proved by the testimony of witnesses personally acquainted with the subject, and sufficiently familiar with it to give an opinion. *Ib.*

213 *a.* Evidence of an unaccepted offer of a certain price for a piece of land is incompetent, for the purpose of showing its value. *Ib.*

(e) **Verdict, and Judgment thereon.**

214. The verdict of a jury by which the location of a way by commissioners is altered, is sufficiently certain if it gives the commencement and termination and the courses and distances, so that the actual location of the way by the jury can at any time be readily ascertained. *Merrill* v. *Berkshire*, 11 Pick. 269 (1831).

215. The jury have no authority to lay out the way over the land of any person except the petitioners for the jury; it is therefore not necessary that their verdict should name the owners of the land over which the way is established. *Ib.*

216. The jury cannot lawfully decide that there shall be no road, when the county commissioners have determined that common convenience requires that there should be one. *Ib.*

217. It is the province of the county commissioners to determine the general course and terminations of a highway, and the jury may make only such minor alterations as in their opinion may improve the highway or render it less burdensome to individuals or corporations affected by it. *Ib.*

218. Where the jury alter the course of the highway, they may of necessity assess the damages for such alteration. *Ib.*

219. An appeal lay to the supreme judicial court from the decision of the court of common pleas adjudicating upon the acceptance of the verdict of a jury in the case of laying out a highway, when the decision was founded on matter of law apparent on the record. *Lanesborough* v. *Berkshire*, 22 Pick. 278 (1839).

220. Where several parties over whose respective lands a highway had been laid out by county commissioners, applied for a jury to make alterations in the location and to reassess their damages, and all the cases were submitted to the same jury at the same time, and a verdict was returned confirming the location over the lands of some of the parties and assessing their damages severally, and stating that as to another part of the location the jury could not agree, it was held, that the verdict was a several verdict in each case; and accordingly that it ought to be received and accepted in each case in which the damages were assessed, and that the case in which the jury could not agree ought to be submitted to a new jury. *Ib.* See Gen. Sts. c. 43, § 23.

221. Where several parties aggrieved by the laying out of a highway, join in a petition for a jury, the verdict is in effect several distinct verdicts on the several rights of the parties, and it is competent to the court to accept and affirm the verdict as to one petitioner and set it aside as to another; and where the verdict is set aside as to one of the petitioners, a new jury should be granted him. *Anthony* v. *Berkshire*, 14 Pick. 189 (1833). See Gen. Sts. c. 43, § 23.

222. It is no ground of objection to the acceptance of the verdict of a jury, assessing damages occasioned to adjoining land by the raising or lowering of a highway, that there was no such determination of damages by the selectmen or mayor and aldermen as to authorize the county commissioners to issue a warrant for a jury. But such objection, if relied upon, must be taken before the county commissioners. *Flagg* v. *Worcester*, 8 Cush. 69 (1851).

223. County commissioners cannot object to a verdict assessing land damages, because the jury apportioned the damages to the different joint petitioners instead of awarding a gross sum. *Thayer* v. *Worcester*, 10 Cush. 151 (1852).

224. On a petition for the assessment of damages to the land of "A. B. and wife," damages cannot also be assessed for land held by A. B. in his own right. *Ib.*

224 *a.* A verdict of a jury assessing damages sustained by a party by the laying out of a road over his land, may be set aside for the reason that the damages are excessive. *Harding* v. *Medway*, 10 Met. 465 (1845).

225. An extension, by the jury, of the time allowed to the owner of land taken for a highway to take off his fences, trees, &c., to "the

first day of October next from the acceptance of this verdict," authorizes him, if exceptions are taken to the acceptance of the verdict by the court of common pleas, and overruled by this court, to take off his fences, trees, &c. at any time before the first of October next after such overruling of the exceptions. *Dwight* v. *Springfield*, 6 Gray, 442 (1856).

226. A verdict of a sheriff's jury under a complaint of A. B. and others for damages to land by reason of the laying out of a highway, which states as follows: "We find that the said complainants have sustained damages by means of said laying out of said street or way over or adjoining their land, and the continuance thereof, and we find and allow damages to each of them respectively as follows, to wit, to A. B. nothing," &c. should not be set aside as repugnant or against law, but should be accepted as a verdict that A. B. has sustained no damages for which he is entitled to compensation. *Chace* v. *Fall River*, 2 Allen, 533 (1861).

227. Under a warrant for a sheriff's jury to assess damages, "by reason of the locating, laying out and widening" of a street, a verdict of the jury assessing damages, or assessing no damages, by reason of "laying out" of the street, will be deemed to cover the whole subject matter submitted to them, and may be accepted. *Fowler* v. *Middlesex*, 6 Allen, 92 (1863).

V. Repairing Public Ways; Powers and Duties of Highway Surveyors.

228. Surveyors of highways, as such, have no authority except as to highways on land. *Austin* v. *Carter*, 1 Mass. 231 (1804).

229. The duty of repairing highways within their limits is enjoined on towns in this state, not by the common law, but only by statute. *Commonwealth* v. *Springfield*, 7 Mass. 13 (1810).

230. The duty required of towns to keep highways in repair, extends to defects and obstructions caused by snow. *Loker* v. *Brookline*, 13 Pick. 343 (1833).

231. Towns are not obliged to keep the whole of a highway, from one boundary to the other, free from obstructions and fit for the use of travellers. *Howard* v. *North Bridgewater*, 16 Pick. 189 (1834).

232. A town has no authority, it seems, to erect an embankment or other separate work, wholly detached from a road, for the purpose of facilitating the making, maintenance, or future repair of the road. *Anthony* v. *Adams*, 1 Met. 286 (1840).

233. Towns are bound by law to erect fences or railings on highways only at such places as, without them, would be unsafe or inconvenient for travellers exercising ordinary care. *Collins* v. *Dorchester*, 6 Cush. 396 (1850).

234. It is the duty of cities and towns to keep that part of the street which lies between the carriage-way and the sidewalk in such repair that foot-passengers may cross any part thereof with a reasonable degree of safety, using such care and caution as are adapted to to the nature of the case; and the establishing of raised crossings at proper distances is not a sufficient compliance with this duty. *Raymond* v. *Lowell*, 6 Cush. 524 (1850).

235. A city has a right to erect a barrier across the entrance of a passage way which opens upon and is below the level of a public street, if it is necessary to do so in order to make the street safe and convenient for travellers. *Alger* v. *Lowell*, 3 Allen, 402 (1862).

236. The surveyors of highways had authority to dig down or raise a street, even when there was no provision of statute for compensation of persons whose estates were thereby injured. *Callender* v. *Marsh*, 1 Pick. 418 (1823).

237. If such authority is exercised by them with discretion, and not wantonly, a party injured cannot maintain an action against them. *Ib.* See *Elder* v. *Bemis*, 2 Met. 599; *Benjamin* v. *Wheeler*, 16 Gray, .

238. A surveyor of highways is not liable to the town for damages which the town may be compelled to pay to a person injured by reason of a defect or want of repair existing in a highway through such surveyor's fault or neglect. *White* v. *Phillipston*, 10 Met. 108 (1845).

239. A surveyor of highways has no authority to repair a way at his own expense, and then call upon the town for an indemnity. *Jones* v. *Lancaster*, 4 Pick. 149 (1826). See Gen. Sts. c. 44, §§ 13, 14.

240. Thus, where a surveyor, before his limits were assigned, and without consulting the other surveyors, repaired at his own expense a way, which upon the assignment fell without his limits, it was held, that he was without remedy. *Ib.*

241. Under the Rev. Sts. c. 25, § 13, (Gen. Sts. c. 44, § 13.) the only authority of a surveyor of highways to charge a town for repairs of a road, when the highway tax is insufficient therefor, is by employing other persons to make such repairs; and those persons, and not the surveyor, may recover payment of the town for their labor. *Armstrong* v. *Wendell*, 9 Met. 522 (1845).

242. Where a defect in a highway, for an injury occasioned by which to person or property the town would be liable, is found to

exist on the Lord's day, it is the duty of such town to cause the defect to be repaired immediately, or to adopt measures to guard against the danger, until such repair can be made; and work, labor, or business for this purpose, is a work of necessity within the statute respecting the observance of the Lord's day. *Flagg* v. *Millbury*, 4 Cush. 243 (1849).

243. A town is not bound to keep in repair a cattle pass under a highway therein, such pass being the private way of an adjoining land owner, so that such land owner's cattle may pass through. *Baker* v. *Dedham*, 16 Gray, (1860).

244. A surveyor of highways lawfully removed wood which was placed within the limits of the highway, and notified the owner of the wood where he had put it, and told him he might have it on paying for the removal of it. *Held*, that the owner of the wood could not maintain an action to recover its value from the surveyor. *Plumer* v. *Brown*, 8 Met. 578 (1844).

245. An action for injuries occasioned to land of an abutter by acts done by direction of a surveyor of highways in digging a water-course in a highway, with the approbation of the selectmen, cannot be supported by evidence that the surveyor acted wantonly and with the intention to injure the plaintiff, or that the acts done were not necessary to the repair of the way. *Benjamin* v. *Wheeler*, 8 Gray, 409 (1857). S. C. 16 Gray, (1860).

246. A highway surveyor has no authority to make repairs upon a highway which has been discontinued by the legislature; and does not by making such repairs make his town responsible in damages to a person injured on such highway. *Tinker* v. *Russell*, 14 Pick. 279 (1833). But see now Gen. Sts. c. 44, § 26; *Hayden* v. *Attleborough*, 7 Gray, 338.

247. Although the liability of towns for damages from defects in ways opened and dedicated by their owners to the public use, but not duly laid out and established, is limited by statute, yet the actual repair of such a way by a town is conclusive evidence of its due location. *Hayden* v. *Attleborough*, 7 Gray, 338 (1856).

248. And such repairs made by the surveyors of highways are made by the town. *Ib.*

249. A surveyor of highways cannot recover compensation of the town for his official services. *Sikes* v. *Hatfield*, 13 Gray, 347 (1859).

250. Highway surveyors have no authority to accept a way in behalf of a town. *Reed* v. *Scituate*, 5 Allen, 120 (1862).

See *post*, 280, 309.

VI. Defects and Obstructions in Ways.

(a) Liability of Towns to an Action.

251. No action lies at common law against a town for damages sustained through a defect in a highway in such town. *Mower* v. *Leicester*, 9 Mass. 247 (1812).

252. Towns are liable to an individual for an injury occasioned by an incumbrance in the road (as by large stones left in it) as well as for one occasioned by any other defect in it. *Bigelow* v. *Weston*, 3 Pick. 267 (1825).

253. In St. 1786, c. 81, § 7, giving damages for injuries sustained by reason of a defect in any highway, the term "highway" includes town ways. *Jones* v. *Andover*, 6 Pick. 59 (1828). And see now Gen. Sts. c. 44, § 22.

254. It is no defence to an action for an injury caused by a defect in a highway, that the town used ordinary care and diligence in repairing the road, if by such care the road was not made safe and convenient, but remained defective. *Horton* v. *Ipswich*, 12 Cush. 488 (1853).

255. A city or town is not responsible in damages for the inconvenience and loss of business occasioned to the abutters on a street by incumbrances and obstructions placed in the street for the purpose of repairing it, or by opening a common sewer in the street. *Brooks* v. *Boston*, 19 Pick. 178 (1837).

256. After a highway has been regularly laid out by the county commissioners, and a time fixed for the town to complete it, and it is subsequently opened to the use of the public, the traveller has a right to presume that it has in fact become a highway, and the responsibility of the town for its safe condition thenceforth attaches. *Drury* v. *Worcester*, 21 Pick. 44 (1838).

257. An action cannot be maintained against a town for damages alleged to have been caused to the plaintiff by the obstruction of a road by snow, by reason whereof he was prevented from travelling on the road and from working on his wood lot. *Holman* v. *Townsend*, 13 Met. 297 (1847). See Gen. Sts. c. 44, § 24.

258. An action cannot be maintained against a town to recover damages for trouble, expense and loss of time incurred by the plaintiff in extricating his horses and sleigh from snow suffered by the town to remain upon a highway. *Brailey* v. *Southborough*, 6 Cush. 141 (1850). See Gen. Sts. c. 44, § 24.

259. In an action against the city of Boston, to recover damages for an injury occasioned by a defect in Second Street East, in South Boston, it was held, that in order to render the defendants liable, it was not sufficient to prove that the way complained of had been so

travelled and used as to become a highway *de facto*, but that it must appear, not only that such way has been laid out, but also that the mayor and aldermen, by an official act, had determined, under St. 1803, c. 111, that it should be completed, that is, graded, fitted for travel, and opened for use. *Bowman* v. *Boston*, 5 Cush. 1 (1849).

260. In an action against a town, to recover damages for an injury alleged to have been caused by a defect in a highway, occasioned by the want of a rail or barrier, the town will be liable therefor, if such rail or barrier was necessary for the proper security of travellers, and would have prevented the happening of the injury complained of. *Palmer* v. *Andover*, 2 Cush. 600 (1849).

261. The liability of a city or town for an injury occasioned by a defect in a street or way, is not varied or discharged, if the defect is occasioned by the exercise of the right of an adjoining owner of land, to use the street or way for some private purpose, not inconsistent with the right of the public. *Bacon* v. *Boston*, 3 Cush. 174 (1849).

262. Notice to a town of a defect in a highway may be inferred from the notoriety of the defect, and its continuance for such a length of time as to lead to the presumption that the proper officers of the town knew, or, with proper vigilance and care, might have known of it. *Reed* v. *Northfield*, 13 Pick. 94 (1832).

263. The only remedy to which a party injured in consequence of a defect in a public highway is entitled, against the city or town bound to keep the same in repair, is the remedy provided by statute; and under the Rev. Sts. c. 25, § 22, where the defect has not existed for twenty-four hours, the party injured thereby is not entitled to damages. *Brady* v. *Lowell*, 3 Cush. 121 (1849). But see Gen. Sts. c. 44, § 22.

264. In computing the time of twenty-four hours, during which a defect in a highway must have existed, in order to render the town liable for an injury occasioned thereby, Sunday is to be included. *Flagg* v. *Millbury*, 4 Cush. 243 (1849).

265. If an injury is caused by reason of the elevation of one edge of a plank, which is laid over an open space left for the passage of water in a public street, and this is found to be an actionable defect, it is enough to authorize a verdict for the plaintiff if the plank has been split, loose, liable to change and unsafe for twenty-four hours before the accident, or if the city authorities had reasonable notice of its unsafe condition, although the position of the plank which was the immediate cause of the accident had continued only for a short time. *Winn* v. *Lowell*, 1 Allen, 177 (1861).

266. A town placing at sunset, around a well opened in the highway, such barriers as to make it safe for the night to persons using ordinary care, is not responsible for an injury suffered during the same night, by a foot passenger, by reason of the removal of such barriers, unless the town had notice of such removal, and of the way having been thereby rendered unsafe. *Doherty* v. *Waltham*, 4 Gray, 596 (1855).

267. Where the owners of land in a city open and dedicate it to the public use, as a footway, placing a fence across it, which allows foot passengers to pass, but is dangerous to horses and carriages, the city, whether it has accepted the way or not, is not liable for an injury occasioned by the fence to a horse and carriage, although driven with ordinary skill and care. *Hemphill* v. *Boston*, 8 Cush. 195 (1851).

268. The obligation of a town to make roads safe and convenient for travellers continues where such roads are crossed by railroads at grade, except so far as the necessary use of the crossing by the railroad may prevent it, and subject to such specific directions as may be given by the county commissioners. *Davis* v. *Leominster*, 1 Allen, 182 (1861).

269. If the proprietors of a railroad, acting within the scope of their lawful authority, construct a cattle guard in their road, at a place where it crosses a highway on the same level; and the town erect and maintain a sufficient and proper barrier against such cattle guard, up to the railroad, and as far as can be done without impeding the passage of cars on the same; the town is not responsible for an injury sustained by a traveller on the highway, in consequence of his falling into the cattle guard, without any fault or neglect on his part. *Jones* v. *Waltham*, 4 Cush. 299 (1849).

270. A town is not responsible for a defect or want of repair in a bridge, whereby a public highway passes over a railroad, the proprietors of which are bound by law to keep the bridge in repair. *Sawyer* v. *Northfield*, 7 Cush. 490 (1851).

271. A town is not liable for injuries done to a traveller on the highway, by a locomotive engine run by a railroad corporation on a track illegally laid across the highway. *Vinal* v. *Dorchester*, 7 Gray, 421 (1856).

272. By St. 1830, c. 4, establishing the Boston & Lowell Railroad Corporation, it is provided (§ 11) that if the railroad should cross any highway, it should be so constructed as not to impede the safe and convenient use of such highway. Where an excavation was made by such corporation in a highway for the purpose of constructing the railroad across it, and an injury was sustained by a person travelling on the highway, in the evening, in

consequence of being thrown into the excavation, it was held, that the town in which such highway was situated was liable to an action for such injury, although the town had given notice to the superintendent of the work on the railroad that a barrier must be put up for the protection of travellers on the highway, and such superintendent had promised that this should be done. *Currier* v. *Lowell*, 16 Pick. 170 (1835).

273. The want of a railing at the side of a highway, necessary to the security of travellers, is a "deficiency" in the way, within the meaning of Rev. Sts. c. 25, § 26 (Gen. Sts. c. 44, § 26). *Hayden* v. *Attleborough*, 7 Gray, 338 (1856).

274. A town is not liable for damages sustained by a traveller upon a highway by reason of a telegraph post erected within the limits of the highway by an electric telegraph company, in a place prescribed by the selectmen of the town. *Young* v. *Yarmouth*, 9 Gray, 386 (1857).

275. A town is liable for injuries occasioned to a traveller using due care, by a ditch dug in the highway by an aqueduct corporation under license from the selectmen, and left open twenty-four hours. *Merrill* v. *Wilbraham*, 11 Gray, 154 (1858).

276. An individual cannot maintain an action against a town for suffering a cattle pass under a highway, which is his private way, to be out of repair, so that his cattle cannot safely pass through. *Baker* v. *Dedham*, 16 Gray, (1860).

277. If the expense of keeping a bridge in repair is imposed by statute upon several towns and a railroad company jointly, with a provision that the municipal authorities of one of the towns shall have the care and superintendence of it, and shall employ all services necessary in the care of it, no action lies against said town in favor of the railroad company, to recover for damages sustained by the latter in consequence of a defect in the bridge. *Malden & Melrose Railroad* v. *Charlestown*, 8 Allen, 245 (1864).

278. If a travelled way, either public or private, over private lots adjoining a public street in which an excavation has been made, and leading into that street, has been so much used by persons having occasion to pass, for a long time before and after the existence of the excavation, as to become known as a common way for travel and to make it reasonably necessary for the city, in the exercise of due and proper care, to provide a barrier for the purpose of preventing travellers who come over such way from the adjacent lots, and use due care, from falling into the excavation in the street, and the city have unreasonably neglected to erect such barrier, they are guilty of negligence and are liable for an injury happening to a traveller in the street by reason thereof. *Burnham* v. *Boston*, 10 Allen, 290 (1865).

279. A rope stretched across a highway, above the ground, and attached at each end to objects which are outside of the limits of the highway, and in temporary use, is not a defect or want of repair in the highway for which a city is liable to a traveller who receives an injury from coming into collision with it while it is in motion from human agency. *Barber* v. *Roxbury*, 11 Allen, (1865).

280. A surveyor of highways may recover against his town for damages happening to him through a defect in the highways within his own district, unless the defect arose from his own neglect. *Wood* v. *Waterville*, 4 Mass. 422 (1808). See *post*, 309.

281. A person who travels on the Lord's day, neither from necessity nor charity, cannot maintain an action against a town for an injury received by him, while so travelling, by reason of a defect in a highway which the town is by law obliged to repair. *Bosworth* v. *Swansey*, 10 Met. 363 (1845). *Jones* v. *Andover*, 10 Allen, 18 (1865).

282. A husband, whose wife has been injured by reason of a defect in a highway, cannot maintain an action against the town obliged by law to repair the same, to recover for medical and other expenses incurred, or for the loss of his wife's services, in consequence of such injury. *Harwood* v. *Lowell*, 4 Cush. 310 (1849).

283. A traveller upon a highway, who stops and ties his horse outside of the limits of the highway, using due care, cannot, if the horse gets loose and runs upon the highway, and suffers an injury from a defect therein, maintain an action against the town for such injury. *Richards* v. *Enfield*, 13 Gray, 344 (1859).

284. A town is liable for an injury occasioned by a defect in a highway which the town is bound to repair, to an elephant driven over it with due care, if in the opinion of the jury an elephant, at the time and place and under the circumstances of the accident, was an animal which it was reasonably proper to take over a highway kept for the reasonable use of the public. *Gregory* v. *Adams*, 14 Gray, 242 (1859).

285. A police officer is not the servant of the city which appoints him, in any such sense as to take away his right of action against it for an injury sustained by reason of a defective highway. *Kimball* v. *Boston*, 1 Allen, 417 (1861).

286. A town is not liable in damages to one who, while stopping in the highway for

the purpose of conversation, leans against a defective railing, and is injured by reason of its insufficiency. *Stickney* v. *Salem*, 3 Allen, 374 (1862).

287. One who lives upon and is acquainted with the condition of a way which has never been formally dedicated to the public, or accepted or treated by the city in which it lies as a public way, but which was constructed by a private corporation upon its own land for its own use and convenience and the use and convenience of tenants occupying its houses upon both sides thereof, and who has seen a sign, "Private way," at one end thereof, cannot sustain an action against the city for an injury sustained by reason of a defect therein while in the use of ordinary care, although the way opens into a public street, and has been open to public travel for more than twenty years without interruption, and the city has not closed up the entrance to the same or in any way given notice that it was dangerous. *Durgin* v. *Lowell*, 3 Allen, 398 (1862).

288. No action lies against a city which is bound to keep a bridge in repair, to recover damages sustained by reason of a defect therein, by an inhabitant of the city who, at the time of receiving the injury complained of, was driving across the same at a rate faster than a walk, in violation of a city ordinance, although he did not know of the existence of the ordinance. *Heland* v. *Lowell*, 3 Allen, 407 (1862).

289. No action lies to recover damages for the obstruction of a highway, against a city which is bound to keep it in repair, by an individual whose place of business thereby becomes more difficult to reach, his business injured, the delivery of articles which he has sold and the gathering in of his crops more expensive, his houses less desirable for tenants, and his rents diminished in value, if other persons suffer damages from the same cause, similar in kind, though less in degree. *Willard* v. *Cambridge*, 3 Allen, 574 (1862).

290. A person who, while using a highway simply for the purpose of play, meets with a personal injury by reason of a defect therein, cannot maintain an action to recover damages therefor against the city or town which is bound to keep the same in repair. *Blodgett* v. *Boston*, 8 Allen, 237 (1864).

291. Payment of a sum of money "in full payment and satisfaction for all claim for damages and costs" in a suit against a corporation for an injury sustained by the plaintiff therein by reason of falling into a trench alleged to have been dug by its servants in a public highway, is a bar to a subsequent action for the same injury against the town which was bound to keep the highway in repair. *Brown* v. *Cambridge*, 3 Allen, 474 (1862).

As to Sidewalks.

292. Sidewalks, when a part of the public streets, as in the city of Boston, are to be kept in a safe and convenient state of repair for public use; and a sidewalk in the city of Boston, six and a half feet in width, should be so constructed and fitted for use, through its entire width, as to be safe and convenient. *Bacon* v. *Boston*, 3 Cush. 174 (1849).

293. The act of 1833, c. 128, respecting the streets of Boston, and the city ordinance passed in pursuance thereof, authorizing the surveyors of highways to regulate the width and height of sidewalks, and to accept and bind the city to maintain the same, when built and relinquished to the city by the abutters, do not exonerate the city, when a sidewalk has been thus built, accepted and relinquished, from its liability, under the Rev. Sts. c. 25, § 22, (Gen. Sts. c. 44, § 22,) for defects therein. *Ib.*

294. The city of Boston is required to keep the sidewalks within its duly established streets in good repair and clear of snow and ice, so that they shall, at all seasons of the year, be safe and convenient for persons travelling and passing thereon. And the city is in no degree exonerated from its obligations in these particulars in consequence of the adoption of ordinances requiring the owners of buildings adjoining the sidewalks to keep the sidewalks free from snow and ice, though such ordinances are valid, and relieve the city of expense in the performance of these duties. *Kirby* v. *Boylston Market Association*, 14 Gray, 249 (1859).

295. The projection of the movable grating of a culvert, from one to two inches above the edge of the sidewalk against which it rests, is not a defect which shows such a want of ordinary care on the part of the city as will make them responsible for an injury occasioned by stumbling over the grating. *Raymond* v. *Lowell*, 6 Cush 524 (1850). See *ante*, 234.

296. A city is liable to pay damages to a person who receives an injury by the fall of an awning projected over the sidewalk of a street by the owner of a building, if the awning be dangerous to travellers for the space of twenty-four hours before the injury happens. *Drake* v. *Lowell*, 13 Met. 292 (1847). See *Day* v. *Milford*, 5 Allen, 98 (*post*, 348).

297. A city is not liable for an injury caused to a foot passenger on a sidewalk which the city is bound to keep in repair, by the falling of an overhanging mass of snow and ice from the roof of a building not owned by the city, although it has so overhung the highway for more than twenty-four hours

before the accident. *Hixon* v. *Lowell*, 13 Gray, 59 (1859).

See *post*, 324, 326, 333, 334, 348, 360, 374, 375, 382, 383, 387.

As to Defects out of the Travelled Path.

298. Obstructions in a highway, though not on the travelled part, are defects for injuries caused by which towns are responsible under the statute, whether placed there by the owner of the soil over which the highway is laid, or others. *Snow* v. *Adams*, 1 Cush. 443 (1848).

299. Towns are not obliged to keep the whole of a highway, from one boundary to the other, free from obstructions and fit for the use of travellers. *Howard* v. *North Bridgewater*, 16 Pick. 189 (1834).

300. A town is not liable for obstructions and defects in portions of the highway not a part of the travelled path, and not so connected with it that they would affect the safety or convenience of those travelling on the highway and using the travelled part. *Kellogg* v. *Northampton*, 4 Gray, 65 (1855).

301. A town is not liable for an injury sustained by a party using the road for the purpose of passing to or from his private way or path, or his own land, caused by a defect within the limits of the highway as located by law, but outside the part of the road used for public travel. *Ib.*

302. A town is liable for injuries received by reason of a defect without the limits of the located way, if it is so near the way as to render travelling there dangerous, and there is nothing to warn travellers of it. *Hayden* v. *Attleborough*, 7 Gray, 338 (1856).

303. An action against a town, to recover damages for an injury received by reason of a defect or want of repair in a highway which the town is by law obliged to repair, cannot be maintained by a party who goes out of the highway, because of the defect therein, into the adjoining land, and there receives an injury. *Tisdale* v. *Norton*, 8 Met. 388 (1844).

304. Where a traveller on a highway, while in the exercise of ordinary care, received an injury in consequence of driving his wagon against a post; and it appeared that the line of the highway was not indicated by any visible objects; that the post, which occasioned the injury, was near the true line of the highway, and within the limits of the general course and direction of the travel, and where travellers were accustomed to pass, and rendered the travelling dangerous; that there was nothing to indicate that the post was not within the way intended for public travel; and that the town, though they had reasonable notice of the course of the travel, and that the post was dangerous to travellers, suffered it to remain an unreasonable time: It was held, that the town was liable for the injury sustained by the plaintiff. *Coggswell* v. *Lexington*, 4 Cush. 307 (1849).

305. A town is not liable for an injury occasioned to a traveller passing from a public highway to a railroad station through a road opened by the proprietors of the railroad for that purpose, by a block of stone, lying within the limits of the highway, as located, and obstructing the entrance to the road to the station, if it does not obstruct the road bed of the highway. *Smith* v. *Wendell*, 7 Cush. 498 (1851).

306. A town is not liable for an injury sustained by a traveller while straying outside of the limits of the highway, when the whole highway and the land next adjoining are safe and convenient to travel upon; nor are towns obliged to maintain fences merely to keep travellers from straying out of the highway. *Sparhawk* v. *Salem*, 1 Allen, 30 (1861).

307. A large vehicle used as a daguerrean saloon, standing partly within the limits of a highway, but outside of and several feet from the travelled path, is not a defect in the highway which will entitle a traveller to recover against a town damages for the injuries sustained by him, if his horse, while driven by himself, is frightened thereby, and becomes unmanageable, and runs for some distance, and upon an embankment, so that the carriage is broken, and himself thrown upon the ground and injured. *Keith* v. *Easton*, 2 Allen, 552 (1861).

308. An action lies against a city to recover damages for an injury sustained by reason of the want of a railing at a point so near to a declivity outside of the limits of the street as to make the street dangerous for travellers, although the injury is not received by passing down the declivity directly from the street itself. *Alger* v. *Lowell*, 3 Allen, 402 (1862).

See *ante*, 283; *post*, 388.

(b) Where the Plaintiff's Negligence or other Causes concur.

309. A surveyor of highways sustaining damage from a defect in the highway within his district, which arises from his own neglect, has no remedy against the town for such damage. *Wood* v. *Waterville*, 5 Mass. 294 (1809).

310. But he may recover damages for such injury, if the defect did not arise from his own neglect. *Wood* v. *Waterville*, 4 Mass. 422 (1808).

311. One who is injured by an obstruction placed unlawfully in a highway, cannot maintain an action for damages, if it appears that he did not use ordinary care, by which the

obstruction might have been avoided. *Smith* v. *Smith*, 2 Pick. 621 (1824).

312. A traveller, in order to be entitled to recover damages of a town, for loss caused by a deficiency in a road, is not obliged to look far ahead in order to guard against obstacles which ought not to be suffered to exist. *Thompson* v. *Bridgewater*, 7 Pick. 188 (1829).

313. Thus, where a person travelling with a horse and wagon might, from an eminence in the road, have seen that a causeway at a considerable distance, which he intended to pass over, was covered with water, but when he descended the hill the causeway was out of sight until he had proceeded too far either to turn back or go on with safety, it was held, that he had not been guilty of negligence; and as he then used ordinary care in endeavoring to extricate his horse from the danger, but without success, he was entitled to recover for damages thereupon incurred. *Ib.*

314. The fact that a person injured through a defect in a highway, had previous knowledge of the defect, is not conclusive evidence of negligence on his part. *Reed* v. *Northfield*, 13 Pick. 94 (1832).

315. The facts that the person injured was an inhabitant of the town in which the highway was situated, and knew of the defect, but omitted to give notice of it to the town, have no bearing on the question of the town's liability for the injury sustained. *Ib.*

316. In an action against a town for an injury sustained by the overturning of the plaintiff's carriage on a highway in such town, the burden of proof is on the plaintiff to show that he was driving with ordinary skill and diligence at the time when the accident happened. *Adams* v. *Carlisle*, 21 Pick. 146 (1838).

317. In an action for an injury to the plaintiff alleged to have been occasioned by the defendant's negligence in driving upon the highway, the burden of proof is on the plaintiff, not only to show negligence and misconduct on the part of the defendant, but ordinary care and diligence on his own part. *Lane* v. *Crombie*, 12 Pick. 177 (1831).

318. In an action against a town for an injury occasioned by a defect in a highway, the question whether or not there was negligence, or want of ordinary care, on the part of the plaintiff, is to be determined by the jury, under all the circumstances of the case. *Bigelow* v. *Rutland*, 4 Cush. 247 (1849).

319. Where a person who had occasion to cross in the daytime from one side of a street to the other, selected for that purpose a portion of the street which, having been necessarily and properly appropriated for a drain, was covered by an iron grating, and, in attempting to cross over the grating, fell and was injured, there being no reason for attempting to cross at that place rather than at any other part of the street; it was held, that the passenger, in attempting to cross at that particular spot, was not in the exercise of ordinary care, and could not therefore recover damages of the city for the injury so suffered. *Raymond* v. *Lowell*, 6 Cush. 524 (1850).

320. A person travelling on a highway obstructed with snow, must use ordinary care in determining whether to proceed or return; and if guilty of negligence in proceeding, he cannot recover for any injury received from the defect in the way to which his negligence in any way contributed. *Horton* v. *Ipswich*, 12 Cush. 488 (1853).

321. If the horse driven by the plaintiff runs in consequence of a defect in the road, the plaintiff is bound to use ordinary care as well after as before the horse begins to run. He cannot abandon himself to needless alarm or give up all proper control of his horse in consequence of the peril to which he is exposed, but must use such care as a person of ordinary prudence and discretion would exercise if placed in similar circumstances and exposed to a like danger. *Brooks* v. *Petersham*, 16 Gray, (1860).

322. And it is an error to instruct the jury, that "the mere want of prudent management on the part of the plaintiff or his companion after the horse began to run, or the mere fact that he imprudently seized the reins and turned the horse from the road, would not exonerate the defendants." *Ib.*

323. Common prudence requires of a person of poor sight greater care in walking upon the public streets, and in avoiding obstructions, than is required of persons of good sight; and if it appears that the plaintiff's eyesight was poor and weak, the omission so to instruct the jury, in compliance with the request of the defendants, is sufficient ground for a new trial. *Winn* v. *Lowell*, 1 Allen, 177 (1861).

324. If a man, while not exercising ordinary care himself, receives an injury by falling into a cellar way dug through a sidewalk, he cannot recover damages therefor against a city, although the city may have been in fault in not erecting a barrier to guard the opening. *Fallon* v. *Boston*, 3 Allen, 38 (1861).

325. In an action to recover damages for a personal injury sustained by reason of a defective way, it is no error to refuse to instruct the jury that if the plaintiff was familiar with the place where the accident occurred, it was his duty to use more care in passing there than if he was wholly ignorant of its condition, or to avoid the place altogether, if in-

structions were given that the burden of proof was on him to show that he used reasonable care, adapted to the circumstances of the case, and that if he was familiar with the place, they should take this fact into consideration, and determine whether on account of it he ought to have used increased care in passing over it, or to have avoided it altogether. *Smith* v. *Lowell*, 6 Allen, 39 (1863).

326. A person who voluntarily attempts to pass over a sidewalk which he knows to be very dangerous, by reason of ice upon it, when he might easily avoid it, cannot maintain an action against the town which is bound to keep the way in repair, to recover for injuries sustained by falling on the ice. *Wilson* v. *Charlestown*, 8 Allen, 137 (1864).

327. This court cannot decide, upon a bill of exceptions, that driving a safe horse, with a tight rein, at night, at his usual speed of ten miles an hour, by a skilful driver, over a wide and level road, with which he is familiar, and over which he has passed in safety within an hour without perceiving any obstruction, is such a want of ordinary care as to prevent a recovery for an injury sustained from a defective highway. *Reed* v. *Deerfield*, 8 Allen, 522 (1864).

328. This court cannot decide, upon a bill of exceptions, that riding a safe horse on a dark night, bareback and without martingales, over a familiar road, by a person accustomed to the use of horses and to that horse, and turning out upon meeting a carriage, show such want of ordinary care as to prevent a recovery for an injury sustained by reason of a defective highway. *Stevens* v. *Boxford*, 10 Allen, 25 (1865).

328 *a*. If, in an action to recover damages for an injury sustained from a collision with a wagon left standing in a highway by the defendant, the evidence shows that the plaintiff had seen the obstruction there on the day of the accident, that he was accustomed to drive horses, and that the accident happened while he was driving a gentle horse in a dark evening on a slow trot, looking out on one side of the horse for a blanket which he had shortly before lost from his wagon, and his companion was looking for the blanket on the other side, and neither of them saw the defendant's wagon before the collision, it cannot be held as a matter of law that the plaintiff was so careless as to preclude his recovery, but the question should be submitted to the jury. *Fox* v. *Sackett*, 10 Allen, 535 (1865).

329. In order to recover of a town for injuries sustained from a defect in its highway, the traveller must not only drive with due care and skill, but must be using a proper horse and vehicle, with strong and suitable harness; and if there be any defect in these particulars, and such defect contributes to the disaster, the town is not liable, although the way be defective. The reason is, that it is impossible to know what proportion of the damage is occasioned by one, and what by the other, or whether there would have been any damage at all but for the traveller's own default. Shaw, C. J., in *Murdock* v. *Warwick*, 4 Gray, 180 (1855).

330. Therefore, if the vicious habits of the plaintiff's horse contributed to the injury, the plaintiff cannot recover. *Ib.*

331. If there is evidence tending to show that the accident happened in consequence of the youth and vicious conduct of the plaintiff's horse, the defendants have no ground of exception to a ruling by the judge that "ordinary care requires a person driving on the highway to do so with a horse which will not, when exposed to ordinary objects and noises upon and along the highway, become unmanageable by a driver of ordinary skill and prudence;" and that, "if a vicious or untrained condition of the horse for ordinary public travel contributed with the insufficiency of the rail to produce the injury, the plaintiff cannot recover." *Bliss* v. *Wilbraham*, 8 Allen, 564 (1864).

332. In an action against a bridge corporation to recover damages for an injury sustained by the plaintiff in consequence of the lamps of the bridge not being lighted, as required by law, it was held, that the burden of proof was on the defendants, to show that there was no negligence on their part in this respect. *Worster* v. *Canal Bridge*, 16 Pick. 541 (1835).

333. The liability of a city or town for an injury occasioned by a defect in a street or way, is not varied or discharged, if the defect is occasioned by the exercise of the right of an adjoining owner of land to use the street or way for some private purpose, not inconsistent with the right of the public, as by constructing a cellar window opening into a sidewalk, within the limits of a street. *Bacon* v. *Boston*, 3 Cush. 174 (1849).

334. A city is not liable for an injury suffered by slipping and falling upon a sidewalk, from the combined effect of the unsafe condition of the sidewalk and of the like condition of steps without the limits of the highway. *Rowell* v. *Lowell*, 7 Gray, 100 (1856).

335. A town is not liable to a person injured by the combined effect of a defect in the highway and the negligence of a third person. *Kidder* v. *Dunstable*, 7 Gray, 104 (1856).

336. A city is not liable for an injury caused by the combined effect of the unsafe condition of a highway and the unlawful or careless act of a third person. *Shepherd* v. *Chelsea*, 4 Allen, 113 (1862).

337. An action lies against a city to recover damages for an injury sustained by being pushed from a public street down an unguarded and dangerous declivity by a crowd, if it was not done through the wilful act or negligence of the crowd, or of any person therein. *Alger* v. *Lowell*, 3 Allen, 402 (1862).

338. Driving a sleigh without the bells required by Rev. Sts. c. 51, §§ 2, 3, (Gen. Sts. c. 77, §§ 3, 4,) does not make the driver liable, nor exempt the town from liability, for injuries caused by collision with his sleigh upon a defective highway, unless his neglect contributes in some degree to the accident. *Kidder* v. *Dunstable*, 11 Gray, 342 (1858). See *Counter* v. *Couch*, 8 Allen, 436.

See *ante*, 271, 283; *post*, 371, 379.

Direct and Proximate Cause.

339. The action given by Rev. Sts. c. 25, § 22, (Gen. Sts. c. 44, § 22,) must be for a damage sustained in using the road, with due care and skill. The damage for which the statute gives a remedy, must be one of which the defect in the highway is the direct and proximate cause, and therefore damage sustained in consequence of not being able to use a highway, because of snow negligently suffered to remain thereon, cannot be recovered under it. *Holman* v. *Townsend*, 13 Met. 297 (1847). *Brailey* v. *Southborough*, 6 Cush. 141 (1850). See Gen. Sts. c. 44, § 24.

340. So an owner of land, who is prevented from a convenient access thereto by reason of a defect in the highway, and thereby sustains damage, is not entitled to recover the same of the town liable to keep such highway in repair. *Smith* v. *Dedham*, 8 Cush. 522 (1851).

341. A town is liable for an injury occasioned by a defect in a highway, where the primary cause of the injury is a pure accident, as, for example, the failure of some part of a carriage; provided the accident occur without the fault or negligence of the party injured, and be one which common prudence and sagacity could not have foreseen and provided against; and provided also, that the injury would not have been sustained but for the defect in the highway. *Palmer* v. *Andover*, 2 Cush. 600 (1849).

342. If a traveller, in the exercise of ordinary care and prudence, voluntarily leaps from his carriage, because of its near approach to a dangerous defect in the highway, and thereby sustains an injury, the town is liable, although the carriage does not come in actual contact with the defect. *Lund* v. *Tyngsboro*, 11 Cush. 563 (1853). See *Ingalls* v. *Bills*, 9 Met. 1.

343. If a horse, drawing a vehicle, though driven with due care, becomes frightened and excited by reason of the striking of the vehicle against a defect in the highway, frees himself from the control of his driver, runs, and at the distance of fifty rods from the defect knocks down a person on foot in the highway, who is using reasonable care, the city or town bound to keep the highway in repair is not responsible to such person for the injury so occasioned to him, though no other cause intervene between the defect and the injury. (Thomas, J. dissenting.) *Marble* v. *Worcester*, 4 Gray, 395 (1855).

344. If a horse, going off a highway by reason of a defect therein, falls upon a fence, and, in being removed from the fence with reasonable care and skill, suffers injury, the town is liable for such injury. *Tuttle* v. *Holyoke*, 6 Gray, 447 (1856).

345. A loaded wagon, while the driver was using reasonable care, was strained and injured by a defect in the highway, and the driver stopped and examined it, and then proceeded on his journey, and after passing over a rough and muddy road, and while on a smooth and level road, the axletree broke, and he was thrown from the wagon and injured. *Held*, that the accident to the driver could not be considered to have resulted directly and immediately from the existence of the defect in the highway, and that the town was not responsible for the injury to him. *Jenks* v. *Wilbraham*, 11 Gray, 142 (1858).

346. An action lies against a city to recover damages for an injury sustained by being pushed from a public street down an unguarded and dangerous declivity by a crowd, if it was not done through the wilful act or negligence of the crowd, or of any person therein. *Alger* v. *Lowell*, 3 Allen, 402 (1862).

347. A town is not responsible in damages if a horse, being frightened by an accident, breaks away from his driver and escapes from all control, and afterwards while running at large meets with an injury through a defect in a highway. *Davis* v. *Dudley*, 4 Allen, 557 (1862).

348. A town is liable, under Gen. Sts. c. 44, § 22, to pay damages to a person who receives an injury by the fall of an awning projected over the sidewalk of a street by the owner of a building, if the awning has been, for the space of twenty-four hours before the happening of the injury, so frail that in the winds, rains and snows ordinarily occurring in this climate it was likely to fall, and did fall, from such cause, although the direct cause was snow which fell thereon less than twenty-four hours before. *Day* v. *Milford*, 5 Allen, 98 (1862).

See *ante*, 307.

(c) **Evidence, Trial, Damages.**

349. It seems, that if the inhabitants of a town, in making a county road, deviate from the true location, they are estopped, in an action against them for an injury occasioned by its being out of repair, to deny their liability to maintain it as they have made it. *Williams* v. *Cummington*, 18 Pick. 312 (1836).

350. The erection and support of a bridge by a town, and the use of it by the public, for thirty-eight years, is sufficient proof of its existence as a highway, on the presumption of a laying out, a grant or a dedication, to render the town liable for an injury occasioned by its being out of repair. *Ib.* And see Gen. Sts. c. 44, § 26.

351. In an action against a town for an injury sustained by the overturning of the plaintiff's carriage on a highway in such town, the burden of proof is on the plaintiff to show that he was driving with ordinary skill and diligence at the time when the accident happened. *Adams* v. *Carlisle*, 21 Pick. 146 (1838).

352. The facts that the person injured was an inhabitant of the town in which the highway was situated, and knew of the defect, but omitted to give notice of it to the town, have no bearing on the question of the town's liability for the injury sustained. *Reed* v. *Northfield*, 13 Pick. 94 (1832).

353. In the trial of an action against a city for an injury occasioned by a defect in a street therein, the presiding judge, having instructed the jury that what was a defect in a highway which would render a town or city liable for an injury occasioned thereby, was a "practical question, to be determined by the jury in view of the circumstances of each particular case," added, by way of illustration, "that a different state of repair would be required in a city, where a large amount and variety of travel was constantly passing, from that in a country place, where the state of things in this respect was different." It was held, that this illustration was a proper comment on the law. *Fitz* v. *Boston*, 4 Cush. 365 (1849).

354. Where a jury were instructed that towns were not ordinarily bound by law to fence their roads, but were afterwards instructed that towns were bound to erect fences or railings at places which would otherwise be unsafe or inconvenient for travellers exercising ordinary care; it was held, that there was no legal exception to the instruction. *Collins* v. *Dorchester*, 6 Cush. 396 (1850).

355. The refusal of the presiding judge to rule, at the trial of an action against a town for damages occasioned by a defect in a highway, that in order to maintain the action the defect must be of such a nature that the town would have been liable to indictment therefor, is not open to exception. *Goldthwait* v. *East Bridgewater*, 5 Gray, 61 (1855).

356. In an action to recover damages of a town for injuries received from a defect within the located limits of a highway but without the travelled path, if the judge instruct the jury generally that the defendants are liable for a failure to keep the highway at that place safe and convenient for travel, without more particularly defining such liability for defects without the travelled path, though requested by the defendants so to qualify the instructions, the defendants are entitled to a new trial. *Kellogg* v. *Northampton*, 4 Gray, 65 (1855).

357. It is a question of fact for the jury, and not of law for the court, whether a town has used ordinary care in the construction of its roads, and whether the latter are reasonably safe. *Hall* v. *Lowell*, 10 Cush. 260 (1852).

358. It is no defence to an action for an injury caused by a defect in a highway, that the town used ordinary care and diligence in repairing the road, if by such care the road was not made safe and convenient, but remained defective. *Horton* v. *Ipswich*, 12 Cush. 488 (1853).

359. The damages recoverable against a town, under Rev. Sts. c. 25, § 22, (Gen. Sts. c. 44, § 22,) are for an injury to the person or property only, and not merely on account of a risk or peril, which caused fright and mental suffering; but, where an actual injury to the person is sustained, however small, which causes mental suffering, that suffering is a part of the injury, for which the town is liable in damages. *Canning* v. *Williamstown*, 1 Cush. 451 (1848).

360. On the trial of an action against the city of Boston, for an injury sustained by the plaintiff, in consequence of falling into a cellar window opening into a sidewalk within the limits of a public street, the existence of similar apertures in various other parts of the city, in great numbers, and for a long time, will not authorize the jury to find that such apertures are not actionable obstructions. *Bacon* v. *Boston*, 3 Cush. 174 (1849).

361. In an action against a town or city, to recover damages for an injury occasioned by a defect in a highway in that part thereof lying between the carriage-way and the sidewalk, the defendants may show, as having a bearing upon the question of ordinary care, that in other towns and cities inequalities in the surface of that part of the highway are of common occurrence; but evidence that such inequalities are not deemed to be a portion of the highway, required to be reduced to a level and kept in repair for the use of foot

passengers, is inadmissible. *Raymond* v. *Lowell*, 6 Cush. 524 (1850).

362. If, in an action against a town to recover damages for an injury sustained by reason of a defective highway, the alleged defect consists in a gutter running obliquely across the highway, it is competent for the defendants to show, upon the question of ordinary care, that a great many gutters equally deep crossed the streets in the same manner, in the same town, or the towns near it. *Packard* v. *New Bedford*, 9 Allen, 200 (1864).

363. In an action against a town to recover damages for an injury occasioned by a defect in a highway, evidence is not admissible on the part of the plaintiff to show that another person, before the injury complained of, received a similar injury, at or near the same place, and from the same alleged defect, without any negligence on his part. *Collins* v. *Dorchester*, 6 Cush. 396 (1850).

364. On the trial of an action against a town for an injury occasioned by a defect in a highway, when one of the defects relied upon by the plaintiff is the insufficient width of the way, evidence that other persons with their vehicles had previously, when the way was in the same condition as at the time of the plaintiff's injury, passed or met other vehicles at the same place, without collision or accident, and had room to spare on each side, is inadmissible to show that the way was not defective in point of width. *Aldrich* v. *Pelham*, 1 Gray, 510 (1854).

365. In such action evidence is admissible of measurements of the width of the way and of the travelled part thereof, taken nine months after the accident occurred, if it is accompanied by proof that no material change has taken place in the way since the accident, which can affect the accuracy of the measurements. *Brooks* v. *Petersham*, 16 Gray, (1860).

366. In an action against a town to recover damages for an injury sustained by reason of a defect in a road, reports of committees appointed by the town to inquire into the facts of the case, and votes of the town accepting such reports, are not admissible in evidence against the town, if such reports do not set forth facts which show the liability of the town, and if such votes neither acknowledge any liability nor direct any settlement with the plaintiff at the town's expense. *Dudley* v. *Weston*, 1 Met. 477 (1840).

367. Reports of committees of a town, relating to the condition of a highway, and the votes of the inhabitants thereupon, are not competent evidence, in an action against the town for an injury occasioned by a defect in such highway, of an admission by the town that the highway in question was defective. *Collins* v. *Dorchester*, 6 Cush. 396 (1850).

368. A person having sustained injuries from an alleged defect in a highway, the report of a committee subsequently duly chosen by the town, that the way was unsafe for travellers, although duly accepted by the town, is not evidence against the town in an action brought to recover for the injuries. *Wheeler* v. *Framingham*, 12 Cush. 287 (1853).

369. Evidence that the duly elected surveyors of highways of a town made repairs upon a way, within six years before the time of an accident from a defect therein, is competent and conclusive evidence of repairs by the town, to establish its liability for the damages resulting from the accident; although it also appears by the plaintiff's evidence that the records of the laying out of the way as a public highway were insufficient. *Hayden* v. *Attleborough*, 7 Gray, 338 (1856).

370. In an action to recover of a town damages sustained by reason of a defect in a part of the highway, which has been so wrought and repaired by the town for public travel as to induce the public to pass over it, the town cannot introduce evidence that that part of the highway was originally wrought for the accommodation of the abutters. *Kellogg* v. *Northampton*, 8 Gray, 504 (1857).

371. A traveller on a highway which had been rendered unsafe by recent freshets and was undergoing repairs, upon coming at sunset to a bridge which had been thus made impassable, crossed at a ford indicated by wagon ruts, and after proceeding for some distance on his journey received an injury from a defect in the highway, and brought an action against the town for damages. *Held*, that the state of the bridge and ford was not conclusive evidence that the traveller was not using ordinary care at the time of the injury, but must be submitted to the jury with the other evidence in the case. *Rindge* v. *Coleraine*, 11 Gray, 157 (1858).

372. In an action against a town for injuries sustained from a defect in a highway, evidence that other persons than the plaintiff passed and repassed the place in safety is inadmissible for the town. *Kidder* v. *Dunstable*, 11 Gray, 342 (1858).

373. Evidence that a highway was in the usual condition of other country roads is inadmissible in defence of an action against a town for damages from a defect therein. *Ib.*

374. In an action against a city to recover damages for an injury sustained from falling into a plumber's furnace left in the sidewalk in a street, evidence is inadmissible to show that the same furnace was left upon the sidewalk for several hours on the day before the accident occurred, or that the police officer

whose duty it was to pass through that street was accustomed to pass through the street daily during the time in which the furnace was placed in the street on the day of the accident. *Donaldson* v. *Boston*, 16 Gray, (1860).

375. In such action, it having been proved that a number of citizens passed through the street while the furnace was standing upon the sidewalk, the jury were instructed that in order to prove reasonable notice to the defendants of the alleged defect, it must appear that the officers of the city having charge of the streets, such as the mayor and aldermen, superintendent of streets, or policemen, had actual notice of the defect, or that a defect which had obstructed travel had continued so long or been so notorious, that if such officers had done their duty, or citizens passing had done their duty, they would have known it; and that the jury might consider whether the obstruction to travel was of such a nature that if citizens passing had seen it they would have been likely to have informed such officers forthwith of its existence. *Held*, that the instructions were in accordance with the law, and sufficiently favorable to the plaintiff. *Ib.*

376. In a suit against a town for an injury sustained by reason of a defective highway, the opinion of a witness as to the state of repair of a road at a period between two and three months before the accident is incompetent. *Hutchinson* v. *Methuen*, 1 Allen, 33 (1861). See *ante*, 365.

377. If an injury is caused by reason of the elevation of one edge of a plank, which is laid over an open space left for the passage of water in a public street, and this is found to be an actionable defect, it is enough to authorize a verdict for the plaintiff if the plank has been split, loose, liable to change and unsafe for twenty-four hours before the accident, or if the city authorities had reasonable notice of its unsafe condition, although the position of the plank which was the immediate cause of the accident had only continued for a short time. *Winn* v. *Lowell*, 1 Allen, 177 (1861).

378. If the plaintiff, in an action against a town for an injury sustained by reason of a defective highway, has introduced no evidence except his own testimony, and by his own testimony has definitively fixed the place of the accident and the circumstances under which it occurred, and the defendants, in reply, have introduced witnesses to show that the accident which caused the injury occurred at a different place in the highway, where no defect had been shown to exist, and under different circumstances, the interference of the presiding judge to check an argument of the plaintiff's counsel to the jury, that the defendants were liable even if the injury was received under the circumstances testified to by the defendants' witnesses, furnishes no ground of exception. *Clark* v. *Lowell*, 1 Allen, 180 (1861).

379. If, in an action against a city to recover damages for an injury sustained by reason of a defective highway, there is evidence that the plaintiff was intoxicated at the time of the accident, and the judge has instructed the jury that he could not recover if anything else than the negligence of the city contributed to cause the accident, or if it occurred in any respect through his own negligence, and that if he was intoxicated that was a circumstance to be considered by them as bearing upon the question of due care on his part, no exception lies to his refusal to instruct them that a city is not bound to keep its streets safe and convenient for intoxicated persons, or that if he was intoxicated at the time of the accident they are to presume he was negligent. *Alger* v. *Lowell*, 3 Allen, 402 (1862).

380. Under a declaration alleging simply a want of repair in a way, it may be proved that the way was defective by reason of the want of a railing to protect travellers from going down a declivity just outside of the limits of the way. *Ib.*

381. Payment of a sum of money "in full payment and satisfaction for all claim for damages and costs" in a suit against a corporation for an injury sustained by the plaintiff by reason of falling into a trench alleged to have been dug by its servants in a public highway, is a bar to a subsequent action for the same injury against the town which was bound to keep the highway in repair; and a written receipt for the money, showing that it was received in full payment and satisfaction for all claim for damages and costs in that suit, cannot be controlled or varied by parol evidence. *Brown* v. *Cambridge*, 3 Allen, 474 (1862).

382. If, in an action against a city to recover damages for an injury sustained by reason of a defective way, the alleged defect in which consisted of ice and snow upon a sidewalk, a witness for the plaintiff has described the condition of the sidewalk at the time of the injury, he may be asked on cross-examination if the ice and snow were not removed from the sidewalk as well as it could conveniently be done by a man with a shovel. *O'Neill* v. *Lowell*, 6 Allen, 110 (1863).

383. If, in an action to recover for damages sustained by falling upon the ice on a sidewalk, it becomes a question whether the defendants had taken reasonable pains to remove the ice, the plaintiff may show that in other

places on the same sidewalk, similarly situated, ice had been removed with a shovel only. *Shea* v. *Lowell*, 8 Allen, 136 (1864).

384. If, in an action to recover for an injury sustained by reason of a defective way, it becomes a material question whether the plaintiff's horse had a habit of shying at the time of the accident, the defendants, after introducing evidence of instances of his shying before that time, may also prove similar instances afterwards. *Todd* v. *Rowley*, 8 Allen, 51 (1864).

385. In an action to recover for injuries to a horse, sustained in consequence of a defect in a highway, the plaintiff is entitled to recover for the diminution, occasioned by the injury, in the market value of the horse at the commencement of the action, and, in addition, such sums as the plaintiff has paid out in reasonable attempts to cure him, with a reasonable compensation for his own services in attempting to cure him, and a reasonable sum as compensation for the loss of the use of the horse while under such treatment; provided that the whole damages allowed do not exceed the value of the horse. *Gillett* v. *Western Railroad*, 8 Allen, 560 (1864).

386. In an action against a town to recover damages for an injury sustained by reason of a defective bridge, a witness cannot properly be asked by the defendants, how the bridge compared, on the day of the accident, in respect to its safety and state of repair, with other bridges of like character on roads of like amount of travel. *Bliss* v. *Wilbraham*, 8 Allen, 564 (1864).

387. If, in an action against a city to recover damages for an injury sustained by reason of a defective way, the defect alleged is ice on a sidewalk, and the defendants have been allowed to prove that rain had fallen and frozen shortly before the time of the accident, so that all the sidewalks in the city were covered with ice, evidence is inadmissible, in their behalf, to prove the steps actually taken by them to remedy the defect. *Payne* v. *Lowell*, 10 Allen, 147 (1865).

388. In an action against a town to recover for a personal injury sustained by the plaintiff, while riding on horseback upon a highway, by going off a bank where there was no railing, the defendants asked the court to instruct the jury that if the plaintiff's horse passed the bank wall in safety, and, while proceeding in the adjoining field, stepped on ice and slipped down, and thus injured the plaintiff, he could not recover. The judge gave this instruction, and added that if the horse, by reason of the want of a railing, went over the bank wall, and immediately, and while under the same impulse or impetus, slipped on ice in the field and fell, thereby injuring the plaintiff, the town would be liable. *Held*, that the defendants had no ground of exception. *Stevens* v. *Boxford*, 10 Allen, 25 (1865).

389. In an action to recover damages for an injury sustained by reason of a defective way, the defendants may prove that the plaintiff, at the time of receiving the injury, was travelling in violation of the statutes for the observance of the Lord's day, without specially averring that as a ground of defence in the answer. *Jones* v. *Andover*, 10 Allen, 18 (1865). See *ante*, 281.

390. A person violates those statutes who travels on the Lord's day for the purpose of supplying fresh meat to marketmen, whom his master has agreed to supply therewith, although he could not do this, in addition to his other work, on Monday morning, and his master, by reason of illness, is unable to do it himself. *Ib.*

See *ante*, 282.

(d) Indictments against Towns.

391. The inhabitants of a town, where a bridge or road has been recently built or laid out without any authority, are under no obligation to repair such bridge or road. *Commonwealth* v. *Charlestown*, 1 Pick. 180 (1822).

392. In an indictment for not repairing a highway it is not necessary to set out the *termini*. *Commonwealth* v. *Newbury*, 2 Pick. 51 (1824).

393. Where a turnpike corporation had ceased for several years to demand toll, and a town way was in due form of law laid out over the turnpike road and accepted by the town, it was held, that the town was indictable for not keeping the way in repair. *Commonwealth* v. *Petersham*, 4 Pick. 119 (1826).

394. An indictment against the town of N. B. for not repairing a highway, alleged that there was a highway, leading from a meeting-house in the town of B. to the dividing line between B. and N. B. and thence in N. B. to the meeting-house in N. B., and that the defendants allowed "a certain part thereof, consisting of twenty rods in length," to be out of repair. It was held, that the indictment was defective, inasmuch as it was left uncertain in which of the towns the unrepaired part of the highway lay. *Commonwealth* v. *North Brookfield*, 8 Pick. 463 (1829).

395. Where the line between two towns, situated in different counties, is the centre of a highway, and one of the towns is indicted for not repairing the same, and submits to the payment of a fine, which is laid out in repairing the road, such town cannot recover one

half of the money so paid, against the other town, in an action for money paid to the use of the latter. *Middleborough* v. *Taunton*, 2 Cush. 406 (1848).

396. If a town has neglected to repair a part of a road which it was its duty to maintain, it is no defence to an indictment for the neglect, to show that this part would be of no immediate practical use, because a portion of a bridge with which the road connects, and which the town is not obliged to maintain, has been swept away and has not been rebuilt. *Commonwealth* v. *Deerfield*, 6 Allen, 449 (1863).

See *ante*, 14, 38, 60; *post*, 400; INDICTMENT.

(e) Liability of Individuals for Obstructions; Civilly and Criminally.

Civilly.

397. A railroad corporation was authorized to construct its railroad across a highway, and in the progress of the work it became necessary from time to time to remove certain barriers, which were placed by the corporation across the highway for the protection of travellers, but were adopted by the town in which the highway was situated, and in consequence of the neglect of the workmen to replace the barriers at night a traveller sustained an injury, and subsequently, under St. 1786, c. 81, recovered double damages against the town. It was held, that the railroad corporation was bound to cause the barriers to be replaced at night, although its charter contained no express provision on this point; as otherwise an accident might have happened before the town had notice, actual or constructive, and no one would have been liable for the damages. *Lowell* v. *Boston & Lowell Railroad*, 23 Pick. 24 (1839).

398. *Held*, also, that the corporation was responsible for the negligence of such workmen, although they were employed by an individual who had contracted to construct this portion of the railroad for a stipulated sum, the work being done by the direction of the corporation. *Ib.*

399. *Held*, also, that an action might be sustained against the corporation by the town for indemnity, but that the town could recover only single damages, and that the corporation was not liable for the costs and expenses of the action brought against the town by such traveller, it not appearing that such action was defended at the request of the corporation or for its benefit. *Ib.*

400. A mill owner placed a dam across the outlet of a pond, and thereby caused the water to overflow a road near the bank of the pond. The town which was obliged by law to repair the road, repaired it, and caused a bank wall to be built on the shore of the pond, out of the line of the road, to protect the road against the action of the water. *Held*, that the town could recover from the mill owner the expense incurred in repairing the road, and building the wall, with interest from the time of demanding payment from the mill owner, but not the costs of an indictment against the town for not seasonably repairing the road. *Andover* v. *Sutton*, 12 Met. 182 (1846).

401. A town which has been compelled to pay damages for an injury from a defect in a highway, occasioned by a nuisance placed therein by an individual, may recover of the latter the damages so paid. *Lowell* v. *Short*, 4 Cush. 275 (1849).

402. Where a town was compelled to pay damages for an injury resulting from a defect in a highway, occasioned by the want of repair of a cellar way constructed in the sidewalk, and leading to a building adjoining thereto, which was in the occupation of a tenant, it was held, that the occupant and not the owner was liable to the town for such damages. But if, in such case, there had been an express agreement between the landlord and the tenant, that the former should keep the premises in repair, then, to avoid circuity of action, the landlord would be liable in the first instance. *Lowell* v. *Spaulding*, 4 Cush. 277 (1849). See *Kirby* v. *Boylston Market Association*, 14 Gray, 249.

403. A verdict and judgment against a city in an action for personal injuries occasioned by a defect within the limits of a highway, are conclusive evidence in a subsequent action by the city against a tenant of the land, (who had notice of the pendency of the former action and of the city's intention to hold him responsible for all damages recovered therein, and had opportunity to furnish evidence, and testified at the trial, although he was not requested to and did not take upon himself the defence of that action,) that the highway was defective, that the person was injured there, while using due care, and of the amount of the injury; but not of the tenant's liability to keep the place in repair, nor of his having neglected to do so, nor of such negligence having been the sole cause of the injury. *Boston* v. *Worthington*, 10 Gray, 496 (1858).

404. If a town have paid a reasonable and just sum as damages to one who has been injured, while using due care, by reason of an obstruction in a highway, they may recover the same of the person who placed such obstruction in the highway, although no action has been brought against them by the person injured. The question whether the sum so paid was reasonable and just is to be determined by the jury upon the evidence. *Swansey* v. *Chace*, 16 Gray, (1860).

405. It is no defence to an action by a town against a person who has placed an obstruction in a highway, to recover damages paid to a person who has been injured by reason thereof, that such obstruction had existed in the highway more than two days before the injury was sustained, and that the town were negligent in not removing the same. *Ib.*

406. The owner of a building, who has leased the lower story for shops, and portions of the upper story for various purposes, including one or two rooms to the town in which the building is situated, and has himself remained in possession of the residue thereof, is, in the absence of an express agreement with tenants to the contrary, responsible for the safety of an awning erected along the whole front of the building, for the benefit of the shops. *Milford* v. *Holbrook*, 9 Allen, 17 (1864).

407. If in such case the owner has had due notice, he may be held liable to the town for damages which they have been compelled to pay to one who has suffered an injury by reason of the falling of the awning, through a defect; and the occupants of the shops need not be joined as defendants. *Ib.*

408. A notice by the town to such owner, of an action brought against them to recover damages for an injury sustained "on the sidewalk in front of or near Union Block, so called, in Milford," (that being the name of his building,) requesting him to defend the same, and stating that, if the town was liable, he was responsible to them, because the injury, if it occurred, must have occurred through his negligence, sufficiently connects the defendant and his property with the alleged injury. *Ib.*

409. In such action by the town against such owner, after such notice, the verdict and judgment against the town are conclusive evidence of the existence of a defect in the highway, the injury to the individual while he was in the exercise of due care, and the extent of the injury. *Ib.*

410. Where several persons were engaged in playing a game of ball in the public highway, and a traveller lawfully passing thereon was accidentally struck by the ball, it was held, that all the persons so engaged were liable in trespass; provided that from the width of the road, and the number of persons usually passing thereon for the ordinary purposes of travel, the game was of such a character as to be likely to endanger the safety of travellers and passengers, and provided that the individual by whom the ball was thrown was acting in the usual manner of persons engaged in such game. *Vosburgh* v. *Moak*, 1 Cush. 453 (1848).

411. The owner of a building, leased in several tenements, who is bound to make all necessary repairs, and has control of the passage ways and doors for that purpose, and who keeps the keys and opens and closes the doors of portions of the building at times fixed by the occupants, is not relieved from liability for injuries caused by defects in the building or by the falling of snow and ice therefrom. *Kirby* v. *Boylston Market Association*, 14 Gray, 249 (1859).

412. The owner of a building is liable for injuries resulting from obstructions caused or created by him in the adjoining sidewalk; but not for injuries resulting from defects in the sidewalk, or from accumulations by natural causes of snow and ice thereon, although the sidewalk forms part of the highway, and he is obliged by the ordinances of the city to keep the sidewalk clear and in good repair. *Ib.*

413. A railroad company has no right to use a highway as a part of its freight yard; but it has a right to pass and repass over a highway in making up its trains and shifting its cars, provided this is done only to a reasonable extent and in a reasonable manner, without encroaching upon the rights of others who have an equal right to use it. *Gahagan* v. *Boston & Lowell Railroad*, 1 Allen, 187 (1861).

414. When, in a suit against a railroad company for an injury received while passing along a highway, an issue is made upon the unreasonable or negligent conduct of the company in the use of the highway at the time complained of, its usage at other times has no legitimate bearing upon this issue, and evidence respecting such usage is incompetent. *Ib.*

415. In an action by an infant child to recover for personal injuries occasioned, as she contended, by the defendants' pushing a railroad car upon her while she was in a highway along which the railroad track was laid, no exception lies to a refusal to instruct the jury, upon the request of the plaintiff, that, if these facts were true, the defendants, by obstructing the highway with the car, were making an unlawful use thereof, and were liable for any injury to her resulting from such unlawful use, if the railroad track was not placed there by the defendants, and it is not proved that the highway was in fact obstructed by moving the car upon it; or to an instruction by the judge that the jury were not required to determine whether or not there was an existing highway there. *Lawler* v. *Northampton Gas Light Co.* 2 Allen, 307 (1861).

416. The lessee of a building, who has employed a carpenter to repair an awning which extends from the building over a public way, with no special contract as to the terms, price or time of doing the work, is liable for

an injury sustained by one who is lawfully using the way, by reason of the carelessness of the carpenter in making the repairs. *Brackett* v. *Lubke*, 4 Allen, 138 (1862).

Criminally.

417. An indictment lies against an individual for a nuisance erected by him on a town way. *Commonwealth* v. *Gowen*, 7 Mass. 378 (1811).

418. A party who obstructs a highway is amenable to the public in an indictment, whether any person be injured or not, but he is not liable to an action by an individual, unless such individual suffers in his person or property by means of the obstruction. PARKER, C. J., in *Smith* v. *Smith*, 2 Pick. 623 (1824).

419. A town may acquire a right of way by grant; and exclusive uninterrupted user by the inhabitants for twenty years unexplained, is evidence of a grant; but such way will be a private way, and an obstruction upon it will not be indictable as a nuisance. *Commonwealth* v. *Low*, 3 Pick. 408 (1826).

420. The statutes for the support and regulation of mills will not justify or excuse the erection of a dam in such manner as to overflow a public highway already appropriated and in actual use, and thereby render it impassable. *Commonwealth* v. *Stevens*, 10 Pick. 247 (1831).

421. Where a mill owner, who has a grant of a right to flow certain lands, suffers his mill and dam to go to decay, and ceases to flow the land, and a highway is then made across the land, he cannot, by afterwards granting his mill privilege and right to flow, authorize his grantee to overflow such highway by means of a new mill dam on the site of the old one; and his grantee, if he so overflow the highway, is punishable for a nuisance. *Commonwealth* v. *Fisher*, 6 Met. 433 (1843).

422. An indictment lies for continuing within the limits of a highway certain buildings previously erected therein, although that portion of the highway which was covered by them was not within the travelled path, and a bank six or seven feet in height had been removed for the purpose of placing the buildings where they stood. *Commonwealth* v. *Wilkinson*, 16 Pick. 175 (1834).

423. It is an indictable offence at common law to place and continue, within the established limits of a highway, a wall, or stones, or anything which obstructs the full enjoyment, by the public, of an easement coëxtensive with those limits, although such wall, stones, or other thing, be not placed or continued within that part of the highway which can be safely used for travel. The common law, as to nuisances in a highway, is not repealed or altered by the Rev. Sts. c. 24, § 61 (Gen. Sts. c. 46, § 1). *Commonwealth* v. *King*, 13 Met. 115 (1847).

424. A railroad corporation, constructing their railroad across a highway without lawful authority, are liable to indictment for a nuisance. *Commonwealth* v. *Nashua & Lowell Railroad*, 2 Gray, 54 (1854). *Commonwealth* v. *Vermont & Massachusetts Railroad*, 4 Gray, 22 (1855). *Commonwealth* v. *Old Colony & Fall River Railroad*, 14 Gray, 93 (1859).

425. The confirmation, by statute, of the illegal location of a railroad in a highway, is no ground for arresting judgment on an indictment for a nuisance by such obstruction, on which the proprietors of the railroad have been convicted before the passage of the statute. *Commonwealth* v. *Old Colony & Fall River Railroad*, 14 Gray, 93 (1859).

426. On the trial of an indictment for a nuisance in a road, caused by digging a ditch across it, the defendant introduced evidence that, at a remote period, a similar ditch, useful for draining certain meadow lands, was in the same place, and had been afterwards filled up; and he contended that the nuisance with which he was charged was a mere removal of a preëxisting nuisance. It was held, that if the road had been used for more than forty years without the incumbrance of a ditch, the right to reopen it had been lost. *Commonwealth* v. *Belding*, 13 Met. 10 (1847).

427. When a party, who is indicted for obstructing a road, gives evidence that when he obstructed it, he opened a new and convenient way on his own land, which was used for seven or eight years, and until a bridge which he built in the new way was carried off by a flood, such evidence does not show an abandonment of the old road, nor furnish any defence to the indictment. *Ib.*

428. The refusal of a city to fulfil an agreement which they have made with the owner of land bounding on a street, to set back the fence and grade the land, in consideration of a release of all damages for a widening of the street, is no defence to an indictment of the agent of such owner for a nuisance in replacing the fence in its former position so as to obstruct the street; although the owner was an infant and a *feme covert* at the time of making the release. *Commonwealth* v. *Smyth*, 14 Gray, 33 (1859).

429. The officers of an agricultural society, who have unlawfully fixed and defined bounds for the purpose of exhibiting horses in a public highway, have no right to obstruct public travel thereon, although there is sufficient room for public travel on the other parts of the highway; and they may be convicted of assault and battery, if without legal process

they have arrested a person within such bounds, who, when directed to fall back, refused to do so, and without malice or unlawful intent struck the horse of a marshal of the society, although he was wilfully and maliciously in the highway for the purpose of obstructing the exhibition of horses there. *Commonwealth* v. *Ruggles*, 6 Allen, 588 (1863).

See *ante*, 23, 74; *post*, 438.

VII. Rights of the Public and of Land Owners in the Soil of Public Ways.

430. Upon the location of a highway, the public acquire an easement not lawfully to be interrupted by the owner of the land; but the soil and freehold remain in the owner for every purpose of use or profit consistent with such easement. He may maintain ejectment for it; and he may sink a watercourse below the surface, covering it so that the highway remains safe and convenient for passengers. *Perley* v. *Chandler*, 6 Mass. 454 (1810).

431. The owner of the soil is entitled to the herbage growing upon a highway. *Stackpole* v. *Healy*, 16 Mass. 33 (1819). *Adams* v. *Emerson*, 6 Pick. 57 (1827).

432. When a highway is laid out, the title of the owner of the land taken is not thereby divested. The fee remains in him and descends to his heirs, subject to an easement in the public during the continuance of the highway. When the highway is discontinued the owner holds the land free from incumbrance. *Perley* v. *Chandler*, 6 Mass. 454 (1810). *Harrington* v. *Berkshire*, 22 Pick. 266 (1839).

433. The owner of the soil over which a turnpike passes may maintain an action against a stranger who ploughs up the land, not for the purpose of mending the road. *Robbins* v. *Borman*, 1 Pick. 122 (1822). See *Brainard* v. *Clapp*, 10 Cush. 9.

434. When a public way is unlawfully obstructed, any individual who wishes to use it in a lawful way, may remove the obstruction. He may even enter upon the land of the party erecting or continuing the obstruction, for the purpose of removing it, doing as little damage as possible to the soil and buildings. *Arundel* v. *M'Culloch*, 10 Mass. 70 (18 3).

435. The public have no right to depasture their cattle upon the highway. *Stackpole* v. *Healy*, 16 Mass. 33 (1819).

436. As to the right of the public to move buildings through the streets, see *Day* v. *Green*, 4 Cush. 437 (1849).

437. If a highway is located over watercourses, either natural or artificial, the public cannot shut them up, but may make a road over them by the aid of bridges. *Perley* v. *Chandler*, 6 Mass. 454 (1810). *Rowe* v. *Granite Bridge*, 21 Pick. 344 (1838).

438. But when a way has been located over private land, if the owner should afterwards open a watercourse across the way, it will be his duty, at his own expense, to make and keep in repair a way over the watercourse, for the convenience of the public; and if he should neglect to do it, he may be indicted for the nuisance; and upon the conviction, the nuisance may be abated by filling up the watercourse, if he shall not make a convenient way over it. *Perley* v. *Chandler*, 6 Mass. 454 (1810).

439. A town which is obliged to maintain a highway, through which a canal has been constructed, not being the owner of the soil, is not entitled to damages under a statute providing for the assessment of damages to the owners of the land through which the canal passes. *Millbury* v. *Blackstone Canal Co.* 8 Pick. 473 (1829).

440. County commissioners, having adjudged a town way to be of common convenience and necessity, located it and made their return, which was duly recorded; an order was thereupon passed by them, requiring the town to complete the way, but allowing the proprietor of the land to remove all property not required for the construction of the way. It was held, that the town way did not become such by the mere force of the adjudication that it was of common convenience and necessity; and that a person breaking down the fence for the purpose of passing over such way, after the expiration of the time allowed to the proprietor of the land for the purpose of removing the property, but before the road was constructed, was liable to an action of trespass by such proprietor. *Loker* v. *Damon*, 17 Pick. 284 (1835).

441. It seems, that the town could not in such case legally break down the fence in order to construct the road, before the expiration of the time allowed to the proprietor for the purpose of removing the property, provided there were growing crops on the soil, to the protection of which the fence was necessary. *Ib.*

442. The owner of the soil over which a town way passes cannot maintain trespass against a person placing logs, stones and timber thereon. *Mayhew* v. *Norton*, 17 Pick. 357 (1835).

443. It is not a trespass upon the owner of the soil of a street in a populous town, to erect buildings and fences on the line of the street with doors and gates so constructed as, when opened, to swing over it; or, in constructing such buildings, to place within the limits of the street building materials and the earth dug from the cellar, provided the street is

not improperly obstructed and such materials and earth are removed within a reasonable time; or to spread earth on the street for the purpose of improving it as a way; or to allow horses and carriages occasionally to stand in such street against or near a house. *O'Linda* v. *Lothrop*, 21 Pick. 292 (1838).

444. The possession and fencing, for more than twenty years, by one holding no conveyance thereof, of land in South Boston, over which a street was laid out by the selectmen under St. 1803, c. 111, but which has not been ordered to be completed, is not such an adverse possession as to affect the right of the mayor and aldermen of Boston to complete the street. *Henshaw* v. *Hunting*, 1 Gray, 203 (1854).

445. One who lays out a street through his land, and then grants all the lots bounding on the street, except one, may maintain an action of tort, in the nature of trover, against either of the grantees, for taking earth from the street, not necessary to the construction or repair of the street. *Phillips* v. *Bowers*, 7 Gray, 21 (1856).

446. The title of the owner of land bounding upon a highway is presumed to extend to the centre of the way. *Rice* v. *Worcester*, 11 Gray, 283, note (1858). But this presumption is rebutted by the production of a deed from which he derives his title, granting the land to the side of the way only. *Smith* v. *Slocomb*, 11 Gray, 280 (1858).

447. The use, by the owner of land bounded on the side of a highway, of the land between his own and the travelled part of the way, by moving a wall, planting trees, cutting brushwood and digging up the soil, for fifteen years, gives no right to maintain an action of tort in the nature of trespass *quare clausum fregit*, for the interruption of such use and possession by another person. *Ib.*

448. An action of tort lies against a city to recover damages occasioned by the obstruction, owing to negligence on the part of the city, of a natural watercourse, through a culvert under a highway, although the plaintiff is the owner of the land on both sides of the highway. *Parker* v. *Lowell*, 11 Gray, 353 (1858). See Actions, 44.

449. A private individual may be held liable as a trespasser by the owner of land over which there is a public highway, for acts done to the injury of the latter in widening or repairing the highway, outside of the travelled limits thereof; although a highway surveyor might properly have done the same acts. *Hollenbeck* v. *Rowley*, 8 Allen, 473 (1864).

See *ante*, 25, 161, 191, 225; *post*, 452.

VIII. Limits and Boundaries of Ways; Fences, &c.

450. St. 1786, c. 67, § 7, (Gen. Sts. c. 46, § 1,) provides that where fences have been erected fronting upon or against any highway, of which the breadth or quantity is not known nor can be made certain by the records, or by any other boundaries, and such fences have been maintained for more than forty years, they shall be deemed the true ancient boundaries thereof. Under this statute it was held, that a fence near a highway was only *prima facie* evidence of the boundary, it being for the jury to determine from the nature and value of the soil, the nearness of the fence to the highway, and from all the other circumstances, whether it was a fence "fronting upon or against" the highway, within the meaning of the statute. *Sprague* v. *Waite*, 17 Pick. 309 (1835).

451. The erection of a pound by a town within the limits of a highway does not change the limits of the highway. *Ib.*

452. Where the travelled path upon a public highway which had been established by user merely, separated into two tracks, thus leaving a triangular strip in the middle, over which the travel had never passed, partly on account of a declivity, and partly on account of some obstructions which had been placed there, it was held, that it was a question of fact to be determined upon consideration of all the circumstances, whether such land had been appropriated to public use as a highway, although not actually prepared for travel at the time when the highway was first used; and that the owner of the soil would have the benefit of the rule that his private right was not to be incumbered by the public unless it appeared satisfactorily that it had been appropriated to public use. *Ib.*

453. In the case of a highway established by user, the jury may be authorized by the circumstances to find that its limits extend beyond the travelled path. *Hannum* v. *Belchertown*, 19 Pick. 311 (1837). See *Sprague* v. *Waite*, 17 Pick. 309.

454. The selectmen of a town viewed a highway, in company with the owners of the adjoining lands, and ordered the fence against the highway to be moved back. The fence was accordingly moved back, and was continued more than twenty years in the place where it was then put. *Held*, that the fence, so moved and continued, was, under Rev. Sts. c. 24, § 61, (Gen. Sts. c. 46, § 1,) to be deemed and taken as the true boundary of the highway; there being no records or monuments by which the boundary could be made certain. *Plumer* v. *Brown*, 8 Met. 578 (1844).

455. A fence fronting on a highway for more

than twenty years is not to be deemed and taken to be the true boundary thereof, (Gen. Sts. c. 46, § 1,) if the original boundary can be made certain by ancient monuments, although such monuments are not now in existence. *Wood* v. *Quincy*, 11 Cush. 487 (1853).

456. A straight line drawn through the centre of a Virginia fence which has been continued for more than twenty years fronting on a highway, the boundaries of which cannot be otherwise ascertained, is to be deemed the true boundary; and there is no presumption that the land enclosed between that line and the angles of the fence next the highway was not intended to be dedicated to public use. *Holbrook* v. *McBride*, 4 Gray, 215 (1855).

457. A fence fronting on a highway and continued for more than twenty years is conclusive evidence of the true boundary thereof, if the same is not known and cannot be made certain by records or monuments. *Pettingill* v. *Porter*, 3 Allen, 349 (1862).

458. Maintaining a fence within the limits of a highway for forty years, under a claim of right, gives to the owner an absolute right, under the statutes of this commonwealth, to continue it there, as against the public. *Cutter* v. *Cambridge*, 6 Allen, 20 (1863).

459. If there is no competent record evidence of the laying out of a highway, and it appears that surveyors have been unable to ascertain the boundaries accurately, evidence of the existence of a fence substantially in the same place for more than twenty years, upon the side of the highway, is competent for the purpose of fixing the boundary line. *Hollenbeck* v. *Rowley*, 8 Allen, 473 (1864).

460. The provisions of St. of 1848, c. 192, (Gen. Sts. c. 43, § 88,) requiring county commissioners, mayors and aldermen and selectmen to cause stone bounds or other monuments to be erected at the *termini* and angles of all roads laid out by them, are merely directory, and not necessary to be complied with, to make a location valid; and compliance therewith need not be stated on the record of the laying out of the road. *Monterey* v. *Berkshire*, 7 Cush. 394 (1851).

IX. Railroad Crossings; Sidewalks in the Cities of Lowell and Charlestown.

461. The St. of 1857, c. 287, concerning the laying out of highways across railroads, applies to a petition for the laying out of a highway, pending at the time of its passage. *Old Colony & Fall River Railroad* v. *Plymouth*, 11 Gray, 512 (1858).

462. Under the St. of 1857, c. 287, an adjudication by county commissioners, laying out a highway across a railroad, which does not state whether the highway is to be carried over, or under, or on a level with the railroad, or show that special notice was given to the railroad corporation, is erroneous, and will be quashed on *certiorari*, although the railroad corporation actually appeared and were heard before the commissioners. *Ib.*

463. A railroad corporation is entitled to damages for land taken by the laying out of a public highway across its railroad, subject to its use for said road, and for the expense of erecting and maintaining railroad signs and cattle guards at the crossing, and of flooring the same and keeping it in repair; but not for any increased liability from accidents, for the increased expense of ringing the bell, or for its liability to be ordered by the county commissioners to build a bridge for the highway over its track. *Old Colony & Fall River Railroad* v. *Plymouth*, 14 Gray, 155 (1859).

464. In assessing damages occasioned to a railroad corporation by the location of a highway across its track, supposed benefit by an increase of travel on the railroad cannot be set off. *Ib.* *Boston & Maine Railroad* v. *Middlesex*, 1 Allen, 324 (1861).

465. A railroad company has no right to use a highway as a part of its freight yard; but it has a right to pass and repass over a highway in making up its trains and shifting its cars, provided this is done only to a reasonable extent and in a reasonable manner, without encroaching upon the rights of others who have an equal right to use it. *Gahagan* v. *Boston & Lowell Railroad*, 1 Allen, 187 (1861).

466. The obligation of a town to make roads safe and convenient for travellers continues where such roads are crossed by railroads at grade, except so far as the necessary use of the crossing by the railroad may prevent it, and subject to such specific directions as may be given by the county commissioners. *Davis* v. *Leominster*, 1 Allen, 182 (1861).

467. Under Rev. Sts. c. 24, § 13, (Gen. Sts. c. 43, §§ 19, 20; c. 63, §§ 57–59,) county commissioners have final jurisdiction of the question whether a highway which crosses a railroad shall be laid out over, under, or on a level with it. *Boston & Maine Railroad* v. *Middlesex*, 1 Allen, 324 (1861).

468. Under Rev. Sts. c. 39, § 69, town or city authorities had no power to lay out a highway across a railroad, on a level therewith; and a railroad company is not estopped from objecting to the exercise of such power by an agreement made by it with former owners of the land, which contained a stipulation for a right of way, to be used by such

owners and their assigns, at the place where the highway was afterwards laid out. *Boston & Maine Railroad* v. *Lawrence*, 2 Allen, 107 (1861). See now Gen. Sts. c. 63, §§ 57-59.

469. Under Gen. Sts. c. 63, § 59, the mayor and aldermen of a city, or selectmen of a town, have no authority to lay out a way across any portion of the land, not exceeding five rods in width, which has been taken by a railroad corporation for their railroad, unless permission so to do has been granted by the county commissioners. *Commonwealth* v. *Haverhill*, 7 Allen, 523 (1863).

See *ante*, 207, 269-272, 277, 397-399, 424, 425; Railroads.

Sidewalks in the Cities of Lowell and Charlestown.

470. The authority of the city council of Lowell to lay out streets within the city, (under St. 1836, c. 128,) is not like that of selectmen to lay out town ways, but is like that of county commissioners to lay out highways. And, therefore, if said city council lay out a street by an order apparently regular and formal, a party who has an easement in the land over which the street is laid cannot, in an action against him to recover the expense of a sidewalk constructed on the side of such street, by order of the city council, successfully object that all persons interested had not due notice of the intention to lay out the street; but, in order to raise this question, he must resort to a writ of *certiorari*. *Lowell* v. *Hadley*, 8 Met. 180 (1844).

471. An assessment on the owner of buildings in the city of Lowell, for the expense of a sidewalk constructed on a street in front of the buildings, by order of the city council, pursuant to the authority given by the city charter and ordinances, is constitutional and valid. *Ib.*

472. The city council of Lowell, by an ordinance, directed a sidewalk on W Street to be constructed by the superintendent of streets, 796 feet in length, and 8 feet in width, of brick and edge stones in front of occupied lots, and of timber and planks in front of vacant lots. The sidewalk over a part of the length in front of H.'s lot was built, in consequence of his request, of flagstones, in three rows, with paving stones between; and in some other places it was built of flagstones and paving stones, across private entrances to yards, with the assent of the immediate abutters, but without asking H.'s consent. In one place near H.'s lot, the sidewalk was made but seven feet wide, and between his lot and one of the most frequented streets in the city, for a length of sixty-three feet, the sidewalk varied from that width regularly to seven and a half feet, and for a further length of sixty-eight feet increased gradually from seven and a half feet to eight feet in width. In a remote and comparatively unfrequented part of W Street, the sidewalk, for a little more than forty feet in length, was made considerable less than eight feet wide. H. was not asked to consent, and did not consent to these alterations. *Held*, in a suit against H. to recover the expense of the sidewalk constructed in front of his lot, (which expense was admitted by him not to be unreasonable in amount,) he was bound to pay it, notwithstanding the departure from the city ordinance in the construction of the sidewalk. *Ib.*

473. The city ordinance of Lowell, c. 16, § 3, which requires the superintendent of streets to make a report to the auditor of accounts of the expense incurred in building a sidewalk, "within ten days from the finishing of the sidewalk," is merely directory; and his omission so to do furnishes no defence to an action brought against the owner of a lot in front of which a sidewalk is built, to recover the expense of building it. *Ib.*

474. A city ordinance having provided that previous to the assessment of the expenses of building a sidewalk upon the abutters, the city auditor should give notice in writing to each person reported to him as liable to be assessed, of his intention to make an assessment, appointing a time and place at which all persons might appear and be heard in relation to the assessment; it was held, that the giving of such notice was a condition precedent to the validity of the assessment, which was not complied with by notifying all the abutters, except one, of the time and place at which they might be heard, and afterwards notifying the remaining abutter of a different time and place, at which he might be heard. *Lowell* v. *Wentworth*, 6 Cush. 221 (1850).

475. The city council of Lowell were authorized by the city charter to cause permanent sidewalks to be constructed on the streets in front of buildings, at the expense of the owners, and temporary sidewalks in front of vacant lands, at the expense of the abutters or of the city, which sidewalks, when accepted by the council, should be afterwards maintained at the expense of the city. In the year 1838, the city council caused a sidewalk of plank to be constructed in front of the defendant's building, and assessed the expense thereof upon him, but it did not appear that this sidewalk was ever expressly accepted. In 1849 the city council caused the wooden sidewalk to be removed, and its place to be supplied by one of brick and stone. It was held, that the first sidewalk was a permanent

one, within the meaning of the charter, and that the city could not charge the defendant with the expense of the second. *Lowell* v. *French*, 6 Cush. 223 (1850).

476. The city of Lowell cannot recover of a land owner an assessment for building a sidewalk on a street in that city, unless the city council have prescribed the materials of which the sidewalk should be constructed, as required by the revised ordinances of the city, c. 17, § 4; which order should appear from the journal kept by the city clerk, and cannot be presumed. *Lowell* v. *Wheelock*, 11 Cush. 391 (1853).

477. If the order of the city council requires the sidewalk to be built on the side of a certain street, the city cannot recover an assessment for building a sidewalk four feet from the side of such street. *Ib.*

478. The charter of the city of Lowell having provided for the construction of sidewalks in front of buildings, "at the expense of the owners thereof," (St. 1836, c. 128, § 9,) the remedy of the city to recover the cost of sidewalks of such owners is at common law, by action, and is not taken away by a statute (St. 1847, c. 82, § 5) giving to the city a lien on the real estate of such owners for such cost. *Lowell* v. *Wyman*, 12 Cush. 273 (1853).

479. Under St. 1855, c. 11, concerning sidewalks in the city of Charlestown, if the mayor and aldermen have ordered that a section of a street shall be graded and covered with gravel and that the gutters therein shall be paved, owners of adjoining land cannot be required to construct sidewalks in front of their land until after such grading, covering with gravel, and paving, has been completed. *Charlestown* v. *Stone*, 15 Gray, (1860).

X. Of the Remedies for Irregularities in Laying out and Completing Ways; and of some other Matters.

480. This court will not prohibit the county commissioners from working a road during the pendency of a petition for a *certiorari* on account of supposed errors in their proceedings, but, after notice of the pendency of such petition, the commissioners, if they proceed with the making of the road, do so at their own risk. *Adams, Petitioners*, 10 Pick. 273 (1830).

481. On *certiorari* this court may quash one part of the proceedings of county commissioners and affirm the other part, where the two parts are independent of and unconnected with each other. *Commonwealth* v. *West Boston Bridge*, 13 Pick. 195 (1832).

482. Whether, where a petition for a new highway is presented to the county commissioners by certain private individuals, and the county commissioners order that no further proceedings shall be had upon the petition, the petitioners merely as such are warranted in applying to this court for a writ of *mandamus* to the county commissioners, *quære*. *Wellington, Petitioner*, 16 Pick. 87 (1834).

483. Upon an application for a *mandamus* to commissioners of highways, commanding them to construct and finish a highway, alleged to have been insufficiently made, but which the commissioners had already accepted as completed, it was held, that a *mandamus* would not lie, the question of the sufficiency of the construction of the road being submitted by law to the judgment of the commissioners. *Rice* v. *Middlesex*, 13 Pick. 225 (1833).

484. When a town way is laid out by county commissioners over land which A. has conveyed to B. by a deed not recorded, and B. does not make known to the commissioners his title and claim for damages, although he has an opportunity to do so, and they award damages to A. and not to B., a writ of *certiorari* will not be issued on the petition of B., for the purpose of quashing the commissioners' proceedings. *Brown* v. *Essex*, 12 Met. 208 (1846).

485. It is no sufficient ground for issuing a *certiorari* to revise the proceedings of county commissioners in laying out a highway, that the public necessity and convenience did not require the same to be laid out; or that a submission of the matter to a jury would not afford the petitioners any effectual remedy; or that the commissioners increased the damages of the land owners, on the hearing of a petition for a discontinuance of the way. *Kingman* v. *Plymouth*, 6 Cush. 306 (1850).

486. *Certiorari* will not lie to remove to the supreme judicial court the record of the proceedings of a town in the location and establishment of a town or private way. *Robbins* v. *Lexington*, 8 Cush. 292 (1851). But *certiorari* will lie to the mayor and aldermen of Boston, to remove their proceedings in the location of ways in Boston; because the powers of the mayor and aldermen, in such cases, are like those of county commissioners. *Ib.* *Parks* v. *Boston*, 8 Pick. 218 (1829). *Stone* v *Boston*, 2 Met. 220 (1841). And see *Dwight* v. *Springfield*, 4 Gray, 107.

487. The owner of land over which a street is laid out by a city council, who objects at the hearing before them to the regularity of the proceedings, and gives written notice to the city, before the commencement of the construction of the street, that he intends to take legal measures to protect his rights, is

not guilty of laches in waiting six months, until the next term of this court for the same county, before he petitions for a *certiorari*. *Dwight* v. *Springfield*, 4 Gray, 107 (1855).

488. Under Gen. Sts. c. 145, § 9, this court have power, in issuing a writ of *certiorari* to vacate irregular proceedings by county commissioners, to order further proceedings by them to correct the irregularity. *Lowell* v. *Middlesex*, 6 Allen, 131 (1863).

489. A writ of *certiorari* will not be issued to correct the proceedings of county commissioners, who, after having adjudged that a road should be constructed, and having laid it out over a portion of the route proposed, have rescinded their adjudication on the ground that public necessity does not require the construction of the road over the remainder of the route. *Thorpe* v. *Worcester*, 9 Gray, 57 (1857).

490. The board of aldermen of a city laid out and accepted a public highway, awarded damages to land owners, and fixed a time for them to remove buildings. A land owner appealed from the award of the board of aldermen to the county commissioners, and obtained a new award of damages from a jury, whose verdict was accepted by the court of common pleas. The order for the removal of buildings had been previously revoked and due notice given of such revocation, and the order accepting the street was afterwards also revoked, before any entry was made upon the land or possession thereof taken for the purpose of constructing the highway. *Held*, that under Sts. 1842, c. 86, and 1847, c. 259, the land owner was not entitled to a warrant of distress for the damages given by the jury, and that an order of the county commissioners issuing such a warrant should be quashed on *certiorari*. *New Bedford* v. *Bristol*, 9 Gray, 346 (1857).

491. Want of notice to one owner of land over which a street is laid out by a city is no ground for issuing an injunction against the completion of the street at the suit of another land owner. *Nichols* v. *Salem*, 14 Gray, 490 (1860).

492. A city assessed to an individual over whose land they had laid out a street so as to compel the removal of his buildings, a certain sum in lieu of all damages for the removal of said buildings. *Held*, that his remedy, if aggrieved, was by petition for a jury, and not by injunction. *Ib.*

493. A city which, after laying out a street, unreasonably delays to complete it, is liable to indictment for the neglect, but not to injunction against completing the street. *Ib.*

494. The record of county commissioners establishing a town way, and reciting that it was made to appear to them that the selectmen of the town, on petition, had unreasonably neglected to lay out the same, can only be avoided by a petition for *certiorari*; and, until so avoided, the order of the commissioners will justify an entry by the town upon the land appropriated, for the purpose of constructing the way. *Durant* v. *Lawrence*, 1 Allen, 125 (1861).

495. The adoption of a city charter, after proceedings for the establishment of a town way have been commenced before county commissioners, does not oust them of their jurisdiction to pass an order, before the city government is organized, for the construction of the way; and such order is valid, if addressed to the town of L. instead of the city of L. *Ib.*

496. In a suit by a land owner against the city for damages for constructing such way in pursuance of the order of the commissioners, it is not necessary to prove in defence a final acceptance of the way. *Ib.*

497. An action to recover of a town the damages assessed by county commissioners, on laying out a town way over the plaintiff's land, cannot be maintained, if it is commenced before the land is entered upon, and possession thereof taken, for the purpose of constructing the way, although the way is constructed before the action comes to trial. And on the trial of such action, thus commenced, the defendants may give evidence that the commissioners, by mistake, awarded damages to the plaintiff, not only for his own land, but also for the lands of others, to whom they awarded no damages; and that those others have since sought and obtained damages of the defendants for the laying out of the way over their lands. *La Croix* v. *Medway*, 12 Met. 123 (1846).

498. The owner of land over which a street has been laid out by the city council of a city, under authority conferred upon them by the city charter, may maintain an action to recover the damages awarded therefor, although the defendants have not entered upon or taken possession of the land for the purpose of constructing the street. *Shaw* v. *Charlestown*, 3 Allen, 538 (1862).

499. St. 1853, c. 315, (Gen. Sts. c. 43, § 84,) which imposes upon owners of lots abutting on any street or way which then was or thereafter should be opened over any private land by the owners thereof, and dedicated to or permitted to be used by the public before being accepted and laid out according to law, the duty of grading such street or way at their own expense, in such manner as the safety and convenience of the public shall, in the opinion of the mayor and aldermen of the city, or selectmen of the town, require; and which authorizes the mayor and aldermen, or

selectmen, to cause the same to be so graded, and to assess the expenses thereof upon the owners of such abutting lots, and to create by such assessment a lien upon their respective lands, if upon notice they refuse or neglect to grade the same in manner aforesaid, or to close the same from public use, is unconstitutional and void. *Morse* v. *Stocker*, 1 Allen, 150 (1861). *Barrett* v. *Cambridge*, 10 Allen, 48 (1865).

500. The making and regulation of streets in the city of Boston is provided for exclusively by special statutes; consequently a by-law containing a provision for removing snow in the streets, differing from the provisions in the general statute of 1786, c. 81, concerning the laying out and regulation of highways, is not repugnant to this statute, as that statute is not in force in Boston. *Goddard, Petitioner*, 16 Pick. 504 (1835).

501. An act of the legislature providing that the expense of building a particular bridge shall be borne in part by the county within which it is situated, when by the operation of the general laws of the Commonwealth the expense would be borne wholly by the town within which it is situated, is not unconstitutional. *Norwich* v. *Hampshire*, 13 Pick. 60 (1833).

502. The owner of land bordering on a stream, whether navigable or not, may maintain an action of tort against a town laying out a highway and bridge across the stream, to recover any special damage occasioned to his land by the bridge being so built or afterwards altered by a third person for his own benefit with the permission or assent of the town, as to obstruct the course of the stream more than it would otherwise be obstructed; although the bridge is built over a tide mill, the owners of which have acquired a prescriptive right to obstruct the water in a less degree. *Lawrence* v. *Fairhaven*, 5 Gray 110 (1855). See ACTIONS, 20, 43, 44; OFFICERS, 43; RAILROADS, 26 *a*.

503. If a private way is opened, leading from a public street, and prepared for use in the same manner as a public street, and with nothing to show that it is not such, the public may lawfully travel over it, although it is closed at one end. *Danforth* v. *Durell*, 8 Allen, 242 (1864).

See *ante*, 3, 16, 18, 32, 64, 113, 134, 470.

TABLE

OF THE

CASES REFERRED TO IN THIS DIGEST.

A.

	PAGE.
Abington v. Boston, 4 Mass. 312,	18
—— (Jewell v.) 2 Allen, 592,	74
—— v. North Bridgewater, 23 Pick. 170,	17, 56
Adams, Petitioners, 10 Pick. 273,	135
—— v. Adams, 13 Pick. 384,	23
—— (Anthony v.) 1 Met. 284,	2, 8, 14, 115
—— v. Carlisle, 21 Pick. 146,	121, 124
—— v. Emerson, 6 Pick. 57,	131
—— v. Farnsworth, 16 Gray,	3, 87
—— v. Frothingham, 3 Mass. 352,	65
—— (Gregory v.) 14 Gray, 242,	118
—— v. Hampden, 13 Gray, 439,	28
—— v. ——, 16 Gray,	28
—— v. Moulton, 7 Pick. 286,	19
—— v. Nantucket, 11 Allen,	84
—— (Parker v.) 12 Met. 415,	12
—— (Snow v.) 1 Cush. 443,	120
—— (Tash v.) 10 Cush. 252,	7, 9
—— (Williams v.) 3 Allen, 171,	30
—— v. Wiscasset, 5 Mass. 328,	51
Aiken (Hastings v.) 1 Gray, 163,	11
Aldrich v. Aldrich, 8 Met. 102,	86, 88
—— v. Pelham, 1 Gray, 510,	125
Alexander v. Pitts, 7 Cush. 503,	90
Alfred (Sayward v.) 5 Mass. 244,	51
Alger v. Lowell, 3 Allen, 402,	115, 120, 123, 126
Allen (Baker v.) 21 Pick. 382,	94
—— (Brookfield v.) 6 Allen, 585,	50, 53, 63
—— (Call v.) 1 Allen, 137,	77
—— (Commonwealth v.) 11 Met. 403,	12
—— v. Metcalf, 17 Pick. 208,	34
—— (Shattuck v.) 4 Gray, 540,	74
—— v. Taunton, 19 Pick. 485,	7, 14
—— v. Turner, 11 Gray, 436,	9
—— v. Westport, 15 Pick. 35,	74
Alvord v. Collin, 20 Pick. 418,	84, 86, 89
Amesbury (Amesbury Woollen Co. v.) 17 Mass. 461,	78, 80
—— (Boston v.) 4 Met. 278,	29, 56
Amesbury W'n Co. v. Amesbury, 17 Mass. 461,	78, 80
Amherst (Granby v.) 7 Mass. 1,	18, 39
—— v. Shelburne, 11 Gray, 107,	62
—— v. ——, 13 Gray, 341,	39, 40
Anderson (Colman v.) 10 Mass. 105,	86
Andover v. Canton, 13 Mass. 547,	38, 39, 41, 58
—— v. Chelmsford, 16 Mass. 236,	48
—— v. Easthampton, 5 Gray, 390,	62
—— (Jones v.) 6 Pick. 59,	116
—— (—— v.) 9 Pick. 146,	99
—— (—— v.) 10 Allen, 18,	118, 127
—— (Palmer v.) 2 Cush. 600,	117, 123
—— (Salem v.) 3 Mass. 436,	50, 54
—— v. Sutton, 12 Met. 182,	128
Andrews v. Worcester Ins. Co. 5 Allen, 65,	87
Anthony v. Adams, 1 Met. 284,	2, 8, 14, 115
—— v. Anthony, 6 Allen, 408,	22
—— v. Berkshire, 14 Pick. 189,	114
Appleton (Barre Turnpike v.) 2 Pick. 430,	109
—— v. Hopkins, 5 Gray, 530,	5, 87, 88
Armstrong v. Wendell, 9 Met. 522,	115
Arundel v. M'Culloch, 10 Mass. 70,	102, 131
Ashby v. Lunenberg, 8 Pick. 563,	59
Athearn (Commonwealth v.) 3 Mass. 285,	33
Athol v. Watertown, 7 Pick. 42,	48
Attleborough (Hayden v.) 7 Gray, 338,	104, 116, 118, 120, 125
—— v. Mansfield, 15 Pick. 19,	55
—— v. Middleborough, 10 Pick. 378,	48
—— (Seekonk v.) 7 Pick. 155,	61
—— (Wrentham v.) 5 Mass. 430,	47, 54
Auburn (Worcester v.) 4 Allen, 574,	48, 50, 57

	PAGE.
Augusta (Embden v.) 12 Mass. 307,	58
—— (Kupfer v.) 12 Mass. 185,	15
—— (Sidney v.) 12 Mass. 316,	59
Austin v. Carter, 1 Mass. 231,	115
—— v. Murray, 16 Pick. 121,	27, 36
Avery v. Stewart, 1 Cush. 496,	104, 106

B.

Babbitt v. Savoy, 3 Cush. 530,	3
Bacon v. Boston, 3 Cush. 174,	117, 119, 122, 124
Badger (Doane v.) 12 Mass. 69,	105
Bailey (Pedrick v.) 12 Gray, 161,	32, 36
—— (Sprague v.) 19 Pick. 436,	84, 86, 94
Baker v. Allen, 21 Pick. 382,	94
—— v. Boston, 12 Pick. 184,	14, 27
—— v. Dedham, 16 Gray,	116, 118
Baldwin v. Fitchburg, 8 Pick. 494,	77, 81
Bancroft v. Lynnfield, 18 Pick. 566,	3, 8, 32
Banker (Saltonstall v.) 8 Gray, 195,	77
Barber v. Roxbury, 11 Allen,	118
Barnard v. Graves, 13 Met. 85,	89
Barnes (Shute v.) 2 Allen, 598,	98
—— v. Springfield, 4 Allen, 488,	96, 109
Barnicoat v. Folling, 3 Gray, 134,	11
Barre v. Greenwich, 1 Pick. 129,	32, 44
Barre Turnpike v. Appleton, 2 Pick. 430,	109
Barrett v. Cambridge, 10 Allen, 48,	93, 137
Barry v. Lowell, 8 Allen, 127,	2, 75
Bartlett (Tasker v.) 5 Cush. 359,	75
Bassett v. Porter, 4 Cush. 487,	88, 94
Bassit v. Glover, 1 Dane Ab. 137,	23
Batchelder v. Salem, 4 Cush. 599,	74
Bates v. Boston, 5 Cush. 93,	79, 81, 91
—— v. Boston & N. Y. Central Railroad, 10 Allen, 251,	75
—— v. Plymouth, 14 Gray, 163,	34, 37
Bath v. Bowdoin, 4 Mass. 452,	44
—— v. Freeport, 5 Mass. 325,	54
Battelle (Welles v.) 11 Mass. 477,	34, 70, 81, 84
Baxter (Parker v.) 2 Gray, 185,	90
Beale (Commonwealth v.) 5 Pick. 514,	25, 64
Bean (—— v.) 14 Gray, 52,	35, 37
—— (Sargent v.) 7 Gray, 125,	85, 90
Becket (Shaw v.) 7 Cush. 442,	92
Belcher v. Farrar, 8 Allen, 325,	27
Belchertown v. Dudley, 6 Allen, 477,	42
—— (Hannum v.) 19 Pick. 311,	105, 132
—— v. Randall, 7 Cush. 478,	72
Belding (Commonwealth v.) 13 Met. 10,	105, 130
Belfast v. Leominster, 1 Pick. 123,	55
Belgrade v. Sidney, 15 Mass. 523,	44
Bell (Colerain v.) 9 Met. 499,	9
Bellingham (Milford v.) 16 Mass. 108,	42
—— v. West Boylston, 4 Cush. 553,	44
Belmont (Frost v.) 6 Allen, 152,	8, 9
Bemis (Elder v.) 2 Met. 599,	115
Benjamin (Pierce v.) 14 Pick. 356,	88, 89
—— v. Wheeler, 8 Gray, 409,	116
—— v. ——, 16 Gray,	115, 116
Bennett v. Clemence, 6 Allen, 10,	107

	PAGE.
Bennett (Kilburn v.) 3 Met. 199,	87
Benoit v. Conway, 10 Allen, 528,	16, 94
Benson (Stacey v.) 18 Pick. 496,	77
Bentley (Canton v.) 11 Mass. 441,	50, 61
Berkley v. Somerset, 16 Mass. 454,	40
—— v. Taunton, 19 Pick. 480,	49
Berkshire (Anthony v.) 14 Pick. 189,	114
—— (Castle v.) 11 Gray, 26,	107
—— (Commonwealth v.) 8 Pick. 343,	98, 99
—— (Great Barrington v.) 16 Pick. 572,	78
—— (Harrington v.) 22 Pick. 266,	131
—— (Hawkins v.) 2 Allen, 254,	107, 109, 113
—— (Holden v.) 7 Met. 561,	106
—— (Lanesborough v.) 22 Pick. 278,	110, 114
—— (Merrill v.) 11 Pick. 269,	107, 108, 110, 111, 114
—— (Monterey v.) 7 Cush. 394,	133
—— (New Marlborough v.) 9 Met. 423,	97
Berlin v. Bolton, 10 Met. 115,	48
Bernardston (Dalton v.) 9 Mass. 201,	40, 50
—— (Westminster v.) 8 Mass. 104,	58, 60
Berry (Commonwealth v.) 5 Gray, 93,	71
—— (Garrigan v.) 12 Allen,	12
Besse v. Dyer, 9 Allen, 151,	7
Bigelow v. Bridge, 8 Mass. 274,	10
—— v. Randolph, 14 Gray, 541,	2
—— v. Rutland, 4 Cush. 247,	121
—— v. Weston, 3 Pick. 267,	116
Billerica v. Chelmsford, 10 Mass. 394,	47
—— (Townsend v.) 10 Mass. 411,	50, 54, 59
Billings (Dickinson v.) 4 Gray, 42,	94
Bills (Ingalls v.) 9 Met. 1,	123
Bishop v. Fahay, 15 Gray,	17
—— v. Rochester, 11 Allen,	16
Blackburn v. Walpole, 9 Pick. 97,	84
Blackstone, (Blackstone M'f Co. v.) 13 Gray, 488,	79
—— v. Seekonk, 8 Cush. 75,	41
—— v. Taft, 4 Gray, 250,	1
Blackstone Canal Co. (Millbury v.) 8 Pick. 473,	131
Blackstone Manuf. Co. v. Blackstone, 13 Gray, 488,	79
Blake (Brackett v.) 7 Met. 335,	5, 34
Blanchard v. Stearns, 5 Met. 298,	20, 21
Blandford v. Gibbs, 2 Cush. 39,	20
Bliss v. Wilbraham, 8 Allen, 564,	122, 127
Blodgett v. Boston, 8 Allen, 237,	119
Blossom v. Cannon, 14 Mass. 177,	84
Boardman (Williams v.) 9 Allen, 570,	5
Bolton (Berlin v.) 10 Met. 115,	48
Borman (Robbins v.) 1 Pick. 122,	131
Boston (Abington v.) 4 Mass. 312,	18
—— v. Amesbury, 4 Met. 278,	29, 56
—— (Bacon v.) 3 Cush. 174,	117, 119, 122, 124
—— (Baker v.) 12 Pick. 184,	14, 27
—— (Bates v.) 5 Cush. 93,	79, 81, 91
—— (Blodgett v.) 8 Allen, 237,	119
—— (Boston & Sandwich Glass Co. v.) 4 Met. 181,	78, 81, 92
—— (Boston Water Power Co. v.) 9 Met. 199,	70, 91
—— (Bourne v.) 2 Gray, 494,	91
—— (Bowman v.) 5 Cush. 1,	100, 117

PAGE.
Boston v. Brazer, 11 Mass. 447, 101
——(Brooks v.) 19 Pick. 174, 75, 111, 116
——(Burnham v.) 10 Allen, 290, 118
——(Cabot v.) 12 Cush. 52, 82
——(Charlestown v.) 13 Mass 469, 40
——(Child v.) 4 Allen, 41, 76
——(Cochrane v.) 4 Allen, 177, 83
——(Commonwealth v.) 16 Pick, 442, 97
——(Cook v.) 9 Allen, 393, 2, 12
——(Crockett v.) 5 Cush. 182, 97, 102
——(Danvers v.) 10 Pick. 513, 39
——v. Dedham, 4 Met. 178, 43, 44, 56
——(Donaldson v.) 16 Gray, 126
——(Dorr v.) 6 Gray, 131, 92
——(Downer v.) 7 Cush. 277, 75
——(Dunham v.) 12 Allen, 16, 66
——(Dwight v.) 12 Allen, 78, 86, 93
——(Erskine v.) 14 Gray, 216, 108
——(Fallon v.) 3 Allen, 38, 121
——(Fernald v.) 12 Cush. 574, 102
——(Field v.) 10 Cush. 65, 80
——(First Church in Boston v.) 14 Gray, 214, 113
——(Fitz v.) 4 Cush. 365, 124
——(Foster v.) 22 Pick. 33, 101, 112
——(Freeman v.) 5 Met. 56, 70
——(Glover v.) 14 Gray, 282, 100
——(Goddard v.) 20 Pick. 407, 108
——(Gray v.) 15 Pick. 376, 78
——(Hancock v.) 1 Met. 122, 98
——(Harback v.) 10 Cush. 295, 95
——(Hemphill v.) 8 Cush. 195, 103, 104, 117
——(Howe v.) 7 Cush. 273, 89, 91
——(Huckins v.) 4 Cush. 543, 80
——(Kimball v.) 1 Allen, 417, 2, 118
——(Knowles v.) 12 Gray, 339 74
——(Lee v.) 2 Gray, 484, 82
——(Loring v.) 7 Met. 409, 71
——(—— v.) 12 Gray, 209, 106, 108
——(Mead v.) 3 Cush. 404, 70
——(Melcher v.) 9 Met. 73, 79
——v. Moore, 3 Allen, 126, 10
——(—— v.) 8 Cush. 274, 95
——(Munigle v.) 3 Allen, 230, 107
——(Otis v.) 12 Cush. 44, 82
——(Paine v.) 4 Allen, 168, 113
——(Parker v.) 1 Allen, 361, 96
——(Parks v.) 8 Pick. 218, 97, 135
——(—— v.) 15 Pick. 198, 107, 110, 111
——(Patterson v.) 20 Pick. 159, 111
——(—— v.) 23 Pick. 425, 112
——(Peirce v.) 3 Met. 520, 5, 87
——(Pool v.) 5 Cush. 219, 70
——(Preston v.) 12 Pick. 7, 80, 91
——(Revere v.) 14 Gray, 218, 108
——(Roberts v.) 5 Cush. 198, 74
——(Rossire v.) 4 Allen, 57, 21, 66
——v. Sears, 22 Pick. 122, 37
——(—— v.) 1 Met. 250, 82
——v. Schaffer, 9 Pick. 415, 1, 5
——v. Shaw, 1 Met. 130, 75

PAGE.
Boston v. Simmons, 9 Cush. 373, 102
——(Smith v.) 7 Cush. 254, 107
——(—— v.) 1 Gray, 72, 68
——(Stone v.) 2 Met. 220, 97, 98, 135
——(Swett v.) 18 Pick. 123, 78
——(Thayer v.) 19 Pick. 511, 1, 32
——(Thorndike v.) 1 Met. 242, 19, 82
——v. Tileston, 11 Mass. 468, 4
——(Tower v.) 10 Cush. 235, 96
——(Tremont Bank v.) 1 Cush. 142, 79
——(Trustees of the Greene Foundation v.) 12 Cush. 54, 81, 85
——(Valentine v.) 22 Pick. 75, 103, 105
——v. Wells, 14 Mass. 384, 43
——v. Westford, 12 Pick. 16, 29
——v. Weston, 22 Pick. 211, 30, 51
——v. Weymouth, 4 Cush. 538, 49, 69
——v. Worthington, 10 Gray, 496, 128
——(Wright v.) 9 Cush. 233, 76, 91
Boston & Lowell Railroad (Commonwealth v.) 12 Cush. 254, 99
——(Gahagan v.) 1 Allen, 187, 129, 133
——(Lowell v.) 23 Pick. 24, 128
Boston & Maine Railroad v. Cambridge, 8 Cush. 237, 79
——v. Lawrence, 2 Allen, 107, 68, 134
——v. Middlesex, 1 Allen, 324, 113, 133
——(Parker v.) 3 Cush. 107, 66
——(Whittaker v.) 7 Gray, 98, 68
Boston & N. Y. Central Railroad (Bates v.) 10 Allen, 251, 75
——(Mears v.) 5 Gray, 371, 2
Boston & Providence Railroad, (Roxbury v.) 6 Cush. 424, 67
——(—— v.) 2 Gray, 460, 68
Boston & Sandwich Glass Co. v. Boston, 4 Met. 181, 78, 81, 92
Boston & Worcester Railroad (Gardiner v.) 9 Cush. 1, 67
Boston Manuf. Co. v. Newton, 22 Pick. 22, 78, 80
Boston Mill Corp. (Rust v.) 6 Pick. 158, 69
Boston Water Power Co. v. Boston, 9 Met. 199, 79, 91
——(Taylor v.) 12 Gray, 415. 105
Bosworth (Inglee v.) 5 Pick. 498, 84
——v. Swansey, 10 Met. 363, 118
Bourne v. Boston, 2 Gray, 494, 91
Boutelle v. Nourse, 4 Mass. 431, 63
Bowdoin (Bath v.) 4 Mass. 452, 44
Bowers (Phillips v.) 7 Gray, 21, 132
——v. Suffolk Manuf. Co. 4 Cush. 332, 103, 104
Bowley v. Walker, 8 Allen, 21, 106
Bowman v. Boston, 5 Cush. 1, 100, 117
Boxborough (Groton v.) 6 Mass. 50, 43
——(Harvard v.) 4 Met. 570, 47
——(Mead v.) 11 Cush. 362, 18, 83
Boxford (Stevens v.) 10 Allen, 25, 122, 127
Boylston v. Clinton, 1 Gray, 619, 42
——v. Groton, 4 Gray, 282, 44
——(New Braintree v.) 24 Pick. 164, 46
——v. Princeton, 13 Mass. 381, 41

PAGE.
Boylston (West Boylston *v.*) 15 Mass. 261, 45
Boylston Market Association (Kirby *v.*) 14 Gray, 249, 119, 128, 129
Brackett *v.* Blake, 7 Met. 335, 5, 34
—— *v.* Lubke, 4 Allen, 138, 130
—— (Nickerson *v.*) 10 Mass. 212, 26
Bradford *v.* Randall, 5 Pick. 496, 75, 86
—— (West Newbury *v.*) 3 Met. 428, 48, 49
Bradley *v.* Heath, 12 Pick. 163, 33
Brady *v.* Lowell, 3 Cush. 121, 117
Brailey *v.* Southborough, 6 Cush. 141, 116, 123
Brainard *v.* Clapp, 10 Cush. 9, 131
—— *v.* Connecticut River Railroad, 7 Cush. 506, 67
Braintree *v.* Hingham, 17 Mass. 432, 60
—— (Newton *v.*) 14 Mass. 382, 41
—— (Quincy *v.*) 5 Mass. 86, 58
—— (Randolph *v.*) 4 Mass. 315, 26
—— (Williams *v.*) 6 Cush. 399, 52
Braman (Sherman *v.*) 13 Met. 407, 23
Brazer (Boston *v.*) 11 Mass. 447, 101
Brewer *v.* New Gloucester, 14 Mass. 216, 1
—— *v.* Tyringham, 14 Pick. 196, 30
Brewster *v.* Dennis, 21 Pick. 233, 42, 49
—— *v.* Harwich, 4 Mass. 278, 6
Bridge (Bigelow *v.*) 8 Mass. 274, 10
Bridgeton (Harrison *v.*) 16 Mass. 16, 6
Bridgewater *v.* Dartmouth, 4 Mass. 273, 60
—— (East Bridgewater *v.*) 2 Pick. 572, 46
—— (Mitchell *v.*) 10 Cush. 411, 108
—— (Thompson *v.*) 7 Pick. 188, 121
—— *v.* West Bridgewater, 9 Pick. 55, 46
Briggs *v.* A Light Boat, 7 Allen, 287, 37
—— *v.* Murdock, 13 Pick. 305, 34, 70
—— *v.* Rochester, 16 Gray, 83
Brigham (Munroe *v.*) 19 Pick. 368, 30
Brightman *v.* Grinnell, 9 Pick. 14, 23
Brighton, (Dover *v.*) 2 Gray, 482, 43
Brimblecom (Commonwealth *v.*) 4 Allen, 584, 17
Bristol (District Attorney *v.*) 14 Gray, 138, 65
—— (Ellis *v.*) 2 Gray, 370, 19
—— (Haskell *v.*) 9 Gray, 341, 98, 109
—— (Monagle *v.*) 8 Cush. 360, 109
—— (New Bedford *v.*) 9 Gray, 346, 109, 136
—— (Westport *v.*) 9 Allen, 203, 97, 98, 110
Brookfield *v.* Allen, 6 Allen, 585, 50, 53, 63
Brookline (Loker *v.*) 13 Pick. 343, 115
Brooks *v.* Boston, 19 Pick. 174, 75, 111, 116
—— *v.* Petersham, 16 Gray, 121, 125
—— (Wilson *v.*) 14 Pick. 341, 38
Brown's case, 8 Pick. 504, 30
Brown *v.* Cambridge, 3 Allen, 474, 119, 126
—— *v.* Essex, 12 Met. 208, 108, 135
—— *v.* Lowell, 8 Met. 172, 109
—— (Plumer *v.*) 8 Met. 578, 116, 132
—— *v.* Worcester, 13 Gray, 31, 104, 108, 113
Bruce *v.* White, 4 Gray, 345, 23
Brunswick *v.* Dunning, 7 Mass. 445, 33
Buckfield *v.* Gorham, 6 Mass. 445, 44
Buckland *v.* Charlemont, 3 Pick. 173, 40

PAGE.
Buffum (Farnum *v.*) 4 Cush. 260, 89
Bulkley *v.* Williamstown, 3 Gray, 493, 83
Burgis (Dillingham *v.*) 16 Mass. 58, 46
Burlington (Lexington *v.*) 19 Pick. 426, 45
—— (Wood *v.*) 1 Met. 493, 38
Burnham *v.* Boston, 10 Allen, 290, 118
—— (Libby *v.*) 15 Mass. 144, 84
—— *v.* Webster, 5 Mass. 266, 63
Burns (Davies *v.*) 5 Allen, 349, 70
Butler *v.* Charlestown, 7 Gray, 12, 3
—— *v.* Hubbard, 5 Pick. 250, 6
Butterfield *v.* Melrose, 6 Allen, 187, 25
Buttrick *v.* Lowell, 1 Allen, 172, 1
Buzzell (Commonwealth *v.*) 16 Pick. 153, 31
Byron *v.* Crippen, 4 Gray, 312, 25

C.

Cabot *v.* Boston, 12 Cush. 52, 82
Calder *v.* Haynes, 7 Allen, 387, 10
Caldwell *v.* Eaton, 5 Mass. 403, 88
Call *v.* Allen, 1 Allen, 137, 77
Callender *v.* Marsh, 1 Pick. 418, 115
Cambridge (Barrett *v.*) 10 Allen, 48, 93, 137
—— (Boston & Maine Railroad *v.*) 8 Cush. 237, 79
—— (Brown *v.*) 3 Allen, 474, 119, 126
—— *v.* Cambridge Railroad, 10 Allen, 50, 69
—— *v.* Charlestown, 13 Mass. 501, 47, 54, 63
—— *v.* Charlestown Branch Railroad, 7 Met. 70, 66
—— (Commonwealth *v.*) 20 Pick. 267, 63
—— (—— *v.*) 4 Met. 35, 63
—— (Cutter *v.*) 6 Allen, 20, 101, 133
—— (Farwell *v.*) 11 Gray, 413, 112
—— *v.* Lexington, 1 Pick. 506, 41
—— (Little *v.*) 9 Cush. 298, 80
—— *v.* Middlesex, 6 Allen, 134, 76
—— (Pierce *v.*) 2 Cush. 611, 79
—— (Stone *v.*) 6 Cush. 270, 99
—— (Union Railway *v.*) 11 Allen, 69
—— (Watson *v.*) 15 Mass. 286, 39, 51
—— (—— *v.*) 18 Pick. 470, 29, 51
—— (Willard *v.*) 3 Allen, 574, 119
Cambridge Railroad (Cambridge *v.*) 10 Allen, 50, 69
Campbell *v.* Race, 7 Cush. 408, 103
Canal Bridge, (Worster *v.*) 16 Pick. 541, 122
Canning *v.* Williamstown, 1 Cush. 451, 124
Cannon (Blossom *v.*) 14 Mass. 177, 84
Canton (Andover *v.*) 13 Mass. 547, 38, 39, 41, 58
—— *v.* Bentley, 11 Mass. 441, 50, 61
—— *v.* Dorchester, 8 Cush. 525, 42
Capen *v.* Glover, 4 Mass. 305, 80
Cargill *v.* Wiscasset, 2 Mass. 547, 51
Carlisle (Adams *v.*) 21 Pick. 146, 121, 124
Carnoe *v.* Freetown, 9 Gray, 357, 82
Carter (Austin *v.*) 1 Mass. 231, 115
Castle *v.* Berkshire, 11 Gray, 26, 107
Caswell (Taunton *v.*) 4 Pick. 275, 26
Caverly *v.* Lowell, 1 Allen, 289, 35

PAGE.
Central Bridge v. Lowell, 4 Gray, 474, 103
—— v. ——15 Gray, 98, 103, 113
Chace v. Fall River, 2 Allen, 533, 115
—— (New Bedford v.) 5 Allen, 28, 53
—— (Swansey v.) 16 Gray, 128
Chandler (Perley v.) 6 Mass. 453, 102, 111, 131
Chapman v. Lowell, 4 Cush. 378, 15
Charlemont (Buckland v.) 3 Pick. 173, 40
—— v. Conway, 8 Pick. 408, 48, 55, 84
Charlestown v. Boston, 13 Mass. 469, 40
—— (Butler v.) 7 Gray, 12, 3
—— (Cambridge v.) 13 Mass. 501, 47, 54, 63
—— (Commonwealth v.) 1 Pick. 180, 102, 127
—— v. Groveland, 15 Gray, 38, 50
—— (Malden & Melrose Railroad v.) 8 Allen, 245, 2, 118
—— v. Middlesex, 3 Met. 202, 102
—— v. ——, 1 Allen, 199, 79, 93
—— (Middlesex Railroad v.) 8 Allen, 330, 78
—— (Shaw v.) 3 Allen, 538, 136
—— (Sherman v.) 8 Cush. 160, 74
—— v. Stone, 15 Gray, 135
—— (Tufts v.) 4 Gray, 537, 112
—— (Warren v.) 2 Gray, 84, 5
—— (Watson v.) 5 Met. 54, 29, 62
—— (Wilson v.) 8 Allen, 137, 122
Charlestown Branch Railroad (Cambridge v.) 7 Met. 70, 66
Charlton (Southbridge v.) 15 Mass. 248, 46, 54
Chase (Commonwealth v.) 6 Cush. 248, 17, 34
—— v. Lowell, 7 Gray, 33, 4, 32
—— v. Merrimack Bank, 19 Pick. 564, 1
Chatham (Orleans v.) 2 Pick. 29, 42
Cheever v. Merritt, 5 Allen, 563, 87, 91
Chelmsford (Andover v.) 16 Mass. 236, 48
—— (Billerica v.) 10 Mass. 394, 47
Chelmsford Co. v. Demarest, 7 Gray, 1, 10
Chelsea (Green v.) 24 Pick. 71, 66
—— v. Malden, 4 Mass. 131, 39
—— (Shepherd v.) 4 Allen, 113, 122
—— (Winnisimmet Co. v.) 6 Cush. 477, 85, 93
Chenery v. Holden, 16 Gray, 17
—— v. Waltham, 8 Cush. 327, 18, 82
Cheney (Claflin v.) 4 Pick. 118, 19
Cheshire v. Howland, 13 Gray, 321, 10, 87, 94
—— (Smith v.) 13 Gray, 318, 2
Chester (Fisk v.) 8 Gray, 506, 18
—— (Monson v.) 22 Pick. 385, 43
Chicopee v. Hampden, 16 Gray, 86
—— v. Whately, 6 Allen, 508, 18, 19, 49, 50
Child v. Boston, 4 Allen, 41, 76
Choate v. Rochester, 13 Gray, 92, 50
Christ Church v. Pope, 8 Gray, 140, 20
Church (Wilson v.) 1 Pick. 23, 63
Claflin v. Cheney, 4 Pick. 118, 19
—— v. Hopkinton, 4 Gray, 502, 7
Clapp (Brainard v.) 10 Cush. 9, 131
Clark v. Commonwealth, 4 Pick. 125, 12
—— v. Great Barrington, 11 Pick. 260, 5, 72
—— v. Lowell, 1 Allen, 180, 126
—— (Middleborough v.) 2 Pick. 28, 50, 61

PAGE.
Clark (Snow v.) 9 Gray, 190, 88
Clarksburgh (Mount Washington v.) 19 Pick. 294, 42, 49
Clary (Commonwealth v.) 8 Mass. 72, 20, 78
Clemence (Bennett v.) 6 Allen, 10, 107
Cleverly v. Towle, 3 Allen, 39, 24
Clinton (Boylston v.) 1 Gray, 619, 42
Cobb v. Kingman, 15 Mass. 197, 5
Cochrane v. Boston, 4 Allen, 177, 83
Codding v. Mansfield, 7 Gray, 272, 70
Coffin v. Field, 7 Cush. 355, 24, 25
—— v. Nantucket, 5 Cush. 269, 25
—— (Russell v.) 8 Pick. 142, 77
—— v. Vincent, 12 Cush. 98, 24
Coggswell v. Lexington, 4 Cush. 307, 120
Colburn v. Ellis, 7 Mass. 89, 86
—— v. Swett, 1 Met. 232, 27, 64
Colerain v. Bell, 9 Met. 499, 9
—— (Donelson v.) 4 Met. 430, 4
—— (Petersham v.) 9 Allen, 91, 60
—— (Rindge v.) 11 Gray, 157, 125
—— (Smith v.) 9 Met. 492, 52
Collin (Alvord v.) 20 Pick. 418, 84, 86, 89
Collins v. Dorchester, 6 Cush. 396, 115, 124, 125
Colman v. Anderson, 10 Mass. 105, 86
Commonwealth v. Allen, 11 Met. 403, 12
—— v. Athearn, 3 Mass. 285, 33
—— v. Beale, 5 Pick. 514, 25, 64
—— v. Bean, 14 Gray, 52, 35, 37
—— v. Belding, 13 Met. 10, 105, 130
—— v. Berkshire, 8 Pick. 343, 98, 99
—— v. Berry, 5 Gray, 93, 71
—— v. Boston, 16 Pick. 442, 97
—— v. Boston & Lowell Railroad, 12 Cush. 254, 99
—— v. Brimblecom, 4 Allen, 584, 17
—— v. Buzzell, 16 Pick. 153, 31
—— v. Cambridge, 20 Pick. 267, 63
—— v. ——, 4 Met. 35, 63
—— v. Charlestown, 1 Pick. 180, 102, 127
—— v. Chase, 6 Cush. 248, 17, 34
—— (Clark v.) 4 Pick. 125, 12
—— v. Clary, 8 Mass. 72, 20, 78
—— v. Cooley, 10 Pick. 36, 28
—— v. Coombs, 2 Mass. 489, 102, 110
—— v. Curtis, 9 Allen, 266, 36
—— v. Dedham, 16 Mass. 141, 30, 72
—— v. Deerfield, 6 Allen, 449, 128
—— v. Dow, 10 Met. 382, 17
—— v. Dracut, 8 Gray, 455, 58, 63
—— v. Dugan, 12 Met. 233, 65
—— v. Fahey, 5 Cush. 408, 27
—— v. Farren, 9 Allen, 489, 32
—— v. Fisher, 6 Met. 433, 130
—— v. Gammons, 23 Pick. 201, 12
—— v. Gay, 5 Pick, 44, 35
—— v. Gee, 6 Cush. 174, 5
—— v. Gibney, 2 Allen, 152, 71
—— v. Gowen, 7 Mass. 378, 130
—— v. Griffith, 2 Pick. 11, 75
—— v. Hampden, 2 Pick. 414, 28

PAGE.
Commonwealth v. Hartford & New Haven Railroad, 14 Gray, 579, 68
—— v. Hastings, 9 Met. 259, 65
—— v. Haverhill, 7 Allen, 523, 103, 134
—— v. Higgins, 4 Gray, 34, 65
—— (Howard v.) 13 Mass. 221, 64
—— v. Howes, 15 Pick. 231, 64
—— v. Hoxey, 16 Mass. 385, 17
—— v. James, 1 Pick. 375, 13
—— (Jones v.) 15 Gray, 17
—— v. King, 13 Met. 115, 130
—— v. Low, 3 Pick. 408, 130
—— v. Lowell Gas Light Co. 12 Allen, 80
—— v. McCarron, 2 Allen, 157, 31
—— v. Middlesex, 9 Mass. 388, 111
—— v. Nashua & Lowell Railroad, 2 Gray, 54, 68, 130
—— v. Newbury, 2 Pick. 51, 103, 127
—— v. Nichols, 10 Allen, 199, 31
—— v. Norfolk, 5 Mass. 437, 110
—— v. Northampton, 2 Mass. 116, 71, 72
—— v. North Brookfield, 8 Pick. 463, 127
—— v. O'Connor, 7 Allen, 584, 65
—— v. O'Donnell, 1 Allen, 593, 31
—— v. Old Colony & Fall River Railroad, 14 Gray, 93, 68, 105, 130
—— v. Petersham, 4 Pick. 119, 127
—— v. Phillipsburg, 10 Mass. 78, 30
—— v. Phœnix Bank, 11 Met. 135, 5, 87
—— v. Porter, 1 Gray, 480, 17, 71
—— v. Presby, 14 Gray, 65, 65
—— v. Reed, 1 Gray, 472, 31
—— v. Rice, 9 Met. 253, 22
—— v. Robertson, 5 Cush. 438, 12
—— v. Roxbury, 8 Mass. 457, 106
—— v. ——, 9 Gray, 451, 10, 11, 30
—— v. Ruggles, 6 Allen, 588, 131
—— v. Runnels, 10 Mass. 520, 71
—— v. Ryan, 5 Mass. 90, 31
—— v. Sawin, 2 Pick, 547, 97
—— v. Sheffield, 11 Cush. 178, 72
—— v. Silsbee, 9 Mass. 417, 20
—— v. Slack, 19 Pick. 304, 28
—— v. Smyth, 14 Gray, 33, 130
—— v. Springfield, 7 Mass. 13, 115
—— v. Stevens, 10 Pick. 247, 130
—— v. Stockbridge, 13 Mass. 294, 102
—— v. Stodder, 2 Cush. 562, 11
—— v. Temple, 14 Gray, 69, 69
—— v. Thompson, 12 Met. 231, 26
—— v. Tucker, 2 Pick. 44, 106
—— v. Turner, 1 Cush. 493, 36
—— v. Upton, 6 Gray, 473, 27
—— v. Vermont & Mass. Railroad, 4 Gray, 22, 68, 130
—— v. Waite, 11 Allen, 32
—— v. Walton, 17 Pick. 403, 31
—— v. Weiher, 3 Met. 445, 98
—— v. West Boston Bridge, 13 Pick. 195, 135
—— v. Western, 1 Pick. 136, 106

PAGE.
Commonwealth v. Wilkinson, 16 Pick. 175, 130
—— v. Worcester, 3 Pick 462, 12, 13, 31, 35
Congdon (Reidell v.) 16 Pick. 44, 6
Connecticut River Railroad (Brainard v.) 7 Cush. 506, 67
—— (Springfield v.) 4 Cush. 63, 6, 67
Converse v. Jennings, 13 Gray, 77, 90
Conway (Benoit v.) 10 Allen, 528, 16, 94
—— (Charlemont v.) 8 Pick. 408, 48, 55, 84
—— v. Deerfield, 11 Mass. 327, 42, 43, 54
Cook v. Boston, 9 Allen, 393, 2, 12
Cooley (Commonwealth v.) 10 Pick. 36, 28
—— v. Granville, 10 Cush. 56, 8
Coolidge v. Williams, 4 Mass. 140, 26, 66
Coombs (Commonwealth v.) 2 Mass. 489, 102, 110
Copeland (Norton v.) 2 Gray, 414, 72
Cornville (Mitchell v.) 12 Mass. 332 51
Cotton v. Pocasset Manuf. Co. 13 Met. 429, 75
Couch (Counter v) 8 Allen, 436, 123
Counter v. Couch, 8 Allen, 436, 123
Crapo v. Stetson, 8 Met. 393, 87, 88
Crawshaw v. Roxbury, 7 Gray, 374, 71
Crippen (Byron v.) 4 Gray, 312, 25
Crockett v. Boston, 5 Cush. 182, 97, 102
Crombie (Lane v.) 12 Pick. 177, 121
Cross (Flanders v.) 10 Cush. 514, 79, 85, 90
Crowell v. Goodwin, 3 Allen, 535, 90
Cummings (Spear v.) 23 Pick. 224, 73
Cummington v. Springfield, 2 Pick. 394, 38
—— v. Wareham, 9 Cush. 585, 62
—— (Williams v.) 18 Pick. 312, 103, 105, 124
Currier v. Lowell, 16 Pick. 170, 118
Curtis (Commonwealth v.) 9 Allen, 266, 36
—— v. Pembroke, 11 Allen, 4
Cushing v. Newburyport, 10 Met. 508, 8, 73
—— v. Stoughton, 6 Cush. 389, 3
Cushman (Greenfield v.) 16 Mass. 393, 61
Cutter v. Cambridge, 6 Allen, 20, 101, 133

D.

Dagget (Richards v.) 4 Mass. 539, 80
Dalton v. Bernardston, 9 Mass. 201, 40, 50
—— v. Hinsdale, 6 Mass. 501, 50, 53, 58
Damon v. Granby, 2 Pick. 345, 15, 33, 65
—— (Loker v.) 17 Pick. 284, 131
Dana v. Hardwick, 10 Met. 208, 47
—— (Palmer v.) 9 Met. 587, 57, 59
—— (Petersham v) 12 Mass. 428, 41
—— (Sutton v.) 4 Pick. 117, 45
—— (—— v.) 1 Met. 383, 47
Danforth v. Durell, 8 Allen, 242, 137
—— v. Williams, 9 Mass. 324, 87
Danvers v. Boston, 10 Pick. 513, 39
—— v. Essex, 2 Met. 185, 97
—— (Fowler v.) 8 Allen, 80, 7, 9
—— (Osborn v.) 6 Pick. 98, 91
—— (Page v.) 7 Met. 326, 31
—— (Salem Iron Co. v.) 10 Mass. 514, 78, 80
Dartmouth (Bridgewater v.) 4 Mass. 273, 60
—— v. Lakeville, 7 Allen, 284, 58

	Page.
Dartmouth (Westport *v.*) 10 Mass. 341,	44
Davenport (Houghton *v.*) 23 Pick. 235,	87
Davies *v.* Burns, 5 Allen, 349,	70
Davis *v.* Dudley, 4 Allen, 557,	123
—— (Hill *v.*) 4 Mass. 140,	63
—— *v.* Leominster, 1 Allen, 182,	117, 133
Day *v.* Green, 4 Cush. 433,	11, 33, 37, 131
—— *v.* Milford, 5 Allen, 98,	119, 123
—— *v.* Otis, 8 Allen, 477,	71
Dean *v.* Lindsey, 16 Gray,	23
Dearborn (Fales *v.*) 1 Pick. 345,	12
Dedham (Baker *v.*) 16 Gray,	116, 118
—— (Boston *v.*) 4 Met. 178,	43, 44, 56
—— (—— *v.*) 8 Met. 513,	30, 56
—— (Commonwealth *v.*) 16 Mass. 141,	30, 72
—— (Doggett *v.*) 2 Mass. 564,	51
—— (Franklin *v.*) 18 Pick. 544,	39
—— *v.* Natick, 16 Mass. 135,	41
—— (Smith *v.*) 8 Cush. 522,	123
Deerfield (Commonwealth *v.*) 6 Allen, 449,	128
—— (Conway *v.*) 11 Mass. 327,	42, 43, 54
—— *v.* Delano, 1 Pick. 465,	61
—— *v.* Greenfield, 1 Gray, 514,	57, 61, 62
—— (Leverett *v.*) 6 Allen, 431,	42
—— (Reed *v.*) 8 Allen, 522,	122
Deer Isle *v.* Eaton, 12 Mass. 327,	53
Delano (Deerfield *v.*) 1 Pick. 465,	61
Demarest (Chelmsford Co. *v.*) 7 Gray, 1,	10
Dennis (Brewster *v.*) 21 Pick. 233,	42, 49
Dickenson *v.* Fitchburg, 13 Gray, 546,	110, 111, 113
Dickinson *v.* Billings, 4 Gray, 42,	94
Dighton *v.* Freetown, 4 Mass. 539,	41
—— (Somerset *v.*) 12 Mass. 383,	40
Dill *v.* Wareham, 7 Met. 438,	26
Dillingham *v.* Burgis, 16 Mass. 58,	46
—— *v.* Snow, 5 Mass. 547,	84
District Attorney *v.* Bristol, 14 Gray, 138,	65
Dix (Goodhue *v.*) 2 Gray, 181,	12
Doane *v.* Badger, 12 Mass. 69,	105
—— *v.* Eldridge, 16 Gray,	10
—— (Macomber *v.*) 2 Allen, 541,	5, 34
Dodds *v.* Henry, 9 Mass. 262,	33
Doggett *v.* Dedham, 2 Mass. 564,	51
—— (Ingraham *v.*) 5 Pick. 451,	94
Doherty *v.* Waltham, 4 Gray, 596,	117
Dolan (Lovejoy *v.*) 10 Cush. 495,	12
Donaldson *v.* Boston, 16 Gray,	126
Donelson *v.* Colerain, 4 Met. 430,	4
Dorchester (Canton *v.*) 8 Cush. 525,	42
—— (Collins *v.*) 6 Cush. 396,	115, 124, 125
—— (Vinal *v.*) 7 Gray, 421,	117
Dorr *v.* Boston, 6 Gray, 131,	79, 92
Dover *v.* Brighton, 2 Gray, 482,	43
Dow (Commonwealth *v.*) 10 Met. 382,	17
—— *v.* Sudbury, 5 Met. 73,	92
Downer *v.* Boston, 7 Cush. 277,	75
Downey (Libby *v.*) 5 Allen, 300,	64
Dracut (Commonwealth *v.*) 8 Gray, 455,	58, 63
Drake (Hays *v.*) 6 Gray, 387,	94
—— *v.* Lowell, 13 Met. 292,	119
Drake *v.* Stoughton, 6 Cush. 393,	3
Dresden (Readfield *v.*) 12 Mass. 316,	54
Drury *v.* Natick, 10 Allen, 169,	95
—— *v.* Worcester, 21 Pick. 44,	116
Dudley (Belchertown *v.*) 6 Allen, 477,	42
—— (Davis *v.*) 4 Allen, 557,	123
—— (Gaskill *v.*) 6 Met. 546,	1
—— *v.* Weston, 1 Met. 477,	125
Dugan (Commonwealth *v.*) 12 Met. 233,	65
Duncan (Fellows *v.*) 13 Met. 332,	5
Dunham *v.* Boston, 12 Allen,	16, 66
Dunnell Manuf. Co. *v.* Pawtucket, 7 Gray, 277,	78, 92
Dunning (Brunswick *v.*) 7 Mass. 445,	33
Dunstable (Kidder *v.*) 7 Gray, 104,	122
—— (—— *v.*) 11 Gray, 342,	12, 123, 125
Durant *v.* Lawrence, 1 Allen, 125,	136
Durell (Danforth *v.*) 8 Allen, 242,	137
Durgin *v.* Lowell, 3 Allen, 398,	104, 119
Dwight *v.* Boston, 12 Allen,	78, 86, 93
—— *v.* Hampden, 7 Cush. 533,	107
—— *v.* ——, 11 Cush. 201,	112
—— *v.* Springfield, 4 Gray, 107,	97, 100, 135, 136
—— *v.* ——, 6 Gray, 442,	110, 115
Dyer (Besse *v.*) 9 Allen, 151,	71

E.

Eames *v.* Johnson, 4 Allen, 382,	94
—— *v.* New England Worsted Co. 11 Met. 572,	27
East Bridgewater *v.* Bridgewater, 2 Pick. 572,	46
—— (Goldthwait *v.*) 5 Gray, 61,	124
—— (North Bridgewater *v.*) 13 Pick. 303,	40, 41
Eastern Railroad (Newburyport Turnpike *v.*) 23 Pick. 326,	66
—— (Webber *v.*) 2 Met. 147,	112
East Granville (Gibbons *v.*) 4 Allen, 508,	73
Easthampton (Andover *v.*) 5 Gray, 390,	62
—— (Southampton *v.*) 8 Pick. 380,	48, 84
Easton (Keith *v.*) 2 Allen, 552,	120
—— (Randolph *v.*) 23 Pick. 242,	56
—— (—— *v.*) 4 Cush. 557,	49
East Sudbury *v.* Sudbury, 12 Pick. 1,	49, 55, 59
—— (—— *v.*) 15 Mass. 260,	46
—— *v.* Waltham, 13 Mass. 460,	49
Eaton (Caldwell *v.*) 5 Mass. 403,	88
—— (Deer Isle *v.*) 12 Mass. 327,	53
—— *v.* Middlesex, 7 Gray, 109,	99
—— (Worcester *v.*) 13 Mass. 371,	65
Edgartown (Marshpee *v.*) 23 Pick. 156,	60
—— *v.* Tisbury, 10 Cush. 408,	41, 42, 60
Edgecumbe (Freeport *v.*) 1 Mass. 459,	60
Egremont (Joyner *v.*) 3 Cush. 567,	84, 92
Ela *v.* Smith, 5 Gray, 121,	71
Elder *v.* Bemis, 2 Met. 599,	115
Eldridge (Doane *v.*) 16 Gray,	10
Ellis *v.* Bristol, 2 Gray, 370,	19
—— (Colburn *v.*) 7 Mass. 89,	86
Elwell (Lexington, &c. Railroad *v.*) 8 Allen, 371,	10
—— (Northampton *v.*) 4 Gray 81,	1

PAGE.
Embden *v.* Augusta, 12 Mass. 307, 58
Emerson (Adams *v.*) 6 Pick. 57, 131
—— *v.* Newbury, 13 Pick. 377, 15, 32
—— *v.* Wiley, 7 Pick. 68, 105
Endicott, Petitioner, 24 Pick. 339, 107
Enfield (Richards *v.*) 13 Gray, 344, 118
Erskine *v.* Boston, 14 Gray, 216, 108
Essex (Brown *v.*) 12 Met. 208, 108, 135
—— (Danvers *v.*) 2 Met. 185, 97
—— (Gloucester *v.*) 3 Met. 375, 110
—— (Marblehead *v.*) 5 Gray, 451, 103
—— (Newburyport *v.*) 12 Met. 211, 85, 93
—— (Peabody *v.*) 10 Gray, 97, 81
—— (South Danvers *v.*) 1 Allen, 25, 63

F.

Fahay (Bishop *v.*) 15 Gray, 17
Fahey (Commonwealth *v.*) 5 Cush. 408, 27
Fairhaven (Lawrence *v.*) 5 Gray, 110, 2, 137
Fales *v.* Dearborn, 1 Pick. 345, 12
Fallon *v.* Boston, 3 Allen, 38, 121
Fall River (Chace *v.*) 2 Allen, 533, 115
Farnsworth (Adams *v.*) 16 Gray, 3, 87
Farnum *v.* Buffum, 4 Cush. 260, 89
Farr *v.* Flood, 11 Cush. 24, 50
Farrar (Belcher *v.*) 8 Allen, 325, 27
—— (Winthrop *v.*) 11 Allen, 28
Farren (Commonwealth *v.*) 9 Allen, 489, 32
Farwell *v.* Cambridge, 11 Gray, 413, 112
Faxon (Stetson *v.*) 19 Pick. 147, 105
Fay, Petitioner, 15 Pick. 243, 22
Fellows *v.* Duncan, 13 Met. 332, 5
Fernald *v.* Boston, 12 Cush. 574, 102
Ferry (Palmer *v.*) 6 Gray, 420, 16, 53
Field *v.* Boston, 10 Cush. 65, 80
—— (Coffin *v.*) 7 Cush. 355, 24, 25
—— *v.* Jacobs, 12 Met. 118, 24
Fields (Folger *v.*) 12 Cush. 93, 25
First Church in Boston *v.* Boston, 14 Gray, 214, 113
Fish (Sandwich *v.*) 2 Gray, 298, 9
Fisher (Commonwealth *v.*) 6 Met. 433, 130
Fisk *v.* Chester, 8 Gray, 506, 18
Fiske *v.* Lincoln, 19 Pick. 473, 38, 52
—— (Lyman *v.*) 17 Pick. 231, 18, 83
—— *v.* Needham, 11 Mass. 452, 4
Fitchburg (Baldwin *v.*) 8 Pick. 494, 77, 81
—— (Dickenson *v.*) 13 Gray, 546, 110, 111, 113
—— (Leicester *v.*) 7 Allen, 90, 44
—— *v.* Winchendon, 4 Cush. 190, 18, 48, 83
Fitz *v.* Boston, 4 Cush. 365, 124
Flagg *v.* Millbury, 4 Cush. 243, 116, 117
—— *v.* Worcester, 8 Cush. 69, 110, 114
—— *v.* ——, 13 Gray, 601, 2, 75
Flanders *v.* Cross, 10 Cush. 514, 79, 85, 90
Fleming (Wendell *v.*) 8 Gray, 613, 9
Fletcher *v.* Lowell, 15 Gray, 33
Flood (Farr *v.*) 11 Cush. 24, 50
Folger *v.* Fields, 12 Cush. 93, 25
—— *v.* Hinckley, 5 Cush. 263, 23

PAGE.
Folger *v.* Worth, 19 Pick. 108, 105
Folling (Barnicoat *v.*) 3 Gray, 134, 11
Foote (Griggs *v.*) 4 Allen, 195, 102
Foster *v.* Boston, 22 Pick. 33, 101, 112
—— (Hayden *v.*) 13 Pick. 492, 88
—— (Henshaw *v.*) 9 Pick. 312, 19
—— *v.* Worcester, 16 Pick. 71, 62
Fowler *v.* Danvers, 8 Allen, 80, 7, 9
—— *v.* Middlesex, 6 Allen, 92, 114, 115
Fox *v.* Sackett, 10 Allen, 535, 122
Framingham (Wheeler *v.*) 12 Cush. 287, 125
Frankfort (Haliburton *v.*) 14 Mass. 214, 2, 7
Franklin *v.* Dedham, 18 Pick. 544, 39
—— (Hallock *v.*) 2 Met. 558, 106
—— (Vermont & Mass. Railroad *v.*) 10 Cush. 12, 67
—— (Westborough *v.*) 15 Mass. 254, 46
Freeland *v.* Hastings, 10 Allen, 570, 7, 9, 14, 86
Freeman *v.* Boston, 5 Met. 56, 70
—— *v.* Kenney, 15 Pick. 44, 10, 94
Freeport (Bath *v.*) 5 Mass. 325, 54
—— *v.* Edgecumbe, 1 Mass. 459, 60
Freetown (Carnoe *v.*) 9 Gray, 357, 82
—— (Dighton *v.*) 4 Mass. 539, 41
—— (Plymouth *v.*) 1 Pick. 197, 41
—— *v.* Taunton, 16 Mass. 52, 41
French (Lowell *v.*) 6 Cush. 223, 135
—— *v.* Quincy, 3 Allen, 9, 65
Frost *v.* Belmont, 6 Allen, 152, 8, 9
Frothingham (Adams *v.*) 3 Mass. 352, 65
Fullam *v.* West Brookfield, 9 Allen, 1, 14
Fuller *v.* Groton, 11 Gray, 340, 8
—— *v.* Melrose, 1 Allen, 166, 9
—— *v.* Plymouth, 15 Pick. 81, 108

G.

Gahagan *v.* Boston & Lowell Railroad, 1 Allen, 187, 129, 133
Gammons (Commonwealth *v.*) 23 Pick. 201, 12
Gardiner *v.* Boston & Worcester Railroad, 9 Cush. 1, 67
Garrigan *v.* Berry, 12 Allen, 12
Gaskill *v.* Dudley, 6 Met. 546, 1
Gates *v* Neal, 23 Pick. 308, 21
—— (Smith *v.*) 21 Pick. 55, 24
Gay (Commonwealth *v.*) 5 Pick. 44, 35
Gee (—— *v.*) 6 Cush. 174, 5
George *v.* Mendon, 6 Met. 497, 84, 85
Georgetown (Perley *v.*) 7 Gray, 464, 1
Gerry *v.* Stoneham, 1 Allen, 319, 7, 85, 93
Gibbons *v.* East Granville, 4 Allen, 508, 73
Gibbs (Blandford *v.*) 2 Cush. 39, 20
—— *v.* Hampden, 19 Pick. 298, 93
—— (Weston *v.*) 23 Pick. 205, 3
Gibney (Commonwealth v.) 2 Allen, 152, 71
Gillett *v.* Western Railroad, 8 Allen, 560, 127
Gilmore *v.* Holt, 4 Pick. 258, 23, 34
Gloucester *v.* Essex, 3 Met. 375, 110
—— *v.* Gloucester, 19 Pick. 542, 81
Glover (Bassit *v.*) 1 Dane Ab. 137, 23

	PAGE.
Glover *v.* Boston, 14 Gray, 282,	100
—— (Capen *v.*) 4 Mass. 305,	80
Goddard, Petitioner, 16 Pick. 504,	35, 36, 64, 137
—— *v.* Boston, 20 Pick. 407,	108
—— *v.* Worcester, 9 Gray, 88,	101
Goff *v.* Rehoboth, 12 Met. 26,	33
Goldthwait *v.* East Bridgewater, 5 Gray, 61,	124
Goodell Manuf. Co. *v.* Trask, 11 Pick, 514,	78
Goodhue *v.* Dix, 2 Gray, 181,	12
Goodrich *v.* Lunenburg, 9 Gray, 38,	85
Goodwin (Crowell *v.*) 3 Allen, 535,	90
—— *v.* Marblehead, 1 Allen, 37,	106
—— (Tracy *v.*) 5 Allen, 409,	10
Gore (Harvard College *v.*) 5 Pick. 369,	19
Gorham (Buckfield *v.*) 6 Mass. 445,	44
—— (Westbrook *v.*) 15 Mass. 160,	43
Goshen (Parsons *v.*) 11 Pick. 396,	8, 15
—— *v.* Richmond, 4 Allen, 458,	40, 57
Goulding (Wheeler *v.*) 13 Gray, 539,	64
Gowdy (Levy *v.*) 2 Allen, 320,	64
Gowen (Commonwealth *v.*) 7 Mass. 378,	130
Granby *v.* Amherst, 7 Mass. 1,	18, 39
—— (Damon *v.*) 2 Pick. 345,	15, 33, 65
Granger (Rising *v.*) 1 Mass. 47,	88
Granite Bridge (Rowe *v.*) 21 Pick. 344,	131
Granville (Cooley *v.*) 10 Cush. 56,	8
—— (West Springfield *v.*) 4 Mass. 486,	44
Graves (Barnard *v.*) 13 Met. 85,	89
Gray *v.* Boston, 15 Pick. 376,	78
—— *v.* Kettell, 12 Mass. 160,	80
—— (Walpole *v.*) 11 Allen,	4
Great Barrington *v.* Berkshire, 16 Pick. 572	78
—— (Clark *v.*) 11 Pick. 260,	5, 72
—— *v.* Lancaster, 14 Mass. 253,	45
—— *v.* Tyringham, 18 Pick. 264,	41
Green *v.* Chelsea, 24 Pick. 71,	66
—— (Day *v.*) 4 Cush. 433,	11, 33, 37, 131
Greene (Holmes *v.*) 7 Gray, 299,	18
—— *v.* Monmouth, 7 Mass. 467,	60
Greenfield *v.* Cushman, 16 Mass. 393,	61
—— (Deerfield *v.*) 1 Gray, 514,	57, 61, 62
Greenleaf (Little *v.*) 7 Mass. 236,	80, 91
Greenwich (Barre *v.*) 1 Pick. 129,	32, 44
Gregory *v.* Adams, 14 Gray, 242,	118
Griffin *v.* Rising, 11 Met. 339,	21
Griffith (Commonwealth *v.*) 2 Pick. 11,	75
Griggs *v.* Foote, 4 Allen, 195,	102
Grinnell (Brightman *v.*) 9 Pick. 14,	23
Groton *v.* Boxborough, 6 Mass. 50,	43
—— (Boylston *v.*) 4 Gray, 282,	44
—— (Fuller *v.*) 11 Gray, 340,	8
—— *v.* Lancaster, 16 Mass. 110,	59
—— *v.* Shirley, 7 Mass. 156,	44
Groveland (Charlestown *v.*) 15 Gray,	38, 50
—— *v.* Medford, 1 Allen, 23,	38, 53, 57
—— (North Andover *v.*) 1 Allen, 75,	47
Grover *v.* Pembroke, 11 Allen,	4, 16
H.	
Hadley (Lowell *v.*) 8 Met. 180,	99, 134
Hadley *v.* Peabody, 13 Gray, 200,	5
—— *v.* Middlesex, 11 Cush. 394,	109
Hadsell *v.* Hancock, 3 Gray, 526,	4, 32
Haliburton *v.* Frankfort, 14 Mass. 214,	2, 7
Halifax (Pope *v.*) 12 Cush. 410,	8
Hall *v.* Hall, 3 Allen, 5,	88
—— *v.* Kent, 11 Gray, 467,	64
—— *v.* Lowell, 10 Cush. 260,	124
—— *v.* Middlesex, 10 Allen, 100,	80, 86
Hallock *v.* Franklin, 2 Met. 558,	106
Hallowell *v.* Harwich, 14 Mass. 186,	54, 59
—— (—— *v.*) 14 Mass. 184,	54
Hamilton *v.* Ipswich, 10 Mass. 506,	39
—— (Salem *v.*) 4 Mass. 676,	45
—— (Woodbury *v.*) 6 Pick. 101,	7
Hampden (Adams *v.*) 13 Gray, 439,	28
—— (—— *v.*) 16 Gray,	28
—— (Chicopee *v.*) 16 Gray,	86
—— (Commonwealth *v.*) 2 Pick. 414,	28
—— (Dwight *v.*) 11 Cush. 201,	112
—— (Gibbs *v.*) 19 Pick. 298,	93
—— (Norwich *v.*) 4 Gray, 172,	6
—— (Springfield *v.*) 10 Pick. 67,	104
—— (Taylor *v.*) 18 Pick. 309,	98
—— (Wilbraham *v.*) 11 Pick. 322,	97
Hampshire (Norwich *v.*) 13 Pick. 60,	137
Hancock *v.* Boston, 1 Met. 122,	98
—— (Hadsell *v.*) 3 Gray, 526,	4, 32
—— *v.* Hazzard, 12 Cush. 112,	9
Hannum *v.* Belchertown, 19 Pick. 311,	105, 132
Hanover (Scituate *v.*) 7 Pick. 140,	40
—— (—— *v.*) 16 Pick. 222,	42
—— (Simmons *v.*) 23 Pick. 188,	8
—— (South Scituate *v.*) 9 Gray, 420,	2
—— *v.* Turner, 14 Mass. 227,	53
Hanson (Hawes *v.*) 9 Allen, 134,	53
—— *v.* Pembroke, 16 Pick. 197,	46
Hapgood (Jennison *v.*) 10 Pick. 77,	18
—— (Lincoln *v.*) 11 Mass. 350,	20
Harback *v.* Boston, 10 Cush. 295,	95
Harding *v.* Medway, 10 Met. 465,	109, 114
Hardwick (Dana *v.*) 10 Met. 208,	47
—— *v.* Raynham, 14 Mass. 363,	40
—— (Tyler *v.*) 6 Met. 470,	85, 87
Hardy *v.* Waltham, 3 Met. 163,	7
—— *v.* Yarmouth, 6 Allen, 277,	81
Harman *v.* New Marlborough, 9 Cush. 525,	81
Harpswell (Topsham *v.*) 1 Mass. 518,	60
Harrington *v.* Berkshire, 22 Pick. 266,	131
—— *v.* Harrington, 1 Met. 404,	99
—— *v.* Worcester, 6 Allen, 576,	91
Harris *v.* Marblehead, 10 Gray, 40,	73
—— *v.* Whitcomb, 4 Gray, 433,	21
Harrison *v.* Bridgeton, 16 Mass. 16,	6
Hartford & New Haven Railroad (Commonwealth *v.*) 14 Gray, 379,	68
Hartwell *v.* Littleton, 13 Pick. 229,	34, 70, 73
Harvard *v.* Boxborough, 4 Met. 570,	47
—— (Newbury *v.*) 6 Pick. 1,	39
—— (Withington *v.*) 8 Cush. 66,	28, 69, 92

PAGE.
Harvard College v. Gore, 5 Pick, 369, 19
Harwich (Brewster v.) 4 Mass. 278, 6
—— v. Hallowell, 14 Mass. 184, 54
Harwich (—— v.) 14 Mass. 186, 54, 59
Harwood v. Lowell, 4 Cush. 310, 118
Haskell v. Bristol, 9 Gray, 341, 98, 109
—— v. Moody, 9 Pick. 162, 64
Haskins (Holyoke v.) 5 Pick. 20, 18
Hastings v. Aiken, 1 Gray, 163, 11
—— (Commonwealth v.) 9 Met. 259, 65
—— (Freeland v.) 10 Allen, 570, 7, 9, 14, 86
—— (Hinckley v.) 2 Pick. 162, 99, 103
Hatfield (Sikes v.) 13 Gray, 347, 116
—— (Winchendon v.) 4 Mass. 123, 41
Haven v. Lowell, 5 Met. 35, 15
Haverhill (Commonwealth v.) 7 Allen, 523, 103, 134
—— (Noyes v.) 11 Cush. 338, 90, 92
Hawes v. Hanson, 9 Allen, 134, 53
Hawkins v. Berkshire, 2 Allen, 254, 107, 109, 113
Hay (Stevens v.) 6 Cush. 229, 10
—— (Sweetser v.) 2 Gray, 49, 10
Hayden v. Attleborough, 7 Gray, 338, 104, 116, 118, 120, 125
—— v. Foster, 13 Pick. 492, 88
Haynes (Calder v.) 7 Allen, 387, 10
—— v. Wells, 6 Pick. 462, 37, 53
Hays v. Drake, 6 Gray, 387, 94
Hayward v. North Bridgewater, 5 Gray, 65, 110
Hazzard (Hancock v.) 12 Cush. 112, 9
Healy v. Root, 11 Pick. 389, 64
—— (Stackpole v.) 16 Mass. 33, 131
Heard (Simonds v.) 23 Pick. 120, 14
Heath (Bradley v.) 12 Pick. 163, 33
Heland v. Lowell, 3 Allen, 407, 119
Hemphill v. Boston, 8 Cush. 195, 103, 104, 117
Henry (Dodds v.) 9 Mass. 262, 33
Henshaw v. Foster, 9 Pick. 312, 19
—— v. Hunting, 1 Gray, 203, 100, 103, 132
Higgins (Commonwealth v.) 4 Gray, 34, 65
—— (Smith v.) 16 Gray, 34
Higginson v. Nahant, 11 Allen, 98, 99
Hildreth v. Lowell, 11 Gray, 345, 1, 35, 75, 76
Hill v. Davis, 4 Mass. 140, 63
Hinckley (Folger v.) 5 Cush. 263, 23
—— v. Hastings, 2 Pick. 162, 99, 103
Hingham (Braintree v.) 17 Mass. 432, 60
—— v. South Scituate, 7 Gray, 229, 57
Hinsdale (Dalton v.) 6 Mass. 501, 50, 53, 58
Hiram (Paris v.) 12 Mass. 262, 38, 44, 54, 58
Hixon v. Lowell, 13 Gray, 59, 120
Hobbs v. ——, 19 Pick. 405, 103
Holbrook v. McBride, 4 Gray, 215, 133
—— (Milford v.) 9 Allen, 17, 129
Holcomb v. Moore, 4 Allen, 529, 98
Holden v. Berkshire, 7 Met. 561, 106
—— (Chenery v.) 16 Gray, 17
Holland (Sturbridge v.) 11 Pick. 459, 38, 55
Hollenbeck v. Rowley, 8 Allen, 473, 132, 133
Holman v. Townsend, 13 Met. 297, 116, 123

PAGE.
Holmes v. Greene, 7 Gray, 299, 18
Holt (Gilmore v.) 4 Pick. 258, 23, 34
—— v. Sargent, 15 Gray, 105, 107
Holyoke v. Haskins, 5 Pick. 20, 18
—— (Tuttle v.) 6 Gray, 447, 123
Hood v. Lynn, 1 Allen, 103, 7
Hopkins (Appleton v.) 5 Gray, 530, 5, 87, 88
Hopkinton (Claflin v.) 4 Gray, 502, 7
—— v. Upton, 3 Met. 165, 42
—— (Walpole v.) 4 Pick. 357, 358, 45, 55, 59
Horton v. Ipswich, 12 Cush. 488, 116, 121, 124
Houghton v. Davenport, 23 Pick. 235, 87
Hovey (Mill Dam Foundery v.) 21 Pick. 417, 75
Howard v. Commonwealth, 13 Mass. 221, 64
—— v. North Bridgewater, 16 Pick. 189, 115, 120
—— v. Proctor, 7 Gray, 128, 86, 87, 90
Howe v. Boston, 7 Cush. 273, 89, 91
—— (Pickard v.) 12 Met. 198, 23, 24
Howes (Commonwealth v.) 15 Pick. 231, 64
Howland (Cheshire v.) 13 Gray, 321, 10, 87, 94
Hoxey (Commonwealth v.) 16 Mass. 385, 17
Hubbard (Butler v.) 5 Pick. 250, 6
Huckins v. Boston, 4 Cush. 543, 80
Humphrey v. Kingman, 5 Met. 162, 20, 21
Hunting (Henshaw v.) 1 Gray, 203, 100, 103, 132
Huse v. Lowell, 10 Allen, 149, 33, 74
Hutchings v. Thompson, 10 Cush. 238, 50
Hutchinson v. Methuen, 1 Allen, 33, 126
—— (South Reading v.) 10 Allen, 68, 51
Hyde v. Middlesex, 2 Gray, 267, 112

I.

Ide (Lothrop v.) 13 Gray, 93, 88, 94
Ingalls v. Bills, 9 Met. 1, 123
Inglee v. Bosworth, 5 Pick. 498, 84
Ingraham v. Doggett, 5 Pick. 451, 94
Ipswich (Hamilton v.) 10 Mass. 506, 39
—— (Horton v.) 12 Cush. 488, 116, 121, 124
—— (Salem v.) 10 Cush. 517, 38, 47
—— v. Topsfield, 5 Met. 350, 42
Ireland v. Newburyport, 8 Allen, 73, 37, 53

J.

Jacobs (Field v.) 12 Met. 118, 24
James (Commonwealth v.) 1 Pick. 375, 13
Jaquith v. Richardson, 8 Met. 213, 12
Jenks v. Wilbraham, 11 Gray, 142, 123
Jennings (Converse v.) 13 Gray, 77, 90
—— v. Tisbury, 5 Gray, 73, 105
Jennison v. Hapgood, 10 Pick. 77, 18
—— v. Roxbury, 9 Gray, 32, 3, 62
—— v. West Springfield, 13 Gray, 544, 63
Jewell v. Abington, 2 Allen, 592, 74
Jewett (McAneany v.) 10 Allen, 151, 17
Johnson (Eames v.) 4 Allen, 382, 94
—— v. Mills, 10 Cush. 503, 10
—— (Putnam v.) 10 Mass. 488, 20
—— v. Wyman, 9 Gray, 186, 106
Jones v. Andover, 6 Pick. 59, 116

	PAGE.
Jones v. Andover, 9 Pick. 146,	99
—— v. ——, 10 Allen, 18,	118, 127
—— v. Commonwealth, 15 Gray,	17
—— v. Lancaster, 4 Pick. 149,	115
—— (Parker v.) 1 Allen, 270,	23
—— v. Percival, 5 Pick. 487,	105
—— v. Scituate, 11 Allen,	16
—— v. Waltham, 4 Cush. 299,	117
Josselyn (Pierce v.) 17 Pick. 415,	25
Joyner v. Egremont, 3 Cush. 567,	84, 92

K.

Kean v. Stetson, 5 Pick. 492,	97, 102
Keith v. Easton, 2 Allen, 552,	120
—— (Worcester v.) 5 Allen, 17,	109
Kellogg v. Northampton, 4 Gray, 65,	120, 124
—— v. ——, 8 Gray, 504,	125
Kempton (Stetson v.) 13 Mass. 272,	7, 84
Kenney (Freeman v.) 15 Pick. 44,	10, 94
Kent (Hall v.) 11 Gray, 467,	64
Kettell (Gray v.) 12 Mass. 160,	80
Keyes v. Westford, 17 Pick. 273,	14
Kidder v. Dunstable, 7 Gray, 104,	122
—— v. ——, 11 Gray, 342,	12, 123, 125
Kilburn v. Bennett, 3 Met. 199,	87
Kimball v. Boston, 1 Allen, 417,	2, 118
King (Commonwealth v.) 13 Met. 115,	130
—— v. Whitcomb, 1 Met. 328,	89
Kingman (Cobb v.) 15 Mass. 197,	5
—— (Humphrey v.) 5 Met. 162,	20, 21
—— v. North Bridgewater, 2 Cush. 426,	3
—— v. Plymouth, 6 Cush. 306,	135
Kingsbury v. Quincy, 12 Met. 99,	72
Kirby v. Boylston Market Association, 14 Gray, 249,	119, 128, 129
Kirkland v. Whately, 4 Allen, 462,	83
Kittredge v. Newbury, 14 Mass. 448,	51
Knowles v. Boston, 12 Gray, 339,	74
Kupfer v. Augusta, 13 Mass. 185,	15

L.

La Croix v. Medway, 12 Met. 123,	136
Lakeville (Dartmouth v.) 7 Allen, 284,	58
Lamphere (Nye v.) 2 Gray, 295,	64
Lancaster (Great Barrington v.) 14 Mass. 253,	45
—— (Groton v.) 16 Mass. 110,	59
—— (Jones v.) 4 Pick. 149,	115
—— (Shirley v.) 6 Allen, 31,	40
—— v. Sutton, 16 Mass. 112,	46
Lane v. Crombie, 12 Pick. 177,	121
Lanesborough v. Berkshire, 22 Pick. 278,	110, 114
—— v. New Ashford, 5 Pick. 190,	59
—— v. Westfield, 16 Mass. 74,	41
Lawler v. Northampton Gas Light Co. 2 Allen, 307,	129
Lawrence (Boston & Maine Railroad v.) 2 Allen, 107,	134
—— (Durant v.) 1 Allen, 125,	68, 136
—— v. Fairhaven, 5 Gray, 110,	2, 137
—— (Middlesex Manuf. Co. v.) 1 Allen, 339,	10
Lawrence (Sanderson v.) 2 Gray, 178,	24
Learned (Medford v.) 16 Mass. 215,	53
Lee v. Boston, 2 Gray, 484,	82
—— v. Lenox, 16 Gray,	49
—— v. Templeton, 6 Gray, 579,	80, 92, 93
—— v. ——, 13 Gray, 476,	92
—— (Waldron v.) 5 Pick. 323,	86
Leicester v. Fitchburg, 7 Allen, 90,	44
—— (Mower v.) 9 Mass. 247,	116
—— v. Rehoboth, 4 Mass. 180,	60
Lenox (Lee v.) 16 Gray,	49
—— (Osborn v.) 2 Allen, 207,	17
Leominster (Belfast v.) 1 Pick. 123,	55
—— (Davis v.) 1 Allen, 182,	117, 133
Leonard v. New Bedford, 16 Gray,	81
—— (Norton v.) 12 Pick. 152,	77
Leverett v. Deerfield, 6 Allen, 431,	42
Levy v. Gowdy, 2 Allen, 320,	64
Lexington v. Burlington, 19 Pick. 426,	45
—— (Cambridge v.) 1 Pick. 506,	41
—— (Coggswell v.) 4 Cush. 307,	120
—— v. Mulliken, 7 Gray, 280,	25, 35
—— (Robbins v.) 8 Cush. 292,	135
—— (West Cambridge v.) 2 Pick. 536,	55
Lexington, &c. Railroad v. Elwell, 8 Allen 371,	10
Leyden (Worden v.) 10 Pick. 24,	51
Libby v. Burnham, 15 Mass. 144,	84
—— v. Downey, 5 Allen, 300,	64
Light Boat (Briggs v.) 7 Allen, 287,	37
Lincoln (Fiske v.) 19 Pick. 473,	38, 52
—— v. Hapgood, 11 Mass. 350,	20
—— v. Worcester, 8 Cush. 55,	91, 93
Lindsey (Dean v.) 16 Gray,	23
Little v. Cambridge, 9 Cush. 298,	80
—— v. Greenleaf, 7 Mass. 236,	80, 91
Littleton (Hartwell v.) 13 Pick. 229,	34, 70, 73
Locks & Canals v. Lowell, 7 Gray, 223,	75
—— (Riddle v.) 7 Mass. 187,	1
Loker v. Brookline, 13 Pick. 343,	115
—— v. Damon, 17 Pick. 284,	131
Lombard v. Oliver, 3 Allen, 1,	21
—— v. ——, 7 Allen, 155,	21
Loring v. Boston, 7 Met. 409,	71
—— v. ——, 12 Gray, 209,	106, 108
Lothrop v. Ide, 13 Gray, 93,	88, 94
—— (O'Linda v.) 21 Pick. 292,	132
Lovejoy v. Dolan, 10 Cush. 495,	12
Low (Commonwealth v.) 3 Pick. 408,	130
Lowell (Alger v.) 3 Allen, 402,	115, 120, 123, 126
—— (Barry v.) 8 Allen, 127,	2, 75
—— v. Boston & Lowell Railroad, 23 Pick. 24,	128
—— (Brady v.) 3 Cush. 121,	117
—— (Brown v.) 8 Met. 172,	109
—— (Buttrick v.) 1 Allen, 172,	1
—— (Caverly v.) 1 Allen, 289,	35
—— (Central Bridge v.) 4 Gray, 474,	103
—— (—— v.) 15 Gray,	98, 103, 113
—— (Chapman v.) 4 Cush. 378,	15
—— (Chase v.) 7 Gray, 33,	4, 32

PAGE.
Lowell (Clark *v.*) 1 Allen, 180, 126
—— (Currier *v.*) 16 Pick. 170, 118
—— (Drake *v.*) 13 Met. 292, 119
—— (Durgin *v.*) 3 Allen, 398, 104, 119
—— (Fletcher *v.*) 15 Gray, 33
—— *v.* French, 6 Cush. 223, 135
—— *v.* Hadley, 8 Met. 180, 99, 134
—— (Hall *v.*) 10 Cush. 260, 124
—— (Harwood *v.*) 4 Cush. 310, 118
—— (Haven *v.*) 5 Met. 35, 15
—— (Heland *v.*) 3 Allen, 407, 119
—— (Hildreth *v.*) 11 Gray, 345, 1, 35, 75, 76
—— (Hixon *v.*) 13 Gray, 59, 120
—— (Hobbs *v.*) 19 Pick. 405, 103
—— (Huse *v.*) 10 Allen, 149, 33, 74
—— (Locks & Canals *v.*) 7 Gray, 223, 75
—— (Meeting-house in Lowell *v.*) 1 Met. 538, 79
—— *v.* Middlesex, 3 Allen, 546, 93
—— *v.* ——, 3 Allen, 550, 94
—— *v.* ——, 6 Allen, 131, 78, 94, 136
—— *v.* Morse, 1 Met. 473, 1
—— (—— *v.*) 7 Met. 152, 34
—— *v.* Oliver, 8 Allen, 247, 14, 77, 86
—— (O'Neill *v.*) 6 Allen, 110, 126
—— (Parker *v.*) 11 Gray, 353, 4, 132
—— (Payne *v.*) 10 Allen, 147, 127
—— (Raymond *v.*) 6 Cush. 524, 2, 115, 119, 121, 125
—— (Rowell *v.*) 7 Gray, 100, 122
—— (Shea *v.*) 8 Allen, 136 127
—— *v.* Short, 4 Cush. 275, 128
—— *v.* Simpson, 10 Allen, 88, 33, 35
—— (Smith *v.*) 6 Allen, 39, 122
—— *v.* Spaulding, 4 Cush. 277, 128
—— (—— *v.*) 23 Pick. 71, 7
—— *v.* Wentworth, 6 Cush. 221, 37, 134
—— *v.* Wheelock, 11 Cush. 391, 135
—— (Winn *v.*) 1 Allen, 177, 117, 121, 126
—— *v.* Wyman, 12 Cush. 273, 135
Lowell Gas Light Co. (Commonwealth *v.*) 12 Allen, 80
Lowell Savings Bank *v.* Winchester, 8 Allen, 109, 16, 94
Lubke (Brackett *v.*) 4 Allen, 138, 130
Lund *v.* Tyngsboro, 11 Cush. 563, 123
Lunenburg (Ashby *v.*) 8 Pick. 563, 59
—— (Goodrich *v.*) 9 Gray, 38, 85
—— (Shirley *v.*) 11 Mass. 379, 61
—— (Williams *v.*) 21 Pick. 75, 84, 85
Lyman *v.* Fiske, 17 Pick. 231, 18, 83
Lynde *v.* Melrose, 10 Allen, 49, 2, 91
Lynn (Hood *v.*) 1 Allen, 103, 7
—— *v.* Newburyport, 5 Allen, 545, 59
Lynnfield (Bancroft *v.*) 18 Pick. 566, 3, 8, 32

M.

McAneany *v.* Jewett, 10 Allen, 151, 17
McBride (Holbrook *v.*) 4 Gray, 215, 133
McCarron (Commonwealth *v.*) 2 Allen, 157, 31
M'Culloch (Arundel *v.*) 10 Mass. 70, 102, 131

PAGE.
Macomber *v.* Doane, 5 Allen, 541, 5, 34
Malden (Chelsea *v.*) 4 Mass. 131, 39
Malden & Melrose Railroad *v.* Charlestown, 8 Allen, 245, 2, 118
Mansfield (Attleborough *v.*) 15 Pick. 19, 55
—— (Codding *v.*) 7 Gray, 272, 70
—— (Norton *v.*) 16 Mass. 48, 46, 55
—— *v.* Pembroke, 5 Pick. 449, 43
—— *v.* Stoneham, 15 Gray, 3
Marble *v.* Worcester, 4 Gray, 395, 123
Marblehead *v.* Essex, 5 Gray, 451, 103
—— (Goodwin *v.*) 1 Allen, 37, 106
—— (Harris *v.*) 10 Gray, 40, 73
—— (Walpole *v.*) 8 Cush. 528, 41
Marlborough *v.* Rutland, 11 Mass. 483, 54
—— (Southborough *v.*) 24 Pick. 166, 43
Marsh (Callender *v.*) 1 Pick. 418, 115
Marshfield (Thomas *v.*) 10 Pick. 364, 65
Marshpee *v.* Edgartown, 23 Pick. 156, 60
Mayhew *v.* Norton, 17 Pick. 357, 131
Mead *v.* Boston, 3 Cush. 404, 70
—— *v.* Boxborough, 11 Cush. 362, 18, 83
Mears *v.* Boston & N. Y. Central Railroad, 5 Gray, 371, 2
Medford (Groveland *v.*) 1 Allen, 23, 38, 53, 57
—— *v.* Learned, 16 Mass. 215, 53
Medway (Harding *v.*) 10 Met. 465, 109, 114
—— (La Croix *v.*) 12 Met. 123, 136
—— *v.* Milford, 21 Pick. 349, 56
Meeting-house in Lowell *v.* Lowell, 1 Met. 538, 79
Melcher *v.* Boston, 9 Met. 73, 79
Melody *v.* Reab, 4 Mass. 471, 25, 64
Melrose (Butterfield *v.*) 6 Allen, 187, 25
—— (Fuller *v.*) 1 Allen, 166, 9
—— (Lynde *v.*) 10 Allen, 49, 2, 49
Mendon (George *v.*) 6 Met. 497, 84, 85
—— *v.* Worcester, 10 Pick. 235, 110
Merriam (Nourse *v.*) 8 Cush. 11, 73
Merrick *v.* Work, 10 Allen, 544, 25
Merrill *v.* Berkshire, 11 Pick. 269, 107, 108, 110, 111, 114
—— *v.* Wilbraham, 11 Gray, 154, 118
Merrimack Bank (Chase *v.*) 19 Pick. 564, 1
Merritt (Cheever *v.*) 5 Allen, 563, 87, 91
Metcalf (Allen *v.*) 17 Pick. 208, 34
—— (Taft *v.*) 11 Pick. 456, 34, 94
Methuen (Hutchinson *v.*) 1 Allen, 33, 126
Middleborough (Attleborough *v.*) 10 Pick. 378, 48
—— *v.* Clark, 2 Pick. 28, [illegible], 61
—— (New Bedford *v.*) 16 Gray, 57
—— (Pelham *v.*) 4 Gray, 57, 43
—— *v.* Plympton, 19 Pick. 489, 39
—— *v.* Rochester, 12 Mass. 363, 40, 50
—— *v.* Taunton, 2 Cush. 406, 128
—— (—— *v.*) 12 Met. 35, 48, 49
Middlesex (Boston & Maine Railroad *v.*) 1 Allen, 324, 113, 133
—— (Cambridge *v.*) 6 Allen, 134, 76
—— (Charlestown *v.*) 3 Met. 202, 102
—— (—— *v.*) 1 Allen, 199, 79, 93
—— (Commonwealth *v.*) 9 Mass. 388, 111

	PAGE.
Middlesex (Eaton v.) 7 Gray, 109,	99
—— (Fowler v.) 6 Allen, 92,	114, 115
—— (Hadley v.) 11 Cush. 394,	109
—— (Hall v.) 10 Allen, 100,	80, 86
—— (Hyde v.) 2 Gray, 207,	112
—— (Lowell v.) 3 Allen, 546,	93
—— (—— v.) 3 Allen, 550,	94
—— (—— v.) 6 Allen, 131,	78, 94, 136
—— (Rice v.) 13 Pick. 225,	135
—— (Wayland v.) 4 Gray, 500,	79, 96
—— (Williams v.) 4 Met. 76,	29
—— (Woburn v.) 7 Gray, 106,	112
Middlesex Manuf. Co. v. Lawrence, 1 Allen, 339,	10
Middlesex Railroad v. Charlestown, 8 Allen, 330,	78
Middleton (Topsfield v.) 8 Met. 564,	56
Milford v. Bellingham, 16 Mass. 108,	42
—— (Day v.) 5 Allen, 98,	119, 123
—— v. Holbrook, 9 Allen, 17,	129
—— (Medway v.) 21 Pick. 349,	56
—— (Nelson v.) 7 Pick. 18,	8, 92
—— (Worcester v.) 18 Pick. 379,	62
Millbury v. Blackstone Canal Co. 8 Pick. 473,	131
—— (Flagg v.) 4 Cush. 243,	116, 117
—— (Torrey v.) 21 Pick. 64,	7, 85, 92
Mill Dam Foundery v. Hovey, 21 Pick. 417,	75
Miller v. Post, 1 Allen, 434,	32
—— v. Somerset, 14 Mass. 396,	51
—— (Springfield v.) 12 Mass. 415,	65
Mills (Johnson v.) 10 Cush. 503,	10
Mitchell v. Bridgewater, 10 Cush. 411,	108
—— v. Cornville, 12 Mass. 332,	51
—— v. Tibbetts, 17 Pick. 298,	20
Moak (Vosburgh v.) 1 Cush. 453,	129
Monagle v. Bristol, 8 Cush. 360,	109
Monmouth (Greene v.) 7 Mass. 467,	60
Monson v. Chester, 22 Pick. 385,	43
—— v. Palmer, 8 Allen, 551,	41, 57
—— v. Williams, 6 Gray, 416,	53
Monterey v. Berkshire, 7 Cush. 394,	133
Moody (Haskell v.) 9 Pick. 162,	64
—— v. Newburyport, 3 Met. 431,	34
Moore v. Boston, 8 Cush. 274,	95
—— (—— v.) 3 Allen, 126,	10
—— (Holcomb v.) 4 Allen, 529,	98
Morse v. Lowell, 7 Met. 152,	34
—— (—— v.) 1 Met. 473,	1
—— (Natick v.) 8 Cush. 191,	72
—— v. Stocker, 1 Allen, 150,	104, 137
Moulton (Adams v.) 7 Pick. 286,	19
Mount Washington v. Clarksburgh, 19 Pick. 294,	42, 49
Mower v. Leicester, 9 Mass. 247,	116
Mowry (Uxbridge v.) 9 Allen, 94,	74
Mulliken (Lexington v.) 7 Gray, 280,	25, 35
Munigle v. Boston, 3 Allen, 230,	107
Munroe v. Brigham, 19 Pick. 368,	30
Murdock (Briggs v.) 13 Pick. 305,	34, 70
—— v. Warwick, 4 Gray, 180,	122
Murray (Austin v.) 16 Pick. 121,	27, 36

N.

	PAGE.
Nahant (Higginson v.) 11 Allen,	98, 99
—— (Simmons v.) 3 Allen, 316,	6
Nantucket (Adams v.) 11 Allen,	84
—— (Coffin v.) 5 Cush. 269,	25
—— (Ruggles v.) 11 Cush. 433,	26
—— (Vincent v.) 12 Cush. 103,	4, 9
Nashua & Lowell Railroad (Commonwealth v.) 2 Gray, 54,	68, 130
Nason v. Whitney, 1 Pick. 140,	84
Natick (Dedham v.) 16 Mass. 135,	41
—— (Drury v.) 10 Allen, 169,	95
—— v. Morse, 8 Cush. 191,	72
Neal (Gates v.) 23 Pick. 308,	21
—— (Webb v.) 5 Allen, 575,	95
Needham (Fiske v.) 11 Mass. 452,	4
—— v. Newton, 12 Mass. 452,	54, 60
Nelson v. Milford, 7 Pick. 18,	8, 92
New Ashford (Lanesborough v.) 5 Pick. 190,	59
New Bedford v. Bristol, 9 Gray, 346,	109, 136
—— v. Chace, 5 Gray, 28,	53
—— (Leonard v.) 16 Gray,	81
—— v. Middleborough, 16 Gray,	57
—— (Packard v.) 9 Allen, 200,	125
—— (Russell v.) 5 Gray, 31,	108, 109
—— v. Taunton, 9 Allen, 207,	37, 58
New Braintree v. Boylston, 24 Pick. 164,	46
Newbury (Commonwealth v.) 2 Pick. 51,	103, 127
—— (Emerson v.) 13 Pick. 377,	15, 32
—— v. Harvard, 6 Pick. 1,	39
—— (Kittredge v.) 14 Mass. 448,	51
Newburyport (Cushing v.) 10 Met. 508,	8, 73
—— v. Essex, 12 Met. 211,	85, 93
—— (Ireland v.) 8 Allen, 73,	37, 53
—— (Lynn v.) 5 Allen, 545,	59
—— (Moody v.) 3 Met. 431,	34
—— (Willard v.) 12 Pick. 227,	7, 33
Newburyport Turnpike v. Eastern Railroad, 23 Pick. 326,	66
—— v. Upton, 12 Mass. 575,	77, 81
New England Worsted Co. (Eames v.) 11 Met. 572,	27
New Gloucester (Brewer v.) 14 Mass. 216,	1
New Marlborough v. Berkshire, 9 Met. 423,	97
—— (Harman v.) 9 Cush. 525,	81
New Salem, Petitioners, 6 Pick. 470,	98
—— v. Wendell, 2 Pick. 341,	55
Newton (Boston Manuf. Co. v.) 22 Pick. 22,	78, 80
—— v. Braintree, 11 Mass. 382,	41
—— (Needham v.) 12 Mass. 452,	54, 60
—— (Rand v.) 6 Allen, 38,	114
—— v. Randolph, 16 Mass. 426,	60
Nichols (Commonwealth v.) 10 Allen, 199,	31
—— v. Salem, 14 Gray, 490,	136
Nickerson v. Brackett, 10 Mass. 212,	26
Nightingale, Petitioner, 11 Pick. 168,	21
Niles v. Patch, 13 Gray, 254,	106

PAGE.
Norfolk (Commonwealth *v.*) 5 Mass. 437, 110
—— (Porter *v.*) 5 Gray, 365, 85, 93
—— (White *v.*) 2 Cush. 361, 108
Northampton (Commonwealth *v.*) 2 Mass. 116, 71, 72
—— *v.* Elwell, 4 Gray, 81, 1
—— (Kellogg *v.*) 4 Gray, 65, 120, 124
—— (—— *v.*) 8 Gray, 504, 125
Northampton Bank (Smith *v.*) 4 Cush. 1, 81, 90
Northampton Gas Light Co. (Lawler *v.*) 2 Allen, 307, 129
North Andover *v.* Groveland, 1 Allen, 75, 47
Northbridge (Upton *v.*) 15 Mass. 237, 40
North Bridgewater (Abington *v.*) 23 Pick. 170, 17, 56
—— *v.* East Bridgewater, 13 Pick. 303, 40, 41
—— (Hayward *v.*) 5 Gray, 65, 110
—— (Howard *v.*) 16 Pick. 189, 115, 120
—— (Kingman *v.*) 2 Cush. 426, 3
North Brookfield (Commonwealth *v.*) 8 Pick. 463, 127
Northfield (Reed *v.*) 13 Pick. 94, 105, 117, 121, 124
—— (Sawyer *v.*) 7 Cush. 490, 67, 117
—— *v.* Taunton, 4 Met. 433, 58, 60
Norton *v.* Copeland, 2 Gray, 414, 72
—— *v.* Leonard, 12 Pick. 152, 77
—— *v.* Mansfield, 16 Mass. 48, 46, 55
—— (Mayhew *v.*) 17 Pick. 357, 131
—— (Randolph *v.*) 16 Gray, 42
—— (Tisdale *v.*) 8 Met. 388, 120
Norwich *v.* Hampden, 4 Gray, 172, 6
—— *v.* Hampshire, 13 Pick. 60, 137
Nourse (Boutelle *v.*) 4 Mass. 431, 63
—— *v.* Merriam, 8 Cush. 11, 73
Noyes *v.* Haverhill, 11 Cush. 338, 90, 92
Nye *v.* Lamphere, 2 Gray, 295, 64

O.

Oakham *v.* Rutland, 4 Cush. 172, 42
—— *v.* Sutton, 13 Met. 192, 49, 50, 57
O'Connor (Commonwealth *v.*) 7 Allen, 584, 65
Odiorne *v.* Wade, 5 Pick. 421, 105
O'Donnell (Commonwealth *v.*) 1 Allen, 593, 31
Old Colony & Fall River Railroad (Commonwealth *v.*) 14 Gray, 93, 68, 105, 130
—— *v.* Plymouth, 11 Gray, 512, 133
—— *v.* ——, 14 Gray, 155, 133
O'Linda *v.* Lothrop, 21 Pick. 292, 132
Oliver (Lombard *v.*) 3 Allen, 1, 21
—— (—— *v.*) 7 Allen, 155, 21
—— (Lowell *v.*) 8 Allen, 247, 14, 77, 86
O'Neill *v.* Lowell, 6 Allen, 110, 126
Opinion of the Justices, 7 Mass. 523, 19, 77
——, 15 Mass. 537, 19
——, 3 Pick. 517, 19
——, 11 Pick. 538, 20, 38
——, 23 Pick. 547, 19
——, 1 Met. 572, 38
——, 1 Met. 580, 20, 38, 71, 78
——, 5 Met. 587, 19, 20

PAGE.
Opinion of the Justices, 5 Met. 591, 20
——, 10 Gray, 613, 70
Orange *v.* Sudbury, 10 Pick. 22, 39, 58
—— (Sutton *v.*) 6 Met. 484, 45
Orleans *v.* Chatham, 2 Pick. 29, 42
Osborn *v.* Danvers, 6 Pick. 98, 91
—— *v.* Lenox, 2 Allen, 207, 17
Otis *v.* Boston, 12 Cush. 44, 82
—— (Day *v.*) 8 Allen, 477, 71
Otis Co. *v.* Ware, 8 Gray, 509, 93
Oxford (Shutesbury *v.*) 16 Mass. 102, 58
—— (Ward *v.*) 8 Pick. 476, 55

P.

Packard *v.* New Bedford, 9 Allen, 200, 125
Page *v.* Danvers, 7 Met. 326, 31
Paine *v.* Boston, 4 Allen, 168, 113
Palmer *v.* Andover, 2 Cush. 600, 117, 123
—— *v.* Dana, 9 Met. 587, 57, 59
—— *v.* Ferry, 6 Gray, 420, 16, 53
—— (Monson *v.*) 8 Allen, 551, 41, 57
Paris *v.* Hiram, 12 Mass. 262, 38, 44, 54, 58
Parker *v.* Adams, 12 Met. 415, 12
—— *v.* Baxter, 2 Gray, 185, 90
—— *v.* Boston, 1 Allen, 361, 96
—— *v.* Boston & Maine Railroad, 3 Cush. 107, 66
—— *v.* Jones, 1 Allen, 270, 23
—— *v.* Lowell, 11 Gray, 353, 4, 132
Parks *v.* Boston, 8 Pick. 218, 97, 135
—— *v.* ——, 15 Pick. 198, 107, 110, 111
Parsons *v.* Goshen, 11 Pick. 396, 8, 15
—— *v.* Pettingell, 11 Allen, 26
Patch (Niles *v.*) 13 Gray, 254, 106
Patterson *v.* Boston, 20 Pick. 159, 111
—— *v.* ——, 23 Pick. 425, 112
Pawtucket (Dunnell Manuf. Co. *v.*) 7 Gray, 277, 78, 92
Payne *v.* Lowell, 10 Allen, 147, 127
Payson *v.* Tufts, 13 Mass. 493, 77, 81
Peabody *v.* Essex, 10 Gray, 97, 81
—— (Hadley *v.*) 13 Gray, 200, 5
Pease *v.* Smith, 24 Pick. 122, 94
Pedrick *v.* Bailey, 12 Gray, 161, 32, 36
Peirce *v.* Boston, 3 Met. 520, 5, 87
Pelham (Aldrich *v.*) 1 Gray, 510, 125
—— *v.* Middleborough, 4 Gray, 57, 43
Pembroke (Curtis *v.*) 11 Allen, 4
—— (Grover *v.*) 11 Allen, 4, 16
—— (Hanson *v.*) 16 Pick. 197, 46
—— (Mansfield *v.*) 5 Pick. 449, 43
—— *v.* Plymouth, 12 Cush. 351, 99
Percival (Jones *v.*) 5 Pick. 487, 105
Perkins *v.* Weston, 3 Cush. 549, 74
Perley *v.* Chandler, 6 Mass. 453, 102, 111, 131
—— *v.* Georgetown, 7 Gray, 464, 1
Perry *v.* Worcester, 6 Gray, 544, 2, 35
Peters *v.* Westborough, 20 Pick. 506, 52
Petersham (Brooks *v.*) 16 Gray, 121, 125
—— *v.* Coleraine, 9 Allen, 91, 60
—— (Commonwealth *v.*) 4 Pick. 119, 127

PAGE.
Petersham v. Dana, 12 Mass. 428, 41
Pettingell (Parsons v.) 11 Allen, 26
Pettingill v. Porter, 3 Allen, 349, 133
Phillips v. Bowers, 7 Gray, 21, 132
Phillipsburg (Commonwealth v.) 10 Mass. 78, 30
Phillipston (White v.) 10 Met. 108, 115
Phipps's case, 2 Pick. 394, note, 38
Phœnix Bank (Commonwealth v.) 11 Met. 135, 5, 87
Pickard v. Howe, 12 Met. 198, 23, 24
Pickering v. Shearer, 11 Gray, 153, 105
Pierce v. Benjamin, 14 Pick. 356, 88, 89
—— v. Cambridge, 2 Cush. 611, 79
—— v. Josselyn, 17 Pick. 415, 25
Pitts (Alexander v.) 7 Cush. 503, 90
Plumer v. Brown, 8 Met. 578, 116, 132
Plymouth (Bates v.) 14 Gray, 163, 34, 37
—— v. Freetown, 1 Pick. 197, 41
—— (Fuller v.) 15 Pick. 81, 108
—— (Kingman v.) 6 Cush. 306, 135
—— (Old Colony & Fall River Railroad v.) 11 Gray, 512, 133
—— (—— v.) 14 Gray, 155, 133
—— (Pembroke v.) 12 Cush. 351, 99
—— (Sturtevant v.) 12 Met. 7, 108
—— (Taunton v.) 15 Mass. 203, 40
—— (Taylor v.) 8 Met. 462, 25
—— (Williams v.) 11 Allen, 16
Plympton (Middleborough v.) 19 Pick. 489, 39
—— v. Woburn, 11 Gray, 415, 113
Pocasset Manuf. Co. (Cotton v.) 13 Met. 429, 75
Pool v. Boston, 5 Cush. 219, 70
Pope (Christ Church v.) 8 Gray, 140, 20
—— v. Halifax, 12 Cush. 410, 8
Porter (Bassett v.) 4 Cush. 487, 88, 94
—— (Commonwealth v.) 1 Gray, 480, 17, 71
—— v. Norfolk, 5 Gray, 365, 85, 93
—— (Pettingill v.) 3 Allen, 349, 133
Portland (Windham v.) 4 Mass. 384, 42, 44
Post (Miller v.) 1 Allen, 434, 32
Powers v. Ware, 2 Pick. 451, 6
Pratt (Sale v.) 19 Pick. 191, 66
Presby (Commonwealth v.) 14 Gray, 65, 65
Preston v. Boston, 12 Pick. 7, 80, 91
Princeton (Boylston v.) 13 Mass. 381, 41
—— (Watson v.) 4 Met. 599, 84, 93
—— v. West Boylston, 15 Mass. 257, 45, 50
—— v. Worcester, 17 Pick. 154, 99
Proctor (Howard v.) 7 Gray, 128, 86, 87, 90
Putnam (Green v.) 8 Cush. 21, 66
—— v. Johnson, 10 Mass. 488, 20

Q.

Quincy v. Braintree, 5 Mass. 86, 58
—— (French v.) 3 Allen, 9, 65
—— (Kingsbury v.) 12 Met. 99, 72
—— (Wood v.) 11 Cush. 487, 133

R.

PAGE.
Race (Campbell v.) 7 Cush. 408, 106
Rand v. Newton, 6 Allen, 38, 114
Randall (Belchertown v.) 7 Cush. 478, 72
—— (Bradford v.) 5 Pick. 496, 75, 86
Randolph (Bigelow v.) 14 Gray, 541, 2
—— v. Braintree, 4 Mass. 315, 26
—— v. Easton, 23 Pick. 242, 56
—— v. ——, 4 Cush. 557, 49
—— (Newton v.) 16 Mass. 426, 60
—— v. Norton, 16 Gray, 42
Raymond v. Lowell, 6 Cush. 524, 2, 115, 119, 121, 125
Raynham (Hardwick v.) 14 Mass. 363, 40
—— v. Rounseville, 9 Pick. 44, 64
Reab (Melody v.) 4 Mass. 471, 25, 64
Readfield v. Dresden, 12 Mass. 316, 54
Reading v. Tewksbury, 2 Pick. 535, 48
Reed (Commonwealth v.) 1 Gray, 472, 31
—— v. Deerfield, 8 Allen, 522, 122
—— v. Northfield, 13 Pick. 94, 105, 117, 121, 124
—— v. Scituate, 5 Allen, 120, 3, 116
Rehoboth (Goff v.) 12 Met. 26, 33
—— (Leicester v.) 4 Mass. 180, 60
—— (Seekonk v.) 8 Cush. 371, 61
—— (Somerset v.) 6 Cush. 320, 42
—— (Westborough v.) 4 Cush. 185, 47
Reidell v. Congdon, 16 Pick. 44, 6
Revere v. Boston, 14 Gray, 218, 108
Rice (Commonwealth v.) 9 Met. 253, 22
—— v. Middlesex, 13 Pick. 225, 135
—— v. Worcester, 11 Gray, 283, note, 132
Richards v. Dagget, 4 Mass. 539, 80
—— v. Enfield, 13 Gray, 344, 118
Richardson (Jaquith v.) 8 Met. 213, 12
Richmond (Goshen v.) 4 Allen, 458, 40, 57
Riddle v. Locks & Canals, 7 Mass. 187, 1
Rindge v. Coleraine, 11 Gray, 157, 125
Rising v. Granger, 1 Mass. 47, 88
—— (Griffin v.) 11 Met. 339, 21
Robbins v. Borman, 1 Pick. 122, 131
—— v. Lexington, 8 Cush. 292, 135
—— v. Townsend, 20 Pick. 345, 48
—— v. Weston, 20 Pick. 112, 30, 51
Roberts v. Boston, 5 Cush. 198, 74
Robertson (Commonwealth v.) 5 Cush. 438, 12
Rochester (Bishop v.) 11 Allen, 16
—— (Briggs v.) 16 Gray, 83
—— (Choate v.) 13 Gray, 92, 50
—— (Middleborough v.) 12 Mass. 363, 40, 50
—— (Shelburne v.) 1 Pick. 470, 59
Root (Healy v.) 11 Pick. 389, 64
Rossire v. Boston, 4 Allen, 57, 21, 66
Rounseville (Raynham v.) 9 Pick. 44, 64
Rowe v. Granite Bridge, 21 Pick. 344, 131
Rowell v. Lowell, 7 Gray, 100, 122
Rowley (Hollenbeck v.) 8 Allen, 473, 132, 133
—— (Todd v.) 8 Allen, 51, 127
Roxbury (Barber v.) 11 Allen, 118

PAGE.

Roxbury *v.* Boston & Providence Railroad, 6 Cush, 424. 67
—— *v.* ——, 2 Gray, 460, 68
—— (Commonwealth *v.*) 8 Mass. 457, 106
—— (—— *v.*) 9 Gray, 451, 10, 11, 30
—— (Crawshaw *v.*) 7 Gray, 374, 71
—— (Jennison *v.*) 9 Gray, 32, 3, 62
—— (Williams *v.*) 12 Gray, 21, 83
Ruggles (Commonwealth *v.*) 6 Allen, 588, 131
—— *v.* Nantucket, 11 Cush. 433, 26
Rumford *v.* Wood, 13 Mass. 199, 75
Runnels (Commonwealth *v.*) 10 Mass. 520, 71
Russell *v.* Coffin, 8 Pick. 142, 77
—— *v.* New Bedford, 5 Gray, 31, 108, 109
—— (Tinker *v.*) 14 Pick. 279, 106, 116
Rust *v.* Boston Mill Corp. 6 Pick. 158, 69
Rutland (Bigelow *v.*) 4 Cush. 247, 121
—— (Marlborough *v.*) 11 Mass. 483, 54
—— (Oakham *v.*) 4 Cush. 172, 42
Ryan (Commonwealth *v.*) 5 Mass. 90, 31

S.

Sackett (Fox *v.*) 10 Allen, 535, 122
Sale *v.* Pratt, 19 Pick. 191, 66
Salem *v.* Andover, 3 Mass. 436, 50, 54
—— (Batchelder *v.*) 4 Cush. 599, 74
—— *v.* Hamilton, 4 Mass. 676, 45
—— *v.* Ipswich, 10 Cush. 517, 38, 47
—— (Nichols *v.*) 14 Gray, 490, 136
—— (Shrewsbury *v.*) 19 Pick. 389, 48
—— (Sparhawk *v.*) 1 Allen, 30, 120
—— (Stickney *v.*) 3 Allen, 374, 119
—— (Wade *v.*) 7 Pick. 333, 29, 51
Salem Iron Co. *v.* Danvers, 10 Mass. 514, 78, 80
Saltonstall *v.* Banker, 8 Gray, 195, 77
Sanderson *v.* Lawrence, 2 Gray, 178, 24
Sandwich *v.* Fish, 2 Gray, 298, 9
Sargent *v.* Bean, 7 Gray, 125, 85, 90
—— (Holt *v.*) 15 Gray, 105, 107
Savoy (Babbitt *v.*) 3 Cush. 530, 3
Sawin (Commonwealth *v.*) 2 Pick. 547, 97
Sawyer *v.* Northfield, 7 Cush. 490, 67, 117
—— (Stow *v.*) 3 Allen, 515, 53
Sayward (Alfred *v.*) 5 Mass. 244, 51
Schaffer (Boston *v.*) 9 Pick. 415, 1, 5
Schlessinger (Worcester *v.*) 16 Gray, 30
Scituate *v.* Hanover, 7 Pick. 140, 40
—— *v.* ——, 16 Pick. 222, 42
—— (Jones *v.*) 11 Allen, 16
—— (Reed *v.*) 5 Allen, 120, 3, 116
—— (Underwood *v.*) 7 Met. 214, 51, 52
Sears *v.* Boston, 1 Met. 250, 82
—— (—— *v.*) 22 Pick. 122, 37
Seekonk *v.* Attleborough, 7 Pick. 155, 61
—— (Blackstone *v.*) 8 Cush. 75, 41
—— *v.* Rehoboth, 8 Cush. 371, 61
—— (Uxbridge *v.*) 10 Pick. 150, 54, 58
Shattuck *v.* Allen, 4 Gray, 540, 74
Shaw *v.* Becket, 7 Cush. 442, 92
—— (Boston *v.*) 1 Met. 130, 75

PAGE.

Shaw *v.* Charlestown, 3 Allen, 538, 136
Shea *v.* Lowell, 8 Allen, 136, 127
Shearer (Pickering *v.*) 11 Gray, 153, 105
—— *v.* Shelburne, 10 Cush. 3, 53, 63
—— (Wilson *v.*) 9 Met. 504, 89
Sheffield (Commonwealth *v.*) 11 Cush. 178, 72
Shelburne (Amherst *v.*) 11 Gray, 107, 62
—— (—— *v.*) 13 Gray, 341, 39, 40
—— *v.* Rochester, 1 Pick. 470, 59
—— (Shearer *v.*) 10 Cush. 3, 53, 63
Shepherd *v.* Chelsea, 4 Allen, 113, 122
Sherman *v.* Braman, 13 Met. 407, 23
—— *v.* Charlestown, 8 Cush. 160, 74
Shirley (Groton *v.*) 7 Mass. 156, 44
—— *v.* Lancaster, 6 Allen, 31, 40
—— *v.* Lunenburg, 11 Mass. 379, 61
—— *v.* Watertown, 3 Mass. 322, 39
Short (Lowell *v.*) 4 Cush. 275, 128
Shrewsbury *v.* Salem, 19 Pick. 389, 48
Shute *v.* Barnes, 2 Allen, 598, 98
Shutesbury *v.* Oxford, 16 Mass. 102, 58
Sidney *v.* Augusta, 12 Mass. 316, 59
—— (Belgrade *v.*) 15 Mass. 523, 44
Sikes *v.* Hatfield, 13 Gray, 347, 116
Silsbee (Commonwealth *v.*) 9 Mass. 417, 20
Simmons (Boston *v.*) 9 Cush. 373, 102
—— *v.* Hanover, 23 Pick. 188, 8
—— *v.* Nahant, 3 Allen, 316, 6
Simonds *v.* Heard, 23 Pick. 120, 14
Simpson (Lowell *v.*) 10 Allen, 88, 33, 35
Skinner (Wild *v.*) 23 Pick. 251, 23, 24
Slack (Commonwealth *v.*) 19 Pick. 304, 28
Slocomb (Smith *v.*) 11 Gray, 280, 132
Smith *v.* Boston, 7 Cush. 254, 107
—— *v.* ——, 1 Gray, 72, 68
—— *v.* Cheshire, 13 Gray, 318, 2
—— *v.* Colerain, 9 Met. 492, 52
—— (Commonwealth *v.*) 9 Mass. 107, 30
—— *v.* Dedham, 8 Cush. 522, 123
—— (Ela *v.*) 5 Gray, 121, 71
—— *v.* Gates, 21 Pick. 55, 24
—— *v.* Higgins, 16 Gray, 34
—— *v.* Lowell, 6 Allen, 39, 122
—— *v.* Northampton Bank, 4 Cush. 1, 81, 90
—— (Pease *v.*) 24 Pick. 122, 94
—— *v.* Slocomb, 11 Gray, 280, 132
—— *v.* Smith, 2 Pick. 621, 121, 130
—— *v.* Wendell, 7 Cush. 498, 120
Smyth (Commonwealth *v.*) 14 Gray, 33, 130
Snow *v.* Adams, 1 Cush. 443, 120
—— *v.* Clark, 9 Gray, 190, 88
—— (Dillingham *v.*) 5 Mass. 547, 84
Somerset (Berkley *v.*) 16 Mass. 454, 40
—— *v.* Dighton, 12 Mass. 383, 40
—— (Miller *v.*) 14 Mass. 396, 51
—— *v.* Rehoboth, 6 Cush. 320, 42
Southampton *v.* Easthampton, 8 Pick. 380, 48, 84
Southborough (Brailey *v.*) 6 Cush. 141, 116, 123
—— *v.* Marlborough, 24 Pick. 166, 43
Southbridge *v.* Charlton, 15 Mass. 248, 46, 54

	PAGE.
Southbridge (Stedman *v.*) 17 Pick. 162,	105
——— (Walker *v.*) 4 Cush. 199,	52
——— *v.* Warren, 11 Cush. 292,	43
South Danvers *v.* Essex, 1 Allen, 25,	63
South Reading *v.* Hutchinson, 10 Allen, 68,	51
South Scituate *v.* Hanover, 9 Gray, 420,	2
——— (Hingham *v.*) 7 Gray, 229,	57
Southwick (Westfield *v.*) 17 Pick. 68,	37, 54, 61
Sparhawk *v.* Salem, 1 Allen, 30,	120
Spaulding *v.* Lowell, 23 Pick. 71,	7
——— (——— *v.*) 4 Cush. 277,	128
Spear *v.* Cummings, 23 Pick. 224,	73
Sprague *v.* Bailey, 19 Pick. 436,	84, 86, 94
——— *v.* Waite, 17 Pick. 309,	105, 106, 132
——— *v.* Worcester, 13 Gray, 193,	2
Springfield (Barnes *v*) 4 Allen, 488,	96, 109
——— (Commonwealth *v.*) 7 Mass. 13,	115
——— *v.* Connecticut River Railroad, 4 Cush. 63,	6, 67
——— (Cummington *v.*) 2 Pick. 394,	38
——— (Dwight *v.*) 4 Gray, 107,	97, 100, 135, 136
——— (——— *v.*) 6 Gray, 442,	110, 115
——— *v.* Hampden, 10 Pick. 67,	104
——— *v.* Miller, 12 Mass. 415,	65
——— *v.* Wilbraham, 4 Mass. 493,	40
——— *v.* Worcester, 2 Cush. 52,	28, 59
Stacey *v.* Benson, 18 Pick. 496,	77
Stackpole *v.* Healy, 16 Mass. 33,	131
State Lunatic Hospital *v.* Worcester, 1 Met. 437,	107, 110
Stearns (Blanchard *v.*) 5 Met. 298,	20, 21
——— (Sudbury *v.*) 21 Pick. 148,	20
——— (Thayer *v.*) 1 Pick. 109,	34
——— (——— *v.*) 1 Pick. 482,	84
Stedman *v.* Southbridge, 17 Pick. 162,	105
Sterling (Templeton *v.*) 15 Mass. 253,	43
——— (West Boylston *v.*) 17 Pick. 126,	56
——— (Worcester *v.*) 5 Gray, 393,	62
Stetson (Crapo *v.*) 8 Met. 393,	87, 88
——— *v.* Faxon, 19 Pick. 147,	105
——— (Kean *v.*) 5 Pick. 492,	97, 102
——— *v.* Kempton, 13 Mass. 272,	7, 84
——— (Wales *v.*) 2 Mass. 146,	106
Stevens *v.* Boxford, 10 Allen, 25,	122, 127
——— (Commonwealth *v.*) 10 Pick. 247,	130
——— *v.* Hay, 6 Cush. 229,	10
Stewart (Avery *v.*) 1 Cush. 496,	104, 106
Stickney *v.* Salem, 3 Allen, 374,	119
Stockbridge (Commonwealth *v.*) 13 Mass. 294,	102
——— *v.* West Stockbridge, 12 Mass. 399,	41
Stocker (Morse *v.*) 1 Allen, 150,	104, 137
Stoddard (West Roxbury *v.*) 7 Allen, 169,	66
Stodder (Commonwealth *v.*) 2 Cush. 562,	11
Stone *v.* Boston, 2 Met. 220,	97, 98, 135
——— *v.* Cambridge, 6 Cush. 270,	99
——— (Charlestown *v.*) 15 Gray,	135
Stoneham (Gerry *v.*) 1 Allen, 319,	7, 85, 93
——— (Mansfield *v.*) 15 Gray,	3
Stoughton (Cushing *v.*) 6 Cush. 389,	3
——— (Drake *v.*) 6 Cush. 393,	3
Stow *v.* Sawyer, 3 Allen, 515,	53
——— (Sudbury *v.*) 13 Mass. 462,	47
Sturbridge *v.* Holland, 11 Pick. 459,	38, 55
——— (Wilbraham *v.*) 6 Cush. 61,	50
——— *v.* Winslow, 21 Pick. 83,	62
Sturtevant *v.* Plymouth, 12 Mass. 7,	108
Sudbury (Dow *v.*) 5 Met. 73,	92
——— *v.* East Sudbury, 15 Mass. 260,	46
——— (——— *v.*) 12 Pick. 1,	49, 55, 59
——— (Orange *v.*) 10 Pick. 22,	39, 58
——— *v.* Stearns, 21 Pick. 148,	20
——— *v.* Stow, 13 Mass. 462,	47
Suffolk Manuf. Co. (Bowers *v.*) 4 Cush. 332,	103, 104
Sutton (Andover *v.*) 12 Met. 182,	128
——— *v.* Dana, 4 Pick. 117,	45
——— *v.* ———, 1 Met. 383,	47
——— (Lancaster *v.*) 16 Mass. 112,	46
——— (Oakham *v.*) 13 Met. 192,	49, 50, 57
——— *v.* Orange, 6 Met. 484,	45
——— *v.* Uxbridge, 2 Pick. 436,	39
Swampscott (Walcott *v.*) 1 Allen, 101,	1
Swan's case, 16 Mass. 220,	30
Swansey (Bosworth *v.*) 10 Met. 363,	118
——— *v.* Chace, 16 Gray,	128
Sweetser *v.* Hay, 2 Gray, 49,	10
Swett's case, 20 Pick. 1,	30
Swett *v.* Boston, 18 Pick. 123,	78
——— (Colburn *v.*) 1 Met. 232,	27, 64

T.

	PAGE.
Taft (Blackstone *v.*) 4 Gray, 250,	1
——— *v.* Metcalf, 11 Pick. 456,	34, 94
Tash *v.* Adams, 10 Cush. 252,	7, 9
Tasker *v.* Bartlett, 5 Cush. 359,	75
Taunton (Allen *v.*) 19 Pick. 485,	7, 14
——— (Berkeley *v.*) 19 Pick. 480,	49
——— *v.* Caswell, 4 Pick. 275,	26
——— (Freetown *v.*) 16 Mass. 52,	41
——— *v.* Middleborough, 12 Met. 35,	48, 49
——— (——— *v.*) 2 Cush. 406,	128
——— (New Bedford *v.*) 9 Allen, 207,	37, 58
——— (Northfield *v.*) 4 Met. 433,	58, 60
——— *v.* Plymouth, 15 Mass. 203,	40
——— *v.* Westport, 12 Mass. 355,	54
——— (Upjohn *v.*) 6 Cush. 310,	15
Taylor *v.* Boston Water Power Co. 12 Gray, 415,	105
——— *v.* Hampden, 18 Pick. 309,	98
——— *v.* Plymouth, 8 Met. 462,	25
Temple (Commonwealth *v.*) 14 Gray, 69,	69
Templeton (Lee *v.*) 6 Gray, 579,	80, 92, 93
——— (——— *v.*) 13 Gray, 476,	92
——— *v.* Sterling, 15 Mass. 253,	43
Terry (Wilson *v.*) 9 Allen, 214,	19, 83
——— (——— *v.*) 11 Allen,	83
Tewksbury (Reading *v.*) 2 Pick. 535,	48
Thayer *v.* Boston, 19 Pick. 511,	1, 32
——— *v.* Stearns, 1 Pick. 109,	34
——— *v.* ———, 1 Pick. 482,	84
——— *v.* Worcester; 10 Cush. 151,	109, 114

PAGE.
Thomas *v.* Marshfield, 10 Pick. 364, 65
Thompson *v.* Bridgewater, 7 Pick. 188, 121
—— (Commonwealth *v.*) 12 Met. 231, 26
—— (Hutchings *v.*) 10 Cush. 238, 50
Thorndike *v.* Boston, 1 Met. 242, 19, 82
Thorpe *v.* Worcester, 9 Gray, 57, 97, 136
Tibbetts (Mitchell *v.*) 17 Pick. 298, 20
Tileston (Boston *v.*) 11 Mass. 468, 4
Tinker *v.* Russell, 14 Pick. 279, 106, 116
Tisbury (Edgartown *v.*) 10 Cush. 408, 41, 42, 60
—— (Jennings *v.*) 5 Gray, 73, 105
Tisdale *v.* Norton, 8 Met. 388, 120
Tobey *v.* Wareham, 2 Allen, 594, 86, 93
Todd *v.* Rowley, 8 Allen, 51, 127
Topsfield (Ipswich *v.*) 5 Met. 350, 42
—— *v.* Middleton, 8 Met. 564, 56
Topsham *v.* Harpswell, 1 Mass. 518, 60
Torrey *v.* Millbury, 21 Pick. 64, 7, 85, 92
Tower *v.* Boston, 10 Cush. 235, 96
Towle (Cleverly *v.*) 3 Allen, 39, 24
Townsend *v.* Billerica, 10 Mass. 411, 50, 54, 59
—— (Holman *v.*) 13 Met. 297, 116, 123
—— (Robbins *v.*) 20 Pick. 345, 48
—— *v.* Walcutt, 3 Met. 152, 34, 87
Tracy *v.* Goodwin, 5 Allen, 409, 10
Trask (Goodell Manuf. Co. *v.*) 11 Pick. 514, 78
Tremont Bank *v.* Boston, 1 Cush. 142, 79
Trull *v.* Wheeler, 19 Pick. 240, 10
Truro (Wellfleet *v.*) 5 Allen, 137, 43
—— (—— *v.*) 9 Allen, 137, 43
Trustees of the Greene Foundation *v.* Boston, 12 Cush. 54, 81, 85
Tucker (Commonwealth *v.*) 2 Pick. 44, 106
Tufts *v.* Charlestown, 4 Gray, 537, 112
—— (Payson *v.*) 13 Mass. 493, 77, 81
Tukey (Wright *v.*) 3 Cush. 290, 103
Turner (Allen *v.*) 11 Gray, 436, 9
—— (Commonwealth *v.*) 1 Cush. 493, 36
—— (Hanover *v.*) 14 Mass. 227, 53
Tuttle *v.* Holyoke, 6 Gray, 447, 123
Tyler *v.* Hardwick, 6 Met. 470, 85, 87
Tyngsboro (Lund *v.*) 11 Cush. 563, 123
Tyringham (Brewer *v.*) 14 Pick. 196, 30
—— (Great Barrington *v.*) 18 Pick. 264, 41

U.

Underwood *v.* Scituate, 7 Met. 214, 51, 52
Union Railway *v.* Cambridge, 11 Allen, 69
Upjohn *v.* Taunton, 6 Cush. 310, 15
Upton (Commonwealth *v.*) 6 Gray, 473, 27
—— (Hopkinton *v.*) 3 Met. 165, 42
—— (Newburyport Turnpike *v.*) 12 Mass. 575, 77, 81
—— *v.* Northbridge, 15 Mass. 237, 40
Uxbridge *v.* Mowry, 9 Allen, 94, 74
—— *v.* Seekonk, 10 Pick. 150, 54, 58
—— (Sutton *v.*) 2 Pick. 436, 39
—— (Webster *v.*) 13 Met. 198, 61

V.

PAGE.
Valentine *v.* Boston, 22 Pick. 75, 103, 105
Vandine, Petitioner, 6 Pick. 187, 28, 35
Vermont & Massachusetts Railroad (Commonwealth *v.*) 4 Gray, 22, 68, 130
—— *v.* Franklin, 10 Cush. 12, 67
Vinal *v.* Dorchester, 7 Gray, 421, 117
Vincent (Coffin *v.*) 12 Cush. 98, 24
—— *v.* Nantucket, 12 Cush. 103, 4, 9
Vinton *v.* Vinton, 17 Mass. 342, 25
—— *v.* Welsh, 9 Pick. 87, 64
Vosburg *v.* Moak, 1 Cush. 453, 129

W.

Wade (Odiorne *v.*) 5 Pick. 421, 105
—— *v.* Salem, 7 Pick. 333, 29, 51
Waite (Commonwealth *v.*) 11 Allen, 32
—— (Sprague *v.*) 17 Pick. 309, 105, 106, 132
—— *v.* Woodward, 10 Cush. 143, 19
Walcott *v.* Swampscott, 1 Allen, 101, 1
Walcutt (Townsend *v.*) 3 Met. 152, 34, 87
Waldron *v.* Lee, 5 Pick. 323, 86
Wales *v.* Stetson, 2 Mass. 146, 106
Walker (Bowley *v.*) 8 Allen, 21, 106
—— *v.* Southbridge, 4 Cush. 199, 52
—— (Worcester *v.*) 9 Gray, 78, 35, 37, 65
Wall (Wheeler *v.*) 6 Allen, 558, 79
Walpole (Blackburn *v.*) 9 Pick. 97, 84
—— *v.* Gray, 11 Allen, 4
—— *v.* Hopkinton, 4 Pick. 357, 45
—— *v.* ——, 4 Pick. 358, 55, 59
—— *v.* Marblehead, 8 Cush. 528, 41
—— *v.* West Cambridge, 8 Mass. 276, 61
Waltham (Chenery *v.*) 8 Cush. 327, 18, 82
—— (Doherty *v.*) 4 Gray, 596, 117
—— (East Sudbury *v.*) 13 Mass. 460, 49
—— (Hardy *v.*) 3 Met. 163, 7
—— (Jones *v.*) 4 Cush. 299, 117
—— (Waltham Bank *v.*) 10 Met. 334, 79
Waltham Bank *v.* Waltham, 10 Met. 334, 79
Walton (Commonwealth *v.*) 17 Pick. 403, 31
Ward *v.* Oxford, 8 Pick. 476, 55
Ware (Otis Co. *v.*) 8 Gray, 509, 93
—— (Powers *v.*) 2 Pick. 451, 6
—— *v.* Wilbraham, 4 Pick. 45, 61
—— *v.* Williamstown, 8 Pick. 388, 59
Wareham (Cummington *v.*) 9 Cush. 585, 62
—— (Dill *v.*) 7 Met. 438, 26
—— (Tobey *v.*) 2 Allen, 594, 86, 93
Warren *v.* Charlestown, 2 Gray, 84, 5
—— (Southbridge *v.*) 11 Cush. 292, 43
Warwick (Murdock *v.*) 4 Gray, 180, 122
Watertown (Athol *v.*) 7 Pick. 42, 48
—— (Shirley *v.*) 3 Mass. 322, 39
—— *v.* White, 13 Mass. 477, 26
Waterville (Wood *v.*) 4 Mass. 422, 118, 120
—— (—— *v.*) 5 Mass. 294, 33, 120
Watson *v.* Cambridge, 15 Mass. 286, 39, 51

	Page.
Watson *v.* Cambridge, 18 Pick. 470,	29, 51
—— *v.* Charlestown, 5 Met. 54,	20, 62
—— *v.* Princeton, 4 Met. 599,	84, 93
Wayland *v.* Middlesex, 4 Gray, 500,	79, 96
Webb *v.* Neal, 5 Allen, 575,	95
Webber *v.* Eastern Railroad, 2 Met. 147,	112
Webster (Burnham *v.*) 5 Mass. 266,	63
—— *v.* Uxbridge, 13 Met. 198,	61
Weiher (Commonwealth *v.*) 3 Met. 445,	98
Welles *v.* Battelle, 11 Mass. 477,	34, 70, 81, 84
Wellfleet *v.* Truro, 5 Allen, 137,	43
—— *v.* ——, 9 Allen, 137,	43
Wellington, Petitioner, 16 Pick. 87,	13, 102, 135
Wells (Boston *v.*) 14 Mass. 384,	43
—— (Haynes *v.*) 6 Pick. 462,	37, 53
Welsh (Vinton *v.*) 9 Pick. 87,	64
Wendell (Armstrong *v.*) 9 Met. 522,	115
—— *v.* Fleming, 8 Gray, 613,	9
—— (New Salem *v.*) 2 Pick. 341,	55
—— (Smith *v.*) 7 Cush. 498,	120
Wentworth (Lowell *v.*) 6 Cush. 221,	37, 134
Westborough *v.* Franklin, 15 Mass. 254,	46
—— (Peters *v.*) 20 Pick. 506,	52
—— *v.* Rehoboth, 4 Cush. 185,	47
West Boston Bridge (Commonwealth *v.*) 13 Pick. 195,	135
West Boylston (Bellingham *v.*) 4 Cush. 553,	44
—— *v.* Boylston, 15 Mass. 261,	45
—— (Princeton *v.*) 15 Mass. 257,	45, 50
—— *v.* Sterling, 17 Pick. 126,	56
—— (Willington *v.*) 4 Pick. 101,	51
West Bridgewater (Bridgewater *v.*) 9 Pick. 55,	46
Westbrook *v.* Gorham, 15 Mass. 160,	43
West Brookfield (Fullam *v.*) 9 Allen, 1,	14
West Cambridge *v.* Lexington, 2 Pick. 536,	55
—— (Walpole *v.*) 8 Mass. 276,	61
Western (Commonwealth *v.*) 1 Pick. 136,	106
Western Railroad (Gillett *v.*) 8 Allen, 560,	127
—— (Worcester *v.*) 4 Met. 564,	79
Westfield (Lanesborough *v.*) 16 Mass. 74,	41
—— *v.* Southwick, 17 Pick. 68,	37, 54, 61
Westford (Boston *v.*) 12 Pick. 16,	29
—— (Keyes *v.*) 17 Pick. 273,	14
Westminster *v.* Bernardston, 8 Mass. 104,	58, 60
West Newbury *v.* Bradford, 3 Met. 428,	48, 49
Weston (Bigelow *v.*) 3 Pick. 267,	116
—— (Boston *v.*) 22 Pick. 211,	30, 51
—— (Dudley *v.*) 1 Met. 477,	125
—— *v.* Gibbs, 23 Pick. 205,	3
—— (Perkins *v.*) 3 Cush. 549,	74
—— (Robbins *v.*) 20 Pick. 112,	30, 51
Westport (Allen *v.*) 15 Pick. 35,	74
—— *v.* Bristol, 6 Allen, 203,	97, 98, 110
—— *v.* Dartmouth, 10 Mass. 341,	44
—— (Taunton *v.*) 12 Mass. 355,	54
West Roxbury *v.* Stoddard. 7 Allen, 169,	66
West Springfield *v.* Granville, 4 Mass. 486,	44
—— (Jennison *v.*) 13 Gray, 544,	63
West Stockbridge (Stockbridge *v.*) 12 Mass. 399,	41
Weymouth (Boston *v.*) 4 Cush. 538,	49, 69
Whately (Chicopee *v.*) 6 Allen, 508,	18, 19, 49, 50
—— (Kirkland *v.*) 4 Allen, 462,	83
Wheeler (Benjamin *v.*) 8 Gray, 409,	116
—— (—— *v.*) 16 Gray,	115, 116
—— *v.* Framingham, 12 Cush. 287,	125
—— *v.* Goulding, 13 Gray, 539,	64
—— (Trull *v.*) 19 Pick. 240,	10
—— *v.* Wall, 6 Allen, 558,	79
—— *v.* Worcester, 10 Allen, 591,	2, 69, 76
Wheelock (Lowell *v.*) 11 Cush. 391,	135
Whitcomb (Harris *v.*) 4 Gray, 433,	21
—— (King *v.*) 1 Met. 328,	89
White (Bruce *v.*) 4 Gray, 345,	23
—— *v.* Norfolk, 2 Cush. 361,	108
—— *v.* Phillipston, 10 Met. 108,	115
—— (Watertown *v.*) 13 Mass. 477,	26
Whiting (Williams *v.*) 11 Mass. 424,	19
Whitney (Nason *v.*) 1 Pick. 140,	84
Whittaker *v.* Boston & Maine Railroad, 7 Gray, 98,	68
Wilbraham (Bliss *v.*) 8 Allen, 564,	122, 127
—— *v.* Hampden, 11 Pick. 322,	97
—— (Jenks *v.*) 11 Gray, 142,	123
—— (Merrill *v.*) 11 Gray, 154,	118
—— (Springfield *v.*) 4 Mass. 493,	40
—— *v.* Sturbridge, 6 Cush. 61,	50
—— (Ware *v.*) 4 Pick. 45,	61
—— (Worcester *v.*) 13 Gray, 586,	49, 57
Wild *v.* Skinner, 23 Pick. 251,	23, 24
Wiley (Emerson *v.*) 7 Pick. 68,	105
Wilkinson (Commonwealth *v.*) 16 Pick. 175,	130
Willard *v.* Cambridge, 3 Allen, 574,	119
—— *v.* Newburyport, 12 Pick. 227,	7, 33
Williams *v.* Adams, 3 Allen, 171,	30
—— *v.* Boardman, 9 Allen, 570,	5
—— *v.* Braintree, 6 Cush. 399,	52
—— (Coolidge *v.*) 4 Mass. 140,	26, 66
—— *v.* Cummington, 18 Pick. 312,	103, 105, 124
—— (Danforth *v.*) 9 Mass. 324,	87
—— *v.* Lunenburg, 21 Pick. 75,	84, 85
—— *v.* Middlesex, 4 Met. 76,	29
—— (Monson *v.*) 6 Gray, 416,	53
—— *v.* Plymouth, 11 Allen,	16
—— *v.* Roxbury, 12 Gray, 21,	83
—— *v.* Whiting, 11 Mass. 424,	19
Williamstown (Bulkley *v.*) 3 Gray, 493,	83
—— (Canning *v.*) 1 Cush. 451,	124
—— (Ware *v.*) 8 Pick. 388,	59
—— *v.* Willis, 16 Gray,	87, 91
Willis (Williamstown *v.*) 16 Gray,	87, 91
Willington *v.* West Boylston, 4 Pick. 101,	51
Wilson *v.* Brooks, 14 Pick. 341,	38
—— *v.* Charlestown, 8 Allen, 137,	122
—— *v.* Church, 1 Pick. 26,	63
—— *v.* Shearer, 9 Met. 504,	89
—— *v.* Terry, 9 Allen, 214,	19, 83
—— *v.* ——, 11 Allen,	83
Winchendon (Fitchburg *v.*) 4 Cush. 190,	18, 48, 83

PAGE.
Winchendon v. Hatfield, 4 Mass. 123, 41
Winchester (Lowell Savings Bank v.) 8 Allen, 109, 16, 94
Windham v. Portland, 4 Mass. 384, 42, 44
Winn v. Lowell, 1 Allen, 177, 117, 121, 126
Winnisimmet Co. v. Chelsea, 6 Cush. 477, 85, 93
Winslow (Sturbridge v.) 21 Pick. 83, 62
Winthrop v. Farrar, 11 Allen, 28
Wiscasset (Adams v.) 5 Mass. 328, 51
—— (Cargill v.) 2 Mass. 547, 51
Withington v. Harvard, 8 Cush. 66, 28, 69, 92
Woburn v. Middlesex, 7 Gray, 106, 112
—— (Plympton v.) 11 Gray, 415, 113
Wood v. Burlington, 1 Met. 493, 38
—— v. Quincy, 11 Cush. 487, 133
—— (Rumford v.) 13 Mass. 199, 75
—— v. Waterville, 4 Mass. 422, 118, 120
—— v. ——, 5 Mass. 294, 33, 120
Woodbury v. Hamilton, 6 Pick. 101, 7
Woodward (Waite v.) 10 Cush. 143, 19
—— v. Worcester, 15 Gray, 50
Worcester v. Auburn, 4 Allen, 574, 48, 50, 57
—— (Brown v.) 13 Gray, 31, 104, 108, 113
—— (Commonwealth v.) 3 Pick. 462, 12, 13, 31, 35
—— (Drury v.) 21 Pick. 44, 116
—— v. Eaton, 13 Mass. 371, 65
—— (Flagg v.) 8 Cush. 69, 110, 114
—— (—— v.) 13 Gray, 601, 2, 75
—— (Foster v.) 16 Pick. 71, 62
—— (Goddard v.) 9 Gray, 88, 101
—— (Harrington v.) 6 Allen, 576, 91
—— v. Keith, 5 Allen, 17, 109
—— (Lincoln v.) 8 Cush. 55, 91, 93
—— (Marble v.) 4 Gray, 395, 123
—— (Mendon v.) 10 Pick. 235, 110
—— v. Milford, 18 Pick. 379, 62
—— (Perry v.) 6 Gray, 544, 2, 35

PAGE.
Worcester (Princeton v.) 17 Pick. 154, 99
—— Rice v.) 11 Gray, 283, note, 132
—— v. Schlessinger, 16 Gray, 30
—— (Sprague v) 13 Gray, 193, 2
—— (Springfield v.) 2 Cush. 52, 28, 59
—— (State Lunatic Hospital v.) 1 Met. 437, 107, 110
—— v. Sterling, 5 Gray, 393, 62
—— (Thayer v.) 10 Cush. 151, 109, 114
—— (Thorpe v.) 9 Gray, 57, 97, 136
—— v. Walker, 9 Gray, 78, 35, 37, 65
—— v. Western Railroad, 4 Met. 564, 79
—— (Wheeler v.) 10 Allen, 591, 2, 69, 76
—— v. Wilbraham, 13 Gray, 586, 49, 57
—— (Woodward v.) 15 Gray, 50
—— (Worcester Ins. Co. v.) 7 Cush. 600, 79
—— (Worcester Savings Inst. v.) 10 Cush. 128, 79
Worcester Ins. Co. (Andrews v.) 5 Allen, 65, 87
—— v. Worcester, 7 Cush. 600, 79
Worcester Savings Inst. v. Worcester, 10 Cush. 128, 79
Worden v. Leyden, 10 Pick. 24, 51
Work (Merrick v.) 10 Allen, 544, 25
Worster v. Canal Bridge, 16 Pick. 541, 122
Worth (Folger v.) 19 Pick. 108, 105
Worthington (Boston v.) 10 Gray, 496, 128
Wrentham v. Attleborough, 5 Mass. 430, 47, 54
Wright v. Boston, 9 Cush. 233, 76, 91
—— v. Tukey, 3 Cush. 290, 103
Wyman (Johnson v.) 9 Gray, 186, 106
—— (Lowell v.) 12 Cush. 273, 135

Y.

Yarmouth (Hardy v.) 6 Allen, 277, 81
—— (Young v.) 9 Gray, 386, 118
Young v. Yarmouth, 9 Gray, 386, 118

INDEX

TO

CITY DOCUMENTS.

INDEX

TO THE

CITY DOCUMENTS,

FROM 1834 TO 1865*.

Aged and Indigent Females. 1849, Doc. 19 — Petition of a Committee of the Benevolent Associations, praying for a site whereon to erect an asylum for.

Aldermen. 1845, Doc. 37 — Opinion of C. B. Goodrich, on the powers and duties of, on the death of the Mayor; 1845, Doc. 43—Opinion of J. P. Rogers concerning the authority of Chn. of the Board to draw drafts in the event of the decease, inability, or absence of the Mayor; 1846, Doc. 17 — Rept. on expediency of paying a salary to; 1846, Doc. 31 — Rept. on same; 1853, Doc. 92 — Proceedings at their last meeting in 1853; 1856, Doc. 78 — Proceedings at their last meeting in 1856; 1857, Doc. 85 — Proceedings at their last meeting in 1857; 1858, Doc. 67 — Proceedings at their last meeting in 1858; 1859, Doc. 79 — Proceedings at their last meeting in 1859; 1860, Doc. 106 — Proceedings at their last meeting in 1860; 1861, Doc. 81 — Proceedings at their last meeting in 1861; 1862, Doc. 105 — Proceedings at their last meeting in 1862; 1863, Doc. 113 — Proceedings at their last meeting in 1863; 1864, Doc. 100 — Proceedings at their last meeting in 1864.

Aliens. 1837, Doc. 16 (Com. Council) — Account of Inspectors of alien passengers; 1850, Doc. 24 — Monthly return of the number of alien passengers received at the House of Industry.

Almshouses. 1835, Doc. 15 (Com. Council) — Rept. of Artemas Simonds; 1851, Doc. 70 — Final rept. on the erection of a new almshouse at Deer Island; 1852, Doc. 17 — Rept. concerning a new almshouse at Deer Island.

Amusement, public places of. 1852, Doc. 13—Rept. on memorial of Francis Parkman and others respecting.

Appropriations. 1834, Doc. 10 (City Council) — Rept. on auditor's estimates for the next financial year; 1835, Doc. 11 (Com. Council) — Rept. on auditor's estimates for the next financial year; 1836, Doc. 2 (Com. Council) — Rept. on auditor's estimates for the next financial year; 1837, Doc. 5 (Com. Council) —Rept. on auditor's estimates for the next financial year; 1838, Doc. 14 — Rept. on auditor's estimates for the next financial year; 1839, Doc. 17 — Rept. on auditor's estimates for the next financial year; 1840, Doc. 4—Rept. on communication of auditor relative to additional appropriations; 1840, Doc. 10 — Rept. on auditor's estimates for the next financial year; 1841, Doc. 11 — Rept. on auditor's estimates for the next financial year; 1842, Doc. 11—Rept. on auditor's estimates for the next financial year; 1843, Doc. 15—Rept. on auditor's estimates for the next financial year; 1844, Doc. 11— Rept. on auditor's estimates for the next financial year; 1845, Doc. 16—Rept. on auditor's estimates for the next financial year; 1846, Doc. 15 — Rept. on auditor's estimates for the next financial year; 1847, Doc. 17 — Rept. on auditor's estimates for the next financial year; 1848, Doc. 14 — Rept. on auditor's estimates for the next financial year; 1849, Doc. 17 — Rept. on auditor's estimates for the next financial year; 1850, Doc. 10 — Rept. on auditor's estimates for the next financial year; 1851, Doc. 18 — Rept. on auditor's estimates for the next financial year; 1852, Doc. 19 — Rept. on auditor's estimates for the next financial year; 1853, Doc. 17 — Appropriations, loans, and transfers; 1853, Doc. 22 — Rept. on auditor's estimates for the next financial year; 1854, Doc. 13 — Additional appropriations for Paving; 1854, Doc. 17 — Additional appropriations for Common; 1854, Doc. 20 — Additional appropriations for Institutions at So. Boston and Deer Island; 1854, Doc. 23 — Additional appropriations for incidentals; 1854, Doc. 34 — Rept. on auditor's estimates for the next financial year; 1854, Doc. 38 — Transfers; 1854, Doc. 67 — Additional appropriations for South and East Boston Grammar Schools; 1854, Doc. 71 — Additional appropriations for incidentals and claims; 1855, Doc. 7 — Additional appropriations for Sewers and Drains; 1855, Doc. 11 — Additional appropriations for Lamps; 1855, Doc. 17 — Additional appropriations for Public Buildings; 1855, Doc. 21 — Rept. on auditor's estimates for the next financial year; 1855, Docs. 62 and 63 — Additional appropriations for Grammar School Houses; 1855, Doc. 64 — Additional appropriations for Public Buildings; 1856, Doc. 9 — Additional appropriation for Paving; 1856, Doc. 17 — Additional appropriation for Lamps; 1856, Doc. 18 — Additional appropriations for Paving, Fire, and Health Depts.; 1856, Doc. 21 — Transfers; 1853, Doc. 27 — Rept. on auditor's estimates for the next financial year; 1856, Doc. 54 — Additional appropriation for Public Lands; 1856, Doc. 60 — Additional appropriation for Assessors Dept.; 1856, Doc. 63 — Appropriations for No. Charles St. Bridge; 1856, Doc. 66 — Additional appropriation for Paving; 1856, Doc. 70 — Additional appropriation for Albany St. Bridge; 1856, Doc. 71 — Additional appropriation for Public Lands; 1857, Doc. 5 — Additional appropriation for Paving; 1857, Doc. 6 — Additional appropriation for Common and Public Squares; 1857, Doc. 7 — Additional appropriation for Cemeteries; 1857, Doc. 8 — Additional appropriation for Bridges; 1857, Doc. 13 — Annual appropriation for Public Library; 1857, Doc. 15 — Additional appropriation for Paving; 1857, Doc. 17 — Rept. on the state of the appropriation

---

* This index embraces all the regular documents, numbered and bound together at the end of each year. They are arranged in alphabetical and chronological order.

for Paving; 1857, Doc. 20 — Additional appropriation for the Board of Health; 1857, Doc. 24 — Additional appropriation for the Fire Dept.; 1857, Doc. 32 — Rept. on auditor's estimates for the next financial year; 1858, Doc. 18 — Rept. on auditor's estimates for the next financial year; 1858, Doc. 40 — Additional appropriation for Common and Squares; 1858, Doc. 42 — Additional appropriation for Public Lands; 1858, Doc. 44 — Additional appropriation for widening streets; 1858, Doc. 53 — Additional appropriation for Bridges; 1858, Doc. 54 — Additional appropriation for Schools; 1858, Doc. 56 — Additional appropriation for Public Buildings; 1858, Doc. 58 — Additional appropriation for Mt. Hope Cemetery; 1858, Doc. 62 — Rept. on the illegality of making expenditures beyond appropriations; 1859, Doc. 14 — Additional appropriation for Public Buildings; 1859, Doc. 15 — Additional appropriation for Sewers; 1859, Doc. 16 — Rept. and ordinance concerning expenditures beyond appropriations; 1859, Doc. 19 — Additional appropriation for Public Buildings; 1859, Doc. 22 — Rept. on auditor's estimates for the next financial year; 1859, Doc. 29 — Application for an additional appropriation for Land Commissioners; 1859, Doc. 48 — Additional appropriation for Lands; 1859, Doc. 57 — Additional appropriation for Public Buildings; 1859, Doc. 60 — Additional appropriation for Smallpox Hospital; 1859, Doc. 67 — Additional appropriation for Bridges; 1859, Doc. 68 — Application for an additional appropriation for Lands; 1860, Doc. 7 — Additional appropriation for Common and Squares; 1860, Doc. 8 — Additional appropriation for Engine Houses; 1860, Doc. 14 — Additional appropriation for Sewers; 1860, Doc. 18 — Appropriations for Steam Fire Engines and Houses; 1860, Docs. 19 and 20 — Additional appropriations for the Eliot & Quincy Schools; 1860, Doc. 22 — Additional appropriation for the Market; 1860, Doc. 26 — Additional appropriation for Paving; 1860, Doc. 28 — Additional appropriation for the Fire Dept.; 1860, Doc. 33 — Additional appropriation for Public Buildings; 1860, Doc. 35 — Rept. on auditor's estimates for the next financial year; 1860, Doc. 37 — Additional appropriation for Internal Health Dept.; 1860, Doc. 40 — Additional appropriation for Lands; 1860, Doc. 73 — Additional appropriation for Public Buildings; 1860, Doc. 76 — Additional appropriation for the Public Garden; 1860, Doc. 81 — Additional appropriation for the Harbor; 1860, Doc. 80 — Additional appropriation for Public Buildings; 1860, Doc. 82 — Additional appropriation for the widening of Tremont St.; 1860, Doc. 87 — Additional appropriation for Land Commissioners; 1860, Doc. 92 — Additional appropriation for Public Buildings; 1860, Doc. 99 — Additional appropriations for Sewers; 1861, Doc. 19 — Rept. on auditor's estimates for the next financial year; 1861, Doc. 22 — Additional appropriation for Sewers; 1861, Doc. 28 — Additional appropriation for Lands; 1861, Doc. 54 — Additional appropriation for Paving; 1861, Doc. 57 — Additional appropriation for Paving; 1861, Doc. 70 — Additional appropriation for Paving; 1862, Doc. 10 — Rept. on the expediency of making quarterly appropriations; 1862, Docs. 19, 20, 21, 22, 23, 25, 26, 28 — Additional appropriations for Public Buildings, Lamps, Overseers of the Poor, Cemeteries, Police, Printing, Public Lands, and Grammar Schools; 1862, Doc. 31 — Rept. on auditor's estimates for the next financial year; 1862, Doc. 54 — Additional appropriation for City Hospital; 1862, Doc. 73 — Appropriation for the Common; 1862, Doc. 76 — Additional appropriation for Public Lands; 1863, Doc. 8 — Additional appropriation for Fire Dept.; 1863, Doc. 23 — Appropriation for widening Lindall St.; 1863, Doc. 29 — Additional appropriation for the City Hospital; 1863, Doc. 32 — Additional appropriations for Lamps, Bells, and Clocks; 1863, Doc. 33 — Additional appropriation for the Fire Dept.; 1863, Doc. 38 — Rept. on the auditor's estimates for the next financial year; 1863, Doc. 40 — Additional appropriations for the Health Dept.; 1863, Doc. 41 — Appropriation for a new Primary School House in Chardon St.; 1863, Doc. 66 — Additional appropriation for Public Lands; 1863, Doc. 85 — Additional appropriation for the Common; 1863, Doc. 88 — Additional appropriation for the Fire Dept.; 1863, Doc. 104 — Additional appropriation for Cemeteries; 1864, Doc. 8 — Additional appropriation for Sewers; 1864, Doc. 9 — Additional appropriation for Bridges; 1864, Doc. 14 — Additional appropriation for the Fire Dept.; 1864, Doc. 17 — Additional appropriation for Lands; 1864, Doc. 18 — Additional appropriation for the City Hospital; 1864, Doc. 19 — Additional appropriation for Public Buildings; 1864, Doc. 22 — Additional appropriation for the Fire Dept.; 1864, Docs. 25, 26, 27 — Additional appropriations for Printing, Health, and Lamps; 1864, Docs. 31, 32 — Additional appropriation for Harbor and Fire Dept.; 1864, Doc. 36 — Rept. on auditor's estimates for the next financial year; 1864, Doc. 72 — Additional appropriation for the Fire Dept.; 1864, Docs. 74, 75 — Additional appropriations for City Stables and City Hospital.

ARCHITECT, CITY. 1863, Doc. 62 — An ordinance in relation to

ARMORIES. 1846, Doc. 33 — Rept. on unoccupied rooms suitable for armories over Faneuil Hall, etc; 1852, Doc. 53 — Rept. on the subject of an armory for the Light Dragoons; 1853, Doc. 25 — Rept. of the Committee on armories; 1853 Doc. 72 — Report on petition of the Mechanic Riflemen to be refunded money paid for rent of armory.

ASSESSORS. 1844, Doc. 5 — Report of Committee to whom was referred so much of the Mayor's address as related to; 1856, Doc. 19 — Nomination of asst. assessors; 1864, Doc. 82 — Rept. of Committee on the assessor's dept.

AUDITOR. 1834, Doc. 5 (City Council) — Rept. of auditor on expenses for printing, and salaries of City and County Officers; 1834, Doc. 10 (Com. Council) — Twenty-second annual rept. of receipts and expenditures; 1835, Doc. 17 (Com. Council) — Twenty-third annual rept. of receipts and expenditures; 1836, Doc. 11 (Com. Council) — Twenty-fourth annual rept. of receipts and expenditures; 1857, Doc. 25 (Com. Council) — Twenty-fifth annual rept. of receipts and expenditures; 1838, Doc. 36 — Twenty-sixth annual rept. of receipts and expenditures; 1839, Doc. 31 — Twenty-seventh annual rept. of receipts and expenditures; 1840, Doc. 19 — Twenty-eighth annual report of receipts and expenditures; 1841, Doc. 20 — Twenty-ninth annual rept. of receipts and expenditures; 1842, Doc. 15; Thirtieth annual rept. of receipts and expenditures; 1843, Doc. 20 1-2 — Thirty-first annual rept. of receipts and expenditures; 1844, Doc. 17 — Thirty second annual rept. of receipts and expenditures; 1845, Doc. 22 — Thirty-third annual rept. of receipts and expenditures; 1846, Doc. 20 1-2 — Thirty-fourth annual rept. of receipts and expenditures; 1847, Doc. 34 — Thirty-fifth annual rept. of receipts and expenditures; 1848, Doc. 29 — Thirty-sixth annual rept. of receipts and expenditures; 1849, Doc. 35 — Thirty-seventh annual rept. of receipts and expenditures; 1850, Doc. 21 — Thirty-eighth annual rept. of receipts and expenditures; 1851, Doc. 49 — Thirty-ninth annual rept. of receipts and expenditures; 1852, Doc. 36 — Fortieth annual rept. of receipts and expenditures; 1853, Doc. 45 — Forty-first annual rept. of receipts and expenditures; 1854, Doc. 59 — Forty-second annual rept. of receipts and expenditures; 1855, Doc. 49 1-2 — Forty-third annual rept. of receipts and expenditures; 1856, Doc. 48 — Forty-fourth annual rept. of receipts and expenditures; 1857, Doc. 54 — Forty-fifth annual rept. of receipts and expenditures; 1858, Doc. 29 — Forty-sixth annual rept. of receipts and expenditures; 1859, Doc. 41 — Forty-seventh annual rept. of receipts and expenditures; 1860, Doc. 56 — Forty-eighth annual rept. of receipts and expenditures; 1861, Doc. 53 — Forty-ninth annual rept. of receipts and expenditures; 1862, Doc. 58 — Fiftieth annual rept. of receipts and expenditures; 1863, Doc. 78 — Fifty-first annual rept. of receipts and expenditures; 1864, Doc. 65 — Fifty-second annual rept. of receipts and expenditures.

AWNINGS. 1854, Doc. 35 — Rept. on the memorial of S. S. Holton and others in relation to, etc.

BACK BAY. 1849, Doc. 36 — Rept. on the memorial of D. Sears *et als.*, in relation to the flats west of Charles St.; 1849, Doc. 48 — Rept. on the memorial of D. Sears in relation to the flats west of Charles St.; 1850, Doc. 14 — Rept. in relation to the drainage of Back Bay; 1850, Doc. 34 1-2—Rept. on the drainage of Back Bay; 1851, Doc. 71—Rept. on the drainage of the northwesterly section of the city; 1853, Doc. 63—Rept. on Back Bay lands, with the proposition of the State Commissioners; 1854, Doc. 15—Proposal from the State Commission on lands; 1854, Doc. 124—Rept. on; 1857, Doc. 59—Indenture between the Commonwealth, the Boston Water Power Co. and the City; 1859, Doc. 42—Message of the Mayor announcing the award of the Commissioners; 1860, Doc. 50—Rept. of the City Engineer on the direction, grades, and sewerage of streets; 1860, Doc. 70—Rept. on the drainage of; 1861, Doc. 25—First rept. of the special committee on improvements of; 1861, Doc. 79—First joint rept. of the Committee and Commissioners on; 1862, Doc. 56—Third rept. of Committee, and second joint rept. of the Committee and Commissioners on; 1863, Doc. 81—Rept. of the joint special Committee, with rept. of the Commissioners; 1863, Doc. 94—Rept. of City Engineer on streets, grades, and drainage; 1863, Doc. 102—Proposed amendment to the order in relation to; 1864, Doc. 23—Rept. on the sewerage and grade of the Back Bay lands; 1864, Doc. 54—Contract with J. E. & N. Brown; 1864, Doc. 99—New tripartite indenture between the City of Boston, the Commonwealth of Massachusetts, and the Water Power Co.

BARK. 1839, Doc. 23—Rept. and ordinance regulating the sale and admeasurement of; 1840, Doc. 7—Rept. on ordinance relating to the admeasurement of; 1854, Doc. 112—An ordinance in relation to.

BATES, JOSHUA. 1864, Doc. 79—Proceedings of the City Council in relation to the death of.

BATHING. 1860, Doc. 105—Rept. on public bathing houses.

BELLS. 1862, Doc. 51—An ordinance in relation to the ringing of church bells.

BEQUESTS. 1838, Doc. 26—Rept. on the property devised to the city by Ambrose S. Courtis; 1860, Doc. 63—Rept. on Elisha Goodnow's bequest to the Free City Hospital.

BOSTON, ENGLAND. 1851, Doc. 63—Seals and documents from; 1856, Doc. 35—Communication of the Mayor relative to the visit of the President of the Common Council to.

BOWLING ALLEYS. 1851, Doc. 41—Acceptance of an act relating to; 1853, Doc. 69—Rept. of Committee on.

BRIDGES. 1854, Doc. 84—An ordinance in relation to So. Boston bridges; 1855, Doc. 51—An ordinance in relation to bridges; 1855, Doc. 54—City Solicitor's opinion respecting the right of the East Boston free bridge; 1856, Doc. 46—Rept. on Albany St. bridge; 1856, Doc. 47—Rept. on East Boston free bridge; 1857, Doc. 34—An ordinance relating to bridges.

BROADWAY RAILROAD. See *Street Railways.*

BUILDINGS. 1839, Doc. 15—Report on the petition of Theodore Washburn and others for a repeal of the law in regard to the erection of wooden buildings; 1854, Doc. 85—An ordinance in relation to buildings; 1863, Doc. 36—An ordinance in relation to buildings.

BUILDINGS, PUBLIC. 1840, Doc. 8—Rept. on what alterations should be made in the manner of making contracts for the erection and alteration of. 1843, Doc. 25—Ordinance concerning the sale of. 1847, Doc. 2—Statement of the names of delinquent tenants of public buildings, together with the amount of rents due; 1851, Doc. 21—Annual rept. of Supt.; 1852, Doc. 8—Annual rept. of Supt.; 1853, Doc. 53—Rept. of Supt.; 1854, Doc. 8—Annual rept. of Supt.; 1854, Doc. 104—An ordinance in relation to; 1855, Doc. 15—Annual rept. of Supt.; 1856, Doc. 6—Annual report of Supt.; 1857, Doc. 11—Annual rept. of Supt.; 1858, Doc. 6—Annual rept. of Supt.; 1859, Doc. 7—Annual rept. of the Supt.; 1859, Doc. 18—Rept. and order relative to the alterations in the County building in Court Square; 1860, Doc. 10—Annual rept. of Supt.; 1861, Doc 10—Annual rept. of Supt.; 1862, Doc. 8—Annual rept. of Supt.; 1863, Doc. 9—Annual rept. of Supt.; 1864, Doc. 13—Annual rept. of Supt.

BURYING-GROUNDS. 1849, Doc. 28—Rept. and ordinance relative to; 1849, Doc. 51—Rept. on so much of the Mayor's address as related to interments out of the city; 1849, Doc. 59—Additional rept. on same; 1850, Doc. 39—Rept. on the subject of intra-mural burials.—See *Cemeteries.*

CAMBRIDGE RAILROAD. See *Street Railways.*

CEMETERIES. 1849, Doc. 54—Grand Jury's Communication respecting the Cemetery at South Boston; 1857, Doc. 72—An ordinance in relation to Mt. Hope Cemetery; 1859, Doc. 10—Annual rept. of the Trustees of Mt. Hope Cemetery; 1860, Doc. 16—Annual rept. of the Trustees of Mt. Hope Cemetery; 1861, Doc. 16—Annual rept. of the Trustees of Mt. Hope Cemetery; 1862, Doc. 13—Annual rept. of the Trustees of Mt. Hope Cemetery; 1863, Doc. 16—Annual rept. of the Trustees of Mt. Hope Cemetery; 1863, Doc. 37—An ordinance in relation to Mount Hope Cemetery; 1863, Doc. 74—Mayor's communication in relation to the Cemetery at Gettysburg; 1863, Doc. 106—Rept. on the Mass. Cemetery at Gettysburg, with oration of Edward Everett; 1864, Doc. 15—Sixth annual rept. of the Trustees of Mt. Hope Cemetery; 1864, Doc. 73—Rept. on abolishing the Board of Trustees of Mt. Hope Cemetery; 1864, Doc. 83—Ordinance in relation to Mt. Hope Cemetery; 1864, Doc. 96—An ordinance in relation to Mt. Hope Cemetery.

CENSUS. 1850, Doc. 42—Rept. in relation to a census of the City of Boston; 1851, Doc. 60—Rept. of a special committee on the census taken in May, 1850, and also a comparative view of the population of Boston in 1850, with the births, marriages, and deaths, in 1849 and 1850, by Jesse Chickering, M. D.; 1855, Doc. 69—Census as taken May, 1855, with analytical and sanitary observations, by Josiah Curtis, M. D.

CHARTER, CITY. 1834, Doc. 6 (City Council)—Rept. on alterations relative to the mode of election, and the powers of the School Committee; 1837, Doc. 21 (Com. Council)—Rept. on revision for the action of the inhabitants thereon; 1838, Doc. 5—Statement of changes proposed, and reasons therefor; 1841, Doc. 5—Rept. on expediency of amending; 1841, Doc. 7—Amendments which were made and adopted to the revised draft; 1842, Doc. 2—Amendments to revised draft of; 1845, Doc. 4—Rept. upon revision of, with amendatory act; 1848, Doc. 16—Rept. of Commissioners on revision of; 1852, Doc. 15—Order submitted by Mr. Hobart respecting the Mayor and Aldermen; 1854, Doc. 27—Charter revised; 1854, Doc. 58—Rept. on Revised City Charter; 1856, Doc. 62—Report concerning alterations in; 1860, Doc. 78—Rept. on amendments to; 1862, Doc. 15—Rept. on amendments to; 1862, Doc. 18—Proposed amendments to; 1864, Doc. 78—Rept. on proposed amendments to.

CHELSEA. 1856, Doc. 26—Rept. on the petitions of John Fenno, and others, for the annexation of Chelsea to Boston.

CHIMNEYS. 1854, Doc. 86—An ordinance in relation to.

CHOLERA. 1848, Doc. 39—Rept. of Board of Consulting Physicians on the subject of; 1849, Doc. 23—Rept. on so much of the Mayor's address as related to; 1849, Doc. 66—Rept. on the Asiatic Cholera, together with the report of the City Physician on the Cholera Hospital; 1861, Doc. 14—Communication from Dr. H. G. Clark, transmitting the rept. of Drs. Buckingham and Hodges on the Cholera Hospital at Fort Hill, in 1854.

CITY COUNCIL. 1840, Doc. 3—Joint rules and orders; 1845, Doc. 1—Address of Alderman Parker to; 1845, Doc. 42—Opinions of Richard Fletcher, C. P. Curtis, and C. G. Loring, on powers and duties of, on demise of the Mayor; 1854, Docs. 2 and 3—First and second repts. on rules and orders; 1855, Doc. 3—Rept. on rules and orders; 1856, Doc. 16—Amendments to joint rules and orders; 1861, Doc. 2—Rept. on joint rules and orders.

CITY HALL. 1837, Doc. 7 (Com. Council)—Rept. on the disposition of the Court House, and the expediency of providing additional accommodations for the officers of the city government; 1838, Doc. 17—Report on the expediency of erecting a new City Hall; 1853, Doc. 31—Majority and minority repts. on the subject of a new building for the use of the City Government, and Public Library; 1856, Doc. 31—Rept. on alterations and additions; 1857, Doc. 42—Rept. of Committee on Public Buildings relative to a new City Hall; 1858, Doc. 8—Rept. relative to a new City Hall (reprint of Doc. 42, 1857); 1860, Doc. 44—Majority rept. on the enlargement of; 1862, Doc. 44—Rept. of the Committee on Public Buildings on the erection of a new City Hall; 1862, Doc. 104—Proceedings at the laying of the corner stone of the new hall.

CLAIMS. 1851, Doc. 65—Rept. of Committee on accounts, on the bills of Alden Gifford, and Healey & Spaulding; 1852, Doc 54—Rept. on petition of H. L. Cummings to be compensated for damages sustained while in the service of the city; 1854, Doc. 47—Rept. on Benson Leavitt's claim for performing the duties of Mayor in 1845; 1855, Doc. 49—Rept. on claims of Charles Chipman and S. & H. Ames for damages on account of the failure of the city to execute its contracts; 1855, Doc. 74—General rept. of the joint standing Committee on.

COAL. 1840, Doc. 7—Rept. on ordinance relating to admeasurement of; 1855, Doc. 36—An ordinance in relation to weighers of; 1855, Doc. 37—Rules and regulations for the construction of coal holes; 1855, Doc. 42—Regulations in regard to coal holes; 1863, Doc. 82—Rules and regulations in relation to coal holes.

COINS. 1837, Doc. 3 (City Council)—Rept. on the petition of Wm. Lawrence, that the city would provide some substitute for the smaller denominations of.

COMMITTEES. 1843, Doc. 24—Joint resolutions on the duties of; 1857, Doc. 23—Ordinance to provide a clerk of; 1860, Doc. 27—Ordinance in relation to a clerk of; 1861, Doc. 21—Rept. on the prerogatives and duties of the Committee on Public Instruction; 1861, Doc. 30—Rept. on the duties of the Committee on Institutions; 1864, Doc. 49—Rept. on the duties of the Committee on Public Instruction.

COMMON. 1843, Doc. 23—Rept. of Com. on Public Lands on the title under which acquired; 1852, Doc. 62—An ordinance in relation to; 1854, Doc. 87—An ordinance in relation to; 1861, Doc. 75—An ordinance in relation to; 1863, Doc. 27—An ordinance in relation to.

COMMON COUNCIL. 1835, Doc. 4 (Com. Council)—Rept. on rules and orders for the regulation of proceedings; 1839, Doc. 1—Rules and orders; 1840, Doc. 3—Rules and orders; 1846, Doc. 37—Reply of G. S. Hillard, President, to a vote of thanks; 1847, Doc. 26—Resolutions, &c., on the resignation of G. S. Hillard, President; 1847, Doc. 49—Reply of Benjamin Seaver, President, to a vote of thanks; 1848, Doc. 47—Reply of Benj. Seaver, President, to a vote of thanks; 1849, Doc. 67—Reply of Benj. Seaver, President, to a vote of thanks; 1850, Doc. 52—Reply of Francis Brinley, President, to a vote of thanks; 1851, Doc. 78—Reply of Francis Brinley, President, to a vote of thanks; 1852, Doc. 74—Reply of H. J. Gardner, President, to a vote of thanks; 1853, Doc. 93—Reply of H. J. Gardner, President, to a vote of thanks; 1854, Doc. 127—Reply of A. H. Rice, President, to a vote of thanks; 1855, Doc. 72—Reply of Wm. A. Bell, President, *pro tem.*, to a vote of thanks; 1855, Doc. 75—Reply of Jos. Story, President, to a vote of thanks; 1858, Doc. 65—Reply of S. W. Waldron, President, to a vote of thanks; 1860, Doc. 104—Reply of J. P. Bradlee, President, to a vote of thanks; 1861, Doc. 78—Reply of J. P. Bradlee, President, to a vote of thanks; 1862, Doc. 102—Reply of Joshua D. Ball, President, to a vote of thanks; 1863, Doc. 112—Reply of Geo. S. Hale, President, to a vote of thanks; 1864, Doc. 97—Reply of Geo. S. Hale, President, to a vote of thanks.

COPLEY, JOHN SINGLETON. 1859, Doc. 45—Painting of Charles I. before Parliament, presented to the city.

CORONERS. 1856, Doc. 76—Rept. on Coroner's bills.

CORRECTION, HOUSE OF. 1834, Doc. 13 (City Council)—Rept. of Committee; 1834, Doc. 2 (Com. Council)—Semi-annual rept. of overseers; 1837, Doc. 23 (Com. Council)—Rept. of Inspectors of Prisons; 1838, Doc. 21—Rept. of Inspectors; 1838, Doc. 32—Rept. on health, cleanliness, &c.; 1839, Doc. 4—Rept. of Inspectors; 1839, Doc. 22—Rept. of Inspectors; 1839, Doc. 28—Rept. on health, cleanliness, &c.; 1840, Doc. 2—Rept. of Inspectors; 1840, Doc. 21—Rept. of Inspectors; 1840, Doc. 24—Communication from overseers and master in relation to performance of medical duties; 1840, Doc. 26—Rept. of Standing Committee of Common Council; 1841, Doc. 4—Rept. of Inspectors; 1841, Doc. 18—Rept. of Inspectors; 1841, Doc. 27—Rept. of Standing Committee of Common Council; 1842, Doc. 5—Rept. of Inspectors; 1842, Doc. 16—Rept. of Inspectors; 1842, Doc. 25—Communication from Moses Grant in relation to; 1843, Doc. 2—Rept. of Inspectors; 1843, Doc. 20—Rules and regulations; 1843, Doc. 21—Rept. of Inspectors; 1844, Doc. 2—Rept. of Inspectors; 1844, Doc. 19—Rept. of Inspectors; 1845, Doc. 3—Rept. of Inspectors; 1845, Doc. 25—Rept. of Inspectors; 1846, Doc. 3—Rept. of Inspectors; 1846, Doc. 24—Rept. of Inspectors; 1847, Doc. 4—Rept. of Inspectors; 1847, Doc. 31—Rept. of Inspectors; 1848, Doc. 3—Rept. of Inspectors; 1848, Doc. 33—Rept. of Inspectors; 1849, Doc. 6—Rept. of Inspectors; 1849, Doc. 40—Rept. of Inspectors; 1850, Doc. 3—Rept. of Inspectors; 1850, Doc. 28—Rept. of Inspectors; 1851, Doc. 7—Rept. of Inspectors; 1851, Doc. 50—Rept. of Inspectors; 1852, Doc. 3—Rept. of Inspectors; 1852, Doc. 20—An act in relation to; 1852, Doc. 43—Rept. of Inspectors; 1853, Doc. 11—Rept. of Inspectors; 1853, Doc. 56—Rept. of Inspectors; 1854, Doc. 9—Rept. of Inspectors; 1854, Doc. 63—Rept. on a new house of correction; 1854, Doc. 66—City Solicitor's opinion concerning contracts; 1854, Doc. 68—Rules and regulations; 1854, Doc. 78—Rept. on removal to Deer Island; 1854, Doc. 81—Rept. of Inspectors; 1855, Doc. 23—Rept. of Inspectors; 1855, Doc. 24—Rules and regulations of; 1855, Doc. 50 1-2—Rept. of Inspectors; 1855, Doc. 65—Rept. on the expediency of placing the institution under the management of a Board of Commissioners; 1856, Doc. 13—Income and expenditures for ten years; 1856, Doc. 14—Rept. of Inspectors; 1856, Doc. 24—Removal of; 1856, Doc. 42—Majority and minority repts. on workshops; 1856, Doc. 58—Rept. of Inspectors; 1857, Doc. 33—An act to establish a Board of Directors of Public Institutions; 1857, Doc. 57—Rept. concerning a Board of Directors of Public Institutions; 1857, Doc. 64—Rept. of Inspectors; 1858, Doc. 14—Rept. of the Board of Directors; 1858, Doc. 19—Rules and regulations; 1858, Doc. 25—Rept. of Inspectors; 1858, Doc. 49—Rept. of Inspectors; 1858, Doc. 59—Rules and regulations for the internal govt. of; 1859, Doc. 32—Annual rept. of the Board of Directors; 1859, Doc. 35—Rept. of Inspectors; 1859, Doc. 65—Rept. of Inspectors; 1860, Doc. 25—Annual rept. of the Board of Directors; 1860, Doc. 54—Rept. of Inspectors; 1860, Doc. 91—Rept. of Inspectors; 1861, Doc. 15—Rules and regulations; 1861, Doc. 20—Annual rept. of the Board of Directors; 1861, Doc. 66—Rept. of Inspectors. 1862, Doc. 7—Annual rept. of the Board of Directors; 1862, Doc. 40—Ordinance establishing a Board of Directors, and defining their duties; 1862, Docs. 79 & 80—Repts. of the Inspectors; 1862, Doc. 84—An ordinance in relation to the Board of Directors; 1863, Doc. 17—Annual rept. of the Board of Directors; 1863, Doc. 73—Rept. of Inspectors; 1863, Doc. 93—Rept. of Inspectors; 1864—Annual rept. of the Board of Directors; 1864, Doc. 35—Rept. of Special Committee on alleged abuses.

COURTS. 1849, Doc. 8—Rept. on the reorganization of the Courts in the County of Suffolk; 1849, Doc. 34—Rept. on the act to establish the Superior Court of the City of Boston; 1851, Doc. 34—Rept. on an order respecting the salary of the senior justice of the Police Court; 1853, Doc. 83—Removal of the Police Court to the new Jail yard; 1855, Doc. 12—Petition of C. B. Goodrich, and others, for the establishment of a new Court; 1855, Doc. 20—An act to establish a new Court in Suffolk County; 1855, Doc. 53—City Solicitor's opinion in relation to the establishment of a new Court in Suffolk County.

COURT HOUSE. 1837, Doc. 7 (Com. Council)—Rept. on disposition of, and expediency of providing additional accommodations; 1840, Doc. 9—Rept. on expediency of altering the old County Court Ho., School St., for the purposes of a City Hall; 1840, Doc. 17—Rept. on disposition of the Court Ho. on School

St.; 1860, Doc. 69—Rept. on the alteration of the Court Ho., Court Sq.

CRIERS. 1854, Doc. 88—An ordinance in relation to; 1861, Doc. 41—Rept. on City Crier's house.

DEBT, CITY. 1834, Doc. 3 (City Council)—Rept. on reduction; 1834, Doc. 8 (City Council)—Rept. on public loans and reduction of debt; 1834, Doc. 12 (City Council)—Amt. of debt falling due the present financial year, and amt. to be placed to the credit of the Committee on reduction; 1835, Doc. 2 (Com. Council)—Rept. relative to the collection of debts due the city; 1835, Doc. 5 (Com. Council)—Rept. on rate of interest paid, bank in which deposits are made, &c.; 1835, Doc. 10 (Com. Council)—Rept. relative to the collection of debts due the city; 1836, Doc. 3 (Com. Council)—Amt. of debt falling due, and amt. to be received applicable to the extinguishment of the same; 1839, Doc. 9—Liquidation of the debt, with amt. of the available city property; 1839, Doc. 12—Rept. on the expediency of appropriating $50,000, annually, for the reduction of the debt; 1840, Doc. 13—Rept. in regard to duties of the Committee on reduction of, etc.; 1842, Doc. 14—Rept. on reduction; 1845, Doc. 20—Rept. on reduction; 1845, Doc. 44—Rept. on reduction; 1846, Doc. 34—Rept. on reduction; 1849, Doc. 65—Rept. on reduction; 1850, Doc. 49—Rept. on reduction; 1851, Doc. 79—Rept. on reduction; 1852, Doc. 68—Rept. on reduction; 1853, Doc. 82—Rept. on reduction; 1854, Doc. 122—Rept. on reduction; 1855, Doc. 68—Rept. on reduction; 1856, Doc. 75—Rept. on reduction; 1857, Doc. 83—Rept. on reduction; 1858, Doc. 66—Rept. on reduction; 1859, Doc. 78—Rept. on reduction; 1860, Doc. 100—Rept. on reduction; 1861, Doc. 77—Rept. on reduction; 1862, Doc. 100—Rept. on reduction; 1863, Doc. 110—Rept. on reduction; 1864, Doc. 87—Rept. on reduction.

DEEDS. 1860, Doc. 32—Rept. concerning the registry of.

DEER ISLAND. 1847, Doc. 30—Rept. on the expediency of removing one or more of the Institutions, now located at South Boston, to Deer Island.

DOCKS. 1862, Doc. 96—Rept. of the Committee on Claims, on the subject of the Summer Street Dock.

DOGS. 1854, Doc. 89—An ordinance in relation to.

DORCHESTER AVENUE RAILROAD. See *Street Railways*.

EASTERN AVENUE. 1861, Doc. 58—Rept. of joint Special Committee on; 1861, Doc. 73—Opinion of the City Solicitor upon the construction of; 1862, Doc. 60—Rept. of the joint Special Committee on; 1862, Doc. 82—City Solicitor's opinion on; 1862, Doc. 92—Opinion of the Harbor Commissioners on; 1862, Doc. 98—Rept. on submitting a deed of transfer.

EASTERN RAILROAD WHARF. 1855, Doc. 27—Rept. and order relative to the purchase of.

ECONOMY. 1856, Doc. 5—Order to insure the most rigid economy in the different depts. of the City Government.

ELECTIONS. 1835, Doc. 12 (Com. Council)—Opinion of City Solicitor on elections and returns; 1843, Doc. 30—Rept. of joint Committee on the law regulating elections, and the qualification of voters; 1844, Doc. 4—Rept. of joint Committee on same; 1844, Doc. 16—Qualification of voters,—opinion of City Solicitor; 1845, Doc. 17—Rept. on certificates of members elected to serve in the Common Council; 1852, Doc. 61—Rept. on the petition of B. F. Cook, *et al.*, concerning the returns of ward officers; 1854, Doc. 90—An ordinance in relation to; 1858, Doc. 41—City Solicitor's interpretation of the word "district," in the amendments to the Constitution, as applied to elections.

ELECTIONS CONTESTED. 1835, Doc. 1 (Com. Council)—Rept. on remonstrance of Saml. Chessman and others, against the election of the sitting members from Ward 3; 1835, Doc. 6—(Com. Council)—Rept. on remonstrance of Saml. Chessman and others relative to the election in Ward 3, with City Solicitor's opinion on elections and returns; 1837, Doc. 2 (Com. Council)—Rept. on remonstrance of S. G. Shipley and others, against John Boles, Jason D. Battles, and Asa B. Snow, returned as members from Ward 3; 1839, Doc. 9—Rept. of majority of the Committee on the remonstrance of D. Nickerson and others, against the return of members of the Com. Council from Ward 12; 1839, Doc. 10—Minority rept. on same; 1843, Doc. 4—Rept. on remonstrance against the right to seats in the Council of persons returned from Ward 1; 1851, Doc. 3—Remonstrance of Osmyn Brewster and others against the right to seats of A. Abbott and T. Sprague; 1851, Doc. 11—Majority rept. on remonstrance from Ward 3; 1851, Doc. 12—Minority rept. on same; 1853, Docs. 3 & 4—Majority and minority repts. on remonstrance of G. L. Blaney and others in regard to election in Ward 3; 1853, Doc. 8—Majority and minority repts. on remonstrance of Charles Mayo and others in regard to elections in Wards 1 & 11; 1859, Doc. 36—Rept. on contested seats in Ward 12; 1860, Doc. 17—Rept. on contested seats of members of the Common Council from Ward 1; 1861, Doc. 7—Rept. on the petition of Joseph F. Paul, for a seat in the Board of Aldermen; 1862, Doc. 16—Rept. on the right of Daniel D. Kelley to a seat in the Board of Aldermen; 1863, Docs. 20 & 21—Majority and minority repts. of the Committee on the case of John C. Tucker, Ward 3; 1863, Doc. 42—Rept. on the election in Ward 10; 1863, Doc. 44—Minutes of the evidence in the case of John C. Tucker, Ward 3; 1864, Doc. 30—Rept. of Committee on the election in Ward 3.

ENGINEER, CITY. 1848, Doc. 38—An ordinance relating to; 1858, Doc. 47—Expenses of dept. for five years preceding Oct. 31, 1858; 1863, Doc. 26—An ordinance establishing a Committee on the dept. of.

ESTIMATES for the Financial year. See appropriations.

EULOGIES. 1864, Doc. 25 1-2—On General Andrew Jackson, July 9, 1845, by Pliny Merrick; 1849, Doc. 35 1-2—On the life, character, and public services of James K. Polk, July 25, 1849, by Levi Woodbury, LL. D.; 1850, Doc. 26—On the life and character of Zachary Taylor, Aug. 15, 1851, by Josiah Quincy, jr.

EXPENDITURES.—See *Auditor*.

FANEUIL HALL. 1845, Doc. 15—An ordinance in addition to an ordinance providing for the appt. of a Supt.; 1851, Doc. 25—Resolutions of Common Council concerning the refusal of the Mayor and Aldermen to allow the use of the hall for the reception of Daniel Webster; 1851, Doc. 26—Correspondence between the President of the Common Council and Daniel Webster in relation to the refusal of Faneuil Hall; 1851, Doc. 31—Rept. on the invitation to Daniel Webster to speak in Faneuil Hall; 1851, Doc. 33—City Solicitor's opinion in regard to the charge of Faneuil Hall; 1852, Doc. 31—Address of Daniel Webster, May 22d, 1852; 1852, Doc. 48—Rept. of Committee on Public Buildings concerning; 1853, Doc. 16—Rept. on improving interior of; 1854, Doc. 91—An ordinance in relation to.

FANEUIL HALL MARKET. 1842, Doc. 24—Rept. and ordinance in relation to; 1843, Doc. 5—Ordinance for the regulation of; 1843, Doc. 9—An ordinance for the regulation of; 1851, Doc. 9—Quarterly rept. of clerk; 1851, Doc. 62—Rept. of Special Committee on; 1852, Doc. 21 and 22—Maj. and min. repts, on market leases; 1852, Doc. 49—An ordinance in relation to; 1854, Doc. 92—An ordinance in relation to; 1854, Doc. 119—Rept. in relation to the sale of; 1854, Doc. 128—Rept. of Special Committee on the sale of; 1855, Doc. 32—Rept. on so much of Mayor's address as related to the improvement of; 1855, Doc. 44—City Solicitor's opinion on alterations in; 1855, Doc. 56—Rept. on sale of provisions, etc.; 1857, Doc. 48—Rept. and ordinance relative to; 1857, Doc. 79—Rept. on regulations of; 1858, Doc. 35—An ordinance extending the limits of; 1859, Doc. 30—Rept. and ordinance in relation to; 1860, Doc. 59—Rept. on the enlargement of.

FERRIES, EAST BOSTON. 1856, Doc. 28—Rept. on tolls; 1857, Doc. 68—Rept. of Special Committee on; 1857, Doc. 80—Final rept. on the purchase of the property and franchise of; 1858, Doc. 12—Rept. of Committee on; 1858, Doc. 23—Opinion of the City Solicitor; 1858, Doc. 61—Rept. on the purchase of the property and franchise of; 1859, Doc. 21—Final rept. on the purchase of; 1859, Doc. 39—Rept., resolve, and order, for the purchase of; 1859, Doc. 61—Final rept. on the purchase of the property of; 1860, Doc. 65—Rept. on establishing tolls;

1860, Doc. 74—An order to purchase; 1860, Doc. 83—Rept. on; 1860, Doc. 96—Rept. on the free passage of school children 1861, Doc. 71—Rept. on so much of the Mayor's address as related to; 1862, Doc. 32—An act concerning; 1862, Doc. 83—Rept. of sub-Committee on; 1862, Doc. 95—Rept. upon a subsidy to; 1863, Doc. 18—Annual statement of the East Boston Co.; 1863, Doc. 22—Annual return of the People's Co.; 1863, Doc. 69—Rept. of joint Special Committee on tolls; 1864, Doc. 16—Annual statement of the East Boston Co.; 1864, Doc. 44—Rept. of Committee to ascertain the daily travel over; 1864, Doc. 53—Rept. on tolls; 1864, Doc. 81—Rept. on a night boat to East Boston.

FINANCE. 1854, Doc. 93—An ordinance in relation to.

FIRE. 1834, Doc. 4 (City Council)—Act for the protection of the City of Boston against; 1837, Doc. 18 (Com. Council)—Rept. on ordinance for preventing and extinguishing; 1852, Doc. 66—Rept. concerning further protection of life and property.

FIRE ALARMS. 1851, Doc. 20—Communication from Dr. W. F. Channing, respecting a system of; 1851, Doc. 42—Rept. concerning a uniform system of; 1851, Doc. 74—Rept. of Committee on Telegraphic Fire Alarms; 1853, Doc. 76—Ordinance; 1855, Doc. 52—An ordinance in relation to; 1861, Doc. 61—Rept. on extension of system to East Boston.

FIRE ARMS. 1854, Doc. 95—An ordinance in relation to.

FIRE DEPARTMENT. 1835, Doc. 1 (City Council)—Rept. on Fire Dept., and the difference existing between the two boards; 1835, Doc. 3 (Com. Council)—Rept. on Mayor's communication in relation to the Chief Engineer; 1835, Doc. 8 (Com. Council)—Rept. on proposed alterations in the dept.; 1837, Doc. 18 (Com. Council)—Rept. on ordinance establishing; 1838, Doc. 24—First annual rept. of Chief Engineer; 1839, Doc. 24—Second annual rept. of Chief Engineer; 1840, Doc. 22—Rept. of Chief Engineer; 1841, Doc. 22—Fourth annual rept. of Chief Engineer; 1842, Doc. 21—Fifth annual rept. of Chief Engineer; 1842, Doc. 22—Rept. on organization, with an ordinance; 1842, Doc. 23—Amendments proposed to an ordinance in relation to; 1843, Doc. 22—Sixth annual rept. of Chief Engineer; 1844, Doc. 20 1-2—Seventh annual rept. of Chief Engineer; 1845, Doc. 30—Eighth annual rept. of Chief Engineer; 1845, Doc. 33—Rept. on a petition for an amendment to the ordinance, so that companies may elect their own officers; 1846, Doc. 25—Ninth annual rept. of Chief Engineer; 1847, Doc. 36—Tenth annual rept. of Chief Engineer; 1848, Doc. 36—Eleventh annual rept. of Chief Engineer; 1849, Doc. 47—Twelfth annual rept. of Chief Engineer; 1850, Doc. 8—Rules and regulations of the department; 1850, Doc. 33—Thirteenth annual rept. of Chief Engineer; 1851, Doc. 13—Rept. on the Board of Engineers; 1851, Doc. 32—Rept. on the reorganization of the dept.; 1851, Doc. 43—Ordinance establishing; 1851, Doc. 53—Fourteenth annual rept. of Chief Engineer; 1852, Doc. 14—Rept. and ordinance; 1852, Doc. 45—Rept. on a misunderstanding between dept. of this and other cities; 1852, Doc. 46—Fifteenth annual rept. of Chief Engineer; 1852, Doc. 70—An ordinance; 1853, Doc. 61—Sixteenth annual rept. of Chief Engineer; 1853, Doc. 76—An ordinance; 1854, Doc. 28—Order concerning dept. fund; 1854, Doc. 36—Rept. on Steam Fire Engines; 1854, Doc. 65—Seventeenth annual rept. of Chief Engineer; 1854, Doc. 94—An ordinance in relation to; 1855, Doc. 50—Eighteenth annual rept. of Chief Engineer; 1855, Doc. 58—An ordinance in relation to; 1856, Doc. 56—Nineteenth annual rept. of Chief Engineer; 1857, Doc. 28—Rept. on parade of; 1857, Doc. 67—Twentieth annual rept. of the Chief Engineer; 1857, Doc. 69—Majority and minority repts. on the Steam Fire Engine—Miles Greenwood; 1858, Doc. 37—Rept. on public trials of Steam Fire Engines; 1858, Doc. 45—Twenty-first annual rept. of Chief Engineer; 1859, Doc. 12—An ordinance in relation to; 1859, Doc. 59—Twenty-second annual rept. of Chief Engineer; 1860, Doc. 48—An ordinance providing for preventing and extinguishing fires, and establishing a dept.; 1861, Doc. 17—Twenty-third annual rept. of Chief Engineer; 1861, Doc. 24—An ordinance in relation to; 1861, Doc. 35—Amendments to the ordinance on; 1861, Doc. 39—Rules for the government of the apparatus; 1861, Doc. 64—An ordinance in relation to; 1862, Doc. 35—Twenty-fourth annual rept. of the Chief Engineer; 1862, Doc. 94—Rules for the distribution of the fire apparatus; 1863, Doc. 84—Twenty-fifth annual rept. of the Chief Engineer; 1864, Doc. 24—Twenty-sixth annual rept. of Chief Engineer; 1864, Doc. 43—Rules for the distribution of the fire apparatus.

FRANKLIN FUND. 1853, Doc. 26—Rept. of the Committee appointed to examine the accounts of the Treasurer of.

FREE STONE. 1862, Doc. 70—Regulations for the survey of.

FORT HILL. 1838, Doc. 29—Inquiry into the city's right to certain lands on; 1854, Doc. 52—Petition of the Fort Hill corporation, for the acceptance of their act of incorporation.

FOUNTAINS. 1852, Doc. 62—An ordinance in relation to.

GALLOP'S ISLAND. 1850, Doc. 23—Rept. on removal of gravel from.

GARDENS, PUBLIC. 1850, Doc. 18—Rept. on so much of the Mayor's address as related to; 1851, Doc. 22—Rept. concerning an appropriation for improving; 1859, Doc. 63—Rept. on improvement of; 1860, Doc. 57—Rept. of the Committee on; 1861, Doc. 65—Rept. of the Committee on; 1861, Doc. 75—An ordinance in relation to.

GAS. 1834, Doc. 7 (City Council)—Rept. on lighting streets with gas instead of oil; 1839, Doc. 6—Rept. relative to the expense of lighting the streets with gas instead of oil; 1852, Doc. 39—Rept. concerning the erection of a gasometer in Mason St.; 1854, Doc. 61—Rept. on the Shawmut and Suffolk Gas Companies, with order; 1856, Doc. 25—Contract with Boston Gas Light Co.; 1860, Docs. 41 & 42—Majority and minority repts. on the Suffolk and Shawmut Cos.; 1864, Doc. 29—Rept. of the Inspector of Gas, for the month of February; 1864, Doc. 38—Rept. of the Inspector of Gas, for the month of March; 1864, Doc. 48—Rept. of the Inspector of Gas, for the month of April; 1864, Doc. 57—Rept. of the Inspector of Gas, for the month of May.

GRAIN. 1860, Doc. 12—Head measurer's rept. for 1859.

GRAND JURY. 1852, Doc. 55—Rept. on the right of the Grand Jury to make official visits to public institutions of the city.

HACKNEY CARRIAGES. 1855, Doc. 13—Rept. on fares.

HANCOCK HOUSE. 1863, Doc. 56—Rept. on the preservation of.

HARBOR. 1846, Doc. 5—Memorial of Boston Marine Society concerning islands in the harbor, with rept. of Lieut.-Col. Thayer on same; 1846, Doc. 22—Rept. on memorial of Marine Society, and documents accompanying same; 1852, Doc. 33—Communication from City Solicitor respecting; 1853, Doc. 60—Rept. of joint Standing Committee for 1852; 1853, Doc. 87—Duties of City Engineer respecting; 1854, Doc. 96—An ordinance in relation to; 1859, Doc. 64—Mayor's communication in relation to a scientific survey of; 1860, Doc. 34—United States Commissioner's communication in relation to Mystic pond and river; 1860, Doc. 37—Preliminary rept. of the U. S. Commissioners on; 1860, Doc. 88—Rept. on the survey of the inner harbor; 1860, Doc. 97—Second rept. of the U. S. Commissioners on; 1861, Doc. 12—Special rept. (third) of the U. S. Commissioners on the relation of Mystic pond and river to the harbor; 1861, Doc. 62—Fourth rept. of U. S. Commissioners; 1861, Doc. 63—Fifth rept. of the U. S. Commissioners; 1862, Doc. 92—Opinion of the U. S. Commissioners on the effect of the construction of the eastern avenue on the harbor; 1863, Doc. 35—Fifth rept. of the U. S. Commissioners; 1863, Doc. 53—Sixth rept. of the U. S. Commissioners; 1863, Doc. 71—Rept. on petition of A. R. Tewksbury, in relation to the purchase of certain lands on Point Shirley; 1863, Doc. 79—Rept. on the petition of Benj. Wheeler's heirs, to take ballast from Winthrop beaches; 1863, Doc. 80—Rept. on the petition of A. R. Tewksbury, for leave to sell accretions, &c., on the beaches at Points Shirley and Winthrop; 1863, Doc. 107—Rept. on petition of Benj. Wheeler's heirs, to take ballast within the harbor lines; 1863, Doc. 108—Communications of Benj. A. Gould, published in the *Daily Advertiser;* 1863, Doc. 111—

Rept. on protection of the head lands; 1864. Docs. 33 & 34—Seventh and Eighth repts. of the U. S. Commissioners; 1864, Doc. 42—Communication from A. Boschké, in relation to the Islands.

HARBOR MASTER. 1848, Doc. 37—Rept. for the year ending Oct. 2, 1848; 1850, Doc. 37—Rept. for the year ending Oct. 1, 1850; 1862, Doc. 29—An act concerning.

HAY SCALES. 1854, Doc. 97—An ordinance in relation to.

HEALTH. 1849, Doc. 31—Ordinance establishing a Board of Health; 1853, Doc. 23—Ordinance establishing the office of Supt.; 1854, Doc. 7—Annual rept. of Supt.; 1854, Doc. 39—Majority and minority repts. relative to charges preferred against the Supt.; 1854, Doc. 40—Third rept. relative to same; 1854, Doc. 73—Rept. on petition of Lewis Rice and others, in regard to house offal; 1854, Doc. 98—An ordinance in relation to; 1855, Doc. 6—Annual rept. of Supt.; 1855, Doc. 45—An act in relation to offensive trades; 1856, Doc. 4—Annual rept. of Supt.; 1857, Doc. 4—Annual rept. of Supt.; 1857, Doc. 25—An ordinance in relation to; 1858, Doc. 4—Annual rept. of Supt.; 1859, Doc. 4—Annual rept. of Supt.; 1859, Doc. 33—An ordinance in relation to; 1859, Doc. 62—An ordinance in relation to; 1860, Doc. 5—Annual rept. of Supt.; 1861, Doc. 6—Annual rept. of Supt.; 1862, Doc. 5—Annual rept. of Supt.; 1862, Doc. 47—An ordinance in relation to; 1862, Doc. 69—Rept. on nuisance at Ward's wharf; 1863, Doc. 5—Annual rept. of Supt.; 1863, Doc. 39—An ordinance in relation to; 1863, Doc. 51—An ordinance in relation to; 1864, Doc. 4—Annual rept. of Supt.

HIGHWAYS. 1854, Doc. 10—Rept. on the expediency of choosing any persons, other than the Mayor and Aldermen, surveyors of highways. See *Streets.*

HOSPITAL, CITY. 1849, Doc. 56—Rept. on the expediency of establishing a City Hospital; 1857, Doc. 37—Rept. on the establishment of; 1857, Doc. 78—An ordinance in relation to; 1860, Doc. 63—Rept. on Elisha Goodnow's bequest to; 1860, Doc. 67—Rept. on so much of the Mayor's address as related to; 1861, Doc. 34—Rept. with plans and estimates; 1861, Doc. 69—Second rept. on; 1862, Doc. 75—Rept. and estimates on; 1862, Doc. 88—An ordinance in relation to; 1863, Doc. 63—An ordinance relating to the funds of; 1863, Doc. 86—Memorial of the Trustees; 1864, Doc. 40—Proceedings at the dedication; 1864, Doc. 45—Rules and regulations.

INDUSTRY, HOUSE OF. 1834, Doc. 11 (City Council)—Eleventh annual rept. of the Directors; 1834, Doc. 13 (City Council)—Rept. on the condition of, at the close of the year; 1835, Doc. 7 (Com. Council)—Rept. on the accommodations; 1835, Doc. 13 (Com. Council)—Twelfth annual rept. of Directors; 1835, Doc. 14 (Com. Council)—Sentences of the Police Court to the Institution, and the effect of such commitments upon it; 1836, Doc. 5 (Com. Council)—Thirteenth annual rept. of the Directors; 1837, Doc. 8 (Com. Council)—Fourteenth annual rept. of the Directors; 1837, Doc. 11 (Com. Council)—Rules and regulations; 1837, Doc. 23 (Com. Council)—Rept. of the Inspectors of Prisons; 1838, Doc. 7—Communication from the Directors, in relation to juvenile offenders; 1838, Doc. 16—Fifteenth annual rept. of the Directors; 1838, Doc. 21—Rept. of Inspectors; 1838, Doc. 32—Rept. on health, cleanliness, &c.; 1839, Doc. 4—Rept. of Inspectors; 1839, Doc. 21—Sixteenth annual rept. of the Directors; 1839, Doc. 22—Rept. of Inspectors; 1839, Doc. 28—Rept. on health, cleanliness, &c.; 1840, Doc. 2—Rept. of Inspectors; 1840, Doc. 12—Seventeenth annual rept. of the Directors; 1840, Doc. 21—Rept. of Inspectors; 1840, Doc. 24—Communication from the Directors and Supt., in relation to the performance of medical duties; 1840, Doc. 26—Rept. of Standing Com. of Common Council on; 1841, Doc. 4—Rept. of Inspectors; 1841, Doc. 13—Eighteenth annual rept. of the Directors; 1841, Doc. 18—Rept. of Inspectors; 1841, Doc. 27—Rept. of Standing Com. of Common Council on; 1842, Doc. 5—Rept. of Inspectors; 1842, Doc. 13—Nineteenth annual rept. of Directors; 1842. Doc. 16—Rept. of Inspectors; 1842, Doc. 25—Communication by Moses Grant, in relation to; 1843, Doc. 2—Rept. of Inspectors; 1843, Doc. 17—Annual rept. of Directors; 1843, Doc. 21—Rept. of Inspectors; 1844, Doc. 2—Rept. of Inspectors; 1844, Doc. 14—Rept. of Directors; 1844, Doc. 19—Rept. of Inspectors; 1845, Doc. 3—Rept. of Inspectors; 1845, Doc. 19—Rept. of Directors; 1845, Doc. 25—Rept. of Inspectors; 1846, Doc. 3—Rept. of Inspectors; 1846, Doc. 19—Rept. of Directors; 1846, Doc. 24—Rept. of Inspectors; 1847, Doc. 4—Rept. of Inspectors; 1847, Doc. 22—Rept. of Directors; 1847, Doc. 31—Rept. of Inspectors; 1848, Doc. 3—Rept. of Inspectors; 1848, Doc. 10—Rept. concerning the enlargement of; 1848, Doc. 17—Rept. of Directors; 1848, Doc. 33—Rept. of Inspectors; 1849, Doc. 6—Rept. of Inspectors; 1849, Doc. 25—Rept. of Directors; 1849, Doc. 40—Rept. of Inspectors; 1850, Doc. 3—Rept. of Inspectors; 1850, Doc. 12—Rept. of Directors; 1850, Doc. 24—Rept. of alien passengers received; 1850, Doc. 28—Rept. of Inspectors; 1851, Doc. 7—Rept. of Inspectors; 1851, Doc. 27—Annual rept. of Directors; 1851, Doc. 50—Rept. of Inspectors; 1852, Doc. 3—Rept. of Inspectors; 1852, Doc. 26—Rept. of Directors; 1852, Doc. 43—Rept. of Inspectors; 1853, Doc. 11—Rept. of Inspectors; 1853, Doc. 30—Rept. of Directors; 1853, Doc. 56—Rept. of Inspectors; 1854, Doc. 9—Rept. of Inspectors; 1854, Doc. 45—Rept. of Directors; 1854, Doc. 81—Rept. of Inspectors; 1855, Doc. 28—Rept. of Inspectors; 1855, Doc. 38—Rept. of Directors; 1855, Doc. 50 1-2—Rept. of Inspectors; 1855, Doc. 65—Rept. on the expediency of placing the institutions under a Board of Commissioners; 1856, Doc. 13—Income and expenditures for ten years; 1856, Doc. 14—Rept. of Inspectors; 1856, Doc. 38—Rept. of Directors; 1856, Doc. 58—Rept. of Inspectors; 1857, Doc. 27—Rept. of Committee on institutions on the present condition of; 1857, Doc. 33—An act to establish a Board of Directors of Public Institutions; 1857, Doc. 40—Rept. of Directors; 1857, Doc. 57—Rept. concerning the Board of Directors of Public Institutions; 1857, Doc. 64—Rept. of Inspectors; 1857, Doc. 75—Rept. on the sale of the old buildings belonging to; 1858, Doc. 14—Rept. of the Board of Directors; 1858, Doc. 19—Rules and regulations; 1858, Doc. 25—Rept. of Inspectors; 1858, Doc. 49—Rept. of Inspectors; 1859, Doc. 32—Annual rept. of the Board of Directors; 1859, Doc. 35—Rept. of Inspectors; 1859, Doc. 65—Rept. of Inspectors; 1860, Doc. 25—Annual rept. of the Board of Directors; 1860, Doc. 54—Rept. of Inspectors; 1860, Doc. 91—Rept. of Inspectors; 1861, Doc. 15—Rules and regulations; 1861, Doc. 20—Annual rept. of the Board of Directors; 1861, Doc. 66—Rept. of Inspectors; 1862, Doc. 7—Annual rept. of the Board of Directors; 1862, Doc. 40—An ordinance establishing a Board of Directors, and defining their duties; 1862, Docs. 79 & 80—Repts. of Inspectors; 1862, Doc. 84—An ordinance in relation to the Board of Directors; 1863, Doc. 17—Annual rept. of the Board of Directors; 1863, Doc. 73—Rept. of Inspectors; 1863, Doc. 98—Rept. of Inspectors; 1864, Doc. 10—Annual rept. of the Board of Directors; 1864, Doc. 66—Rept. on amended rules.

INSTITUTIONS. See Houses of *Correction, Reformation and Industry, and Lunatic Hospital.*

INSURANCE. 1856, Doc. 68—Minority rept. relative to the insurance by the city of losses by fire.

INTELLIGENCE OFFICES. 1848, Doc. 30—Rept. of Committee on Licenses, on the subject of; 1848, Doc. 34—Resolves in relation to.

INTERNATIONAL EXCHANGES. 1849, Doc. 46—Rept. in relation to donations received from Paris, and the proceedings of the City Government upon the subject of International Exchanges.

JAIL. 1834, Doc. 13 (City Council)—Rept. on the condition of; 1837, Doc. 2 (City Council) Rept. on removal from Leverett st. to Bellevue; 1837, Doc. 23 (Com. Council)—Rept. of the Inspectors of Prisons; 1838, Doc. 21—Rept. of Inspectors; 1839, Doc. 4—Rept. of Inspectors; 1839, Doc. 14—Rept. on removing the Jail in Leverett st., and erecting a new one in South Boston; 1839, Doc. 22—Rept. of Inspectors; 1840, Doc. 2—Rept. of Inspectors; 1840, Doc. 21—Rept. of Inspectors; 1841, Doc. 4—Rept. of Inspectors; 1841, Doc. 18—

Rept. of Inspectors; 1841, Doc. 25—Rept. on so much of the Mayor's address as related to; 1842, Doc. 5—Rept. of Inspectors; 1842, Doc. 6—Majority and minority repts. on Jail in Leverett St.; 1842, Doc. 16—Rept. of Inspectors; 1843, Doc. 2—Rept. of Inspectors on; 1843, Doc. 7—Rept. of Committee on so much of the Mayor's address as related to the erection of a new County Jail; 1843, Doc. 8—Minority rept. on same; 1843, Doc. 21—Rept. of Inspectors; 1843, Doc. 31—Rept. of Committee on subject of a new Jail; 1844, Doc. 2—Rept. of Inspectors; 1844, Doc. 19—Rept. of Inspectors; 1845, Doc. 3—Rept. of Inspectors; 1845, Doc. 18—Rept. on subject of erecting a new Jail; 1845, Doc. 23—Rept. concerning plans and estimates for a new Jail; 1845, Doc. 24—Rept. concerning the location and erection of a new Jail; 1845, Doc. 25—Rept. of Inspectors; 1845, Doc. 34—Rept., plans, &c., for the proposed new Jail; 1845, Doc. 36—Dr. Luther V. Bell's letter on building, heating, and ventilating; 1846, Doc. 3—Rept. of Inspectors; 1846, Doc. 24—Rept. of Inspectors; 1847, Doc. 4—Rept. of Inspectors; 1847, Doc. 31—Rept. of Inspectors; 1848, Doc. 3—Rept. of Inspectors; 1848, Doc. 8—City Solicitor's opinion on the jurisdiction of the Mayor and Aldermen in providing a suitable Jail for Suffolk County; 1848, Doc. 24—Sheriff's rept. of the number of persons confined therein for the last ten years; 1848, Doc. 33—Rept. of Inspectors; 1849, Doc. 6—Rept. of Inspectors; 1849, Doc. 22—Rept. of Committee on the purchase of Jail lands; 1849, Doc. 40—Rept. of Inspectors; 1850, Doc. 3—Rept. of Inspectors; 1850, Doc. 6—Rept. on erection of a new Jail; 1850, Doc. 28—Rept. of Inspectors; 1851, Doc. 7—Rept. of Inspectors; 1851, Doc. 50—Rept. of Inspectors; 1851, Doc. 61—Rept. on the erection of a new Jail; 1852, Doc. 3—Rept. of Inspectors; 1852, Doc. 43—Rept. of Inspectors; 1853, Doc. 11—Rept. of Inspectors; 1853, Doc. 32—Rept. on the petition of Nathl. Hammond and others, in regard to the Jail lands; 1853, Doc. 39—Rept. on Jail lands, with Mr. Bonney's amendment; 1853, Doc. 40—Majority and minority repts. on Jail lands; 1853, Doc. 56—Rept. of Inspectors; 1854, Doc. 9—Rept. of Inspectors; 1854, Doc. 70—Rept. on Jail lands; 1854, Doc. 79—Rept. relative to purchase of Jail lands, by Rev. John McElroy; 1854, Doc. 81—Rept. of Inspectors; 1855, Doc. 28—Rept. of Inspectors; 1855, Doc. 59 1-2—Rept. of Inspectors; 1856, Doc. 14—Rept. of Inspectors; 1856, Doc. 36—Reprint of No. 32, 1853, on Jail lands; 1856, Doc. 44—Rept. on petition of John B. Fitzpatrick, relative to Jail lands; 1856, Doc. 58—Rept. of Inspectors; 1857, Doc. 64—Rept. of Inspectors; 1858, Doc. 25—Rept. of Inspectors; 1858, Doc. 49—Rept. of Inspectors; 1859, Doc. 35—Rept. of Inspectors; 1859, Doc. 65—Rept. of Inspectors; 1860, Doc. 54—Rept. of Inspectors; 1860, Doc. 91—Rept. of Inspectors; 1861, Doc. 66—Rept. of Inspectors; 1862, Docs. 79 & 80—Repts. of Inspectors; 1863, Doc. 73—Rept. of Inspectors; 1863, Doc. 93—Rept. of Inspectors.

JUNK SHOPS. 1839, Doc. 13—Rept. on conditions and restrictions under which licenses should be granted, with ordinance.

LANDS, PUBLIC. 1834, Doc. 2 (City Council)—Rept. on the appointment of a supt., and the management of the lands; 1834, Doc. 9 (City Council)—Rept. on the petition of Cornelius Coolidge, to re-convey certain lands back to the city, and have an execution against him stayed; 1834, Doc. 7 (Com. Council)—Another rept. on same; 1836, Doc. 8 (Com. Council)—Rept. on the disposition of land and buildings on Leverett St., used as a Jail; 1838, Doc. 18—Rept. on the petition of Saml. Greeley and others, for a grant of land on the "Neck" for the erection of a Chapel for the "Benevolent Fraternity of Churches;" 1840, Doc. 20—Rept. on expediency of amending the ordinance, so as to make it the duty of the Supt. of Pub. Lands to take charge of the erection and repairs of all public buildings; 1843, Doc. 18—Annual rept. of Supt.; 1843, Doc. 23—Rept. of Committee on remonstrance against the sale of lands west of Pleasant St.; 1843, Doc. 23 1-2—Opinion of the City Solicitor on same; 1843, Doc. 28—Rept. on lands contiguous to Boston and Providence Railroad; 1843, Doc. 29—Rept. on the claim of the City to land occupied by the State for an arsenal; 1844, Doc. 3—Rept. on expediency of altering the present organization of the Committee on, with an ordinance; 1846, Doc. 6—An ordinance for the care and management of; 1846, Doc. 30—An ordinance for the care and management of; 1847, Doc. 10—Rept. on the situation of the public lands, particularly those east of Harrison av.; 1847, Doc. 28—An ordinance authorizing the sale of lands purchased by, or conveyed to the city for the purpose of introducing water; 1848, Doc. 46—Rept. on the mode of preparing the lands for sale; 1849, Doc. 32—Rept. respecting the grading of City lands at South Boston; 1849, Doc. 45—Rept. in relation to the estimates of the value of the lands owned by the City; 1850, Doc. 19—Rept. on the petition of Ebenezer Stevens and J. Shackford Kimball; 1850, Doc. 20—An ordinance concerning; 1850, Doc. 25—Rept. on the subject of grading the City lands between First and Fourth Sts.; 1851, Doc. 35—Rept. of Supt.; 1851, Doc. 47—Rept.,—expenditures of Committee on Public Lands; 1851, Doc. 75—Rept. of Supt.; 1852, Doc. 11—Rept. on petition of J. S. Tyler, and others, for inducements to build on land purchased of the City; 1852, Doc. 62—An ordinance in relation to; 1852, Doc. 72—Rept. of Supt.; 1853, Doc. 13—Rept. on so much of the Mayor's address as related to public lands; 1853, Doc. 32—Rept. on petition of Nathl. Hammond and others, in regard to the Jail lands; 1853, Doc. 34—Rept. of Supt.; 1853, Doc. 33—Rept. of sales and contracts; 1853, Doc. 39—Rept. on Jail lands, with Mr. Bonney's amendment; 1853, Doc. 40—Majority and minority rept. on Jail lands; 1853, Doc. 51—Communication of City Engineer, transmitting a plan of City lands in So. Boston; 1853, Doc. 52—Rept. on petition of Abbott Lawrence, and others, in relation to North Market St.; 1853, Doc. 80—Rept. on petition of C. C. Conley; 1853, Doc. 81—Rept. of Commissioners; 1853, Doc. 85—Rept. of Supt.; 1854, Doc. 29—Rept. and order respecting public lands in the City proper; 1854, Doc. 30—Rept. and order respecting sale of lands in So. Boston; 1854, Doc. 70—Rept. on Jail lands; 1854, Doc. 79—Rept. relative to purchase of Jail lands, by Rev. John McElroy; 1854, Doc. 105—An ordinance in relation to; 1854, Doc. 121—Annual rept. of Commissioners; 1854, Doc. 123—Annual rept. of Supt.; 1855, Doc. 29—An ordinance to abolish the public land commission; 1855, Doc. 70—Rept. of Supt.; 1856, Doc. 36—Reprint of No. 32, 1853, on Jail lands; 1856, Doc. 44—Rept. on petition of John B. Fitzpatrick, relative to Jail lands; 1856, Doc. 57—Rept. of Supt.; 1856, Doc. 65—An ordinance concerning; 1856, Doc. 77—Rept. of Supt.; 1857, Doc. 29—An ordinance concerning; 1857, Doc. 35—Supt's. quarterly rept.; 1857, Doc. 38—Order authorizing the City to take mortgages; 1857, Doc. 51—Rept. on certain proposals to purchase City lands; 1857, Doc. 55—Supt's. quarterly rept.; 1857, Doc. 68—Rept. of the Supt.; 1857, Doc. 74—An ordinance in relation to; 1857, Doc. 84—Rept. of Supt.; 1858, Doc. 31—Supt's. quarterly rept.; 1858, Doc. 39—Supt's. quarterly rept.; 1859, Doc. 3—Supt's. annual rept.; 1859, Doc. 25—Supt's. quarterly rept.; 1859, Doc. 44—Supt's. quarterly rept.; 1859, Doc. 55—Supt's. quarterly rept.; 1860, Doc. 3—Supt's. annual rept.; 1860, Doc. 55—Supt's. quarterly rept.; 1860, Doc. 71—New conditions of sale; 1860, Doc. 75—Supt's. quarterly rept.; 1861, Doc. 4—Annual rept. of Supt.; 1861, Doc. 23—Quarterly rept. of Supt.; 1861, Doc. 37—Quarterly rept. of Supt.; 1861, Doc. 60—Quarterly rept. of Supt.; 1862, Doc. 6—Annual rept. of Supt.; 1862, Doc. 34—Quarterly rept. of Supt.; 1862, Doc. 53—Quarterly rept. of Supt.; 1862, Doc. 74—Quarterly rept. of Supt.; 1863, Doc. 4—Annual rept. of Supt.; 1863, Doc. 28—An order concerning the land between the Providence Railroad dépôt and the Water Power Co.'s lands; 1863, Doc. 48—Quarterly rept. of the Supt.; 1863, Doc. 67—Quarterly rept. of Supt.; 1863, Doc. 87—Supt's. quarterly rept.; 1864, Doc. 12—Annual rept. of Supt.; 1864, Doc. 39—Ordinance abolishing the Board of Land Commissioners; 1864, Doc. 60—Quarterly rept. of the Supt.

LEASES. 1840, Doc. 14—Auditor's schedule of all leases of City property; 1847, Doc. 23—Auditor's schedule of leases; 1849,

Doc. 30 — Auditor's schedule of leases; 1851, Doc. 36 — Auditor's schedule of leases; 1852, Docs. 20 & 21 — Majority and minority repts. on market leases; 1852, Doc. 28 — Auditor's schedule of leases; 1853, Doc. 41 — Auditor's schedule of leases; 1854, Doc. 56 — Auditor's schedule of leases; 1855, Doc. 39 — Auditor's schedule of leases; 1856, Doc. 23 — Faneuil Hall leases; 1856, Doc. 29 — City Solicitor's opinion on Faneuil Hall leases; 1856, Doc. 40 — Auditor's schedule of leases; 1856, Doc. 41 — Faneuil Hall leases; 1856, Doc. 43 — Majority and minority repts. on Faneuil Hall leases; 1857, Doc. 56 — Auditor's schedule of leases; 1858, Doc. 32 — Auditor's schedule of leases; 1859, Doc. 34 — Auditor's schedule of leases; 1860, Doc. 66 — Auditor's schedule of leases; 1861, Doc. 29 — Auditor's schedule of leases; 1862, Doc. 57 — Auditor's schedule of leases; 1863, Doc. 58 — Auditor's schedule of leases; 1864, Doc. 52 — Auditor's schedule of leases.

Liberty Tree. 1850, Doc. 4 1-2 — Communication of Hon. David Sears relative to.

Library, Public. 1848, Doc. 15 — Act authorizing the City to establish; 1851, Doc. 51 — Communication from the Mayor transmitting to the City Council a communication from Edward Everett, and a catalogue of the books presented by him to the library; 1851, Doc. 79 — Rept. of the Committee on; 1852, Doc. 10 — Message of the Mayor relative to; 1852, Doc. 37 — Rept. of the Trustees; 1852, Doc. 57 — An ordinance in relation to; 1853, Doc. 31 — Majority and minority repts. on the subject of a new building for the use of the City Govt. and Public Library; 1853, Doc. 73 — First annual rept. of the Trustees; 1854, Doc. 21 — Rept. of Committee; 1854, Doc. 75 — Second annual rept. of the Trustees; 1854, Doc. 114 — An ordinance in relation to; 1854, Doc. 120 — An ordinance establishing a Board of Commissioners on the erection of a building for; 1855, Doc. 19 — An ordinance in addition to an ordinance relative to the erection of a building; 1855, Doc. 22 — First rept. of the Commissioners on the erection of a building; 1855, Doc. 26 — An ordinance in addition to an ordinance establishing a Board of Commissioners for the erection of a building; 1855, Doc. 57 — Third annual rept. of the Trustees; 1855, Doc. 59 — Rept. of Commissioners on the erection of a building; 1855, Doc. 60 — Proceedings on laying the corner stone; 1856, Doc. 45 — Fourth rept. of the Commissioners on the erection of a building; 1856, Doc. 61 — Fourth annual rept. of the Trustees; 1856, Doc. 69 — Fifth rept. of the Commissioners on the erection of a building; 1857, Doc. 70 — Communication from the Mayor, transmitting a memorial from the Trustees relative to a change in the ordinance; 1857, Doc. 71 — Fifth annual rept. of the Trustees; 1857, Doc. 81 — Rept. of the Committee on a modification of the ordinance in relation to; 1858, Doc. 46 — Sixth annual rept. of the Trustees; 1859, Doc. 45 — Presentation of Copley's picture of Charles I. before Parliament; 1859, Doc. 66 — Seventh annual rept. of the Trustees; 1860, Doc. 90 — Eighth annual rept. of the Trustees; 1861, Doc. 68 — Ninth annual rept. of the Trustees; 1862, Doc. 77 — Rept. on the petition of Wm. Dwight and others (non-residents) for privileges in; 1862, Doc. 85 — Tenth annual rept. of the Trustees of; 1863, Doc. 65 — An ordinance in relation to; 1863, Doc. 76 — A proposed ordinance in relation to; 1863, Doc. 97 — Eleventh annual rept. of the Trustees; 1864, Doc. 80 — Rept. on the opening on Sunday; 1864, Doc. 92 — Twelfth annual rept. of the Trustees.

Licenses. 1856, Doc. 64 — Rept. on petition of the proprietors of the Music Hall; 1861, Doc. 43 — Rept. on licenses for non-resident truckmen.

Lighters. 1852, Doc. 34 — An ordinance in relation to the weighing of; 1852, Doc. 59 — An ordinance in relation to weighing; 1853, Doc. 18 — Rept. on petition of Patrick Daley and others; 1854, Doc. 33 — An ordinance in relation to weighing and marking; 1854, Doc. 115 — An ordinance in relation to; 1860, Doc. 31 — An ordinance in relation to.

Liquors. See *Spirituous Liquors.*

Lumber. 1842, Doc. 10 — Rept. on fees received by Surveyor General of; 1847, Doc. 45 — An ordinance in addition to an ordinance regulating the survey and admeasurement of lumber brought to the city by water; 1849, Doc. 11 — Rept. and ordinance relating to the office of Surveyor General; 1853, Doc. 38 — Ordinance in relation to the survey of; 1853, Doc. 46 — Rept. on election of Surveyor General of; 1854, Doc. 99 — An ordinance in relation to; 1855, Doc. 14 — Annual rept. of Surveyor General; 1858, Doc. 22 — An ordinance in relation to the survey of; 1859, Doc. 11 — An ordinance in relation to the survey of.

Lunatic Hospital. 1839, Doc. 8 — Rept. on a system for the organization and government of the hospital lately erected at South Boston; 1839, Doc. 26 — Rept. and ordinance in relation to; 1840, Doc. 16 — First annual rept. of Superintendent; 1840, Doc. 24 — Rept. on the administration and conduct of the establishment, and on an inquiry as to the manner in which the medical duties of the other establishments in South Boston are performed; 1841, Doc. 19 — Second annual rept. of Superintendent; 1841, Doc. 26 — Rept. on alterations in the ordinance relating to, and also on the condition and expense of; 1842, Doc. 5 — Rept. of Inspectors; 1842, Doc. 16 — Rept. of Inspectors; 1842, Doc. 17 — Third annual rept. of Superintendent; 1842, Doc. 18 — Rept. of the Board of Visitors on duties of Supt., Steward, and Matron; 1842, Doc. 19 — An ordinance relating to; 1843, Doc. 2 — Rept. of Inspectors; 1843, Doc. 21 — Rept. of Inspectors; 1843, Doc. 27 — Rept. of Supt.; 1843, Doc. 32 — Rept. on employment of patients, by the erection of suitable workshops, or otherwise; 1844, Doc. 2 — Rept. of Inspectors; 1844, Doc. 19 — Rept. of Inspectors; 1844, Doc. 22 — Fifth annual rept. of Supt.; 1845, Doc. 2 — An ordinance in addition to an ordinance relating to; 1845, Doc. 3 — Rept. of Inspectors; 1845, Doc. 25 — Rept. of Inspectors; 1845, Doc. 31 — Rept. of the Supt.; 1846, Doc. 3 — Rept. of Inspectors; 1846, Doc. 24 — Rept. of Inspectors; 1846, Doc. 35 — First annual rept. of Board of Visitors, with seventh rept. of Supt.; 1847, Doc. 4 — Rept. of Inspectors; 1847, Doc. 31 — Rept. of Inspectors; 1847, Doc. 48 — Rept. of Board of Visitors and Supt.; 1848, Doc. 3 — Rept. of Inspectors; 1848, Doc. 33 — Rept. of Inspectors; 1848, Doc. 49 — Rept. of Board of Visitors and Supt.; 1849, Doc. 6 — Rept. of Inspectors; 1849, Doc. 10 — Rept. of Board of Visitors and Supt.; 1849, Doc. 40 — Rept. of Inspectors; 1849, Doc. 62 — Rept. of the Board of Visitors and Supt.; 1850, Doc. 3 — Rept. of Inspectors; 1850, Doc. 28 — Rept. of Inspectors; 1850, Doc. 48 — Rept. of Board of Visitors and Supt.; 1851, Doc. 7 — Rept. of Inspectors; 1851, Doc. 45 — An ordinance in relation to; 1851, Doc. 50 — Rept. of Inspectors; 1851, Doc. 72 — Rept. of Board of Visitors and Supt.; 1852, Doc. 3 — Rept. of Inspectors; 1852, Doc. 43 — Rept. of Inspectors; 1852, Doc. 69 — Rept. of Board of Visitors and Supt.; 1853, Doc. 11 — Rept. of Inspectors; 1853, Doc. 56 — Rept. of Inspectors; 1853, Doc. 58 — Rept. on a new Hospital; 1853, Doc. 70 — Rept. on so much of the Mayor's address as related to a new Hospital; 1853, Doc. 86 — Annual rept. of Board of Visitors and Supt.; 1854, Doc. 9 — Rept. of Inspectors; 1854, Doc. 42 — Rept. on a new Hospital; 1854, Doc. 69 — Rept. on a new Hospital; 1854, Doc. 81 — Rept. of Inspectors; 1854, Doc. 126 — Annual rept. of Board of Visitors and Supt.; 1855, Doc. 28 — Rept. of Inspectors; 1855, Doc. 50 1-2 — Rept. of Inspectors; 1855, Doc. 65 — Rept. on the expediency of placing the institutions under a Board of Commissioners; 1856, Doc. 8 — Annual rept. of Board of Visitors and Supt.; 1856, Doc. 14 — Rept. of Inspectors; 1856, Doc. 58 — Rept. of Inspectors; 1857, Doc. 33 — An act to establish a Board of Directors of public institutions; 1857, Doc. 57 — Rept. concerning the Board of Directors of public institutions; 1857, Doc. 64 — Rept. of Inspectors; 1858, Doc. 14 — Rept. of the Board of Directors; 1858, Doc. 19 — Rules and regulations; 1858, Doc. 25 — Rept. of Inspectors; 1858, Doc. 49 — Rept. of Inspectors; 1858, Doc. 55 — An ordinance in relation to the admission of patients for compensation; 1859, Doc. 32 — Annual rept. of the Board of Directors; 1859, Doc. 35 — Rept. of Inspectors; 1859, Doc. 65 — Rept. of Inspectors; 1860, Doc. 25 — Rept. of the Board of Directors; 1860, Doc. 54 — Rept. of Inspectors; 1860, Doc. 91 — Rept. of Inspectors; 1861, Doc. 15 — Rules and regulations; 1861, Doc. 20 — Annual rept. of the Board of Directors; 1861,

Doc. 52 — Rept. on the communication of John Hatton, charging the Supt. with neglect of duty; 1861, Doc. 66 — Rept. of Inspectors; 1862, Doc. 7 — Annual rept. of the Board of Directors; 1862, Doc. 40 — An ordinance establishing a Board of Directors, and defining their duties; 1862, Docs. 79 & 80 — Repts. of the Inspectors; 1862, Doc. 84 — An ordinance in relation to the Board of Directors; 1833, Doc. 11 — Memorial of the Board of Directors in relation to; 1863, Doc. 17 — Annual rept. of the Board of Directors; 1863, Doc. 73 — Rept. of Inspectors; 1863, Doc. 91 — Communication from the Board of Directors in relation to; 1863, Doc. 98 — Rept. of Inspectors; 1864, Doc. 10 — Annual rept. of the Board of Directors.

LYING-IN HOSPITAL. 1858, Doc. 20 — An order authorizing the Committee on Public Buildings to sell the estate on Springfield St.; 1858, Doc. 21 — Memorial of the Trustees respecting the disposition of their former institution on Springfield St.

MARBLE. 1854, Doc. 51 — An ordinance in relation to the survey of; 1854, Doc. 117 — An ordinance in relation to; 1862, Doc. 70 — Regulations for the survey of.

MARKETS, PUBLIC. 1848, Doc. 48 — Rept. on petition of John Albee, *et als.*, for more public markets. See *Faneuil Hall Market.*

MAYOR. 1838, Doc. 2 — Inaugural address of Samuel A. Eliot, January 1, 1838; 1839, Doc. 2 — Inaugural address of Samuel A. Eliot, January 7, 1839; 1839, Doc. 3 — Address of Samuel A. Eliot to the School Committee, January, 1839; 1840, Doc. 1 — Inaugural address of Jonathan Chapman, January 6, 1840; 1841, Doc. 2 — Inaugural address of Jonathan Chapman, January 4, 1841; 1841, Doc. 9 — Address of Jonathan Chapman to the City Council, on their first taking possession of the City Hall, School St., March 18, 1841; 1842, Doc. 1 — Inaugural address of Jonathan Chapman, January 3, 1842; 1843, Doc. 1 — Inaugural address of Martin Brimmer, January 2, 1843; 1844, Doc. 1 — Inaugural address of Martin Brimmer, January 1, 1844; 1845, Doc. 7 — Inaugural address of Thomas A. Davis, Feby. 27, 1845; 1845, Doc. 37 — Opinion of C. B. Goodrich, in regard to the powers and duties of the Board of Aldermen, on the death of the Mayor; 1845, Doc. 33 — Opinion of Richard Fletcher on the authority of the City Council to elect a Mayor *pro tempore;* 1845, Doc. 42 — Opinions of Richard Fletcher, C. P. Curtis, and C. G. Loring, concerning the powers and duties of the City Council upon the demise of the Mayor; 1845, Doc. 43 — Opinion of J. P. Rogers on the authority of the Chairman of the Board of Aldermen, in the event of the decease, inability, or absence of the Mayor; 1845, Doc. 43 1-2 — Address and proceedings at the funeral of Thomas A. Davis, Nov. 1845; 1846, Doc. 1 — Inaugural address of Josiah Quincy, Jr., January 1, 1846; 1847, Doc. 1 — Inaugural address of Josiah Quincy, Jr., Jany. 4, 1847; 1848, Doc. 1 — Inaugural address of Josiah Quincy, Jr., January 3, 1848; 1849, Doc. 1 — Inaugural address of John P. Bigelow, January 1, 1849; 1850, Doc. 1 — Inaugural address of John P. Bigelow, January 7, 1850; 1851, Doc. 1 — Inaugural address of John P. Bigelow, January 6, 1851; 1851, Doc. 80 — Address of John P. Bigelow to the Board of Aldermen on retiring from office; 1852, Doc. 1 — Inaugural address of Benjamin Seaver, January, 1852; 1853, Doc. 1 — Inaugural address of Benjamin Seaver; January 3, 1853; 1853, Doc. 92 — Address of Benjamin Seaver to the Board of Aldermen on retiring from office; 1854, Doc. 5 — Inaugural address of J. V. C. Smith, January 16, 1854; 1855, Doc. 1 — Inaugural address of J. V. C. Smith, January 1, 1855; 1856, Doc. 1 — Inaugural address of Alexander H. Rice, January 7, 1856; 1857, Doc. 1 — Inaugural address of Alexander H. Rice, January 5, 1857; 1857, Doc. 85 — Address of Alexander H. Rice to the Board of Aldermen at their final meeting in 1857; 1858, Doc. 1 — Inaugural address of Frederic W. Lincoln, Jr., January 4, 1858; 1858, Doc. 67 — Address of Frederic W. Lincoln, Jr., to the Board of Aldermen at their final meeting in 1858; 1859, Doc. 1 — Inaugural address of Frederic W. Lincoln, Jr., January 3, 1859; 1859, Doc. 79 — Address of Frederic W. Lincoln, Jr., to the Board of Aldermen at their final meeting in 1859; 1860, Doc. 1 — Inaugural address of Frederic W. Lincoln, Jr., January 2, 1860; 1860, Doc. 106 — Address of Frederic W. Lincoln, Jr., to the Board of Aldermen at their final meeting in 1860; 1861, Doc. 1 — Inaugural address of Joseph M. Wightman, January 7, 1861; 1861, Doc. 81 — Address of Joseph M. Wightman to the Board of Aldermen at their final meeting in 1861; 1862, Doc. 1 — Inaugural address of Joseph M. Wightman, January 6, 1862; 1862, Doc. 33 — An ordinance to establish the office of Clerk to the Mayor; 1862, Doc. 55 — Veto message of Joseph M. Wightman on the proposed ordinance on public institutions; 1862, Doc. 63 — Veto message of Joseph M. Wightman on the salary bill; 1862, Doc. 104 — Address of Joseph M. Wightman at the laying of the corner stone of the City Hall, Dec. 22, 1862; 1862, Doc. 105 — Address of Joseph M. Wightman to the Board of Aldermen at their final meeting in 1862; 1863, Doc. 1 — Inaugural address of Frederic W. Lincoln, Jr., January 5, 1863; 1863, Doc. 113 — Address of Frederic W. Lincoln, Jr., to the Board of Aldermen at their final meeting in 1863; 1864, Doc. 1 — Inaugural address of Frederic W. Lincoln, Jr., January 4, 1864; 1864, Doc. 100 — Address of Frederic W. Lincoln, Jr., to the Board of Aldermen at their final meeting in 1864; 1864, Doc. 101 — Remarks of F. W. Lincoln, Jr., to the School Committee, Dec. 27, 1864.

MESSENGER, CITY. 1852, Doc. 56 — An ordinance establishing office of; 1854, Doc. 113 — An ordinance in relation to.

METROPOLITAN RAILROAD. See *Street Railways.*

MIDDLESEX RAILROAD. See *Street Railways.*

MILITIA. 1863, Doc. 100 — Rept. of the Special Committee on militia organizations.

MILK. 1859, Doc. 37 — An ordinance in relation to the inspection of; 1862, Doc. 49 — Rept. of the inspector of; 1863, Doc. 49 — Rept. of the Inspector; 1864, Doc. 37 — Rept. of the Inspector.

MOUNT HOPE CEMETERY. See *Cemeteries.*

MUNICIPAL REGISTER. 1841, Doc. 1 — Rules and orders of the City Council, City Officers, ordinances, laws, etc.; 1842, Doc. 3 — Same; 1843, Doc. 3; 1844, Doc. 6; 1845, Doc. 9; 1846, Doc. 2; 1847, Doc. 3; 1848, Doc. 4; 1849, Doc. 2; 1850, Doc. 2; 1851, Doc. 2; 1852, Doc. 1 1-2; 1853, Doc. 2; 1854, Doc. 1; 1855, Doc. 2; 1856, Doc. 2; 1857, Doc. 2; 1858, Doc. 2; 1859, Doc. 2; 1860, Doc. 2; 1861, Doc. 3; 1862, Doc. 2; 1863, Doc. 2; 1864, Doc. 2.

NUISANCES. 1863, Doc. 60 — Rept. in relation to the nuisance created by Henry Sperry, in erecting buildings on the Back Bay below grade; 1863, Doc. 96 — Rept. on the petition of the Rowe's wharf corporation, in regard to the nuisance created by the emptying of the sewer into the South Dock. See *Health.*

OFFICERS, CITY. 1850, Doc. 40 — An ordinance in relation to; 1854, Doc. 100 — An ordinance in relation to; 1855, Doc. 33 — An ordinance in relation to contracts with; 1856, Doc. 12 — An ordinance in relation to; 1857, Doc. 16 — An ordinance in relation to bonds of; 1860, Doc. 61 — An ordinance in relation to bonds of.

OIL. 1863, Doc. 50 — An ordinance to regulate the storage of petroleum, earth-oil, benzole, &c.

OMNIBUSES. 1852, Doc. 42 — Communication of Chief of Police respecting omnibus routes; 1863, Doc. 57 — Rept. on the petition of J. H. Hathorne, for an extension of omnibus routes.

ORATIONS. 1837, Doc. 26 (Com. Council) — Jonathan Chapman, before the City Govt., July 4, 1837; 1838, Doc. 35 — Rev. Hubbard Winslow, July 4, 1838; 1839, Doc. 30 — Ivers J. Austin, July 4, 1839; 1840, Doc. 18 — Thomas Power, July 4, 1840; 1841, Doc. 17 — George T. Curtis, July 5, 1841; 1842, Doc. 20 — Horace Mann, July 4, 1842; 1844, Doc. 19 1-2 — Peleg W. Chandler, July 4, 1844; 1845, Doc. 23 1-2 — Charles Sumner, July 4, 1845; 1846, Doc. 23—Fletcher Webster, July 4, 1846; 1847, Doc. 29 1-2—Thos. G. Cary, July 5, 1847; 1848, Doc. 27 — Joel Giles, July 4, 1848; 1849, Doc. 37 — Wm. W. Greenough, July 5, 1849; 1850, Doc. 21 1-2 — E. P. Whipple, July 4, 1850; 1851, Doc. 47 1-2 — Chas. Theo. Russell, July 4, 1851; 1853, Doc. 55 1-2 — Timothy Bigelow, July 4, 1853; 1854, Doc. 62 1-2 — Rev. A. L. Stone, July 4, 1854; 1855, Doc. 40 1-2 — Rev. A. A. Miner, July 4, 1855; 1856, Doc. 41 1-2 — Edward G. Parker, July 4, 1856; 1858, Doc. 13 1-2 — John S. Holmes, July 5, 1858; 1859, Doc. 50 — George Sumner, July 4, 1859; 1859, Doc. 50 1-2 — Edward Everett, at the inauguration of the statue of Daniel Webster, Sept. 17, 1859; 1860, Doc. 62 — Edward Everett, July 4, 1860 — 1861, Doc. 46 — Theophilus Parsons, July 4, 1861; 1862, Doc. 59 — Geo. Ticknor Curtis, July 4, 1862; 1863, Doc. 68 — Oliver Wendell Holmes, July 4, 1863; 1863, Doc. 106 — Edward Everett, at Gettysburg, Pa., Nov. 19, 1863; 1864, Doc. 64 — Thomas Russell, July 4, 1864; 1864, Doc. 88 — Wm. R. Alger, July 4, 1857. See *Eulogies*.

ORDINANCES. 1848, Doc. 5 — Rept. on the origin and progress of the commission on the revision of the city ordinances; 1848, Doc. 16 — Rept. of Commissioners on the revision of; 1849, Doc. 58 — Rept. of Commissioners on the revision of; 1850, Doc. 36 — An ordinance in relation to the Revised Ordinances; 1850, Doc. 44 — Rept. on the revision of; 1851, Doc. 24 — Rept. concerning ordinances, &c., passed in secret session of the Board of Aldermen; 1854, Doc. 83 — Rept. on revised ordinances; 1854, Doc. 101 — An ordinance in relation to; 1863, Doc. 99 — General rept. on the revision of the ordinances, by T. C. Amory, Jr.

PARENT WASHINGTON TOTAL ABSTINENCE SOCY. 1846, Doc. 13 — Rept. on a petition for aid.

PAUPERS. 1852, Doc. 30 — Rept. concerning foreign paupers.

PAWNBROKERS. 1856, Doc. 33 — Ordinance in relation to; 1862, Doc. 45 — Ordinance in relation to; 1862, Doc. 68 — Rept. and order for the regulation of.

PHYSICIAN, CITY. 1849, Doc. 50 — First quarterly rept.; 1849, Doc. 66 — Rept. on the cholera hospital; 1853, Doc. 9 — Quarterly rept.; 1853, Doc. 68 — Quarterly rept.; 1853, Doc. 79 — Communication proposing a sanitary survey, in view of the approach of the cholera; 1855, Doc. 35 — Ordinance in relation to; 1855, Doc. 41 — Ordinance in relation to; 1856, Doc. 32 — Annual rept.; 1857, Doc. 9 — Quarterly rept.; 1858, Doc. 33 — Quarterly rept.; 1859, Doc. 9 — Annual rept.; 1860, Doc. 77 — Quarterly rept.; 1861, Doc. 14 — Communication from Dr. H. G. Clark, transmitting documents relative to the Cholera Hospital at Fort Hill, in 1854; 1863, Doc. 7 — Annual rept.; 1864, Doc. 5 — Annual rept.; 1864, Doc. 61 — Quarterly rept.

PLACARDS. 1853, Doc. 24 — Ordinance in relation to; 1854, Doc. 116 — Ordinance in relation to.

POLICE AND WATCH. 1834, Doc. 4 (Com. Council) — An ordinance prescribing the duties of the Chief Marshal; 1834, Doc. 9 (Com. Council) — Annual rept. of the City Marshal; 1837, Doc. 15 (Com. Council) — Message of the Mayor in relation to; 1840, Doc. 25 — Rept. on the subject of altering the hour of setting the watch, and also upon increasing the pay of the members; 1849, Doc. 21 — Quarterly rept. of City Marshal; 1849, Doc. 64 — Rept. of the City Marshal for the year; 1850, Doc. 43 — Rept. on watch and police departments; 1851, Doc. 5 — Annual rept. of City Marshal; 1851, Doc. 28 — Quarterly rept. of City Marshal; 1851, Doc. 48 — Quarterly rept. of City Marshal; 1851, Doc. 55 — Quarterly rept. of City Marshal; 1851, Doc. 66 — Rept. of Special Com. on Watch and Police Depts.; 1852, Doc. 5 — Annual rept. of City Marshal; 1852, Doc. 35 — Ordinance in relation to; 1852, Doc. 63 — Rept. on Watch and Police Depts.; 1853, Doc. 9 — Annual rept. of the Chief; 1853, Doc. 28 — Ordinance on the union of the Police and Watch Depts.; 1853, Doc. 42 — Ordinance providing for the organization; 1853, Doc. 47 — Rept. on organization; 1853, Doc. 78 — Ordinance; 1854, Doc. 4 — Annual rept. of the Chief; 1854, Doc. 24 — Rept. on Police and Watch Depts.; 1854, Doc. 31 — Rules and regulations; 1854, Doc. 48 — City Solicitor's opinion on the subject of police; 1854, Doc. 50 — Rept. on the pay of Police and Watch; 1854, Doc. 102 — An ordinance in relation to; 1855, Doc. 4 — Rept. of Chief, for seven months, to Jan 1, 1855, under the new organization; 1855, Doc. 31 — An ordinance in relation to the union of the Watch and Police; 1855, Doc. 73 — Annual rept. of the Chief; 1856, Doc. 52 — Quarterly rept. of the Chief; 1856, Doc. 78 — Rept. of Committee on Ordinances, on the appointment of Special Police Officers; 1857, Doc. 10 — Annual rept. of the Chief; 1858, Doc. 5 — Annual rept. of the Chief; 1858, Doc. 88 — Rept. on a uniform for; 1859, Doc. 6 — Annual rept. of the Chief; 1859, Doc. 26 — Quarterly rept. of the Chief; 1859, Doc. 43 — Quarterly rept. of the Chief; 1860, Doc. 4 — Annual rept. of the Chief; 1860, Doc. 29 — Rept. on the powers and duties of Police; 1860, Doc. 51 — Rept. on the alleged criminalities in the dept.; 1860, Doc. 58 — Rept. of the Chief; 1860, Doc. 79 — Amendments to the regulations; 1860, Doc. 93 — Rept. on a resolve of the City Council of Cambridge, relative to the conduct of the officers at the Fourth Station; 1861, Doc. 9 — Annual rept. of the Chief; 1862, Doc. 3 — Annual rept. of the Chief; 1862, Doc. 68 — Rept. on Special Police Officers, and Street Stands; 1862, Doc. 81 — Revision of the ordinance on; 1863, Doc. 6 — Annual rept. of the Chief; 1863, Doc. 14 — Argument of Thos. C. Amory, Jr., before the Committee of the Legislature, on the subject of a Metropolitan Police; 1863, Doc. 30 — Ordinance in relation to; 1864, Doc. 6 — Annual rept. of the Chief.

POOR, OVERSEERS OF. 1834, Doc. 1 (Com. Council) — Account of receipts and expenditures; 1837, Doc. 6 (Com. Council) — Mayor's communication specifying amt. of funds, investments, appropriations, &c.; 1859, Doc. 27 — Rept. on so much of the Mayor's address as related to; 1863, Doc. 15 — Rept. on the estimates of; 1863, Doc. 55 — Rept. of the Committee on the communication from; 1863, Doc. 103 — Rept. on a communication asking an appropriation for aid to the poor having no legal settlement; 1864, Doc. 21 — Rept. of the Committee on so much of the Mayor's address as related to; 1864, Doc. 55 — An ordinance relating to; 1864, Doc. 70 — Rept. on the organization of the Board; 1864, Doc. 77 — Quarterly rept.; 1864, Doc. 91 — Rept. on recommending a relief building; 1864, Doc. 95 — Rept. on a building for.

POPULATION. See *Census*.

PORT PHYSICIAN. 1841, Doc. 24 — An ordinance in addition to an ordinance to establish the office of; 1849, Doc. 27 — Rept. on the expediency of abolishing the office.

PRESIDENT OF THE UNITED STATES. 1851, Doc. 19 — Communication from, in relation to the rescue of a fugitive slave; 1851, Doc. 44 — Reply to the invitation of the city authorities to visit Boston.

PRINTING, CITY. 1846, Doc. 27 — Rept. on the petitions of George Coolidge and Bense, Morgan, & Ewer, asking to be appointed printers for the city; 1854, Doc. 103 — Ordinance in relation to; 1863, Doc. 95 — Majority and minority repts. on the petition of the city printers for increased compensation.

PRISON DISCIPLINE. 1847, Doc. 11 — Mr. George Sumner's letter to the Mayor, on the subject of Prison Discipline in France.

PROPERTY, CITY. 1859, Doc. 77 — Estimate of the value of the real estate belonging to the City of Boston, May 1, 1859.

PROVIDENT ASSOCIATION. 1857, Doc. 76 — Communication from the Mayor in relation to the memorial of; 1857, Doc. 77 — Rept. of Committee on Public Buildings on the memorial of.

QUARANTINE. 1841, Doc. 16 — Rept. on alterations necessary in the ordinance relating to Quarantine, and Rainsford Island; 1850, Doc. 27 — Communication from the consulting physicians respecting quarantine regulations; 1857, Doc. 41 — Opinion of consulting physicians on quarantine regulations.

QUINCY, JOSIAH. 1864, Doc. 59 — Proceedings of the City Council on the death of.

RAILROADS. 1855, Doc. 55 — City Solicitor's opinion in regard to assessing damages resulting from railroad locations. See *Street Railways*.

RAILROAD JUBILEE. 1851, Doc. 81 — Celebration upon the opening of railroad communication between Boston and Canada.

RAINSFORD ISLAND. 1841, Doc. 3 — Rept. on the connection of the City of Boston with, etc.; 1843, Doc. 11 — Rept. on expediency of removing hospital establishment from; 1847, Doc. 37 — Solicitor's opinion of the tenure by which the city holds possession of.

RECEIPTS. See *Auditor*.

RECRUITING. 1862, Doc. 86 — Rept. in relation to the payment of bounties; 1862, Doc. 103 — Correspondence between the Mayor and Major Rogers in relation to the quota of Boston;

1863, Doc. 89—Rept. on the organization of a Committee on recruiting; 1863, Doc. 93—Rept. on a system for recruiting.

REFORMATION, HOUSE OF—1834, Doc. 13 (City Council)—Rept. on the condition; 1834, Doc. 6 (Com. Council)—Quarterly rept. of Directors; 1834, Doc. 8 (Com. Council)—Memorial of the Directors, relative to the erection of a new edifice; 1837, Doc. 14 (Com. Council)—Receipts and expenditures; 1837, Doc. 23 (Com. Council)—Rept. of Inspectors of Prisons; 1838, Doc. 7—Communication from the Directors in relation to juvenile offenders; 1838, Doc. 8—Rept. of Directors concerning the management of; 1838, Doc. 21—Rept. of Inspectors; 1838, Doc. 32—Rept. on health, cleanliness, &c.; 1839, Doc. 4—Rept. of Inspectors; 1839, Doc. 22—Rept. of Inspectors; 1839, Doc. 28—Rept. on health, cleanliness, &c.; 1840, Doc. 2—Rept. of Inspectors; 1840, Doc. 6—Rept. of Directors on the effect of confining children of both sexes in the same building; 1840, Doc. 21—Rept. of Inspectors on; 1840, Doc. 24—Communication from Directors and Supt., in relation to performance of medical duties; 1840, Doc. 26—Rept. of Standing Committee of the Common Council on; 1841, Doc. 4—Rept. of Inspectors; 1841, Doc. 6—Reply of Board of Directors to a communication from the Mayor, in regard to the condition, &c.; 1841, Doc. 14—Rept. on the subject of sending girls to, and whether any change is expedient in the law establishing the institution; 1841, Doc. 18—Rept. of Inspectors on; 1841, Doc. 27—Rept. of the Standing Committee of the Common Council on; 1842, Doc. 5—Rept. of Inspectors; 1842, Doc. 13—Rept. of Directors; 1842, Doc. 16—Rept. of Inspectors on; 1842, Doc. 25—Communication from Moses Grant in relation to; 1843, Doc. 2—Rept. of Inspectors; 1843, Doc. 21—Rept. of Inspectors; 1844, Doc. 2—Rept. of Inspectors; 1844, Doc. 14—Rept. of Directors; 1844, Doc. 19—Rept. of Inspectors; 1845, Doc. 3—Rept. of Inspectors; 1845, Doc. 19—Rept. of Directors; 1846, Doc. 3—Rept. of Inspectors; 1846, Doc. 19—Rept. of Directors; 1846, Doc. 24—Rept. of Inspectors; 1847, Doc. 4—Rept. of Inspectors; 1847, Doc. 22—Rept. of Directors; 1847, Doc. 31—Rept. of Inspectors; 1848, Doc. 3—Rept. of Inspectors; 1848, Doc. 17—Rept. of Directors; 1848, Doc. 33—Rept. of Inspectors; 1849, Doc. 6—Rept. of Inspectors; 1849, Doc. 25—Rept. of Directors; 1849, Doc. 40—Rept. of Inspectors; 1850, Doc. 3—Rept. of Inspectors; 1850, Doc. 12—Rept. of Directors; 1850, Doc. 28—Rept. of Inspectors; 1851, Doc. 7—Rept. of Inspectors; 1851, Doc. 27—Annual rept. of Directors; 1851, Doc. 50—Rept. of Inspectors; 1852, Doc. 3—Rept. of Inspectors; 1852, Doc. 26—Rept. of Directors; 1852, Doc. 43—Rept. of Inspectors; 1853, Doc. 11—Rept. of Inspectors; 1853, Doc. 30—Rept. of Directors; 1853, Doc. 46—Rept. of Inspectors; 1854, Doc. 9—Rept. of Inspectors; 1854, Doc. 45—Rept. of Directors; 1854, Doc. 81—Rept. of Inspectors; 1855, Doc. 28—Rept. of Inspectors; 1855, Doc. 38—Rept. of Directors; 1855, Doc. 50 1-2—Rept. of Inspectors; 1855, Doc. 65—Rept. on the expediency of placing the institutions under a Board of Commissioners; 1856, Doc. 13—Income and expenditures for ten years; 1856, Doc. 14—Rept. of Inspectors; 1856, Doc. 38—Rept. of Directors; 1856, Doc. 58—Rept. of Inspectors; 1857, Doc. 33—Act to establish a Board of Directors of public institutions; 1857, Doc. 40—Rept. of Directors; 1857, Doc. 57—Rept. concerning the Board of Directors of public institutions; 1857, Doc. 64—Rept. of Inspectors; 1858, Doc. 14—Rept. of the Board of Directors; 1858, Doc. 19—Rules and regulations; 1858, Doc. 25—Rept. of Inspectors; 1858, Doc. 49—Rept. of Inspectors; 1859, Doc. 32—Annual rept. of the Board of Directors; 1859, Doc. 35—Rept. of Inspectors; 1859, Doc. 65—Rept. of Inspectors; 1860, Doc. 25—Annual rept. of the Board of Directors; 1860, Doc. 54—Rept. of Inspectors; 1860, Doc. 89—Rept. of the Committee on the rept. of the Inspectors, in regard to the management of; 1860, Doc. 91—Rept. of Inspectors; 1861, Doc. 15—Rules and regulations; 1861, Doc. 20—Annual rept. of the Board of Directors; 1861, Doc. 66—Rept. of Inspectors; 1862, Doc. 7—Annual rept. of the Board of Directors; 1862, Doc. 40—An ordinance establishing a Board of Directors, and defining their duties; 1862, Docs. 79 & 80—Repts. of the Inspectors; 1862, Doc. 84—Ordinance in relation to the Directors; 1863, Doc. 17—Annual rept. of the Board of Directors; 1863, Doc. 73—Rept. of Inspectors; 1863, Doc. 98—Rept. of Inspectors; 1864, Doc. 10—Annual rept. of the Board of Directors; 1864, Doc. 35—Rept. of Special Committee on alleged abuses; 1864, Doc. 66—Rept. on amended rules.

REGISTER. See *Municipal Register*.

REGISTRAR, CITY. 1849, Doc. 33—Ordinance providing for the appointment of; 1850, Doc. 4—Rept. of births, deaths, and marriages, for the year 1849; 1851, Doc. 8—Quarterly rept; 1851, Doc. 10—Annual rept. for 1850; 1852, Doc. 7—Annual rept. for 1851; 1853, Doc. 10—Annual rept. for 1852; 1854, Doc. 12—Annual rept. for 1853; 1854, Doc. 106—Ordinance in relation to; 1855, Doc. 10—Annual rept. for 1854; 1856, Doc. 10—Annual rept. for 1855; 1857, Doc. 14—Annual rept. for 1856; 1858, Doc. 9—Annual rept. for 1857; 1859, Doc. 13—Annual rept. for 1858; 1860, Doc. 85—Annual rept. for 1859; 1863, Doc. 34—Annual rept. for 1862; 1864, Doc. 47—Annual rept. for 1863.

RIOTS. 1834, Doc. 11 (Com. Council)—Rept. on the destruction of the Ursuline Convent at Charlestown, Aug. 11, 1834; 1837, Doc. 12 (Com. Council)—Rept. on the riot in Broad St. on Sunday, June 11, 1837; 1863, Doc. 75—Mayor's communication in relation to the riot caused by the draft for the volunteer forces, July 14, 1863.

RUSSIA. 1864, Doc. 58—Speeches at the banquet in honor of the officers of the Russian Fleet.

SALARIES. 1834, Doc. 5 (Com. Council)—Rept. on salaries for City and County Officers; 1835, Doc. 9 (Com. Council); 1836, Doc. 4 (Com. Council); 1838, Doc. 13; 1839, Doc. 18; 1840, Doc. 11; 1841, Doc. 10; 1842, Doc. 8; 1843, Doc. 14; 1844, Doc. 13; 1845, Doc. 14; 1846, Doc. 12—Repts. on same; 1846, Doc. 17—Rept. on expediency of paying members of the Board of Aldermen a salary; 1846, Doc. 31—Rept. on same; 1847, Doc. 12—Rept. on salaries for City and County Officers; 1847, Doc. 16—Comparative statement of salaries paid by the city for the years 1835-36-40-41-42-43-45-46, and amounts proposed to be paid in 1847; 1848, Doc. 13—Rept. on salaries for City and County Officers; 1849, Doc. 15; 1850, Doc. 9; 1851, Doc. 15—Repts. on same: 1851, Doc. 30—Rept. on salaries of resident and non-resident teachers; 1851, Doc. 56—Salaries of City and County Officers; 1851, Doc. 59—Rept. on salaries of Asst. Teachers of Grammar Schools; 1852, Doc. 60—Rept. on salaries for City and County Officers; 1853, Doc. 33—Rept. on same; 1853, Doc. 54—Salaries of School Teachers; 1853, Doc. 71—Revised salary bill; 1853, Doc. 77—Rept. on salaries of Primary School Teachers; 1854, Doc. 22—Rept. on salaries for City and County Officers; 1855, Doc. 47; 1856, Doc. 39—Repts. on same; 1856, Doc. 51—Salaries of City and County Officers, as passed July 3; 1856, Doc. 53—Salaries of the masters of the Latin, English, High, and Girls' High and Normal Schools; 1857, Doc. 58—Salaries of City and County Officers, as passed; 1857, Doc. 61—Rept. on the salaries of teachers of the Public Schools; 1858, Doc. 10—Rept. on salaries for City and County Officers; 1858, Doc. 27—Salaries of City and County Officers, as revised; 1859, Doc. 24—Rept. on salaries for City and County Officers; 1859, Doc. 46—Salaries of City and County Officers, as revised; 1860, Doc. 39—Rept. on salaries for City and County Officers; 1860, Doc. 64—Salaries of City and County Officers as revised; 1860, Doc. 95—Rept. on the salaries of teachers of sewing in the schools; 1861, Doc. 26—Rept. on salaries for City and County Officers; 1861, Doc. 31—Salaries of City and Port Physicians; 1861, Doc. 51—Salaries of Officers of Institutions; 1862, Doc. 27—Rept. on salaries for City and County Officers; 1862, Doc. 30—Rept. on firemen's pay at East and South Boston; 1862, Doc. 63—Mayor's veto on salary bill; 1863, Doc. 24—Rept. on salaries for City and County Officers; 1863, Doc. 105—Rept. on salaries of School Teachers; 1863, Doc. 109—Salary bill as revised by the City Council; 1864, Doc. 41—Rept.

on salaries for City and County Officers; 1864, Doc. 86 — Salary bill as revised by the City Council.

SCHOOL FOR ADULTS. 1851, Doc. 17 — Rept. on petition of F. T. Gray, and others, in regard to Adult Schools.

SCHOOL, CHARITY. 1853, Doc. 43 — Rept. of Committee on the communication of Samuel Eliot, in regard to the Charity School established in Channing St.

SCHOOL DISTRICTS. 1859, Doc. 31 — Boundaries of the Winthrop, Franklin, Dwight, Brimmer, and Boylston districts.

SCHOOLHOUSES. 1837, Doc. 13 (Com. Council) — Rept. on the erection of a new house for the accommodation of the northern wards; 1843, Doc. 12 — Rept. on the erection of one or more schoolhouses; 1844, Doc. 12 — Communication from the Mayor enclosing a rept. and resolves of the School Committee, relative to the erection of two new schoolhouses; 1842, Doc. 12 — Votes of Committee on Public Buildings, and rept. on condition of out-buildings and use of yards; 1846, Doc. 36 — Rept. relative to cost of land, &c., for the Hancock and Adams Schoolhouses; 1847, Doc. 6 — Rept. on the subject of ventilation of the schoolhouses of the city; 1847, Doc. 7 — Rept. of Primary School Committee on the same subject; 1847, Doc. 9 — Rept. on the expediency of erecting a new schoolhouse upon, or in the immediate vicinity of, South Cove; 1847, Doc. 46 — Rept. relating to the ventilation of schoolhouses; 1847, Doc. 47 — Rept. relative to the closing of one of the furnaces of the Mayhew School; 1850, Doc. 17 — Rept. of the City Auditor, showing the cost of the Grammar and Primary Schoolhouses, and the land occupied by them; 1851, Doc. 39 — Rept. on expenses of warming and ventilating schoolhouses; 1851, Doc. 69 — Rept. on vacant seats in the schoolhouses; 1854, Doc. 41 — Rept. and order for new schoolhouses at South Boston; 1854, Doc. 72 — Rept. of facts relative to the purchase of a schoolhouse in East Boston; 1854, Doc. 118 — Rept. on the subject of the purchase of a new lot in East Boston for a schoolhouse; 1854, Doc. 125 — Majority rept. on the purchase of a lot for a schoolhouse in East Boston; 1855, Doc. 23 — Rept. by Messrs. Woodman & Porter on the East Boston Schoolhouse; 1855, Doc. 24 — Rept. by Messrs. Hinks & Chipman on same; 1855, Doc. 25 — Rept. by Ald. Woodberry on same; 1856, Doc. 74 — Rept. on the Adams Schoolhouse; 1859, Doc. 52 — Rept. in favor of the new Phillips Schoolhouse; 1861, Doc. 13 — Rept. of the Committee on Public Instruction, on plans of Primary Schoolhouses.

SCHOOL, NAUTICAL. 1861, Doc. 33 — Rept. of the Committee on Public Instruction, on the memorial of R. B. Forbes, for the establishment of a Nautical School.

SCHOOLS, PUBLIC. 1836, Doc. 1 (Com. Council) — Rept. on the petition of Saml. Prince and others, for the establishment of a High School for girls; 1836, Doc. 9 (Com. Council) — Rules and regulations; 1837, Doc. 19 (Com. Council) — Rept. on the memorial of the Boston Academy of Music and many citizens, for the introduction of music into the public schools; 1837, Doc. 22 (Com. Council) — Semi-annual rept. on the condition of the Primary Schools; 1838, Doc. 3 — Majority and minority repts. on petitions relative to changes in the distribution of scholars in several of the city schools; 1838, Doc. 6 — Rules of the School Committee; 1838, Doc. 10 — Rept. on the expediency of instituting and requiring semi-annual meetings of the teachers, and examinations of the primary schools; 1838, Doc. 15 — Rules and regulations; 1838, Doc. 19 — Rept. on an order authorizing the Committee to admit any child over seven years of age to the primary schools; 1838, Doc. 22 — Rept. on establishing a model primary school; 1838, Doc. 23 — Rept. on the location, general superintendence, and course of studies pursued in the several schools; 1838, Doc. 29 — Rept. on the erection of a school building on Fort Hill; 1838, Doc. 30 — Rept. on the annual distribution of medals; 1839, Doc. 3 — Address of the Mayor — Samuel A. Eliot — to the School Committee; 1839, Doc. 7 — Rept. on the origin of the Primary Schools, and the authority of the Committee; 1839, Doc. 11 — Rules and regulations; 1841, Doc. 21 — Extracts from the repts. of the Committee appointed to make the annual examinations of the public schools; 1841, Doc. 22 — Rules and regulations; 1843, Doc. 13 — Rept. on the organization of the Primary Schools; 1844, Doc. 18 — Rept. of the School Committee on the semi-annual returns from masters of the Grammar and Writing Schools; 1844, Doc. 27 — Rules and regulations; 1845, Doc. 5 — Rept. on a petition respecting the Wells's School; 1845, Doc. 26 — Rept. of the Visiting Committees on the Public Schools; 1846, Doc. 4 — Rept. relative to the best manner of carrying into effect the requisitions of law, concerning the examination of teachers; 1846, Doc. 7 — Amendments to the law concerning the examination of teachers; 1846, Doc. 8 — Rept. on the appointment of a Supt. of Grammar Schools; 1846, Doc. 23 — Rept. on the petition of colored people, for the abolition of the school for colored children, with the opinion of the City Solicitor; 1846, Doc. 28 — Rept. of the Visiting Committee on the Public Schools; 1846, Doc. 38 — Orders relative to the Primary Schools, with extracts from the rept. of the Standing Committee; 1847, Doc. 7 — Rept. of the Primary School Committee, on the subject of ventilation; 1847, Doc. 14 — Rept. on the subject of establishing the office of Supt. of Public Schools; 1847, Doc. 20 — Rept. on the subject of medals to Grammar Scholars; 1847, Doc. 21 — Rept. on books to be used in the Public Schools during the ensuing year; 1847, Doc. 25 — Rept. on supplying philosophical apparatus for the use of the schools; 1847, Doc. 32 — Rept. on the expediency of establishing another Grammar and Writing School in South Boston; 1847, Doc. 33 — Rept. on measures to enable the School Committee to discharge their duties more effectually; 1847, Doc. 35 — Rept. on an order to consider what changes, if any, can be advantageously made in the system of instruction in the schools, in order to avoid any neglect of the lower classes by the head masters; 1847, Doc. 38 — Rept. on the expediency of recommending the City Council to furnish, at the city's expense, the text-books and implements of instruction used in the Common and Primary Schools; 1847, Doc. 40 — Rept. of the sub-Committee to make the annual examination of the Grammar dept. of the Grammar and Writing Schools; 1847, Doc. 41 — Resolve and order for an Executive Committee of three, for the general supervision of Public Schools; 1848, Doc. 2 — Orders offered in the School Committee relating to Public Schools; 1848, Doc. 6 — Rept. on rules and regulations of the Public Schools; 1848, Doc. 7 — Rept. on instruction in music in the Public Schools; 1848, Doc. 20 — Rept. on the expediency of establishing a High School for girls; 1848, Doc. 23 — Rept. on the expediency of restoring the city medals to the girls' school, and of introducing a system of prizes for the encouragement of pupils in all the classes in the Grammar Schools; 1848, Doc. 25 — Rept. of the Committee on the establishment of a High School for girls; 1848, Doc. 31 — Rept. of the annual examination of the Public Schools; 1848, Doc. 31 — Rept. of the annual examination of the Public Schools; 1848, Doc. 40 — Rept. of a sub-Committee on vacations; 1848, Doc. 41 — Rept. of a sub-Committee on the subject of the admission of pupils; 1849, Doc. 7 — City Solicitor's opinion on the mode of appointing the Primary School Committee; 1849, Doc. 13 — Rept. of the Committee on the High School for girls; 1849, Doc. 14 — Rept. on the memorial of John Green, Jr., *et als.*, relative to the requisite qualifications for membership of the School Committee; 1849, Doc. 39 — Rept. of the annual examination of the Public Schools; 1849, Doc. 42 — Rept. on the petition of colored persons for the abolition of the Smith (colored) School; 1849, Doc. 49 — Rules and regulations; 1849, Doc. 55 — Rept. on the boundaries of the several Grammar School sections; 1850, Doc. 15 — Quarterly rept. of the Executive Committee on Primary Schools; 1850, Doc. 35 — Rept. on so much of the Mayor's address as related to the organization of a Primary School Board; 1850, Doc. 38 — Rept. of the annual examination of the Public Schools; 1850, Doc. 46 — Opinion of the City Solicitor concerning the right of children to attend the Public Schools, whose parents are not citizens of Boston; 1850, Doc. 50 — Rept. of a joint Special Committee upon the expediency of establishing the office of Supt. of Schools; 1851, Doc

4—Rules and regulations; 1851, Doc. 16—Rept. on the appointment of a Supt. of Public Schools; 1851, Doc. 23—Rept. on the appointment of a Supt. of Public Schools, with resolutions prescribing his duties; 1851, Doc. 52—Annual rept. of the examination of the Public Schools; 1851, Doc. 57—Rept. on a revised course of studies for the Grammar Schools; 1851, Doc. 64—Rept. on Phonetic instruction in the Primary Schools; 1851, Doc. 67—Rept. on a revised course of studies for the Grammar Schools; 1851, Doc. 68—Minority rept. on a revised course of studies for the Grammar Schools; 1851, Doc. 73—First semi-annual rept. of the Supt. of Public Schools; 1852, Doc. 4—Communication from the Mayor, upon the organization of the Grammar and Primary School Committees; 1852, Doc. 9—Rept. on the classification and consolidation of the Public Schools; 1852, Doc. 16—Rules and regulations; 1852, Doc. 22—Rept. of the Committee on Public Instruction, on the present organization of the Grammar and Primary School Committees; 1852, Doc. 27—Rept. on the consolidation of Grammar Schools; 1852, Doc. 32—Rept. of a Special Committee on Normal Schools; 1852, Doc. 40—Rept. of a sub-Committee on a plan for organizing a Normal School; 1852, Doc. 47—Semi-annual rept. of the Executive Committee on Primary Schools; 1852, Doc. 50—Rept. on the annual examination of the Public Schools; 1852, Doc. 73—Second annual rept. of the Supt. of Public Schools; 1853, Doc. 12—Rules and regulations; 1853, Doc. 19—Annual rept. of the Executive Committee on Primary Schools; 1853, Doc. 48—Rept. on the consolidation of the Franklin, Johnson, and Winthrop Grammar Schools; 1853, Doc. 62—Semi-annual rept. of the Executive Committee on Primary Schools; 1853, Doc. 65—Rept. on the annual examination of the Public Schools; 1853, Doc. 89—Rept. on the High School for girls; 1853, Doc. 91—Third annual rept. of the Supt. of Public Schools; 1854, Doc. 14—Rules and regulations; 1854, Doc. 32—Annual rept. of the Executive Committee on Primary Schools; 1854, Doc. 43—Rept. on a High School for girls; 1854, Doc. 44—Rept. on a High School for girls (second plan); 1854, Doc. 54—Rept. on the case of a child excluded from one of the Public Schools; 1854, Doc. 61—Semi-annual rept. of the Executive Committee on Primary Schools; 1854, Doc. 74—Rept. of the annual examination of the Public Schools; 1854, Doc. 80—Rept. on the High School for girls; 1855, Doc. 8—Rules and regulations; 1855, Doc. 61—Annual repts. of the Committee and Supt. of Public Schools; 1855, Doc. 66—Rept. on additional male teachers in the Grammar Schools for boys; 1855, Doc. 67—Rept. on High School instruction for girls; 1855, Doc. 71—Action of the School Committee in relation to the children of non-residents; 1856, Doc. 37—Rules and regulations; 1856, Doc. 55—Rept. of the School Committee on text-books; 1856, Doc. 72—Annual repts. of the Committee and Supt. of Public Schools; 1857, Doc. 18—Rules and regulations; 1857, Doc. 43—Rept. on the supervision of Schools for special instruction; 1857, Doc. 44—Rept. on music; 1857, Doc. 45—Rept. of a Special Committee on the rept. of the Supt. of Public Schools; 1857, Doc. 49—Rept. on the attendance of destitute children at school; 1857, Doc. 52—Rept. on an order to pay the expenses of a substitute during the sickness of a teacher; 1857, Doc. 63—Rept. on the communication of Rev. C. F. Barnard, in regard to study out of school hours; 1858, Doc. 11—Annual repts. of the Committee and Supt. of Public Schools; 1858, Doc. 17—Rules and regulations; 1858, Doc. 30—Rept. of the Committee on text-books; 1858, Doc. 34—Rept. on music; 1859, Doc. 23—Annual repts. of the Committee and Supt. of Public Schools; 1860, Doc. 9—Annual repts. of the Committee and Supt. of Public Schools; 1860, Doc. 38—Rules and regulations; 1860, Doc. 86—Annual repts. of the Committee and Supt. of Public Schools; 1860, Doc. 94—Rept. on physical training; 1860, Doc. 96—Rept. on the free passage of children across the East Boston Ferries; 1861, Doc. 33—Rept. on additional accommodations for the Girls' High and Normal School; 1861, Doc. 74—Annual repts. of the Committee and Supt. of Public Schools; 1862, Doc. 67—Rept. on the examination of teachers; 1863, Doc. 31—Rept. on annual exhibitions; 1863, Doc. 52—Rules and regulations; 1863, Doc. 54—Annual repts. of the Committee and Supt. of Public Schools; 1863, Doc. 59—Annual rept. of the Committee on text-books; 1863, Doc. 101—Rept. on instruction in military drill; 1864, Doc. 50—Annual repts. of the Committee and Supt. of Public Schools; 1864, Doc. 56—Rept. on music; 1864, Doc. 71—Rept. on rules and regulations; 1864, Doc. 93—Rept. on gymnastics and military drill; 1864, Doc. 94—Rept. on corporal punishment.

SEALERS OF WEIGHTS AND MEASURES. 1863, Doc. 64—An ordinance in relation to; 1864, Doc. 62—Annual rept. of the Sealer for the Northern District; 1864, Doc. 63—Annual rept. of the Sealer for the Southern District.

SEA WALLS. 1845, Doc. 35—Rept. on expediency of erecting a wall parallel with Harrison avenue.

SECOND-HAND ARTICLES. 1854, Doc. 107—Ordinance in relation to; 1862, Doc. 46—Ordinance in relation to dealers in; 1863, Doc. 12—Ordinance in relation to dealers in.

SEWERS. 1834, Doc. 1 (City Council)—Rept. on the ordinance relative to constructing, repairing, assessing, and collecting dues for; 1837, Doc. 10 (Com. Council)—Rept. on assessing and collecting dues for; 1838, Doc. 12—Rept. on petition of Wm. Foster, and others, for alteration in the ordinance relating to; 1840, Doc. 15—Communication of City Solicitor, and opinion of Sup. Jud. Court, in case of Shaw, *et als.;* 1841, Doc. 12—Rept. on alterations necessary in the ordinance relating to; 1841, Doc. 15—Rept. on, accompanied by an ordinance; 1844, Doc. 8—Rept. of Committee of Aldermen on, with an ordinance; 1857, Doc. 47—Rept. on drainage in Dover St.; 1857, Doc. 73—An ordinance in relation to; 1858, Doc. 23—An ordinance in relation to; 1858, Doc. 50—Rept. of the Committee on; 1858, Doc. 63—Rept. on drainage near Northampton St.; 1858, Doc. 64—Rept. on drainage of Dover St.; 1860, Doc. 11—Annual rept. of Supt.; 1860, Doc. 50—Rept. of City Engineer on sewerage of the Back Bay; 1861, Doc. 11—Annual rept. of Supt.; 1862, Doc. 12—Annual rept. of Supt.; 1862, Doc. 38—Opinion of the Supreme Court in the case of D. W. Child *vs.* City of Boston, for damages caused by the flooding of his house, in Dover St., with water from the Common sewer; 1862, Doc. 62—An ordinance in relation to; 1863, Doc. 13—Annual rept. of Supt.; 1864, Doc. 11—Annual rept. of Supt.; 1864, Doc. 46—Rept. on sewerage at the south end.

SIDEWALKS. 1849, Doc. 20—City Solicitor's communication concerning cellar doors, and defects in sidewalks; 1853, Doc. 90—Rept. on petition of T. C. Leeds, respecting Pearl St. sidewalks. See *Streets.*

SLAVERY. 1851, Doc. 19—Communication from the President of the United States, in relation to the rescue of a fugitive slave.

SMALLPOX. 1837, Doc. 1 (City Council)—Rept. on expediency of establishing another hospital for persons affected with smallpox; 1856, Doc. 30—Memorial of Lemuel Shattuck, in relation to the smallpox; 1861, Doc. 14—Dr. Cheever's rept. on the smallpox hospital established in Albany St., in 1859-60.

SOAPSTONE. 1862, Doc. 70—Regulations for the survey of.

SOLDIERS, AID TO FAMILIES OF. 1861, Doc. 82—First rept. of the joint Special Committee on the fund for soldiers' families; 1861, Doc. 56—Second rept. of the Committee on same; 1861, Doc. 76—Third rept. of the Committee on same; 1863, Doc. 19—Rules and regulations of the Committee; 1864, Doc. 7—Rules and regulations of the Committee.

SOLDIERS, DONATIONS TO. 1862, Doc. 99—Rept. of the Committee on, and rept. of Mrs. H. G. Otis, on the Evans House; 1864, Doc. 51—Rept. of Mrs. H. G. Otis.

SOLICITOR, CITY. 1835, Doc. 6 (Com. Council)—Opinions of John Pickering on certain questions propounded to him by the Committee of the Common Council on Elections; 1835, Doc. 12—Opinion of John Pickering on the legalty of adjourning ward meetings for the election of City Officers; 1837, Doc. 3 (City Council)—Opinion of John Pickering and C. P. Curtis, on the authority of the city to issue certificates for fractional

parts of a dollar; 1837, Doc. 2 (Com. Council) — Two opinions of John Pickering relative to elections; 1838, Doc. 4 — Opinion of John Pickering on the authority of the city to introduce pure water; 1838, Doc. 7 — Opinion of John Pickering on the power to confine minors in the house of reformation, who have not been convicted before a judicial tribunal, and the authority to tax citizens for their support; 1838, Doc. 12 — Opinion of John Pickering on the power to lay common sewers, and assess the expense on all persons entering their private drains into the same; 1838, Doc. 29 — Opinion of John Pickering on the rights of the city to the lands on Fort Hill; 1839, Doc. 20 — Rept. on the expediency of making any alteration in the ordinance providing for the appointment, and prescribing the duties of an Attorney and Solicitor for the city, with draft of an ordinance; 1840, Doc. 15 — Communication from John Pickering upon transmitting the decision of the Supreme Court on the subject of Common Sewers, and the liability of the owners of real estate to contribute to the expenses of the same; 1843, Doc. 4 — Two opinions of John Pickering relative to elections; 1843, Doc. 23 1-2 — Opinion of John Pickering on the power of the City Council to sell any part of the public lands west of Pleasant St. and south of Boylston St.; 1844, Doc. 16 — Opinion of John Pickering on the question whether the third section of the third chapter of the Revised Statutes, relative to the qualification of voters, applies to the City of Boston; 1846, Doc. 11 — Rept. on the amount of money paid for legal services rendered the city since January, 1843; 1846, Doc. 16 — An ordinance providing for the appointment of a City Solicitor, and prescribing his duties; 1846, Doc. 23 — Opinion of P. W. Chandler upon the right of the School Committee of Boston to establish and maintain special Primary Schools for colored children; 1847, Doc. 37 — Statement of P. W. Chandler in regard to the tenure by which the city holds possession of Rainsford Island; 1848, Doc. 8 — Opinion of P. W. Chandler on the question, "Is the duty of providing a suitable jail for the County of Suffolk imposed by law upon the City Council, or upon the Board of Mayor and Aldermen, exclusively;" 1848, Doc. 35 — Opinion of P. W. Chandler on the question, "Does the City Charter confer upon the City Council any power to give annuities or direct donations in money from the City Treasury;" 1848, Doc. 45 — Opinion of P. W. Chandler on the power of the Water Commissioners to establish the water rates; 1849, Doc. 7 — Communication from P. W. Chandler, transmitting the opinion of John Pickering on the mode of appointing the Primary School Committee; 1849, Doc. 20 — Communication from P. W. Chandler, in regard to the decision of the Sup. Jud. Court on an action for damages for an alleged defect in a sidewalk; 1850, Doc. 13 — Opinion of P. W. Chandler upon the request of the Children's Friend Society, for the use of water without charge; 1850, Doc. 46 — Opinion of P. W. Chandler on the right of children, whose parents are not citizens of Boston, to attend school; 1851, Doc. 33 — Opinion of P. W. Chandler in regard to the control of Faneuil Hall; 1852, Doc. 33 — Communication from P. W. Chandler in relation to the outer harbor of Boston; 1852, Doc. 61 — Rept. of P. W. Chandler on the petition of B. F. Cook, *et al.*, on the election returns; 1853, Doc. 3 — Opinion of P. W. Chandler relative to the contested election in Ward 3; 1853, Doc. 8 — Opinion of P. W. Chandler relative to the elections in Wards 1, 3, and 11; 1853, Doc. 17 1-2 — Rept. in the case of E. A. Bourne *vs.* the City of Boston, with the argument of P. W. Chandler for the city; 1853, Doc. 27 — Opinion of P. W. Chandler relative to the expenditure of moneys raised by taxation; 1854, Doc. 48 — Opinion of Geo. S. Hillard on the power of the Common Council in police matters; 1854, Doc. 66 — Opinion of Geo. S. Hillard on the power of the Directors of the House of Correction to make contracts in regard to convict labor; 1855, Doc. 44 — Opinion of Geo. S. Hillard on proposed alterations in the Market House; 1855, Doc. 53 — Opinion of A. A. Ranney on the authority of the General Court to establish a Court for the County of Suffolk, and impose upon the City of Boston, by taxation, the exclusive cost of its maintenance: 1855, Doc. 54 — Communication from A. A. Ranney respecting the right of the East Boston Free Bridge Corporation; 1855, Doc. 55 — Opinion of A. A. Ranney, relative to damages by a railroad location; 1855, Doc. 71 — Opinion of A. A. Ranney on the action of the School Committee in relation to the children of non-residents; 1856, Doc. 7 — Synopsis of payments from 1851 to 1855 for legal services; 1858, Doc. 28 — Opinion of J. P. Healy upon certain questions relative to the East Boston Ferries; 1858, Doc. 38 — Opinion of J. P. Healy on the question, "whether the Common Council have any control over the matter of uniform for the police"; 1858, Doc. 41 — Opinion of J. P. Healy relative to the interpretation of the word "district," in the third article of the amendments to the constitution; 1859, Doc. 21 — Opinion of J. P. Healy in relation to Horse Railroads through the streets; 1860, Doc. 9 — Opinions of J. P. Healy, furnished under orders of the School Committee, printed in the appendix to the annual rept. of the Committee, p. 161; 1860, Doc. 53 — Rept. of the Committee on ordinances, on the expediency of reorganizing the law department of the City Govt.; 1861, Doc. 73 — Opinion of J. P. Healy in regard to private rights affected by the construction of the "Eastern Avenue;" 1862, Doc. 24 — Opinion of J. P. Healy on the authority to exempt from taxation the property left by Abbott Lawrence to be invested in model lodging houses; 1862, Doc. 52 — Opinion of J. P. Healy upon the abatement of taxes assessed upon the Massachusetts Grand Lodge; 1862, Doc. 82 — Opinion of J. P. Healy relative to the proposed "Eastern Avenue;" 1863, Doc. 47 — Opinion of J. P. Healy on the petition of the Massachusetts General Hospital, for the use of Cochituate water at reduced rates; 1863, Doc. 103 — Opinion of J. P. Healy on the rights of the Overseers of the Poor in Boston, in the expenditure of money appropriated by the city.

SOUTH BAY LANDS. 1853, Doc. 35 — Rept. of the Committee, and rept. of the Commissioners on; 1853, Doc. 44 — Rept. of estimated cost of filling; 1854, Doc. 49 — Rept. on so much of the Mayor's address as related to; 1854, Doc. 77 — Rept. of Land Commissioners respecting; 1857, Doc. 82 — Rept. of Joint Special Committee on; 1858, Doc. 26 — Rept. concerning expenses of; 1859, Doc. 47 — Rept. in favor of changing the Evans' contract for filling; 1859, Doc. 51 — Rept. of Committee with the new Evans' contract for filling; 1862, Doc. 50 — Rept. on the purchase of the "ox bow;" 1862, Doc. 78 — Rept. on the contract of Wm. Evans for filling.

SPIRITUOUS LIQUORS. 1842, Doc. 4 — Rept. on so much of Mayor's address as related to laws regulating the sale of spirituous liquors; 1849, Doc. 16 — Rept. on so much of the Mayor's address as related to; 1851, Doc. 58 — Rept. of City Marshal on places where sold; 1852, Doc. 41 — Rept. on the petition of Henry Plympton and others; 1853, Doc. 57 — Majority and minority repts. on petition of Lyman Beecher and others; 1854, Doc. 18 — Majority and minority repts. on so much of the Mayor's address as related to the execution of the laws: 1855, Doc. 40 — Preamble and resolutions in relation to the enforcement of the law against the sale of.

STABLES. 1851, Doc. 41 — Acceptance of the act relating to stables; 1853, Doc. 69 — Rept. of Committee on; 1858, Doc. 36 — Rept. on proposed removal of city stables to South Bay lands; 1858, Doc. 51 — Rept. on the removal of the city stables; 1861, Doc. 36 — Rept. on papers of the City Council of 1860, concerning the construction of the city stables; 1862, Doc. 101 — Rept. of the Committee on Internal Health on the city stables.

STATUES. 1859, Doc. 50 1-2 — Proceedings at the inauguration of the statue of Daniel Webster; 1859, Doc. 63 — Rept. on the expediency of aiding in the erection of an equestrian statue of Washington.

STEAM ENGINES. 1845, Doc. 17 — An act regulating the use of, and resolution adopting the same; 1853, Doc. 67 — Rept. on the remonstrance against the erection of a steam planing mill on the corner of Cambridge and Charles Sts.

STREETS. 1834, Doc. 3 (Com. Council) — Orders laying out and widening certain streets; 1835, Doc. 16 (Com. Council) — Ordinance in relation to obstruction of, by carts, carriages, or other vehicles; 1838, Doc. 27—Rept. with ordinance; 1838, Doc. 31—Ordinance in addition to an ordinance in relation to; 1839, Doc. 27—Rept. on damages for laying out and widening; 1840, Doc. 5—Rept. on making application to the legislature for an alteration of the City Charter in relation to, etc.; 1843, Doc. 10—Rept. and ordinance relative to paving and repairs; 1843, Doc. 16—Rept. and ordinance in relation to; 1843, Doc. 19—Rept. on widening Fleet St.; 1844, Doc. 7—Ordinance to prevent obstructions in; 1844, Doc. 10—Rept. of joint Committee on subject of providing by ordinance for the prevention of obstructions; 1844, Doc. 15—Ordinance in relation to obstructions; 1844, Doc. 20—Rept. on city's rights to streets, lanes, alleys, squares, and other public places in Ward 12; 1844, Doc. 21—Rept. on a petition for an alteration in the ordinance relating to obstructions, with an ordinance; 1844, Doc. 28—Order for the City Marshal to notify certain persons that they have encroached upon streets in South Boston; 1845, Doc. 6—Rept. on a petition on the subject of unaccepted streets; 1845, Doc. 8—Ordinance prohibiting coasting in; 1845, Doc. 11—Rept. of joint Special Committee on unaccepted streets; 1845, Doc. 21—An ordinance for the regulation of horses and carriages in; 1845, Doc. 28—Rept. on widening Richmond Street; 1845, Doc. 30—An ordinance for the regulation of horses and carriages in; 1846, Doc. 10—Schedule of sums expended for widening and extending, from 1822 to 1846; 1846, Doc. 29—Statement of amounts paid for widening Richmond and Fleet streets; 1847, Doc. 24—An act to prevent obstructions in the streets, and to regulate coaches and other vehicles; 1847, Doc. 42—Rept. of Commissioners appointed to ascertain and fix the grades of streets and highways at South Boston; 1848, Doc. 11—An ordinance concerning injurious practices in the streets; 1848, Doc. 19—An act to prevent obstructions in the streets; 1848, Doc. 21—An act to prevent unlawful and injurious practices in the streets; 1849, Doc. 44—An order concerning obstructions in the streets, and to regulate coaches, &c.; 1849, Doc. 60—Rept. on the petition that O St. be laid out according to a plan of South Boston, by Mather Withington; 1850, Doc. 11—Rept. on a petition for laying out a new street opposite Florence St.; 1850, Doc. 30—An ordinance in relation to streets; 1850, Doc. 34—W. P. Parrott's communication on the grade of streets south of Dover, and west of Suffolk; 1851, Doc. 6—Quarterly rept. of Supt.; 1851, Doc. 29—Quarterly rept. of Supt.; 1851, Doc. 77—Rept. on the subject of a railroad track along the marginal streets; 1852, Doc. 2—Rept. of Supt. on expenditures; 1852, Doc. 38—Rept. concerning the widening of Exchange St.; 1852, Doc. 52—Rept. in reference to an additional appropriation for paving dept.; 1853, Doc. 6—Annual rept. of Supt.; 1853, Doc. 15—Rept. on extension of Warren St.; 1853, Doc. 29—Ordinance in relation to the Supt.; 1853, Doc. 37—Rept. on remonstrance of Thos. Wigglesworth against the numbering of Franklin St.; 1853, Doc. 59—An act concerning the grades of streets and ways; 1853, Doc. 84—Encroachments by private persons; 1854, Doc. 6—Annual rept. of Supt.; 1854, Doc. 14 1-2—Communication of Mr. Bonney in relation to a joint Committee on; 1854, Doc. 62—Rept. and orders in relation to the Mt. Washington avenue corporation; 1854, Doc. 109—An ordinance in relation to streets; 1855, Doc. 5—Annual rept. of Supt.; 1856, Doc. 3—Annual rept. of Supt.; 1856, Doc. 15—Proposed act in relation to laying out and discontinuing certain streets in Boston; 1856, Doc. 34—Ordinance in relation to; 1857, Doc. 3—Annual rept. of Supt.; 1857, Doc. 39—Rept. and order from the Land Commissioners, relative to laying out certain streets, passage-ways, and a square on the South Bay territory; 1857, Doc. 60—Majority rept. on the extension of Devonshire St.; 1857, Doc. 62—Minority rept. on same; 1858, Doc. 3—Annual rept. of Supt.; 1858, Doc. 43—Rept. on the extension of Albany St.; 1858, Doc. 48—Rept. on the extension of Albany St.; 1859, Doc. 5—Annual rept. of Supt.; 1859, Doc. 54—Rept. on the widening of Water St.; 1859, Doc. 73—Second rept. on widening Water St.; 1860, Doc. 6—Annual rept. of Supt.; 1860, Doc. 15—Loan for widening North St.; 1860, Doc. 46—Rept. on raising the grade of Tremont St.; 1860, Doc. 47—Rept. on raising the grade of Dover St.; 1860, Doc. 50—Rept. of the City Engineer on the direction, grade, &c., of the Back Bay streets; 1860, Doc. 68—Rept. on the widening of North St.; 1860, Doc. 72—Rept. on the widening of North St.; 1861, Doc. 5—Annual rept. of Supt.; 1861, Doc. 27—Rept. on the improvement of Dover St.; 1861, Doc. 42—Rept. on the improvement of Albion St.; 1862, Doc. 4—Annual rept. of the Supt.; 1862, Doc. 39—Rept. on the widening of Union St.; 1862, Doc. 48—An ordinance in relation to; 1862, Doc. 68—Rept. and order in relation to fruit stands in; 1862, Doc. 91—Rept. on the grading of Dover St.; 1862, Doc. 93—Rept. on the subject of raising Emerald and Village sts.; 1862, Doc. 97—Closing rept. of the Committee on streets; 1863, Doc. 3—Annual rept. of Supt.; 1863, Doc. 25—An ordinance in relation to; 1863, Doc. 43—Proposed amendments to the ordinance; 1863, Doc. 45—An ordinance in relation to; 1863, Doc. 81—Rept. of joint Special Committee on Back Bay streets, with rept. of Commissioners; 1863, Doc. 94—Rept. of City Engineer on Back Bay streets, grades, drainage, &c.; 1863, Doc. 114—Final rept. of the Committee on streets; 1864, Doc. 3—Annual rept. of Supt.; 1864, Doc. 23—Rept. on grade, &c., Back Bay lands; 1864, Doc. 46—Rept. on grade, &c., at the South End; 1864, Doc. 67—Reprint of Doc. 20, 1844, on South Boston sts.; 1864, Doc. 84—Rept. on fast driving in the sts.; 1864, Doc. 98—Final rept. of the Committee on sts.

STREET RAILWAYS. 1851, Doc. 77—Rept. on the subject of a railroad track along the marginal streets; 1853, Doc. 49—Rept. on Metropolitan Railroad, with act annexed; 1853, Doc. 50—Rept. on Cambridge Railroad with act annexed; 1853, Doc. 64—Majority rept. adverse to the location of the Metropolitan; 1853, Doc. 66—Minority rept. in favor of the location of the Metropolitan; 1854, Doc. 37—An act in addition to an act to incorporate the Metropolitan; 1854, Doc. 46—An act in addition to an act to incorporate the Cambridge; 1854, Doc. 53—Petition for the acceptance of the act of incorporation of the Boston and Chelsea; 1854, Doc. 55—Petition for the acceptance of the act of incorporation of the Middlesex; 1854, Doc. 57—Petition for the acceptance of the act of incorporation of the Dorchester avenue; 1854, Doc. 60—Rept. accepting the acts of incorporation of the Chelsea, Middlesex, and Dorchester avenue; 1856, Doc. 49—Location of Cambridge; 1856, Doc. 50—Extension of the location of the Metropolitan; 1856, Doc. 67—Petition of the Broadway Co. for approval of their Charter; 1857, Doc. 36—Order concerning the Middlesex; 1857, Doc. 46—Regulations for the government of; 1857, Doc. 53—Charter of the Broadway Co.; 1857, Doc. 65—Proposed location of the Metropolitan at So. Boston; 1858, Doc. 15—Rept. of the Committee on the location of the Broadway; 1858, Doc. 52—Rept. on acceptance of the Suffolk charter; 1859, Doc. 17—Rept. on locating a turnout for the Metropolitan; 1859, Doc. 58—Rept. on the proposed meeting of the railways at a central point; 1859, Doc. 70—Additional location of the Metropolitan; 1859, Docs. 71 and 72—Majority and minority repts. on additional location of the Middlesex; 1859, Doc. 74—Additional location and turnout for the Dorchester; 1859, Doc. 75—Additional location for the Broadway; 1859, Doc. 76—Location of the Suffolk; 1860, Doc. 21—City Solicitor's opinion on; 1860, Doc. 43—Rept. on the extension of the Broadway; 1860, Doc. 52—Mayor's message in relation to the location of the Broadway; 1860, Doc. 60—Additional location of the Cambridge; 1860, Doc. 84—New location granted to the Cambridge, and a portion of the old rescinded; 1860, Doc. 101—Rept. on the permanent location of the Metropolitan in Harrison av.; 1860, Doc. 102—Rept. on the location of the Metropolitan at the north end; 1860, Doc. 103—Rept. on the location of the Suffolk; 1861, Doc. 40—Location of the Broadway; 1861, Doc. 44—Minority rept. on the location of the Broadway; 1861, Doc. 45—Rept. on the location of the Suffolk; 1861, Doc. 47—Location of the Broadway; 1861, Doc. 48—Rept. on the location of the Metropolitan at the west end; 1861, Doc. 49—Location of the Metropolitan in Harrison av. and Dover St.; 1861, Doc. 50 — Rept. on location of the Cambridge; 1861, Doc. 55 — Second location of the Suffolk; 1861, Doc. 59 — Third location of the Suffolk; 1861, Doc. 72 — Fourth location of the Suffolk (printed, but not reported to the Board of Aldermen): 1861, Doc. 80 — Rept. of the Committee on a ticket commutation system; 1862, Doc. 14 — Rept. on the use of tracks; 1862, Doc. 41 — Rept. and order in relation to the connection of the tracks of the Suffolk with the tracks of the Metropolitan; 1862, Doc. 42 — Rept. and order in regard to the East Boston Wharf Company's tracks to connect with the Eastern Railroad; 1862, Doc. 43 — Rept. on location of the Suffolk; 1862, Doc. 64 — Rept. on location of the Suffolk; 1862, Doc. 65 — Rept. on location of the Cambridge; 1862, Doc. 66 — Rept. on location of the Middlesex; 1862, Doc. 71 — Rept. on location of the Suffolk; 1862, Doc. 72 — Rept. on location of the Cambridge; 1862, Doc. 87 — Additional locations of the Metropolitan; 1862, Doc. 90 — Rept. on location of the Suffolk; 1863, Doc. 61 — Rept. on location of the Metropolitan; 1863, Doc. 70 — Rept. on Union Freight Railway; 1863, Doc. 72 — Rept. on location of the Suffolk; 1863, Doc. 77 — Rept. on the number of cars on Washington St.; 1863, Doc. 83 — Memorial of the Broadway Co., remonstrating against the petitions of the Suffolk and Dorchester avenue companies; 1863, Doc. 92 — Ninth location of the Suffolk; 1864, Doc. 69 — Additional location of the Broadway; 1864, Doc. 85 — Location of the Metropolitan; 1864, Doc. 89 — Location of the Metropolitan; 1864, Doc. 90 — Location of the Broadway.

STREET STANDS. 1862, Doc. 68 — Rept. in relation to persons standing in the street to sell articles.

SUFFOLK COUNTY. 1860, Doc. 98 — Rept. of a Joint Special Committee on the relations of Boston to Suffolk County.

SUFFOLK RAILROAD. See *Street Railways.*

TAXES. 1836, Doc. 6 (Com. Council) — Ordinance respecting the assessment and collection of; 1836, Doc. 12 (Com. Council) — List of persons, &c., taxed on $25 and upwards; 1838, Doc. 34 — List of persons, &c., taxed on $25 and upwards; 1839, Doc. 13 — List of persons, &c., taxed on $25 and upwards; 1840, Doc. 23 — List of persons, &c., taxed on $25 and upwards; 1841, Doc. 8 — List of persons, &c., taxed on $25 and upwards; 1842, Doc. 7 — List of persons, &c., taxed on $25 and upwards; 1842, Doc 9 — Rept. on assessment of valuation of estates, and oaths to be administered to assessors; 1843, Doc. 9 — List of persons, &c., taxed on $25 and upwards; 1844, Doc. 9 — List of persons, &c., taxed on $25 and upwards; 1844, Doc. 23 — Rept. on the ordinance concerning the assessment and collection of; 1845, Doc. 10 — List of persons, &c., taxed on $25 and upwards; 1845, Doc. 13 — Rept. on alterations of the ordinance concerning assessment and collection of; 1846, Doc. 14 — List of persons, &c., taxed on $25 and upwards; 1847, Doc. 13 — List of persons, &c., taxed on $25 and upwards; 1847, Doc. 15 — Rept. on the expediency of amending the ordinance concerning the assessment and collection of; 1848, Doc. 9 — Rept. on measures to improve the method of assessing, abating, and collecting; 1848, Doc. 9 (extra) — An ordinance concerning assessment, abatement, and collection of; 1848, Doc. 12 — List of persons, &c., taxed on $25 and upwards; 1848, Doc. 26 — List of outstanding taxes, amounting to $5 and over, for years 1845-46-47; 1849, Doc. 12 — List of persons, &c., taxed on $25 and upwards; 1850, Doc. 5 — List of persons, &c., taxed on $6,000 and upwards; 1851, Doc. 14 — List of persons, &c., taxed on $6,000 and upwards; 1852, Doc. 12 — List of persons, &c., taxed on $6,000 and upwards; 1852, Doc. 64 — Rept. on petition of James Parker to have taxes refunded; 1853, Doc. 14 — List of persons, &c., taxed on $6,000 and upwards; 1853, Doc. 17 1-2 — Rept. of case of Ezra A. Bourne *vs.* City of Boston; 1853, Doc. 27 — City Solicitor's opinion in relation to the expenditure of moneys raised by taxation; 1854, Doc. 26 — List of persons, &c., taxed on $6,000 and upwards; 1854, Doc. 76 — Rept. on the increase of taxes; 1854, Doc. 110 — An ordinance in relation to; 1855, Doc. 16 — Rept. on so much of the Mayor's address as related to; 1855, Doc. 18 — List of persons, &c., taxed on $6,000 and upwards; 1856, Doc. 22 — List of persons, &c., taxed on $6,000 and upwards; 1857, Doc. 19 — An ordinance in relation to; 1857, Doc. 26 — An ordinance concerning assessment and collection of; 1857, Doc. 31 — List of persons, &c., taxed on $6,000 and upwards; 1858, Doc. 13 — List of persons, &c., taxed on $10,000 and upwards; 1859, Doc. 20 — List of persons, &c., taxed on $10,000 and upwards; 1860, Doc. 30 — List of persons, &c., taxed on $10,000 and upwards; 1861, Doc. 18 — List of persons, &c., taxed on $10,000 and upwards; 1862, Doc. 24 — Rept. on proposed abatement of taxes on property left by Abbott Lawrence to be invested in model lodging houses; 1862, Doc. 37 — List of persons, &c., taxed on $10,000 and upwards; 1862, Doc. 52 — Rept. on petition of the Mass. Grand Lodge for abatement of tax; 1862, Doc. 89 — An ordinance in relation to the assessment and collection of; 1863, Doc. 46 — List of persons, &c., taxed on $10,000 and upwards; 1864, Doc. 28 — List of persons, &c., taxed on $10,000 and upwards.

THEATRES. 1850, Doc. 31 — Rept. in relation to the safety of audiences in case of fire.

TIMEPIECES. 1853, Doc. 75 — Communication of Prof. E. N. Horsford, respecting the regulation of; 1853, Doc. 88 — Rept. of Committee on Fire Alarms, on the regulation of.

TREASURY. 1845, Doc. 39 — Rept. of a joint Standing Committee on; 1848, Doc. 35 — Solicitor's opinion on the power of the City Council to confer annuities or direct donations in money from; 1850, Doc. 22 — Rept. on the Treasurer's accounts; 1852, Doc. 25 — Rept. on the accounts of the late Treasurer, James C. Dunn.

TREES. 1860, Doc. 23 — Rept. on removal of the trees from Tremont Street.

TRUANCY. 1846, Doc. 18 — Rept. on the subject of, in the Public Schools; 1849, Doc. 9 — Rept. in regard to truants from the Schools, and vagrant children; 1852, Doc. 58 — Officer's rept. in relation to; 1852, Doc. 71 — Rept. on the administration of the statute and ordinance in relation to; 1853, Doc. 21 — Officer's quarterly rept.; 1853, Doc. 55 — Officer's quarterly rept.; 1862, Doc. 61 — Ordinance concerning; 1863, Doc. 90 — Ordinance concerning. See *Vagrant Children.*

TRUCKS, &c. 1849, Doc. 43 — An order concerning the licensing of trucks, drays, &c.

UNION FREIGHT RAILWAY. See *Street Railways.*

URINALS. 1859, Doc. 53 — Rept. on the subject of establishing urinals, closets, and lavatories in different parts of the city.

URSULINE CONVENT. 1834, Doc. 11 (Com. Council) — Rept. on the destruction of the Convent at Charlestown, Aug. 11, 1834.

VAGRANT CHILDREN. 1837, Doc. 3 (Com. Council) — Rept. on the memorial of John Tappan and others respecting; 1837, Doc. 4 (Com. Council) — Rept. on intermediate schools for; 1837, Doc. 17 (Com. Council) — Rept. on the memorial of C. F. Barnard and others upon the subject. See *Truancy.*

VAULTS. 1863, Doc. 82 — Rules and regulations in relation to.

WARDS. 1838, Doc. 20 — Rept. on authorizing a new division; 1838, Doc. 25 — Rept. on division of the city, with ordinance; 1838, Doc. 20 — Ordinance on division; 1847, Doc. 18 — Petition of inhabitants of Ward 12, concerning wants of said ward; 1848, Doc. 28 — Rept. on petition that East Boston might form an independent ward; 1850, Doc. 16 — Rept. on the subject of a new division of the wards; 1860, Doc. 24 — Rept. on a new division of the wards.

WARD MEETINGS. 1862, Doc. 36 — An ordinance in relation to.

WARD ROOMS. 1861, Doc. 67 — Rept. and ordinance in relation to the use of, for political meetings.

WASHINGTON, GEORGE. 1859, Doc. 69 — Rept. on the expediency of aiding in the erection of an equestrian statue of.

WATCH. See *Police and Watch.*

WATER. 1834, Doc. 12 (Com. Council) — Rept. of Loammi Baldwin, Engineer, on the subject of introducing pure water into the city; 1836, Doc. 7 (Com. Council) — Rept. on introducing water into the city; 1836, Doc. 10 (Com. Council) — Rept. of R. H. Eddy, Engineer, on the introduction of soft water; 1837, Doc. 1 (Com. Council) — Rept. on the introduction of water, with an order; 1837, Doc. 9 (Com. Council) — Providing funds to cover the expense of introducing water; 1837, Doc. 24 (Com. Council) — Rept. of Danl. Treadwell, J. F. Baldwin, and Nathan Hale, on a plan for supplying the city with water; 1838, Doc. 1 — Order under which the Water Commissioners were appointed; 1838, Doc. 4 — Rept. on the introduction of water, accompanied by the opinion of the City Solicitor; 1838, Doc. 9 — Communications from R. H. Eddy and L. M. Sargent, with evidence, etc., before the House of Commons, relative to the introduction of water into London; 1838, Doc. 11 — Resolve pertaining to the Boston Hydraulic Co., and plan to supply the city with water; 1838, Doc. 33 — Rept. on the introduction of water, with revised estimates of the Commissioners; 1839, Doc. 5 — Rept. of J. F. Baldwin, giving reasons for dissenting from the opinion of the other Commissioners; 1839, Doc. 19 — Rept. on the introduction of water; 1839, Doc. 25 — Rept. on the introduction of water; 1839, Doc. 29 — Statement of the evidence before the Legislature; 1843, Doc. 6 — Rept. on petition of Jas. C. Odiorne, for leave to bring into the city and distribute the water of Spot Pond; 1844, Doc. 24 — Rept. of Commissioners on the expense of bringing water from Long Pond; 1844, Doc. 24 1-2 — Rept. of Commissioners on an order to devise a plan for supplying the city with; 1844, Doc. 25 — Rept. of joint Special Committee on the introduction of; 1844, Doc. 26 — Rept. of same Committee, with resolve and order; 1845, Doc. 12 1-2 — Proceedings before Committee of the Legislature, on the petition of the city for leave to introduce water from Long Pond; 1845, Doc. 27 — Petition of Stockholders of Spot Pond Aqueduct Co.; 1845, Doc. 29 — Rept. on a petition concerning a subscription on the part of the city to the capital of the Spot Pond Aqueduct Co.; 1845, Doc. 40 — Rept. on the proposition to sell Spot Pond to the city; 1845, Doc. 41 — Rept. of the Commissioners on the sources from which a supply may be obtained; 1846, Doc. 14 1-2 — An ordinance to regulate the proceedings of the Commissioners for supplying the city with; 1846, Doc. 20 — First monthly rept. of Commissioners; 1846, Doc. 21 — Rept. on arrangements necessary to procure funds to pay for the introduction of; 1846, Doc. 26 — First quarterly rept. of Standing Committee on; 1846, Doc. 32 — Rept. of Standing Committee on the petition of Josiah Bradlee, and others, relative to the Jamaica Pond Aqueduct, with rept. of Water Commissioners on same; 1847, Doc. 5 — Second quarterly rept. of the Standing Committee on water; 1847, Doc. 8 — Rept. of joint Standing Committee on petition of Silas P. Barnes; 1847, Doc. 19 — Rept. on petition of Luther Mann, and others; 1847, Doc. 27 — Rept. of the joint Standing Committee on; 1847, Doc. 28 — An ordinance to regulate the proceedings of the Water Commissioners; 1847, Doc. 29 — Rept. on a petition praying for the purchase of a part of Dorchester heights, to be used for the purpose of a reservoir and public square; 1847, Doc. 30 — Rept. of the Committee on Finance, on the progress made in negotiating a loan; 1847, Doc. 43 — An order authorizing the Commissioners to purchase lands and water sights, erect dams, &c., for forming reservoirs to serve as a substitute for the water which may be diverted from Concord River; 1847, Doc. 44 — Semi-annual rept. of Water Commissioners; 1848, Doc. 18 — Rept. of consulting physicians on the action of Cochituate water upon mineral substances; 1848, Doc. 22 — Rept. on petition that the water may be carried to East Boston; 1848, Doc. 32 — Rept. of Commissioners on the best material for distribution water pipes, and the most economical mode of introducing water into private houses; 1848, Doc. 42 — An ordinance in addition to an ordinance to regulate the proceedings of the Commissioners; 1848, Doc. 43 — Rept. of the Committee on water, and counter rept. concerning the schedule of water rents; 1848, Doc. 44 — Rept. of the Committee on water on the purchase of Jamaica Pond Aqueduct; 1848, Doc. 45 — City Solicitor's opinion on the power of the Commissioners to establish the water rents; 1848, Doc. 50 — Account of the celebration on the introduction of the water of Lake Cochituate; 1849, Doc. 3 — Schedule of water rates established by the Water Commissioners; 1849, Doc. 4 — Rept. of the Commissioners respecting the progress of the water works; 1849, Doc. 5 — Rept. of Commissioners, stating the number of hydrants provided for extinguishing fires; 1849, Doc. 18 — Rept. of Commissioners on work to be done, and expenditures required; 1849, Doc. 24 — Rept. on the expediency of carrying the water of Long Pond to East Boston; 1849, Doc. 26 — An ordinance in addition to an ordinance to regulate the proceedings of the Commissioners; 1849, Doc. 29 — Rept. on the act of the Legislature for supplying the city with water; 1849, Doc. 38 — Rept. of Commissioners relative to reservoirs, &c.; 1849, Doc. 41 — Engineer's rept. in relation to taking water to East Boston; 1849, Doc. 53 — Rept. concerning charges for water supplied to fountains; 1849, Doc. 57 — Rept. on a plan of organization of the water dept.; 1849, Doc. 61 — Rept. of the number of persons, other than laborers, employed by the Commissioners; 1849, Doc. 63 — An ordinance establishing the Cochituate Water Board; 1849, Doc. 68 — Final report of the Commissioners; 1850, Doc. 3 1-2 — Final rept. of Commissioners, W. Hale, J. F. Baldwin, and T. B. Curtis; 1850, Doc. 7 — Quarterly rept. of the Water Board; 1850, Doc. 13 — City Solicitor's opinion on the right to give water to the Children's Friend Society; 1850, Doc. 29 — Tariff for 1851; 1850, Doc. 32 and 32 1-2 — Ordinance providing for the care and management of the water works; 1850, Doc. 41 — An ordinance in relation to water rates; 1850, Doc. 45 — Annual rept. of the Cochituate Water Board; 1850, Doc. 51 — Rept. upon examining the books and accounts of the Water Board; 1851, Doc. 37 — Rept. of Water Board on an Aqueduct to Deer Island; 1851, Doc. 38 — Communication from the Water Board respecting the purchase of the Boston Aqueduct; 1851, Doc. 40 — Rept. of Com. on water, concerning the power of the Water Board to purchase the franchise of the Jamaica Pond Aqueduct Co.; 1851, Doc. 46 — Rept. from Water Board stating that they have purchased the property of the Aqueduct Corporation; 1851, Doc. 54 — Rept. of Water Board on petition of R. Frothingham, Jr.; 1852, Doc. 6 — Annual rept. of Cochituate Water Board; 1852, Doc. 24 — Rept. in relation to supplying the fountain in Louisburg square; 1852, Doc. 51 — Rept. on the daily consumption of water; 1852, Doc. 67 — Rept. on water loan; 1853, Doc. 7 — Annual rept. of Water Board; 1853, Doc. 20 — Reprint of annual rept. for 1851; 1853, Doc. 74 — Repts. and ordinance in relation to water rates; 1854, Doc. 11 — An ordinance in relation to water rates; 1854, Doc. 16 — Annual rept.; 1854, Doc. 19 — An ordinance relating to the water works; 1854, Doc. 25 — Rept. of Water Board on rates; 1854, Doc. 82 — An ordinance to establish water rates; 1854, Doc. 111 — An ordinance in relation to; 1855, Doc. 9 — Annual rept. of Water Board; 1855, Doc. 30 — Majority and minority repts. of Committee on water works; 1855, Doc. 43 — An ordinance in relation to; 1855, Doc. 48 — An ordinance in relation to; 1856, Doc. 11 — Annual rept. of Water Board; 1857, Doc. 12 — Annual rept. of Water Board; 1857, Doc. 50 — Rept. of Water Board on the subject of a new main pipe; 1858, Doc. 7 — Annual rept. of Water Board; 1858, Doc. 16 — An ordinance concerning the waste of water; 1858, Doc. 24 — An ordinance to establish water rates; 1858, Doc. 57 — Communication of the Water Board, relative to a supply for a skating pond; 1858, Doc. 60 — An ordinance in relation to water rates; 1859, Doc. 8 — Annual rept. of Water Board; 1859, Doc. 40 — Communication from the Water Board, on the route of the new main pipe; 1859, Doc. 49 — Rept. of Water Board on the flowage of meadows on Sudbury river; 1859, Doc. 56 — Communication from the Water Board, with an ordinance to revise the water rates; 1860, Doc. 13 — Annual rept. of Water Board; 1860, Doc. 45 — Rept. of the Water Board on laying the new main; 1861, Doc. 8 — Annual rept. of the Water Board; 1862, Doc. 9 — Annual rept. of the Water Board; 1862, Doc. 11 — Rept. of the Water Registrar on the waste by hopper closets; 1862, Doc. 17 — An ordinance providing for the care and management of the water works; 1863, Doc. 10 — Annual rept. of the Water Board; 1863, Doc. 47 — Rept. of the Committee on the reduction of the rates for the Mass. General Hospital; 1864, Doc. 20—Annual rept. of the Water Board; 1864, Doc. 63—Rept. on the petition to have water pipes laid in Lawrence St., said st. being below grade; 1864, Doc. 76—Request of the Cochituate Water Board for a new reservoir.

WEBSTER, DANIEL. 1851, Doc. 25—Resolutions of the Common Council concerning a refusal of the Mayor and Aldermen to allow the use of Faneuil Hall for the reception of; 1851, Doc. 26—Letter of, to the President of the Common Council; 1851, Doc. 31—Reply to the invitation to speak in Faneuil Hall; 1852, Doc. 31—Address in Faneuil Hall, May 22, 1852; 1859, Doc. 50 1 2—Inauguration of the statue of.

WHARVES. 1852, Doc. 44—Rept. on the sale of the city wharf; 1852, Doc. 65—Final rept. on the disposition of the City Wharf; 1856, Doc. 59—Rept. on the sale of the North Wharf; 1857, Doc. 22—Rept. on the sale of the North Wharf; 1857, Doc. 30—Rept. on the sale of the North Wharf.

WINDOWS. 1844, Doc. 7—Rept. on alterations in the law regulating the projection of, into the streets.

WOOD. 1839, Doc. 23—Rept. and ordinance regulating the sale and admeasurement of; 1840, Doc. 7—Rept. on an ordinance relating to the admeasurement of, etc.; 1854, Doc. 112—An ordinance in relation to.

www.ingramcontent.com/pod-product-compliance
Lightning Source LLC
LaVergne TN
LVHW021304110826
845150LV00003B/473

* 9 7 8 1 4 2 5 5 6 0 5 4 6 *